THE

RELIGION

OF

JAVA

THE
RELIGION
OF
JAVA

CLIFFORD
GEERTZ

THE UNIVERSITY OF CHICAGO PRESS
CHICAGO AND LONDON

The University of Chicago Press, Chicago 60637
The University of Chicago Press, Ltd., London

90 89   6 7

International Standard Book Number: 0-226-28510-3
Library of Congress Catalog Card Number: 75-18746

For the Wedono,

the Modin,

and my *abangan* Landlord

Nuwun Pangestunipun Sedaja Kalepatan Kula

Foreword

THIS IS the first of a series of descriptive monographs about various aspects of contemporary life in an actual and in many respects typical place in east central Java. For obvious reasons, the names given to locations and persons are fictitious, but the descriptions are based on direct observation.

The other monographs in this series will report on Village Life and Rural Economy (Robert Jay), The Market (Alice Dewey), Administrative Organization (Donald Fagg), Family Organization and Socialization (Hildred Geertz), and The Chinese Community (Edward Ryan).

The field work on which these monographs are based was conceived as a team project, a concerted effort by students of sociology and anthropology to study a segment of what was known to be a highly complex society. The decision to publish separately the reports of the various investigators is due partly to practical considerations, but it is also based on the nature of the phenomena. Since the complexity of even this small segment of Javanese society compelled each investigator to limit his observations to one set of institutions, a truly *joint* general report would not have been feasible, however desirable.

For a fuller and more balanced view of Javanese society, reading of all the reports is of course recommended; but each report has been written in such a way that the specialist can comprehend the relationship between his interest and the whole. For instance, the student interested in, say, farm economy, will find sufficient background in Dr. Jay's monograph to comprehend how peasant farming is related to other aspects of Javanese life.

Because of the nature of its subject matter, the present report by Dr. Clifford Geertz provides perhaps a wider view of Javanese life than the others, and it is therefore fitting that it should be the first to appear.

DOUGLAS OLIVER

Cambridge, Mass.
1959

vii

Acknowledgments

As THE research project upon which this work is based has extended over a six-year period, both in Indonesia and in the United States, the number of people who have given valuable assistance toward the successful completion of it are literally legion. Here, I can mention but a few of those to whom I am indebted.

To Alice Dewey, Donald Fagg, Rufus Hendon, Jane Hendon, Robert Jay, Anne Jay, Edward Ryan, and Anola Ryan, fellow members of the field team, I have a debt which is both professional and personal. Having exchanged ideas and data with them almost continually over the past several years, it is not easy to separate out in the following what is originally my own and what originally I learned from them, although for the general pattern of organization and analysis I am, of course, alone responsible. Particularly my wife, Hildred Geertz, also a member of the group, has shaped the development of this work in every phase, from the collection of the data, through the analysis of it, to the actual writing of the book.

To the Center for International Studies, Massachusetts Institute of Technology, which administered the grant which was provided by the Ford Foundation, I am also grateful. In particular, Dr. Douglas L. Oliver, who originated the research project, Dr. Max Millikan, director of the Center, and Mr. Richard Hatch, publications director, have been very helpful throughout the course of the project.

Selecting Indonesians to whom to offer explicit thanks is an even more difficult task, for kindness, patience, and helpfulness to us was almost universal among the hundreds of people with whom we had dealings in that country. Our official hosts were the Indonesian Government and the National University of Gadjah Mada in Djogjakarta, and I wish to thank in this connection Mr. Suwanto, Cultural Attaché of the Indonesian Embassy at the time the original arrangements for the project were made, Professor Sardjito, President of the University of Gadjah Mada, Mr. Abdur Rachman, then Secretary to the Resident of Kediri, and R. M. Soemomihardjo, the District-Officer of "Modjokuto." To the other, necessarily more obscure, Indonesians, in Modjokuto and elsewhere, who in countless ways aided my work, I am very grateful, and hope that in some way this book may contribute to the realization of their aspiration to build a strong, stable, prosperous, and democratic "New Indonesia."

CLIFFORD GEERTZ

Berkeley
1959

CONTENTS

xi

PART FOUR: Conclusion: Conflict and Integration

Introduction

MODJOKUTO,* the small town in east central Java within which this study was made, lies at the extreme eastern edge of a great irrigated rice plain through which a rambling, circular-swinging river flows northward toward the Java Sea. A half-day's drive from Surabaja, the Republic of Indonesia's second largest city and best port, Modjokuto marks the point at which the flat, fertile countryside begins to tilt upward toward the cluster of active volcanoes which tower over it to the east and whose periodic eruptions provide much of its fertility.

A commercial, educational, and administrative center for eighteen surrounding villages, the town has a population of almost 20,000, of whom about 18,000 are Javanese, 1,800 Chinese, and the remainder a handful of Arabs, Indians, and other minorities. Its spatial form is determined by the juncture of three poorly paved secondary roads, one from Surabaja, the provincial capital, one from the regional capital fifteen miles to the west, and one from a large inland city on the other side of the eastern mountains.

The town is surrounded on three sides by thousands of small mud-walled rice fields, most of them not more than twenty-five yards square. Flooded in the rainy season by means of an age-old irrigation system of gullies, springs, and water traps improved by Dutch-introduced cement dams and steel sluice gates, these fields are cultivated almost entirely in rice for six months of every year. In the dry season, which is pronounced in East Java, the land does not lie fallow but is planted in maize, soybeans, peanuts, onions, peppers, or sweet potatoes—usually two or three of these in turn. Almost all land-holdings are small—under three acres—and although there is, particularly near the town, considerable sharecrop tenancy, the landlords in-

*This description of the town was published earlier in essentially the same form as part of my article, "Religious Belief and Economic Behavior in a Central Javanese Town: Some Preliminary Considerations," *Economic Development and Cultural Change,* Vol. 4, No. 2 (January, 1956), pp. 138–158.

1

volved are not absentee nor are their holdings any larger, with one or two not very dramatic exceptions, than those of the peasants themselves.

On the fourth side of Modjokuto, the southwest, lies either forest or dry, broken, largely unirrigable land on which, in the early part of this century, an extensive plantation system in coffee, rubber, and sugar was built up. Dutch-owned, Dutch-managed, and Javanese-worked, this network of plantations and sugar mills had a heavy impact on the economy of Modjokuto before the war. As the town was founded only toward the latter half of the nineteenth century, the interaction between the small-scale, intensive wet-rice farming system practiced by the independent Javanese peasant and the large-scale, extensive cash-crop estate agriculture of the Dutch shaped the economic history of the region almost since the beginning.

The Dutch are gone from Modjokuto now, their estate and factory system shaken by the depression and shattered by the war and revolution. What remains is a peasantry very used both to money and to foreign goods, tremendous underemployment both rural and urban, and an overcomplex economic system in which the Chinese minority controls the main streams of trade. The Chinese form the heart of the economic circulatory system of Modjokuto, pressing goods, many of them imported, down through its arteries, pulling back goods, the greater part of them agricultural, through its veins, and passing them on to the large urban centers for further distribution. Javanese commercial activity becomes relevant only between the ends of the two channels—where they braid out into a complex network of tiny, doubled-over, and marvelously interwound economic capillaries reaching into the small crevices of native life.

There are two business districts, both of them lined with small, open-front, wooden stores, almost all Chinese-run. Inside the stores one finds hardware, home furnishings, various types of food, jewelry, false teeth, automobile and bicycle parts, building materials, textiles, and drugs—from sulfa to such promising herbs as crocodile tongue and cat's beard. Even more important in terms of economic power, the Chinese control the trade in dry-season crops grown in Javanese fields, and their mills process the rice from those fields (although for the past few years a great part of the actual buying has been done under government contract and, nominally, under government control). They own almost all the trucking, almost all the string-and-bailing-wire jitneys which carry a great proportion (with the busses and the train) of inter-local travel, and almost all the bicycle rickshaws which, Javanese-pedaled, provide the bulk of passenger transport within the town. The larger small-scale factories in town and outside it—rice, lumber, soda pop, bread, charcoal—are, with a few notable exceptions, in Chinese hands. Chinese own the movie and the theater where Javanese plays are given, and they manage the carnival when it comes to town. They are prevented from totally dominating the economy by only one restriction: they are forbidden, by a Dutch law continued into the Republican period, to hold farm land.

The Javanese stores, almost all of them marginal, number about a dozen, most of them in the secondary business section. The core of native-run commercial life is the market, where each day hundreds of professional or semi-professional Javanese salesmen and speculators, both men and women, bargain vigorously in a desperate attempt to earn a living or part of a living from small-scale, person-to-person trade. Textiles, daily food supplies, and dry-season crops probably form the bulk of the business; but buttons, dried fish, mats, baskets, perfumes, religious books, cooked food and hot coffee, chairs and tables, nails, ready-made clothing, meat, patent medicines, leather goods, parasols, pots and pans—in fact, almost everything portable—are each day passed from hand to hand to someone's (usually small) profit.

In the market you can have your hair cut, your bicycle fixed, and your pants mended while you wait. For an Indonesian quarter you can rent a spot under a tree or a wooden shed and sell cigarettes for a cent more than you just paid for them in a Chinese store across the street. You can buy a basket of corn in the morning and sell it at noon, never leaving the market—getting your profit out of the slight rise in price which takes place every day as the market day wears on. (If you are a friend or a paying acquaintance of the man who runs the scales, you may make something out of the greater weight the corn has when you sell it than when you bought it.) Or, for two rupiahs a day (and a few hundred rupiahs capital), you can become one of the aristocrats of the market with a three-meters wide stall of your own, selling imported and domestic textiles for as much more than they are worth as you can wheedle an unwary peasant into paying. For the Modjokuto Javanese, whether buyer or seller, the market is the very model of commercial life, the source of nearly all his ideas of the possible and the proper in economic behavior.

Aside from petty commerce, three other nonagricultural activities play an important part in the Javanese sector of the economy: simple manual labor, independent craft and repair work, and white-collar office work. The manual laborers, if they find work at all, may be employed by the Chinese in their rice mills, lumber yards, or other enterprises; by the government fixing roads, building irrigation dams, or sweeping streets; or by one of the scattered "here today, gone tomorrow" Javanese cottage industries. A great many are employed on the narrow-gauge railroad which runs four short passenger trains a day from the regional capital through Modjokuto to connect with the main Surabaja line fifteen miles northward. Many, too, are servants of the richer townsmen, although the departure of the Dutch has markedly reduced job opportunities in this field. The independent artisans—carpenters, chauffeurs, bricklayers, blacksmiths, watchmakers, barbers, tailors—are spread unevenly throughout the town, for they work mostly in their own homes, accepting jobs as they come fitfully to them, and drifting uneasily into unskilled occupations if forced to by economic pressure.

The white-collar clerks, teachers, and government officials form the intellectual and social elite of Modjokuto, inheritors of a political tradition in which the ability to read and write was confined to a hereditary court class born to rule and venerated for doing so. Many of the old caste marks of the literati are nearly gone now—the variously colored parasols symbolizing rank, the deep bow of the inferior to touch the knee of the standing superior, the proclamation of pedigree through the use of court title, the tongue-tied shame of the peasant in the presence of the government official—but the general attitude of respect and subservience on the part of the uneducated toward the educated remains.

The number of the educated has been increasing rather rapidly of late with the post-revolutionary expansion of the school system. In Modjokuto there are a half dozen six-grade government elementary schools, a government technical school at the junior high level, three private junior high schools, a government school for elementary teachers, and scattered other private schools including Chinese and Catholic elementary schools. Further, each of the surrounding villages has a school of its own, and there is still a number of old-style religious schools in the area which have recently been semi-modernized. The result of this sudden florescence of educational activity is that teachers, on the one hand, and advanced students, on the other, form two of the most clearly defined and dynamic social groups within the society, perhaps the two groups who are least closely bound to the Javanese past and whose relationships with the rest of the society are the most ambiguous.

There are two major government offices in Modjokuto, for it is the capital both of a district (kewedanan)* and a subdistrict (ketjamatan). The subdistrict, the lowest level to which the wholly appointive national bureaucracy reaches, administers eighteen villages all lying within ten miles of town. The district administers five contiguous subdistricts, including that of Modjokuto itself, and is in turn subordinate to the regional (kebupaten) government, the capital of which is the nearby city of Bragang. In addition, the regional headquarters of the central government police force is in Modjokuto rather than in Bragang, as are also the government pawnshop and the government hospital for the area. Offices concerned with the repair of roadways, the building and maintenance of irrigation systems, the improvement of agriculture, and the administration of the market further swell the total of white-collar workers employed or underemployed by the government, as do the post office and the office of the local representative of the Ministry of Religion.

These five major occupational types—farmer, petty trader, independent artisan, manual laborer, and white-collar clerk, teacher, or administrator—represent the Javanese population of Modjokuto, grouped according to their economic activity. The crystallized typology of work patterns reflects the underlying organization of the economic system of the town of which it is an outcome. Similarly, the same population grouped according to their world outlook—according to their religious beliefs, ethical preferences, and political ideologies—yields three main cultural types which reflect the moral organization of Javanese culture as it is manifested in Modjokuto, the general ideas of order in terms of which the Javanese farmer, laborer, artisan, trader,

---

* The spelling of Indonesian words conforms to the current official orthography. Javanese words are spelled in accordance with the system currently employed by Balai Pustaka (a publishing agency of the Ministry of Education) in its publications in that language. This is identical with the orthography of Th. Pigeaud's *Javaans-Nederlands Handwoordenboek* (Groningen, n.d.), except that *oe* is replaced by *u*. Arabic words are also spelled in accordance with the Javanese system.

or clerk shapes his behavior in all areas of life. These are the *abangan, santri,* and *prijaji.*

There are, it seems to me, three main social-structural nuclei in Java to-day: the village, the market, and the government bureaucracy—each of them taken in a somewhat more extended sense than is common.

The Javanese village is as old as the Javanese, for it is likely that the first Malayo-Polynesian peoples to come to the island already possessed knowl-edge of agriculture. The evolution of the Javanese village to its present form has at each stage been regulated and expressed by a more or less unified re-ligious system, itself, of course, evolving too. In the days before the Hindus, who began to come to the island around 400 A.D. or before, it seems likely that the sort of "animism" common still to many of the pagan tribes of Malaysia comprised the whole of the religious tradition; but this tradition has proved, over the course of the centuries, remarkably able to absorb into one syncretized whole elements from both Hinduism and Islam, which followed it in the fifteenth century. Thus today the village religious system commonly consists of a balanced integration of animistic, Hinduistic, and Islamic ele-ments, a basic Javanese syncretism which is the island's true folk tradition, the basic substratum of its civilization; but the situation is more complex than this, for not only, as we shall see, do many peasants not follow this syncretism, but many townsmen—mostly lower-class displaced peasants or sons of displaced peasants—do. The *abangan* religious tradition, made up primarily of the ritual feast called the *slametan,* of an extensive and intricate complex of spirit beliefs, and of a whole set of theories and practices of curing, sorcery, and magic, is the first subvariant within the general Javanese religious system which I shall present below, and it is associated in a broad and general way with the Javanese village.

The second major social substructure, the market, must be taken in a broad sense to include the whole network of domestic trade relationships on the island. For the most part, the inter-local aspects of this trade are in Chinese hands, the more local aspects in Javanese hands, although there is a good deal of overlap. The association of the Javanese trading element with a more puristic version of Islam than is common in Java stretches back to the introduction of the Mid-Eastern religion into the island, for it came as part of a great trade expansion, stimulated ultimately by the rise of the Age of Exploration in Europe, along the Java Sea. The coming of the Dutch crushed the lively Javanese trade which had sprung up in the north coast ports—Surabaja, Gresik, Tuban, and others—as part of this expansion, but the trading culture did not wholly die; it persisted, although much changed and weakened, down to the present. The rise of reformist move-ments in Indonesian Islam in the early part of this century as part of the general nationalist movement which in 1945 finally brought Indonesia her freedom from Dutch rule revivified and further sharpened the sense for a purer Islam, less contaminated with either animism or mysticism, among the small-trader element in Javanese society.

The purer Islam is the subtradition I have called *santri.* Although in a broad and general way the *santri* subvariant is associated with the Javanese trading element, it is not confined to it, nor are all traders, by far, adherents of it. There is a very strong *santri* element in the villages, often finding its leadership in the richer peasants who have been able to make the pilgrimage to Mecca and set up religious schools upon their return. The market is, on the other hand, especially since the war and the disappearance of the Dutch demand for servants and manual workers, clogged with swarms of small *abangan* traders attempting to make a marginal living, although the greatest number of the larger and more vigorous traders are still *santris*. The *santri* religious tradition, consisting not only of a careful and regular execution of the basic rituals of Islam—the prayers, the Fast, the Pilgrimage—but also of a whole complex of social, charitable, and political Islamic organizations, is the second subvariant of the general Javanese religious system which I shall present below.

The third is the *prijaji. Prijaji* originally referred only to the hereditary aristocracy which the Dutch pried loose from the kings of the vanquished native states and turned into an appointive, salaried civil service. This white-collar elite, its ultimate roots in the Hindu-Javanese courts of pre-colonial times, conserved and cultivated a highly refined court etiquette, a very complex art of dance, drama, music, and poetry, and a Hindu-Buddhist mysticism. They stressed neither the animistic element in the over-all Javanese syncretism as did the *abangans,* nor the Islamic as did the *santris,* but the Hinduistic. In this century, the ascendant social and political position of this group so far as the native Javanese society is concerned (the Dutch of course occupied the genuinely dominant position until the revolution) has been weakened, access to the bureaucracy has become easier for the low-born but well educated, and an increasing number of nongovernmental "white collar" jobs has appeared. Further, it was upon this "bureaucratic" group that the Dutch had their most direct acculturating influence, leading ulti-mately to the production of the highly secularized, Westernized, and, com-monly, somewhat anti-traditional political elite of the Indonesian Republic. As a result, the traditional court culture has weakened. Nevertheless, the *prijaji* variant not only remains quite strong among certain of the conservative ele-ments in the society but also plays a basic role in shaping the world view, the ethics, and the social behavior of even the most Westernized element in the still dominant white-collar group. The refined politesse, the high art, and the intuitive mysticism all remain highly characteristic of Java's social elite; and, although somewhat attenuated and adjusted to changed conditions, the *prijaji* style of life remains the model not only for the elite but in many ways for the entire society.

Abangan, representing a stress on the animistic aspects of the over-all Javanese syncretism and broadly related to the peasant element in the popu-lation; *santri,* representing a stress on the Islamic aspects of the syncretism and generally related to the trading element (and to certain elements in the peasantry as well); and *prijaji,* stressing the Hinduist aspects and related to the bureaucratic element—these, then, are the three main subtraditions I shall describe. They are not constructed types, but terms and divisions the Javanese themselves apply. They indicate the way the Javanese in Modjokuto themselves perceive the situation, as will, I hope, be apparent from the extensive quotations from my field notes which I have included in the text. All these quotations are, perhaps, not absolutely necessary for the simple description of Modjokuto religion, but it seems to me that one of the characteristics of good ethnographic reporting—and this essay claims to be nothing more than a report —is that the ethnographer is able to get out of the way of his data, to make himself translucent so that the reader can see for himself something of what the facts look like and so judge the ethnographer's summaries and generalizations in terms of the ethnographer's actual perceptions.

Java—which has been civilized longer than England; which over a period of more than fifteen hundred years has seen Indians, Arabs, Chinese, Portuguese, and Dutch come and go; and which has today one of the world's densest populations, highest development of the arts, and most intensive agricultures—is not easily characterized under a single label or easily pictured in terms of a dominant theme. It is particularly true that in describing the religion of such a complex civilization as the Javanese any simple unitary view is certain to be inadequate; and so I have tried in the following pages to show how much variation in ritual, contrast in belief, and conflict in values lie concealed behind the simple statement that Java is more than 90 per cent Moslem. If I have chosen, consequently, to accent the religious diversity in contemporary Java—or more particularly in one given town-village complex in contemporary Java—my intention has not been to deny the underlying religious unity of its people or, beyond them, of the Indonesian people generally, but to bring home the reality of the complexity, depth, and richness of their spiritual life.

Part One

THE "ABANGAN" VARIANT

Chapter 1

The *Slametan*
Communal Feast
as a Core Ritual

AT THE center of the whole Javanese religious system lies a simple, formal, undramatic, almost furtive, little ritual: the *slametan* (also sometimes called a *kenḍurèn*). The *slametan* is the Javanese version of what is perhaps the world's most common religious ritual, the communal feast, and, as almost everywhere, it symbolizes the mystic and social unity of those participating in it. Friends, neighbors, fellow workers, relatives, local spirits, dead ancestors, and near-forgotten gods all get bound, by virtue of their commensality, into a defined social group pledged to mutual support and cooperation. In Modjokuto the *slametan* forms a kind of social universal joint, fitting the various aspects of social life and individual experience together in a way which minimizes uncertainty, tension, and conflict—or at least it is supposed to do so. The altered form of twentieth-century urban and suburban life in Java makes it rather less efficient as an integrating mechanism and rather less satisfying as a religious experience for many people; but among the group here described as *abangan*—the more traditionalized peasants and their proletarianized comrades in the towns—the *slametan* still retains much of its original force and attraction.

A *slametan* can be given in response to almost any occurrence one wishes to celebrate, ameliorate, or sanctify. Birth, marriage, sorcery, death, house moving, bad dreams, harvest, name-changing, opening a factory, illness, supplication of the village guardian spirit, circumcision, and starting off a political meeting may all occasion a *slametan*. For each the emphasis is slightly different. One part or another of the total ritual is intensified and elaborated; another part is toned down. The mood changes somewhat, but the underlying structure of the ritual remains the same. There is always the special food (differing according to the intent of the *slametan*); there is always incense, the Islamic chant, and the extra-formal high-Javanese speech of the host (its content, too, naturally, varying with the occasion); and there is always the polite,

11

embarrassed, muted manner which suggests that, despite the brevity and lack of drama the ritual displays, something important is going on.

The *Slametan* Pattern

MOST *slametans* are held in the evening, just after the sun has gone down and the evening prayer—for those who perform it—is done. If the occasion is, say, a name-changing, a harvest, or a circumcision, the host will have employed a religious specialist to determine an auspicious day according to a numerological interpretation of the Javanese calendrical system; if it is a death or a birth, the event itself determines the timing. The day is spent in preparing the food. The women do this: for a small feast only those of the household itself, for a large one a wider range of kin ties may be drawn upon. The ceremony itself is all male. The women remain *mburi* (behind—i.e., in the kitchen), but they inevitably peek through the bamboo walls at the men, who, squatted on floor mats *ngarepan* (in front—i.e., in the main living room) perform the actual ritual, eating the food the women have prepared.

The men invited are all close neighbors, since to a *slametan* one invites all those who live in the immediate area around one's own house. The basis of within a short distance from one's house in any direction must be invited and selection is entirely territorial: relative or not, friend or not, anyone who lives must come. They are called together by a messenger of the host (most often one of his children) only five or ten minutes before the *slametan* is to begin, and they must drop everything and come immediately. Despite this apparently haphazard procedure, almost everyone turns up, because during the period just after sunset almost everyone in Modjokuto is at home, people are usually aware—although no one may have actually said anything about it—that a *slametan* is about to be given a good while before it actually occurs and so expect the messenger, and the Javanese has a kind of punctuate sense of time which makes it easy for him to shift sharply from one kind of activity to another with very little transition.

Upon arrival each guest takes a place on the floor mats, squatting in the formal Javanese sitting posture called *sila* (with legs folded inward and crossed in front of the body and with the trunk ramrod stiff). The room slowly fills with the odor of the burning incense, and there is a little subdued small talk as people drift in and seat themselves (there is no special order) in a large circle around the food, which has already been placed in the center. When all have arrived and the circle is complete, the ceremony begins.

The host opens the ceremony with a speech in very formal high-Javanese. First, he expresses his profound gratitude for his neighbors' attendance. He regards them, he says, as witnesses to the purity and the nature of his intentions and to the fact that he is holding the required rite in order to realize these excellent intentions, and he hopes they will share in any benefit the ceremony brings. Second, he states these intentions: he presents the specific reason for the *slametan*—his daughter is seven months pregnant, it is the

Prophet's birthday, or whatever. Next, he gives the general reason for the rite. This is always the same: to secure for himself, his family, and his guests that peculiarly negative state of bodily and mental equanimity the Javanese call *slamet,* from which the ritual takes its name. To this end he petitions the spirits of the village, young and old, male and female. Lastly he begs pardon for any errors he may have made in his speech or anything he may have said which disturbed anyone, and for the inadequacy of the food he is serving. Through the whole speech he speaks in an even, rhythmic, mechanical cadence, and at each pause the audience responds with a solemn *"inggih"*—"yes."

When the host has completed the *udjub,* as this formal introductory speech is called, he asks someone present to give the Arabic chant-prayer. Actually, most of those assembled do not know how to chant, but the host always makes certain that someone who does is present. On a special occasion he may even invite the *modin,* the official village religious specialist, to give the prayer, but usually he will just invite a friend who he knows has attended a religious school for a period and can chant short Arabic prayers (whose meaning, however, he is almost never able to understand). Fragments from the Koran, most often the *Alfatékah,* the short prayer which precedes the Koran proper, are usually used, although some people may know special prayers. The prayer leader recites the prayer or Koranic passage while the other guests sit with their palms turned upward toward the sky and their faces lifted as though awaiting a gift from God; or, alternatively, they stare down into their palms and may even bury their faces in them. At each pause in the leader's chant they utter *"amin"* (amen), and when he is finished they rub the palms of their hands on their faces as though they were attempting to wake themselves from a sleep. For his trouble the prayer leader receives a small token payment called the *wadjib.*

The preliminaries completed, the singsong cadence of the Arabic chant having been balanced against the regular, mechanical rhythms of the Javanese speech, the serving of the food begins. Each participant (except the host, who does not eat) receives a cup of tea and a banana-leaf dish into which is put a sample of each sort of food from the center of the floor. The fare is much better than average: usually there are several kinds of meat, chicken, or fish, plus variously colored or molded rice or rice porridge, each variety with a meaning which the participants may or may not remember. (In giving the *udjub* the host often tells what each food means as part of his declaration of intentions.) The food is not served by the host but by one or two of the guests, who hop into the middle of the circle and fill the various dishes. When everyone has his filled dish, the host bids them eat. They scoop the rice and meat up with their fingers, eating hurriedly and quietly—for it is believed to be bad luck to talk while eating. After about a half-dozen scoopfuls or about five minutes, they one by one stop eating, and when all have stopped they ask permission to "follow my own will" (*nuwun sakersa*) and, receiving it, depart for home, crouching so as not to tower over the seated host, about ten or fifteen minutes after they have come. Most of their food remains uneaten. It is taken home, wrapped in the banana-leaf dishes, to be eaten in the privacy of their houses in company with their wives and children. With their departure, the *slametan* ends.

The Meaning of the *Slametan*

THIS, then, is the basic core ritual in that part of Modjokuto society in which the *abangan* world-view is most prominent. On some occasions, beginning a journey, for example, it may comprise the entire ceremony; on others, such as a wedding, it may be so brief and covered over by other and more elaborate kinds of ritual and ceremonial behavior that if you do not watch closely you will miss it altogether; and on yet others—death, for example—the exigencies of the situation may demand that whole parts be dropped out. Since all, or nearly all, *abangan* ceremonies are, nevertheless, in one sense variations on this underlying ritual theme, an understanding of the meaning of the *slametan* to those who give them brings with it an understanding of much of the *abangan* world-view and provides a key to the interpretation of their more complex ceremonies.

Why do Javanese hold *slametans?* When I asked this question of an old bricklayer, he gave two reasons: "When you give a *slametan,* nobody feels any different from anyone else and so they don't want to split up. Also a *slametan* protects you against the spirits, so they will not upset you." This tendency to state the implications of social behavior in psychological terms, according to its ultimate effect on the individual's emotional equilibrium, and to state those implications negatively, is characteristic. At a *slametan* everyone is treated the same. The result is that no one feels different from anyone else, no one feels lower than anyone else, and so no one has a wish to split off from the other person. Also, after you have given a *slametan* the local spirits will not bother you, will not make you feel ill, unhappy, or confused. The goals are negative and psychological—absence of aggressive feeling toward others, absence of emotional disturbance. The wished-for state is *slamet,* which the Javanese defines with the phrase "*gak ana apa-apa*"—"there isn't anything," or, more aptly, "nothing is going to happen (to anyone)."

But since something might happen, and almost inevitably does, the *abangan,* aware of this, personifies the possibility of unforeseen bad fortune in terms of spirit beliefs and attempts to deal with the spirits by means of the *slametan.* In Java, said one of my informants with the usual Javanese sense for cultural relativism, the spirits are unusually disturbing: "I don't know how it is in America, but here they are always upsetting one." The reason for this, no doubt, is that there are more of them in Java—all around the house (especially the toilet), at every unusual point in the landscape, around cemeteries, at old Hindu ruins; and the woods are full of them. Thus the incense and the aroma of the food at the *slametan* are considered as food for the spirits in order to pacify them so they will not disturb the living. As a Javanese put it:

At a *slametan* all kinds of invisible beings come and sit with us and they also eat the food. That is why the food and not the prayer is the heart of the *slametan*. The spirit eats the aroma of the food. It's like this banana. I smell it but it doesn't disappear. That is why the food is left for us after the spirit has already eaten it.*

* This passage and others similarly employed without source reference throughout the text are transcriptions from the author's field notes.

Chapter 2   Spirit Beliefs

A YOUNG carpenter, rather more systematic about such things than Javanese generally are, told me that there were three main kinds of spirits: *memedi* (literally, frighteners), *lelembut* (literally, ethereal ones), and *tujul*.

Memedis merely upset people or scare them, but they do not usually do serious damage. Male *memedis* are called *gendruwo* and female ones *wéwé* (married to the *gendruwos,* they are always seen carrying small children on their hips in shawls, just like human mothers). *Memedis* are usually encountered at night in especially dark or lonely places. Often they will take the form of parents or other relatives, dead or alive—sometimes, even, of one's own children. The carpenter remembered that a few years ago there was a little boy lost in the neighborhood. They looked high and low for him for a whole week. When they finally found him he was hiding under the back of the house and was too frightened to talk because he had seen a *gendruwo* which had taken the form of his father. Evidently his "father" had been sitting up in the top of a tree and had urinated on the boy. Actually, said the carpenter, he need not have been so frightened; these spirits are largely harmless and merely like to scare you.

Lelembuts, in contrast to *memedis,* can make one ill or drive one crazy. The *lelembuts* enter the individual's body, and if one is not treated by a native Javanese curer (called a *dukun*) one will die. Western doctors can't do anything for madness or sickness caused by *lelembuts;* only *dukuns* can. A *dukun* can often tell where *lelembuts* have gone into the body and pull them out by massaging just that place—for example, the foot, or the arm, or the small of the back. Since *lelembuts* are not visible at all, they do not assume the appearance of relatives, but they are very dangerous to human beings.

Lastly, the *tujuls* are spirit children, "children who are not human beings." The carpenter pointed to two three-year-old children standing there listening to our conversation and said: "*Tujuls* look just like these kids, only they

16

aren't human but are spirit children." They don't upset and frighten people or make them sick; quite the contrary, they are very much liked by human beings, for they help them become rich. If one wants to communicate with them, he must fast and meditate and then after a while he will be able to see them and to employ them for his own uses. If one wants to get rich, he sends them out to steal money. They make themselves invisible and travel great distances in a short time and so have no difficulty finding money for one.

Another kind of *tujul* is called a *mentèk*. These are also small children, and they wear no clothes; some people say they are the *tujuls'* cousins. *Menteks* live in the rice fields. "Suppose," said the carpenter, "you and I have rice fields. I have a *mentèk,* which I got through fasting and meditation. I send him to take the grains out of your rice and put them in mine. Then later when the harvest comes your stalks are empty and mine are full and doubly fat.* Of course, this is not a nice thing to do. Later, after I died, I would have to face God and be punished for this. But while you're living it's nice to have a *tujul* of your own."

There is no doctrine in these matters. The carpenter's views are his own, and, although they are roughly typical, the details about spirits vary from individual to individual. There is much discussion and dispute about the spirit world, and, while there is general agreement on the reality and importance of supernatural beings (called, as a class, *bangsa alus*), each individual seems to have some ideas of his own as to their exact nature and some personal experiences to prove it. *Abangan* spirit beliefs in Modjokuto are not part of a consistent, systematic, and integrated scheme, but are rather a set of concrete, specific, rather sharply defined discrete images—unconnected visual metaphors giving form to vague and otherwise incomprehensible experiences.

Memedis: Frightening Spirits

Memedis are the most easily understandable of Javanese spirits for Westerners, because they are almost exactly equivalent to our "spooks." In fact, some show signs of having been borrowed from European sources: the *djrangkong,* who is a man "with his flesh off," i.e., a skeleton; or the *wedon,* a spiritual being covered with a white sheet like our ghosts. The *memedi* who kept adding salt to an informant's food for three months, the disembodied pair of hands at which the same man threw a plate of hot peppers, and the ghost whose shadow remained on the wall even after the light had been turned off may also owe something to our cultural tradition. But others have a distinctly Indonesian flavor: the *panaspati,* whose head is where his genitals should be and who walks on his hands, breathing fire; the *djims,* the more Islamic spirits who pray five times a day, wear prayer robes, and chant in Arabic; the *pisatjis* ("wanderers"), small children without parents or fixed abode who are con-

---

* Properly speaking, *mentèk* is the name of a rice disease.

sequently always on the lookout for human beings to live in; the *uwils,* who are only rarely encountered nowadays but who are said to be former Buddhist soldiers; the *sétan gundul* ("bald devils"), who have all their hair shaved off except for a *kutjung,* the specially cut "topknot" that small boys used to wear in the old days, a custom now almost wholly abandoned.

One of the best-defined and generally agreed upon variety of spirits is the *sundel bolong*—"prostitute with a hole in her." A *sundel bolong* is a beautiful naked woman, but her loveliness is marred by the fact that she has a large hole through the middle of her back. She has long black hair which hangs down over her buttocks and so conceals the hole. Opinions seem to differ as to whether or not she is attractive to men. Some say that when a man sees her he is immediately frightened and runs away. Others say that on the contrary she is very attractive and usually asks the man to go off with her, an offer very difficult to reject. If he goes, however, she castrates him.

Gendruwos, the commonest type of *memedi,* are generally more playful than harmful and enjoy playing practical jokes on people, such as prodding women in the buttocks (especially when they are praying), removing a person's clothes from the house and throwing them into the river, tossing rocks onto the roof all through the night, jumping out big and black from behind a tree near the cemetery, and so forth. When Pak Paidin fell off the bridge on which he was working, he knew a *gendruwo* had pushed him, for after he landed in the water the spirit pinned his arms behind him and spoke to him (in classical literary Javanese; *gendruwos* always speak archaically, said Paidin), asking solicitously if he was all right. Evidently the spirit had no evil intentions.

But *gendruwos,* fun-loving as they may be, are not always harmless. Often they will appear in the form of a parent, grandfather, child, or sibling and say, "Hey, come along with me." If one obeys, he will then become invisible. Then the real relatives, missing the victim and suspecting what has happened, will go about beating on hoes, sickles, pots, and so forth, making as much noise as they can. The *gendruwo,* upset by all this racket, will then offer the victim some food. If he eats it, he will remain invisible; if he refuses it, he will become visible again and his relatives will be able to find him. One day, in the neighborhood across the street from my house, a boy was missing and it was thought he had been snatched by a *gendruwo,* and so the people went around making a terrible racket. It turned out finally, however, that he had hitched a ride into a nearby town and had not been spiritually kidnapped at all.

Sometimes the *gendruwos* will take even more serious liberties. They will adopt the form of a woman's husband and sleep with her, she being none the wiser. Then there will be children of these unions who will be monsters. There was one in Modjokuto—a large, black, and curiously misshapen child who lived to be sixteen and then died. All in all, *gendruwos,* despite their generally pleasant dispositions, are not to be trifled with, and one should not even talk about them—although everyone does—for they may overhear and become annoyed. No one, child or adult, in the household with which my wife and I lived would dare go to the toilet alone after sundown for fear of *gendruwos.*

Lelembuts: Possessing Spirits

WHAT the carpenter called *lelembuts* (but others might as easily claim are *gendruwos, sétans, ḍemits,* or *djims*), the kind of spirits which enter and possess one, are a rather more serious affair, for an encounter with them may end in sickness, insanity, or death. The kind of complex difficulties one can get into in dealing with this sort of spirit is exemplified by an experience of the family with whom I boarded. A few years before I arrived, they attempted to chop down a clump of bamboos in the back yard of their house. They were aware that some *lelembuts* lived in the bamboos, but Pak Ardjo, the head of the household, sprinkled some salt on them the night before and recited a short spell, hoping that would take care of the matter. The men hired to cut the trees were forewarned and extremely careful, but, unknown to them, one of the trees fell on an invisible earthenware pot owned by one of the spirits and broke it. Some of the spirits who were living there and who were *santris* (Moslems) had a big prayer house to say their prayers in; and the earthenware pot was one of those large pots the *santris* use to wash their feet and hands in before they pray.* The breaking of their pot made the *santri* spirits very angry, and they gave one of the workmen a crack on the back of the head. He felt the blow and immediately went home, but by the time he arrived there he was crazy, raving on and on in a meaningless manner. That night he had a dream in which he met the village spirit of a nearby village who told him that a group of young men were coming after him, but, if he ducked through the legs of the village spirit toward the north, the young men, who were really the *lelembuts,* going south, would miss him. He did, and they did, and the next day he was well.

Javanese theory of possession is rather highly developed. *Lelembuts,* say some, always enter the body from underneath through the feet. (That is why people wash their feet before praying in the mosque, one man told me. It is also why it is better to heat one's feet over the stove before visiting a woman with a newborn child, because infants are particularly liable to a kind of spirit seizure called *sawanen.*) Others, probably the larger group, hold that

---

* This ascription of religious and social differentiation to the spirits is not atypical. One informant, discussing *djims,* said: "There are two kinds: the Islamic, who live in the mosques and *langgars* (prayer houses), and the non-Islamic, who live just anywhere. A *djim* will enter the body of a person if it should happen the body of that person is empty. Emptiness isn't caused by the *djim,* it's just sort of an accident. For instance, if a person is startled, confused, mixed up, and doesn't know where he is, he becomes empty and the *djim* can enter him easily. If an *abangan* person is entered by an Islamic *djim,* he can then chant even though before he couldn't. But *abangan djims* don't enter *santris;* they don't dare. . . . There are many Islamic *djims* in Mecca, and some *hadjis* (pilgrims to the Holy City) bring them back with them to help them get rich. This is why *hadjis* are the richest people in the whole world."

spirits always enter through the head. That is why a baby's fontanel must be kept covered with a mixture of onions, hot peppers, and mashed coconut (the "hot" food "startles" the spirit, who is thus frightened off), and why people who are feeling slightly indisposed rub lime on their foreheads.

A mere faint, lasting less than ten minutes, is not usually considered to be a possession. A rub on the face with a sarong of the victim's mother will usually suffice to bring the victim around. For seizures lasting longer, one elderly man, a hospital worker and my best informant on these matters, classified the varieties of possession into six types. Others might list fifteen, or, more likely, lump them all into one complex and ill-defined category.

His first type was *kesurupan,* which is derived from a root which means "to come in," "to enter (something)," but also has the secondary meaning "sunset." This, perhaps, reflects the belief that the period during which the sun is setting is an especially dangerous one so far as the spirits are concerned, for, like the Javanese themselves, the spirits are all out wandering about and visiting their friends at this time and one is likely to run into one in the street. (But twelve noon and twelve midnight are unusually dangerous times too.) *Kesurupan* is the common or garden variety of possession and accounts for the great majority of cases. A *dukun* (curer) is called (or, failing that, an old man, such as the informant himself, who knows about these matters) and addresses the stricken one: "What is your name? Where is your home? Why have you come here? What do you want?" These questions are addressed to the inhabiting spirit, who answers through the mouth of the possessed: "My name is Kijaji Bendok. My home is on the bridge in front of the market. I came here to eat and drink." The spirit involved here is a *santri,* because *kijaji* is the title given to Koran scholars and teachers, men comparable to the Mid-Eastern *ulama.* But the *lelembut* could as likely be an *abangan,* in which case he might be called Sapu Djagad (sweeper of the world), or a *prijaji,* with a name like Radèn Baku Sentot, *radèn* being a Javanese court title. These are all well-known *lelembut* names. Having heard the spirit, the *dukun* will reply: "I will give you something to eat and drink, but when you are finished eating and drinking you must quickly go home again." According to Javanese ideas, said the informant, the *lelembuts* drink liquor, rice wine usually, and eat incense. When he is through, the spirit will say out of his victim's mouth: "All right, I'll go home now." Then the victim will shake three times or so rather violently, will go suddenly weak, and faint. When he recovers, he will remember nothing of what has gone on.

The second type, *kampir-kampiran,* means literally "to take a flying visit to someone," "to come from a long distance and stop in briefly at a friend's while on the way somewhere else." Thus *kampir-kampiran* as a possession is the same as *kesurupan* except that the spirit is not from a local bridge or bamboo clump but is, say, a spirit from the Indian Ocean on his way to a large volcano to the east of Modjokuto who just happened to bump into the victim on the street. *Kampel-kampelan* is also similar except that the victim is not so obviously sick. He walks around and behaves more or less as usual, but acts rather oddly at times. For example, if Parto (the informant) comes back from the Hindu ruins just to the north of Modjokuto and begins to hit his little boy, something he never otherwise does, his wife will say to him. "You must have been entered by a spirit at the ruins." This kind of possession is mild, and usually a good bath will cure it.

Sétanan is like *kampel-kampelan* except more serious. One is still walking around and not severely ill, but it takes a *dukun* to get the spirit out of him. The *dukun* will discover where one got the *sétan* and tell him to make certain kinds of offerings in order to be rid of it. The offering (*ulih-ulih* or *sadjèn*) usually consists of flowers, incense, perhaps certain kinds of leaves. The *sétan* eats this and leaves his victims in peace. *Kedjiman* is the same except that, whereas the *sétans* are Javanese and *abangan, djims* are Arabs and *santri*. These can stay a very long time. The man who has them is not sick, but is odd and behaves curiously. For example, he may eat an extraordinary lot, or, on the contrary, go very long without eating. His senses may be abnormally sharp and he may think a lot, often with greater cleverness than usual.

Kemomong, the last type, is a kind of voluntary devil's pact. A man, usually someone who does not believe in God, becomes friends with a *sétan* —such as the one on the market bridge mentioned above—and the *sétan* enters him, a voluntary partnership on both sides. The man then becomes half crazy but may develop certain powers, say of curing, which he evidently feels are worth the cost; or he may merely do it for the experience of it, much as Brataséna, the shadow-play hero, once died on purpose merely because he had never been dead and wanted to see what it felt like.

Tujuls: Familiar Spirits

Tujuls are another matter. Although some people say they can be gotten just by fasting and meditation, and others argue that you need not do even that ("It all depends on the *tujul;* if he wants to help you he will, if he doesn't he won't, no matter what you do"), most people think one has to make a kind of devil's pact to get a *tujul* to do one's bidding. The three people in the town of Modjokuto most universally held to be in possession of a *tujul*—a wealthy butcher, a very *nouveau riche* woman textile trader who prospered rather suddenly during the Japanese occupation, and an old-line *hadji* businessman who had been quite rich in the years before the war but who had not prospered since—were all said to have made such a pact. Each of them journeyed to various Hindu ruins lying in a great circle around Modjokuto, one in each of the directions: Borobodur to the west, Penataran to the south, Bongkeng to the east, and the grave of Sunan Giri, a Javanese culture hero, near Gresik to the north. At each of these ruins they swore an oath that if the spirit would give them a *tujul* they would deliver a magically killed human sacrifice for the spirit of the ruins each year—either a close relative or a friend. Later, it was generally agreed, these sorcery-practicing *tujul*-owners would have a very slow and difficult death: their breath would come shorter and shorter, they would have continued pain and a prolonged high fever, and would have a tortuously slow time leaving the world.

Dying by inches is perhaps a small enough price to pay, because once one has a *tujul* the money flows in. The *tujuls* are able to steal with no chance of detection; and all one needs do for them in return is to give them a place to sleep and to put out for them each evening a little rice mush, which, since they are children (they are said to skip and hop in little circles when walking, as tiny children will), is their natural food. In town the *tujuls* steal money— the butcher's *tujul* was vigorously accused (out of his hearing, of course) of stealing money from the women traders in the small market in our neighborhood at least once during my stay, but in the villages they are more likely to steal rice. One quite common rice thief of this sort is called *gebleg* because, though it is in the form of a chicken, it shuffles its feet heavily when it walks (making the sound *bleg-bleg-bleg*). It stuffs the rice up under its wings and walks back to its owner; then it flaps its wings, and the rice falls out into the owner's granary.

People who are accused of having *tujuls* fit quite easily into a single social type. They are always rich, often having become so quite suddenly, and, usually but not always, they are misers; they wear old clothes, bathe in the river with the poverty-stricken coolies, and eat corn and cassava—a poor man's dish—rather than rice, while all the time (it is said) their house is full of gold bars. Also, they often seem to be deviant socially. They talk loudly, are aggressive, lack manners, are sloppy dressers, and have a quite un-Javanese habit of blurting out to people just what is on their minds. The woman trader is of this sort. Before the war, said an informant (male), she was calm and withdrawn like Javanese women usually, but then all of a sudden she got rich, and now she is like a wild animal.

One of the most famous *tujul* owners in the Modjokuto area is an old *hadji* who lives in a village a few miles to the east of town. The richest man out that way, he is also the most miserly. He acquired his *tujuls* through the usual pact—promising to deliver four dead people to the spirits each year. He seeks his victims everywhere; he even looked for them in Mecca. The odd thing is that, although he has been doing this for years, it was only discovered in 1951 by another man—something of a dealer in the occult himself—who developed countermagic against the *hadji*. He gathered together thirty-three students and taught them special magical techniques for defeating *tujuls*. One Friday midnight the students attacked the *tujuls* of the *hadji,* but the latter called in reinforcements from among the spirits at the various ruins. The attacking students wore black spectacles in order to see the spirits and used flashlights as weapons, for where there is light there can be no spirits of any kind. The *tujuls* threw a *tjakra* (a magical ring-shaped weapon, used by Krishna in the Mahabharata) at the students but did not kill them, and, although the struggle was hard, the four victims were not taken. Now, it is said, every Friday midnight this struggle continues. People who see the students fighting think that they are mad because they strike the empty air. The first battle took place in the *hadji*'s front yard, but now the war seems to move about from place to place.

Demits: Place Spirits

THERE are numerous versions of the Javanese creation myth, *Babad Tanah Djawi.** In the one related to me by a shadow-play puppeteer in the village just to the north of Modjokuto the story opens with Semar, the wonderfully comic and wise shadow-play clown and the greatest of Javanese culture heroes, speaking with a powerful Hindu-Moslem priest, the first of Java's long line of colonizers. The priest asks Semar: "Tell me the story of Java in the times before there were any men." Semar replies that in those days the whole island was covered with primeval forest except for the small patch of rice fields he himself cultivated at the foot of Mount Merbabu (a volcano in Central Java), where he lived peacefully tilling the soil for ten thousand years. "What are you?" asked the startled priest. "Are you a man? Your age is tremendous! I never knew a man ten thousand years old before! It is not possible! You can't be a man. Even the Prophet Adam only lived one thousand years! What kind of being are you? Confess the truth!"

"In truth," says Semar, "I am not a man, I am the guardian spirit—the ḍanjang—of Java. I am the oldest spirit of Java, and I am the king and ancestor of all spirits, and through them of all men. But," he continues in a changed tone, "I have also a question to ask you. Why are you ruining my country? Why have you come here and driven my children and grandchildren out? The spirits, overcome by your greater spiritual power and religious learning, are slowly being forced to flee into the craters of the volcanoes or to the depths of the Southern Sea. Why are you doing this?" And the priest replies: "I have been ordered by the king of Rome ['An Arab country west of India,' explained the puppeteer] to fill this island with human beings. I am to clear the forest for rice fields, to set up villages, and to settle twenty thousand families here as colonists. This is the will of my king, and you cannot stop it. But those of the spirits who will protect us may continue to live in Java; I will tell you what you must do." He then proceeds to outline the entire prospective history of Java down to modern times and describes Semar's own role in the process, which is to be a spiritual advisor and magical supporter of all the kings and princes to come—that is, to continue to be Java's chief ḍanjang.

Thus, in this version at least, what the Javanese have in *Babad Tanah Djawi* ("the clearing of Java") is not so much a creation myth as what might be called a colonization myth, which, considering Java's history of successive "invasions" of Hindus, Moslems, and Europeans, is not surprising. To

---

* There is extant a written semi-historical legend entitled *Babad Tanah Djawi* composed at the beginning of the seventeenth century in the court of the Mataram kingdom of Central Java, evidently to legitimize Mataram's ruling dynasty. A myth of the same name is still recounted orally in the countryside, but the versions of it are not always in very close concordance with the written *Babad Tanah Djawi*.

mbabad is to clear a tract of wilderness and turn it into a village complete with surrounding rice fields, to create a small island of human settlement amid a great sea of forest-dwelling spirits, although nowadays it is also used for the general preparation (plowing, raking, and so on) of a rice field which one must do at the beginning of the rice-growing cycle each year. The picture the myth presents is one of an incoming flow of migrants pushing back the harmful spirits into the mountains, uncultivated wild places, and the Indian Ocean as they move from the north coast to the south, all the while adopting some of the more helpful ones as protectors of themselves and their new settlements.

The usual name for a spirit with a fixed abode who may support the wishes of men is *demit,* although here again people are not consistent but tend to use such words as *demit, danjang, lelembut,* and *sétan* in both a wide and narrow sense, to indicate spirits in general and to indicate certain fairly definite subtypes of them in particular. *Demits* in the narrow sense live in holy places called *pundèns,** which may be marked by a small Hindu ruin (perhaps one little broken statue), a large banyan tree, an old grave, a nearly hidden spring, or some such topographical peculiarity.

There are a number of such *pundèns* in the Modjokuto area at various oversized or misshapen trees or at the various Hindu temple ruins scattered around, but by far the most famous, most often worshipped, and reputedly the most powerful is one in the dead center of the town of Modjokuto, at the edge of the public square (*alun-alun*). His name is *mBah Buda,* literally "Grandfather Buddha," but the "Buddha" does not refer to Gautama, but merely to the fact that the shrine where he lives is marked with a Hindu-Buddhist relic.

The shrine, enclosed by a solid white fence, lies at the foot of a massive banyan tree and consists of a small foot-high stone statue of Ganesha, the Hindu elephant-god of wisdom; and there is a story that goes with it. A long time ago, "in the Buddhist time," the Sultan of Solo, the great court city of Central Java, was warring with the King of Madura. The Sultan of Solo was winning, and he pursued the fleeing Madurese king north and east toward the latter's homeland. En route he stopped at Modjokuto, then still an unsettled forest lying between the two kingdoms, to rest his troops. Thus the town which is here called Modjokuto got both its name—for its actual name is said to derive from an Old-Javanese word meaning "resting place"—and its shrine—for the king left the Ganesha to mark the place under the great banyan tree where he rested. Whatever its origin, however, the Ganesha is now certainly occupied by a *demit.* Once when it was taken to Bragang, some fifteen miles away, it returned under its own power. On another occasion a Dutch controleur (the lowest-ranking European official in the colonial bureaucracy) stationed in Modjokuto who kicked the Ganesha—evidently to show his disdain for the devices of the heathen—died within a week of a broken neck, and within the year his whole family followed him to the grave.

---

* Strictly speaking, a *pundèn* is anything toward which one offers reverence for *pundi,* the root, means to praise or offer reverence. Thus a magical dagger or a grave of a hero may be a *pundèn.* Some of the *pundèns* in the Modjokuto area were such (mythical) burial places of heroes from the Hindu-Javanese times.

If one wants *mBah Buda* to do something for him, he must go to the shrine —though some say one can do this part at home—and beg pardon and forgiveness from the *ḍemit* and promise to give a *slametan* in the *ḍemit's* honor if his request is fulfilled. What is crucial for success is to want one's wish badly enough, to want it with an unmovable and single mind and think of nothing else until it is granted. One petitioner compared it to crying for something as a child does: "You don't cry outside, but inside, within your heart; you have to want it so much that you'll die if you don't get it; and if you do want it badly enough and keep at it long enough you will most certainly get it." What one usually wants is restored health either for oneself or close relatives, or perhaps to find a lost object or to insure someone's safety on a long trip. There is a difference of opinion as to whether one can wish for such things as success at cards, a new gong for one's *gamelan* orchestra, or the love of another man's wife, some people holding that *mBah Buda* responds only to "serious" requests; but it is clear that people ask for some rather unexalted blessings on occasion:

> In connection with this [a discussion of divorce] Sutinah [the informant] told me about a time when she gave a *slametan* to *mBah Buda* when her older sister was still married to her second husband, and she said to the sister: "If you get a divorce and there isn't too much trouble connected with it and everything is smooth and easy, then I'll give a *slametan* to *mBah Buda*." Later, after the divorce, she gave the *slametan* and sent some of it [the food] to her sister too, with a note saying, this is the *slametan* for you-know-what.

The *slametan* one gives the *ḍemit* after one has gained his wish (should one forget to do so, a black snake with white arrow marks on his back will crawl between one's legs and remind him) should be given on a special day— the day on which Friday of the Western seven-day week coincides with *Legi* of the Javanese five-day market week, a coincidence which occurs every thirty-five days.

The *slametan* is a simple one of rice, a little chicken or fish, soybean-cake, and so on, plus some flowers. One can either take it to the shrine oneself or send a child with it, and most people do the latter. At the shrine the child gives the food to the caretaker, telling him what the offering is for—what the "intention" is. The caretaker takes the food, burns incense, and spreads the flowers on the Ganesha's head. Next he gathers up some of the old flowers others have brought and makes them up into a little packet which he gives to the child. This is taken home and mixed with water, and the person who gave the *slametan* either drinks it or uses it as a salve for purposes of general welfare or over-all *slamet*. People who find it awkward to cook up the rice can buy the flowers in the market for an Indonesian quarter and give one rupiah to the caretaker for the rice. The food is given out to the poor who crowd around the shrine waiting for it (anyone who is "brave" enough to ask for it, the caretaker said), but every time I watched this ritual it seemed that the caretaker, admittedly not very well-off himself, got the lion's share of the food, which was considerable. On a good day I have seen over fifty people, some of them from twenty miles away, giving a *slametan* to *mBah Buda*.

Ḍanjangs: Guardian Spirits

Ḍanjang is commonly but another name for ḍemit (jang is a Javanese root meaning "spirit"). Like ḍemits, ḍanjangs live in special places called pundèns; like ḍemits, they respond to people's pleas for help and receive vowed slametans in return; and like ḍemits, they never harm people but seek only to protect them. Unlike ḍemits, however, some ḍanjangs are considered to be spirits of actual historic figures now deceased: the founders of the village to which they are attached, the men who were the first to mbabad (i.e., clear) the land. Each village usually has one major ḍanjang.* This ḍanjang désa, when still a man, came to the village when it was but wilderness, cleared it, and distributed the land to his followers, family, and friends, becoming the first village headman (lurah). When he died he was buried, usually near the center of the village, and his grave thereupon became a pundèn, and he continues to watch over his village's welfare. (Sometimes, however, there is no specific grave for the founding ḍanjang.) Certain people may still regard themselves as his descendants, and he is said to determine magically who shall be village chief by controlling the movements of a special kind of political spirit called a pulung (most people say he actually is the pulung):

He said that there was a kind of "spiritual stuff" called a pulung which, visible and shaped like a moon, descends on the chosen candidate for village chief. Only village chiefs and the king of the entire country have pulungs (the latter's being much larger), which shows that the position of a lurah is more important than that of a bupati or wedono [heads of a regency and a district, respectively]. When one lurah dies or goes out of office, his pulung leaves him and searches for the new lurah. (It sometimes momentarily goes abroad and is visible while he is in office when something special is up or the village is in danger.) The candidates often sit in the village square, and the pulung hovers over them choosing the one that is most pure. Lurah candidates sometimes give a slametan at the ḍanjang's grave in order to attract the pulung. There is one pulung for every village. It stays with the lurah until he dies or no longer acts nobly. In the latter case it leaves him, his village becomes sick, famished, disorderly; people will no longer obey the chief. Soon he is forced to resign, and the man to whom the pulung has gone becomes the lurah. I asked him what had happened to the pulung that used to go to the king, and he said he thought it had gone to Djakarta and that Bung Karno [the President of the Republic] had the king's pulung now.

The area over which the ḍanjang désa has power is called the kumaran. Kumara (or kemara) means a voice out of the blue, a voice coming out of nothing, as when two weeks after a famous ḍukun has died one will suddenly

* Sometimes the ḍanjang is considered to be merely a vague protective spirit, resident in a larger tree or some other natural phenomenon, who was a guardian of the area before human beings arrived, and is distinguished from the founder of the village, who is called the tjikal-bakal. Usually, however, the two are merged and the term ḍanjang désa ("village ḍanjang") is used to refer to a single founder-guardian spirit. There may, however, be secondary ḍanjangs (or ḍemits) in the village besides the main one.

hear his voice without any visible source for it. Thus the *kumaran* includes all the space above the village from which one could hear the sound of a human voice speaking on the ground. In addition, the four corners of the village are sometimes held to be occupied by protective spirits, also often called *ḍanjang* and conceived of as spirit sons of the main *ḍanjang,* who finds his permanent home in the center of the village.

In the town of Modjokuto itself, the *ḍanjang désa* is a thief, Maling Kandari, buried in the old cemetery to the east of the center of town. But, in line with the general decadence of village political structure in the urban setting, he does not play a very important role in the minds of most townsmen. Only a few older, lower-class people seem to know much about him, and then only that he gained his control over the town area through trickery, deceit, and traffic with evil spirits.

In the villages, interest in the *ḍanjang désa* is greater. For example, in Sumbersari, the village immediately to the north of Modjokuto, the name of the *ḍanjang* is mBah Nur Wakit. Nur Wakit came to Sumbersari from the west, from Djogjakarta in Central Java. The King of Bragang, who was then ruling the area (in the story; actually the last King of Bragang had died three hundred years before Sumbersari was founded), granted him the uncleared land. He placed his wife in the dead center of the area he had been granted, protected her only by a thin fence of banana leaves, and instructed her that no matter what occurred she was not to move a muscle but to sit unmoved where he had placed her. He then ran around the entire village to determine its borders. A great typhoon blew up and the rain came in torrents; all the trees fell down and the land was cleared without anyone's lifting an axe. Nur Wakit's wife, seated immobile while trees fell all about her, was unharmed.

Nur Wakit, in addition to being the first *lurah,* was also a *kijaji,* an Islamic religious scholar and teacher. After a while his teaching duties grew so great that he turned the job of *lurah* over to his son, but when the latter drafted some of Nur Wakit's students to work his own land for him, Nur Wakit cursed him blind. Although by birth Nur Wakit was a *radèn mas*—that is, a noble—he did not like to mix with *prijajis;* he thought them too proud and haughty, which is why he went out to the countryside to live among the common people. Like most ardent *santris,* he disapproved of the *gamelan* (the Javanese percussion orchestra) and the *wajang* (the shadow-play), and during the time he was *lurah, gamelans* were unable to produce any sound in Sumbersari. Even today a man who holds a *wajang* is likely to fall sick or grow poor as a result. Almost all the *lurahs* in Sumbersari have been *santris,* the villagers say (just as in town they were reputed to have all been thieves), and those few who have been *abangans* have lasted only a year or two. That these considerations are not merely theoretical in the minds of people today can be seen from the following note from an *abangan* informant:

> Just two months ago there was [a special ceremony for an only child at which a *wajang* is traditionally given] in Tempel [a village]. . . . There wasn't any *wajang* because *wajangs* aren't allowed in Tempel because the *ḍanjang* is a *santri;* so instead they had a *kentrung* [another kind of entertainment in which a man recites stories]. . . . If you have a *wajang* in Tempel you will get

poor; that is what happened to her father-in-law . . . and to a man named Pak Setro, who had *wajangs* in spite of the prohibition.*

Nur Wakit finally died in 1889 and was buried in the center of the village, at the very spot on which his wife had waited while he cleared the land and where he had later built his religious school. Like any good *ḍanjang,* however, he still guards his village. Every so often he emerges from his grave, taking the form of a pure white tiger, in order to warn the village of an impending epidemic, flood, or other disaster. At these times, one may glimpse him just for a moment, digging like a cat with his front paws at the crossroads. He never attacks anyone, for his purpose is to warn the inhabitants of the approaching trouble; as soon as he is certain he has been seen, he disappears. He digs briefly at each crossroads to make certain someone sees him, and then he goes to the home of the *lurah*—perhaps in a dream—and tells him what kind of magic to make in order to protect the village against the threatened disaster. Satisfied that his village is safe, he returns to his grave.

The Meaning of Spirit Beliefs

Bangsa alus, memedi, gendruwo, lelembut, sétan, djim, ṭujul, ḍemit, ḍanjang —this flood of bald children, white tigers, and foot-shuffling chickens—provide for those who believe in their existence a set of ready-made answers to the questions posed by puzzling experiences, symbolic pictographs of the imagination within whose framework even the anomalous seems inevitable. Has Older Sister Suwarni just recovered from a week of splitting headaches? It is because when she squatted down on the toilet there was a *lelembut* already seated there—in his anger and chagrin he slapped her across the eyes. Has Hadji Abdullah, having lost a brother and a wife within the year, now suddenly gotten rich? The combination of circumstances strongly suggests a *ṭujul.* The spirit world is the social world symbolically transformed: *prijaji* spirits lord it over *abangan* ones, Chinese spirits open stores and exploit the natives, and *santri* spirits spend their time in praying and thinking up ways to make things difficult for unbelievers.

But, despite the confusions, contradictions, and discontinuities of *abangan* spirit beliefs, they present also a wider and more general meaning than the isolated explanations of unhealing wounds, psychological fugues, and improbable bad luck might lead one to expect. They depict the triumph of culture over nature, human and nonhuman. As Javanese culture advances and the heavy tropical forest turns into rice fields and house lands, the spirits retreat to the remaining woods, the volcano cones, and the Indian Ocean (where Lara Kidul, the Queen of the South Sea and perhaps Java's most powerful

---

* In a neighboring village west of Modjokuto the *ḍanjang* is an *abangan* who was particularly fond of drinking gin and smoking opium. In that village a *wajang* brings good luck, and Arabic music, a favorite *santri* amusement, brings misfortune.

single *lelembut,** waits to carry off to the depths of the ocean anyone who is foolhardy enough to wear green near her home). Similarly, as an individual becomes more civilized in the Javanese pattern, he is less likely to be empty, confused, and disoriented, and thus prey to be entered by a spirit:

> Parto said that people who are easy for *sétans* and other such to enter are people who do not believe in God, who never fast, and who don't have any order in their lives; for the souls of these people are said to be empty and thus easy for the *sétans* to enter. People with a very strong belief in God and who "know order" are not easily entered by *sétans, demits,* and other such threats to individual well-being.

In this context the *slametan* represents a reassertion and reinforcement of the general cultural order and its power to hold back the forces of disorder. The *slametan* concentrates, organizes, and summarizes the general *abangan* ideas of order, their "design for living." In a subdued dramatic form, it states the values that animate traditional Javanese peasant culture: the mutual adjustment of interdependent wills, the self-restraint of emotional expression, and the careful regulation of outward behavior. And it is at just those points in Javanese life when the need for the statement of these values is greatest, when the spirits and the nonhuman disorder they represent are most threatening, that the *slametan* tends to occur.

* In the areas along the southern seacoast of Java there is a highly developed cult of Lara Kidul, but in the Modjokuto area her importance is only marginal.

Chapter 3   The *Slametan* Cycles

Slametans FALL into four main types: (1) those centering around the crises of life—birth, circumcision, marriage, and death; (2) those associated with the Moslem ceremonial calendar—the birth of the Prophet, the ending of the Fast, the Day of Sacrifice, and the like; (3) that concerned with the social integration of the village, the *bersih désa* (literally: "the cleansing of the village"— i.e., of evil spirits); and (4) those intermittent *slametans* held at irregular intervals and depending upon unusual occurrences—departing for a long trip, changing one's place of residence, taking a new personal name, illness, sorcery, and so forth.

Before considering these several types in detail, some mention must be made of two factors common to all: first, the underlying principle of timing *slametans* and, second, their economic significance.

Pétungan: The Javanese Numerological System

BIRTH *slametans* are fixed in time by the accident of birth, and death *slametans* by the accident of death; but the Javanese remove both these events from the realm of chance by ascribing them to the will of God, which fixes precisely the span of each man's life. When Brataséna, the *wajang* hero, appears in heaven after having died on purpose in the story mentioned earlier, Batara Guru, king of all the gods, admonishes him for his presumptuousness in dying before the time divinely set for him and sends him packing back into the world of men. Circumcision and marriage ceremonies—as well as residence changes and the like—would seem necessarily to be set by the will of men, but here too the purely adventitious is avoided and a wider ontological order invoked by means of a system of numerological divination called *pétungan* or "counting."

At the base of this often quite involved system lies one of the most fundamental Javanese metaphysical concepts: *tjotjog*. To *tjotjog* means to fit, as a
key does in a lock, as an efficacious medicine does a disease, as a solution does
an arithmetic problem, as a man does to the woman he married (if he doesn't,
they get divorced). If your opinion agrees with mine, we *tjotjog;* if the clothes
I wear are proper for my class standing, they *tjotjog;* if the meaning of my
name fits my character (and if it brings me good luck), it is said to be *tjotjog*.
Tasty food, comfortable surroundings, gratifying outcomes are all *tjotjog*. In
the broadest and most abstract sense two separate items *tjotjog* when their
coincidence forms an aesthetic pattern. It implies a contrapuntal view of the
universe in which what is important is what natural relationship the separate
elements—space, time, and human motivation—have to one another, how
they must be arranged in order to strike a chord and avoid a dissonance.

As in harmony, the ultimately correct relations are fixed, determinate, and
knowable, and so religion, like harmony, is ultimately a science, no matter
how much of an art its actual practice may be. The *pétungan* system provides
a way of stating these relationships and thus of tuning one's own actions to
them, of avoiding the kind of disharmony with the general order of nature
which can only bring misfortune.

Suppose one wishes to change his residence. He can't just up and move;
he must first take into account two important variables: the direction in which
he will be moving and the day on which he wishes to move. The direction is
usually one of the cardinal directions, for Javanese villages and towns tend
to be laid out, as are the individual houses, streets, and rice fields within them
(except on mountain sides where it is not possible), more or less in alignment
with the major compass points. Space is square, and one moves through it
rectangularly: people tell you to move your chair a little to the west or to
pass the peppers to the man on your east. After two hours on a bus winding
along a mountain road, I was requested to exit by the north door. Javanese
dread to be mixed up about directions, and a person confused or dizzy or
slightly off is said to be someone who does not know where north is.

Time, on the other hand, is, as has been mentioned, pulsative: a given
period of time is a result of the coincidence of days in the five- and seven-
day cycles, and, in the more elaborate *pétungan* systems, of these days with
one of the thirty seven-day *wukuh* weeks, one of the twelve Moslem lunar
months, and one of the eight *windu* years. In moving, then, one *tjotjogs* the
direction of movement with numbers attached to the days.

I then asked Ardjo [my landlord] how he had decided what day would be a
good one for us to move in on. He said each day has a number (*neptu*):
Monday 4, Sunday 5, Tuesday 3, Wednesday 7, Thursday 8, Friday 6, Saturday 9; *Legi* 5, *Paing* 9, *Pon* 7, *Wagé* 4, *Kliwon* 8. You add these. Thus we
came on *Saptu-Wagé,* which is 9 for Saturday, plus 4 for *Wagé,* giving 13.
Then, whether this number is good is dependent upon the direction in which
you are moving. We were moving south to north, so it was all right. He finds
out which numbers are good for which directions by consulting records inherited from his parents. He said he had "half memorized" them but still
always checked, for if he made a mistake the troubles which followed would

be his fault. He said that moving is the thing of very first importance for the Javanese, "number one." Not so for the Dutch, though—they don't believe in it. When Ardjo's father was transferred here from Tebing (he was, like Ardjo, a railroad worker), his Dutch superior was transferred too. Ardjo's father figured out the correct day to move but the Dutch boss, being haughty, felt it would be beneath his dignity to go on the same day as his Javanese inferior and so waited for two more days. Ardjo's father told him that that was a bad day to go south and something terrible would happen to him, but the Dutchman said that was just "empty talk," and then six months after he moved he died.

For the more reflective of the *prijajis* these number systems for the days are empirical descriptions of the ultimate order of nature. They are said to have come out of the inner consciousness of some famous mystic and to have been handed down generation to generation, often secretly, from teacher to chosen pupil. But for the *abangans* they tend to be explained once more in terms of a spirit, the so-called *naga dina* or "snake of the day."* Someone moving the wrong way on the wrong day is said to be either bitten by the snake of the day or eaten by him.

There are also snakes of the week, month, and year. For example, here is a chart of the directions permitted by the *naga wulan,* the snake of the Moslem lunar months:

North: Sawal
       Sela
       Besar

West: Redjeb   East: Sura
      Ruwah   Sapar
      Pasa   Mulud

South: Bakdamulud
       Djumadilawal
       Djumadilakir

Thus, in *Sawal, Sela,* and *Besar,* one should move north or go on an important trip in that direction; in *Redjeb, Ruwah,* and *Pasa* one should go west; and so on. One uses *naga wulan* for more serious occasions—a long trip, say, to Djakarta or Surabaja—while *naga dina* are mostly used for movements within the town. *Naga taun,* the snake of the year, is concerned with really momentous journeys, such as trips outside Java.

The *naga dina* are naturally the least powerful and can sometimes be deceived. For example, if one wishes to go south on the wrong day for it, he can start off north, throwing the *naga* off his trail, turn west and then south, circling his destination and finally coming in, apparently correctly, northward. Few people would venture this for the months, however, and even with the

---

* Here too, however, excessively literal interpretations are to be avoided. When I asked an old woman who had told me that I had fallen sick because I had entered Modjokuto originally on the wrong day and so had been "eaten by the snake of the day," what such a snake looked like and how one came into contact with them, she said: "Don't be silly—you can't see Wednesday, can you?"

days it is risky, for the snake may see through your tricks. The father of one of my informants finally died after having been desperately ill with tuberculosis for several years, and the informant attributed his death to his having moved west on the wrong day even though the evasion method had been applied and he had started off to the east. When I protested that his father had been nearly moribund for over a year, he said, "Sure, but he was sick for three years and he didn't die; we moved house and immediately he died."

A rather more complicated system in use by some people in Modjokuto employs a diagram such as this:

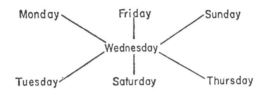

Here we have a somewhat more general system, in that it can tell one whether anything he intends to do is likely to be a good idea or not. First one figures the number of the day on which he is doing the divination—e.g., in the system quoted earlier, by far the most widespread in Modjokuto, *Saptu-Wagé* was 13. So he takes 13 corn kernels and drops them one by one on each day in order (beginning with Monday). When he has run out of all 13, he picks up all the kernels lying on the day on which he has just dropped the last kernel and continues until he comes to rest on another day, and so forth. Eventually he will land with a final kernel on a day on which no kernels remain. This day is the one on which it would be the most unwise to carry out the contemplated action, while the day on which the greatest number of kernels lies when the process has been completed is the most propitious one. Another system merely lists the months and gives the days and dates which are propitious and those which are not: in *Sawal,* Friday is a good day for almost anything, and the second of the month is too; on the ninth and twentieth one is better off sitting at home. One man I knew had a chart with days, months, and *wukuh* weeks all interlaced with various other variables to produce a quite refined predictive instrument.

Systems of this complexity are usually the property of a specialist; the average person will usually go to a *ḍukun* when he wishes to divine something. Before the war, it is claimed, this was even truer than now. Such systems are said to have been very secret then, handed down from teacher to pupil with much care; it is only lately that they have been diffused among the common people. I rather doubt this, but the possession of a *pétungan* system somewhat different from those of one's neighbors and accounted superior to them even today gives one an edge over others in the business of living, and one's private system is often guarded with great care. Such people, who tend often to be curers as well, are consulted about all kinds of personal problems and for just a general prognosis:

Pak Tjipto (a *ḍukun,* one of the best-known curers in Modjokuto) asked me when I was born (the days; he was not interested in the month or year), and so I said *Rebo-Pon* and (my wife) *Djumuwat-Legi* and that we were married on *Saptu-Wagé.* Well, he said, *Rebo* is 7, *Pon* is 7, and that makes 14. *Djumuwat* is 6, *Legi* 5, which makes 11. Eleven plus 14 is 25. *Saptu* is 9. *Wagé* 4 or 13. Thirteen and 25 are 38. Subtract 3 times 10 or 30 and you get 8. Subtract 3 more for 5 and then 3 more giving 2. This is good. If you get 1 or 0 it is not good and people fight and often get divorced. . . . . He said *Djumuwat-Legi,* my wife's birthday, was better than mine, *Rebo-Pon,* so I should follow her decisions and not she mine. If I did things "according to my own will," I would certainly go wrong, and she should be the head in the family.

Pétungan systems are used to decide in which direction to enter a house when one wishes to rob it without being discovered, to pick the side of a cock-ring on which to sit in order to win all one's bets, to predict whether one will succeed or not in trade on a given day, to choose the correct medicine for a disease, to analyze someone's character, to determine the proper day for circumcisions and weddings (usually down to the very hour at which the ceremony ought to occur), and to decide whether a prospective marriage is likely to work out. For this last, the birthday of the bride and groom are added up, almost always by a *ḍukun,* to see if they *tjotjog;* if they do not, the wedding does not occur, at least in traditional circles where this belief is still quite strong. In some cases there may be a conflict when the bride's and groom's families or their *ḍukuns* use different systems, and I know of such a case in which the wedding—after months of argument—did not take place; but usually this sort of problem is avoided by deferment to the system employed by the bride's family. Also, people are not above using *pétungan* as a way out of a difficult situation, as in the case of the woman who told a suitor for her daughter's hand whom she found unacceptable generally that his date was not *tjotjog* when in fact it was.

I know of at least one case in which a couple were finally allowed to marry over the protests of their parents despite incompatible birthdates; and some people just marry and hope for the best, blaming whatever misfortune occurs on the lack of fit. In general, however, even fairly urbanized families often still hold firmly to the system—as can be seen in the following case, where the problem was one of the timing of the wedding ceremony rather than incompatible birthdates:

Rahman told me about his cousin, Mutallip, who was supposed to get married to a girl in Bragang (a small city not far from Modjokuto) last week. He has known this girl for years, and they were school friends, and they have been engaged for nearly three years. The girl already works somewhere, and they have been waiting for Mutallip to get some steady job in Djakarta, where he now lives. . . . He finally found one as a secretary of a former cabinet minister, and this made it possible for him to get married. The date was set by the father-in-law and everything was made ready. The day of the wedding, last Saturday, came and the bridegroom didn't arrive from Djakarta until late in the day. He said after he arrived that he had been going from person to person in Djakarta, the cabinet minister included, to borrow money for his fare here. This excuse was taken as reasonable by his aunt, Bu Merto. But the trouble was that the wedding was set for 11:00 A.M. at the latest and he arrived at 11:15. The father-in-law said that it was too late, the propitious moment had passed, and any wedding after that time would not be right. Mutallip and his father, Pak Rijadi, seemed to think the fifteen minutes or half-hour weren't very important, but the father-in-law was steadfast. Mutallip didn't talk to the father-in-law directly, but just to his father and fiancée. He was quite angry and said that unless they were married this week he would not have the money to come all the way from Djakarta again for a long time, probably a year. This meant marry now or wait a year. The father-in-law didn't give in, and Mutallip went back to Djakarta.

Costs of *Slametans*

THE giving of *slametans,* of course, costs money, but it is difficult to make an estimate of how much, not only because people do not keep records of such expenditures but also because figures giving amounts of money in a foreign currency are often quite meaningless or misleading even if one knows the exchange rate. This is true not merely because the official rate (about 11.3 rupiahs to the dollar in Indonesia) may be unrealistic, but also because even the free rate (about 30 to 1 in 1953) reflects the differences not between the buying power of the two currencies as the average man perceives them but between the wealth of the two countries taken as a whole. Thus, no matter how enlightening it may be for the analysis of world income distribution,. to take the 30 to 1 ratio and say that a man who in Indonesia makes 600 rupiahs a month is comparable to a man making $20 a month in the United States is sociologically preposterous, for the 600-rupiah man is actually moderately well off so far as standard of living within the Javanese context is concerned.

To estimate the economic significance of their religious celebrations from the point of view of the Javanese themselves, in order to give a valid notion to the Western reader of the actual sums of Javanese wealth involved, demands what might be called a comparative phenomenology of currency. One must find a divisor for Indonesian currency which gives a result which reflects, even if only very roughly, some realistic notion of what rupiah notations of wealth mean in terms of buying experience, social status, and relative well-being as we are familiar with them—a divisor which translates Indonesian economic perceptions into American ones, insofar as that is at all possible.

In attempting to find such a divisor it must not be forgotten that the distribution of available wealth within the two countries among the various social groups and classes is quite remarkably different: many fewer people are "moderately well-off" there than here. Moreover, there is a great difference in the over-all total of available wealth, with the result that, for example, because of the lack of large-scale domestic industrial production, many goods accessible to even relatively poor Americans—automobiles, for example—are very much less accessible to even fairly well-off Indonesians.

In this context, then, I think, mainly on the basis of a common-sense comparison of my own experiences in the United States and in Modjokuto, that a divisor of three is a realistic one. Thus the man who earns 600 rupiahs can be compared to a man who earns $200 here in general terms of the view both he himself and others around him hold of his economic and social position; and a soft drink that sells for 30 cents in Indonesia could probably be had for a dime in the United States. Therefore, when I say a fairly simple *slametan* in Modjokuto will cost about 30 rupiahs, it would be highly incorrect to conclude that this is comparable in any phenomenological sense to an expenditure of one dollar in the United States; ten dollars would give more of the feel of the thing.

Preliminaries completed, the following gives some figures on the cost of different *slametans* actually given while I was in Modjokuto (figures marked with an asterisk are estimates):

Type of Slametan	Cost (Rp)
"Dream" *slametan* (urban laborer; as it was the end of the month, no rice included)	3
Megengan (policeman)	5
Name-changing	15
Pasaran for baby (policeman)	20
Moving	30
Megengan	40
Maleman	75
Moving	90
Maleman (policeman)	100*
Tingkeban (a wholly rural peasant; includes two goats at Rp 160; the return from *buwuhs* was Rp 250)	600*
Wedding (urban laborer; *buwuhs* totaled Rp 1,000*)	700*
Funeral (mediumly well-off town family)	1,345*
Wedding (railroad conductor)	1,500*
Circumcision (urban laborer)	1,500*
Wedding (very well-to-do) (The *tajuban*—in which the participants contribute money before each turn with the dancer and the gin glass—at this wedding brought in Rp 1,475. In addition there were many expensive gifts from both Indonesians—one group of 36 officials gave a present worth Rp 700—and Chinese)	5,000

In the case of the funeral in the list above, which cost an estimated Rp 1,345, an itemization of the expenses is available. The expenditure for the funeral proper were as follows (Rp):

Coins given out to mourners	40
Muslin winding sheet	40
Grave marker (bought ready-made from a Chinese; this would never be done in a village)	45
Rental of litter	5
Planks (the wood was bought)	30
Flowers	15
Food (in addition to that brought by the guests)	60*
Cigarettes for guests (this is an item in all *slametans*)	45
TOTAL for the funeral proper	Rp 280*

In sequel to the funeral, these expenses (in Rp) were incurred:

Seven days of chanting at prayer house	35
Third-day *slametan*	100
Seventh-day *slametan*	130
Fortieth-day *slametan* (about 40 people in attendance)	200*

This was as far as the informant had reached in the cycle of death *slametans*. The addition to the expenses itemized above of extrapolated estimates of Rp 150 for the first- and second-year *slametans* and Rp 300 for the thousandth-day *slametan* gives an estimated total expenditure, for the entire series of ceremonies, of Rp 1,345.

Chapter 4   The *Slametan* Cycles: Birth

JAVANESE RITES of passage describe an arc running from the fussy, detailed little gestures surrounding birth to the large, often rather elaborate feasts and entertainments accompanying circumcision and marriage to the muted, emotionally constricted rituals of death. In all, the *slametan* provides the skeleton; what varies is the intensity, mood, and complexity of the special symbolism of the occasion. The rites emphasize both the continuity and the underlying identity of all aspects of life and the special transitions and phases through which it passes.

Tingkeban

AROUND birth four major *slametans* and a variable number of minor ones cluster. The major ones are given at seven months of pregnancy (*tingkeban;* this one is only held when the child is the first for either the mother or the father or both), at birth itself (*babaran* or *brokokan*), five days after birth (*pasaran*), and seven months after birth (*pitonan*). Other *slametans* may or may not be given at three months in the first pregnancy (*telonan*), the first month after birth (*selapanan*), and one year after (*taunan*). Some people hold *slametans* each month after birth for a year or two sporadically into the adulthood of the child, but this practice is widely variable and such *slametans* are generally small and unimportant ones.

The timing, it should be noted, is not by Western thirty-day months but by the Javanese month of thirty-five days. The Javanese combine their own five-day market week (*Legi, Paing, Pon, Wagé, Kliwon*) with the Western-Moslem seven-day week (*Minggu, Senén, Selasa, Rebo, Kemis, Djumuwat, Setu*). They originally had a seven-day week of their own as well as various others, and the present one is merely a case of Islamic names replacing native ones. As seven times five is thirty-five, there are thirty-five possible separate days (*Minggu-Legi . . . Senén-Paing . . . Djumuwat-Legi, Setu-Paing . . . Setu-Kliwon*), and this cycle forms the "month." Actually, however, these "months" are not fixed and absolute units as ours are but merely the length of time between any one singled-out day and its next occurrence thirty-five days later.

If one asks a Javanese when he was born, he always knows: *Setu-Paing,* for example. The difficulty is that he almost never knows the month or year, and he doesn't care. If he is born on *Djumuwat-Legi,* then his *selapanan* or "one-month birthday" is *Djumuwat-Legi* the next time it comes around. His seven-month birthday (*pitonan*) will fall on the seventh *Djumuwat-Legi* after the one on which he was born. Javanese calendrical time is pulsative, not spatial like ours.* When the cogs of the calendar click together in a certain combination, it is time for a certain ceremony to be held, a journey to be begun, or a medicine to be taken. It is perhaps in part a result of this that Javanese life seems to fluctuate between what might be called full and empty time: moments, hours, or days of busy, crowded, intense activity alternate with periods in which people seem to do nothing much at all but wait for something to happen to them.

Except in those comparatively few cases where a three-month pregnancy *slametan* has been given or where a woman who has already had a child has married a man who has not, the *tingkeban* represents the introduction of the Javanese woman into motherhood. Because of the relative indefiniteness of the time of conception, the *tingkeban* is not held on a fixed day corresponding to that on which the pregnancy began, but always on the closest Saturday to the beginning of the seventh month of pregnancy insofar as that can be estimated.

It is held at the home of the mother-to-be's mother, and a special *slametan* is prepared with the following major elements, which I give with a few of their meanings, along with another warning that it is never possible to get complete agreement among informants on all these things:

(1) A dish of rice for each guest with white rice on the top, yellow underneath. The white rice symbolizes purity, the yellow love. This should be served in a banana-leaf basket held together with a steel needle (kings and nobles are said to have used gold ones in the "old days") so that the child will be strong and sharp of mind.

(2) Rice mixed with grated coconut and a whole stuffed chicken. This is intended both to honor the Prophet Muhammad and to secure *slamet* for all the participants in the feast and for the unborn child. Usually there is included here an offering to *Dewi Pertimah* (literally: "The Hindu Goddess, Fatimah"—i.e., Muhammad's daughter with a Hindu title!) of two bananas joined at the base.

(3) Seven small pyramids of white rice mainly symbolizing the seven months of pregnancy, but often various other "intentions" are added, such as to honor the seven days of the week, the seven layers of heaven, and the like.

(4) Eight (sometimes nine) round balls of rice shaped with the fist to symbolize the eight (or nine) *Walis*—the legendary bringers of Islam to Indonesia—and particularly to honor Sunan Kalidjaga, the most famous and

* The Western calendar is, of course, used by the larger businesses and the agencies of the Indonesian government.

most powerful of the *walis*, who is usually credited with founding the shadow play, the *slametan*, and *abangan* religion in general.

(5) A large rice pyramid, called the "strong" pyramid because it is made of sticky glutinous rice, the intent of which is to make the child strong and to honor the *danjang* of the village.

(6) Some food plants which grow below the ground (such as cassava) and some which grow hanging above (such as fruits), the first to symbolize the earth and the latter the sky, each of which is conceived as having seven levels.

(7) Three kinds of rice mush: plain white, red (made so by adding coconut sugar), and a combination of the two: white around the outside and red in the center of the dish. The white represents the "water" of the mother, the red the "water" of the father, and their mixture (called *bubur sengkala* —literally, "misfortune porridge") is considered especially efficacious for preventing the entrance of harmful spirits of any kind.

(8) *Rudjak legi*, a very spicy concoction of various fruits, peppers, spices, and sugar. This is the most important so far as the *tingkeban* is concerned, and the most distinctive; most of the other elements occur in other *slametans*, but *rudjak* occurs only here. It is said that if the *rudjak* tastes "hot" or "spicy" to the prospective mother she will have a girl, but if it tastes flat to her she will have a boy.

These are only a few of the major elements of the *tingkeban* and of the interpretations that go with them. A learned *abangan* informant, especially an older one, could list half a hundred *slametan* foods, each with a special method of preparation, a special symbolic meaning, and intended for a special recipient. What is immediately striking even in these few examples, however, is the rich mixture of Islamic, Hindu-Buddhist, and native spirits, deities, and culture heroes into one grand syncretism. Hindu goddesses rub elbows with Islamic prophets and both of these with local *danjangs;* and there is little sign that any of them are surprised at the others' presence.

In the half-hour *udjub* (introductory speech) to one *tingkeban* which I attended, an old man of about seventy-five dedicated food and good intentions to the Prophets Adam and Eve, to the Prophet Muhammad, his wife, his children, and his Companions; to the *danjang* of the village and to *his* children standing guard at the four corners of the village; to the twin guardian spirits of the man involved in the ceremony, which came (as do those of every Javanese) originally from the remains of his navel cord and from the amniotic fluid of his mother and which follow him around the rest of his life; to the five senses (seeing, hearing, feeling, smelling, and *talking*) and the four directions; to the ancestors of everyone present; to Nini Tawek, the angel who guards the Javanese kitchen and to whom the women give a small offering before every *slametan;* to God under both his Javanese and Arabic names (Pangéran and Allah); to the spirits living in the rafters of the house; to some spirit blacksmiths pounding out magical daggers (*kris*) and spears (*tumbak*) in a nearby volcano crater; to the animals that crawl along like snails and the animals which run along like ants (so they would stay out of the food); to "mother earth," not further defined; to Sunan Kalidjaga and the other *walis;* to Baginda Ilijas and Baginda Chilir, guardians of the land

and the water respectively; and to the as yet unborn child fasting and meditating in his mother's womb. And then he closed with the Moslem Confession of Faith: "There is no god but God, and Muhammad is His Prophet!"

A shorter and perhaps more typical *udjub,* at least within the town where people are satisfied with a briefer treatment, was dictated to me by an informant in the usual exalted Javanese employed for this purpose:

> My brothers, now that all of you whom I have invited, young and old, have arrived, I will speak, giving the intentions of my son Mertowirjo. This married couple wishes, with all respect, on this day of the seven-day week and of the five-day week, *Setu-Paing,* to seek well-being (*slamet*), and deeply wishes and begs that they may not be harmed by anything and that nothing will happen to them and that no hindrances at all will occur. Therefore I offer praise to the *danjang* who founded this village, who cleared it from the forest and who guards it day and night. May he give us well-being and may he protect us from all dangers. My first intention is to dedicate the coconut rice and the whole chicken as food for the Prophet Muhammad and his wife, children, and Companions Abu Bakar, Umar, Usman, and Ali. For this reason they are asked to dine with us and are asked to give forgiveness, and we hope that this *tingkeban* will bring well-being to the as yet unborn child from this seventh month in the womb until it is born. The round balls of rice I give in honor of Sunan Kalidjaga and eight *walis.* I hope that we shall all be given pardon and well-being and that we shall be safe from all dangers, and that the as yet unborn child from this seventh month in the womb until it is born will have well-being. The seven pyramids of rice I give in honor to the seven days of the week, the five market days, the thirty weeks (*wukuh;* one *wukuh* has seven days), the twelve months, and the eight *windu* (eight named years make up a *windu* cycle and are sometimes each called a *windu* as well). May this *Setu-Paing* bring us all well-being. And in order to aid the realization of my intentions I give honor to the Prophet Ilijas, who guards the earth, and the Sultan Chilir, who guards the water. May the water in which this married couple later will be bathed protect them from all dangers and hindrances, and may the dirt which will be washed off them cause them no harm, and may nothing happen to them. The dish of white and yellow rice is in honor of the seven months the child has already passed in the womb.* May he have well-being until his birth. The white rice porridge is from the mother, the red rice porridge is from the father—may they insure the child's well-being until his birth. The red and white rice porridge, may it protect us against all the misfortunes which have already fallen upon us and all those which have not yet fallen upon us. May those which have not yet fallen be prevented from doing so by Allah, and may those which have already fallen be blown away on the wind. If I have omitted anything, if my speech has had faults in it, if there has been anything that has disturbed anyone's emotions, I beg pardon from you, my brothers, old and young.

In the *tingkeban,* as in all *slametans,* in addition to the food itself, the joint offering to both the spirits and one's neighbors, there is a special offering for the spirits taken in their totality: the *sadjèn.* More or less constant in its

---

* Actually it is only six. People say that the ceremony is given at the beginning of the seventh month rather than at the end so that the excitement will not be so likely to cause a miscarriage.

composition, the *sadjèn* appears in nearly all Javanese ceremonies and often appears by itself without a ceremony. Peasants often put *sadjèns* at one corner of the rice field when plowing, planting, transplanting, weeding, or harvesting. Someone who has, say, dreamed of a dead person will, if he feels the event not serious enough for a *slametan,* put a *sadjèn* out on the crossroads. And many Modjokuto *abangans* still follow the ancient custom of putting them out in various room corners and doorways around the house each Thursday evening, which by Javanese reckoning is part of Friday since sunset marks the beginning of a new day. The *sadjèn,* the meaning of whose separate items is largely lost, is—along with the spell—the simplest and most elemental of Javanese religious acts and as such finds a place in almost every aspect of their daily life.

In a *tingkeban* given in a village about fifteen miles from Modjokuto the rather elaborate *sadjèn* was composed of the following items:

a miniature hair comb
another, finer-type comb
a tiny box fashioned from cardboard
a model mirror, made from a fragment of glass pasted onto some newspaper
a paper of pins
some traditionally woven Javanese thread
a wooden shuttle used in weaving (this is special to the *tingkeban*)
a tiny water jug of Mid-Eastern type
various types of flowers, spices, and medicinal herbs from the garden (ten
    kinds)
a tiny piece of incense
a mixture of betel nut
a plug of tobacco
18.5 cents (this should be in old coins, but these are rarely available now)
a little rice
an egg (also special to the *tingkeban*)

All this was placed in a large banana-leaf basket lined with bananas and put to one side of where the *slametan* guests sat.

When the *slametan* part of the *tingkeban* is completed, the *sadjèn* is presented to the *ḍukun baji* (midwife), who conducts the ceremony which follows and who, traditionally, finally aids in the birth itself. Nowadays, however, the *ḍukun baji* who officiates at the *tingkeban* is not always the one who conducts the birth, and even those people who later have their babies in a hospital sometimes give a *tingkeban* with a *ḍukun baji*. This pattern is quite general: for a shadow play a *sadjèn* is prepared and given to the puppeteer; at the marriage the *ḍukun mantèn* (marriage specialist) receives it; and at the ceremony initiating the harvest the *ḍukun wiwit* (literally, "opening specialist") gets it. At the *tingkeban* the *ḍukun mantèn* who originally officiated at the couple's wedding may preside rather than the prospective *ḍukun baji;* one of my informants claimed to have had both at his *tingkeban*.

When the introductory speech is completed, the *donga* (Arabic prayer) given, and the food tasted and wrapped up for carrying home, the ceremony for the *tingkeban* proper begins. A tub of water strewn with flower petals is prepared, the water taken, theoretically, from seven different springs. It is said that it is in such a bath that gods and goddesses always bathe, and so the married couple are momentarily viewed as divine, and scoopfuls of this water are poured over them by the *ḍukun,* who chants a spell (*djapa*):

In the name of God, the Merciful, the Compassionate!
My intention is to bathe this husband and wife,
I *tingkeb* them with water from seven springs.
May all their descendants have well-being from this day forward.
This is necessary because of Allah (may He be exalted!).
The creation of Allah.

The Javanese string from the *sadjèn* is then produced, the woman tying it loosely about her waist. The man takes a Javanese dagger (*kris*), lifts it high above his head to honor it, and then cuts loose the string, coming up from below and inside it, so as to cut it toward himself. The *kris* is then stored away. In a *tingkeban* I saw, a *kris* belonging to the wife's mother's ancestors was used, and it was said that the *kris* had no other modern use except in *tingkebans.*

While the man is accomplishing this task, the *ḍukun* chants another *djapa:*

In the name of God, the Merciful, the Compassionate!
My intention is to cut open a young unopened leaf [i.e., the string, sometimes
    an actual leaf is used],
But I really am not cutting open a leaf—
I am cutting open the way for the baby to emerge.
I limit you [the baby] to nine months
Of meditation in your mother's womb.
Come out easy, go in easy,
Easy, easy, by the will of Allah.

Next the weaving shuttle is dropped by the *ḍukun* inside the woman's sarong. It is caught at the bottom by the husband's mother in a shawl of the type in which Javanese babies are carried about on their mother's hip, and she carries it off as though it were a real child. The mother of the husband will joke, speaking to the cradled shuttle, saying, "Oh, my grandson," while the mother of the woman will say, "Oh, my granddaughter." The first is supposed inevitably to desire a boy, the second a girl descendant. Two green coconuts on which have been drawn Djanaka and Sumbadra, the male shadow-play hero and his wife, who the Javanese say are the two most beautiful people who ever lived, are placed in front of the husband. He takes one slash at each of them with a large knife. If both split, it means there will be a very easy birth, no trouble at all. If only one splits, then the unsplit one tells the sex of the child (a male if Djanaka, etc.). If neither splits, then the birth will be difficult and may not come off well at all. Various other gestures, such as dropping an egg down through the woman's sarong, throwing a water jug out the door (both of them breaking), and the like are often added to symbolize an easy birth.

Now the woman engages in a clothes-changing routine. She puts on one sarong after another, pulling out the previous one from underneath. Each

time the crowd cries out amid much hilarity, "Oh no, that is not proper," until
she reaches the seventh and last one, the so-called *toh watu.* A *toh watu,*
properly speaking, is a mark on a stone which cannot be erased. As a sarong,
a *toh watu* is a special type made of heavy cotton which will not fade and
thus symbolizes the lasting relationship between the mother and the child
throughout life, their life-long inseparability. The efficacy of a mother's
sarong for bringing a person out of a faint has already been mentioned, but
the symbolization of mother-child relations in terms of the mother's clothing
is even more general.

> The old lady said that wherever I went I should always take one or two
> pieces of my mother's clothing with me. This would keep me *slamet.* She
> said that if I was upset or dizzy and I laid my head on my mother's pillow I
> would recover. She said all this was because when I was an embryo I medi-
> tated in my mother's cave for nine months. She said this was just like regular
> religious meditation. The foetus doesn't eat or sleep, just meditates and learns
> about spiritual things. Later, when the child is instructed in spiritual things,
> one always reminds him of this: "You were nine months in my cave," and so
> forth. That is why, said the old woman, a person can never talk back to his
> mother (he may to his father, a very little bit), because he meditated in her,
> and why I should have a couple of pieces of my mother's clothes with me
> whenever I travel if I wanted to be sure and be *slamet.*

A similar belief is connected with a girl's first menses. The sarong she is
wearing when she first menstruates is never washed or worn again, but kept.
Later, if the girl has a sick child, she wraps him in this sarong and he will
get well, this being held to be more effective treatment than one can get from
either a *dukun* or a Western-trained doctor.

The *tingkeban* ritual finally closes with the wife, assisted by the husband,
selling *rudjak legi,* a kind of spicy-sweet fruit juice, to all those present for
a token payment. No one I talked to seemed to remember what the meaning
of this act was, although some said that the mother would use the money
collected to buy medicine for the baby.* In general, conscious awareness of
the meaning of the various elements in *abangan* rituals varies rather widely
from person to person; and while some people are much interested in religious
detail and love to discuss it, others merely do what they are told to do by
those who "know," caring little about the ultimate significance of what they
are doing.

To have a child without a *tingkeban* is said to *ngebokné* him, i.e., make
a carabao out of him, and to say this about someone's child is a serious insult, insinuating that the child's parents are mere animals and "don't know
human order." Nevertheless, sometimes if a woman has lost three or four
children in childbirth or before, her husband may take an oath, "*Jèn kowé
meteng manèh, tak-kebokné*" ("If you get pregnant again, I will treat the
child as a carabao"), and says he will hold no *tingkeban,* and no other birth
slametans either. This is a rather serious thing to do, for not only does it
leave one unprotected against the spirits but it also leaves one open for later

---

* No other preparation for the baby's arrival, such as making clothes or cradles,
etc., are approved of; this is "presupposing God" and brings misfortune.

criticism if the child grows up intractable, as it would be likely to do in such a case. But a man in our neighborhood whose wife was ill during pregnancy swore thus and all came off well.

Babaran

JUST before the birth, some people have a small *slametan* with just the household members attending, the main feature of which is a dish of rice meal with a peeled banana in the middle of it to symbolize an easy birth, but this *slametan* is as often ignored as given, even by fairly strict *abangans*. In any case, when the labor pains begin, the *ḍukun baji* is called and immediately upon arrival puts out a *sadjèn* by the mother's bed and another in the toilet (because the spirits in the toilet do not like the smell of the blood associated with birth). Then she rolls out a sleeping mat on the floor, sits the mother on it, and begins to massage her, chanting a spell for her well-being:

> In the name of God, the Merciful, the Compassionate!
> My intention is to roll out a sleeping mat
> And set a loosely woven basket on it [i.e., the mother].
> Grandfather Spirit of Modjokuto, Grandmother Spirit of Modjokuto!
> Open the door to heaven,
> Close the door to hell.
> The devils and other evil spirits, may they go away.
> The male ancestor spirits say that nothing will happen,
> The female ancestor spirits say that nothing will happen.
> Wherever you wander, you may be safe,
> May you be safe from dangers both from above and from below,
> Wherever you wander or go, little mother,
> Who are about to bear a child.

After the child has been born, the *ḍukun* employs the traditional bamboo knife (*welad*) to cut the umbilical cord.

> In the name of God, the Merciful, the Compassionate!
> The bamboo knife
> Which I am about to use to cut the skin and flesh,
> The skin of the newborn baby.
> "Your inlaid metal decorations are what?" [she questions the knife]
> "It is metal with magical power!" [the knife replies]
> May you [the baby] feel no pain, may it be usual,
> Usual by the will of Allah
> . . . .
> Be cool, be cool—hit by my white saliva,
> May the white blood [of the child] gather with the white blood,
> May the black blood gather with the black blood,
> The red blood with the red blood.
> May the flesh [of the umbilical cord] close up,

May the veins narrow and the skin grow together,
Grow together by the will of God.
May the bones join with the bones,
The flesh with the flesh,
The skin with the skin,
The blood in the bones with the blood in the bones,
The veins with the veins.
May the flesh close up, the veins narrow, the skin grow together,
The blood coagulate, -ate, -ate, by the will of Allah.

She then rubs *kunir* (tumeric), the Javanese all-purpose herb, onto the wound and ties the cord.

The baby is washed, and then the mother; and there are spells for both of these performances too. The umbilical cord and afterbirth are wrapped in white muslin, put into a jug, salted, and buried outside the house, in front if the child is a boy, in back if it is a girl, although some people bury both in front, the boy to the left of the door, the girl to the right. A little wicker fence is erected around the spot or a broken earthware pot is inverted over it to keep dogs or other animals from digging it up, and a small candle is kept burning over it for thirty-five days in order to prevent evil spirits from disturbing it.

In the name of God, the Merciful, the Compassionate!
Father Earth, Mother Earth,
I am about to leave in your care the birthcord of the baby.
Thus the baby itself I leave behind [i.e., I don't bury it],
Only the umbilical cord do I leave in your care.
Don't bother the baby,
This is necessary because of Allah.
If you do bother him, you will be punished by God.
Cast away the childhood illnesses from the baby,
This too is necessary because of Allah.
Birthcord, thus I leave you in someone else's care.
Little baby, don't oppose your father,
Or you will be punished by Allah.

The burying of the umbilical cord is a serious matter. One woman blamed the death of her child, in convulsion after forty days of life, on the fact that the *dukun* did not put enough salt in the umbilical cord when she buried it, and so it "came up" and the child died. The cord and afterbirth, coming as it does after the birth of the child, is considered to be his spirit younger brother, while the amniotic fluid which precedes him (it is thrown out up into the air) is considered to be his spirit older brother. For the first thirty-five days they remain near the child and protect him against illness, the first under the ground, the other in the sky. Afterwards they may wander, but they remain one's guardian spirits. It takes, however, extended mental concentration, fasting and wakefulness—what the Javanese call *tapa*—to get into contact with them. Sometimes the bamboo knife and the *kunir* herb medicine are considered spirit brothers and protectors too, giving each person four, but this is less common.

Lastly, the *dukun* places the baby on a low table and slaps the table three times to startle the baby so that he will be accustomed to such surprises and less likely to be severely startled later in life and thus less easily made ill, for such sudden upset is one of the main causes of sickness in both the child and the adult. At the same time, the *dukun* introduces the child into the life of men:

In the name of God, the Merciful, the Compassionate!
My intention is to startle the baby,
Born from the womb of his mother.
"Little baby" [she addresses him], "what gifts have you brought?"
"Body and breath" [he answers], "health,
And a fixed religious duty [i.e., Islam]."
There is no god but God, and Muhammad is His Prophet!
Jaallah, Jaallah, Jaallah.

She then strikes the table three times with the flat of her hand and recites in Arabic the Moslem Confession of Faith:

I declare truly that there is no god but God,
And I declare truly that Muhammad is His Prophet.

That evening a small *slametan,* called *babaran,* is held, marked by the presence of a whole chicken egg, because before one is born he is an egg. With this the complex of spells and rituals immediately around birth is completed.

Pasaran

FIVE days after the first *slametan* for the new-born baby is held, a somewhat larger one, the *pasaran,* takes place, at which, among other things, the child is named. The father, theoretically, has the final say on the child's name, and he usually gives the name to the child in the *udjub* speech at the *slametan.* (He may, however, honor his own father and father-in-law by allowing them to perform this act.) To a large extent names are determined by the social category into which the family falls.

Parto talked about naming: There are three types of names one uses, depending on what group one is in: village names, noble or *prijaji* names, and *santri* names. Village boys are sometimes just named after the day on which they are born, for example, Senèn or Paing. Or they have simple names such as Sidin or Sirin. Girls have the same names, only in the feminine form: Sidinah. Boys of very high *prijajis* usually have either Djoko- or Bambang- in front of their names, and girls will have Endang-. Like Djokosentono; *Sentosa* means strong. Or Bambang Suwarno. Of for a girl, Endang Suwarni. For *santris* the first name is often Muhammad or Abdul. Like Muhammad Taha, Abdul Mutallip. For girls, Sitti: Sitti Aminah. . . . I asked him what if village people used *prijaji* names, and he said no one would because people would laugh at them and they would feel ashamed. Even a name like Sasro wouldn't be used; it would be shifted to Sastro for a lower *prijaji,* that is, "one who works in an office but doesn't have a title." The village people wouldn't even dare this, but would use Setro; instead of Sastrodihardjo they would be Setrodiredjo. He said that among the village people the names may be spelled (and pronounced) differently according to whether a man is a *santri* or not. An *abangan* would call his child Kalil, a *santri* Cholil; the *abangan* Katidjah, the *santri* Chotizah. Sometimes the village Christians will use the names of the Christian prophets, Daniel, Musa, etc. But high Christians, like those around Modjokuto, will use *prijaji* names.

As Javanese change their names rather readily—after a severe illness, at marriage, after returning from the pilgrimage to Mecca, on getting a new job, on the birth of their child—any social mobility or shifts of allegiance are easily adjusted for. Perhaps the most common single name for young *abangan* boys in Java is Slamet, often as a result of a childhood illness during which the name was changed as a curative measure. These categories do not hold absolutely, but they are clear enough in the minds of the people so that when I mentioned a high official I knew whose name was Paidjan (a definitely *abangan* name), the man to whom I was speaking (a *santri*) said, "*Wah,* this is indeed a new era—before the revolution you would never have found a *prijaji* with a name like Paidjan; he would have changed it." Most still do.

Strictly speaking, the timing of the *pasaran* depends upon when the stub of the baby's umbilical cord falls off. If it is not off by the fifth day, the *pasaran* should be postponed to the sixth day or even the seventh. This rarely occurs, however, and I never encountered a *pasaran* held on other than the fifth day. In the old days people used to bring in *santris* to chant from eight o'clock until midnight each night after birth until the cord fell off, but this is rarely practiced now, if at all—certainly never in town. Another old practice which has disappeared, at least in the Modjokuto area, is the singing of long Javanese poems at the *pasaran;* now people play cards instead. Evidently this poem-singing used to occur at other *slametans* too in the years before the war, but one never hears it now.

The food at the *pasaran* is nearly the same as that of the *tingkeban,* minus the *rudjak legi,* and with the addition of various little between-meal snacks from the market (fish chips, popcorn, candied rice, etc.). These rather taste-less tidbits on which the Javanese seem forever to be nibbling are called *djadjan,* and they seem to turn up almost everywhere one Javanese sits down to chat with another. If a friend drops in casually off the street—as is the custom—they are served; at weddings, official government banquets, and political meetings they are served; and they are what are sold in all the dozens of little coffee shops that are scattered around town where each day hundreds of people sit and talk about nothing very much for hours on end. Thus *djadjan* is a natural symbol of the kind of social interaction the Javanese love best; a stiffly correct and mechanically polite formality on the one hand (most marked among the *prijajis*), and a kind of mildly in-tense haphazard hubbub on the other (most marked among the *abangans*). That it is the latter meaning that is intended in the *pasaran* is clear, for the *djadjan* must be bought in the market itself, not in a store or along the wayside. It is hoped, people say, that the child will grow up liking the crowds, the helter-skelter, and the constant buzz of joking conversation the Javanese call *ramé,* which finds its prime exemplification in the market.

Many of the magical practices traditionally associated with the *pasaran* are still carried out. A thread, again woven in the traditional manner (though it is available now in the stores), is strung all around the house just under the eaves to keep out evil spirits. At each of the four corners are put pointed pineapple leaves and a plant with tendrils for a similar purpose. Two of these corners are painted black with ashes and two white with a kind of chalk. Then one takes an old, ruined broom and puts various hot spices and peppers on the bristles; this is called the *tumbak séwu* ("a thousand spears"). Next a draw-board from a loom is painted in alternate black and white stripes with ashes and chalk. These are put under the mother's bed,* along with the *sadjèn* with various foods, such as betel nut, which the spirits like. A spirit who then tries to enter the house will first be held back by the string. If he gets by that he will be confused by the black and white corners and get stuck on the pointed pineapple leaves or caught in the tendrils. If this doesn't stop him, the thousand spears will stab him or the loom-board will crush him. If he survives even this, he will probably eat the *sadjèn* and go away satisfied; if not, the limits of human ingenuity have been reached and one can only hope. Thirty-five days after birth all these things are taken down and there is another *slametan,* the *selapanan,* with roughly the same food as on the fifth day, but without the *djadjan* from the market.

Pitonan

FEWER and fewer people seem to be holding the three-month *slametan,* and if they do, it is a small affair.** But the seven-month *slametan*—or *pitonan*—is still rather widely given, although it is beginning to become somewhat less important.

The major food here is a kind of rice-meal pudding called *djenang,* which is set out in seven colors. It is colored nowadays with dye bought in the stores, but traditionally with various herbs. Also there is a large rice pyramid with seven small pyramids around it and a large plate of mixed vegetables with seven small ones around it, besides the usual array of rice balls, three kinds of mush, and the like. Here, as in the *tingkeban,* however, the ceremony rather overshadows the *slametan* proper.

---

* The mother is almost certainly up and around by five days; one tries to get up as quickly as possible after childbirth so the blood will flow as rapidly as possible.

** For small *slametans* it is quite common to have only three or four people in and to send the rest of the food around to the neighbors' houses wrapped in the traditional banana-leaf baskets—a pattern called *tondjokan* (or *berkat*). Even when a *slametan* feast is of normal size, however, *tondjokan* baskets may be sent in addition to honor more distant neighbors or friends. For example, as a symbol of respect, a railroad worker who is having a *pasaran* may send a *tondjokan* to his boss.

Directed by the midwife, as are all postnatal ceremonies, the rite begins with the waking of the baby at cockcrow or around four in the morning and his being placed in the nest of a chicken along with the chicken—a cock for a boy, a hen for a girl. This chicken is later carefully protected and never killed and eaten, for the longer it lives the longer the child's life will probably be. The child is then presented with a shallow bamboo basket in which have been placed yellow-colored rice and some coins. If he throws this rice and money around, as he usually does, it means he will later in his life be a spendthrift; if he does not, then he will be thrifty. Then the baby is allowed for the first time in his life to put his feet on the ground and, having come down to earth, he is handed a severed chicken's foot to remind him that he, like the lowly chicken, will have to scratch for his food throughout the whole of his life.

Following this the *slametan* proper is held. In contrast to almost all other *slametans,* the *pitonan* must be held in the morning before twelve noon. When this has been completed, the child is washed in a tub of flower water. Leading up to the tub is a ladder (or banana-tree trunk) with seven rungs in it, and on each rung is placed a bowl of rice porridge, the first one colored red, the second white, the third red, and so on, the red again symbolizing the father, the white the mother. The child steps on each of these in turn until he reaches the tub, inevitably squalling, and is bathed by the *dukun.* Little snips of hair are cut by each guest from the baby's head and thrown on the ground with some money, which is used for medicine for him. This whole gesture is usually omitted now that children no longer grow the topknot, *kutjung,* for its purpose was to initiate that process.

After the bath, the baby is powdered with yellow powder, is dressed in brand new clothes, draped with flowers, and sits down to a miniature *slametan* to which a number of neighboring children between the ages of about four and six are invited. This kind of play *slametan*—called a *pantjakan* (literally, "newcomer")—serves as a kind of initiation for the child into traditional Javanese religious practices, his first introduction to a rite he will perform many many times more before he dies. The child is then presented a tray on which has been placed a number of symbolic objects indicating occupations or character traits: pencil (teacher or clerk—clever); rice (peasant—industrious); money (trader—rich); mirror (actor—vanity); knife (soldier—brave). The child's future occupation and character are then predicted on the basis of which two items he takes from the tray, although people with wishes for class advancement are not above directing him toward the pencil.

For the mother, too, the *pitonan* is not without meaning, for she is released from the postnatal taboos which hem her in for the first seven months after birth: sleeping sitting up with her back propped against a board; bathing in the early afternoon (i.e., before sunset) in a special tub set up in the kitchen (the regular bath being infested with spirits); applying regular herb salves and ointments several times a day; and numerous food taboos, many of which begin before birth. For most families the *pitonan* completes the *slametan* cycle focused on birth, although some give another small one at twelve months.

Chapter 5

The *Slametan* Cycles:
Circumcision and Marriage

Circumcision: *Sunatan*

ALTHOUGH SOME SORT of circumcision may have been practiced in Java before the beginning of the Islamic period in the sixteenth century, almost no traces of such a pre-Moslem initiation rite are today apparent in Modjokuto. The ceremony celebrating the circumcision has been largely patterned after the marriage ceremony, with the subtraction of those elements pertaining to the actual joining of the couple. Thus the food at the *islaman* (circumcision, also called *sunatan*) and *kepanggihan* (marriage) *slametans* is identical, and both rites provide the primary occasions for conspicuous spending in Javanese and social life. Elaborate hired entertainment—a shadow play and percussion orchestra, a Western-type orchestra complete with female vocalist, or a traveling drama or dance troupe—is often presented. As many as two hundred people may be fed at a secular reception following the *slametan* (which is, in any case, confined to eight or ten participants); and guests are expected either to bring presents or to give money. In a sense, both marriage and circumcision are puberty rites for the Javanese, the first for girls, the second for boys, and should be viewed in this light as a linked pair of coming-of-age ceremonies, one for each sex.*

Most Javanese boys are circumcised sometime between the ages of ten and fourteen, although I knew one *santri* whose five-year-old had just had the operation. Most Modjokuto boys are circumcised separately, but sometimes groups of two or three brothers, cousins, and neighbors are taken at one time.

Traditionally the operation was performed by a specialist called a *tjalak* (or *bong*) who was often also either a barber, a butcher, or a curer. Nowa-

* It is reported that around Surakarta in Central Java incision is sometimes practiced on eight-year-old girls, but this ceremony does not occur in Modjokuto.

days many urbanites have the operation performed at a hospital by a male nurse (*mantri*), but the great majority probably still employ a *tjalak* if only because it is cheaper. The local office of the Ministry of Religious Affairs in Modjokuto had eleven *tjalaks* officially registered for the subdistrict. The most active of these was also a curer and a *hadji,* who had learned the skill from his father, and who, although he owned about two acres of rice land, said that his practice brought in the greater part of his income (he charged from twenty to fifty rupiahs, depending upon the distance from Modjokuto, where he lives, and, I imagine, upon the class standing of the client). Under government health regulations he is required to apply an antiseptic, which is furnished by the Ministry of Health. As he put it, "My father used to chant and cut. Now I chant, cut, and apply the medicine. It's just the same, it makes no difference."

After a *pétungan* system has been applied and an auspicious day chosen a *slametan* is given the evening before the circumcision is to take place.* This *slametan,* called the *manggulan,* is exactly the same as the one given the evening before a wedding (*midadarèni*). It includes nearly all the foods mentioned earlier plus rice pressed out flat onto a large tray until it forms a wafer-thin disk. This rice disk is intended to symbolize the idea that everyone at the *slametan* is free of secret feelings of envy, hate, jealousy, and the like; that everyone's emotions have been flattened out to the point where all present are calm, peaceful, and undisturbed "within." Also, there is in addition to the usual three kinds of porridge—red, white, and mixed— a fourth. Made from pounded rice husks, it is called *paru-paru*—literally, "lungs." Javanese believe, or many of them do, that the seat of life is in the human breath—which, however, they also connect with the beating of the heart—and so *paru-paru* is to honor "the spirit of life within the breath of the person being circumcised or married."

Various *sadjèns* are put around in the house corners, the toilet, the rice bin, and so on for the *sétans;* and after the *slametan* is over, the boy is given a lukewarm herb medicine and massaged by a *ḍukun pidjet* (a masseuse) and covered with a yellow powder.

The next morning he soaks in a tub of water for an hour or so and then dresses. He wears a new white muslin cloth under his sarong, and after he has been circumcised he sits on new white muslin as well. Another *sadjèn* is prepared for the spirits, the boy reads the Confession of Faith, and is circumcised by the *tjalak,* who uses a knife called *wesi tawa,* literally, "iron you can't feel." If the boy faints, his mother rubs his face with her sarong. When the operation is completed, he is laid on a low bed and his mother steps across him three times, demonstrating that she, too, is free of any hidden feelings toward the boy which might hamper the necessary process of his growing emotionally away from her toward manhood. This state of weakened emotional investment in one's immediate environment, or self-

---

* A boy may not be circumcised on any day on which either of his parents or any of his four grandparents died. No circumcision can take place during the month of the Fast, whereas the months of *Besar, Mulud, Djumadilakir, Redjeb,* and *Ruwah* are especially favorable ones. Similar conditions hold for weddings.

induced distance and disciplined aloofness from all events in the transient world of men—they call it having a "flaccid heart"—is among the most valued of Javanese feeling patterns: *iklas*.

That evening the feast and entertainment take place, and the boy may find himself, pale, wan, and in not a little pain, forced to sit immobile atop a great pile of pillows through the greater part of a night-long shadow play. Nevertheless, the general opinion is that only a small percentage of children fear the ritual, and in fact many request their parents to hold it before the latter think the child is really old enough to stand it, or, perhaps, before the parents can afford it.

> Sutrisno (aged about 11), her son, wants to be circumcised this year and as a matter of fact started up a campaign of his own, telling his grandmother and various aunts that he was going to be circumcised this month and for them to give him new clothes. This embarrassed Minah very much when they came to her and asked what day this would be, because she has no money now and will have to put it off for some months, till after the rice harvest, when she and her relatives will have rice.

Marriage: *Kepanggihan*

UNTIL recently in Java, most first marriages were arranged by the parents of the bride and groom. Even when a boy had some ideas of his own as to which girl he would prefer to marry, he would work for his aims through the good auspices of his parents—if he could convince them of the wisdom of his choice. This is still the pattern among many of the more traditional and "old-fashioned" groups, but the pattern of romantic love is making rapid and steady encroachments in contemporary Modjokuto. Among the educated, Dutch-influenced, upper class of the town one even finds engagement ceremonies now and then in which gold wedding bands are exchanged between a man and his fiancée. Called *tukar tjintjin* ("to exchange rings"), a term borrowed from Indonesian, the new (to a Javanese) national language spoken mainly in the cities and larger towns, this ring ceremony seems so far to be largely confined to the student group, who tend to have long engagement periods as a result of their extended schooling.

For most people, even though in a great number of the cases the boy and girl have already come to an understanding of their own in the matter, the old *lamaran* pattern of formal request by the groom's parents to the bride's is still carried out, at least in form.

In the *lamaran* the groom's family visits the bride's family and engages in an elaborate version of the kind of hyper-correct empty formalism in the practice of which the Javanese are past masters. The father of the boy may open matters with a remark such as, "Frost in the morning means rain in the evening," by which he means to communicate that the problem he has come to discuss is a "cool" one, i.e., a simple one which should stir up no strong feelings. Slowly and in similarly metaphorical manner, he arrives at the point and says he would like to become in-laws with his host, to marry his son to the latter's daughter. There will be much false protesting at this point by the host that his daughter is spoiled, that although she is an adult she acts like a child, and the host would find her highly unwelcome as a daughter-in-law, and so on. At length—after perhaps two or three such visits—the matter will be settled one way or the other. A meeting is then arranged at the girl's house at which the groom, the bride, and all the would-be parents-in-law are present. Called the *nontoni*—"the looking (over)"—the occasion is marked with the same strained pretense: the conversation is about everything but marriage; the girl, rigid with shyness, serves the boy tea without speaking to him, and he views her out of the corner of his eye to see (in the traditional case, this would be the first time they had seen each other) what he is getting. If he likes what he sees, he says so on the way home to his parents, and the marriage is set.

The marriage ceremony is called the *kepanggihan* ("the meeting") and is always held at the home of the bride. All parents, the theory goes, have an inescapable obligation to provide one major festival for each of their children; for the boys this is their circumcision, for the girls their marriage. As the parents of the bride are paying for the wedding, they will usually try to wait until after the next harvest before holding the ceremony; but if the boy is in a hurry, he can help pay for part of the ceremony.* Failing this, he can get an official marriage at the mosque and skip the *abangan* part of the celebration for six months or so until he gets enough money together to hold it. This is quite often done, especially among the poorer urban groups.

The boy traditionally had to give two bridal gifts to the girl: the *paningset*, usually clothes and jewelry, given, often with a *slametan* for the bride's parents, after the wedding has been finally decided upon; and the *sasrahan*—traditionally a buffalo or ox and house furniture, but now usually reduced, when it is given at all, to a few kitchen utensils—which is presented to the girl at marriage. Both of these bridal gifts are rare in Modjokuto today.

Since one is supposed always to marry off one's daughters in descending age order and this is commonly done, although not always, the first and last wedding ceremonies given by a household are usually rather more elaborate than those given for other daughters. The ceremony for the first daughter is called *bubak*, which has roughly the same meaning as *babak*: to clear land or open up virgin territory. The ceremony for the youngest daughter is called the *pundjung tumplek* or, rather freely, "the completed honors."

I shall describe the marriage ceremony in the fullest form in which it appears, but I shall include no practice not carried out on the occasion of at least one wedding I saw during the time I was in Modjokuto. It must be remembered not only that ceremonies for middle daughters are usually somewhat less elaborate, but also that various people omit various parts of the ceremony pretty much at will. At some weddings little more than necessary is done: the bride and groom go to the mosque and pronounce the

---

* *Mulud* and *Besar* are the two best months for weddings, and when one of these immediately follows the harvest a tremendous number of weddings takes place.

Moslem Confession of Faith, return home to shake each other's hand, and hold a secular reception for their guests.

As in the *islaman*, the *slametan* for a wedding is given the evening before the actual ceremony. Called the *midadarèni*, except for the traditional prayer that the bride and groom will prove to be as inseparable from one another as are the male and female Moluccan crabs, it is identical to the *manggulan* given before the circumcision ceremony. Only the bride is present at the *midadarèni*, and if the groom, having come from afar, has already arrived in the neighborhood, he is kept hidden from her, for they are not supposed to see one another before the actual meeting.

After the *slametan*, the bride is dressed in very simple clothes. If the house is of the old-fashioned type which has a ceremonial bedroom in the center (the *senṭong tengah*—only about five houses in all of Modjokuto still have these), the girl is seated in front of it; if not, then just the center of the house will do. Here she sits perfectly immobile for about five hours until midnight, during which time an angel comes down and enters her, remaining until five days after the wedding. Thus it is that all brides look so much more beautiful on their wedding day than on any other.

While the girl is seated there, her mother performs the ritual of the buying of the *kembang majang*—"blossoming flower(s)." The *kembang majang* are large composite plants. Their stems are made of banana-tree trunk, their "blossoms" of scalloped tree leaves of various types, and they are wrapped with green coconut branches. They represent the virginity of the bride and the groom, two being constructed for each of them. If the man has been married before, only two *kembang majang* are made; if the girl has been married, no *kepanggihan* need be held at all. The person who has made the *kembang majang*, usually an older man, sits on the floor with them, and the mother of the bride pretends she is a guest:

MOTHER: May I come in?
HOST: Please do.
MOTHER: Is this a rich and fertile village?
HOST: Yes, this is a rich and fertile village. What village are you from?
MOTHER: I am from the village Sidowareg.
HOST: My, but you have come a great distance! What do you want?
MOTHER: I want something very much: I will beg for it by weeping. My child wants a *kembang majang*.
HOST: Yes, we have them here. but are you sure you wish to buy them? They are expensive.
MOTHER: Yes, I will buy them. How much do they cost?
HOST: Oh, the price is two and a half rupiahs.

The mother then pays the money, places the *kembang majang* by the girl, and the evening is over.

The actual wedding comes the next morning. For this day the *pétungan* system is applied to each hour to discover whether it is good or bad and so that the various parts of the ceremony are timed to occur at the right moment. At one of these auspicious times in the early forenoon the groom goes off with his entourage to the office of the *naib*, the government religious official empowered to legitimize and register marriages. The entire company is led by the *modin,* the village religious official, whom the boy has notified of his plans several days in advance and who has consequently checked to be sure the boy is not already married and then arranged the appointment with the *naib.* Although there is one *modin* for each village (as well as, usually, several assistant *modins*), there is but one *naib* for each subdistrict, and his office is in the subdistrict capital. In the Modjokuto subdistrict the capital is Modjokuto town, and the *naib* serves eighteen villages within a radius of about fifteen miles; and so the trip, usually accomplished in a long train of horse carts gaily decorated with green coconut leaves, red and white bunting, and numerous Indonesian flags, may be a relatively long one.*

The bride does not usually go along on this trip to the *naib*'s office (sometimes humorously referred to as "going on the Pilgrimage"), but is represented by her legal guardian under Moslem law, her *wali.* A girl's *wali* is her nearest living male relative in her paternal line—either her father, father's brother, brother, or paternal grandfather. If her paternal relatives are all dead or very distant from the scene of the marriage, then the *naib* himself may act as her *wali,* in which case he is called a *wali hakim* or "court-appointed guardian." The girl, her *wali,* and the *modin* typically visit the *naib* a few days before the actual marriage without much fanfare. Nowadays, when the pretense that the boy and girl have never met until their wedding day is almost universally transparent, the girl may just go a few minutes before the boy with a wedding procession of her own made up of women.

At the *naib*'s office, which in Modjokuto is located at the main mosque, the *wali* formally requests the *naib* to marry his daughter to the boy. The *naib* asks the boy whether he wishes to marry the girl. Then the boy is requested to repeat the Confession of Faith word by word after the *naib,* first in Arabic (about which many people, able only roughly to approximate the Arabic pronunciation, feel very embarrassed) and then in Javanese. The *naib* informs the boy that if he does not feed his wife, sleep with her, or provide her a place to live in, or if he abandons her for three months with no information as to his whereabouts, the girl will be entitled to demand a divorce from him. The *naib* chants a prayer in Arabic, which the assembled, seated in the usual palm-upwards, face-raised prayer posture, punctuate with appropriate amens; sees that the groom gives the *wali* the five-rupiah *mas kawin* ("marriage gold") for the girl demanded by Moslem law; and concludes the services by pronouncing the boy and absent girl man and wife. For the *santris* this is the crucial part of the marriage, that which makes it official in the eyes of God (and of the government, which regards the *idjab,* as this ceremony is called, as the legal marriage ceremony for everyone except Christians); and they never fail to mention this fact in the speech to the guests at the reception which follows. For the *abangans,* however, the really important part of the ceremony is yet to come.

Back at the home of the bride the festivities are about to begin. Yellow

---

* Wealthier people in the town of Modjokuto usually pay the *naib* about 25 rupiahs to come to them, but this is beyond the means of the poorer class of townsmen and all but the very well-to-do village people.

coconut branches have been bent in a half-circle arc over the entrance to the quarter to indicate to all who pass by that a family within "has work" (*duwé gawé*)—i.e., is having a marriage or a circumcision. A special extension of the roof has been built out over the yard to shelter the guests, who sit there sipping coffee, nibbling *djadjan,* and exchanging pleasantries. Inside the house the girl is being dressed either by her female relatives or by a woman expert called the *tukang paras.*

Traditionally the bride (*mantèn*) dressed as a princess, the groom (also called *mantèn*) as a prince, and each marriage re-enacted a royal marriage. The girl wore a black blouse trimmed with flowers and a very fine sarong from one of the great court centers. Her face was made yellow with powder; little black points, looking like so many widow's peaks, were painted along the top edge of her forehead, and her mouth was colored a bright red. Three necklaces of silver or of flowers hung across her chest, and silver ornaments were placed on her ears, silver armlets on her arms. The boy (also dressed by the *tukang paras*) wore a new sarong, too, and a black coat trimmed in yellow. On his head was placed a Javanese turban to which was attached a large jeweled brooch. He too was draped with flowers, and in his belt was stuck a huge, flower-covered *kris,* a conscious symbolization of the phallus. In the old days a high *prijaji* marrying a girl of lower standing (usually as a second wife) would not come to the wedding in person but just sent his *kris.* This now obsolete pattern got a curious reactivation while I was in Modjokuto. When a boy from the north coast failed to show up at his wedding at the girl's home in Modjokuto, the distressed and extremely ashamed bride's family satisfied the *naib* by producing a letter from the boy stating his intentions and then married the girl to his photograph.

In Modjokuto the traditional dressing pattern is now found, for the most part, only among the *prijajis*—the two most elaborate examples of it during my stay being the weddings of the daughter of the district officer and the daughter of a retired assistant director of the government pawnshop. Whatever they did in the past—and it appears rather doubtful that this pattern at its most elaborate ever extended to the villages to any large degree—*abangan* girls in Modjokuto now wear Western dresses (for which they still get sharply criticized as practicing *tjara njonjah-njonjah*—i.e., the way of the Dutch women and their big-city imitators) or, more commonly, somewhat better-quality clothes of the same style as the average Javanese woman wears every day, with flowers and the like added. The *abangan* boy appears in a Western jacket, a sarong, and the small black overseas cap, the *pitji,* that has become the prime symbol of nationalism so far as dress is concerned. *Santri* girls, especially those in town, wear pure white gowns, something like our wedding gowns, and the Moslem head shawl or *kuḍung,* while the man wears Western clothes topped by the *pitji.* Village *santri* girls wear the shawl with usual Javanese dress.

Now things are ready for the actual meeting. An old sarong belonging to the girl is laid down outside in front of the house where they will meet, the spot having been determined by *pétungan* and the direction from which the boy will approach having been fixed by considering the *naga dina.* On

top of this sarong a brass bowl containing flower water and a chicken egg
are placed, and under it a yoke for a pair of oxen. A special *sadjèn* offering
to be placed at the *sentong tengah* (or its equivalent) is prepared containing
soybeans, green beans, yellow beans, onions, pepper, a small piece of batik
cloth in a little bamboo tube, rice, money, various herbs, a mirror, two
bunches of bananas, a green coconut with the husk off, an egg, a tiny water
jug filled with water and with the spout plugged up, and a small kerosene
lamp. Similar *sadjèns* may be placed in dangerous places around, a coconut
is thrown into the well, and the *ḍukun mantèn* goes about sprinkling water over
which he has chanted a spell so that none of the family's property will be
lost, broken, or stolen during the ceremony.

At the chosen moment the girl emerges from the house, followed by two
virgin girls carrying the *kembang majang,* and the boy advances from outside,
followed by two virgin boys carrying his *kembang majang.* Both the bride
and the groom have a small package of betel nut in their hands, and as they
draw near they throw these at one another, the theory being that the one
who hits the other first with the betel will be the dominant partner in the
marriage. There is an unwritten rule that the girl is supposed to see to it
that she loses this contest, which she seems invariably to do.

When they come face to face and are standing on the girl's discarded
sarong (symbolizing her nakedness before her husband and her willingness to
prostrate herself before him), either the girl performs the traditional gesture
of obeisance from an inferior to a superior—the *sembah*[*]—or they will
simply touch palms in the Islamic handshake (*salaman*). One would be likely
to encounter a *sembah* only in a *prijaji* wedding nowadays, and *santris* invariably employ only the *salaman*.

This act completed, the two virgin girls and the two virgin boys exchange
their mock plants diagonally with one another, crossing in front of the
couple, which symbolizes the mutual relinquishment of virginity by the bride
and groom. The girl kneels, breaks the egg on the boy's foot (the white
symbolizing her loss of purity, the yolk the breaking of the hymen), and
then washes his feet in the flower water. This latter act, which symbolizes
her subservience to her husband, is often eliminated nowadays as inconsistent
with contemporary notions as to the equal status of men and women.

The girl then rises, turns facing the house again, and takes her place
next to the boy, standing with him on the double ox yoke, symbolizing their
inseparability and the fact that only two people, those actually involved, ever
know what really goes on between man and wife. Sometimes each then takes
a sip of flower water from a coconut dipper offered by the wife's mother,
and a shawl is circled around the wife's mother, her daughter, and her son-in-
law as if she were cradling them both in a *sléndang,* the shawl a mother
uses to carry her baby around on her hip until the child can walk. This
latter gesture is intended to suggest that the bride's mother has adopted the

---

[*] The palms are pressed together with fingers extended upwards and thumbs pressed
to the nose, while the unturned head is moved in a strictly horizontal plane, first to
the right and then to the left. The gesture, which has been called "the horizontal nod,"
is usually performed in a crouching position.

groom as her child along with the bride, and the former that she will continue to nurse them both.

The bride and groom now return to the house, where they are seated in front of the *sentong tengah* (or its equivalent), there to remain immobile except for a few ritual acts and the greeting of the guests as they file by. Immobility is associated with spiritual force in Javanese minds. To sit absolutely quiet, without food or sleep, and with your whole mind concentrated on a single imaginary point until it is empty of all thought and sensation—to *tapa*—is the major road to inward strength and outward power. Thus, as the ancient kings sat as rigid as a bronze Buddha during their inauguration or whenever their country was in serious danger, and as the great shadow-play heroes practiced long *tapa* feats before engaging in either love or war, so the unborn child, the just circumcised boy, the newly married couple, and the recently deceased corpse display that trance-like immobility that signifies spiritual power.

As the *ḍukun mantèn,* who has conducted affairs since the beginning of the ceremony, seats the bride and groom, he (or she) chants a spell:

> In the name of God, the Merciful, the Compassionate!
> My intention is to seat the bride and groom.
> Male guardian spirit, female guardian spirit of
>   Sumbersari [the village],
> The land of mBah Nur Wakit [the name of the guardian spirit],
> This is the place of birth of the bride.
> May she stay fixed in position with her husband, by the will of Allah!
> O, forty-four angels, come and help guard the bride and groom!
> I see her from the front—she looks like a princess;
> I see her from the left, she looks likes Sembadra
>   [the beautiful first wife of Ardjuna, the shadow-play hero];
> I see her from the right, she looks like Srikandri
>   [the beautiful second wife of Ardjuna];
> From behind she looks like an angel.
> Jaullah, Jaullah, Jaullah.

Following this chant a *slametan* is held with a layer of yellow rice on top of a layer of white—for love and purity—in each person's banana-leaf dish. The bride and groom eat from one another's dish, but they do not finish their food. The boy's dish is inverted over the girl's to make one unit which remains in place by the *sentong tengah* for five days. When it begins to smell, which is likely to be soon in the tropics, it indicates that the girl is no longer a virgin and the consummation of the marriage has taken place, but only the immediate family members are allowed to inspect this omen.

For the first daughter a special ceremony is performed at this time. (There is some conflict as to whether it ought properly to be held the night before, but in the single case I saw it was held after the *kepanggihan*). Two large painted earthenware vessels are brought out and placed on either side of the couple. Inside one of the vases is old rice, old soy beans, old money, and old vegetable seeds; in the other there are various kinds of *djadjan*— fish chips, popcorn, and so forth—and rice. The father of the bride opens one vase and takes a piece of *djadjan* out and gives it to the mother of the bride, who announces in a loud voice the name of the *djadjan* and takes a bite of it. The father asks: "How does the *djadjan* I just gave you taste?" The mother replies: "It is tasty, sweet, and altogether pleasant." They go through this process several times until there is no more *djadjan,* and then the father takes out the rice and asks his wife: "What is this, Mother [i.e., of the bride]?" "Oh, that's rice, Father." Father: "Oh, this is my wealth; receive it!" Wife: "Yes, Father, I receive it with freedom and happiness in my heart. I will use it to secure well-being for your daughter from this day forward. I receive it gladly." The father pours the rice into her upturned sarong hem and she carries it into the kitchen and mixes it with the rice the guests will later eat.

The *dukun mantèn* then comes forward and the old money, seeds, and so forth are poured into the hem of his sarong; he pours them into the hem of the groom; and the groom pours them into the hem of the bride, symbolizing the fact that the groom is willing to surrender all his riches to the bride. The *dukun* meanwhile chants a spell:

> In the name of God, the Merciful, the Compassionate!
> My intention is to make as one the bride and groom.
> I do not separate them from wealth, I separate them from sickness,
> Old money, old rice, old seeds, old soybean.
> The male ancestors say nothing will happen,
> The female ancestors say nothing will happen,
> Grandfather spirit, you witness that I make the bride and groom as one.
> May they be able to adjust to one another,
> May the two separate bodies come to know one another!
> The male ancestors say nothing will happen,
> The female ancestors say nothing will happen.
> Wherever you go, may you be safe [*slamet*],
> Safe, by the will of Allah.

The *kembang majang* are now thrown on the roof, the bridal couple greet each guest in turn, and the ceremony is completed—although the entertainment, shadow play or whatnot, may continue all through the night.

Following the ceremony, if traditional ways are followed strictly, the couple remain incommunicado for five days at the home of the bride's mother and then move to the groom's house until the thirty-fifth day after marriage. It never occurs that way in Modjokuto any more. Some couples remain for the five-day period at the bride's home, but hardly ever without any guests as they are supposed to do. Many people have a *slametan* following the ceremonial procession from the bride's house to the groom's, and in some cases this may be quite large.* One of the most elaborate feasts—complete with hired dancers—that I saw in Modjokuto was given by a somewhat ambitious *prijaji* for his son on such an occasion, as the boy had been married in Solo in Central Java and his father was anxious not to miss an opportunity to have a dinner party to which he could invite local people of

---

* This *slametan* is called the *kirab* (literally: to shake off dirt as a chicken will, or as a wet dog shakes off water), or the *penindjoan* ("the visit").

importance. But people remain at the groom's house only a night or two, and the 35-day *slametan* is never held now so far as I could tell.

For a bride who has not yet menstruated there is added to the regular marriage rites a special ceremony called the *djago-djagoan.* A friend of the groom, a boy, makes a large white cock (*djago*) out of papier-mâché or muslin and puts Chinese money (the kind with a hole in it), rice, and an egg inside. He then carries it—followed by a long train of clowning young comrades of the groom all crowing like cocks—in a *sléndang,* as though it were a baby, around town, ending up at the groom's house. Then, after the *kepanggihan,* the girl is made to sit on the cock. If the egg breaks it means she has menstruated but has not told anyone. If it does not break, the bride is called a *mantèn pangkon,* a "lap bride," for, although the boy may hold the girl on his lap, he cannot sleep with her. This ceremony is still quite common in Modjokuto and the villages around it.

Social and Economic Aspects of Circumcision and Wedding Ceremonies

THE Javanese call holding a wedding or circumcision ceremony *duwé gawé,* literally "to have work," and claim it to be a prize example of a value they call *rukun,* best translated perhaps as "traditionalized cooperation." The qualifier "traditionalized" is necessary not only because *rukun* is rather more talked about than practiced in Modjokuto today but also because in its correct meaning it refers to specific and concrete practices of labor and capital exchange—in house building, in rice field cultivation, and in irrigation, road building, and other village work—rather than to a general valuation of cooperation as an abstract concept applicable in all contexts of life and completely generalizable—a fact not always taken into account by those who prescribe Western cooperatives for Java's economic ills or argue for the natural social democracy of Javanese village life.

Rukun, as a value, ties together a group not of oversocialized primitive communists but of rather self-contained peasant materialists with a clear realization of where their own interests lie; and it does so not so much by appealing to vague notions of universal brotherhood as by defining actual modes, means, and forms of specifically limited inter-individual cooperation within clearly defined social contexts. As a ceremony, the *duwé gawé* comes as close to generalizing and summarizing these separate obligations to *rukun* as any other institution in traditional Javanese society, for the social function of religious ritual is just to provide such understandable generalizations and summaries of approved social practices in symbolic form. But in what might be called its material aspect—the manner in which the food, entertainment, and spiritual power it mobilizes are organized, financed, and consumed—it provides a clear example of the form these obligations take in actual practice.

On the consumption side, the secular aspects of a wedding or circumcision are usually quite set off from the directly religious aspects. The ceremony proper is most often held in the morning, and one invites only one's near neighbors (plus, in the case of a wedding, perhaps a few of one's closer friends and relatives).

The actual *slametan* food was the usual. . . . and when the time came, the oldest boy went around to the neighbors and invited them. The Setros—real urbanites who lived in the center of Modjokuto town—didn't even know the names of a good number of these neighbors. I asked Pak Setro why he didn't invite his friends instead of these people he doesn't know very well. He said: "If there is ever any trouble you don't go far off looking for your friends, you go to the man next door. So, if you have *slametans,* you invite your neighbor so as to make friendly relations with him so that if you do have trouble the neighbor will help you."

But in the evening, when the secular feast is held and the entertainment presented, one invites as many guests as one wishes and can afford.

Went last night to the Sosro wedding reception. Rather elaborate—catered by Kiet's, the Chinese bakery, with very elaborate food, including a kind of Western meat-and-potato dish. Just about everybody who is anybody was there, and they were divided, the men anyway (the women as usual were in the inside room where the bride and groom were sitting), into about five spatially distinct groups. All the high *prijajis,* about a dozen, headed by the subdistrict officer, were up in the southwest corner of the room in the best seats. All the *santris* of both [of the two main Moslem political] parties came in more or less en bloc and sat in the southeast corner. Thus the Javanese dancers (hired from a local dance school) performed in between these two groups. . . . In the northwest corner, across the aisle from the *prijajis,* were mostly Chinese; and in the southwest corner, across the aisle from the *santris,* was a band of about 40 young men, evidently friends of the groom from Surabaja. . . . who went home in a body about 10 o'clock. Between them and the Chinese were some somewhat lower *prijajis* (mostly teachers), some older *abangan* men, and so forth. All in all, maybe 150 people, not counting perhaps half that many women inside. The whole reception was one of the fanciest I'd seen, with *gamelan,* dancers, fine food, and all.

The above notes record, of course, one extreme; but that was not an isolated case. One elderly *prijaji* hired the local equivalent of the town hall to hold his shadow play in and must have drawn five or six hundred people and fed them all; and the subdistrict officer had large receptions on two successive evenings, one with dancers and one with a shadow play. Even relatively poor people will give fairly elaborate receptions, as can be seen from the following note describing a reception given by a fairly poor railroad worker who lived in a two-room bamboo shack near me:

Went to a wedding at Pak Reso's in the *kampong* across the road. . . . The women sat inside in the front room. The men sat outside at small square tables in a thatched bamboo shelter erected for the purpose and were served one cup of coffee (one only—one man was given a second cup by accident, and it was taken back) and small *djadjan* of various kinds. There was a seven-piece band, all string (bass, violins, guitars, etc.), complete with a female singer with pearls and thin voice, and the effect of the whole thing, with lanterns, tables, and all, was like a night club. The girl sang Indonesian popular songs, as did some of the other members of the otherwise all-male band. It was rather dull, nobody talking very much, and after a while people began playing cards at a few tables. (Card-playing continued all night. Gambling is always a prime feature at such receptions; at fancy weddings you may find Chinese-run roulette wheels.)

Even for the near-destitute some sort of reception must be arranged, as this description of a circumcision celebration held by a family in which the father had no work (he also was seriously ill with tuberculosis) shows:

Inside the house the women were sitting chatting. This was an extremely simple affair—one strand of palm leaves over the door, no furniture, just mats to sit on, nothing fancy in the way of *djadjan*. mBok Mun and her sister explained to me that the boy came to them less than a week ago and said, "I want to be circumcised this week." They answered: "Why not wait till after the harvest?" and he is supposed to have said no, he didn't want too much fuss. So they borrowed or got money somehow and had it now. The boy said he was getting ashamed of being so old (he is about 12). . . . The boy came in to sit in a chair prepared for him and, with much advice from everyone about keeping his sarong from touching his penis and keeping his legs spread, sat in state there. They let his local playmates come in and sit around him. . . . I went home and ate, and when I got back later the front room was packed with about 40 people playing cards (and they had all been served food). The card playing continued all through the night, but there was no other entertainment.

A better idea of the sacrifice these people had made to give this reception can be gained from a later interview with the same family:

I went to see mBok Mun down the street. Her husband had gone out to look at the water situation in one of her sister's rice fields. Her husband only works here and there nowadays, mainly because he is sick, I guess. He gets work once in a while from whomever happens to need someone—three or four days a week if he is lucky; if not, less. Evidently family fortunes have gone steadily downhill in the last couple of years. He used to be a sharecropper with two oxen of his own. One ox he sold to marry off his eldest daughter. . . . The other ox he sold a while later to circumcise his oldest son. mBok Mun seemed to think it absolutely necessary to give these big *duwé gawé* affairs and regarded their coming as a kind of natural affliction. . . . She said her husband might have to go off somewhere else to look for work and leave her home alone, but she is too old to worry about that anymore. She said things were very tough, and that as far as she could see there was much more unhappiness in the world than there was happiness.

Having shown something of the range of variation in the patterns of expenditure of wealth at the *duwé gawé,* it remains next to show where this wealth comes from and how it is mobilized. A man giving such a feast has a number of sources of support. He can draw on the labor of his relatives and, especially if he is wealthy and of high status to start with, friends. He can spend money out of his own savings, as mBok Mun did when she sold her oxen, or borrow, at ruinous rates of interest, from either friends or moneylenders. Finally, he receives a small cash payment called a *buwuh*, from all those who attend the feasts. Almost always a man will draw on all these sources, although he will avoid borrowing if it is at all possible—which is rare.

The ability to call on others for labor is perhaps the feastgiver's greatest economic asset. For the *slametan* this is traditionally confined to his relatives, for the ideal pattern is that a set of kin prepares a *slametan* and a set of neighbors consumes it. At a *slametan* in a village near Modjokuto, the following people worked for two days to prepare the *slametan* and the various meals which surrounded it: the wife of the younger brother of the pregnant girl (the occasion was a *tingkeban*); the father's younger sister and the sister of her husband; her older sister (she came from another village nearby); two of her nieces; the wife of her younger brother; the mother-in-law of her older sister; and two neighbors she had known since childhood. The attached males butchered the goat, built the shelter for the guests, and so forth. Thus in the village context this pattern still holds up, at least to a degree, as it does among many of the poorer townspeople.

In such a situation an exact reciprocality is maintained. Each person who worked for the pregnant girl and her husband had the right to call on them for a day's work for a similar purpose at a later date, and such obligations, no matter how complex they become, are remembered. Evidently, also, there are variations in the ability of different families to cooperate internally.

> Talking about *rukun* again, she said that some families are more able to *rukun* than others. The family of her sister-in-law, the wife of Prijo, are very *rukun*, and if any one of the ten people in the family who live around there has a feast, everyone chips in about 50 rupiahs. But Minah's in-laws—none of them will do that. They will help in the kitchen, but they will never contribute any money.

The more elaborate town weddings tend to draw not merely on relatives but also on a larger group of friends, neighbors, and, most particularly since the revolution, fellow women's-club members. For *santris* the group of women belonging to the ladies' auxiliaries of the two Islamic political parties forms a kind of rotating work force for one another's weddings and circumcisions; for the *prijajis* the women's nationalist organization Perwari forms a similar group; and for some *abangans* women's groups connected with the labor unions play a similar role. In these arrangements the reciprocality may not be exact, especially between people of differing status. Thus, for example, the wife of the district officer, who had about 50 people working in her kitchen for three days before her daughter's wedding, would be expected to work, if at all, in return for only a select handful of the highest-status women. But a general equivalence of contribution is expected even if among the more exalted it often approaches the merely symbolic.

As for spending from their own savings, people may, like mBok Mun, sell capital equipment such as bicycles, textiles, or jewelry, or they may merely pawn it. Pawning may seem on the surface more like borrowing than spending out of savings, and insofar as interest must be paid to the pawnshop (which is government-owned and -run), perhaps it is. But from the Javanese point of view, such items as bicycles, textiles, and gold jewelry (which is sold by the Chinese goldsmith complete with a ticket saying how much he will give in pawn for it if the purchaser brings it back to him) are often seen primarily as claims on stored cash, as we see credits in a bankbook. Since people know how much they can pawn various items for, expensive textiles and jewelry sometimes serve almost entirely this notational purpose, being very seldom worn. They are, in fact, purchased in the first place with the expressed purpose that the buyer is trying to build up a pawnable surplus for use in circumcising and marrying off his children. Oxen, goats, chickens, and the like are often purchased with the intent to raise them and then sell them when the time comes for a ceremony; and petty clerks in town will often buy a quarter of an acre or so of village land and rent it out for a similar purpose.

Very little Javanese saving, then, is in the form of cash or bank credit; most of it is in hard goods. One method by which cash may be saved more directly is through the various cooperative savings societies, of which there are literally dozens around town. People form these among their friends, neighbors, fellow club members, fellow workers, and in fact in almost every conceivable social group. Each person puts in, say, five rupiahs a week. (Among the wealthy, the weekly contribution may be as much as 50 rupiahs.) Each week lots are drawn, and the "winner" gets (if there are ten people in the society, which is about average) 50 rupiahs, such money being quite often used for *slametans*. This system also appears in the popular burial societies. Each person contributes so much a month, and his family receives a set sum—to be used to pay for his funeral—at his death. The same general principle is applied to the buying of plates, glasses, and other utensils needed for feasts. Each person pays a share of the cost and then can use the equipment when he needs it, paying a small fee to the others if he uses it out of turn.

Borrowing, the third source of possible resources, is, at least verbally, not approved; and for the *slametan* proper it is prohibited, for it makes the ceremony religiously invalid.

> She said it was important not to borrow for a *slametan* because if one does, it won't be valid. The spirits will come and look, but they won't eat. It is better just to take what little rice one has [and add a few simple side dishes] than to give a complicated *slametan* if one doesn't have the money.

Nevertheless, borrowing is just about inevitable for feasts of any size and often leads to quite serious difficulties.

> The village clerk then went home to Sawahredjo [a village near Modjokuto], and in about half an hour he was back dashing in to Ali's and telling us he was on his way to the subdistrict office to report a suicide by hanging, naming the woman and going on. Ali and the clerk both knew the woman. Ali speculated that the cause of the woman's suicide was that back in the month of

Besar she had held a circumcision for which she borrowed money from her friends, and now she couldn't pay it back, and so was embarrassed and killed herself. This was all based on no evidence, so far as I could see, just a surmise, although perhaps there were rumors about her insolvency, the size of the circumcision ceremony being too large, and so on. (Ali's speculation on further investigation turned out to be correct.) Ali said it was better to give a little ceremony within one's means than to borrow from friends and then not be able to pay back.

The fourth major source of wealth for the feast given is the *buwuh,* perhaps the most interesting from the theoretical point of view, since it reveals the value premises upon which the whole *duwé gawé* pattern rests. The *buwuh* is typically a monetary contribution by the guest to the host in return for the food and hospitality he receives. The usual manner of presenting it is to place it in the palm of one's hand and press it secretly in the host's palm on shaking his hand upon departing, at which point the host diffidently hands the giver's wife a small paper sack of *djadjan* tidbits as a symbol of the contribution he has made to the giver during the evening by feeding and entertaining him. Again a sharp sense of reciprocity is involved here.

Lots of weddings coming up, she (the informant) said. She has been invited to one at Ichwan's, one at Abdullah's, and one at the home of a man named Rasdi in Sumbersari. The last one she doesn't know well; so she doesn't have to go and doesn't have to give a *buwuh.* (If she were obligated to give a *buwuh,* she would do so whether she attended the celebration or not; if she did not go, she would send her child with the *buwuh* and receive a bananaleaf dish full of food in return.) As for Abdullah, she knows the wife extremely well, and, besides, the wife gave her a *buwuh* when she had a baby, and so she must go and give a *buwuh* in return. Ichwan is a neighbor; and she feels that, since in a year or so she is going to have a circumcision for her son, Sustrisno, it is rather like "saving" for her to give *buwuhs* to her neignbors. It is very sad when someone gives a ceremony and no one *buwuhs;* and this is because the person himself didn't go to many and didn't give *buwuhs.* The other day she went to a *slametan* given to a niece of her neighbor. Pak Senèn, who had just had a baby, and there was not much giving of *buwuhs.* She had taken her littlest child with her, and he kept eating all the *djadjan;* and so out of shame she gave a *buwuh* although she hadn't intended to.

Evidently the *buwuh* was originally the actual food used at the feast, or a direct replacement for it. Close relatives still often give food instead of money; and at death—which often occurs unexpectedly—everyone contributes rice rather than cash, for the food is immediately needed for the *slametan.* Thus the *buwuh* is, as is the labor contribution, ideally a form of *rukun.*

Nowadays, especially in the town, the *buwuh* is sometimes viewed more cynically as a possible source of profit, and many people are said to hold celebrations mainly in hopes of material gain from the guests' contributions.

He said he had heard that some man in a village some distance from here had hired an acting group for a wedding, and he said the man would probably make lots of profit. He said the *buwuh,* which used to be a matter of *rukun,* particularly in the days when it was not money but goods like food and so forth, has degenerated into a simple money-making proposition on the part of the person giving the *duwé gawé* affair. Most of the time the money coming in is more than what is put out; so the host profits; and so lots of people like to hold feasts now just to make a profit. People say it is too bad if one doesn't have any children of his own to have marriage and circumcision celebrations for, because one loses out on a chance to make some money. He said that *santris* for the most part don't approve of this and don't practice it. (As the informant was himself a *santri,* this is hardly an unbiased observation. However, insofar as *santris* tend to disapprove of large expenditures of wealth in general, there is probably a grain of truth in it.) But for most people now this notion of the *slametan* as a business proposition is a recognized thing. He said Merto, the curer, is a prime practitioner of this sort of thing. Recently he had a marriage in which he used not his own child but a girl borrowed from a poorer relative, and since he did not have much entertainment he must have made an enormous profit.

There is, however, another tendency, somewhat in opposition to this more commercial one. Many people attempt to gain prestige through lavish celebrations, some of them on a truly remarkable scale. Among the *prijajis,* who show this tendency most clearly, the *buwuh* pattern insofar as it concerns money is rejected as crass, and a giving of presents, especially at weddings, replaces it.

We spoke about the difference between village and town patterns of *duwé gawé,* and she said the *buwuh* pattern was different. She said that the people on the Pohredjo row (this is the elite section of town, inhabited almost entirely by *prijajis*) wouldn't accept *buwuh.* They only accept gifts (called *cadeau,* following Dutch usage), and then they note down the price of the gift, and when the giver has a *duwé gawé* they return something of exactly the same value. In the village, on the contrary, one must give a *buwuh,* and if one doesn't he feels ashamed. (Her younger brother said, "You give a *buwuh* because you don't want the other person to be stuck with a tremendous debt, and you figure your turn will come around next time and you'll want to get your *buwuhs.*") . . . . She said in the village the thing is all supposed to even out, but usually the host loses. . . . But she still thought the giving of *buwuhs* was a good thing, because it showed the *rukun* of neighbors and friends. She said that among the police (her husband was a member of the central government police force) at her level (vice constable) and below they accepted *buwuhs,* while above her level they followed what she called the Pohredjo pattern.

Chapter 6

The *Slametan* Cycles: Death

Funerals: *Lajatan*

IN CONTRAST to other rites of passage, all funerals (*lajatan*) are still inevitably conducted by the *modin,* the official religious specialist of the village. A few people call him now and then to lead prayers for birth and circumcision ceremonies (he is almost always a strong *santri*), and in any case he must take the groom down to the *naib's* office for the Islamic part of the marriage ceremony; but it is at death that he really comes into his own as general director of the entire affair.

When there is a death in a family the first thing they do is to send for the *modin,* and the second is to spread the word around the neighborhood that a death has occurred. If death occurs in the late afternoon or during the night, they wait until the next morning to begin the funeral process.

Javanese funerals occur as quickly as possible after death. A man dead at 10 A.M. will be buried by noon or shortly thereafter, and a man dead at 4 P.M. will be in the grave by ten the next morning. Although the family will sometimes delay an hour or so if some relatives are coming from a distance, apparently they rarely delay long enough: these distant relatives never seemed to be on time for any of the funerals I saw. The usual reason given when one asks why there is so much haste is that the spirit of the dead man is flying around loose (it is often conceived of as a bird) until he is buried, and this is dangerous to everyone, especially to the survivors. The sooner he is buried, the sooner his spirit can return to its natural home.

As soon as they receive the news of a death, the neighbors drop whatever they are doing and go off to the house where the death has occurred. (Even salaried workers on the railroad and in the government offices leave immediately on such news.) Each woman brings a tray of rice, which, after a handful of it has been thrown out the door by the bereaved, is immediately cooked for a *slametan.* The men bring tools with which to

68

make grave markers, a litter to carry the body to the grave (in most cases, however, this is rented or provided by the burial society), and wooden supports to put inside the grave. Actually, only a half-dozen or so of the very close neighbors need bring tools; the other men just come and stand around chatting in the yard.

More than any other single passage rite the funeral draws everyone. Class lines, ideological antagonisms, and personal quarrels often modify the strictly geographical attendance at other *slametans,* especially in the town of Modjokuto, but everyone who lives near a dead man and anyone in the town who knew him at all well or is in any way related to him comes to his funeral. Again, one finds the notion that one should go to other people's funerals so they will come to his. When I questioned one man about a burial society to which he belonged, he said that the money one gets at death is only nominal. What is important is that all the members of the society are obligated to come to a member's funeral.

When the *modin* arrives, he strips the corpse, laying a sarong loosely over the genitals, ties the jaw up with a string over the top of the head so it cannot drop open, and ties the feet together. The arms are crossed on the chest, right hand over left, with the tips of the fingers touching the shoulders, and the body is laid with its head to the north, a lamp being sometimes lit above the head. The corpse is then washed by the close relatives and friends of the deceased—preferably (but not necessarily) the women if the deceased is female, the men if male—under the direction of the *modin.* The relatives hold the corpse on their laps while sitting on chairs so the water drenches them and their clothes. This act is called *pangkon,* the same word which is used when one cradles a small child on one's lap, or when the groom cradles the not yet pubescent wife, and as such is a last demonstration of nurturing love by the survivors for the deceased.

The corpse is bathed in the front yard, protected from general view by hastily erected bamboo matting—although people feel free to look over the matting at will. Usually three different kinds of water, each in a different earthenware container, are used: one with flowers in it; one with money, a special kind of tree leaf, and various herbs in it; and one plain, without anything in it. In addition, there is a shampoo for the hair made of burned rice stalks. The *modin* pours the first dipper of water on the corpse, and then the other relatives each take a turn.

Being able to hold one's deceased father, wife, sister, uncle, or whomever on one's lap while he is being washed, is called being *tegel*—able to do something odious, abominable, and horrible without flinching, to stick it out despite an inward fear and revulsion. No one is absolutely required to do this; and if none of the family members or close relatives is *tegel,* the corpse may be laid crossways on three banana-tree trunks. Since they are expected to be *tegel* and if they are not are severely criticized, most people would feel deeply ashamed to withdraw from this duty or to show any strong open emotion while performing it. A young girl I knew was crying slightly when her father died rather suddenly, and her relatives told her she would not be allowed to wash the body if she did not stop crying, which she immediately did. Two reasons are given for the prohibition of tears near the corpse: it makes the atmosphere dark so that the deceased will have great difficulty finding his path to the grave; and it so upsets the deceased that he cannot bear to leave the house.

After the bathing the bathers wash their hands and feet in the water which is left. The orifices of the body are plugged with cotton dipped in perfume, the body is wrapped in white muslin and tied in three places (feet, waist, and top of the head) by the *modin,* and then about a half-dozen *santris* begin to chant the Koran under his leadership. The chant takes place next to the corpse, which has now been placed in the main living room, and lasts from five to ten minutes. Then the body is placed on the litter, a bamboo framework over which brand new textiles have been stretched with strings of flowers laid across them. These textiles are not buried with the corpse; and one of the standing graveyard jokes seems to be to bargain with the man who carries them back from the grave as though he were peddling them.

The litter is carried into the yard, where the descendants (usually children) of the deceased duck back and forth under it three times. This is to indicate that they are *iklas*—that their emotions have been quieted and have been flattened out into a true detachment, that they feel no psychological pain at the departure of the deceased, and that their hearts are already free. A few coins wrapped in paper are then distributed to each person at the funeral to symbolize the same idea: as they can give away money without feeling any remorse, so they can let the deceased go with no wish to cling to him emotionally. (Sometimes, but not always, a few of the guests are given banana-leaf dishes of rice to eat at this time, in which case they get no coins, for the latter are a substitute for the former.) A vessel filled with water is thrown on the ground and broken, also to symbolize *iklas,* and the litter moves off to the graveyard, carried by the men, while the women remain behind at the house, scattering salt so the soul will not come back and disturb them. (Children, except the dead man's own, are kept away from funerals because they are so easily entered by spirits.)

As there is almost always a graveyard within a half mile, the funeral procession is not extended. At the head of it walk the men carrying the homemade wooden grave markers—sharply pointed ones for a male corpse, flat or rounded ones for a female—marked usually only with the name and date of death of the deceased. They are followed by the men carrying the planks for the grave.* Next comes a man carrying a golden or bronze bowl containing yellow rice, turmeric, various coins, flowers, and betel, all of which he strews along the ground as he walks to show the following corpse, borne usually by four to eight men, the way to the grave. Behind the corpse, over whose head is held a parasol to shield it from the sun, comes the body of attending men, rarely less than fifteen, sometimes as many as two hundred.

---

* The grave is prepared during the time the washing and winding are going on. It is dug about three feet wide and about two or three feet deep. In the floor of the excavation a slit-trench just wide and deep enough for the corpse is cut. The planks are placed over the trench after the body has been placed in it so that when the grave is filled no earth falls directly on the corpse.

People change off in the jobs of scattering the rice and flowers, holding the parasol, and bearing the corpse, for it is considered necessary that all male members of the family and very close friends should "feel the weight of the corpse" for at least a short time.

The ceremony at the graveyard is brief. The body is taken off the litter and put into the grave on its side, being handed down to three men standing in the grave. The body is laid to rest on seven stones with its head pointed to the north. The strings on the shroud are loosened and the face exposed so that the cheek touches the earth, and then either the *modin* or some other *santri* jumps down into the grave and shouts the Confession of Faith three times into the dead man's ear. The planks are then laid in place, the dirt pushed into the grave, and the grave markers erected. The *modin* reads the *tèlkim,* a set funeral speech addressed to the deceased, first in Arabic and then in Javanese (some old-fashioned *modins* refuse to translate it, however, regarding this as against the strict tenets of Islam):

> Oh, you are already living in the world of the grave (Moslem corpses remain slumbering in the grave until Judgment Day—a kind of limbo). Do not forget the Confession of Faith. You will shortly be visited by two messengers of God, two angels (Mungkar and Nakir, who visit each new corpse to question him about his faith, etc.). (The angels will say:) "O human being, who is your God and what is your religion, and who is your prophet and what is your religious lodestar, and what is the direction in which you turn to pray, and what has been commanded of you and who are your brothers?" You must answer clearly and forthrightly; you must not be afraid or startled: "The Lord Allah is my God; Islam is my religion; Muhammad is my Prophet; the Holy Koran is my lodestar; I turn toward the Black Stone of Mecca to pray; the five daily prayers are what I have been commanded; all Moslems, men and women, are by brothers." O Pak Tjipto (the name of the deceased), you know already know that the questions of the angels do in fact exist, that life in the grave does in fact exist, that the balancing of good and evil deeds does in fact exist, that heaven and hell indeed do in fact exist, and that the Lord Allah will wake each individual in the grave on Judgment Day is a fact as well.

After this the great mass of mourners goes back to their homes or jobs, but a small group of close neighbors, friends, and relatives returns to the house for a *slametan.* (This group must include all those who actually worked at the funeral—who dug the grave, made the grave markers, etc.). All death *slametans* are marked by two special food symbols: the small round rice-flour pancakes called *apem,* which are the special food of the dead and of one's ancestors;* and a flattened-out disc of rice with two large cones of rice seven or eight inches high. The flattened rice again symbolizes *iklas;* but in addition the contrast between the flat disk and the cones is supposed to suggest the difference between death and life—the flattened-out featurelessness of death and the phallic upward-directedness of life. However, some others say one of the cones is for the living, the other for the dead.

Slametans of exactly the same form, but of increasing size in terms of the

---

* Sometimes one finds *apem* cakes at other *slametans* too, where their intent is always to honor the ancestors; but their real place is in death rituals.

number of guests and the length of the chant, are held three, seven, forty, and one hundred days after death, on the first and second anniversaries of the death, and on the thousandth day after death. Each child of the deceased who maintains a separate household must give the whole series of *slametans*. The last *slametan,* which marks the point at which the body is thought to have decayed entirely to dust, is the most elaborate. One is supposed to kill ritually a dove, goose, or other fowl, which is then washed in flower water, shampooed, and wrapped in muslin exactly as the corpse was. (This ceremony is called the *kékah,* and sometimes occurs at an earlier *slametan,* but in any case only once. It is often omitted altogether nowadays.) The *apem* and the rice-disc symbol of death are omitted; the whole chicken for the Prophet and the various other foods used for *slametans* on happier occasions are re-introduced; and once again one gives out coins to the guests as a symbol of one's final turning from the dead toward the living. After this *slametan* the gap between the dead and the living is absolute, but for one's parents one should go to their grave to strew flowers on each an-niversary of their death, on the day before the Fast begins, when one is ill or when one's children are, and any time one happens to dream of them, for this means that they are hungry and wish to be fed. (One may, if the dream is vivid enough, give a small *slametan* and take some of it to a prayer house and have the *santris* there chant a while for the dead; or one may merely put some food, tea, and flowers at the crossroad.)

After death one also puts out food for the dead—the kind of food the de-ceased especially liked—near the *seṇṭong tengah* spot in the house or by the bed he died in for 40 days after death, and usually a *sadjèn* is added. One I saw included an ancient photograph of the deceased. If one wishes, he may for about 35 rupiahs hire some *santris* to chant in their prayer house an hour or two each night for seven days after death, and even some pretty anti-Islamic people do this. As an old *santri* lady said to me in reference to my vigorously *abangan* landlady, "People like Bu Ardjo hate *santris* like me, but they need us to do their praying for them."

Beliefs and Attitudes concerning Death

THE mode of a Javanese funeral, as one can see from the foregoing description, is not one of hysterical bereavement, unrestrained sobbing, or even of formalized shrieks of grief for the deceased's departure. Rather it is a calm, undemonstrative, almost languid letting go, a brief ritualized relinquishment of a relationship no longer possible. Tears are not approved of and certainly not encouraged; and one sees remarkably few of them. The effort is to get the job done, not to linger over the pleasures of grief. The detailed busy-work of the funeral, the politely formal social intercourse with the neighbors pressing in from all sides, the series of *slametans* stretched out at intervals for almost three years—the whole momentum of the Javanese ritual system—are supposed to carry one through the grief process evenly and without severe emotional disturbance.

Iklas, that state of willed affectlessness, is the watchword, and although it is often difficult to achieve, it is always striven for.

I went to buy a sarong from Mudjito, whose wife died suddenly about two weeks ago. Mudjito was still rather upset about it evidently, smiling a nervous smile from ear to ear and talking about it without a pause for breath from the moment I came in until the moment I left. . . . He said first, as Javanese inevitably do when they "have trouble," "I beg your pardon a thousand times because my wife is not here" (that is, please lighten my burden of grief by giving me your pardon); and I mumbled in return that I was sorry I had not come to see him sooner. He then went on at great length about how he was *iklas,* that it was God that took his wife away, and that he had no right to complain. He said that he was just *iklas* and bent to the will of God (Mudjito was a *santri* and thus more likely to ascribe things to the will of God than an *abangan* would be). There was nothing he could do anyway. When first she died, he could see no reason to go on working (I noticed him already in the store the day after the death, people going in and out paying their respects). What was the point of it? He said that he felt that his wife was not evil and had done no wrong, and he felt that she didn't deserve to die so young. But after a while he began to see that . . . he should be *iklas,* and he slowly talked himself into being *iklas,* and now that he was truly *iklas* he didn't feel anything at all any more. He said that's the way one should feel. One's feeling should be flat, even, always on the same level. One shouldn't go up and down in feeling, very unhappy one minute and very happy the next, but try to keep one's feelings evened out. He said that happiness and unhappiness are irrevocably connected with one another; so, if one is happy now, he will surely be unhappy later on, and one should not indulge himself in either feeling. If one feels happy, one should remember the unhappiness he had before and that he will have again; and if one is unhappy, he should remember the happiness he had before and he will have again later, and so keep his emotions averaged out. This is what he has tried to do. It is the right thing to do. It is wrong to be very sad, depressed, and upset; one should try to keep his feelings without mountains and valleys—on a level plain. He said one shouldn't keep strong emotions locked up in his heart, but *iklas.* "Just like when I sell you this sarong, I should feel I got the right price, and you should too, so that neither of us is upset inside his heart. We must be *iklas* toward it, and that is the way I feel about my wife's death." . . . He said he felt at first as if he would like to die too, but then he talked himself out of it and said he had to carry on to see the children raised.

Sometimes this self-discipline proves to be too difficult and more direct measures need to be applied.

I asked him if he was upset when his mother died a few years ago, and he said no, she was already old; and besides, he had been down to see her about four or five days before she died, and she was very ill, and so he knew she was going to die. So he was not startled by it. . . . He said one doesn't get upset when people are old and sick and then die. How about for babies, I asked. He replied, "Yes, for them you often get very upset. If they are only a month or two old, you don't get very upset,* but if they are already a year or a year and a half old and you have been watching them play around and they are very cute and all and then they die, you can get quite upset." He said that when his youngest child died (evidently not so long ago) at the age of one and a half, his oldest son, who is about 17 or 18, cried solidly for a week, couldn't eat, couldn't sleep or anything. Finally, he went and got a *dukun* for him, and the *dukun* came and gave the boy some magic tea to drink and uttered a spell over the boy enjoining him to forget about the death, which he then did. He stopped crying and ate and slept normally.

Despite deviations such as this, most people do what can only be called a remarkable job of at least not showing their grief.

Death does not seem to hold any overwhelming terrors for most Javanese, and people talk about it directly with little show of anxiety. Once at a funeral of a man whom I did not know and had never seen I was sitting with two old men, one about sixty, the other about seventy. "How old was the deceased?" I asked, somewhat tactlessly trying to find out how much of a blow his death had been to his family. "Was he already old or did he die in middle age?" "Oh," said the sixty-year-old, "he was already quite old; it was already his time to go. He was just a little younger than Pak Paidin here," pointing gracefully with his thumb to the seventy-year-old, to which Pak Paidin immediately agreed without any show of gloom or even graveyard humor, but merely as a man would agree with any simple statement of fact.

Whatever the deeper psychological reasons for this relative equanimity about personal extinction may be, assuming it is real, there are beliefs on the intellectual level to which one might point in partial explanation. One inform- ant insisted that curers can never have any effect on the length of one's life. If one is going to die at thirty, he will die at thirty; if at sixty, sixty. All the *dukun* can do is make life easier for one so that, instead of being ill from one's thirtieth year until one's fated death, at, say, seventy-five, one goes to a *dukun* to be cured and live happily to the day of death. There are variations on this belief in fate, however; for some hold that a man's life will be lengthened if he behaves ethically, and other people (or sometimes the same ones—the logical compatibility of separate beliefs is not usually a serious issue for *abangans*) think that premature death may be the result of sheer accident, sorcery, consorting with evil spirits, taking a false oath, an especially fast pace of living, persistent and prolonged emotional upset, or a sudden trauma of some sort.

But perhaps the major intellectual reason Javanese seem not to fear death so much as some other peoples is that it seems to them to bear the character- istics of that emptiness of emotional and intellectual content, that inner re- straint of the will, that they value so highly.

He talked a little about his attitude toward death. It was all determined ab- solutely by God, so there was no use worrying about it and no use feeling sorry when someone else died. I asked him why some sinners flourished as

* Funerals for infants are almost always abbreviated, and usually only the initial *slametan* and perhaps the three-day *slametan* are held; also, as the baby is innocent, the *tèlkim* speech at the grave is omitted, as it is for children generally.

the green bay tree, and so forth, and he said that he thought God was giving them a chance to understand. He laughed and said, "Yes, you often see old bent-over men who are real sinners." And he said he thought that God keeps them living in hopes they'll finally see the light, whereas the young good ones are all right anyway and so they die early, as a kind of reward, for it is a good thing to be dead. He spoke happily, not in any *weltschmerz* mood. I asked why he thought this, and he said, "Well, when you are dead, you don't want anything: you don't want an auto, you don't want money, you don't want a wife, you don't have any wants at all. Like God—God doesn't need any money, or wife, or auto, does He? Well, that's wonderful, not to want anything; and after you're dead, that's the way it is." I said, "Well, if it is so good being dead, why don't people kill themselves?" He was properly offended at this idea and said, "That would be wrong because it would be from your own will. It is up to God to decide when you should die, not yourself. It is wrong to commit suicide because you are trying to take into your own hands affairs which are properly God's." But he said he was ready to die any time (he was about seventy); he thought it a good state not to want anything, not to need anything, like God, and he seemed to find it rather unimaginable (*mboten masuk akal*—literally, "it doesn't go into the mind") that this didn't seem like an obvious and self-evident proposition to me.

Three separate notions of life after death, again often held concurrently by the same individual, are present in Modjokuto. The first is the Islamic version of the concept of eternal retribution, of punishment and reward in the afterworld for the sins and good deeds in this one. This is, naturally enough, strongest among the *santris,* often—especially among the more modern groups —complete with ideas of hell-fire, the constant moral inspection of the individual by God, and the awfulness of absolute Judgment (but never, of course, original sin, a concept notably absent in Islam). One finds it throughout the society, although usually rather vaguely conceived and only half believed in outside of strictly Moslem circles.

Much more popular with *abangans* is the concept of *sampurna,* which means literally "perfect" or "complete" but which indicates in this context that the individual personality completely disappears after death and nothing is left of the person but dust. (Like many peoples around the world, the Javanese, although they often conceive of the dead as spirits annoying the living or demanding worship from them, never consider seriously what it must be like to be a spirit and never reflect that they will become one themselves. One sometimes hears the idea that spirits of the dead who attack people are those of individuals who have been evil in their lifetime, and sometimes also *sétans* and the like are held to originate partly from this source, although this is as often explicitly denied.)

The third view, which is extremely widely held by all but *santris,* who condemn it as heretical, is the notion of reincarnation—that when a person dies his soul enters shortly thereafter into an embryo on its way to being born. The usual way in which this occurs is that a pregnant woman feels a sudden intense craving for some special food—an orange out of season or a duck egg —and the soul is inside this food and so enters the woman's womb and is reborn as her child. Often but not always reincarnation occurs within the same family, although the relationship may be rather distant and the individual in whom the soul is reincarnated need not necessarily be of the same sex as the deceased. It may be heralded by a dream on the part of the mother or established by a similarity of features in the child and the recently deceased or by a similar birthmark. It is not wise to tell a child when it is still young of whom it is the reincarnation, for this might make the soul within the child ashamed, and he would fall sick. After he is over six or so, it does not matter any more. When I asked people of whom they were the reincarnation, they never seemed to know, although they could almost always tell me of whom their children were reincarnations. Sometimes people hold to the Hindu notion of advancement and regression in the stages of being according to one's deportment while alive; but most *abangans* leave this sort of thing to *prijajis* to reflect upon and use the idea of reincarnation primarily to explain personal peculiarities in their children and strange behavior on the part of an odd animal now and then, such as dogs who fast, as humans often do, on Mondays and Thursdays.

The Javanese have sometimes been said to worship their ancestors, but, except for the vague apostrophes to "the ancestors" taken generally or to one's own ancestors as "grandfathers and grandmothers" in spells and at *slametans,* the burning of incense to "ancestors" on Thursday nights by a few people, and the decoration of family graves now and again, evidence of any kind of ancestor cult is absent in Modjokuto. Javanese claim they reckon kinship ascent eight generations back and have terms for each level (father, grandfather, great-grandfather . . .); but I never knew anyone who knew his ancestors by name back farther than his grandfather, and I have never heard of an ancestor, other than parents, being petitioned by name. Javanese "ancestor worship", in present-day Modjokuto at least, amounts to little more than a pious expression of respect for the dead plus a lively awareness of the necessity of being on good terms with one's own deceased father and mother and of being sure to feed them some rice or flowers when they appear in one's dreams.

Chapter 7

The *Slametan* Cycles: Calendrical, Village, and Intermittent *Slametans*

Calendrical *Slametans*

IN ADDITION to the cycle of *slametans* connected with the points of passage in the life of the individual, there is another cycle, much less elaborated and emphasized, connected with the yearly Moslem calendar.* Having adopted the Islamic pattern of time reckoning by lunar months and the holy days which are attached to it (the orthodox significance of which remain a concern only of *santris*), the Javanese have felt obliged to celebrate its sacred time periods in the only way they know: by giving *slametans*. However, except for the Prophet's Birthday and the complex of *slametans* centering around the Fast,** these ceremonies have remained simple and rather unimportant and are given only sporadically.

The following are calendrical *slametans* which the Javanese recognize:

1 *Sura:* This is a Buddhist rather than a Moslem holiday, and as such it is celebrated only by those who are self-consciously anti-Moslem. With the development since the war of some vigorously anti-Moslem sects and individual religious teachers preaching a return to "original" Javanese customs, *slametans* on 1 *Sura* have perhaps increased slightly in frequency. Some particularly anti-Islamic individuals even fast in *Sura* instead of in *Pasa*, but this is rather rare.

10 *Sura:* In honor of Hasan and Husein, the grandsons of the Prophet,

* The Moslem year has 354 days (355 in leap years) and is divided into twelve lunar months. In the following list of the months, the Arabic names are given, with the popular Javanese names in parentheses: Muharram (Sura), Safar (Sapar), Rabi'u-lawal (Mulud), Rabi'ulachir (Bakdamulud), Djumadilawal (Djumadilawal), Djumadila-chir (Djumadilakir), Radjab (Redjeb), Sja'ban (Ruwah), Ramadan (Pasa), Sjawal (Sawal), Dzulka'idah (Sela), Dzulhidjah (Besar).

** The word *pasa* means "fasting" in general. *Pasa* is also the popular name for the month of Ramadan, during which it is forbidden to eat, drink, or smoke between sunrise and sunset.

who, the story goes, wanted to give a *slametan* for Muhammad when the Prophet was fighting with the infidels. They carried rice (where they got rice in Arabia is not discussed) to the river to wash it, but the horses of the enemy came by and kicked it away into the river. The two boys wept and then picked up the rice and found it mixed with sand and pebbles, but they made porridge of it anyway. Thus this *slametan* is marked by two bowls of porridge—one with pebbles and sand in it for the grandsons to eat, and one with peanuts and bits of fried cassava in it to represent the impurities, which the people eat. Although some people said this essentially *Shi'ite* but locally distorted ritual was still sometimes given, I never saw one in Modjokuto, and it is at any rate quite rare.

12 *Mulud:* The day on which, by agreed convention, the Prophet both was born and died. This *slametan* is called *Muludan* (this and the name of the month itself, *Mulud,* are derived from the Arabic *maulud,* "nativity"). It is marked by a whole stuffed chicken (the insides are taken out, cleaned, and replaced, and the chicken is then tied up), the major offering to the Prophet at all *slametans.* This *slametan* is perhaps the most regularly given of the calendrical *slametans.*

27 *Redjeb:* This *slametan* (called *Redjeban*) celebrates the *Mi'radj,* the one-night ascension of Muhammad to face God. The food is the same as on *Muludan,* and although it is given fairly frequently (always on a very simple scale) very few non-*santris* have much of an idea what its purpose is supposed to be.

29 *Ruwah:* The beginning of the Fast, called *Megengan* (from *pegeng,* "to wean"). This *slametan* is invariably given by all those who have at least one parent dead. (*Ruwah,* the name of the month, comes from the Arabic *arwah,* "souls of the dead.") Like the death *slametans* proper, it is marked by the presence of the rice-flour pancake called *apem,* which is the Javanese food symbol of death. Just before the *slametan* one goes to the cemetery to scatter flowers on the graves of the parents involved, and the dead parents supposedly come to the *slametan* to eat the odor of the food. One also bathes thoroughly to purify oneself for the Fast. The *Megengan* is given, unlike most other *slametans,* just before (rather than after) sunset, and as such marks the last legitimate daylight eating before the Fast.

21, 23, 25, 27, or 29 *Pasa:* The *slametan* held on one of these dates is called *Maleman* (from *malem,* "night, evening") because it is given at night, eating in the daytime being forbidden during *Pasa.* (Relatively few non-*santris,* however, actually observe this prohibition, and people who are not keeping the Fast show no reluctance about eating publicly during the daytime while others are fasting.) One chooses one of these dates either just offhand or by a *pétungan* divination applied to one's birth date. The last date, the 29th, is called *Djagalan*—the Day of the Butcher—because traditionally the butcher spent the other days slaughtering animals for other people's *slametans,* and so the last day was reserved for him alone; but this is no longer observed. Sometimes people say that the 21st, 23rd, and 25th are for "true Moslems" (i.e., *santris*), the 27th for young people, and the 29th for the old; but how widely held this belief is I am not certain. Just about every *abangan* gives a *Maleman* on one or another of these dates. In the villages both *Muludan* and *Maleman* are commonly village-wide celebrations held at the village chief's house, to which all the families of the village bring *slametan* offerings which are then exchanged, much as at the village cleansing celebration to be described later.

1 Sawal: The breaking of the Fast, called *Bruwah.** Yellow rice and a kind of omelet are the special foods. Only people who actually fast are supposed to give this *slametan,* but some non-fasters do so also. The dead are sometimes held to return to earth for this *slametan* too, and people then follow it with another trip to the graves of their parents.

7 Sawal: A small *slametan* called *Kupatan.* The only people who are supposed to give this are those who have had small children who have died—which must include nearly every adult in Java, although this *slametan* is not in fact very frequently given. At seven in the morning one makes *kupats,* which are little packets of glutinous rice, and somewhat similar packets called *lepets.* Some of these are hung outside the door so that the small dead children can return and eat out there without bothering anyone inside.

10 Besar: This is the day honoring Abraham's sacrifice and the day on which the pilgrims gather in Mecca for the re-enactment of the sacrifice. Although the holiday is important to *santris,* who butcher oxen and goats for the poor, the *slametan* is only rarely given. It should be noted that in none of these "Islamic" *slametans* are *sadjèns* prepared—or at least they are not supposed to be.

Muludan, the *slametan* for the birthday of the Prophet, and *Maleman,* the evening *slametan* toward the end of the Fast, are the two most important of the calendrical ceremonies. *Abangans* have a saying: "If you are willing to give the *Maleman* and are willing to give the *Muludan,* you are already a Moslem. If you don't give the *Maleman* and don't give the *Muludan,* you are not of Muhammad's community"—a view of Islamization which is, needless to say, strongly rejected by the orthodox. To say to a man that he "doesn't know *Muludan* (or *Maleman*)" is to say to him that he has no religion and is therefore an animal, a rather serious thing to say to a Javanese, for whom sheer animality is the quintessence of evil. (The only punishment for incest I could ever elicit was that "they would be made to eat grass like animals.")

The exact meaning of *Maleman* is not easy to discover; everyone you meet seems to have a different idea—or no idea at all—about it. I have been told that it was on these days that the Prophet readied his arms and army to return to the war against the infidels, resting on the even-numbered days in between (which are called *trowongan*—"holes, gaps"), and finally returning victoriously to the battlefield on *Rijaja,* the great holiday which ends the Fast. Another rather ingenious gentleman, a puppeteer, told me the Prophet was incarcerated in hell all through the Fast, and toward the end people were expecting him to return and so prepared a feast for him; but on the 21st he didn't come, on the 23rd he didn't come, and so forth, and he finally arrived on *Rijaja.* Some say that it is one of these days—no mortal knows which—that the angels in heaven fix a mortal's fate for the coming year, and so one gives a *slametan* in the hope that they will go easy on him.** Others say that

* This date, 1 *Sawal,* is also the great Javanese holiday *Rijaja,* which is described in the Conclusion of this report.

** This notion is evidently derived from the more general Malaysian-Islamic concept of the *Lailatul Kadar,* the Night of Power. On this night—it is one of the *Maleman* dates, but again no human can predict which one—God sends an angel down to earth, and all who are fortunate enough to be giving a *slametan* on that night will receive great blessings in the coming year.

the Koran began descending on the 21st, continued to do so on the 23rd, and so on, being completely in the hands of Muhammad by *Rijaja*. (Actually, the date that the Koran began to descend is 17 *Pasa,* but only *santris* celebrate this day, and they do so with prayers in the mosque and through sermons.) Pak Parto, my most reliable informant in matters of this sort, said that for *abangans* the *Malemans* represent the first, third, fifth, seventh, and ninth months of pregnancy; *Rijaja* is the birth of the baby; and *Kupatan* represents the burial of the umbilical cord—all of which is ingenious, if nothing else. Still other interpretations of *Maleman* are that people are merely inviting the dead to return on *Rijaja;* it represents the *abangan* method of *zakat-fitrah,* the obligatory giving of alms of *Rijaja;* or it has no meaning whatsoever and represents the pagan love of ritual on the part of the Javanese who are unable or unwilling to embrace the strict simplicities of pure Islam. Stripped of its evaluative elements, this last statement probably comes as close to the truth as any.

Unlike the rites-of-passage *slametans, Muludan, Megengan, Maleman,* and *Bruwah* are given by everyone at the same time, the result being not only that prices in the market go up somewhat but that on those days people go around from *slametan* to *slametan* in a kind of neighborhood trading-off pattern. The neighborhood principle is most strong in these *slametans,* and one rarely invites anyone but the eight or so nearest neighbors, so that one sees small groups of men going about from one house to the next to hold five-minute *slametans* (which, nevertheless, take the women of the house the entire day to prepare), one right after the other. In my case I went to six *slametans* during the *Maleman* period and held my own on the 27th—the composition of the audience being just about the same at each one. One can avoid a little of this by sending out *tondjokans* (or *berkats*)—i.e., *slametan* food wrapped in banana-leaf baskets—to the homes of a few of the more distant people or to relatives living elsewhere whom one wishes to honor.* For a person not to invite someone to his *slametan* who has invited him or who has sent him food, or to ignore a very close neighbor, would be a terrible insult, and seems never to occur (except that sometimes when two people are mutually angry, they will break off all communication entirely, in which case they will be omitted from each other's *slametans*).

In connection with calendrical *slametans* we may discuss the ceremonies surrounding the agricultural cycle. In the town of Modjokuto these rituals are given very seldom and when given are not felt to be of much importance. Even in the countryside they seem no longer to have the importance or show the degree of elaboration ascribed to them by earlier writers. In general, crop *slametans* are given only in connection with the cultivation of rice, not for the cultivation of dry crops, although sometimes someone will put out a small offering in connection with an onion or soybean crop.

When the rice season is approaching, the peasant seeks out an older more knowledgeable man who applies a *pétungan* numerological system to select the correct day on which to "open" (i.e., begin plowing) the land. When this

---

* In the villages this pattern of sending out *tondjokan* food packets is rather more extensive and amounts to a wholesale exchange of food among the various households. This pattern is also sometimes called *wèwèhan,* "mutual gift-sending."

day arrives, a small *slametan* called *wiwit sawah* ("beginning the rice field") is held at midmorning in the field, and anyone who happens to be passing by must be invited to participate. In the evening of the same day a small *slametan* is often held in the peasant's house. Another small *slametan* is sometimes held in the house when the rice is sown in the nurseries, and yet another at the time of transplanting, although both of these are quite commonly omitted. Toward the end of the growing season, after the first weeding has taken place and the rice is beginning to bend over with the weight of its grains, a *tingkeban* or, roughly, "rice pregnancy" *slametan,* is held, also in the house. But the most important crop ceremony is the *slametan metik,* a harvest or first-fruits ritual, and this is still often carried out on a fairly elaborate scale, especially in the villages.

Behind the harvest ritual lies the story of Tisnawati and Djakasudana. Tisnawati, the daughter of Batara Guru, the king of the gods, fell in love with Djakasudana, a mortal. In anger, her father turned her into a rice stalk and, pitying her human husband, who merely sat and gazed sorrowfully at his transformed wife, changed Djakasudana into a rice stalk also. The harvest ritual re-enacts their marriage, and is often referred to as *temantèn pari,* or "rice marriage."* For this ceremony a specialist called a *tukang metik* is employed. (*Metik* means "to pluck.") About a month before the harvest is to occur the *tukang metik* chooses a day by numerology. If he chooses, for example, *Ngahad-Kliwon* (*Ngahad* is another name for *Minggu,* or Sunday), then on the fourth consecutive Ngahad-Kliwon after his computation is made the harvest ceremony takes place, and the harvest itself the day after that. On the day of the ceremony the *tukang metik,* usually accompanied by guests of the owner of the field, circles the field several times, chanting a spell which begs for the forgiveness and blessings of Tisnawati (or mBok Sri) and Djakasudana. Then he burns incense, sets out offerings, and cuts a small number of stalks, depending upon the number of the day (usually 13, for example, in the case of *Ngahad-Kliwon*), these stalks being called the *mantèn* (bride and groom). They are taken back by the *tukang metik,* usually at the head of a procession of the guests, to the rice granary and hung up on the wall, where they remain until that year's rice harvest has been entirely consumed or sold. Back at the house a *slametan* is held. That night the *tukang metik* returns to the field for more offerings, incense, and propitiatory spells, and the next day the harvest takes place, the output of the field having been increased by virtue of the ceremony.

The Village Slametan: *Bersih Désa*

BOTH passage and calendrical *slametans* are oriented toward the sacralization of certain points in time, the former within the life cycle, the latter within

* There is another somewhat similar legend which accounts for the origin of rice in terms of a transformation of a goddess named Déwi Sri into a rice stalk by Wisnu (Vishnu), and this legend is sometimes syncretized with the Tisnawati story so that Tisnawati is called mBok (Mother) Sri. There are also origin stories of a similar nature for other crops, but they are of very little importance.

the yearly round of social activities. The *bersih désa,* or "cleansing of the village" *slametan,* is concerned with sanctifying relationships in space, with defining and celebrating one of the basic territorial units of Javanese social structure—the village. What the village is cleansed of, of course, is dangerous spirits. This is accomplished by giving a *slametan* in which food is offered to the *ḍanjang désa* ("guardian spirit of the village") at the latter's place of burial. In strong *santri* villages the *bersih désa* may take place in the mosque and consist entirely of Moslem prayers. In villages where there is no recognized place of burial for the *ḍanjang* or where the place is inconvenient, the rite may be held at the house of the village headman. To this *slametan* each family in the village is supposed to contribute food, and the adult head of each family is in theory obligated to attend.

The *bersih désa* is always held in *Sela,* the eleventh month of the lunar year, but on different days in different villages according to local tradition. The celebration differs somewhat depending upon the personal characteristics attributed by the people to the *ḍanjang désa.* For example, in one village near Modjokuto the *ḍanjang désa,* whose name is "Bearded Grandfather," is something of a reprobate and so demands that opium be burned for him and that a *tajuban,* a slightly disreputable form of entertainment involving female street dancers (who commonly are also prostitutes) and the ritual drinking of Dutch gin, be given. This is known to be what he wants because once he entered a man who was passing the spring in which he lives and demanded the opium and *tajuban* as the price for returning home and leaving the poor unfortunate man sane again. In another village the *ḍanjang désa* is a more proper and aesthetic type, and for him a shadow play must be given.

In the suburban village in which I lived, the *ḍanjang désa* was, as I have said, a pious *santri* who was buried in the center of the village. Thus the *bersih désa* in that village took the form of a death *slametan* for the *ḍanjang désa* complete with Arabic chanting, *apem* cakes, and so forth. The date for it was fixed—always *Rebo-Legi* in *Sela*—so that people would not forget when it was; but the *modin,* who conducted it the year I was there, said that the night before it was to occur he dreamed that Hadji Abdur, the village's headman, wealthiest citizen, and leading *santri* for over twenty years, as well as a supposed direct descendant of the *ḍanjang désa,* who died during the Japanese occupation, came to him and said, "Now [the *modin*'s name], I am looking for food." This was a sign, said the *modin,* that it was time for the *bersih désa* to be held, for it is directed not only toward the village founder but toward all who have led the village since then.

About 50 or 60 of a possible 500 or so adult men attended the *slametan,* and I counted about 135 trays of food, the surplus being sent by means of small boy messengers by adults too busy or too uninterested to come themselves. Most of the trays were put out by the grave, but about 30 were brought inside the prayer house where the *slametan* proper was held and where all the village officials and leading *santris* were gathered. (In this village it just so happened that, although the village was almost evenly divided between *abangans* and *santris,* with a scattering of *prijajis* near the town, the village government was almost entirely in *santri* hands.) The village chief made a short speech (a local *abangan* made one to the people outside by the grave), explaining who the *ḍanjang* was and the purpose of the *slametan,* and then led an Arabic chant for 15 or 20 minutes. Then each person took a bite or two of the food, the leftovers being given to the hundreds of children crowding around begging for them. Each guest participant took a little food home to put under his pillow or to make into a salve for well-being.

In the town of Modjokuto, where village political structure has rather atrophied and where most upper-class people feel themselves directly under the subdistrict officer rather than the village chief (who is more or less of an invalid anyway), the *bersih désa* is also rather attenuated. It was held at the graveyard, in which all past village chiefs are supposed to have been buried, on the edge of town. Although a rather large number of people came (due mainly to the fact that only one ceremony was held for the whole of Modjo-kuto—some 20,000 people), they were without exception, so far as I could see, all "little people," many of them extremely poor and obviously there in hopes of a free meal. None of the social or political elite of the town was present (though some were said to have sent trays of food), and the cere-mony was very perfunctory. The village chief—it was the first and last time I saw him out of his house during my stay—gave a very brief speech, saying that he was sorry that he was ill and that he could not get around much to see people and hoped that both he and the village would improve in health in the coming year. The *modin* then recited a very brief Arabic prayer, and the ceremony was over almost as soon as it had begun. No one with whom I spoke could name the *ḍanjang désa* or tell me who was buried in the main grave in the center of the yard.

The *bersih désa,* designed originally to integrate people not too unlike one another, sometimes has difficulty doing so in the more urban contexts where geographical proximity is less important than ideological commitment or differences in social status. Thus in the village mentioned above, in which the *ḍanjang désa* demands a *tajuban,* two are given: the first in the afternoon, to which come only peasants, coolies, and other rural or lower-class types; the second in the evening, to which come mostly government officials, clerks, teachers, and the like. Even the ceremony I have recorded for my village seems to symbolize as much conflict as it does harmony.

> The *modin* said that the purpose of the *bersih désa* was to bring well-being to the village. . . . He said there were two interpretations of it. *Abangans* thought that the prayer was to the dead *ḍanjang,* but this was wrong and the worst sin you could commit. Wito gave this interpretation of the ritual in his speech outside, and he, the *modin,* would have prohibited it if he could be-cause this was like having an extra God, and such a sin was never pardoned. The prayer was sent directly to God, he said.

Intermittent *Slametans*

WHAT I shall call "intermittent" *slametans,* those given from time to time for some special occasion or purpose which does not typically recur at any set intervals, are somewhat less common in Modjokuto than the regular ones described above and almost always rather simple affairs. *Slametans* for change of residence, change of name, embarking on a journey, bad dreams, prevention or encouragement of rain, anniversaries of clubs and fraternal organizations, sorcery, curing, and for an only child—all fall within this category. A name-changing *slametan* I gave for myself and my wife is typical. The impetus for it came from the headman of the village next to ours, who decided that our American names were too difficult either to pronounce or to remember.

In the evening the village chief of *Sawahredjo* came by. His rural accent is very thick, but I gathered he had come to name my wife and me. The chief chose the name according, he said, to the appearance of my body (he mentioned another name as being unsuitable, being too "big" for me), my character, and so forth, and came up with Kartopawiro. *Karto* seems to mean something like "orderly," and *pawiro* "manly" or "brave"—all of which is encouraging. He asked me if the name fitted, because if it didn't, it wouldn't be proper. I said it did and that he was undoubtedly an expert in choosing names; and he said, indeed, it was a difficult business to choose a name for a person, for if it didn't fit, bad things would happen. Many people came to him to help them choose a new name that would fit them and bring them good fortune. He said he had learned how to do this from his parents, but not only from them but from all of his ancestors. He said that all my ancestors would come to my *slametan,* and that I could inform them as well as my neighbors of the new name.

Since the *slametan* I gave under the direction of my landlord more or less duplicated the *pasaran* five-days-after-birth ceremony, in a sense I was "re-born" under my new name. A similar pattern occurs sometimes when a marriage does not go well. In order to try to save the marriage, a second ceremony and *slametan* are held, called *bangun nikah*—"to build up a marriage"—in which some of the events of the original ceremony are duplicated on a smaller scale and the same foods prepared for the *slametan.* Sometimes a *slametan* of this sort will be given just because a husband says to his wife, "I'll divorce you," and doesn't mean it. If such a *slametan* were not to be given, then the marriage would probably soon break up.

This pattern of the *slametan* as a defensive reflex against any unusual occurrence—having your house robbed, your child fall from a tree, or an out-size toadstool grow in your backyard—is quite common and is perhaps best seen in the reaction to anxiety dreams.

He said that Javanese believe dreams foretell the future. "If you dream something, it must happen; when—in a year, a month, a week—you can't tell, but it must happen. If you dream about something fearful happening but you don't necessarily know what, you have to give a *slametan* to prevent it. If you see someone giving *slametans* all the time, this may be the reason—because he has had many bad dreams."

Yet another stimulus for the giving of intermittent *slametans* is an adherence to the "heterdox" teachings of some self-appointed religious teacher (*guru*). Thus, for example, one of my informants followed the teachings of a man who claimed that the truly Javanese way to do things was to give a *slametan* on your birthday each 35 days, but no others. Although the informant was unable to avoid the regular *slametans,* as advised, she did add these new *slametans* as extra protection. Influence from Dutch customs— mostly among the *prijajis*—sometimes leads to out-of-the-ordinary *slametans;* some people, for instance, give silver wedding anniversary *slametans* or engagement parties. There are certain traditional occasions for *slametans* which are irregular in occurrence, such as the necessity to give one for an only child so he will not be eaten by the Hindu demon Batara Kala. One must give a *wajang* with this, and its expense prevents it from occurring very frequently nowadays, although sometimes people give it in combination with another occasion, such as a circumcision. Lastly, there are *slametans* which can only be ascribed to the effect of the "new era" in Indonesia; for instance, a beer-crate manufacturer gave a *slametan* in honor of his new diesel wood-sawing machine just imported from Western Germany.

Chapter 8

Curing, Sorcery, and Magic

IF SPIRIT beliefs and *slametans* are two of the most general subcategories of *abangan* religion, the complex of curing, sorcery, and magic centering around the role of the *ḍukun* makes up a third. Strictly speaking, restricting *ḍukuns* to the *abangan* context is not correct, for belief and disbelief in their powers, as well as actual practitioners of the art, are spread throughout Javanese society, among *prijajis* and *santris* as well as *abangan*. But both their greater frequency and their greater everyday importance, and probably a generally greater belief in them, among the *abangans* can justify their being considered here as a predominantly *abangan* phenomenon, with *santri* and *prijaji ḍukuns* being taken as secondary variations.

The *Ḍukun:* Curer, Sorcerer, and Ceremonial Specialist

THERE are all kinds of *ḍukuns: ḍukun baji,* midwives; *ḍukun pidjet,* masseurs; *ḍukun préwangan,* mediums; *ḍukun tjalak,* circumcisors; *ḍukun wiwit,* harvest ritual specialists; *ḍukun temantèn,* wedding specialists; *ḍukun pétungan,* experts in numerical divination; *ḍukun sihir,* sorcerers; *ḍukun susuk,* specialists who cure by inserting golden needles under the skin; *ḍukun djapa,* curers who rely on spells; *ḍukun djampi,* curers who employ herbs and other native medicines; *ḍukun siwer,* specialists in preventing natural misfortune (keeping the rain away when one is having a big feast, preventing plates from being broken at the feast, and so on); *ḍukun tiban,* curers whose powers are temporary and the result of their having been entered by a spirit.

Usually one man is several kinds of *ḍukun;* he may be everything but a midwife, a status reserved to women.* Some types—*ḍukun temantèn,* for example—are not true specialties, usually being taken on rather casually for the particular occasion by any older person who commands the necessary knowledge of tradition. A man who is able in several of these specialties at once is called a *ḍukun bijasa*—"common *ḍukun*"—or just *ḍukun* without a qualifier, and it is he who is the most important. He is the general magical specialist in the traditional society, useful for all that ails one physically or psychologically, predicter of future events, finder of lost objects, insurer of good fortune, and usually not unwilling to practice a little sorcery if that is what one desires.

This type of practitioner is in the typical case the son of a similar practitioner. To be a *ḍukun* is thought to be dangerous to the individual, for the extraordinary power with which he traffics can destroy him if he is not spiritually strong. Since madness is a typical outcome for people who attempt too much along these lines, it is a help to be a descendant of a man with proven ability to support such power, for then one is also likely to have the necessary spiritual resources. But this is not necessarily so. One *ḍukun* I interviewed said that his father had originally tried to teach his specialty to each of the informant's two older brothers, but both of them fell ill, showing that they were not strong enough for it; and so he, the third brother, got his chance to become a *ḍukun.*

Further, although the capacity to be a *ḍukun* is at least in part inherited, the actual ability is not; it is a learned skill. Just what is learned varies somewhat from *ḍukun* to *ḍukun. Prijaji ḍukuns* tend to emphasize ascetic discipline—extended fasts and long periods of wakeful meditation—and to claim that their power is entirely spiritual. *Santris* usually employ chanted passages from the Koran interpreted mystically, or magic bits of carefully drawn Arabic script chewed up and swallowed, or the like; and some *santris* claim that whatever curing "real Moslems" do is based on scientific medical knowledge included in the Koran hundreds of years before it was "discovered" in the West. *Abangan ḍukuns,* finally, tend more to emphasize specific techniques, amulets, spells, herbs, and the like. Admittedly, however, these lines blur; most *ḍukuns* employ something of all these techniques, and some sort of spiritual preparation is necessary in any case.

> He said that when he started being a *ḍukun* he fasted for a hundred days, eating no rice, only leaves off trees, and such things. Another time he did this for a year, for this is the way he gets his power. He said now he just fasts on Monday and Thursday of every week; the rest of the time he can eat as much as he wants. On Monday and Thursday he doesn't eat or drink anything from daybreak to sunset as in the Fast. I asked him why fasting gave him power, and he said, "When you fast your spirit (he didn't use a word, just pointed to his head) goes directly to God. If you don't, it is much more likely to get distracted to the side somewhere."

*Women sometimes, perhaps typically, become *ḍukun tiban* and *ḍukun préwangan,* and quite commonly *ḍukun pidjet* or *ḍukun temantèn,* but almost never any of the others.

Whatever it is that the practitioner learns, he learns from another *dukun,* who is thus his *guru* (teacher); and whatever he learns he and others call his *ilmu* (science). *Ilmu* is generally considered to be a kind of abstract knowledge or supernormal skill, but by the more concrete-minded and "old-fashioned" it is sometimes viewed as a kind of substantive magical power, in which case its transmission may be more direct than through teaching.

On Sunday morning we stopped at the house of Abdul's sister, who had dropped in at our house the day before on her way out to (a nearby village), where their father has been dying for the past ten days. . . . She said what was holding things up was that the breath (which the Javanese regard as the seat of life) was still inside of him and hadn't yet come out. She felt that it was probably trying to come out, trying to come out, and trying to come out, but hadn't yet been able to make it. She felt that it probably had left the stomach and that it was now in the throat and struggling to get free and when it finally did, when it finally came out, he would be dead. . . . Then someone who could bear it and was watching at the right time would attempt to swallow it in order to take over the *ilmu* of the old *hadji.* What one does is wait for the final expulsion of the breath (known by the appearance of saliva at the lips, but the *ilmu* itself has no shape and can't be seen) and then put one's lips to those of the dying man and catch his magical knowledge (*kepinteran*—literally "cleverness") in one's mouth and swallow it. The old man evidently has lots of *ilmu,* as one can tell by how rich he is. He got the power in the first place from a *kijaji* (Koran scholar and teacher) up by the north coast. He went to this *kijaji's* school when he was but a boy, and the *kijaji* taught him the *ilmu,* which involved secret meanings for Koranic passages. The *kijaji* would write down passages and explicate them to the young man and tell him to commit the knowledge to memory and never, ever, to write it down again. This went on for some time, evidently, and then the *hadji* came home and became rich, lived a long time and the like—all due to this *ilmu.* That is why it would be a great loss if it merely escaped into the air and got away and why Abdul, her brother, has been at the bedside more or less continually for the past two or three days.

What a man can do with his *ilmu* more or less depends upon what kind it is. Some *ilmu* is quite specific. There is *ilmu* for causing people in a house one is robbing to sleep soundly, for finding lost objects (some *ilmu* enables one to tell where the object is exactly, other *ilmu* just tells one in which direction it lies), for getting rich, for seeing what is going on in other places, and for becoming invulnerable. This latter *ilmu* was very popular during the revolution. At the time of the battle against the British in Surabaja about a hundred young men setting off to fight were first each given a small glass of tea over which one of Modjokuto's leading *dukuns* had chanted a spell which was supposed to render them invulnerable. There is also *ilmu* for telling where to drill a well so the water will not be foul, where to build a house so the occupants will not sicken, for attracting the affections of someone else's spouse. There is even *ilmu* for predicting world events. One seer gave out that World War III would begin within a year or two, that Russia would occupy almost all of Asia including Indonesia but would be finally defeated by the United States, and that then the United States, England, and Indonesia would be the three major world powers. This man is said to have predicted both the triumph and the downfall of the Japanese in Indonesia.

Other *ilmu* is quite general and consequently rarer, enabling one to do almost anything—fly, disappear, turn into a tiger—but somehow the really powerful practitioners of this sort seem always to have existed in the past, there being a rather general belief that so far as *ilmu* is concerned people are not so skilled as they once were.

I talked to Djojo on the corner the other night about his marvelous grandfather. . . . He said his grandfather was able to disappear magically. Also he could go great distances in a short time. He would walk out of the house and announce to his wife that he was going to Semarang [three or four hundred miles away] and in fifteen minutes he would walk back in, saying he had just come back from Semarang. He had pupils to whom he taught this *ilmu,* but none of them are left now, and the *ilmu* is lost. No one can do these things any more now, said Djojo. . . . His grandfather was arrested once by the Dutch and taken to Bragang and put into jail because of his *ilmu*—all his pupils walking along behind as he was led in. When they returned home, they found him there in the house ready to teach, and it turned out later that he was in both places at once: in jail and in his house teaching. He evidently applied his magical powers in the jail toward freeing prisoners, and so the Dutch thought perhaps it would be better if they just let him go. But now he was stubborn and wouldn't leave. "You sentenced me to seven years," he said, "so I'll stay here seven years. . . ." I asked Djojo whether his grandfather could cure people, and he said, yes, he could. He said that now there are plenty of people who say they can cure people, but they really can't, they are just swindlers deceiving people. I asked Pak Parman (the village's best known *dukun*), and he said, "Oh, he is just a stupid man; he can't do anything and just cheats people out of their money. There was a man out in Sumbersari who could really cure, but he died a few years back and now there is no one."

Today the leading *dukuns* in Modjokuto are all at least middle aged, but none is really old. Of the really well-known ones, three are *abangans;* one is a *santri;* and one, the subdistrict officer, a *prijaji*. All but the subdistrict officer are sons of *dukuns,* and all but him are also small landholders (from one-half to about two acres) who either rent their land to sharecroppers in order to be free to cure or (in one case) work it themselves. Thus no one in Modjokuto makes a living entirely from being a *dukun;* it is at best a part-time specialization. None of the leading *dukuns* is extremely poor, and none, again excepting the subdistrict officer,* is particularly well off. All are members of that peculiar economic category the Javanese call *tjukupan*—they "have enough."

As to personality, nothing seems to set the leading *dukuns* off from their neighbors. They show no unusual character traits and no obvious neurotic behaviors, nor are they considered peculiar by others. With one possible exception there is little sign that these *dukuns* chose their vocations because of frustrated prestige or power drives, for they are not the type of men to whom

---

*The subdistrict officer came to Modjokuto in 1952, and so has no roots there. He practices only among his friends, the upper status people among the *prijajis,* a rather limited group in number; but among them he has a high reputation.

the normal channels to power and prestige are closed; and, in fact, the *dukun* role, although it carries some prestige, also tends to draw suspicion, for some people always suspect the *dukun* of either fakery or sorcery. All in all, it is hard to escape the impression that within the *abangan* context the *dukun* role is a fairly straightforward one which people adopt for fairly understandable reasons: it brings a certain monetary reward, although seemingly not an extremely great one; it carries some prestige, although this is ambivalent at best; and they believe in their own skills and enjoy practicing them successfully.

The impression of "normality" in the *dukun's* role is strengthened by the consideration that, in addition to the five fairly well-known *dukuns,* there are literally dozens much less well-known—mostly *abangans*—whose powers are considered much less but who nevertheless draw part of their income from curing, seeking lost objects, practicing sorcery, and the like. In each neighborhood there always seems to be some man, usually a little older and somewhat more intelligent than the rest, to whom people look for help in the event of illness, theft, and so on, turning to the better known *dukuns* only rarely and in more serious cases. In fact, since almost every adult male knows at least a few spells and may be called upon to try his hand at curing a neighbor, finding a lost ring, or attracting a girl's affections, the role of the *dukun,* although a professional specialty, shades off at the edges into an irregular amateurish practice. If one stays in Modjokuto long enough one will hear just about every man in town referred to as a *dukun* at one time or another, although it will be clear that only certain people are really considered to be very good as *dukuns* and spend very much time at this practice.

Another peculiarity of the *dukun* role is that the reputation of a first-class *dukun* is almost always greater outside of his home region than in it. Really good *dukuns* draw a great part of their clientele from a distance; and it is said that they are more effective with people who are not otherwise acquainted with them, although exactly why this is so no one really seems to know. Many Modjokuto people go off to *dukuns* in other parts of East Java. My landlord went to a man near Malang, some 60 miles to the east, to get some sorcery practiced against a thief; and one old man who had been ill for some time went a hundred miles on the back of a truck to see a *dukun* he had heard about only vaguely, the trip in itself almost killing him. Similarly, the leading *dukuns* in Modjokuto drew many of their patients from as far away as Surabaja, 100 miles to the north, even though they were often thought to be frauds by their closest neighbors. Just how people at this distance know about curers in Modjokuto I never was quite able to discover. Whenever I asked this question of a *dukun,* he assured me that it was God who brought his patients to him.

Finally, there is the problem of the belief in *dukuns.* A partial skepticism about *dukuns* and their ability to do the things they claim to do is nearly universal. Nearly everyone with whom I spoke about the matter in Modjokuto believed in *dukuns* in general, in their possibility; but opinions about the powers of any one given *dukun* living in the area varied tremendously. I heard opinions expressed about each of the leading *dukuns* which ranged from absolute belief to outright accusation of fraud, but I never heard a denial that at least some *ḍukuns* were good, honest, and miraculously powerful.

Also, the concept of *tjotjog*—fittingness—which is so important in numerical divination plays a crucial role here too. A particular *ḍukun* may be very powerful and very clever, but he still may not *tjotjog* with one. There may be no question of his skill—for example, in a case of illness, he may have cured far more difficult cases but if the patient and he do not *tjotjog,* there will be nothing he can do and the patient will remain sick. So, when a man is ill, he tries one *ḍukun* after another until one cures him, never concerning himself about the reasons for their failure, and not necessarily holding it against them that they were unable to help him. It is just the same with Western-trained doctors. People would say earnestly to me: "Sometimes they *tjotjog* and cure you and sometimes they do not. The only difference is that you have to pay a doctor even if you die in his hands, while a good *ḍukun* expects payment only if he succeeds."

Curing Techniques

DESPITE all the wonderful things really powerful *ḍukuns* can do, their real forte, and the basis of their prestige, is their curative powers. As does any medical practice, the *ḍukun*'s treatment has two main aspects or stages: first, diagnosis and selection of the appropriate method of treatment by the practitioner; and second, the actual application of the treatment. Diagnosis can be based on any one of three main methods or any combination of them: numerology (*pétungan*), intuitive insight through meditation, analysis of symptoms.

The general *pétungan* process has already been described. Suffice it to say in this context that the usual method is to take the day on which the individual was born in connection with the day on which he fell sick and by various calculations come up with a number which then corresponds to a form of treatment (usually an herb medicine) and in some cases indicates the cause of the disease as well. This is the most common method of diagnosis, especially among second-rank *ḍukuns,* for it is the quickest and easiest to apply.

The method of intuitive insight through meditation is more difficult, for it takes years of practice. Both cases of it which I encountered were among *prijaji ḍukuns.* The *ḍukun* meditates, going into a near trance and clearing his mind entirely of any "pictures" until he gets an abstract and formless feeling which tells him what the disease is and what the cure should be. Despite the lack of mental pictures, however, the diagnosis and cure may be quite concrete.

> I asked him for an example of someone he had cured. He said there was a woman in (a neaby village) who had had an enlarged swollen stomach for three years. She went to several *ḍukuns,* but none could help her. She went to several doctors, but they all wanted to operate and she wouldn't permit it.

Finally, after three years, she came to Dono (the informant) out at his house with her husband, very desperate. Dono meditated for a while and figured out that the toilet at her house, which had been built just three years before, had been built on land that didn't want it there (because, evidently, spirits were living there); and so he told her that if she moved the toilet over to the other side of the house she would get well. She went home and they moved the toilet. That night she felt as if she collided with two spirits. Dono said they didn't enter her, but it was more as though they were trying to carry her off or something. All night long she was very sick and nearly died, but in the morning her stomach had gone down to normal size, and she was well again. However, when he told her the cure, Dono had told her, too, that she had to be patient and calm and not get depressed or angry for three years afterwards, or the sickness would come back; that she must not get emotionally upset in any way. Unfortunately, she did get upset and often angry, and so in about a year and a half her sickness returned. So she came back to Dono again, but this time, after suitable meditation, he said he couldn't help her at all any more; so she went to the hospital at one of the sugar factories and was operated on, and they took five big containers of water out of her stomach. But it came back again, and at this point her distraught husband came to Dono to see if he couldn't do something for her. Dono meditated again, said no, he couldn't do anything for her, and said she was surely going to die in a week. Exactly a week later she died.

Analysis of symptoms is particularly appropriate to more specific illnesses with well-defined disease pictures and rests on a categorization of such pictures at once elaborate and, seemingly, quite accurate, which is widely diffused among the populace generally. One boy, not a *dukun,* listed 47 separate diseases for me, each with a special name and symptom pattern, in the space of a half hour; and four other informants did almost as well. Among diseases commonly listed are: fever, chills, rheumatism, headache, red eyes with and without pus, boils, infected wounds, pimples on face and hands of adults and adolescents, white blotches on the skin, toothache, running nose, venereal diseases, paralysis, old age, rash (itchy or painful), yaws, smallpox, upset stomach, dysentery (with or without blood in the stools), short breath, gasping breath, tuberculosis (marked by continual coughing and extreme weakness), unclear eyesight, simple-mindedness, insanity (violent or nonviolent), measles, convulsions, malaria (called by that name; alternating fevers and chills), menstruation, frequent urination, tumors (external or at least perceivable to the touch), goiter, piles, swollen jaw, swelling in the groin, broken bones, and burns.

For each of these there are appropriate herbs (which are appropriate to which illnesses differs somewhat from informant to informant and *dukun* to *dukun*), mechanical methods of manipulation (massage, rubbing glass on the skin, bone setting), and specialized techniques such as the insertion of gold needles under the skin or the administration of mercury to be swallowed. The herb pharmacopoeia is very large and elaborate. Since it has been reported on at great length,* it need not be described here except to note that in the

---

* See especially K. Heyne, *De Nuttige Planten van Nederlandsch-Indie* (3 vols., Den Haag, 1927), and R. A. Seno-Sastroamidjojo, *Tentang Obat Asli Indonesia* (Djakarta, 1948).

Modjokuto area the most commonly employed medicinal herbs (they are grown in the house gardens, but may also be bought in Chinese drugstores) are *kunir* (tumeric, *Curcuma longa*), *kentjur* (*Kaempferia galanga*), *kemiri* (*Aleurites triloba*), *djaé* (ginger, *Zingiber officinale*), *lombok* (*chili* pepper, *Capscium annuum*), and *laos* (*Alpinia galanga*). All these and hundreds of others are used for nearly everything, both internally and externally. Turmeric seems to be the most common laxative; *kentjur* is frequently used to settle the stomach; and ginger is common as a salve for rheumatism and headaches. However, as all the informants said, which medicine you use depends on the one that "fits" you, and if one doesn't work, you try another. "Doctors have only two medicines—pills and injections; Javanese have thousands."

When one goes to a *dukun* one gets not only an herb but a spell with it. The *dukun* holds the herb in his hand and chants over it—in Arabic if he is a *santri dukun,* in Javanese if an *abangan*—and then either spits on it or blows on it when treating a child for worms.

> In the name of God, the Merciful, the Compassionate!
> "Grandmother spirit" [the *dukun* addresses the spirits],
> "Grandfather spirit, where are you going?"
> "To the Purwosedjati mountain" [they answer].
> "What are you seeking?"
> "We're seeking dringo herb and onions."
> "Why, whatever for!"
> "We are going to medicate the little baby."
> The harmful worms—may they all die.
> The good worms—may they stay for the whole length of the child's life.
> Ah, the medicine looks black [the *dukun* spits into it]—
> Yes, I am medicating the child.

As it is the spell, or more exactly the spiritual power, of the *dukun* which counts, he does not necessarily have to use an herb if he is powerful enough; and, in fact, perhaps the most common medicine dispensed by *dukuns* is just plain tea over which they have chanted and into which they have spat. This tea is then drunk by the patient or perhaps rubbed on his navel, for many *dukuns* conceive of their function as calling back to the patient the two guardian spirits who were born with him in the amniotic fluid and his umbilical cord. It is these who cure, they argue, by chasing off spirits, not the *dukun;* and the latter's only function is to enable the patient to get in touch with his invisible twin guardians, which he cannot do unaided and which the *dukun* accomplishes for him through his concentration, his chanting, and his application of the tea to the navel. Instead of tea, liquid concoctions made of egg yolk, coconut juice, or mashed vegetables are often used. It is of perhaps some interest that the word for the sipping of such a liquid medicine is the same as for suckling at the breast: *mik.*

Finally, one of the most common curing techniques is the massage or *pidjet.* The massage may be a simple secular massage with no mystical overtones of any sort, but it may also be accompanied by a spell and a spitting:

In the name of God, the Merciful, the Compassionate!
May the Prophet Adam repair [the person],
May Eve order [the person].
Untangle the tangled veins,
Right the dislocated bones,
Make the fluids of the body feel pleasant,
Make everything well again,
Well again, well as at the beginning [i.e., before the sickness].
Health falls with my white spittle [she spits three times on the neck of the
    patient],
Well, well, well, by the will of God.

Many other curing techniques are used. For example, Hadji Rasid was a specialist in what one might call metallic medicines. He gave people mercury to swallow for syphilis, iron filings pounded into a dust for general strengthening, and egg burned black and rubbed with silver for dysentery; but the technique for which he was most famous was *susuk:* injecting small slivers of gold under the skin. These slivers—the Hadji said he had about sixty or so of them in himself, and I knew dozens of people who had been injected by him, the slivers often still being visible under the skin—are injected where the pain is. A man with continual headaches will have them inserted in his forehead; someone with eye trouble will have them put in near the eye; a man with a bad stomach will have them injected near his navel. (For insane or upset people, one inserts them in the stomach also in order to calm their "heart," which is in their stomach.) Rasid's reliance on medicines was perhaps somewhat stronger than other *dukuns'*, and, unlike some others, he charged (Rp 6.50 for the gold slivers; Rp 15 for the mercury treatment, which is also good for making you strong) whether he cured one or not. The way he put it was that he charged only for the medicine but cured for nothing.

In sum, there are three elements in the curing process: the medicine, the spell, and what Malinowski used to call "the condition of the performer"—in this context the spiritual strength of the *dukun,* his ability to so concentrate his mind that the spell reaches the ears of either God or the patient's twin guardian spirits. In Trobriand curing and sorcery Malinowski found the spell the essential part and so called them "magical practices"; among the Azande, Evans-Prichard emphasized the medicine as basic and held the other two aspects secondary. It is of interest that in Java the third, the condition of the performer, is the crucial element.

Then he went on about *dukuns*. I asked him who was a good *dukun* here, and he said Pak Tèn (the subdistrict officer) was the best. He said no, his power was not inherited, his father could not cure, but Pak Tèn had been able to do it since he was 12 years old. It all comes from meditation (*sumèdi*), fasting and not sleeping, and general abstinence. Pak Tèn recently worked over the father of Bu Wirjo. He had a stroke, said the doctors, but they said nothing could be done to help him; he was paralyzed and struck dumb. Pak Tèn said a spell over him, gave him some tea, etc., and he improved. He is not all well, but he can get around and can talk again, and this in spite of the fact that the doctors said he wouldn't be able to. He said that he, Harijo, himself had talents along these lines, and put his lighted cigarette out with his tongue to prove it to me, saying that he had lots of other things equally marvelous he could do, but this would serve as an example. He said he could cure people but only used his powers for his children, for if people knew he could cure they would all come around for treatment, and he wouldn't be free any more and would have no time for himself. He said his powers came from not eating or sleeping much.

Each of the three elements—medicine, spell, and condition of the performer—may be used separately. Medicines may be employed in the home with or without the advice of a *dukun*. Individuals may be cured simply through meditating on their problems and giving them advice to move the toilet, rebury their child's umbilical cord, or sleep with their head at the other end of the bed, without any spells or medicines at all. People may be massaged and chanted over with no medicines and no particular power of concentration necessary on the part of the masseur. But more commonly all three are employed as interdependent parts of a unitary curing method in which the spell and the medicine are energized by the spiritual abilities of the *dukun*. The spell the *dukun* chants reaches God or the guardian twins because the curer's intense mental concentration drives it into their consciousness, and then they act in response to the spell's plea back through the *dukun* as he spits into the medicine to make it really powerful. So each element lends to the others some of its own efficacy, but it is the state of superior spiritual strength in the *dukun*, a state conceived of in psychological terms, upon which the process as a whole depends.

Theory of Disease and Curing

THAT the reputation of *dukuns* as a class is not entirely good is evident from the general belief that they inevitably die a violent death and from the fact that if one asks a curer if he is a *dukun* he always denies it and says he is merely trying to help people.

Went again to see Pak Parman, the "*dukun*" who says he isn't one, because the name indicates someone who takes money and he, Parman, doesn't (he accepts gifts, however), so he should be called a *pitulung* (helper). He said there are many people around who say they can cure, promise to do so for everybody (one sign of a *dukun* is that he tells one he can certainly cure him; Parman never does that—always says maybe he can and maybe he can't), and also claim that it is they themselves who cure you rather than God. But these people are all talking empty talk and just want one's money.

Everyone else in town, however, thought Parman was a *dukun* and called him one, including his chief rival, Hadji Rasid.

He, however, denied he was a *dukun*. He said Parman was, although Parman wouldn't admit it if one asked him. He said the difference between the way he practiced and a *dukun* was this: "A *dukun* tells you the cause of your disease, a *pitulung* just cures it for you." For example, a *dukun* will tell one that the reason for his disease is that a *sétan* has entered him. Rasid considers this unwise from a religious standpoint, for if one tells people *sétans* are what are disturbing them, they will start to fear *sétans*, and the Koran says one is not to fear *sétans,* only God. People should not pay too much attention to *sétans* but ignore them. Though he often knows that a *sétan* is the cause of his patient's sickness, he doesn't tell the patient—just cures him . . . Or a *dukun* will say the reason one is ill is that Pak so-and-so is witching him. Rasid doesn't do this either—although he often can see that a particular patient has been witched—because it often leads to fights with people. He said he used to practice as a *dukun* now and then but learned better from bitter experience. He said once a sick woman came to him and he told her it was her husband who was making her sick. The husband was very angry, and when later he fell sick he blamed Rasid for it, accusing him of sorcery, and it was unpleasant all around. Another difference between *dukuns* and people like him is that *dukuns* have other powers than mere curing; for example, they can find lost things. He doesn't do that—just cures.

And the third most popular *dukun* (and the most notorious money-grubber) had the same story:

He said he is not a *dukun* but merely a *pitulung* (I have never heard this term applied except by a man to himself; for everyone else, this man was a *dukun*). I asked him what the difference was, and he said a *dukun* takes money, but a *pitulung* doesn't—just helps people out. He said he can't always cure people; sometimes he can and sometimes he can't. If he could say for certain, "I can cure you," there would be two gods. As it is, he just supplicates God and sometimes it works and sometimes it doesn't, although he admitted he said spells over three hen's eggs as one of his techniques (the eggs are then eaten or made into a salve) and that he accepted gifts from satisfied patients.

As these excerpts from my notes indicate, there are several factors cluster-ing around the psychological relationship between the *dukun* and his patient which seem to account for the ambivalent attitude most people show toward *dukuns,* for the fact that they regard them both as supportive figures and as threatening ones. The first is the problem of the uncertain outcome of treat-ment, the essential contingency of the curative process involving as it does the possibility that one's hopes for well-being will be frustrated. The second is the degree to which the *dukun* may become involved in his patient's per-sonal life and the necessity from the *dukun*'s point of view for the careful handling of this problem. And the last is the inherent ambiguity of the *dukun*'s power, trafficking as he does both with God and with devils, able to sicken people as well as to cure them, and engaging both in devout supplications to a high God and in dubious contracts with less elevated spirits—*ndukuni* ("to *dukun* someone") means both to cure a person of a disease and to sorcerize a person into having one.

Something of the quality of the relationship between the *dukun* and his client can be seen from the fact that the major alternative term for *dukun* is *tijang sepuh,* which means (in the respectful speech style) "parent"; that the client is usually said to "beg pardon" (*nuwun pangèstu*) from the *dukun;* and that the former is often held to be seeking "advice" and "good counsel" from the latter, "as one does from one's own parents."

I asked her to whom she would go for help if she had some great problem. She asked me what sort of problem, and I said it was up to her; and she said she would go to someone she "looked upon" as a father, such as the curer in a nearby village. They used to go to one near Bragang, but he's dead now. Once when she was very sick, Pak Wirjo went to the Bragang one, "begged forgiveness," and told him about the sickness. He was given a bit of sugar which the curer had prayed over (illustrated by holding a pinch of sugar before her and closing her eyes for a moment). The *dukun* directed him to give it to her to eat. This even though they had already gone to the doctor. Also if she is having money troubles—for instance, she once gave a shadow play and borrowed money from a Chinese for this (before the war). The time for repayment came and she didn't have the money, and the Chinese wouldn't let her extend the period but insisted on her paying up all at once, so she was very troubled and went to this curer and "begged pardon."

Dukuns are quite aware, at least peripherally, that much of their power is psychological; and all Javanese seem to hold that there are two main kinds of disease: one kind, with discoverable physical causes, which is amenable to treatment by Western doctors; and a second kind in which there are no medical findings but still the person is ill, the latter type being the kind *dukuns* are peculiarly competent to cure. Thus Pak Parman said that he was at his best on convulsions and temporary insanity. But if the person with convulsions or the insane man came from parents who were also liable to convulsions or were mentally ill, he very rarely could help them and usually refused even to try. All *dukuns* emphasize the necessity for absolute trust and belief in the *dukun* and ascribe many of their failures to the fact that the patient had inner reservations about the curer's ability. The psychological causation of physical illness is a commonplace.

When Pak Ardjo went to Djakarta to visit his son whose wife had just died, he went by train with the mother of the wife. On the trip he began to feel ill, and by the time he got there he was very sick and spent the entire visit in bed. He said the reason he got sick . . . was that he was angry (*pegel*—anger concealed in the heart; unexpressed, secreted anger) toward the woman whose daughter it was who had died because she seemed not to be grieving at all over her daughter's decease. At every stop almost, she got herself something to eat and ate and ate all the way there (Ardjo did not eat the whole day, he said proudly), and he was angry at her but didn't show it, and this being held inside him was what made him sick.

The connection between emotional stability and physical health is usually put in more concrete form, especially by *abangans*. If one is upset, startled, or severely depressed, one becomes confused and disoriented, and one's soul is then empty and easily entered by the spirits. Sometimes the spirit is held to displace the soul, in which case the curing process is stated in even more metaphorical form:

"When a *sétan* enters you, it chases out your own spirit (he said he didn't know where it went to—just 'away') because it struggles with the *sétan* and loses because your soul is weak, and so you become insane. When you are cured—with the aid of a *dukun*—the soul comes back, struggles with the *sétan;* the *sétan* loses, departs, and you are well again. You have been reorganized," he said.

Among the specialists themselves, particular psychological stresses may be explicitly connected to particular physical symptoms. One *dukun,* something of a *prijaji* actually, said he treated two kinds of diseases: specific ones, such as toothaches, broken bones, upset stomach, and dysentery; and general all-over ones, of which latter type there were four main varieties: dirty blood (*darah kotor*), a shortage or lack of blood (*kurang darah*), an empty soul, perhaps entered by spirits but not necessarily (*djiwa kotong*), and air, "heat," or some other foreign substance inside the body, sometimes induced there magically through sorcery.

The first, dirty blood, he said could be caused in one of two ways. Eating bad food—spoiled or too peppery, or merely food which one is not used to eating—which "startles" your stomach and so makes you upset in the "heart" will dirty your blood. Secondly, continual anger, greed resulting in frequent frustration of your wishes, or secreted emotions like envy or jealousy will upset your "heart" and dirty your blood. The symptoms of dirty blood are general sluggishness, perhaps a rash or boils, alternation between fevers and chills,* and a "dark mind"—i.e., confused and suspicious thought, liability to sudden thrusts of passion.

Lack of blood the *dukun* traced to nagging fear, anxiety, or depression without an obvious cause. This thins out one's blood, leading to a shortage of it. Symptoms are paleness, weakness, and general lassitude of mind—one just lies around and does nothing all day. Lack of blood may also follow as a second stage after dirty blood.

An empty soul, on the other hand, is due to a lack of spiritual discipline— a failure to exercise the soul by fasting, staying awake, and meditation— which leaves one very liable to sudden startle and prey to marauding spirits. The general symptoms are: if a spirit has entered, intellectual disorientation, delirium, strange behavior—in a word, "insanity"; and, if no spirit has yet entered, a general inability to persist in an activity, indirection, aimlessness, and so forth—a kind of loss of inward strength quite often ascribed by older Javanese to younger ones of the rising generation.

> I talked with Tjipto and the old man who takes care of the graveyard for a few minutes. Both were bemoaning the younger generation. The younger generation, they said, are very clever, but they are not very wise. They have a lot of knowledge but no wisdom; they think they know everything and they really don't know anything. In the old days people accepted their lot, were always peaceful in their hearts, and one could count on them. If they said they were going north, they went north in fact; they didn't go south first. Tjipto said that in the old days if he went out of the house and told his wife he was going north and someone invited him to go south, he would refuse because he had said where he was going and his will was set. In those days people did not

---

* This may also, of course, be due to malaria. Since many Javanese hold that malaria is caused by eating newly harvested rice (a view which is reasonable enough, considering that it is at the harvest time that the irrigation streams are beginning to stagnate and thus the mosquitoes multiply), it too is sometimes seen as a "dirty blood" disease.

spend so such time fooling around as they do now. They fasted, slept little, and went in for self-control. They led a much more ordered life. Nowadays people just sit around and talk all the time, stop in at a coffee shop here and a coffee shop there, chit-chat with everyone they meet. They thought this was bad—just following your will of the moment. In the old days people were stronger, and their wills were pure; they were single-minded, and they weren't drawn here and there by irrelevancies. The younger generation are no longer peaceful either, and the result is they don't live so long. There used to be people who lived for 150 to 200 years because they were so peaceful; now at sixty they are already old.

Finally, the last variety of general disease is caused either by air entering the body, by heat entering it, or by foreign objects—nails, glass, human hair—introduced into the stomach by means of sorcery. Air in the body (*masuk angin*) produces symptoms much like our "cold"—coughing, sneezing, and general aches. Heat in the body (*panas mlebu*) leads to somewhat more localized pains. The symptoms of a disease due to sorcery are more violent: vomiting blood, convulsions, and the like. Again, those most liable to sorcery are those who are weak spiritually, but anyone may have air or heat enter merely by sitting in a draft or in wet clothes.

This particular analysis is but one man's view, and it would be unwise to take it as definitive. However, categories like "dirty blood," "lack of blood," "empty soul" are nearly universal and are given interpretations of the same general order as those presented above, although many would dispute details, and the great mass of people have little theory beyond the terms themselves, which they apply more or less haphazardly. At any rate, this *dukun* said that there were for a Javanese two things of chief importance in staying well, and on this I think he would get general assent: watching one's food to make sure it is clean and not too "startling"; exercising one's soul to gain spiritual strength.

On this basis he went further to argue that no *dukun* ever cures a general disease (he may, of course, cure specific ones) but just alleviates it, for he does not touch the underlying cause. For example, if one has a rash caused by dirty blood, the *ilmu* of the *dukun* can make it go away, but the blood will still be dirty, and the rash may later come back, or one may get another symptom to replace it caused by the underlying dirty blood. So it is that one sees people who have a rash cured by a *dukun* only to develop boils; the boils go away, and they get headaches; the headaches vanish, and they are laid up with rheumatism. One can't clean up dirty blood with a spell, he said; only meditation by the patient and a careful diet can do that. However, he admitted rather sadly, some *dukuns* will promise one anything.

The Possessed Curer: *Dukun Tiban*

IF the common *dukun* is protected against the inevitable ambivalence with which the public views the curer of souls in any culture by the social "normality" of his role, by the regularity of the traditionalized procedures he employs, by the strictness of his discipline and the breadth of his learning, by his insistence that he cures only with the aid of God, by his pseudoparental status, and by his own usually sound enough civic reputation—these "bourgeois virtues" balancing off the morally equivocal forces with which he deals and the possibilities for doing evil with which he is presented—the *dukun tiban* has no such protection. He exchanges the social acceptability of the common *dukun*'s practice for the greater power possible in a more simple, direct, and uncircumspect approach to the darker powers.

The roles of the *dukun bijasa* and the *dukun tiban* differ in almost every particular. Where the power of the former is based on learning plus, sometimes, an inherited factor, that of the latter comes suddenly, without any preparation on his part, by "divine stroke" (*tiban* means "fallen," "fallen as a wonder from the skies"). Where almost all of the former are men, perhaps a majority of the latter are women. Where the former seem usually to be psychologically stable and economically secure, the latter are said usually to be at least somewhat unbalanced and to come from among the economically depressed. Where the power of the former is continuing and, relatively speaking, moderate, the power of the latter disappears as suddenly as it comes (usually within a year, almost always within three) and is of much greater intensity while it lasts. Where the former are numerous everywhere, the latter are rare and occur only sporadically (most informants said one seemed to turn up somewhere around Modjokuto about once every five years or so). And where there is at most only a mild skepticism about either the effectiveness or the morality of the practices of the former, there is sharp disagreement concerning both the reality and the ethical character of the forces upon which the *tiban* calls.

The only *dukun tiban* of any importance to appear in the Modjokuto area for the past five or six years "occurred," luckily enough, during the period of field study in the village immediately to the north of town. About the first of November in 1953 (and at the beginning of the Javanese year in the month of *Sura*) a poverty-stricken onion peddler in the town market (her debt-ridden husband owned no land and was reduced to seeking casual farm work wherever he could find it) lost a ring. She looked high and low for it for two or three days with no success. Then one night in a dream she saw a great beam of light come down from heaven and strike the floor. The brick where the light had been focused was broken open and found to contain the ring, and she knew—how, I was never quite able to discover—that if she dipped the ring in home-made medicine she would have the power to cure.

Within a week her fame had spread over the entire Modjokuto area and farther (it was said that the first patients came to her, instructed to do so in dreams, from a distance of 50 to 60 miles). Everyone was discussing her—the general opinion was that she had been entered by an evil spirit—and her miraculous cures of the deaf, the halt, and the blind. One man, unable to unclench his fist for 15 years, could now flex it normally after one treatment. Another person had been cured of blindness, but later said evil things of the *dukun* and the blindness returned. The wife of a well-known religious teacher

—himself something of a curer but ineffective with his wife (*dukuns* are generally held to be unable to cure relatives)—had been cured of a lingering illness. Literally hundreds of people flocked to the new *dukun*'s house for treatment week after week, often from great distances (many of her patients seemed to come from the old plantation areas south and east of Modjokuto), the trade slowly dropping off until by the end of December it was reported that she had lost her power, and some of the people she had cured began to wonder if this meant that they would fall ill again.

During the time her power was at its height the *dukun tiban* held mass curing sessions in her small bamboo house almost every afternoon. There never seemed to be less than ten people crowded into the tiny front room, some paralyzed, some weak and pale, some coughing their lungs out, and all, like the sick everywhere, extremely interested in their own symptoms, which they discussed with one another and with the *dukun* insofar as they could communicate with her at all. One ancient lady complained that she seemed to be forgetting things more and more and losing her eyesight. A rabbity little man said he had been sick to his stomach for two months. (He later told me he had been cured.) Another man had brought his young son, whose eyes had been operated on by Indonesia's most famous eye specialist, a Chinese doctor in Djogjakarta, about a month before, because, he said, despite the operation the boy's eyes were not yet "perfect." There was a young man of about 25 looking deathly ill, who said he didn't know what was wrong with him but he had been too weak and trembling to do much but lie in bed for almost a year. Others had fevers, bloody stools, shooting pains, headaches, or were infertile; and one woman said she had come in order to curb her husband's gambling. My landlord, who accompanied me on one occasion to see what the *dukun* could do for his tuberculosis (he later assured everyone that the *dukun* had told him what was wrong with him without asking him, although I saw him describe his symptoms to her), said that many people visited the *dukun tiban* to get rich or to be successful in the market, but I could never get anyone to admit such a purpose to me.

The *dukun,* an extremely hyperactive woman of about 30 who suckled an infant through part of one of her performances, moved nervously and fitfully among this crowd, paying only minimal attention to individuals; now chanting bits of the Confession of Faith, punctuated with cries of *Allahu Akbar* ("God is most Great"); now grasping someone's hand ("How many fingers do I have?"—"Which is better, left or right?") and commanding them to rub tea on their foreheads or stomachs; now throwing out such cryptic fragments as "Your parents enter your soul and the devils go out," "I seek only good, not evil," and "God is inside me" (pointing to her chest); now firing questions suddenly at people such as, "Do you choose the way of life or the way of death?" (The correct answer if you are ill is "the way of death"; if you seek riches, "the way of life") and, "Is it better to be rich or poor?" ("rich"); now going out back to the kitchen, where an assembly line of female relatives was brewing pots full of a yellow-green medicine made of eggs and herbs, into each batch of which they dipped the magic ring, then emerging again to bid each patient drink a glassful of this concoction in a single gulp; now greeting new arrivals with *assalam alaikum* (an Arabic salutation meaning "peace be unto you") and a string of formal Javanese greeting phrases (she spoke, however, a very low Javanese all of the time); now presenting departing patients with a banana-leaf package of lime, water, and flowers on which they were to sleep and with which they were to rub themselves, collecting Rp 1.10 from them and telling them that when they were cured they were obligated to present her with a coconut (toward the middle of her period of power her back yard was filled with what must have been 150 coconuts) and a raw egg (to replace the one in the medicine).

So she went on unceasingly, hour after hour, ever-moving, ever-talking in her curious whining tone, half argumentative and defensive, half explanatory and exhortatory, stringing one magical sentence after another in such a disordered profusion that even the Javanese understood her only once in a while, with a physical stamina which, given the heat, smoke, and sweaty dampness of the room, was quite astounding. It seemed to me at the time as though she were calling on all her reserves of strength and gathering up all the spells, medicines, and magical techniques of which she had ever heard in a last desperate attempt to heal both herself and her patients. She seemed in the throes of an undisciplined spasm of the kind of trans-human force that in the regular *dukun* is regularized, rationalized, and carefully controlled. She seemed, in fact, definitely unbalanced.

Toward the middle of the second month of her power, I think because she felt her power was slipping, although she never said this, she gave a large *slametan* to which she invited everyone whom she had cured, although of course only those nearby were able to come—about 20 or 30 people. The *slametan* was a usual one, marked by two large cones of rice representing, the *dukun* said in her *udjub* speech (she was the only woman I have ever seen participate directly in a *slametan*), her hope that her power would continue. She said that despite what anyone might have said she had used her power not for self-gratification or for money but to help people, and that she had cured many people. She said that if her power left her she would immediately stop curing and not deceive people. She said that her power came from God, from her dead parents, and from the *danjang* of the village, and not from evil spirits. She told her guests that with this *slametan* they no longer had any obligations toward her as a result of her having cured them; they owed her nothing more. (In addition to the coconut and the money they had been obligated to pay her for a cure, people of very serious ailments, or ailments they took to be serious, would be likely to give more elaborate presents as a sign of gratitude and as an insurance that the cure would last. The *dukun* managed to build a new brick outhouse and purchase two goats with her fees, and she had definitely improved her general economic position with her practice.)

All in all, she seemed much more subdued than usual. Although after the *slametan* she rose to her usual phrenetic heights at a few points in curing a new patient or two, the continually heightened excitement of the earlier visits seemed gone and she looked tired and discouraged. Two or three weeks later I heard her power was gone. The last time I saw her was at a village election a few months before I left Modjokuto, when, although she pushed her way up among the *prijaji* election observers on the front platform, she seemed quite quiet and withdrawn. People to whom I talked were not much impressed with her, saying they had never believed in her in the first place, that most of her supposed cures had relapsed, and that she had been dealing with evil spirits; they made jokes about her sitting among the *prijajis,* when she was just a little ignorant village girl.

This woman being the only *ḍukun tiban* I ever saw, I am hardly in a position to argue that her case is absolutely typical even though my informants said that most *tibans* were as odd and peculiar as she and operated in a similar manner. As for *ḍukun préwangan,* who are also said to be unstable and untrained and to be mostly women, I have never seen or heard of one around Modjokuto, although many people assured me that they occur from time to time in other parts of Java. These are mediums who become possessed by the spirits of the dead at will, enabling one to present petitions to one's deceased relatives directly.

Secondary Curing Methods: Magic, Drugs, and Western Medicine

IN addition to the *ḍukuns, tiban* or common, to whom they have access, Modjokuto Javanese have two other possible sources of help in the face of disease: home curing and the more or less scientific Western-type medical care provided by the two hospitals in town.

The home curing methods are several. There are various kinds of amulets, such as small daggers worn inside the belt or pebbles strung around one's neck. There are packaged medicines of the "good for all that ails you" type, which traveling salesmen are forever hawking in the market or the town square. There are Chinese drugs, such as ground dragon's tongue, which can be purchased at the local Chinese drugstores (while one waits they are mixed up by the druggist (*singsèh*), to whom one has described his symptoms). There are the special time-honored techniques for specific diseases (e.g., polliwogs rubbed on the skin for measles). And there are the peculiar, all-purpose protectors the Javanese call *djimats.* Commonly, a *djimat* is a written amulet, usually in Arabic and often made by the more old-fashioned Koranic scholars for their followers. They not only cure but also may be worn, like amulets generally, as invulnerability charms or as instruments of sorcery. The term *djimat* also tends to be used for a "snips and snails" kind of medicine in which otherwise repulsive substances, particularly waste products from one's own body, are ingested, worn, or hung over the doorway. The following is a fair sample:

> He described another of these *djimats* to me. When the baby is newly born, the palms of its hands are wet with a kind of white oil. One blots this up with a tiny piece of kapok. Soon afterwards the baby will have his first bowel movement. "The faeces are always black," said Wirjo, "like black rice por-

ridge. You keep this and put the kapok in it. In a day or so the stub of the umbilical cord falls off, and you add that to the collection. On the thirty-fifth day he gets his first haircut, and you put the clippings in the collection too, and you save the whole business, and later when the child is about 15 years old (if he is ill, or for general protection against illness, or general spiritual strength), you go out and buy him a gold ring which is the same weight as all this stuff and then he wears the ring and eats the stuff (he can put it in a banana to make it go down easier) and the child will be strong. He won't have to go to a specialist, for he has his own *djimat*."

The patent medicines, with their supposed scientific legitimacy, their appeal to the Javanese conviction that the West, whatever its spiritual drawbacks, has discovered the technological key to all the material problems of life, and the extreme simplicity of applying them ("take two spoonfuls for tuberculosis, three for indigestion"), stand halfway between the indigenous curing system and the intrusive system of Western-type medical care institutionalized in the town's two hospitals, its three Western-trained doctors, and its group of locally trained male nurses (*mantri*). Patent medicines are advertised in the newspapers and sold in the stores, but the most vivid hawking of them is by the traveling medicine men who can be found three or four times a week at the center of a large crowd in the town square and almost every day in the market.

I took a walk in the morning. There was a man in the town square under the sacred banyan tree selling patent medicine. He was dressed in Western style with a white shirt, polka-dot brown and yellow tie, two-tone shoes, and slicked-down hair. About 25 to 30 years old, he spoke with great rapidity, all in Indonesian. He said his medicine was good for everything from heart trouble, coughing (he coughed as an example), and stomach ailments to insanity. He said he was from Djakarta and in Djakarta all the government leaders used this medicine regularly. He said in America too they used it and mentioned something about Eisenhower. He had pictures from *Life* magazine and various medical journals, all in glorious Technicolor, spread on the ground. He said that when one eats all the food goes into the stomach and gets all messed up. He put some food in a glass of liquid and showed how repulsive it looked after a while. Americans, he said, and Djakarta people are always cleaning out their stomachs, but Indonesians may go two, three, four years without doing so. He said the medicine was made in Djakarta, not by stupid people, but by clever ones—specialists in chemistry. He said that if one's blood gets dirty, this affects all the parts of the body—the lungs (he coughed, wheezed; showed pictures of X-rays of chest); the head (he picked up a cutaway picture of the skull). It gives one smallpox (he had a picture of that); bowel trouble (he gave imitation of someone trying to evacuate and not being able to do so; he had a picture of the bowels, too). It disturbs a woman's menstruation (he gave an imitation of a groaning woman, "Oh, my husband! . . . Oh!"); and it causes syphilis (he had a picture of a diseased penis all shrunken up). He went on about syphilis, saying that it spreads from the penis to the face, and one loses his nose and has to get a rubber nose, called an "atom" nose, and when one is riding along in a *betjak* (bicycle rickshaw) and it stops, the nose flies off. He also had a picture of a model all cut open in various parts, saying that if one didn't take his medicine, later the doctor would cut him up. He pulled out a small bottle of penicillin and quoted how much it cost compared to his one-rupiah medicine. He demonstrated his medicine, which was a crystal which fizzed in water, and then sold a dozen or more packages, packed up, and went off.

The three doctors* and two hospitals in the small town of Modjokuto are certainly not typical for Java. It is rather the accidental result of three circumstances. One of the two main East Java hospitals of the *Handelsvereniging Amsterdam* (HVA), the huge prewar Dutch plantation concern, happens to be located in Modjokuto. Mainly because a building was available, the government hospital for the whole of the Bragang area comprising four districts and hundreds of thousands of people happens to be located in Modjokuto rather than in Bragang, the capital city of the area, as it normally would be. And the man who was the government doctor is now past retirement age and has been replaced in the hospital itself by an imported Austrian doctor, but, owing to the shortage of doctors in Indonesia generally, continues to travel around the rural areas holding clinics and still maintains some of his private practice within the town itself. As a result, Modjokuto is something of a medical center; but for most *abangans* this can hardly be said to be of much importance in their life, except insofar as it provides them with jobs as launderers, janitors, gardeners, and ambulance drivers.

Only a few of the higher-status people of some wealth go to the HVA hospital in any case, unless they happen to be employees of the company, for the fees for private patients are exorbitant. The government's hospital maintains a daily clinic for a flat fee of one-half rupiah, and many people in the town itself (but relatively few outside of it) go to it each day; but the patient-doctor ratio is so extremely large and the financial resources of most people with which to pay for any extended medical care so sharply limited that only minimal treatment is possible. As a result, the main contact that most people in the Modjokuto area have with the hospitals and with rational scientific medicine is through the male nurses called *mantri*.

Generally trained for simple laboratory work or pharmacy, the *mantris* are forbidden by law to dispense medicines, but as a matter of fact they do so quite freely. For many people, going to a *mantri* has replaced or supplemented going to a *dukun,* with the result that the *mantris* are carrying a rather striking amount of the medical load in Java these days and have become a modernized version of the traditional curing specialist. Where the *dukun* has spells and herbs, the *mantri* has pills and injections, and there is apparently little greater scientific understanding of illness in the latter case than in the former. The *mantri* has become the agent for the Javanese reinterpretation of Western medicine and has simply been added to the traditional armory of curing means available to the average Javanese.

People everywhere tend to face a crisis such as illness with all the cultural resources upon which they can call and to interpret what they are doing in terms of the categories which they learned as children; and so the Javanese

---

* Of the three doctors, one was an Indonesian from Sumatra who received his medical education in France, the second was an Austrian trained in Austria, and the third was a Javanese who studied medicine in Djakarta.

flails at his health difficulties with any stick his culture gives him and sees imported methods as but new elements in an age-old pattern. *Dukuns,* herbs, patent medicines, *mantris,* and doctors—all get called into play in a desperate attempt to alter an impossible situation, but somehow in the end the vivid word pictures of the *dukun* give him an edge on his new-fangled competitors.

mBok Minah, the woman who lives next door, has a granddaughter, Ti, aged about two, who has been sick for the past two weeks—so seriously that at one point she was given up for dead. They said she had a very high fever and nothing much else in the way of symptoms. At the height of the fever her nose bled. Now the fever has subsided, but the little girl has regressed to babyhood —only suckles and won't talk, although it is evident she understands what is said to her. She is completely flaccid, won't respond to people, just looks at them. If she isn't fed, she makes no indication she is hungry. . . . Pak Ardjo (our landlord) said a *dukun* had discovered that the child was possessed by spirits, and everyone seems to agree with this diagnosis. While she had the fever, many kinds of herb remedies were tried, every neighbor suggesting a different one. The child was taken to the *mantri,* Pak Wisto, who "injected" her and gave her some cough medicine (although she had no cough). Several Chinese medicines from the drugstores were tried, and the famous Chinese patent medicine "Tiger Balm" was rubbed on her. She was at length taken to Pak Harso (the semi-retired government doctor), who said he could find no illness. This was after the fever had subsided. In between times several *dukuns* were called but all without change. After all this, Pak Ardjo suggested a *dukun* who works on the railroad, and the man came and said a spell over some salt and spread it on the child and went out back to examine the river. He then said the trouble was that the child had played or urinated in the river without the parents noticing it and had upset the games of four little spirit children, who live 15 yards up the river in the clump of bamboo trees behind the house, and the spirit children were angry and made her sick. The spirit children didn't actually enter the sick child, being too small and weak to do so, but just stood by her side pressing up against her. If they did enter her, she would die. The reason she was so sick was that there were four of these spirit children after her. . . . The notion that it was urinating in the river that caused the trouble is a common one and had been advanced as a theory by some of the women around her before the *dukun* himself came.

Sorcery

THERE is an underside to everything, and so far as Javanese curing and magical practices are concerned the underside is sorcery. Sorcery, like curing, is largely in the hands of specialists. If one wants to sorcerize someone, one has to hire a *dukun* to do it. Most *dukuns* will deny that they practice sorcery, but evidently it is not hard to find one who will do it if the price is right—about a hundred rupiahs for visiting someone not too far away with a relatively severe sickness, and up to several hundreds for a death. The only defense against sorcery is to get a better *ḍukun,** one whose spiritual strength is greater than that of the *ḍukun* one's enemy has employed against him. A struggle between *ḍukuns,* on a mystical plane of course, then takes place, and if one's *ḍukun* is indeed stronger than his adversary's, he will turn the latter's magic back upon him, and the enemy will fall ill with the disease he has wished on one. In either case, the *ḍukuns,* like contending lawyers in a civil suit, remain unharmed.

There are several different types of sorcery, all of which bear a family resemblance one to the next, but true witches, able to harm others as a result of a purely natural ability and without ritual manipulation, seem not to exist among the Javanese. The general term for sorcery is *sikir* or *sihir,* and the three most virulent varieties are *tenung, djènggès,* and *santèt.*

The symptoms of *tenung* sorcery are such as vomiting blood, violent sickness in the stomach, or a raging fever, without any traceable cause. The *ḍukun*'s performance (an informant told me; with one exception I have never seen witchcraft performed) consists of a kind of Black-Mass mock *slametan.* The *ḍukun* sits chanting spells in the center of a half-circle of *sadjèns*—food offerings for the evil spirits—pleading for the destruction of his victim. The *sadjèns* consist of unbroken pieces of incense and opium mostly, although various other things of which *sétans* are especially fond, such as mirrors, may be added. If one intends to kill the victim rather than merely sicken him, one must break the incense into small bits and wrap it in white muslin tied in three places as though it were a corpse, and one can chant a little *tahlil* (the chanting one does at funerals) if he wishes.

In *djènggès* a similar rite is performed, except that objects such as nails, hair, broken glass, and pieces of iron and needles are added to the *sadjèns.* The *ḍukun* spells his spell and concentrates upon his evil intent and by so doing is able to persuade the spirits to induce the objects into the stomach of the victim, who will hear a sudden explosion all around him and then fall dreadfully sick. Sometimes a long piece of wire may be employed which is induced into the victim's arm or leg, thereby paralyzing him. This seems to be the most common form of serious sorcery, and observed cases of it were reported to me by about a half-dozen people, including one of the town doctors (the Javanese). He said a seriously ill woman came into the hospital only a year or so before, but he could find nothing wrong with her. The X-ray revealed bits of glass, metal, and hair in her stomach, which were then removed by a stomach pump and which are still in the hands of the police. The woman had refused to marry a young man to whom her parents had betrothed her, and she accused him of the sorcery. The doctor said that his Western training had made him skeptical of sorcery, and in 30 years or so of practice all over Indonesia he had not seen a case until this one, but now he had changed his mind and felt perhaps it was possible after all.

The term *santèt* is also sometimes used for inducing foreign objects into

* But a well-practiced soul is valuable as a general protective measure. As in the case of ordinary illness resulting from entry by spirits, a man who often fasts, stays awake, and meditates is very difficult to harm. Of course, if he does enough of this, he is probably himself a *ḍukun* by simple virtue of the fact.

the stomach of the victim, but, strictly speaking, it refers to the kind of sorcery in which the *dukun* must actually approach the victim and rub pepper grains (or something of the sort) against him while repeating a spell soundlessly in his mind. The victim then contracts incurable diarrhoea.

Agreement on terms is far from complete, but other kinds of sorcery—all on a similar pattern—include being able to make a person come to a set place against his will (*gendam*) and various sorts of love magic (one man outlined four types of increasing strength to me) to attract reticent men (or women) to one's bed (*guna*):*

> He said his father had told him that his (the informant's) uncle, now dead, was once in love with a girl, but she wouldn't have him. So he went to a *dukun*, who advised him to fast for seven days in a room with all the windows and doors shut. He did this, turning somewhat black in the process; but the girl began to go in large circles around him in the market when he returned to sell again; and finally they were married. Unfortunately, this hard-earned marriage lasted only a few months, and then they were divorced.

There is also thieves' magic, which causes people to sleep deeply while being relieved of their valuables (*sirep*).

> After the alarm had been given that my landlord had been robbed, people came running over from all directions. Everyone's immediate reaction was that there must have been some magic operating. The thief must have been able to *sirep*, cast a charm so that everyone slept unusually soundly that night. Bu Mudojo, the seamstress from across the street, said she couldn't keep her eyes open after nine the night before.

And there is sorcery which compels the victim to do whatever one commands him to do (*nuraga*), for which the following is a suitable spell:

> As the head of the carabao hangs down,
> Stiff as a sea-shell,
> May Pak Sastro lower his head as my servant,
> Bow down as though he were the servant of my penis.

The satanic pacts for the purpose of gaining riches described earlier also fall into the category of sorcery in Javanese minds, as does the ability of some people to turn others into animals by means of the proper rites.

> He talked about sorcery and people doing evil to others by magical means. He said: "People can also turn into animals. What you do is you and your wife work it together with the aid of a *dukun*. You get wrapped up in white muslin like a corpse and lie on the table with an oil-candle lamp by you. Then you can become a wild boar (you leave your apparently dead body behind you lying on the table), and if you go to someone's outhouse and smell the waste water coming out of it, their money will flow out of it too, and you can get it." If the boar should happen to get into trouble, say be surrounded by village people who are out to capture him, then the lamp will begin to flicker, and if the wife stays awake and is faithful, she will blow the candle out, which will cause the boar to disappear right in front of the eyes of the village people and return to the "corpse."

* *Guna,* like all these terms, is often used to apply to sorcery generally, of whatever type.

Accusations of witchcraft are common enough, but they are never made openly and directly against anyone; they are only whispered to others as malicious gossip or discussed rather abstractly as hypotheses to account for peculiar behaviors. Thus a woman whose third marriage to the same man had just ended the same way the first two had—with his losing all their money at cards—when asked why on earth she had married him again anyway said matter-of-factly that she supposed she had been sorcerized. When the first village-chief election in my village was declared invalid by the government, many people ascribe it to the successful employment of a *ḍukun* by the losing candidate. One man told me that two years after his wife had died suddenly he discovered that an old enemy of his had sorcerized her. When I asked if he were now going to sorcerize the culprit in return or do anything else to him, he said, no, that was all in the past now. His main interest in the sorcery notion seemed to be mainly as an explanation of something for which he could not otherwise account.

In many instances the immediate suffering from sorcery is psychologically real and the accusations fervent. A young man whose proposal of marriage had been turned down blamed his very severe depression over the matter on the fact that the girl had not been content just to turn him down but had got a *ḍukun* after him as well; and he spent a few weeks eating in the pitch dark, praying for three hours every night (he was a *santri*) and, I suspect, getting a *ḍukun* friend of his to send out a few counterimprecations against the girl. Even in cases of this sort where the hurt is real and immediate, accusations are never expressed directly to the assumed culprit, nor is a public charge made; gossip to all one's neighbors is the typical pattern.

Bu Min drew me over to her house. (She was a neighbor of ours, as were the people she accused.) She showed me two glasses of water, one for each of her deceased parents, that she had prepared. Also with them were a glass of coffee and a box of the makings for betel-nut chew. She said there should also be a cigarette for the dead father. Then, having sat me down, she began whispering to me at a great rate, and finally I figured out what she was saying to me. She had been sick for 27 months now, she said—head aching, itch, fever—all due to the sorcerizing of the coffee shop owner, Nur, and his wife. They were doing this because they were evil and because they wanted her to get out of the house (it belonged to them) and because she had more money than they and could have nicer clothes. She said they went to a *ḍukun* in (a village about 20 miles away) and had this done. She described the way of doing it—four persons sitting in a square with one in the middle who chanted, and with a fire. She said that if one paid a hundred rupiahs the *ḍukun* would guarantee that the victim would die within 24 hours with a great swollen stomach. She herself had gone to a *kijaji* (Koran teacher) who had given her three "letters," at a cost of 25 rupiahs, which were written in Arabic and which said, he told her, that she was being sorcerized by these people and which had also magic words which would make a counter-effect. These "letters" were wrapped in a little cloth bundle with thread tied around it—she said she got them that way —and she kept it tied to the end of her waist band. She had also been fasting —had eaten no rice, only cassava—and stayed up as much of the night as she could—until 4 A.M. or so. . . . She also showed me, in each corner of the house, a sort of cactussy plant with big thorns which was to keep the spirits away that were being sent her by the evil coffee shop owner and his wife.

Sorcery, then, as the Javanese conceive of it, tends to be practiced on neighbors, friends, relatives, and other acquaintances fairly close at hand. Of course, the dukun employed may be a distant one and so be attacking someone far away from where he is performing his rite, but the actual instigator of the deed is always someone near at hand. Unlike some other peoples, Javanese do not accuse outsiders of sorcery: "The enemies of the people in Tebing live in Tebing," I was told when I asked a man who had told me that there was much sorcery in this nearby town if the people there ever sorcerized the people in Modjokuto.

Secondly, sorcery is always practiced for a specific reason, never for sheer malevolence. It seems to follow no definite kin or class lines, but instead there seems to be a tendency for a man to accuse another of sorcerizing him if he, the victim, conceives of himself as having either frustrated the wishes of the attacker or angered him in some way.

Finally, there is no way in which sorcery can be established as a public crime or even a tort. In all the cases of sorcery of which I heard, I never discovered a case in which direct confrontation by the victim of the accused took place or where any general open accusation was made or any claim for punishment or damages instituted even informally—there being no formal procedures for doing so in any case. Sorcery is a mystical act to be mystically combatted. Although one may gossip about it and make secret accusations to one's heart's content (which will in most cases get back to the accused in one fashion or another), any open attempt to organize public opinion against an accused sorcerer would be almost certain to fail. Similarly, one finds no private individuals in Modjokuto with a wide reputation for instigating sorcery. Although some dukuns are suspected as all-too-willing agents, even these are in no way socially ostracized.

In certain circumstances sorcery may be a near-legitimate, though still morally questionable, act, as in the case of my landlord, who had been robbed twice in a single month, a really terrible blow to him both financially and psychologically:

Pak Ardjo has taken steps against the thief who has come in twice in the last month. When the thief's handiwork was discovered, Pak Ardjo was very strict that no one disturb the traces, and later he put a plank across the threshold of the door which had been dug by the thief so that no one's footprints would disturb the dirt. He also found a footprint of the man in the back yard, which he covered with a pot so that it wouldn't be disturbed. Then the next day after the theft (i.e., the second one) he went away overnight, and it turned out later that he had gone to Malang, a large city about 60 miles to the east, to visit a famous dukun there. He took with him to this dukun a bit of the dirt from the place where the thief had been digging and a bit of the dirt from the footprint of the thief, plus the hat that the thief had left behind him at his work. When he came back from the dukun, he had his wife set up a charcoal stove with burning coals in it and with an earthenware pot over it. Then he rigged up a sort of support on which to hang within the pot where it was hot from the fire the hat of the thief, which was rolled up in the shape of a sausage and covered with white cloth to represent the muslin of death. This sausage looked rather like the wrapped-up body of a man, and Pak Ardjo said that was what it was. This was all covered with a lid and hidden behind the door and the fire has been kept going day and night to this day (about a month after the theft). Pak Ardjo says, with no little satisfaction, that as a result of this the thief is in a high fever; he can't sleep, he tosses to and fro, and he can't go out of his house and reap the benefits of his theft. The thief can get well only if he comes to Pak Ardjo and begs his pardon, and then Pak Ardjo will take the equipment back to the *dukun* and have a spell said over it again to remove the sorcery. (This idea that one can remove a sorcery spell by begging pardon of the instigator is general, but I never heard of anyone who ever did it.) Pak Ardjo said that he had to pay the *dukun* 25 rupiahs, which is the flat rate, plus 50 rupiahs for a *slametan* which the *dukun* held—the same *slametan* which is held for a dead person. On top of this were the expenses of the trip. He said this kind of magic is evil except when one is in the right, as he is; but he asked us not to tell anyone about it, for they might misunderstand his motives.

Chapter 9

Permai:
A Modern *Abangan* Cult

IN ADDITION to the distinction between *abangan, santri,* and *prijaji* which I have been stressing, there is a second distinction to be made without which much religious belief and behavior in Modjokuto is extremely difficult to interpret. This is the distinction between *kuna* (or *kolot*) and *modèren. Kuna* means old-fashioned, traditional, the ancient way. *Modèren* means exactly what it sounds like—modern; and the contrast between the very Javanese word and the second term, which strictly speaking is not Javanese at all but Dutch borrowed by way of Indonesian, gives something of the contrast between religious, ideological, and moral beliefs to which the terms refer. For *kuna* people the ways of their fathers are good enough, and the temptations of the present a snare and a delusion; for *modèren* people, mostly but not entirely clustered in the town, there is a need to reform the beliefs of the past to make them consonant with what they take to be the demands of the present. That such reform should paradoxically sometimes take the form of a return to a supposed earlier and purer form of belief considered to be more adequate than the degenerations which followed it is not so surprising in the light of anthropological studies of revivalist religious movements in different parts of the world, or, in fact, in the light of our own religious history; our prophets, too, condemn the present in terms of the past.

The *kuna-modèren* contrast appears most sharply among the *santris,* where it has led to a serious internal rift within the group, but it cuts across the entire society and all the categories, giving rise among the *abangans* to one of its most interesting manifestations—a politico-religious sect in which "original" Javanese religious beliefs are fused with a nationalistic Marxism which enables its adherents both to support Communist political policy in Indonesia and to purify *abangan* rituals of even the remnant of

Islam still contained in them. This sect, Permai,* represents an attempt to lend contemporary relevance to traditional *abangan* beliefs, to give Javanese spirit ideas, *slametan* practices, and curing techniques a meaning within a social context far different from that in which they arose, and, so far as its leaders are concerned, to reap some political advantages from this transformation.

On the national scene, Permai is a political party with members in the parliament, a central organization, and a platform. The general nature of the latter may be ascertained from the following excerpt from the statement of the Permai position in an official almanac of political parties published by the government Ministry of Information in 1951:**

> Thus the "common people"† are those who, although oppressed, exploited, and despised, still have belief in their own power, which they organize in order to oppose and evict, indeed to shatter, imperialism and capitalism, and to destroy all arbitrary oppression and exploitation. The common people . . . is that group in society composed of those who have indeed become poor and despised, but who still respect themselves as human beings who must live in the world and are conscious of their rights. With this consciousness there arises a flaming will to claim those rights.

In Modjokuto this aspect of things is largely confined to the leaders, one of whom, a young, highly urbanized man, was said by one of the members of the party to be "in contact with the Central Governing Board" and may have been a professional organizer. (He left Modjokuto in the middle of my stay.) Among the, for the most part, politically naive *abangans* Permai represents three things: a powerful curing cult; a set of esoteric beliefs patterned on typical *abangan* ones but with special twists and hidden meanings accessible only to the initiates; and a vigorously anti-Islamic social organization composed mainly of town laborers, employed or unemployed, impoverished rural radicals, and estate workers past and present.

Permai, its adherents hold, is based on "pure native science," on "original" Javanese beliefs as they were before they were corrupted with Hindu and, most particularly, Islamic additions. "Each people has its own science," one of the leaders explained. "The Westerners have theirs, the Moslems have theirs, and we Javanese have ours. It fits in with modern life just as well as any other. The trouble is that Indonesians have always tried to be Hindus, or Arabs, or Dutchmen, rather than Indonesians. Now that we are free, we

* Permai is short for Persatuan Rakjat Marhaen Indonesia, which roughly translated means "Organization of the Indonesian Common People." Actually, the short name forms the kind of abbreviating pun of which modern politicized Indonesians seem especially fond; for the contracted form in itself has a meaning. *Permai* is an Indonesian word for "beautiful."

** *Kepartaian di Indonesia* (Djakarta, 1951). The expositions of party programs in this almanac were prepared not by the Ministry of Information but by the respective political parties, and thus represent authoritative statements of their public platforms as of the date of publication.

† Permai uses a special term for "common people," *marhaen;* and the Permai doctrine is known as "Marhaenism."

have to seek the philosophy of our ancestors and throw away all those foreign sciences." Permai anti-Hinduism is merely *pro forma,* and many of the ideas and practices these people take for "original" are Indian in origin, but the opposition to Islam is extremely virulent and well worked out.

He (a Permai member) went into a diatribe against the Moslems. He said there were two kinds of Islam in Indonesia, Arabic Islam, which was foreign, and *Islam lugu* (literally: "starting capital"). This latter was the original religion here, and the other was a foreign importation. Then he went through a point-for-point comparison of the two. He said the Arab Moslems have the five prayer times, but the Javanese Moslems pray just any time; they may pray forty times a day or may not pray at all, depending on the situation. In addition, they can't be seen when they pray. It is an interior thing and nothing is said aloud, it is all in the head, whereas the *santris* pray aloud and move their bodies through the various prayer postures. Secondly, the alms. For the *santris* it is so much once a year, a fixed amount, rice given to the poor. Permai people, he said, regard the banana-leaf baskets of food one gives out at a *slametan* as alms, and they do this all year round; they don't just wait for *Rijaja* (the holiday that ends the Fast). For the *abangans,* if one is eating and a man outside is hungry, one should give him half one's food. The Pilgrimage, he said, is not necessary, in the sense of going to Mecca. For him it is just traveling around, mixing with people and gaining experience, and one can travel anywhere. He said the pilgrims were actually the victims of a colonialist plot. Mecca was owned by the British, and the Dutch, being under the British, then deceived the Javanese into going there and throwing all their money away. . . . For the "original" Javanese it is the way a man behaves that is important, and the mere fact that a man has been to Mecca doesn't make him anything special; he may be doing bad just the same. "In fact," he said, "it takes a lot of money to be a pilgrim, doesn't it? Thus they are mostly rich, which shows they are more dishonest than other people." He said, "Some pilgrims enter Permai, but they have to take off their turbans and become Javanese again. As for the Confession of Faith, the Permai people have their secret word."

To join the organization one must take a secret oath, sealing it by drinking a cup of tea in the presence of other members; and it is said that if a member reveals the secrets of the organization he will sicken and die or go insane. One also learns a secret word, whispered to the novice six months after his initiation in the dead of night, which when pronounced soundlessly over tea enables one to cure illness. Here, evidently, the basis of curing ability has been shifted from individual spiritual discipline to organizational membership as symbolized by the single secret word; for the curing ability is said to be universal among members, and I know of a few cases in which Permai members not otherwise *ḍukuns* have attempted to cure fairly serious diseases by the secret-word method.

In addition there are books, mostly written by the founder of the movement,* with glosses giving esoteric significance to key words in the text—"unlike the Koran, where everything means what it says." The content

* The founder is, as a matter of fact, not a Javanese but a Sundanese from West Java. He is supposed to have come upon the science in the traditional manner—by meditating in the woods.

of the doctrine thus revealed in these otherwise straightforward nationalist pamphlets being secret, I had only partial access to it. In general, it seems to consist of a fusion between modern nationalist ideology, particularly as set forth in the *Pantjasila,* President Sukarno's famous "Five Points" (Monotheism, Nationalism, Humanism, Social Justice, and Democracy), which are the official philosophical base for the new Republic of Indonesia, and such traditional Javanese religious patterns as calendrical divination, food symbolism, and methods of spiritual discipline, plus a new note of explicit moralism designed to combat Moslem moralism on the one hand and to connect up traditional peasant values such as *rukun* ("cooperation" in house building, irrigation, etc.) with Marxist ethics on the other.

All these themes appeared quite clearly in the public meetings Permai held in several villages in the Modjokuto area on or about the first of *Sura,* the beginning of the Javanese New Year, in 1953, a day in itself symbolic of "Javanese" as against "Moslem" belief. In my village, something of a Permai stronghold, this annual meeting was held at the home of a hospital worker. His small bamboo house was decorated for the occasion as though he were marrying off a daughter or circumcising a son. Yellow coconut branches were bent over the gateway, the house was draped with red and white bunting, and a temporary matted-leaf roof extended out over the yard to protect the male guests from the rain. The women sat, as usual, inside the house. On the front porch there was a speaker's stand piled high with various kinds of farm products: corn, cassava, peppers, soybeans, onions. On the front of it hung a large Indonesian flag.

> The meeting opened with a brief *slametan* with rice cones, incense, and all —although there was no Arabic chanting. Pak Min (the hospital worker) went through the usual forms of politesse. He explained that this was a Permai meeting, that Permai was a religious science, and that the intent of this science was to enable everyone to *rukun*—to be able to live together peacefully and to help one another advance in these new times. Wito, the aggressive young leader of the group from Modjokuto, attired in a snappy grey business suit, two-tone shoes, and a loud tie, leapt to his feet at this point and led us in *Indonesia Raya* (the Indonesian national anthem) and in several vigorous shouts of "Freedom" (the slogan of the Indonesian revolution). Min then presented a four-page "special message" from party headquarters in Djakarta, which turned out to be not on political matters but on religious ones. As it was in Indonesian, which I imagine very few people in the audience could follow, the rest of the meeting was largely spent in explicating this text in Javanese. The first speaker to attempt this was a young man dressed in very traditional style—complete with turban, black-and-brown striped jacket, and hand-painted sarong. He looked like a picture in the ethnography books. Very nervous and shy, he spoke in a mechanical mumble and kept getting coached from the sidelines. He explained the meaning of the Javanese months as they were set forth in the text. For example, "*Sura* (the name of the first month) means courage; so we must have courage to do the right." He went through a similar routine with the letters of the Javanese alphabet, each letter starting a sentence of general moral instruction—like "A is for Always wash your face before dinner" in the old primers. In both cases the original sentence in the text

was first quoted in Old Javanese and then translated into Indonesian, and the boy said the sentences were actual sentences written a long time ago by the audience's ancestors and so represented the wisdom of the ancients. He said that this wisdom had been neglected, nay, suppressed in the colonial period, but was now being taught again by Permai. He said this wisdom was still useful today as a "compass," and we shouldn't just ignore it. An older man followed him, explicating a complicated numerical divination system which was also in the original text, but which was so complex that I understood little of it in either language. Next came a lively little man hopping up out of the audience and placing himself back of the speaker's stand with all the farm products on it. He gave a long, very clever (and evidently very funny, because he had the audience in the aisles, though most of the jokes went by me), and seemingly impromptu speech. He snatched up each of the fruits and vegetables in turn and gave a short political-moral sermon on it. "See," he said, "how all these bananas are joined together at the base," holding a bunch aloft. "This is how we must all hang together if we are not to be kicked around. All these crops grow easily in fertile Java, but we, the children of the land in this country, are all still unhappy and hungry because the imperialists steal most of them from us." Lastly, we got Wito. He spoke with a very demagogic delivery. He waved his hands and mopped his brow, paced up and down, shouted and whispered, repeated continually for emphasis, and demanded responses from the audience ("Is there anyone here who is not a man?"—"No!"—"Is there anyone here who is a carabao?"—"No, there isn't anyone!"—"Who here is an ox?"—"No one, there aren't any oxen!"—"Then why, my brothers, should we stand being treated like carabao and oxen?" Nobody seemed to know.) "Indonesians are free now," he cried. "There are no more colonists here. But we are still fighting among ourselves (a reference to the Moslem rebellion then going on in West Java). Why is this? Because we were set one against the other by the Dutch for three hundred years." He attacked the Dutch for not turning over West New Guinea to Indonesia as they promised, attacked Islam for "insulting" womanhood by permitting polygyny, and attacked the Ministry of Religion for not allowing civil marriage for non-*santris* (i.e., a ceremony in which it would not be required to repeat the Moslem Confession of Faith). He went over each point in the *Pantjasila,* giving it a vaguely Marxist political interpretation ("We must demand social justice for the poor as well as the rich!"), and ended his speech after a half hour of intense exertion with a cry of "Freedom!," collapsing exhausted into his chair to receive the only applause of the evening. The meeting closed with a minute's silent meditation during which Wito asked us to concentrate our thoughts to the end that the reactionaries who were trying to take over Indonesia and oppress the common people might not succeed.*

The doctrine concerning "non-Islamic" marriages and funerals is not merely theoretical but has actually led to some of the sharpest open conflicts between *abangans* and *santris* in the Modjokuto area. The marriage argument is perhaps the strongest from an abstract point of view, especially since the government allows Christians to have their own ceremonies. It is also the most difficult to carry out because, in the absence of a government decision either recognizing Permai as an official religion—as Islam and

---

* This is not a direct transcription of my fieldnote on the meeting but a slightly reorganized synopsis of it.

Christianity—or legitimizing completely secular marriages, any Permai members who marry without repeating the Confession of Faith before the subdistrict religious officer (the *naib*) are living in sin, and this stigma is difficult for the rank-and-file members to bear even in the name of anti-Islam or the Rights of the Common Man. A very violent Moslem speaker from Djakarta speaking in a town near Modjokuto got his greatest ovation when he accused Permai and the Indonesian Communist Party (which also supports secular marriage) of intending to raise a generation of bastards in Indonesia.

So, for the moment, Permai is reduced on the marriage question to lobbying in Djakarta. On the local level little can be done, although a few sporadic attempts have been made.

> I asked the religious officer—*modin*—of my village about marriage. Do the Permai people go to the *naib* for that? He said that they tried not to in a nearby village not so long ago. As all the people involved were Permai members, they went to the village chief with a written contract and a tax stamp and wanted him to sign it and bring it in to the subdistrict officer—that being the whole of the ceremony. The subdistrict officer refused to allow this, and so all these people along with the Modjokuto heads of Permai went in and made a big fuss with the subdistrict officer, but didn't get anywhere. He said that the Ministry of Religion recognized only Christian and Islamic marriage ceremonies, and he just carried out government regulations. They went to the district officer and got the same answer. The district officer said he couldn't set up his own country; he had to follow the decrees of the central government.

But the funeral situation is rather different, for the employment of the *modin* at a funeral is not a law but a custom, and, at least theoretically, one is free to use him or not. After Permai leaders complained vigorously about Islamic funerals for non-Islamic corpses to the subdistrict officer, the latter warned all the *modins* in his bailiwick that they would be well advised in cases of Permai death just to take down the name, age, and illness of the deceased and go home. Otherwise, they might get into trouble, and he, the subdistrict officer, would not be responsible for them if they did. The hitch in this logically impeccable abstention doctrine is that since the *modin* is also the technical and the religious specialist in preparing people for burial, the Javanese "undertaker," people are rather lost without his help.

Also, since it is only rarely that someone dies who has been consistent enough to have only Permai people for relatives, under the stress of grief, when people are not much interested in social reform in any case, there is always strong pressure for a traditional funeral. The woman I mentioned earlier as having hanged herself because of debts incurred in giving an over-elaborate circumcision ceremony was married to a Permai man. The second in command of Permai in Modjokuto, a shoe repairman, hurried out to the village where she lived and told the *modin* on duty that the husband was Permai and that he should go home and mind his own business; which the *modin,* mindful of the subdistrict officer's advice, did with all haste. But the husband, broken up enough over his wife's death by her own hand and not wishing to incur any more problems, shortly thereafter came weeping to the *modin*'s home and asked him for God's sake to go through the Islamic routine of bathing, wrapping, and praying over the body; and the *modin,* I imagine with some satisfaction, obliged.

An even more dramatic case of the same conflict occurred in my neighborhood. A young boy of about ten or eleven who was living with his aunt and uncle, the latter a street peddler of iced drinks and a strong Permai member, died very suddenly. The *modin,* following the subdistrict officer's policy, refused to officiate. As a result, the funeral stalled completely, and the boy's body lay all morning in the house without anything being done to prepare it for the grave. After a while a *santri* acquaintance of the uncle—less rigid than most—tried to help out and bathe the body; but he was advised by the *modin* that he was taking on a great responsibility and so hesitated in fear of committing a mortal sin. All the guests just sat around, expressionless as ever, in an atmosphere of growing tension, wondering what would happen next. (Because of the pull of the tradition that all neighborhood people should turn up at a funeral, there were both *abangans* and *santris* present, but they sat separately.)

After about an hour, the father and mother of the child arrived from their home in Surabaja, and, probably in part stimulated by the general disorganization, the mother and aunt soon dissolved into hysterics, the only case of emotional outburst at a funeral I saw in Modjokuto. The *santri* friend of the uncle now approached the father—the *modin,* as a government official, did not feel that he himself should do it—and asked him if he wanted an Islamic funeral. The father, not being Permai, said yes. The *modin* thereupon leapt gleefully back into his role and the funeral was completed in the usual pattern. The third-day *slametan,* however, turned out to be a political meeting of Permai at the uncle's home rather than the usual feast and chanting, and no *santris* were present.

Perhaps the most interesting thing about this whole affair was the fact that at one point the *modin* asked the leaders of Permai to officiate at the funeral, but, lacking confidence, they refused. And they lost yet another test case when the father eventually accepted the Moslem ritual. (When asked if he wanted it, he said, "Of course, I don't hold much with religion, but I'm not a Christian!") Had they accepted, we would have seen a genuine case of ritual change in action. We would have caught the historical process at the elusive point at which things stop being what they were and become something else, where a pattern dissolves and a new one replaces it. In any case, in the Permai movement one sees the *abangan* religious system as it attempts to widen out to include a new social experience, as it readjusts itself in a context where things once held immutable have altered and where more than simple reciprocity and emotional restraint are demanded. It is a religious system designed for a peasant come to town.

Part Two

THE "SANTRI" VARIANT

Chapter 10   *Santri* versus *Abangan*

Islam: A General Introduction

ISLAM is a religion of ethical prophecy. Muhammad's break with tradition was sharp and clear, and his message, or the message of God revealed to him, was essentially one of rationalization and simplification. Where there had been many gods, he preached one; where there had been extensive harems, he preached a four-wife polygamy; where there had been a bottomless self-indulgence, he preached a moderate asceticism, forbidding drinking and gambling. He rejected rich symbolism, simplified ritual, proclaimed the universality of his message, and urged a holy war to spread it among the unbelievers. Although Muhammad saw himself as but a vessel for the word of God, the directions of his religious interests were not transcendental but this-worldly. His reaction to the world of men as he found it was not a radical rejection, a turning away into mysticism with disgust and despair, but a direct attempt at active mastery of it. "From the beginning of his career as a preacher," the British Islamic historian H. A. R. Gibb has written, "his outlook and his judgment of persons and events were dominated by his conceptions of God's government and purposes in the world of men."*

Prophecy, however, is a fleeting thing, for much of its immediacy departs with the prophet. Succeeding generations have read the message Muhammad brought mostly as it has been translated by those who come after him. His followers live now not so much in the brilliant glare of religious innovation as in the half-light of doctrinal orthodoxy, for, as with Christianity, a great swarm of learned doctors—the *'Ulama* ("the knowing")—surrounded the original core of Islam and covered it with a great honeycombed construction of doctrine and law, of exegesis and codification.

The core of Islam rests in the Koran and the Hadith, the Koran being

---

* H. A. R. Gibb, *Mohammedanism* (London, 1949), p. 24.

the collection of the words of Allah spoken by Muhammad during the years 610–622 A.D., and the Hadith collections of short narratives (each called a *hadith*) told by people who knew the Prophet personally during his lifetime and which, handed down through the ages, describe some act or saying of the Prophet which is to be taken as a guide.

Taking the Koran and the Hadith as given, the *'Ulama* piled on top of them the *Shari'a*—the Moslem law, a complex codification of legislation covering almost every field of social life, but particularly emphasizing the domestic. The law has been for Moslems, as Jewish law has been for the Jews, a substitute for the formal church organization they have never been able or willing to erect. Without priests and without popes, the *'Ulama,* a class of experts professionally occupied with the interpretation of the Koran and the Hadith, became the heart and soul of Moslem orthodoxy. The lawyer who is at the same time a teacher has set the form and determined much of the content of Islam.

The multiple legal interpretations of the Koran and the Hadith finally crystallized into four orthodox schools, all considered equally valid and sacred. After the second and third Islamic centuries, no further extension of the Law was permitted; the "gate of *itjihad*" (individual interpretation of the Koran and Hadith) swung shut, and henceforth no scholar, however eminent, could qualify as an authoritative lawmaker. The body of orthodox Islam (called Sunnite Islam after the Arabic *sunna,* "custom"), made up of the contents of the Koran, the Hadith, and the *Shari 'a,* has been fixed since the tenth century A.D.

Islam means "surrender." The world-famous Moslem confession of faith— "There is no god but God and Muhammad is his Prophet"—repeated over and over again by one-seventh of the world's population, states the terms of this surrender. The Confession is the rock bottom of Islam, for anyone who repeats and believes this phrase is a Moslem; and in the nation of equal believers that is Islam no one has the right to call anyone else's faith into question.

Allah, this single God, is Almighty, Self-sustained, and Inscrutable. He decides all according to His Will, which is Incalculable save as He from time to time makes that Will known to mankind through a series of prophets sent to the different races of man. Altogether, twenty-eight prophets are mentioned in the Koran, including Adam, Moses, Jesus (whose divinity is denied), and John the Baptist. All these prophets, as well as others not mentioned (e.g., Buddha), are legitimate, bringing the genuine word of God, and Muhammad is but the special prophet of the Arabs. Nevertheless, there has been an evolution in prophecy toward the final and perfect revelation of Muhammad, the last and Seal of the prophets. All the prophets are but men, including Muhammad; they have no knowledge of the supernatural beyond that revealed to them, no miraculous powers. They have all brought a similar message: "Come ye unto God or be damned."

To avoid an adverse decision on Judgment Day, five ritual acts—the so-called Five Pillars—are obligatory for each believer. The first is the Confession of Faith. The second is the prayers. The prayers are said five times a day: at daybreak, at noon, in the mid-afternoon, after sunset, and in the early evening. They consist of the recitation of a few set Arabic phrases, two to four prostrations toward Mecca, and a few other ritual incantations. The noon prayer on Friday is preferably to be performed in a mosque with at least thirty-nine other Moslems and with a leader to set the pace. Ablution before prayers—a washing of the hands, face, and ankles at least, with sand if no water is available—is strictly enjoined.

Fasting, the third pillar, is prescribed in the month of Ramadan, the ninth month of the lunar year, with complete abstinence from food or drink in the hours of daylight, from the time you can tell a black thread from a white one until you again cannot. The pilgrimage to Mecca (the *hajj*) is prescribed at least once in a lifetime for those who have sufficient wealth to accomplish it (for those who have not, it is forbidden), in the twelfth lunar month *Dhu'l-Hijja*. The fifth pillar is the *zakah,* the religious tax, the proceeds of which are to go to the poor, the needy, debtors, stranded travelers, new converts, religious students having no means of support, and to prosecute the Holy War. Alms suited to the individual purse and given at irregular times to the needy of one's own choosing are also required.

This is the essential substance of Islam, perhaps as simple and easily marketable a religious package as has ever been prepared for export. Lacking a formal church organization by means of which they could enforce orthodoxy, the learned doctors of Islam have of necessity a gradualist position: first the Confession, then the Pillars, later the piety, and after that the learning and the Law. This is the course Islam has taken in Java, where over 90 per cent of the population has confessed to being Sunnites of the *Shafi'ite* law school for four centuries, but where only recently has a large minority of the population come to understand very clearly what it was they were confessing and to make any serious attempt to carry out the commands of God upon which their religion is based.

That serious attempt is the result of a shift in attitude which has not endeared the minority to those of their compatriots for whom the syncretic Islam of Sunan Kalidjaga—the culture-hero, who, after suitable meditation and ascetic practice, is represented to have introduced the shadow play, the percussion orchestra, the *slametan,* and the Koran and the Pillars into Indonesia*—is still the ideal. It is this minority, these "true Moslems," as they call themselves, or "Javanese Arabs," as their enemies call them, to whom the term *santri* (originally applied only to religious students) is given.

The Development of Islam in Indonesia

SNOUCK HURGRONJE, Holland's great Islamic scholar, wrote of Indonesian Islam as he found it in 1892:

---

* Sometimes the non-Islamic elements of this complex—the shadow play and so forth—are said to have been invented by the pre-Islamic culture-hero, Radèn Pandji.

To follow up the image of the five pillars (of Islam), we might say that the pointed roof of the building of Islam is still mainly supported by the central pillar, the confession that there is no god but Allah and that Muhammad is the messenger of Allah, but that this pillar is surrounded with a medley of ornamental work quite unsuited to it which is a profanation of its lofty simplicity. And in regard to the other four, the corner pillars, it might be observed that some of these have suffered decay in the long lapse of time, while other new pillars, which according to the orthodox teaching are unworthy to be supports of the holy building have been planted beside the original five and have to a considerable extent robbed them of their functions.*

Hurgronje was referring specifically to Acheh in northern Sumatra, but his simile would have applied even more aptly to Java, where the pillars were scarcely visible among the buttresses. Aside from a conviction that they were Moslems and that to be a Moslem was in general a good thing, Hurgronje found among the inhabitants of tropical Indonesia little of the desert-dried Near Eastern monotheism he had (perhaps) known in Mecca, where he had lived, a Christian disguised as a Moslem pilgrim. Indonesians, he said, "render in a purely formal manner due homage to the institutions ordained of Allah, which are everywhere as sincerely received in theory as they are ill-observed in practice";** and a generation of scholars echoed him—in despair if they were Islamologists, in triumph if they were ethnologists dedicated to preserving native customs in their pristine beauty.

But Hurgronje was writing at the end of one era and the beginning of a new one. Twenty years after he wrote, Muhammadijah, a vigorously modernist Islamic society, was founded in Djokjakarta, the very center and climax of Hindu-Javanese culture, heralding what the Javanese call "the time of the organizations" and announcing the final arrival on the Indonesian social scene of the self-conscious Moslem, the man not only fond of his religion in theory but also committed to it in practice. The appearance of such a man was not as sudden an occurrence as it looked to some, surprised by signs of life in a religion they had long accounted lacking in either internal dynamism or in basic appeal to what they took to be "the Indonesian soul." Hurgronje, wiser than most and knowing that changes in the sphere of Islamic life and doctrine were taking place even in his time, warned his readers that these changes were so gradual that "although they take place before our eyes they are hidden from those who do not make a careful study of the subject."†

Islam came to Indonesia from India, brought by merchants. Its Mid-

---

* C. Snouck Hurgronje, *The Achehnese* (Leyden, 1906), p. 313.

** *Ibid.* He also noted that "The [indigenous customs] which control the lives of the Bedawins of Arabia, the Egyptians, the Syrians, or the Turks, are for the most part *different* from those of the Javanese, Malays and Achehnese, but the relation of these [customs] to the law of Islam, and the tenacity with which they maintain themselves in despite of that law, is everywhere the same. The customary law of the Arabs and . . . of the Turks differ from the written and unwritten [customary law] of our Indonesians, but they are equally far removed from the revealed law, although they are equally loud in their recognition of the divine origin of the latter" (p. 280).

† *Ibid.*

Eastern sense for the external conditions of life having been blunted and turned inward by Indian mysticism, it provided but a minimal contrast to the mélange of Hinduism, Buddhism, and animism which had held the Indonesians enthralled for almost fifteen centuries. Although it spread—peacefully for the most part—through almost all of Indonesia in a space of three hundred years and completely dominated Java except for a few pagan pockets by the end of the sixteenth century, Indonesian Islam, cut off from its centers of orthodoxy at Mecca and Cairo, vegetated, another meandering tropical growth on an already overcrowded religious landscape. Buddhist mystic practices got Arabic names, Hindu Radjas suffered a change of title to become Moslem Sultans, and the common people called some of their wood spirits jinns; but little else changed.

Toward the middle of the nineteenth century the isolation of Indonesian Islam from its Mid-Eastern fountainhead began to break down. From the Hadhramaut, that barren ground of Moslem medievalism at the southern tip of the Arabian peninsula, came Arab traders in ever increasing numbers to settle in Indonesia and transmit their fine sense for orthodoxy to the local merchants with whom they dealt. And, with the growth of sea travel, Indonesians began to go on the pilgrimage to Mecca in such numbers that by the time Hurgronje lived there in the 1880's the Indonesian colony was the largest and most active in the entire city. "Here," he wrote, "lies the heart of the religious life of the East-Indian archipelago, and the numberless arteries pump thence fresh blood in ever accelerating tempo to the entire body of the Moslem populace in Indonesia."*

At the other end of these arteries, in Java, were rural Koranic schools in which the returning pilgrim taught, if not the content of Islam (for the most part neither he nor his peasant students could understand any Arabic, although they could chant it well enough), at least a sense for the austerity of its form and for the fact that it was different in spirit from the polytheistic mysticism to which the Javanese had been so long accustomed. Around these schools and around the mosques attached to them, a space for orthodoxy was cleared; and those who lived in this clearing—the *santris*—began to see themselves as minority representatives of the true faith in the great forest of ignorance and superstition, protectors of the Divine Law against the pagan crudities of traditionalized custom.

But even in this context the drift toward orthodoxy was slow. Up until about the second decade of this century the various Koranic schools located around the countryside remained independent, mutually antagonistic, mystically tinged religious brotherhoods in which a certain compromise was reached with the religious beliefs of the *abangans* on the one hand and the fears of the colonial government of an organized and socially conscious Islam on the other. It was in the towns, where continued contact with Hadhramaut Arabs, a developing merchant ethic, the growth of nationalism, and modernist influences from the Islamic reform movements of Egypt and India combined

---

* C. Snouck Hurgronje, *Mekka in the Nineteenth Century* (London, 1931), p. 291.

to produce a greater militancy among the explicitly Moslem, that Islam became a living faith in Indonesia.*

With the founding of Muhammadijah by a returned pilgrim in 1912, and
the birth of its political counterpart Sarekat Islam ("The Islamic Union") in
the same year, the awakened sense for orthodoxy spread beyond the towns
to the villages. Conservative organizations arose to combat what they took
to be dangerous departures from the more medieval Islamic doctrines in the
programs of the modernist groups, but, details apart, the recognition that
there was at last a true Islamic congregation in *Indonesia*—a genuine *ummat,*
as Moslems call the community of true believers—was finally inescapable.
Even those who had ignored Hurgronje's warning to make a close study of the
subject could now see that Indonesian Islam had changed and that in almost
every village and town in Java there was a group, often living in a separate
neighborhood, commonly made up of petty traders and richer peasants, to
whom Islam was no longer another mystic science among many but a unique,
exclusivist, universalist religion demanding total surrender to a distant God
and dedicated to an eternal struggle against the unbeliever.

Modjokuto, having been founded in the latter half of the nineteenth century, has a history lying almost entirely within this period in which a self-conscious Moslem community crystallized out from the more general *abangan*
background. The great majority of its prewar trading class and much of its
peasant population having been drawn through migration from the heavily Islamic areas of northern Java—Demak, Kudus, Gresik—where the Moslem tradition brought by the earliest traders never wholly died out, Modjokuto has
experienced each phase of reform and counter-reform within the Islamic community in Indonesia during this century until today perhaps a third of the
population—as a rough estimate—are *santris*. Grouped into their own neighborhoods (less so now than before the war, but still noticeably clustered),
their own political parties, and their own social organizations, and following
their own ritual patterns, this group represents a genuine variant of Modjokuto
culture.

Santri versus *Abangan:* General Differences

COMPARING the *abangan* and *santri* variants of the Modjokuto religious pattern, two very striking general differences, other than their differential evalu-

---

* Actually, a more orthodox version of the Moslem creed has been characteristic
of the peoples of the north coastal areas and of the small urban Javanese trading classes
scattered throughout the larger and smaller towns all over Java since the conversion of
the island to Islam in the fifteenth century. In these groups, where the mercantile
tradition has also remained stronger, Islam has been rather less diluted with mystical
and animistic elements than it was either in the great inland courts, such as those
at Djokjakarta and Surakarta, or in the rice-plain peasant villages of the Solo and
Brantas rivers, where syncretism was, and is, very strong. Thus the recent growth of
Moslem orthodoxy in Java is, in part, a strengthening and widening of this persistent
minority tradition, not a wholly novel development.

ation of Islamic orthodoxy, are immediately apparent. In the first place, *abangans* are fairly indifferent to doctrine but fascinated with ritual detail, while among the *santris* the concern with doctrine almost entirely overshadows the already attenuated ritualistic aspects of Islam.

An *abangan* knows when to give a *slametan* and what the major foods should be—porridge for a birth, pancakes for a death. He may have some ideas as to what various elements in it symbolize (and as often he may not, saying that one has porridge because one always has porridge on such an occasion), but he will be little upset if someone else gives a different interpretation. He is tolerant about religious beliefs; he says, "Many are the ways." If one performs the correct passage rituals, one is not an animal; if one gives the *slametans* in the Fast, one is not an infidel; and if one sends a tray off to the "cleansing of the village," one is not a subversive—and that is enough. If one doesn't believe in spirits or if one thinks God lives in the sun, that's one's own affair.

For the *santri* the basic rituals are also important—particularly the prayers, the conscientious performance of which is taken by *santris* and non-*santris* alike to be the distinguishing mark of a true *santri*—but little thought is given to them; they are simple enough in any case. What concerns the *santris* is Islamic doctrine, and most especially the moral and social interpretation of it. They seem especially interested, particularly the urban "modernist" *santris*, in apologetics: the defense of Islam as a superior ethical code for modern man, as a workable social doctrine for modern society, and as a fertile source of values for modern culture. In the countryside the doctrinal aspect is less marked; there the *santri* ethic remains somewhat closer to the *abangan*. But even in the countryside a *santri* differs from an *abangan* not only in his self-declared religious superiority to the latter, but also in his realization, if only vague, that in Islam the main religious issues are doctrinal; and in any case the rural *santri* follows an urban leadership. For the *santri* the dimensions have shifted. It is not the knowledge of ritual detail or spiritual discipline which is important, but the application of Islamic doctrine to life. The kinds of *santris* vary from those whose difference from their *abangan* neighbors seems to lie entirely in their insistence that they are true Moslems, while their neighbors are not, to those whose commitment to Islam dominates almost all of their life. But, for all, a concern for dogma has to some extent replaced a concern for ritual.

One result of this difference of emphasis is that the curiously detached unemotional relativism that *abangans* evince toward their own religious customs, an attitude not entirely unlike that of the dilettante ethnologist collecting quaint customs among the heathen, tends to be replaced among the *santris* by a strong emphasis on the necessity for unreserved belief and faith in the absolute truth of Islam and by marked intolerance for Javanese beliefs and practices they take to be heterodox.

> I talked to Abdul Manan from the village (some distance away from Modjokuto) where we stayed for a while a few months back. . . . Asked him about *pundèns* (spirit shrines) there, and he said there is one there with the same

name as the one here—*mBah Buda*—just down the street from his place. People give *slametans* there just as here, in order to fulfill a vow that they would do so if cured and so on. He said he as a good Moslem doesn't believe in it, and said he proved this one dark night by taking the statue of a man that was there and carrying it off to the mosque and breaking it into pieces. Nothing happened, he said, which proves it was just a statue. He said there is a statue of an ox there now and people still go on holding *slametans* there as usual, but only those who are too stupid to know any better.

The second obvious way in which the *abangan* and *santri* religious variants differ from one another is in the matter of their social organization. For the *abangan* the basic social unit to which nearly all ritual refers is the household—a man, his wife, and his children. It is the household which gives the *slametan,* and it is the heads of other households who come to attend it and then carry home part of the food to the other members of their families. Even the *bersih désa,* the "cleansing of the village" ceremony, the closest thing to a public or super-household ritual that one can find within the *abangan* system, is but little more than a compound of separate *slametan* contributions from each of the village's households rather than a ritual of the village as a whole; it is food from separate kitchens brought together, rather than food from a common kitchen divided up. Aside from coming with their food, there is little that the participants are called upon to do, and the kind of large-scale religious ritual carried out by special clubs, fraternities, and associations one finds in, say, Melanesia, parts of Africa, or among the American Pueblos is quite foreign to the Javanese tradition. With the exception of Permai, a latter-day development indeed and largely politically inspired at that, there is nothing in *abangan* religious life which could even in the remotest sense be called a church or a religious organization, and there are no temples either. The Javanese peasant, who has so often been held to be a featureless cipher swallowed up in his social whole, actually holds himself rather aloof from it, keeping his thoughts to himself and willing to give others only what tradition assures him they are going to give back to him; and his religion shows it. There is no organic religious community, strictly speaking, among the *abangans:* in contemporary Modjokuto at least, there is only a set of separate households geared into one another like so many windowless monads, their harmony preordained by their common adherence to a single tradition.

For the *santri,* the sense of community—of *ummat*—is primary. Islam is seen as a set of concentric social circles, wider and wider communities— Modjokuto, Java, Indonesia, the whole of the Islamic world—spreading away from the individual *santri* where he stands: a great society of equal believers constantly repeating the name of the Prophet, going through the prayers, chanting the Koran.

Usman (a local Koran teacher, speaking to about twenty mostly illiterate peasants in a small, heavily *santri* village near Modjokuto on the occasion of the Prophet's birthday) gave as usual a series of unrelated commentaries on *hadiths* and Koranic passages. He started by saying, "The world is round, is it not, my brothers? You've seen it on the Nahdatul Ulama (one of the two major Moslem political parties) flag haven't you, and it is round, isn't it? Thus it is different times in different places, so that if it is evening prayer here, perhaps it is already morning prayer in Mecca, and further west in Cairo or Morocco it is already perhaps noon prayer, and there are all gradations in between, in Djokjakarta, in Djakarta, in Pakistan. There are three hundred million Moslems, my brothers, so that every minute of every day someone is saying *Muhammad ar-Rasulullah* (Muhammad, the Prophet of God), someone is saying it around this round globe. And this has been going on, my brothers, for 1,344 years. No one's name has been spoken so often as that of the Prophet, is it not true? If there is someone whose name has been spoken more often I would like to know who he is! We here in Sidomuljo, in a tiny village out in the corner of the countryside, are only a part of a great *ummat Islam;* in Modjokuto, in Djakarta, in Mecca, all over the world right now as we chant our prayers, Moslems just like us are chanting theirs."

Before the power and majesty of God all men are as nothing, and in their nihility they are equal. Cut off by an absolute gulf from direct experience of God and so restricted to the books of prophets, and especially to the Koran and the Hadith, for their knowledge of Him, mankind—a part now, the whole of it later—has bound itself into a legal community, defined by its adherence to a set of objective laws based upon the revelations God has seen fit to communicate to man. There are no priests, because no man is any closer to God or of any greater intrinsic religious worth than any other; but the law must be communicated, interpreted, and administered, and so there are teachers, judges, and officials, and schools, courts, and religious bureaucracies. It is the adherence to an objective, deductive, abstract law that defines a Moslem and defines the Moslem community; and, although in Java, as I imagine elsewhere, the greater flexibility of the inductive, relativistic, pragmatic customary law tends to be in practice more attractive to *santris* as well as *abangans* than the rigid beauties of the Koranic law, the sense for a concrete community regulated by an objective system of law is quite real in *santri* minds.

We got on to Islam and he went over the usual business about the importance of the law as a compass, as a way of choosing between right and wrong. Admittedly, some people who don't know the law are good, but they don't have a sure guide and they may go wrong. Only those who have the Koranic law really can find their way safely through life to the afterlife. He read me a Koranic passage saying that the true Moslem is willing to labor and to sacrifice his money, his property, and all his personal resources for the good of society, to build mosques, schools, and so forth; and he said that this social conscience is obligatory to Moslems. It is like making a suit of clothes, he said. To make clothes that fit and won't fall apart the tailor needs to make measurements. For life, individual and social, we need measurements too, and there are in the Koran and the law.

This concern with the community means that, despite their tremendous interest in doctrine, Modjokuto Moslems never see their religion as a mere set of beliefs, as a kind of abstract philosophy, or even as a general system of values to which as individuals they are committed. Instead, they always conceive of it as institutionalized in some social group: the *santris* in their neighborhood, or all those they consider such in the Modjokuto area, or all Indonesian Moslems, or "the Islamic world." When they speak of Islam, there is almost always in the back of their minds a social organization of some sort in which the Islamic creed is the defining element. It may be a charitable organization, a woman's club, the village mosque committee, a religious school, the local office of the religious bureaucracy, or their political party at either the local, regional, or national level.

These two distinguishing features of the *santri* religious pattern—a concern for doctrine and apology and for social organization—crosscut one another to produce the internal structure of the Moslem community in Modjokuto. On the doctrinal level there is only one major distinction of importance, rather less marked now than it was in the years before the war: that between the "modern" (*modèren*) and the conservative or "old-fashioned" (*kolot*) variants of the creed. From 1912 almost until the war the conflict between those Indonesian Moslems who had been influenced by modernist Islamic reform movements originating in Cairo, Mecca, and, to a far lesser extent, in parts of India, and those who reacted against this influence, was indeed a sharp and bitter one. Today, this once entirely religious conflict has been transformed in part into a political one as the leaders of both groups have come to accept a general and watered-down version of modernism and have shifted their interest more and more towards the ever intriguing question of how they are going to get into power. But the old division still remains. Although many of the leaders of the "old-fashioned" group have abandoned the extreme reactionary position, many of the rank-and-file members have not; and the general distinction between modern *santris,* who accept the twentieth century with enthusiasm and see its complexities as but a challenge to be dealt with, and those who are at best resigned to it and its pitfalls for the pious, is still of fundamental importance within the Modjokuto *ummat.*

On the organizational side, Islam in Modjokuto is focused around four major social institutions: the Moslem political parties and their associated social and charitable organizations; the religious school system; that division of the central-government bureaucracy—largely under the Ministry of Religion—which is concerned with the administration of the Moslem law, the preservation of mosques, and other similar duties; and the more informal kind of congregational organization which focuses around the village mosque and the neighborhood prayerhouse. These four *institutional* structures interweave with one another and with the *modèren* and *kolot* ideological patterns to provide a complex framework for almost all the Moslem religious behavior which takes place in Modjokuto.

Chapter 11　　　　　　The Development of
　　　　　　　　　　　Islam in Modjokuto

THE MODJOKUTO AREA was opened up to settlement around the middle of the nineteenth century. It was originally populated, in the main, from four regions of Java: the so-called Mataram area of Central Java, which includes the court kingdoms of Djokjakarta and Surakarta; the Brantas river valley running north of Modjokuto to Surabaja (Kertosono, Modjoagung, Modjokerto, and Krian); the Kediri plain, spreading out fanwise south of that city to Blitar, Tulungagung, and Trenggalek; and the north coast of Java—Gresik, Rembang, Kudus, Demak, and the Java Sea islands of Bawean and Madura. Migration patterns are, as always, a matter of statistics, but most of Modjokuto's earliest *prijajis* (as well as many of its *abangans*) seem to have come originally from Mataram; a large part of its *abangan* population from the next two areas, the Brantas and Kediri plains; and the bulk of the older *santri* population, with one notable exception, originally from the north coast regions.

　　The first wave of migration from the north coast area consisted of peasants, in part uprooted by the social disorganization, economic distress, and governmental repression following upon the Java War of 1825–1830 and upon the imposition of the forced-crop "Cultivation System" (*Cultuurstelsel*) by the colonial government in 1830. A party of twenty or so families from the Kudus and Demak countryside settled in a village in the district to the immediate north of Modjokuto in about 1860, and a decade or so later moved on en masse, one half of them founding a village in the northeast section of the Modjokuto subdistrict, the other half opening another just to the northwest of the town. (These two villages are still renowned in the Modjokuto area for being about 100 per cent *santri*, for providing an unusual number of prominent Moslem political leaders, and for containing the most fertile and best irrigated land for miles around.) Other rural migrants from Kudus and Demak, some relatives and some not, followed and settled both among these pioneers and at various other points within the subdistrict—usually, but not always, somewhat segregated from the *abangan* settlers who were drifting in at the same time.

There was, then, about 1900, among the peasantry living on the land around the town of Modjokuto (which itself was little more than a government outpost plus about a half-dozen Chinese stores and a small privately-run market, a solid core of displaced north coasters who, having come from an area in which the Islamic aspects of the Javanese religious syncretism had from the beginning been taken rather more seriously than elsewhere, were to form the body of both the Islamic reform movement and the conservative reaction to it when these developed in Modjokuto.

But this is only half the story. About 1910 there began to come into the town of Modjokuto itself, also from the north coast, a group of itinerant Javanese traders in cigarettes, cheap cloth, dried fish, leather goods, and small hardware, men not from the countryside but from the urban trade centers such as Kudus, Gresik, and Lamongan. They were representatives of a petty merchandising tradition stretching back to the sixteenth century when Indian and Malay traders, sailing eastward out of Malacca, first propagated Islam in these northern cities. In the beginning, the attachment of these wandering traders to Modjokuto was minimal; their homes were still to the north. On the road they aped the business methods, the style of life, and the religious customs of the Arabs, who provided them the model for their fly-by-night marginal trading and next to whom they lived, closeted ghetto-like in the crowded all-*santri* barrios which surround the mosque in any Javanese city or town and which are everywhere referred to as the *kauman*. "We dressed in rags, ate one meal a day of rice and corn with no trimmings, and walked for miles peddling our stuff," one old *santri* trader reminisced. "We weren't liked much," he added wryly, "but we all got rich."

As time passed and transportation improved, more and more of these peripatetic traders settled permanently in Modjokuto and made only periodic trips to the northern commercial centers where they had been born. They formed tight little in-groups, residentially segregated as to place of origin, so that neighborhoods in Modjokuto still bear names such as Kudus neighborhood, Gresik neighborhood, and Madura neighborhood; Bawean people, the richest group, lived in the Kauman with the Arabs. In large part their trade was likewise specialized according to place of origin: Kudus men sold cigarettes, Gresik men fish, Bawean men cloth, Madurese small hardware. Stimulated by the boom, crushed by the depression, this group of small businessmen and their descendants were the second element which went into the making of an *ummat* in Modjokuto.

The third element, much smaller in numbers but of perhaps even more crucial significance, consisted of a single bilaterally extended family—what Modjokuto people call "the *penghulu* family." *Penghulu* was the title given before the war by the Dutch government to the highest-ranking mosque official—a somewhat marginal officer in the colonial bureaucracy—at the regency, district, or subdistrict level, who was responsible for the administration of marriage and divorce regulations and for giving advice to those who requested it on other aspects of the Moslem law, such as inheritance.* As in the case of

* Since the war this strictly religious part of the bureaucracy has been expanded, and the man fulfilling the *penghulu*'s functions at the subdistrict level is now called the *naib*.

village headships, high regional administrative posts, and the like, the job of *penghulu* tended after a time to become semihereditary in an informal sort of way and, in addition, the *penghulu* families within a single regency tended to intermarry. In Modjokuto the job of *penghulu* and nearly all the mosque posts under his jurisdiction, of which there were usually five or six, were in the hands of a single family from the time such offices were first established in the town; and this family was related by marriage to the *penghulu* families of practically every other town in the regency, the informal head of this vague kin-group being the chief *penghulu* in the regency capital.

Although this family too can trace its ultimate origins back to Demak, its proximate origins so far as Modjokuto is concerned lie in Modjoagung, a town in the Brantas valley, from whence around the turn of the century one Muhammad Cholifah was moved into Modjokuto by the Dutch and installed as its *penghulu*. He and his descendants monopolized all the government religious posts thereafter, until the postwar period, when political party considerations led to their displacement. Rich (they owned the entire eastern half of the *kauman;* Hadji Hanawi, the richest of the traveling traders, a Bawean native, owned the western half), rather well educated (the last Modjokuto *penghulu* in this line was the only non-*prijaji* Javanese ever to be allowed to attend the elementary school for Dutch children that existed in Modjokuto during the colonial period), and politically powerful throughout the whole region, this family was the top of the social heap within the Modjokuto *ummat* in the years before the war, and as such it provided one of the main arenas within which the modernist-conservative battle was fought out.

These three groups—the *santri* peasants living in the villages, the petty traders settling into the town, and the *penghulu* family, a kind of *santri* aristocracy if that is not a contradiction in terms—were the fixed points around which the Modjokuto *ummat* crystallized. It was, in large part, a bourgeois *ummat* because the peasant *santris* tended to be richer than their *abangan* opposite numbers; because the *penghulu* family, although exalted, could never quite manage, being *santris* after all, full *prijaji* status; and because, of course, the traders represented the best effort of the Javanese to wrest at least a portion of the interurban distributive trade from the hands of the Chinese, an effort still largely unsuccessful. In one sense, it has been the slow growing together of this incipient yeomanry on the one hand and this embyronic middle class on the other, in great part under the leadership of the *penghulu* group, which has provided the content of the reform and counter-reform movements in Modjokuto Islam. It has been the social differences between these groups which have caused the conflicts, and it has been their religious commonalities which have resolved them, insofar as they have been resolved at all.

The Rise of Modernism: 1910–1940

ON the rural side, the crucial institutions of Islam were the pilgrimage and the school. A man worked hard, saved his money and, if a dishonest ticket broker didn't swindle him out of it, went to Mecca. In Mecca he studied with a teacher if he was serious, and took in the sights if he was not; but in either case, when he returned he was considered a scholar and a world traveler, and as often as not he set up a Koran school, called a *pondok* (sometimes also called *pesantrèn* from the original meaning of *santri*—"religious student"), in which the students, young men from six to twenty-five years of age, spent part of every day chanting the Koran and part of it working in the *hadji*'s* fields to support themselves. In the early part of this century there were at one time nearly a dozen such *pondoks* of respectable size around Modjokuto, to several of which were attached cloth-dyeing factories or industries producing cigarettes by hand in which the students also worked. The economic advantages of a religious ethic emphasizing thrift, hard work, and individual effort, plus a form of education which tended to make for a more rational organization of labor than did the traditional exchange-work customs of the *abangans,* have made the term *hadji* synonymous with "rich man" in the Modjokuto area.

In any case, there grew up around Modjokuto a number of these religious schools, still largely concerned with a simple chanting of the Koran, to the meaning of which they had no access, each school separate and independent, a kind of small religion of its own under its own teacher and as often as not antagonistic to all other schools in the area. But by 1915 the influence of developments on the national scene began to be felt in the town of Modjokuto, where a group of traders, schoolteachers, and, at first, government officials, all led by a generally unconventional and fiery *kijaji*** whose *pondok* lay just outside of town, opened a local chapter of Sarekat Islam, the mass Islamic party which had been founded in Central Java just three years before.

This *kijaji,* who was also a *hadji*—and so was called Kijaji Hadji Nazir—was destined to play the leading role at each stage in the developments that followed, to be the leading proponent of and apologist for Islamic modernism, and to be identified with it as no other person in Modjokuto. He was respected and idolized by those who agreed with him, hated and despised by those who did not. It is interesting, then, to note that the description of his character I received from all who knew him, whether they liked him or not, was as atypical in terms of Javanese values as it is possible to be.

I asked him (a vaguely modernist *santri* youth, now studying under Nazir's son) whether he remembered Kijaji Nazir, and he said yes, he certainly did, and that Nazir was a very hard (*keras*) character—sort of like Hadji Zakir (one of Nazir's chief followers, an old trader still living in Modjokuto), only of course with much more brains. Nazir had the courage to argue with anyone, anywhere, even with people more clever than he, bigger and more famous *kijajis* known all over Java. He didn't care; he just plowed right into them. If Nazir was angry he would just show it, even on a train with people around or in public. (All this was said with depreciation by Umar, the informant, my impression being that the general opinion was that Nazir was not very "polite"

* *Hadji* is the title given to a returned pilgrim. Thus a man named Abdul will be called Hadji Abdul after he comes back from Mecca. Actually, he will often change his name entirely and be called, say, Hadji Hasjim.
** A teacher in a *pondok* and any Islamic scholar in general is called a *kijaji*. The *kijajis* in Indonesia are roughly comparable to the Mid-Eastern *'ulama*.

or "genteel"; he not only told his betters off, but he did it directly and showed his feelings in public—all basic sins for the Javanese.) He fought with other local leaders almost all the time and was very outspoken—particularly with the *kijaji* in Tebuireng (the leader of the conservative movement for all of Java, and probably the most famous and respected *kijaji* on the island), and in general people didn't like him. He also worked terribly hard and was very punctual. If one was late to a class he would get very angry. If it was raining and he had a scheduled appointment or class, he would come plowing through the rain just as usual, no matter how far; and if one stayed home because of the rain his wrath knew no bounds. (For just about every other Javanese, not only is punctuality not a virtue but the idea of keeping an appointment when it is raining would appear absurd; the only man who ever kept an appointment with me when it was raining during the whole time I was in Java was Hadji Zakir, Nazir's follower.) He always had to speak his mind directly; and it is said that the heart attack that killed him was caused by the fact that in the Japanese time he was not able to speak out and he bottled it all up inside him and it ruptured his heart.

Nazir, born in Modjokuto in 1886, was a direct descendant of the first wave of Kudus immigrants and the son of an old-time *kajaji* who ran a *pondok* near the town with over a hundred students. His outline autobiography, written for some official purpose during the Japanese occupation, states that he began to chant the Koran regularly at home when he was seven and that by the time he was eleven he was living, studying, and working in a *pondok* some fifty miles away.* At the age of thirteen he was in Mecca—his first of two pilgrimages—with his older brother, where, according to the autobiography, he studied with six different *kijajis* from as many different regions of Java (Djepara, Banjumas, Djombang, Kediri, Kudus, and Patjitan) and, "pressured by an indomitable will," he also got training in the Latin alphabet, mathematics, and "general studies," all of which were no part of the traditional Moslem education of that time.

After four years in Mecca he was back in Java, where he traveled to study at *pondoks* in Madura, Kediri, Sidohardjo, and Surakarta, until eleven years later he entered the "people's movement" Sarekat Islam (SI). His history after this consists of the story of one organization after another, one governing board after another, one national conference after another.

In 1921 he was in the thick of the SI-Red vs. SI-White struggle within the party, then grown to two million on the national scene (and a claimed three thousand in Modjokuto), in which the Communists only narrowly failed in their effort to take over the party and managed to cripple it in the attempt. In 1924 he set up an organization to protect *hadjis* against swindle by dishonest ticket brokers and the like, for which purpose he went to Mecca a second time in 1926 just after the Wahhabi Ibn Saud ejected Sharif Husein. In 1933 he left the party because of a personal difference with the leadership and joined another, but in a few years he was back again. And so it went until,

* As *abangans* with *dukuns*, so *santris* with *pondoks* seem to prefer distant ones to nearer ones, the reason given in this latter case being that it strengthens the self-reliance of the boy to be away from home, and that it is less distracting and easier to concentrate when one studies at a distance from one's relatives.

during the first two years of the Japanese occupation, he seemed to "rest" for the first time in his life—although he admits that he went every Friday to the Modjokuto mosque "to give advice to those who pray there and to encourage them to work ever harder for their ideals." But, as the Japanese policy of favoring the *santri* group against the rest of the population became more evident, he accepted a job in the puppet government, at which point the autobiography ends.

After a year or so he died—perhaps, as my informant suggested, because he was not allowed to express his mind freely. In his intense organizational activity, in his interest in "general studies," in his social consciousness and his concern at the same time for fundamental religious learning, in his eventual deception and manipulation by the Japanese, and in his death in 1944 just as the new free Indonesia was about to come into being, Nazir and his career typify in almost every detail the course and character of the modernist reformation, such as it was, in Javanese Islam.

Along with Nazir in the original Sarekat Islam were Modjokuto's richest *prijaji* landholder (he was also a government meat inspector), a few railroad workers, about a half-dozen tradesmen from the town, one or two other unimportant *kijajis,* and a few government schoolteachers. At this time SI, as the only really mass political party in Java, drew members from among the socially conscious and nationalistically inclined in all groups. Communist labor agitators, aristocratic political idealists, and middle-class realists out to forge political weapons with which to curb Chinese competition rubbed elbows in the same movement.

This harmony ended in the 1921 struggle in which the Communist element, having prepared the ground by capturing several labor unions and by attacking SI's leader, H. O. S. Tjokroaminoto, as dishonest, attempted to turn SI into a thoroughgoing Marxist organization. In practically every chapter of the party there occurred a split between the "White," or anti-Communist, faction and the "Red," a pro-Communist, faction. In Modjokuto, too, this occurred, where Nazir led the White group and a railroad employee named Karman (now a Communist Party chief in the next town north of Modjokuto) led the Reds. After a tremendous struggle, leading at times to fistfights on the floor of the convention, H. Agus Salim, later to be the first foreign minister of the Republic of Indonesia and at that time one of Indonesia's leading modernist, succeeded in pushing through a resolution expelling the Communist group from the central organization of the party. But the damage was done. The government employees and teachers, ever timid in the face of anything involving genuine militancy, fled the movement; and many of the no-nonsense traders, convinced that the party was wasting their valuable time by involving them in a network of purposeless intrigue, quit in disgust. Karman, the Communist leader, attempted to wrest control of the branch from Nazir, offering one of the latter's lieutenants a sizable bribe to desert him, but he failed. When it was all over, SI in Modjokuto was down to a hard core of thirty members.

But the core was hard now, at any rate. It was pure *santri,* and it had added the vigorous anti-Communism which continues to animate much of Islamic politics today. The faithful few managed to raise among themselves

1,000 rupiahs (which would be about 10,000 today) with which to buy a plot of land in the Modjokuto *kauman* just to the rear of the mosque, on which they erected the first modern-style religious school, a *madrasah*, in the Modjokuto area. A *madrasah*, in contrast to a *pondok*, is a school in which part of the time is spent in religious studies and part in general studies. It represents an attempt to modernize the traditional Moslem educational system, to combine the best of two worlds—that of the government schools, which were organized and which taught along Western lines, and that of the Koran-chanting *pondoks*. This compromise, seemingly so moderate, aroused a storm of protest from the old-fashioned religious scholars in the area, who forbade their followers to have anything to do with this infidel institution. Aside from children of SI members, only children of a few of the more flexible urban *santris* and all of the Arab children attended; and the school soon got the name it still bears in the minds of most townspeople—"the Arab school."

Nazir's popularity with the conservative faction was not enhanced when shortly after he founded his school he began the first Moslem boy scout movement in the area, instituted evening courses in Islam in the Modjokuto mosque for women, and began to demand that the Friday sermon in the mosque (*chotbah*), then but an extended Arabic chant on the part of the prayer leader, be translated into Javanese. But the action that sealed his damnation in *kolot* eyes was his institution of circulating religious propaganda meetings in the villages around Modjokuto, in which he and his followers preached an internal mission to the peasant *ummat* and took as their guide one of the most controversial authors in the history of modern Islam, the Egyptian reformer Muhammed Abduh.

Abduh, who died in 1905, taught at Al-Azhar, the great orthodox Moslem university in Cairo, and although, as Gibb has said, "in relation to the traditional orthodox structure he was no innovator,"* he attempted to renovate the structure somewhat by insisting that corrupting influences and practices, such as saint-worship and the cult of holy men, be purified from Islam; that Moslem education be reformed to allow the teaching of modern sciences, geography, and the history and religion of Europe; and that greater attention be given to the holy books of Islam, the Koran and the Hadith, and less to the secondary elaborations erected on top of them. A true puritan, he preached modernization and increased adherence to fundamentals at one and the same time, demanding an Islam that was at once more like that Muhammad preached and practiced and more adequate to the conditions of modern life. Neither the strictness of his doctrine nor the seeming radicalism of it was attractive to those committed to a less aggressive Islam.

> He (a *santri* taxi driver) went, after he got out of the SI *madrasah* in the *kauman*, to Nazir's *pondok* (which the latter had taken over from his father), which he said had seventy people there (mostly from West Java, he being one of the very few from around here) chanting both morning and late afternoon. It had both "general studies" and religion. He said Abduh was used but that he thought him too strict, too much Hell involved. The least little thing and one

* H. A. R. Gibb, *op. cit.,* p. 176.

went to Hell. He said that Abduh was very controversial and most people thought him too strict. He said that the old books one usually read in *pondoks* were not so hard. One sin did not send one to Hell, and they were more patient with people whose Islam was not yet complete and pure. For example, Abduh had just a small number of dedicated and very "pure" followers, very strong religious believers, and would have nothing to do with people whose Islam was not perfect but excluded them from the fold, while the earlier classical authors took people step by step and were quite willing to have "impure" and "imperfect" followers. He said there was much violent opposition to Nazir in those days. All the *kijajis* in the area were after him, and it got pretty hot and heavy for a while.

But the political aspects of Nazir's party interfered with the religious, particularly after the Dutch, frightened by Communist outbreaks in West Java and Sumatra in 1926, began to put pressure on all non-cooperating political parties and officially forbade government officials to belong to them. (In Modjokuto, Karman, the SI-Red leader, and some of his followers were arrested and exiled to New Guinea.) In such a context even attendance at one of Nazir's meetings seemed to most people to be perilously close to sedition, and as a result he was isolated.

In 1931 a branch of Muhammadijah, the Islamic social-welfare organization also centered in Djokjakarta, was founded in Modjokuto. Dedicated not only to the preaching of Abduh's doctrines but also to the practicing of them, this society was, however, concerned entirely with religious problems to the exclusion of political ones, and it pledged cooperation with the colonial government. The combination of political conservatism with religious radicalism appealed to the more educated among the government-employed *penghulu* family and to the Arabs, for whom Indonesian nationalism had no appeal in any case; and so it was a coalition of members of these two groups, plus a local school inspector and a recently arrived *santri* merchant, which began Muhammadijah in Modjokuto. Although Nazir, restrained by his loyalty to Sarekat Islam and political non-cooperation, never joined Muhammadijah, he supported it informally, and many of his relatives and followers were prime movers in it from the beginning.

Muhammadijah built another modern-type school with only one third rather than one half of the time devoted to religious studies, and these taught in Javanese rather than Arabic. They began their own Boy Scouts, erected an orphanage, started a soccer team, set up a woman's auxiliary as well as one for young girls, and introduced evening prayer meetings at which sermons on social and religious matters were given, sometimes by lecturers imported from their large city chapters in Djokjakarta, Solo, and Surabaja. They distributed books carrying the modernist message; initiated such reforms as holding mass prayer meetings in the public square rather than in the mosque on *Rijaja* (the end-of-Fast holiday) and on the Prophet's birthday; and they not only translated the Friday sermon but the Koran as well.

Even more annoying to the rigidly orthodox, they argued for a more flexible use of all four lawbooks in deciding cases rather than a reliance on the Shafi'ite alone. They criticized the giving of *slametans* as wasteful extravagance better applied to good works; attacked *abangan* ritual around death, arguing that Islam allowed only three practices at a funeral: washing, wrapping, and burying the corpse; and declared certain traditional *santri* practices, such as chanting a spell before doing one's prayers to "calm" the heart, to be heterodox. They announced that those still engaged in what they in their unholy ignorance called Islamic mystical practices were certain to end in Hell, and argued that the *pondok* system of education with its reliance on secondary interpretations and its blind chanting of non-understood verses was a medieval anachronism. In sum, they said, "We must go back to the Koran and the Hadith; these are the 'Light of the Prophecy.'"

He (an Indonesian-born Arab, the first secretary and one of the prime movers in Muhammadijah in its earliest days) said there were five people who began Muhammadijah here in town: Mudjito, the school inspector; Rachmat Mussalam, another Arab, now no longer in Modjokuto; Hadji Ustaz, the store-owner; Achmad Muchlas from the *penghulu* family, later to be *penghulu* himself; and Hadji Kasim, another trader. When they first started, the opposition to the organization was intense, particularly from the *kijajis*. The *kolot* Moslems thought Muhammadijah was a new religion which was not really Islam but a false doctrine. He said that after he and the other Muhammadijah people went around speaking in the various villages trying to convince the people, the tension lessened, but it still exists. He said the main content in the sermons was the social application of Islam: the teachings of the Koran and the Hadith relative to village cooperation, morality in village life, and the like, in contrast to the *kolot* chanting and the reservation of reading of the Koran only for very old men who couldn't understand it anyway. What they were trying to do was to bring the Koran down to earth.

Thus the battle shifted onto entirely religious ground; but, as the transcript from my notes shows, the evasion of political problems, did nothing to soften the reaction of the conservatives. In fact, by concentrating its fire upon just those aspects of *santri* practice which seemed most crucially to define orthodoxy to the *kijajis* and their followers (Muhammadijah paid little attention to *abangans* directly; their reform was directed internally to the *ummat* itself), the reliance of the Shafi'ite law and the old-fashioned Koranic school, Muhammadijah exacerbated the conflict tremendously. Tension rose to the point where conservative Moslems would not go to the same mosque with the Muhammadijah members, where even opening a book by Abduh was held to be a mortal sin which would lead to blindness, and where an informant of mine who had founded the only village branch of Muhammadijah in the Modjokuto area (it soon failed; the organization was and is an almost wholly urban phenomenon in Modjokuto) found that none of his old-line friends would speak a word to him for over two years and would cross to the other side of the road when they saw him coming. The conservatives also organized, forming a local chapter of Nahdatul Ulama (abbreviated NU), the Indonesia-wide organization of conservative religious scholars and their followers which had its central headquarters about thirty miles from Modjokuto in what was, under the late Kijaji Hasjim Ashary, perhaps the most famous (as well as one of the largest, having several thousand students at one time) *pondok* in all Java.

NU actually got started in Modjokuto in 1926, a few years before Muhammadijah appeared. Stimulated both by the nearness of the central headquarters and by Nazir's vigorous modernist missionizing, the organization, dedicated to "awakening" rural religious teachers to the threat posed to their way of life by Islamic reformism, drew its original leaders from the leading *kijajis* in the area plus a few town tradesmen who left Nazir's SI because of its modernist turn. Its combination of political adaptablity with religious conservatism, thus avoiding both horns of Nazir's dilemma, had an immediate appeal; and the organization grew to about 15,000 people (a rough estimate by its prewar leader) by 1940, while Muhammadijah remained very small, never having a membership much over forty people. Despite the discrepancy in numbers, however, the two organizations were about an even match, Muhammadijah making up for what it lacked in size by a much tighter organization and a far more aggressive spirit. The intensity of the argument grew, splitting both the urban and rural communities (although the latter was predominantly conservative) and leading finally to a serious split within the *penghulu* family itself and a succession crisis in the government religious bureaucracy.

The second *naib* (i.e., *penghulu*) of Modjokuto, the one who held office the longest and who is regarded as the family's most important recent ancestor, was a polygynist with three wives. By the second he had only one child, but by the first and third he had five apiece. As the first wife was about a generation older than the third, the children of the first were, in general, also a generation or a half-generation older than the children of the third. When this man died in 1919, he was succeeded in office, according to the unwritten rule, by his eldest living son (i.e., a child of his first wife). Since this son, whose name was Kasman, was, like all the other male members in the senior wing of the family, a convinced conservative, he used his office to advance the conservative cause, in which effort he was strenuously opposed by the younger wing of the family, the children of the third wife, all of them modernists and members of Muhammadijah. Kasman not only favored the conservative party in every way in which he was able but he also slowly managed to remove the Muhammadijah members of the family— evidently through intra-family maneuvering, the details of which it is impossible to reconstruct—from the religious office staff. Thus developed a war of generations within the *penghulu* family, an ideological split between half-brothers, that at times grew extremely heated.

Bisri (a son of one of the old *naib*'s sons by the younger wife) said that when his father (now dead) was a young man he was very active in organizations. His spirit was very strong. He was a pioneer of Muhammadijah, and every day he had fights with Kasman about this. At that time Kasman, his half-brother, was *naib* in Modjokuto and senior member of the family, and was opposed by the younger half-brothers and -sisters, including Bisri's father. Once Bisri's father arranged for a *chotbah* (sermon) in the mosque to be translated into Javanese after it had been presented in Arabic, although he knew Kasman was very much opposed to this. When Kasman found out about it, he and Bisri's father had a great fight about it, and Bisri's father left home and went to a *pondok* to live.

Upon the death of Kasman this struggle came to a head when the modernist wing of the family succeeded in convincing the chief *penghulu* in the regency—to whom, as I have said, the Modjokuto family was related by marriage—to appoint (i.e., recommend to the regent for appointment) as *naib,* not the son of Kasman as would be the normal practice, but instead one of his younger half-brothers, the intellectual leader of the modernist wing and a Muhammadijah founder, using as a transparent excuse the fact that Kasman's son was somewhat ailing. The outcry at this was tremendous; and it not only brought the split within the *penghulu* family out into the open (the new *naib's* own mother, an unbeliever in newfangled ways, did not approve of his taking the job) but also divided almost the whole *ummat,* particularly within the town, into two camps. Letters were written to the Indonesian press, petitions were carried to the regency capital, accusations were hurled in both directions, and threats of various kinds were made—but the new *naib* remained in office. With his installation the high-water mark of the *moderen-kolot* conflict was reached, the permanency of Muhammadijah on the local scene was assured, and, since some of the more unbending reactionaries were beginning to age and die, a process of reconciliation began.

The process of reconciliation consisted, on the conservative side, of their slow acceptance of modernist innovations in organization (of which the very founding of Nahdatul Ulama in 1925 had been the first example) and, on the modernist side, of the abandonment of any intensive attempt to force reform interpretations of religious detail upon the *ummat.* NU began to build schools with at least half of the curriculum secular (or to give a few non-religious classes within the *pondoks*); to hold prayer meetings of their own; to set up women's auxiliaries, start boy scouts, and the like.

In this sense the modernists won. But in another, perhaps more fundamental sense, they did not, for they lost or gave up their zeal for Islamic reform just at the point—so it seems to an outsider—when it was beginning to come to some interesting conclusions. Abduh was pushed aside as too radical for everyday use, serious attempts to rethink Islamic problems were abandoned as unlikely to lead to solutions which could gain acceptance in any case, and discussion of details of religious belief and practice was avoided as leading only to useless arguments. "Never discuss different interpretations of Islam," the leader of the modernist political party in Modjokuto told a group of Islamic youth at a meeting I attended in 1954. "It only leads to broken friendships."

The reasons for this compromise were many. The depression hurt the budding middle class of *santri* businessmen, who were modernism's main support and source of élan, perhaps as much as any other group, wiping out many, driving others to the larger cities, and taking much of the heart and all of the optimism out of the rest. In the countryside, the *kijajis* and their peasant followers began to come more into contact with the modern world as new means of communication and transportation multiplied, while at the same time some of their younger sons moved into town to be traders and some of their daughters married into the urban *santri* group, bringing the two groups closer together. (There has been, however, only one marriage between an NU and a Muhammadijah person in the town of Modjokuto; and that occurred during the revolution, people saying that anything could happen then but that it probably wouldn't be permitted now by the families involved.) Also, as the situation stabilized, the greater intensity of the Muhammadijah being matched by the greater numbers of NU, a kind of natural social balance was reached in which compromise more or less occurred of itself.

Other reasons for the rapprochement might include the fact that an atmosphere of intense controversy is foreign and acutely uncomfortable to the Javanese, who tend to prefer adjustment to argument and indirection to open conflict, and the fact that Islamic scholars in the Moslem universities of the Middle East failed to take the next intellectual and doctrinal steps beyond Abduh's pioneering effort, leaving Indonesian modernists with a late-nineteenth-century reform doctrine that seemed irrelevant in a world full of labor unions, large plantations, and falling commodity prices. But perhaps the greatest impetus for the new compromise was the re-entrance of politics onto the scene. As the possibilities for a successful nationalist movement became more apparent, the quest for national self-determination began to occupy the minds and engulf the hearts of the Indonesian elite, leaving precious little time for reflection upon the ultimate contexts of human behavior.

The Japanese Period: 1942–1945

THE Japanese, who for reasons of their own undertook to simplify Indonesian domestic politics, aided the cause of *moḍèren-kolot* reconciliation by forcing all politicized *santris* into a single organization, ultimately called Masjumi (Council of Indonesian Moslem Organizations), and by carrying out a policy of systematic favoritism toward the *santri* element of the population in an attempt to woo them to Greater East Asia Co-Prosperity Sphere ideology. Several of Modjokuto's Moslem leaders, both from Muhammadijah and from Nahdatul Ulama, were taken to Djakarta to be instructed in the Japanese view of world politics and domestic order and returned to Modjokuto to spread the new theories among their neighbors.

Bisri said that during the Japanese period both Jahja (at present chairman of Muhammadijah in Modjokuto) and Achmad Muchlas (the *naib* who triumphed over the conservatives in the case mentioned earlier) were among those who were sent to Djakarta to study as part of the Japanese attempt to win over *santris*. Evidently the attempt wasn't entirely without success, according to Bisri, because later both Jahja and Muchlas voluntarily joined in Bragang the *Barisan Djibaku* ("Human Bomb Corps") which was organized to provide a kamikaze defense against the Americans if they should invade Java. Bisri said he doubted that these men would actually have become kamikazes had the time for it arrived, but they were quite anti-American in those days and pro-Japanese, which he attributed to the lack of political experience on the Moslems' part. He said the Japanese went out of their way never to pressure Islam, and Moslems felt no opposition between their beliefs and those of the Japanese. He said that the men invited to Djakarta in addition to the two Muhammadijah men were mostly *kijajis*. The children, such as he, were also filled with Japanese propaganda, which took very well, even with him, but they really didn't know any better. He said school children voluntarily shaved their heads to be more like the Japanese and wore Japanese-type hats on their own initiative. He said that every morning they had to bow to Japan in school. Asked whether this didn't conflict with Islam, he said no, it was regarded as not being a religious act; there were long discussions at the time whereby it was distinguished from Islamic praying by the slight differences in position and the like. He said the Japanese were careful never to attack Islam.

Moslem leaders of both factions held many of the most important posts in the Japanese-sponsored organizations in Modjokuto. In both Modjokuto and several nearby villages they headed the relief organization for the assistance of people whose sons had been carried off to forced labor in Siam or elsewhere;* and they were appointed to special bureaucratic posts duplicating existing jobs, the duties of which seem to have been concerned mainly with spying on the *prijajis* who held the actual posts. They also toured the villages, spreading Japanese propaganda much as, a few years before, they had spread Islamic propaganda, but now their message displayed a greater uniformity.

Despite these efforts, the deception, especially after the Japanese had been around a year or two and the Javanese could see what "co-prosperity" amounted to, was probably not more than skin deep with most of the *santri* mass, who saw their leaders' peregrinations in a humorous light and, having a peasant's sense for the realities of human motivation, attributed to these leaders purposes rather more materialistic than ideological:

> They (three young *santris*) said Hadji Zakir (Nazir's lieutenant; Nazir himself, along with another of his chief aides, was at the time serving on the puppet "Regional Governing Council" at Regency Headquarters) was one of those sent to Djakarta as a *kijaji* and a "religious expert" to get a course in propaganda and then to be sent here to go around to the villages. (This man, an illiterate, was in no sense a *kijaji*, but he was a vigorous *santri* and middle-rank Moslem political leader in Modjokuto.) They said the Japanese even gave him a special uniform, and that in general the Japanese "raised up" the *santris* as against the rest of the population and favored them, trying to use them, evidently with good success, as agents of their policy. They were taken to Djakarta to be instructed or sent to Bragang (as volunteers) to be kamikazes, where they studied how to be "unafraid to die" for a month and were

---

* The suffering being what it was, the shortages being what they were, and the Japanese having complete control over all categories of consumption goods, many of which were released through this organization, this position was a rather powerful one, and several times I heard the occupants of these posts referred to as the "little dictators" of the Japanese time.

given clothes and extra food. Talkah (one of my informants) thought it just rather funny; and this evidently is what most people thought at the time, perhaps even those who went and participated, because no one thought these people were "unafraid to die," and they didn't prove that they were, later in the revolution. It was a quick way to get permits—e.g., to buy and sell stuff or to travel, which were the real currency during the Japanese occupation and were the crucial things to have if one wanted to get ahead economically; and the Japanese paid off in permits. When I asked about Haslim (a prewar NU leader, still active), they said that he didn't go to Djakarta but did circulate in the villages for the Japanese. They said that the Japanese time was a very hard time; people ate leaves and had almost no clothes—but it was very funny, too. In response to my question, they agreed that the Japanese policy of favoring the Moslems as against other people was evident at the time. There was much discussion then of how Islam fitted in with Japanese orders.

It was the other aspect of Japanese policy, the fusion of the various opposing *santri* social and political groups into one "party," Masjumi, which had the greatest long-run effect on the *ummat*. Masjumi was led on the national level by Wachid Hasjim, son of the *kijaji* who founded Nahdatul Ulama and his father's successor as the organization's head, and by Hadji Mansoer, the prewar Muhammadijah leader.

For the first time, all the old Sarekat Islam stalwarts (it was by now called PSII—Partai Sarekat Islam Indonesia), the NU conservatives, and the Muhammadijah modernists were in a single party. True, the "party" was so controlled by the Japanese authorities as to have little independence of action, but, as in so many areas of national life, the Indonesians were able to learn the techniques involved and forget the content rather quickly. As in newspaper publishing, where they learned the methods of effective layout and production while writing the most primitive kind of propaganda, and in administration, where, in genuinely responsible bureaucratic posts for almost the first time, they learned much about the day-to-day governing of men even though they were operating under a policy more repressive and less concerned with Indonesian welfare than any the Dutch had ever devised, so in political organization they took the form and left the content, learned the techniques of machine politics and forgot their fascist lessons as soon as the Japanese were out of sight. After the heightened solidarity of the revolutionary period passed, a period in which Masjumi played a major role, this new-found unity was in part lost; but the effect of the enforced cooperation had left the various groups both less antagonistic one to the other and more skilled at (as well as infatuated with) political agitation, organization, and intrigue.

The Republican Period: 1945 to the Present

IN Modjokuto the unitary Masjumi was led by representatives of each of the groups—Sarekat Islam, Muhammadijah, and Nahdatul Ulama—with Muhammadijah, having the greatest number of intellectuals, rather dominant. When the Republic of Indonesia was proclaimed on the 17th of August, 1945, two military organizations were incorporated into the party structure. The first, Hizbullah, a guerilla batallion of young men, grew out of a similarly named organization formed by the Japanese to give training in military drill to young Moslems. In Modjokuto (like Masjumi itself, Hizbullah was Indonesia-wide but, also like Masjumi, it had little effective central organization) this group was led by the present head of Muhammadijah—the same man who a year or so before was going to Djakarta for propaganda training and studying to be a kamikaze. The second military group was the Sabilillah, a kind of home guard made up of older men and led, now that Nazir was dead, by Hadji Zakir, the old SI man, which in fact never got around to doing much of anything.

Modjokuto was in Republican territory until the second Dutch "aggression," when it fell to colonial troops, many of the town's finest buildings being destroyed by the scorched-earth tactics of the retreating Indonesians. Most Masjumi leaders retired to secret military headquarters in one or the other of the two villages where the first Kudus migration had ended, the most heavily *santri* villages in the area. Evidently these rather obvious locations were not apparent to the Dutch (although eventually four of the top leaders were captured by the Dutch near Bragang and imprisoned), for these leaders were able for several months to direct sporadic attacks against the Dutch quartered in the town—attacks which evidently were, except as harassments, rather ineffective but in which several young Moslems were killed.

At length, world public opinion, the diplomatic skill of their leaders, and their own remarkable courage brought Indonesians freedom; and Masjumi was transformed from a semi-military revolutionary association to a genuine all-Indonesia political party within a parliamentary context.

In the new atmosphere of freedom, the unity imposed by the Japanese and necessitated by the revolution soon evaporated. Sarekat Islam, now PSII, dissatisfied, among other things, with Muhammadijah dominance within the party, was the first to leave Masjumi. (In Modjokuto, Muhammadijah domination had grown quite noticeable. The Chairman, Vice Chairman, Secretary, and four of seven members of the Governing Council were Muhammadijah people.) A short while later Nahdatul Ulama left for similar reasons and as a result of a conflict with Muhammadijah over who was going to hold the Ministry of Religion. (These decisions to leave Masjumi were, of course, taken by the central governing boards of the parties in Djakarta.) Thus for the first time NU became a genuine political party rather than merely a social organization.

In Modjokuto, but not necessarily elsewhere in Java, where different histories have resulted in different patterns, all this splitting off left the leadership of Masjumi largely in Muhammadijah hands, although almost all of the rank-and-file members around the countryside are not members of Muhammadijah. Although the departure of NU and to a much lesser extent that of PSII (which is a very small though rather activist party, having in Modjokuto only about forty members) weakened Masjumi considerably, it is still the largest Moslem party in Indonesia and thus the second-generation descendants of the original modernists now find themselves at the head of a mass organization, a feat their "fathers" were never able to accomplish in the years before the war. In part this is a result of their moderation in matters of purely religious concern; the rural *santris* are not nearly so suspicious of their orthodoxy as they once were. In part it is an unintended consequence of the formation of the unitary Masjumi in the days of the Japanese and its front-rank role in the revolution. Many people who had never before participated in any Moslem organization were drawn into Masjumi during this period; and these recruits remained loyal to the new party when those who had been NU or SI members before the war withdrew.

In short, the complex history just traced produced in the Modjokuto of 1953–1954 an *ummat* with one minor and two major political parties, plus a modernist-inspired social and charitable organization more or less attached, informally but rather firmly, to one of the parties. There is Partai Sarekat Islam Indonesia (PSII), now rather unimportant, made up of a few surviving warhorses of the original Sarekat Islam, a few of their sons and nephews, and a few new recruits. There is Nahdatul Ulama, now both a social organization and a political party joined into one rather poorly organized whole. There is Masjumi, a mass political party, only slightly better organized, led by the same people who lead Muhammadijah. And there is Muhammadijah itself, still running its schools (it now has half a dozen), its orphanages, and its boy scouts, and still, despite NU criticism, holding prayers in the town square on the Prophet's birthday. It also still has its small but extremely energetic and well-organized membership of about forty people willing to make genuine sacrifices for the organization. But most of its zeal for modernist reform of Islamic religious doctrine has largely evaporated.

When I asked him (the son of Hadji Nazir, the SI founder, who now runs his father's *pondok* and is the only important Masjumi leader in Modjokuto who is not also a member of Muhammadijah) where the influence for his father's political activity had come from, he said from Tjokroaminoto and Agus Salim, whom Nazir evidently knew quite well, from books, and evidently to a degree from Arabs. . . . When I started talking about Abduh, he said that his big influence was in Muhammadijah, which drew the greatest fire from the *kolot,* who called the Muhammadijah people Wahhabis (a fundamentalist Islamic movement in the Middle East, beginning in the nineteenth century and extending, to a degree, into the twentieth), a very scornful term here. Muhammadijah was much more ideologically modern before the war than it is now, he said. When I said that it seemed to me no one cared much about Abduh and his friends any more, he said, "No, not even the Muhammadijah people talk about him any more; everyone is just interested in politics. It seems as though all the old religious problems that exercised everyone before the war are not thought of any more." He said that, although before the war NU people would not pray in the same mosque with Muhammadijah people, the conflict has mostly receded into the background, and in religious matters each person now does as he wishes. Muhammadijah has mostly forgotten the ideological problems; and at any rate, even if individual Muhammadijah people still hold these modernist positions, they aren't interested in proselytizing others any more. There are still traces of differences, but they are much lessened. NU people tell people that Masjumi is Muhammadijah-dominated, he said. "Isn't it?" I asked. He said, "Well, somewhat, maybe;" but pointed to himself. The NU people, he agreed, have pretty much accepted the organizational reforms of the Muhammadijah people such as schools and orphanages and don't care about religious ideologies any more either. "Everyone is interested in politics," he said again; and when I asked why, he said, "They figure if they win in politics they will have no trouble with religion later on."

Chapter 12

Conservative versus Modern: The Ideological Background

ALTHOUGH THE PROGRESS of the reform movement has been halted, at least temporarily, the results of the first phase can be plainly seen in Modjokuto. The conservatives have adopted some of the outward trappings of the modernists; the modernists have become less intense about conservative practices they consider unworthy of Islam. But the doctrinal differences between the two groups persist, and a certain degree of antagonism continues to be manifested concerning them. With the re-emergence of the separate parties since the revolution, the *ummat* has been stabilized, roughly in the form it had reached by the time the Japanese came, embracing a modernism most of the original goals of which have either been accomplished or laid aside as impossible of achievement and a conservatism which is to a great extent old wine in new bottles. Each is somewhat hostile to the other, and they more or less divide up the Islamic community between them. Three transcripts from my notes will convey a sense of the situation in doctrinal terms:

(1) He (the secretary of Muhammadijah) said that Muhammadijah is the organization in Indonesia which has the most buildings, does the most work, and so on. He said they have polyclinics in many big towns and lots of orphanages, schools, and the like as here in Modjokuto. He said there are only forty members in Modjokuto but that they are very close to each other, work well together, and thus have much better results than other groups. He said most people do not want to enter Muhammadijah because they know they would have to contribute time, money, and work. The main difference between NU and Muhammadijah is that the latter is *modèren* and the former *kolot;* Muhammadijah wants to unite East and West, NU wants just the East. NU has many, many members, but not much in the way of results. It shows no progress and is poorly organized.

(2) He (prewar head, now vice chairman of Nahdatul Ulama) said NU is a *kolot* organization; that all the leaders are *kolot*—lots of *kijajis* particularly; and that he himself is *kolot*. Asked whether NU people liked to be called

148

kolot, he said, "Yes, of course they do." I asked him just what he meant by *kolot*. He said, "Well, for example, we like *slametans*, we like the old ways, like wearing wooden sandals and sarongs. We stick to the ways of our parents and grandparents. . . ." I asked him if only the old and village people were *kolot* (because he had mentioned that he was old and that there were lots of old men and village people in NU). How about young townsmen like Rivai (secretary of NU)? Was he *kolot* too? He said, "Yes, it is the heart that is important. A man like Rivai has an old heart; he is old-fashioned inside. All NU people are that way." He mentioned the present Minister of Religion, who is an NU man, and said that even though he dresses in a tie, coat, and long pants, his heart is *kolot;* down deep he is an old-fashioned man.

(3) He (a watchmaker and rank-and-file member of both Masjumi and Muhammadijah) went on to list the various intellectuals with academic titles in Masjumi—Dr. Sukiman, Mr.* Rum, Mr. Jusuf Wibisono, Dr. A. R. Hanifah (all leaders of Masjumi at the national level)—and compared this situation favorably with that of NU, which had only *kijajis* and such, and really no educated men. He said that NU was more interested in religion than Masjumi, and Masjumi more in politics. The NU leaders were undoubtedly deep enough in religion, he said, but they didn't know anything about leading a country.

The contrast, then, between the modernists and conservatives remains, if muted. People still almost inevitably distinguish between the two approaches, choose one and denigrate the other. What is the content of the doctrines involved? How does the *moḍèren* interpretation of Islam differ from the *kolot?* Five pairs of oppositions fairly well sum up the situation:

(1) The *kolot* group tends to emphasize a relationship to God in which the reception of blessings as acts of His Grace and in reward for one's moral uprightness and a sense of the individual career as being entirely fated by His Will are the main features. The *moḍèren* group tends to emphasize a relationship to God in which hard work and self-determination are emphasized.

(2) The *kolot* group tends to hold to a "totalistic" concept of the role of religion in life, in which all aspects of human endeavor tend to take on a religious significance and the boundaries between the religious and the secular tend to be blurred. The *moḍèren* group tends to hold a narrowed notion of religion in which only certain well-defined aspects of life are sacralized and in which the boundary between the sacred and the secular tends to be fairly sharp.

(3) The *kolot* group tends to be less concerned (but still concerned) with the purity of their Islam and more willing to allow non-Islamic rites at least a minor place within the religious sphere. The *moḍèren* group tends to insist upon an Islam purified of any foreign religious matter.

(4) The *kolot* group tends to emphasize the immediately consummatory aspects of religion, to emphasize religious experience. The *moḍèren* group

* *Mr.* (abbreviation of *meester*) is a Dutch academic title used by holders of a master's degree in law.

tends to emphasize the instrumental aspects of religion, to be concerned with religious behavior.

(5) The *kolot* group tends to justify practice by custom and by detailed scholastic learning in traditional religious commentaries. The *modèren* group tends to justify it upon the basis of its pragmatic value in contemporary life and by general reference to the Koran and the Hadith interpreted loosely.

1. Fate versus Self-Determination

MODERNISTS most often sneer at conservative beliefs as "grave and gift" (*kuburan lan gandjaran*) religion, by which they mean that it is largely concerned with life after death and the gaining of blessings from God.

> Both Dullah from Masjumi and Aziz from PSII complained after the NU public meeting at the mosque . . . of NU's exclusive concern with religion and with the afterlife. Dullah said, "This isn't fitting; you have to deal with the situation now"; and Aziz said, "All they are interested in is *kuburan* and *gandjaran*. The village people just love this. They love to hear about how they are going to receive blessings for their goodness and about life beyond the grave. This is the old-time religion, and still very popular." He too, however, doesn't like it. He thinks NU is out of touch with reality.

The *kolot* message is eternally the same: if you will be good, pious, moral people, God will probably reward you with good health, riches, and happiness and, in any case, on Judgment Day He will take you up with Him into heaven. Combined with a belief in the determination of all things by the Will of God, this tends to produce a reliance upon one's moral superiority as the instrument for gaining one's goals rather than action, particularly where action is likely to lead to sticky situations. A man who orders bricks from a brickmaker and pays for them but never gets them resigns himself by saying that it is God's Will and that, anyway, later he, the swindled, will get the *gandjaran* that was intended for the brickmaker.

The usual image which is employed (by modernists and conservatives alike) as a symbol of the determination of man's actions by God's Will is that of the shadow-play puppeteer with his puppets. As the puppeteer manipulates his puppets, so God manipulates men; and as the puppets go into the box at the close of the performance, so men go into the grave at the close of their performance. But although modernists and conservatives both have a lively sense of divine determinism, the manner in which they interpret this doctrine —*takdir*—varies in its emphasis.

> Then I asked him (a young modernist) about *takdir*, and he said that he believed everything was *takdir* and that man's fate was wholly in God's hands. "Well," I said, "why do anything then? Why did the Indonesians bother with the revolution if everything is up to God?" He said, very strenuously, that we are commanded in the Koran to work and strive, to better ourselves. At my objection that this seemed in conflict with *takdir* he said that he sup-

posed that this wish to work and strive is determined by *takdir* too. But he was somewhat perplexed and asked me what Western thinkers thought on the subject; and I reassured him they were not much ahead of him on the problem. He said that it is partly a matter of emphasis. Some people, particularly the older, more *kolot* people, emphasize the *takdir* part of the thing and ascribe everything to that while others, younger people like himself, while still believing in *takdir,* also believe that effort makes a difference. For example, he has often argued with his grandmother on just these very lines. His grandmother will say, for instance, of a relative who is very poor, "Oh, it is just *takdir,* just fate." He will reply, "No, they are just lazy; they don't work hard enough." He said they never agree on this sort of problem.

The difference, then, between the *kolot* and *modèren* positions on the problem of free will is, in the first place, one of the extent to which the doctrine of determination is invoked to explain actual behavior and, in the second place, of the amount of stress put on the Koranic command to work as against that put upon the power of God to determine the details of individual behavior. In the *kolot* view, not only is *takdir* invoked more readily to condone, or at least to explain, moral, biological, or economic failure, but also the balance between the command to work and the sense for *takdir* seems more nearly even. The result is a view of things in which human effort can as a matter of fact really do little or nothing in altering individual destiny, but in which it is necessary to work patiently, whether one gets anywhere that way or not, a patient and peaceful servant of one's divine Master following out the commands He has issued, neither complaining nor questioning.

He (an NU leader) said, "If you believe there is a God and that all things are ordained by God you will be at peace and you won't get angry. People who believe this are very difficult to upset because they know everything is the work of God. . . ." I asked him if this was *takdir,* and he said, "Yes. It is the realization of this that makes you peaceful. You don't worry about being sick or dying because you know all that is in the hands of God." "Then why work?" I asked. He said that the Koran commands one to work. "Everyone has to work; it is sinful not to. It doesn't matter whether you are successful or not; you have to keep on hoeing in your fields even if you never get anywhere and just stay poor. Whether you succeed or not is in the hands of God; what you have to do is obey the command to work."

In the modernist view, however, *takdir* tends to get narrowed to apply only to those occurrences clearly outside any possibility of human control; and the degree to which one responds to the command to work is held to be the main determinant in one's fortunes.

I asked him (a young Masjumi man) about *takdir*. He said that in his opinion everyone is *takdir* exactly the same. God does not *takdir* some people rich and some poor, but everybody is *takdir* with an even chance. Thus those who are poor are poor mainly because they are lazy or stupid or sinful; for example, they gamble. Those who are rich are rich because they work hard and are clever. He said that if, for example, he was well-off, it was not God's Will but a result of his own efforts, and anyone could do the same if only he would try hard enough. He said that it is important, however, to give thanks to God for one's good fortune. When I asked him if sickness was *takdir,* he said that there were two kinds: illnesses due to dirt, malaria, for example, and those which are not and are thus not one's own fault. "The same is true with accidents," he said, unprompted. "If you leave here and walk out in the middle of the street without looking where you are going and you get hit by a truck, that is not *takdir,* it is your own fault. But if the accident was completely beyond your own control, that is *takdir.*"

There are various other compromises and solutions between these two extremes, such as the view that God determines us generally into one of two groups, rich or poor, but that within these effort can make a difference; but in general people tend to lean to one pole or the other: that man should be a pious, patient, steady worker in the service of God and he will receive his blessings, most likely in this life, certainly in the next, or that man should strive for what he wishes, thank God when he gets it, but not employ the doctrine of divine determination as an excuse for his failures.

2. Totalistic versus Narrowed Religion

THE varying range over which the doctrine of *takdir* is applied is in itself an example of the second opposition: the totalistic versus the narrowed view of the scope of religion. The greater percentage of secular studies in modernist schools, the emphasis on non-religious groupings such as peasant associations, labor unions, boy scouts, and sport clubs by the modernists, and the generally much less obviously religious atmosphere in which the modernist groups operate point to the same thing. When a modernist opens a meeting, say the *kolot,* all he does is shout *Bismillah!* ("In the name of God!") and then plunges into a discussion of the budget, returning to Islam only to shout *Alhamdulillah!* ("Thanks be to God!") as the meeting ends. This, says the *kolot* critic wryly, makes the organization Islamic.

The issue here, it need be understood, is not a difference of point of view concerning the importance of religion in relation to the rest of life. For both groups Islamic doctrine is considered to be the fundamental basis for human action in all of its aspects; there is no simple rendering unto Caesar. In that sense, all *santris* are totalistic—in contrast to *abangans* and *prijajis,* for whom religion is only one part of life with its own specific patterns and purposes and more or less equal in prestige with other parts which, in turn, do not need to be justified in any explicitly religious terms. But for the *santris* this latter is just what is involved: how is the secular life to be justified in terms of the religious? While the conservatives have a tendency to regard Islam as providing adequate and explicit directions in all fields of human endeavor from the domestic to the political, the modernists display a greater willingness to allow secular institutions to operate largely independently of a constant harassment by details of religious doctrine as long as their basic relationship to that doctrine is such that there is no obvious reason to condemn them.

I talked with Radjat (an NU member) a while. He discussed the difference between NU and Masjumi and said that their aims were identical but their methods different. For example, both Masjumi and NU want a state based on Islam; but Masjumi argues that people must make the secular state perfect first, or at least some of its leaders, and that they can declare it Islamic later, while NU says Islam first, and that will make the state perfect.* Also, the leadership of NU in contrast to Masjumi is made up of *kijajis* and *pondok* people, people who have in many cases never been to school at all, while Masjumi leaders are mostly educated people. Also, NU puts more emphasis on religion and less on secular affairs; Masjumi emphasizes the secular more than the religious. They are both Moslem, however; it is just a matter of stress.

The tendency for the religious to widen out to engulf the secular, to regard everything as having religious significance, was even stronger in the years before the war, when wearing Western clothes was considered by some conservative leaders to be an infidel practice, the story being told that at one NU conference before the war a famous *kijaji* insisted (unsuccessfully, it must be admitted) that other delegates refrain from wearing neckties. This sort of thing occurs rather seldom now, but it is still not always possible to predict what an old-fashioned *santri* is going to consider anti-Islamic. Movies, playing cards even without gambling, and gym shorts for girls have raised orthodox hackles during the past few years.

3. Syncretic versus Puristic Islam

DESPITE their seeming greater religiosity, the conservatives are somewhat more flexible about both *abangan* rituals on the one hand and *prijaji* mysticism on the other. Their flexibility does not, paradoxically, indicate a greater tolerance; if anything, the conservatives are more likely directly to attack "infidel" practices by non-*santris* than are the modernists, who worry more about heterodoxy within the *ummat* than outside of it. Rather, it is a slightly broader view as to what may be considered Islamic or, if not actually Islamic, at least harmless enough to be legitimately practiced by a "true" Moslem without damaging his religious status. Mysticism can be lent orthodoxy by adopting the rules of one

---

* In other words, Masjumi is willing to work in the present secular republic and feels no necessity for the immediate declaration of an Islamic theocracy, which many Masjumi members privately consider would raise more problems than it would settle. NU, although forced to work under the present secular state, there being no alternative but to rebel (as right-wing Moslems seeking an Islamic state have indeed done in West Java, in South Celebes, and sporadically in North Sumatra), feels that the theocracy should be declared immediately, whereupon reform of the government will follow as a natural consequence of the mere application of the superior political and legal theories of Islam. The Masjumi view just given is not official party doctrine, for neither party would dare come out against an immediate imposition of an Islamic state; it is, however, an accurate summary of the view actually held by the leaders of the party in Modjokuto.

of the Sufi brotherhoods (i.e., "orthodox" Islamic mystic sects); and if the spirits petitioned at a *slametan* are called *djins* and if the Koran chant be somewhat extended, then these little feasts are at worst pleasant gatherings of neighbors, age-old customs of only minor religious significance which it would be a shame to give up.

So, among the *kolot,* the traditional round of *slametans* goes on only somewhat simplified for economy's sake and with the Islamic elements accentuated at the expense of the non-Islamic; but among the *modèren, slametans* often disappear almost completely. A modernist *santri* wedding will often consist entirely of the ceremony at the *naib*'s office, the meeting (the bride most often dressed in a white Western gown to accentuate the secularity of this part of the ceremony), an Islamic sermon addressed to the couple by an older male relative, and a reception. At death a good modernist may merely buy a half-dozen new benches for his group's school and dedicate them to the memory of the deceased. Pregnancy and birth *slametans* tend to be either ignored completely—sometimes on the pretext that they are dangerous to the health of the mother—or extremely simplified. A modernist informant of mine simply killed a small goat for a feast about two weeks after his wife gave birth. Calendrical *slametans* are commonly not given at all because they are considered "Buddhist," the Islamic holidays being celebrated by prayers in the public square and by gifts to the poor. This passage from a poem composed in the early days of Muhammadijah in Modjokuto gives pretty well the modernist attitude to *abangan* religion:

> Many people are thrown in,
> Who die, and then are thrown into the flaming fire.
> Such is the fate of careless thinkers,
> Who guide their behavior by guess.
> The Lord God does not ever forgive
> The sins of idolators, even after death.
> One must pray only to one God!
> Those who pray to wood and stone,
> Who burn incense to ask forgiveness,
> Who place magical bundles here and there to call spirits—
> Indeed, they shall live in continuous misery!

As for mysticism, in any form, it is even more of an anathema to the *modèren.*

Chalifa said that members of the modernist movement, such as himself, thought these people (we were discussing a nearby Moslem mystic brotherhood) were wrong, and that they thought people like him were wrong. He said that they were *kolot,* knew nothing about the science of Islam, and were not interested in helping others. They would go there (to the brotherhood's *pondok*) for a month at a time, leaving their families behind unguarded and uncared for, and were interested only in their own spiritual welfare. He said that he and people like him, whose minds were already opened, who knew the true Islam, should teach it to those who did not. He said also that the *kolot* mystics don't really know much about this world. A good Moslem, he said, must know both this world and the religious life, and not just one or the other. He read to me something he had written in Arabic in his composition book which said that those people who stumble around mumbling the Confession of Faith over and over again are like dead men who can move, like ambulant corpses just waiting to finally die and trying to assure themselves of God's favor but not caring about anyone else.

4. Religious Experience versus Religious Behavior

THE *kolot* side of the fourth opposition, the tendency to emphasize the immediately consummatory aspects of religion, is well enough indicated in the concern with "blessings," with "inner peace," and the relative tolerance towards *abangan* ritual and towards mysticism which have already been discussed. Similarly, the *modèren* side of the equation appears in the emphasis on hard work and religious purity and the concern for social progress which I have ascribed to them. But perhaps the clearest indication of the two groups' differing choice of horns in this particular dilemma is to be seen in their contrasting attitudes toward art.

The *modèren* view is well summed up by this transcript from my notes on a conversation with a twenty-year Muhammadijah veteran:

> Among other things we discussed shadow-plays. He said that he thought that every person ought to see a shadow-play at least once but not more than that. He said the reason people ought to see it once is that it pictures how the world is. The puppeteer moves the puppets around, and it is just like God and His people. If it were not for God, people could not walk or talk. God is the puppeteer of the world. But once is enough to comprehend this; it is of no use to see it again. But Zaini (the informant's wife) said that she had never seen a shadow-play; and when I asked why, she said that good *santris* don't like shadow-plays because they are "just pleasure" and of no use. Zaini said Islam teaches that we should not waste our time in frivolous pursuits. Her husband then said that *tijd is geld* (Dutch for "Time is money"), and that when I came we should always talk about important things, not just engage in small talk.

Just about the only art, aside from chanting, which they do not regard as an art form (and the criticize the extended chants of the *kolot* as being "of no use" also), of which the modernists approve, is moral stories for children. Such stories, emphasizing the virtues of honesty, thrift, hard work, and cleanliness, are evidently frequently related in *santri* households and form an important part of the religious education of the child. But other forms of art appear conspicuously lacking among the modernists. Rather, there seems to be something of an emphasis on sports, most particularly soccer and badminton, which are justified, not in terms of the enjoyment they bring, but on the basis of their body-building and health-preserving functions.

On the other hand, the conservatives, who also have little interest in shadow-plays and court dancing, have managed to build up, largely around the *pondok* system, a fairly lively art adapted from the Arabs which contrasts both with the restrained formality of *prijaji* art and the puritan aesthetics of the modernists. Three art forms are involved: *terbangan,* a special type of elaborated chanting, originally from Persia, in which small drums are beaten and a history of the Prophet Muhammad is chanted, alternate sections in rhymed prose and in poetry (i.e., with a fixed beat and line length); *gambusan,* a Middle-Eastern-type orchestra, consisting of stringed instruments (the *gambus* proper; evidently derived from the Hadhramaut) and various-sized drums (also called *terbang*), to the music of which all-male Arabic dances are danced and secular Arabic songs sung; and, third, a set of strength tests, flesh mortifications, and native "wrestling" exhibitions centering around the famous Indonesian fighting dance, the *pentjak.*

The *terbangan* is usually held in the mosque, most commonly on the Prophet's birthday or other Moslem holidays, and lasts for about two hours. Shorter ones are sometimes held on Friday eves (i.e., Thursday nights) and at *santri* circumcisions and marriages. Modernists tend not only to look down on these celebrations as old-fashioned but also to regard the performance of them in the mosque as sacrilegious.

I asked Dullah and Hadji Muchtar, the Muhammadijah man who works in the *naib*'s office, about the *terbangan* I heard was to be given in the mosque on August 17th (Indonesia's Independence Day; this was evidently the first time this religious art form had been employed on a secular holiday); Muchtar laughed ironically and said, "Oh, we are having a hot time in the mosque from morning to night these days." Dullah said that it was just a play for ignorant village people and was sponsored by NU. For Muhammadijah this kind of thing was absolutely forbidden. The mosque was for praying only and that was all, but the NU people were very orthodox (!) and didn't understand. He said Muhammadijah had tried to prevent it, but evidently was unsuccessful.

As for the *gambusan,* it occurs also at circumcisions and marriages and at "graduation" ceremonies in *pondoks.* It may in fact be held just for the joy of it, with no special occasion; and there were three or four *gambus* orchestras in town made up of young *santris* who used to get together once a week at the home of one of the members to have a kind of jam session. Often, but not always, associated with the music is the singing of catchy Arabic songs (the meanings of which, except in general terms, the singers do not know) and lively Arabic dances, most of them comic, which often include female impersonations. The whole effect, with drum-beating, rhythmic hand-clapping, shouting, and all the skipping back and forth in helter-skelter fashion, provides such a sharp contrast to the usual Javanese formality that it is considered by most people to be rather animalistic and uncivilized. "It is like Africa in Indonesia," one young modernist said disapprovingly.

Pentjak, the fighting dance, is not strictly speaking a wholly *santri* art or one exclusively practiced by *santris;* nor did it originally have any connection with Islam. But for various reasons it has come to be mainly associated with *pondok* culture. Since Sumatra and the other larger "outer islands" of Indonesia have, in general, tended to have a stronger Islamic tradition than

Java and a much weaker Hindu-Buddhist tradition, the *pentjak,* which was always strong there, tended to get associated with Moslem culture. Also, the generally energetic character of the *pentjak* fits better with the pseudo-Arabic culture of the *pondoks* than it does with the more restrained culture of the non-*santris;* and the kind of encapsulated all male—even somewhat homosexual—hairshirt youth society that *pondoks* represent is likely to find art forms emphasizing physical strength, agility, and endurance attractive. (One *santri* who had been at the central NU *pondok* said that the *kijaji* there encouraged *pentjak* so that the students would not wish to play such sports as soccer, which might take them out of the *pondok* sphere and into contact with secular life). In any case, almost all of the skillful *pentjak* performers around Modjokuto are *kolot santris* who have spent long periods in *pondoks;* and about the only place one still sees *pentjak,* a dying art (it had a brief renaissance under the Japanese, who stimulated it in line with their pro-Moslem and military preparedness program—and perhaps because it seemed to them much like their judo), is at "graduation" ceremonies at *pondoks.*

Pentjak is a half-dance, half-fight in which aggressive acts are initiated and developed but not consummated. The two participants strike viciously at one another with their hands and feet, sometimes even wielding knives, but withdraw their blows at what seems like the last possible moment so they do not land. They throw one another to the floor, the victim cooperating in exact rhythm with the attacker; they leap around into formal poses, turning sharply toward and away from one another. All the while the drums beat, the audience shouts. It is a pantomime struggle just on the verge of the actual, and, somewhat as in a bullfight, the beauty and the excitement come from the thinness of the line between art and life. Two fight; one, tired or consistently out-maneuvered, withdraws; and another combatant leaps out from the audience. After five or ten minutes there is another unspoken decision, one of these two retires, and a new challenger faces the victor. This can go on for hours, ten or a dozen young men participating, the mock combat seeming always about to break into actual struggle and open aggression as the antagonists shout and grimace at one another; but it never does.

But *pentjak* is not just an art form. It is at the same time a practical system of self-defense which can be used without the aesthetic restraint when necessary, and a form of spiritual training. Many stories of actual *pentjak* feats in battle are told, and a man near me who beat off a huge knife-wielding thief one night was said to have been able to do so because he was a *pentjak* expert. In the old-time *pondoks,* it is said, there used to be people whose spiritual discipline through *pentjak* was so great that they could knock people down without touching them in a *pentjak* struggle; and a *pentjak* exhibition is still today half viewed as a struggle between two wills, so that a good *pentjak* man causes others to withdraw through his superior spiritual strength as well as his physical agility—these being, in fact, but reverse aspects of each other.

Associated with *pentjak* exhibitions is usually a series of strength tests and flesh mortifications. At a *pondok* "graduation" I attended, young men rolled in thorns, lifted weights, dropped heavy bricks on one another, and climbed slippery poles. It is said that they sometimes lacerate themselves with glass and walk on fire, but I have not seen either. The purpose is again a dual one of physical fitness and spiritual discipline, a kind of mystical sport. In sum: the *terbangan,* the *gambusan,* and the *pentjak* combine to define a quite variant subcultural art style by means of which the austere simplicities of Islam are modified for those for whom religion needs to be more than faith and works and to whom time is more than money.

5. Custom and Scholasticism
versus Pragmatism and Rationalism

FINALLY, there is the opposition between the *kolot* reliance on custom and detailed scholastic learning and the *modèren* group's tendency to take general oughts from the Koran and justify them pragmatically. The strongly *kijaji* leadership of NU means that the scholastic tradition is extremely entrenched there.

> We talked on about NU and Muhammadijah. He (a young modernist) said that NU has all the *kijajis;* in Modjokuto, Muhammadijah does not have one religious expert, one *kijaji.* He said that the reason NU is stronger (i.e., has more members) is that it has a fixed religious line. Most NU positions on religious problems are decided by the big *kijajis,* and the others fall in line. Muhammadijah has none of this. Each man just about decides for himself on the basis of his own interpretation of the Koran. He said that Dullah (a Muhammadijah leader) holds that if one misses a prayer one does not necessarily have to repeat it later; but Pak Ali (Chairman of Masjumi and Vice Chairman of Muhammadijah) doesn't agree with this position—an example of the conflict that exists even within the organization.

The greater reliance on scholastic learning and on custom is not self-contradictory as it might seem, for what often happens is that *kijajis* find for themselves interpretations of the law which will allow them and their followers to practice the customs which they are wont to practice on traditional grounds. The modernists, on the other hand, tend to reject traditional Moslem customs which they feel are not in keeping with the true spirit of Islam—such as the symbolic acts surrounding death, or the short "calming" spell said before a prayer—and to be somewhat unimpressed by what they consider sophistic arguments for such customs by the learned. Thus a modernist scholar pointed out at a Masjumi meeting that people often use *hadiths* rather unfairly. For example, he said, there are three *hadiths* concerning women, one of which puts them higher than men, one of which puts them lower, and one which says they are equal, and that by quoting any one of these one could make a case for almost any position. One must get the spirit of the Hadith in general, all the quotations on this point, he said. As for arguments from secondary religious commentaries, modernists tend merely to say that it is best to stick to the Koran and Hadiths and not be oversubtle.

For the customs they do accept as "fitting" with the Koran and the Hadith, modernists tend almost inevitably to add pragmatic rationalizations. Thus the prayers are justified as being good exercise and healthful (The early morning prayer is said to get one out of bed early in the morning so that one can get right to work and not laze around in bed), circumcision as preventing genital infections, the Pilgrimage as broadening one as travel always does. Western spiritualist writers are quoted in "scientific" support of the existence of the supernatural, prohibition of pork is justified by references to trichinosis, and Western medicine is said to have established that fasting prevents stomach cancer. But the most insistent theme is that Islamic doctrine presages almost all later thought, social or scientific, and thus is extremely functional in a modern context. The Koran is claimed to contain all the necessary rules for modern hygiene and much of modern medicine; adequate astronomy, chemistry, and physics are also claimed to have been included in the Holy Book. One speaker explained the Prophet's speedy journey to Palestine at the time of the *Mi'radj* as being explicable by the fact that he had the secret of atomic power centuries before it was discovered in the West.

It is especially in the realm of social doctrine that the claim for modernity and for the continuing usefulness of Islamic doctrine and law is put most strongly.

> His (a modernist speaker at a meeting in the mosque on the Prophet's birthday) second point was that many times one hears people say that the Islamic law may be all right, but it doesn't fit with the modern world; it can't be made operative in the situation today. . . . He then gave several examples to show that Islamic law was not only as up to date as Western law (he took French law as the quintessence of Western law and made his comparisons with that) but actually preceded it. Take the matter of the notion that all men are equal. This came to the Western world at the end of the eighteenth and the beginning of the nineteenth centuries with the French Revolution and the Declaration of the Rights of Man. Before that, society was sharply divided into aristocrats and commoners. But in the Islamic law this principle is stated (he quoted it), in the Hadith it is stated (he quoted it), and in the Koran it is stated (he quoted it). Second example: women's rights are equal to those of men. This again is in the law, the Hadith, and the Koran; and he quoted them. Thus in both these cases—the equality of men and the equality of men and women—the Islamic law was centuries ahead of the West and fits in with modern ideas. This proves, he said, that the Koran is the Word of God.

Conservative and Modern Islam and the Traditional Javanese Religious Outlook

THESE, then, are the dimensions along which doctrinal distinctions within the Modjokuto *ummat* tend to arrange themselves: a "fated" life versus a "self-determined" one; a "totalistic" view of religion versus a "narrowed" one; a more "syncretic" Islam versus a "pure" one; an interest in "religious experience" versus an emphasis on "the instrumental aspects of religion"; the justification of practice by "custom" and "scholastic learning" versus justification by the "spirit of the Koran and the Hadith" in general and "pragmatically."

It is no accident that the *kolot* side of these equations appears in each case to place them very near to the kind of world view I have already described as *abangan*. The extreme *kolot santri,* despite the fact that he is often called "orthodox," is not actually the most Islamic of Javanese Moslems but the least. It is he who has made the minimum shift from the traditional religious system in which "animistic," Hindu-Buddhist, and Islamic elements found a stable balance toward the situation where Islam and the world view associated with it have been fully taken up into the self, have been internalized in the individual psyche so that they actually control behavior rather than merely putting a gloss on it to hide the values which are really determining individual action.

It is very hard, given his tradition and his social structure, for a Javanese to be a "real Moslem"—to accept fully at the deepest emotional levels a religion which, in the words of H. A. R. Gibb, "set[s] the terms of a new experiment in human religion, an experiment in pure monotheism, unsupported by any of the symbolism or other forms of appeal to the emotions of the common man, which had remained embedded in the earlier monotheistic religions."* The otherness, awfulness, and majesty of God, the intense moralism, the rigorous concern with doctrine, and the intolerant exclusivism which are so much a part of Islam are very foreign to the traditional outlook of the Javanese. Even the modernists, supported as they are in their effort by some marked changes in the forms of social organization, succeed only part of the time in actually organizing their behavior in these terms—but then most Christians are pagans much of the time.

It would be a mistake to draw from this the conclusion—and it has often been drawn—that Islam is really of no importance in Javanese life and that the difference between *abangan* and *santri* is merely one of terms and protestations. For, even among the most *kolot* of *santris,* there has been a crucial shift when a man, propelled by class, occupation, geography, or family history, or, who knows, by an inner psychological need for a different sort of religion from that which his culture offers him, becomes a *santri.* He starts a process of genuine religious conversion which, if it cannot be completed in him, may well be in his children. Even the minimal *santri* has adopted, however vague and ill-understood they may be, several principles which, given time and increased social-structural support, may end in a totally different orientation toward the world: the idea of a distant and powerful God who is concerned with the moral worth of the individual believer; the idea that secular behavior must somehow be justified in terms of religious doctrine; and the idea that among the proposed paths to religious understanding, one is correct and all the others are wrong.

Nor can one simply say that the *kolot*-to-*modèren* scale measures the degree to which these principles have taken hold in the essentially *abangan*

* H. A. R. Gibb, *Mohammedanism* (London, 1949), p. 70.

mentality of the Javanese. Rather, they represent two alternate ways in which these principles can in part be realized in a still mainly non-Moslem social context. The modernist emphasizes the way of radical disassociation from that context and the purification of doctrine within a small group of religious leaders; the conservative tries to work out a halfway covenant with the reigning tradition which will both make his own transition easier and lessen the tension between himself and his neighbors who do not agree with him. It is well to remember, however, that not everyone is so consistent as to choose the same side of each of my oppositions nor is everyone so vigorous as clearly to choose one or the other side in any one of them. There is much indistinctness, ambivalence, and flaccidity of belief; and what one finds is a continuum from the *kolot* to the *modèren* along which people fall, many of them at neither extreme but somewhere in between. Tendencies are only tendencies after all, even if, as here, they are quite striking ones; and when one comes to consider the manner in which these variations in Islamic religious doctrine are institutionalized in Modjokuto, the social form they take, and the social context in which they exist, the picture gets not clearer but fuzzier.

Chapter 13

Patterns of Internal Organization of the *Santri* Community

THERE ARE two main *santri* political parties in Modjokuto, Masjumi and Nahdatul Ulama (NU); one minor one, Partai Sarekat Islam Indonesia (PSII); and one social organization concerned with education and various charitable activities which claims to be nonpolitical but which is in fact indissolubly linked with Masjumi, Muhammadijah. Most generally, Masjumi-Muhammadijah is said by almost everyone to be "progressive" or "modernist," and NU is said to be "conservative" and "old-fashioned." (PSII, in Modjokuto, is usually grouped with the modernist sector.)

It would be simple if one could merely accept this common stereotype and identify *modèren* ideology with Masjumi and *kolot* with NU; but unfortunately the situation is much more complex than this. The relationships between cultural patterns—beliefs, values, and expressive symbols—and the set of social structures in which they are embedded is only rarely one to one, because the general problems of human living to which the cultural, most especially religious, patterns are a response are not the same as the specific social exigencies to which the social structures are a response. Thus in Modjokuto the problems inherent in organizing a mass *ummat* containing old and young, male and female, peasant and trader, educated and illiterate so that the values it holds should have an effect upon the wider society make it nearly impossible that ideological standpoints and political party membership would have any simple relationship. Politics make strange bedfellows in Java as elsewhere.

Taking the Modjokuto *ummat* as a whole, almost everyone in it belongs either to Masjumi or to Nahdatul Ulama, or at least considers himself a follower of one or the other. In contrast to both *abangans* and *prijajis* there are almost no politically neutral *santris*. In comparison with American attitudes the political party plays a much less functionally specific role in the life of Modjokuto *santri* than the Republican and Democratic parties play for most middle-class urban Americans. As in certain rural areas in our Midwest and South and, until recently at any rate, among certain depressed ethnic groups in our cities, political parties for the Javanese *santri* are not merely loose conglomerates of people with similar voting habits. Rather, they are social, fraternal, recreational, and religious organizations within which kinship, economic, and ideological ties coalesce to press a community of people into the support of a single set of social values which are not just concerned with the proper exercise of political power but condition behavior in many different areas of life. To join a Moslem political party is to commit oneself to one or another of the variant interpretations of Islamic social doctrine.

Insofar as the preceding paragraphs are contradictory, their resolution is this: In addition to the fact that the "public reputations" of the two parties, one for conservatism, the other for modernism, tend to bring the conservatives into one and the modernists into the other, other social considerations tend to bring about the reverse. In general, in both parties, the young, the educated, the urban, and the weakly religious tend to be more modern. The coalescence of kinship, economic, and ideological ties in either party is inexact, distorted both by accident—so that the modern-minded son of a *kolot kijaji* may end up an NU leader out of opportunity rather than out of conviction—and by design—so that a modernist may enter NU simply because he thinks he can get a more powerful position there due to the lack of educated leaders. Even geography makes a difference. Certain villages tend to be mainly Masjumi, others mainly NU; and the modern-minded man in an NU village will have to decide for himself whether ideological or neighborhood ties shall predominate.

What this means is that a man who is old, rural, uneducated, and deeply pious is very likely to be strongly *kolot* and very likely to be in NU; a man who is young, urban, and educated (he may or may not be deeply religious) is quite probably in Masjumi; but the loyalties of people in whom these attributes are mixed, such as old, uneducated urbanites, are less easy to predict. When we consider that there are also pressures—such as kinship ties, geographical considerations, and desire for personal power—which may act to make an individual go against the grain, we see that things are not so clearly marked off as the simple fact that even the most backward *santri* peasant knows NU to be "conservative" and Masjumi "progressive" and that he considers himself an adherent of one or the other would lead one to believe.

Political-Religious Leadership

THE various pressures and counter-pressures find, as one would expect, their greatest intensity among the elite of each party. Among the rank and file, conservatism or modernism is likely to be mainly a vague preference on the part of an individual, and he is called *tjondong* ("sympathetic") to one or the other parties, a kind of fellow traveler not altogether clear what the issues are but feeling that one group or the other "fits" (*tjotjog*) better with how he feels about things. But among the leadership, prejudices are more articulate, and so each party has a dual problem; to balance things off among the elite so that a consensus can be found as to just how "conservative" the conservative party is going to be and how "modernist" the modernist; and, second, to attract and hold the masses to their leadership in these terms.

In Modjokuto the leadership conflict is cast in different terms for each party. In NU the conflict is between the younger, more educated, urbanized leaders the party needs in order to operate effectively in the political arena, men whose modernism is often nearly as strong as that of the leaders in Masjumi, and the older, rural *kijajis,* who are more likely to wish to keep NU on its traditionally *kolot* course. The governing board of NU in Modjokuto consists of two groups. There are three or four old-line *kolot* men of about sixty years of age whose main task is to communicate both with the rank and file and with the countryside *kijajis* who are their spiritual preceptors and to convince both of these that the party has not fallen into sinful hands. And there are three or four young men whose job is to chart the party's course in the local political struggle, to give it some semblance of effective organization, and to transmit orders from the central leadership.

Thus while the local leader of the party can say that NU is a very, very conservative party indeed and that its main motto is "Be careful," and can argue that Muhammadijah is much too incautious in religious matters, the secretary of the organization, a young man, can deliver a speech to me that would not sound out of place in the depths of Muhammadijah councils.

He started talking about Islamic education. He said he thought the main reason for the moral crisis now raging in Indonesia was the tremendous inadequacies and the primitiveness of religious education in Indonesia in the Dutch time. He said that the *kijajis* would just chant the Koran and the students just memorize the words. This sounded fine, he said, but none of them know what was in the Koran or what Islam was all about; they weren't really Moslems. The old method of education also led to indifference to religion or later to anti-religious feelings on the part of students when they realized they had been wasting their time. He said the situation was improved some now, but still pretty bad.

As the following of NU is predominantly *kolot,* if not always as outspoken about it as the *kijajis,* the younger leaders seem constantly engaged in an effort to drag an unwilling party along the road to greater modernity.

I went to an NU meeting last night. There were about thirty people present, most of them older men, many of them quite old. Muksim (an old NU leader, one of the founders of NU in Modjokuto) ran the thing. He started the meeting off with an Arabic sentence and went on about the value of Islam, particularly stressing its importance for men about his age, saying "When you die, die Islam." The first speaker (a somewhat younger leader) launched into an attack on the lassitude of NU people. He said that if NU wants an Islamic state they must turn out for the meetings and learn about general things, not just religion, and that they must develop their organization. He said that Moslems in Indonesia comprise 90 per cent of the population* but don't

* I.e., confessed Moslems; *santris* always claim everyone but Christians, Balinese, and outright pagans as Moslems, though many of those they so claim are in fact bitterly anti-*santri.*

have nearly their proper power because they just sit back and don't come to the meetings. (A number of people slept through this speech, and a few slept through almost all of them.) At any rate, his speech turned out to be a plea for the *ummat* to become more active; and he especially decried the showing at the meeting. . . . Muksim then called in Rais, the secretary of NU, who came in from outside the door where he had been waiting. He spoke fifteen minutes, his speech being entirely an exhortation for the rank and file to be more active in NU. He kept saying over and over again that both the leaders and "those who are led" have to participate. He said that they should go out and urge their friends to come, that only 30 people coming when NU was so large was an unhappy state of affairs, and that NU had social responsibilities to meet and couldn't just pay attention to religion. Muksim then talked a while about the comforts of religion to the aged and made his point about dying Islam again. . . . In general NU people (this was the first meeting I attended) here seem much older than Muhammadijah people, and interest in directly religious questions is somewhat more evident. (Two strictly religious speeches are omitted from the above account.) Most of the younger NU people were not there. Others like Rais just came in, made a speech, and left. Some people wore traditional dress; one man had a full beard; and three or four were very old indeed, using canes to walk. Muksim seems more in touch with people than the rest, and I suppose that is why he was in charge.

The older audience and the religious emphasis of that meeting are partly attributable to the fact that it was a meeting for religious propaganda rather than business. But the almost desperate tone with which the younger leaders tried to get the NU rank and file to leave off *kolot* concerns and take a somewhat more modern attitude was typical.

Within the Masjumi leadership the issue is somewhat different. In the first place, all but one of the major Masjumi leaders in Modjokuto are Muhammadijah members and thus strict modernists, and the seventh, the son of H. Nazir, the modernist pioneer, is generally sympathetic to modernism. The issue is not so much between modernism and conservatism as between what one might call a "secularist" approach to modernism and a "pious" approach. By definition, no *santri* can be a secularist; and I have already emphasized the fact that modernists are concerned with a "pure" Islam. Nevertheless, people come at modernism from two angles.

First, there is the deeply pious Moslem whose feelings for the traditions of Islam are as deep as those of any conservative but who, being well-educated, has a painful awareness of the inadequacy of Islam in its full medieval form for modern life. The interest of this sort of man (for example, Nazir's son, learned in several languages, his scholarship in the Koran and Hadith renowned throughout the whole area among modernists and conservatives alike) in modernism is in producing an Islam of which he will not have to feel ashamed in any particular when faced with other modernized creeds such as Christianity, but which will still be Islam and will still fulfill his strong religious needs. The second type of man to whom modernism appeals is one whose main interests are in the secular world but who also feels a need for some religious context for his behavior. He wants a religion which will not continually hamper his activity in modern secular life, which will leave him free to pursue his interests there, but which will still allow him to be a good Moslem and allow him to justify his life in terms of the Koran. The present chairman of Muhammadijah in Modjokuto is such a man. He is more interested in political activity and social work than in religious learning, but he is most certainly not a secularist.

As both Unitarians and Lutherans find a place in Christian reform, so both these types tend to get attracted to Islamic reform; and it is the contrast between the two which one sees in Masjumi-Muhammadijah councils.

> We talked about Usman (Nazir's son). He (the informant was a young Muhammadijah man) said Usman is the most intellectual of the speakers on religious subjects around here; he always get his material out of books like a true scholar. Pak Mul, who does most of the Muhammadijah talking on religious topics, is more down to earth and just takes his examples from everyday life. When I asked him who the Muhammadijah people look to for leadership, he said, "Ali (Chairman of Masjumi; Vice Chairman of Muhammadijah) and Mul do most of the talking on religious subjects along with Hadji Muchtar, who works in the *naib's* office, Dullah (a Muhammadijah leader), H. Ustaz (one of the founders of Muhammadijah and one of its main sources of financial support in Modjokuto), and Iskak (Chairman of Muhammadijah) don't know very much about religion and you rarely hear them talk about it."

The kind of conflict that typically occurs in such a situation is exemplified in the following report, written by another member of our research team, of a Muhammadijah school committee meeting, in which roughly the same people participated as are mentioned in the above note and lined up in respect to a problem just about as one would predict:

> They discussed the separation of the various school classes into boys and girls, deciding finally not to do so but to continue with the present co-educational classes. The argument for separation was all religious, Iskak said, while the arguments against it and the difficulties were all practical. Opposed to the separation were Dullah, H. Ustaz, and Iskak; the supporters were led by H. Muchtar and Mul. One of the practical difficulties was that, since there were more boys than girls, there would be an imbalance. Also, said Iskak, there would be an educational danger, for there would be less competition and thus less good results educationally. He said that it is better for the boys to have the girls present so that they will have to behave above a certain minimum, whereas if they were alone they would be more difficult to handle—an argument on the ideological rather than the practical level which tends to deny the original rationale for separation. Then they discussed whether the religious injunction was absolute or only advisory and decided that it was absolute but only insofar as it was possible of realization.

Also, because of this dual appeal of modernism, Muhammadijah draws for its membership not only upon those who have grown up in a *santri* background which they now feel needs to be adjusted to changed conditions but also upon those people who grow up in a non-*santri* environment and decide upon becoming adults that a reformed Islam is attractive to them. There is a tendency on the part of both these kinds of people, moreover, to want to disassociate themselves from traditional village *santris*.

> I went in the evening to see Rachmad (head of the Muhammadijah high school). I asked him whether his parents had been *santris* and he said no. He never knew about Islam until he went to work for Muhammadijah. He was born and educated in Djember and went to a place near there where the Muhammadijah school was in bad shape, with only a handful of students and no teachers left, and he was asked whether he wanted to teach there. He thought that he would teach only for the experience, but he got more and more involved in it until finally he became a member of Muhammadijah and a *santri*. He was rather uncomfortable with this last term; he said that he wasn't a *santri* like regular village *santris*. He then explained: "With Muhammadijah people you can not tell they are *santris* just by looking at them as you can other *santris*. For example, I look just like anyone else, any other teacher. And Zuhari (a young Kudus-descended religious teacher in the Muhammadijah high school; from a strong *santri* background and rather learned in religion for a young man but quite modernist), for example, is very learned in religion, but you would never know it to look at him. He looks just like a modern young man."

In short, among the NU leadership the conflict is between the need to appease a *kolot* following and still meet the demands a modern political party must meet in order to compete effectively; among the Muhammadijah-Masjumi leadership the conflict is between the desire to modernize Islam and the necessity to make sure that this does not lead to secularism. So, in a sense, the problems in the two elites are parallel: how to interpret Islam so that it can at the same time be both religiously satisfying and socially adequate. The difference lies in the fact that the danger in the first is that social adequacy will be sacrificed to religious satisfaction and the party will lose its political effectiveness, and in the second the danger is that religious validity may be sacrificed to social efficiency, depriving the party of its basis of mass support. It is in this sense that NU may be called "conservative" and Masjumi-Muhammadijah "modern."

Political-Religious Activity

THE fact that NU is in danger of being swallowed by its rank and file and Masjumi of losing its rank and file points to the fact that the crucially difficult problem of organization the two parties face is how to relate the fairly well-organized central structure to the more or less inchoate peasant mass upon which they rely for support. Like the central government bureaucracy, after which they and most other Indonesian political parties are modeled, NU and Masjumi are both built down from the top rather than up from the bottom; and, as in the government bureaucracy, the central organization of the party, in which roles are at least somewhat well defined and allocated (much, much less so in the parties than in the civil bureaucracy), ends at the subdistrict level. That is, the legitimized lines of political hierarchy go no lower down than towns the size of Modjokuto. In the bureaucracy the most important link in the entire set-up is that between the subdistrict officer, as the lowest appointive official in the bureaucracy, and the village chief, elected by his compatriots. Similarly, in party organization the crucial link is between the town-centered party governing board, made up of a group of highly inter-married urbanites forming a very tight unit of their own, and the various local chapters of the party in each village, which, for the most part, have very little internal organization of any sort.

The governing board of either party, resident in the town of Modjokuto (the main major exception being Nazir's son, who is on the Masjumi governing board and resides in a village at the edge of town), keeps in touch with the mass of its following, resident in the seventeen villages surrounding it, in several different ways. Contact is made through holding regular business meetings between the governing board as a group and the leaders of each village chapter about every month or two, at which party strategy is planned, largely by the governing board, but at least within the hearing of the local leaders.

Individual members of the governing board circulate through the villages speaking at local chapter meetings on political topics of national concern. Regular weekly "prayer-meetings" (separate ones for each sex) are held at which religious specialists from each party, but not necessarily from the governing board, speak on Islam, most usually on its social application and its ethical content. In some villages these "prayer-meetings" (called *pengaosan,* which strictly means "a reading of the Koran"; but little Koran-reading, except for five minutes or so at the beginning, gets done now) are joint NU and Masjumi affairs and therefore more or less nonpartisan, each member being responsible for a small sermon on a religious topic in his turn. Even where separate *pengaosans* are held for each party, I have known speakers from the other party to be invited.

Another important method which the town-centered governing boards use in communicating to the rural rank and file is the mass meeting at which important speakers from higher up in the party hierarchy combine with local leaders from Modjokuto to give talks on social and political problems. These meetings are usually held in Modjokuto. (NU sometimes holds them in the villages themselves, but the central location of the town and the peasant view of it as an economic, governmental, and educational center make it more suitable for such "big events.") They are held at either the mosque or the "town hall" and usually scheduled on or near the big Moslem holidays: Idul Fitri, Maulud, and others. Great tides of people swamp the roads to town on such occasions, pouring in from villages as far as two hours away. From about eight in the evening until one in the morning they sit, lie, and stand in disordered profusion on the grass fronting the meeting place, patiently listening to party harangues. Then they ebb home again, much as they flooded in.

An example of the first sort of meeting, one in which the party governing board decides party policy in the presence of all the local leaders in the area, is one held in a village in the Modjokuto area by Masjumi under the chairmanship of Usman, H. Nazir's son, at which were present almost all the members of the governing board and almost all the village leaders. Usman began by giving a report of his recent trip through other parts of East Java, comparing organizational problems in Masjumi in these areas with similar problems faced in the Modjokuto area, outlining solutions tried elsewhere, new ideas, and so on. He also discussed struggles between Masjumi and the Communists in those areas, for both NU and Masjumi are deeply concerned with the "Communist problem," and in some parts of Java open clashes between Moslems and Communists have occurred.

The secretary of the party then outlined in great detail all the political problems which were currently most talked about in Djakarta, the national capital, discussing Masjumi's position on each one and rationalizing it. He discussed problems of the nationalization of oil fields, political struggles within the army, the importing of foreign capital, the organization of the coming general election, the opening of an embassy in the Soviet Union, the fiscal policy of the government, and the proper relation of the Indonesian parliament to the cabinet and the presidency. Following this, the chairman of Muhammadijah, who is also Vice Chairman of Masjumi, discussed ways and means of organization for the coming general election in the Modjokuto area, discussing ward organization, methods of financing the campaign, and canvassing techniques, and reviewing the distribution of party strength over the countryside. An NU meeting of the same type would be less impressive because Masjumi contains a greater number of skillful politicians, but either would establish the fact that modern politics have come to the Indonesian countryside.

Pengaosans, on the other hand, are more concerned with general religious and social doctrine, rather than with specific political problems. Here is a much condensed note on a meeting which lasted about four hours:

After he opened the NU *pengaosan,* Muksim called on a young man to read the Koran. Muskim then said something about the importance of coming to *pengaosan,* even for an old man such as himself who could be said to be just about finished. He had gotten a letter, he said, from an NU man who usually comes to the *pengaosan* almost every week, an old man who now had fallen sick and asked the NU membership to pray for his recovery. Achmad (a young *kijaji* from a nearby district) spoke next. He urged people to come to *pengaosan,* ridiculing people who just sit and pray and don't do anything else. He also ridiculed people who come to *pengaosan* and fall asleep, who don't participate in organizational life but just think about the next world. He said that one must adjust Islam to the modern world without losing its essence. He criticized people who didn't dress neatly, whose hair was uncombed, and whose clothes were disarranged—and he put his hat on sideways in mockery. He said that the Prophet not only prayed but prayed and acted. His speech, which went on for over two hours, was one comic routine after another, each with a moral point. He walked about stiffly to indicate intellectual inflexibility. He imitated a man hearing a bicycle bell and turning his head suddenly to see what was coming and then dodging elaborately to one side— to show that the various senses cooperate one with another: ears hear first, then eyes see, and so on. He imitated fat people and said, "If you eat too much your stomach gets big, your arms get big, but—Thanks be to God!—

your ears stay the same size." He made plays on words, mocked the civil servants (*prijaji*) who think they are better than everyone else (flouncing self-im-
portantly around the platform), and ridiculed people who worship stones and
wood. All of this chatter was strung together like daisies on a chain. His speech
went nowhere and had no organization, but it was marvellously well done. The
meeting was a kind of religious vaudeville in which moral maxims were
dramatized in pantomime. It was also a kind of rally, with speakers exhorting
the listeners in the most general terms to rouse up and do something—come to
pengaosan. But the speakers didn't offer them anything concrete to do.

On the other hand, at a Masjumi *pengaosan* the revivalist atmosphere
might be somewhat lessened and one might even get a kind of scientific
rationale for religion—as in the speech the head of Muhammadijah made at
the women's *pengaosan* of his organization, in which he tried to connect Islam
up with modern psychological theory. But the general pattern is similar in
either case. *Pengaosans,* because they occur weekly and because they are
very popular, are important elements in the social and religious life of both
the rural and urban *ummat* and are more comparable in some ways to our
church services than is the Friday prayer.

The other type of village meeting, in which a single member of the town
governing board attends a local chapter meeting, is more sporadic. The town
member, particularly in the Masjumi case, will usually review the national
political situation in detail as the secretary did at the strategy meeting, and a
local leader will handle the religious sermon. Leaders of the women's sections
of the parties also attend rural women's meetings in a similar capacity, and
sometimes flying squads of four or five urbanites will speak at an extraordinary
meeting in a village on political or religious topics or both. The mass meetings
in town are, however, usually entirely political and often quite demagogic,
although this is a general pattern not confined to the *santri* parties. Leaders
fairly high up on the party hierarchy may speak at such meetings on occasion,
and once during my stay Modjokuto people, rural and urban, flocked to the
regency capital 15 miles away by the thousands to hear Masjumi's most
fiery national leaders speak.

Political-Religious Organization

WHEN one comes to describe the efforts of NU and Masjumi to differentiate
their structure within the villages—to form semi-independent youth groups,
peasant organizations, and labor unions attached to the party, the contrasting
nature of the tasks facing the elite of each party are even more obvious. Organizations of young girls are so fiercely resisted by rural religious leaders that
they exist only in strictly modernist circles within the town. Boy scout organizations, which had a certain popularity before the war, are said to be weaker
now. In the villages the *kijajis* are still at best ambivalent to them; in the towns
all but the younger children think that boy scouts are somewhat beneath their

dignity. As a result both Ansor, the NU scouts, and Hizbul Wathon, the Muhammadijah scouts (PSII scouts are called SIAP), although they are still quite active, holding campouts, jamborees, and the like, are not so strong as the leaders would prefer them to be.

I asked Mul, who is head of Hizbul Wathon, the Muhammadijah scouts, about them. He said that the structure of Islamic and non-Islamic scouts (there is a large secular scout organization in town too) is the same but the basis is different according to whether religious teaching is included or not. He said the aim of scouting is healthy bodies and good character. He said that there are no dues involved, but I gathered that the boys are expected to get a uniform. He said that the scouts are not very popular; parents who don't understand don't want their boys to enter, and many boys, especially older ones, don't want to. Since in the villages the boys are expected to work in the rice fields, most scouts are from the towns. He said that the reason for lack of general interest in scouting is ignorance.

As for the peasant associations and labor unions, the lack of success is even more marked, and none has been able to gain much momentum in the Modjokuto area. The reasons for failure seem different for each party. For NU, the failure has been almost total. Although there are plans on paper, particularly for a peasant organization, and although many of the more modernist leaders of NU are painfully aware of the need for such organizations, nothing has been done. ("All the argument about doctrine doesn't mean a thing," one such leader told me; "the party that first sets up an organization that really does something for the peasant will win any general election easily.") The reason seems to be not only a shortage of effective leaders to carry out such projects but also the traditional Koran teachers with their double influence on the party—politically as advisors to its leadership and religiously as preceptors to its rank and file. They are at best indifferent and at worst hostile to the penetration of the party's secular forms of organization into the villages where their own power is based.

Masjumi's situation is quite different. In the first place, they have a more adequately equipped technical leadership. Secondly, they have made much more hopeful attempts at peasant and labor organization than in NU. For Masjumi, the problem seems to be that there is a marked tendency on the part of the highly organized urban leadership of the party to over-centralize such organizations as are formed, with the result that they become detached from the rural context.

I asked him (a Masjumi village leader) if STII (Sarekat Tani Islam Indonesia, the Masjumi peasant organization) was doing anything in the village, for I had heard from the STII head in Modjokuto that he, Abdul, was head of it in Banjuurip (the village). Abdul said, "Nothing is going on at all, nothing. Next time you see Mahmud (the Modjokuto STII leader) ask him for me why he doesn't pay any attention to the villages." Abdul was quite bitter and was evidently serious about my saying something to Mahmud in order to communicate his feeling to the governing board. He said that they only pay attention to the rice factory STII owns, and that there is no leadership at all provided for the villages. He said that the main problem was poor leadership. When Rusman (leader of STII just after the revolution, when the spirit of the times carried this sort of organization along better than it does now) was running it there was lots of work in the villages around Modjokuto. For example, in Banjuurip they had co-operative rice fields owned by STII and worked by members. Now it has all been sold off to individuals and STII doesn't really exist except in name.

STII in Modjokuto is an instructive example. Originally the organization was concerned with providing storage places for rice for the peasant so that he could avoid price fluctuations and with lending him capital for various small-scale agricultural enterprises. This program led in turn to the founding of a large mechanized rice mill by Rusman, the leader named above, under STII auspices, ostensibly to provide cheap milling for the farmers and to build up the capital of the organization. In time, however, the rice mill absorbed more and more of the energies of the technical leadership of the organization until the local units of STII were neglected and died out. Now STII more or less amounts to the rice mill (they also still own a little sugar land near the mill), which is evidently well-run and profitable but which is by and large indistinguishable in the eyes of the Masjumi peasants from any other privately owned rice mill. In any case, the organization in and around Modjokuto is at the moment quiescent.

Labor organization is an even more difficult problem, for there is the added difficulty that, since estate workers and town laborers, among whom such an organization would be expected to take effect, are heavily *abangan* and leftist, a Moslem labor organization, *santris* being mainly "middleclass" and politically to the right, has some of the same problems a labor union sponsored by the Republican Party in the United States would have. SBII (Sarekat Buruh Islam Indonesia), Masjumi's labor union, is active in areas near Modjokuto, but in Modjokuto itself it is nonexistent.

There is one union, Sarekat Buruh Indonesia (SBI), unaffiliated with any other in Indonesia, which, although it has no formal connection with Masjumi, is led by a Masjumi intellectual. A kind of "Moslem front organization," designed to ease the antagonism of many laborers to Islam in general and Masjumi in particular, SBI is a product of such a unique set of circumstances and so disconnected from all other aspects of Masjumi endeavor in Modjokuto that it need not be further described here except to note that its success seems somewhat due to its very segregation from the centralizing tendencies present in the rest of the leadership. (Its leader is the only member in the Modjokuto area of Achmadijah, the very extreme modernist movement which is regarded by Masjumi and NU people alike as "outside the bounds of Islam.")

The best example of the centralizing tendencies of Masjumi leadership is Muhammadijah, the socio-charitable association the members of which completely dominate that leadership. Muhammadijah is perhaps the most effective private organization from a technical point of view in all of Modjokuto. In contrast with many private groups in Indonesia, it does not merely spout doctrine and plan programs but gets a remarkable amount accomplished; and from a social point of view it is perhaps the most self-contained, consisting for all intents and purposes of thirteen individuals. (The total membership is thirty-seven, but the other fourteen are largely passive.)

> Next was the problem of getting the people of Muhammadijah into a working group. (Iskak, chairman of the Modjokuto branch, was addressing a regional conference of Muhammadijah in a nearby town.) He said that almost all the people who were active in Muhammadijah were the Governing Board; there wasn't any rank and file. Strictly speaking, this is not so, but I gather that he meant there are just two kinds of members in Modjokuto: the totally active and the totally passive ones, and that he didn't think the latter were of much importance. He said there were only forty members altogether anyway. Muhammadijah in Modjokuto, he said, did little active seeking of members and wasn't at all interested in increasing its size. What counted was to get people who would give their all. Then he gave several examples of how Modjokuto wove its active members into a solid group. He said that they had savings societies for both the Governing Board and the teachers in the school which were specifically designed to bring people together.

Muhammadijah activities are of two main types: charitable and educational, each under a special standing committee. Included under the former in Modjokuto's are the organization's orphanage, the distribution of meat to the poor on *Idul Adha,* the "Day of Sacrifice," and its organization of the obligatory poor-offering, the *zakat-fitrah,* due on the end-of-Fast holiday, *Idul Fitri.* Included in the educational activities are a nursery school for pre-school children (taught by the wife of the head of Muhammadijah), a religious school for young girls, a six-grade elementary school, a three-grade junior high school, and a three-grade teachers' school for people who intend to teach in elementary schools.

The orphanage, which is run full-time by a member of Muhammadijah, has sixty children and a staff of six, including a janitor, a cook, and a laundress, in addition to the head, his wife, and a secretary. Children are admitted upon the recommendation of Muhammadijah members or village chiefs, with preference being given those who have neither parents nor other relatives to care for them. At present the orphanage is financed in part by Muhammadijah (contributions being countable as *zakat* for those who give them) and in part by a subsidy of Rp 2.10 per child per month from the government. The Muhammadijah contribution is about one-fourth that of the government but is supplemented by special drives from time to time, as in the case of the collection of two tons of rice from the villages in 1952 in order to buy new mattresses for the children's beds. The children, who are of both sexes, range in age from six to sixteen and are housed in a large well-kept building in the center of town and educated in the Muhammadijah schools. They also learn to pray and to chant the Koran and get general religious training, all of them being members of the Muhammadijah youth organization.

The meat distribution on *Idul Adha* is to commemorate Abraham's sacrifice and is timed to coincide with a similar sacrifice of sheep and goats by the *hadjis* collected near Mecca, for this is the holiday which marks the high-point of the pilgrimage. Various members and friends of Muhammadijah contribute money (or, if rich, an actual ox or goat) with which oxen and goats are bought for the sacrifice. Tickets are distributed to poor families both by Muhammadijah members, who receive suggestions from people outside the organization, and by village chiefs. Each ticket entitles the family to a package of about one kilogram of meat. On *Idul Adha* in 1953 one ox and five goats were sacrificed and about 250 packages of meat were distributed. Most poor people are too ashamed to come themselves but send their children over to the orphanage. Theoretically, this meat distribution should occur in all the villages, but around Modjokuto only Muhammadijah seems to have the energy and ability to organize it.*

The *zakat-fitrah,* however, is collected in many of the villages by the various organizations. Muhammadijah, NU, and PSII collected it in the town; NU and Masjumi collect it in each of the villages in which there is a strong *santri* group. Until Muhammadijah appeared upon the scene in 1931, the *zakat-fitrah* either went uncollected or was collected by the *kijajis, modins,* and other religious figures; and it is said that it did not always get to the people for whom it was intended.

Here, as elsewhere, the Muhammadijah effort was to provide a model of correct and orthodox Islamic practices which the rest of the *ummat,* sunk in ignorance, could copy, a function they still perform within Masjumi.

Later on in the evening when Nur, the son of the Masjumi leader in Sumbersari (a nearby village), came up (to where Muhammadijah was gathered the night before *Idul Fitri* distributing the *zakat*) to get some advice on dividing the *zakat,* he happened to mention that it had not yet been divided up. Rachmad (head of the Muhammadijah high school) angrily said that if it wasn't divided before morning those who were dividing it were the ones who would have committed a sin. It had to be done before morning prayer; that was the law and one couldn't do it just any old way. He, Nur, would have to answer to God for it later, and he should be sure it was done right. Nur backed off, saying that it wasn't really he who was in charge of dividing it up but his father, and that every year something goes wrong. Ali (Chairman of Masjumi, Vice Chairman of Muhammadijah) supported Rachmad, and Nur began to look rather woebegone and just mumbled that village people didn't ever know how to do things right, and every year it went wrong no matter how hard they tried. Then Rachmad softened a little and said that Nur should tell his father that next year he should come up to Modjokuto to Muhammadijah headquarters and get assistance and learn how to do the *zakat* correctly.

The *zakat-fitrah* is set at two and one-half kilograms of rice for each person. Thus a family which has six members will have to give 15 kilograms.** (Strictly, one may not give money, but the organizations keep rice on hand to sell to people who wish to contribute money for convenience' sake.) The *zakat* proper, the general religious tax set at 2.5 per cent of accumulated wealth, which can be paid at any time during the year, is much less systematically collected. Muhammadijah bases much of its collection appeal to

* In 1954 NU began distributing meat on *Idul Adha* for the first time.
** Since these various Moslem taxes have, of course, no civil standing in Indonesia, they are purely voluntary.

the *ummat* on the grounds that contribution to the organization fulfills the *zakat* requirement at least in part. *Kijajis* have traditionally relied on the *zakat* from their villages to help support their *pondoks;* and nowadays political parties are beginning to regard the part of the *zakat* that is supposed to be contributed to the "Holy War" (in Java traditionally taken to mean the building of mosques, etc.) as legitimately employed to help finance their political campaigns. In any case, the payment of the *zakat* in its full form is sporadic at best around Modjokuto.

Charitable efforts aside, it is their school system which is the Muhammadijah pride and joy. Policy is made for the schools by a special education committee which includes almost all the major leaders of the organization. It is financed through contributions from the organization, through tuition fees (which are, however, quite low), and through underpaying the teachers rather markedly. As a result, the perennial problem the education committee faces is to get adequate teachers and hold them; and most of the struggles which go within the organization result from the differing interests of the teacher group among the membership, whose interest is in raising both standards and their salaries, and the trader group,* which is interested in making ends meet.

This conflict has been the dynamic force within Muhammadijah since its founding in Modjokuto. Since the original founders of the organization were for the most part traders, and teachers had to be imported from Djokjakarta and other large Muhammadijah centers (or local youths sent off there to study), there was always a native group and a "foreign" teacher group. As time passed, however, some of the teachers became more and more integrated into the local community; and today the leader of Masjumi and vice-chairman of Muhammadijah is a former teacher in the Muhammadijah high school who was originally imported from Djokjakarta, and the vice-chairman of Masjumi and chairman of Muhammadijah is a local Kudus-descended boy who was sent off to Muhammadijah schools in Djokjakarta to study. The traders still remain active, however, and the mediation between these two groups is still the main concern of the school committee.

Conservative versus Modern: A Balanced Opposition

TO sum up the over-all social organization of the *santri* community in Modjokuto, Masjumi-Muhammadijah on the one hand and Nahdatul Ulama on the other hand are the determinants of the main axis along which the Modjokuto *ummat* is subdivided. Almost without exception, every *santri* considers himself a "follower" of one or the other of these two groups and considers that the first important thing to learn about a stranger is whether

* With only five exceptions, all the members of Muhammadijah are either traders or school teachers; and most of the school teachers are teachers in the Muhammadijah schools. Not all teachers in the Muhammadijah schools, however, are members of the organization.

he is a *santri* at all, and, having ascertained that, whether he is "sympathetic" to Masjumi or NU.

The relation between the two groups being only somewhat hostile, the sense of differences only rarely gets intense enough to blot out the sense of commonality of religious belief throughout the whole *ummat,* a sense strengthened by the nearly universal animosity borne toward *santris* by non-*santris.* It seems that what one has here is a kind of implicit moiety organization based on religious commitment rather than kinship, in which a lesser hostility between two relatively balanced halves of a community acts, paradoxically, as a kind of integrated force to hold the group together in the face of rather more serious external threats to its unity. Thus one finds a kind of fluctuation in perception of the situation by the people involved, in which assertions of unity and solidarity of the entire *ummat* alternate with vigorous emphasis on the differences between its two halves.

The following note on a conversation with a PSII leader may be compared in this connection with earlier notes in which the differences between the various groups were emphasized:

> I went to see Atmilan again and asked him what the differences between PSII and other groups like Masjumi and NU were. He said there weren't any at all; they were all based on Islam. He said that it was all just a matter of roads and was just a result of different people in different parties. That is, some people were in one party because they followed certain leaders, but there were no differences in policy at all; they were all part of *ummat* Islam. I said that many people told me that there were differences. He replied that what they told me wasn't true. Some say NU is *kolot,* Muhammadijah *modèren,* PSII leftist, Masjumi rightist, but his opinion was that there was no difference. He said that it was all a matter of steering the automobile; many wanted to steer, so there had to be many parties. A kind of prima donna theory of Indonesian politics.

There is much to be said for such a theory, particularly in explaining otherwise unpredictable behavior on the part of certain power-hungry members of the elite; but it does little toward explaining the penetration of the two parties deep into the masses and the ever-increasing role they play in the non-political aspects of life among both leaders and followers. As time goes on, the political parties seem to be becoming more and more important as bases of village and town social organization among the *santris,* replacing the old geographical ties with ideological ones (a tendency present but rather less apparent among *abangans* or *prijajis*). Nahdatul Ulama, the purpose of which from the beginning, one leader informed me, was "to wake up the sleeping *kijajis,*" attempting to enclose the traditional religious social forms focusing around the *pondoks* within a modern political party structure with a minimum alteration of such forms; Masjumi-Muhammadijah, trying to replace the old forms by providing town-manufactured models of new possibilities: these are the basic social reference groups for the Modjokuto *santri.*

Chapter 14   The *Santri* Educational System

Abangan RELIGION, so ritualized and so tied to custom, needs no formal training to support it. It can be learned as almost everything else in a peasant's life is learned, casually and concretely, through following out examples set by others; and it persists on the basis of a constant rehearsal of its compacted dramas, woven as they are into the whole rhythm of social and cultural life. *Prijaji* mysticism demands training, but, in the absence of any concern for orthodoxy or any hostility from the society generally, elaborate formal organization of such training is hardly necessary; and, in fact, *prijaji* religious education is quite commonly almost autodidactic. By contrast, a religion which is at once doctrinal and important must almost necessarily rely upon a well-developed formal school system for its propagation and for its maintenance, and "true" Moslems are in a special position. The doctrinal complexity of their creed, its lack of close integration with some of the basic social forms and fundamental attitudes of peasant society, and the hostility to it on the part of most non-*santris* demand that there be a special and persistent effort made to indoctrinate those who wish to be its followers. Religious illiteracy and backsliding, neither of them even meaningful to *abangans,* are central problems for the *ummat,* and the Islamic school system is designed specifically to combat them.

Pondok: The Traditional Pattern

AT the center of the traditional school system lies the *pondok,* also sometimes called *pesantrèn.* A *pondok* consists of a teacher-leader, commonly a pilgrim (*hadji*), who is called a *kijaji,* and a group of male pupils, anywhere from

177

three or four to a thousand, called *santris*.* Traditionally, and still to an extent today, the *santris* live at the *pondok* in cloister-like dormitories, cook their own food, and wash their own clothes. They gain their sustenance by working in the fields of the *kijaji* or other leading Moslems of the community, by craftwork such as cloth-dyeing, cigarette-making, and tailoring, and by contributions of rice and money from their families at home. The *kijaji* is not paid, and the students pay no tuition; all the costs of the institution are borne by pious members of the *ummat* as part of the religious duties included under the *zakat,* the religious tax.

The *pondok* buildings, almost without exception located in the countryside, usually consist of a mosque (*mesdjid*), a house for the *kijaji,* and a set of dormitories for the *santris.* Classes are held in the mosque, where the *kijaji* chants passages from books of religious commentary (and, since the rise of Muhammadijah, increasingly from the Koran and Hadith themselves) and the *santris* echo him, line by line. If the *kijaji* understands Arabic, which is far from always the case, he may comment from time to time on the meaning of certain passages, the *santris* writing his comments in the margins of their books (in Arabic script). If he does not, he can use an Indonesian translation. In any case, it is not the content but the form which is of primary importance so far as the chanting proper is concerned.

The *kijaji* may hold such classes anywhere from one to five hours a day, but there is no required attendance by anyone. (Advanced students may lead the others if the *kijaji* is not present.) One goes if he wishes to, stays away if he does not want to attend. The *pondok* has no fixed schedule, and one may live there without even chanting at all if he so desires, so long as he earns his own keep and is not a behavior problem. People go at their own speed, learning as much or as little as seems necessary to them. When a book is completed one "graduates" for that book; and when a number of people have finished the same book, a ceremony called a *kataman* is held, at which *pentjak, gambus,* and *terbang* amusements are usually presented and various strength contests held. But there are no "grades" in *pondok* either in the sense of "classes" or of "marks," and one does not graduate from the school but merely leaves when one feels like it or has a need to.

Thus people wander in and out of a *pondok,* only having to gain the *kijaji*'s permission, which is easily enough obtained if one has a good reputation. Some stay two weeks, some ten years. Some students move around restlessly from one *pondok* to the next, often traveling great distances from home, spending some time here, some there. (Different *kijajis* often have different specialties. One is good on law, one on astronomy, one on philosophy, and so forth. During the Fast it is traditional for *santris* to spend the month at a different *pondok* from the one at which they have been normally staying, but this too is up to the individual.)

* Thus the term *santri* has a broad and a narrow meaning. In the narrow sense it means "a student in a religious school called a *pondok* or *pesantrèn*," the latter name being constructed on *santri* as a root and so meaning literally "a place for *santris*." In the broad and more common sense of the term *santri* refers to a member of that part of the Javanese population who take their Islam seriously—who pray, go to mosque on Friday and so on.

Although in some ways *pondoks* remind one of monasteries, *santris* are not monks. Married men are not allowed as *santris*, not because there is anything unholy in marriage but merely because the duties and responsibilities of family life conflict with the unregulated pattern of life characteristic of a *pondok*. Both divorced men and widowers may become *santris*. Old bachelors, insofar as there are any in Java, do not usually remain in *pondoks*. (Most *santris* are between the ages of twelve and twenty-five, although I have known some as young as six and as old as thirty-five.) Since being a *santri* is not a life's work, middle-aged or old men in *pondoks,* except as *kijajis,* are decidedly rare.

What one has, then, is not the strictly ruled monastery system of medieval Catholicism, but a system in which each elderly religious scholar is settled into his own academy,* while students come and go more or less casually (although in the *pondok* they are expected to stay there and minimize contact with the secular world), supporting themselves by working, doing as much chanting as they wish, discussing religion with their fellows. There is a marked tendency for *santris* to settle down after a time to one *pondok* and become a follower of its *kijaji*, thus often giving a religious sect atmosphere to *pondoks,* but the rigid organization of Catholic monastery life is notable for its absence. A *santri* is not an apprentice saint; he is merely a young man becoming adult in a religious environment, growing to maturity with the droning chants of Islam echoing in his ears.

But the chants began to echo long before he entered the *pondok*. The typical sequence of religious education of the village *santri* boy begins at about the age of six, with his mother telling him stories from the Moslem tradition (or the Javanese tradition, adapted to Islam), informing him that God created the world and will punish him if he misbehaves, and perhaps teaching him a short prayer or two. At eight or so, sometimes younger, the boy begins accompanying his father (or older brother) to the village mosque, where slowly he learns to imitate his father's actions and memorizes a few of the set phrases used in the praying. But he is not expected to be deeply serious. Islamic services are generally informal enough so that a child running around and paying little attention to what the adults are doing is not very disruptive; even today almost any mosque will have a few children sitting around or playing quietly while adults pray, oblivious of them. Often groups of children are gathered together at one person's house or at several people's houses in turn and taught simple chants.

When the boy is ten or twelve and seems self-reliant, he is finally allowed to go off somewhere to *pondok,* returning home from time to time for short periods (and for circumcision), finally settling down in his own home when his parents have arranged a marriage for him. From then on he does his daily prayers, goes to mosque on Fridays, contributes to the support of *pondoks* if he can afford to, and visits his old *kijajis* from time to time for advice, spiritual counsel, and even for a little curing:

* *Pondoks* are usually declared to be "the property of God" under the rules for Islamic religious foundations (*wakap*).

He (Usman, Nazir's half-modernist *kijaji* son) said that people often went to older *kijajis* for advice, and he mentioned a *kijaji* in Bragang who gives advice to lots of people. He said that in addition to the directly religious aspects of the *pondok* two other things were always associated with the *pondok* in the old days: *pentjak* (the fighting dance) and the *kijaji* as a curer. Mainly the *kijajis* cured people through the use of herbs, but they also prayed. Praying was very important, for the *kijaji* did not want to let the patient think it was just the herbs that cured him and not God, lest the patient become materialistic and think all he needed was the herbs and not God. The way it worked was this: The patient came to the *kijaji*. The *kijaji* would then pray, and while he was praying there would appear in his mind the diagnosis and treatment, which herb to use and where to get it. (He said many *kijaji* grew all kinds of herbs in their gardens, but sometimes the herb had to be secured from a great distance.) After the patient had got the herb the *kijaji* would then pray over it to make it effective. Usman seemed to think curing by *kijajis* was entirely legitimate from the Islamic point of view and quoted to me an American doctor who had said that some sicknesses are of the spirit and must be cured by spiritual means. . . .

The *kijajis*—curers, counselors, teachers, and scholars—were the men of top prestige within the *ummat*. Mostly they were sons of farmers wealthy enough to have sent them on the pilgrimage—or more commonly, to have taken them. An old man of sixty-five who had saved for forty years, burying his money in silver coins under the dirt floor of his house, departing on the pilgrimage with his young son or grandson was a common sight in the years before the war. They might be descendants of a long line of *kijajis* and *hadjis* whose steady accumulation of land over the years had transformed them into small-scale landlords. Religious status and wealth coalesced to produce a class of mutually independent religious intellectuals who both determined doctrine and wielded a social power no less important for being informal and indirect.

He said *kijajis*, when they correct someone's (i.e., a layman's) point of view, never tell him he is wrong but do it by telling a story of long ago from which the individual who is wrong can see that he is wrong without being told so directly. I said: "Don't the *kijajis* sometimes disagree among themselves?" He replied, "Yes, this is so. Sometimes England, France, and America don't agree. Isn't that so—on small things even though basically they are united?" I agreed. "That is the way it is with *kijajis*," he said. "They often disagree over details, but on main issues agree." I said, "Well, how does the layman know which is right?" "He just chooses the *kijaji* he respects and follows him," he replied. He said that some *kijajis* have very great influence because of their learning, and thus people follow them rather than lesser *kijajis* who oppose them.

Langgar and Mosque: The Local *Santri* Commmunity

THE *kijaji* and his *pondok,* then, have formed, and to an extent still form the nucleus of rural Islamic social structure and the climax of *kolot* culture.

Combined on the one hand with the pilgrimage and on the other with the institution of the *langgar* (small prayer-houses, usually attached to individual homes), this part school, part temple, part religious brotherhood both related the Javanese *ummat* to the wider Islamic world and defined the nature of orthodoxy for it. Through the returned *hadji-kijaji,* the concepts of orthodoxy current in the world capital of Islam filtered down to the mass of the *ummat,* first to his *santris,* then to the rest of the population through the mosques and *langgars,* which were the real terminal points of the communication network.

A *langgar* is the same as a mosque except that it is smaller, it is often privately owned (although some *langgars* are public foundations, as are nearly all mosques), and Friday service is not conducted in it. Usually *langgars* are separate buildings to one side of the house of the owner, but sometimes even a room in one's house, from which one has removed all the furniture, may be consecrated as a *langgar.* (As in a mosque, one must enter a *langgar* shoeless; and, of course, one should not conduct secular activities in a *langgar* even if it is but a room in one's house.)

In a *santri* neighborhood or village men will gather in the *langgars* an hour or so each evening after sunset prayer, or perhaps for two or three hours on Thursday evening to pray and chant the chants they learned at *pondok.* As there is generally a *langgar* in such neighborhoods for every twenty-five or thirty households—usually owned by one of the richer peasants—there occurs a crystallization out among the *ummat* attached to the village's mosque of smaller congregations of thirty people or so, made up mainly of older men who have studied at *pondoks* and returned to marry and their younger sons who have not yet gone off to the religious schools. (One does not, however, have to go to the *langgar* nearest one's house; nor is it necessary to attend with absolute regularity, any more than it is at a *pondok.*)

Such was the religious division of labor in the rural *ummat:* the rich man's son went to Mecca to discover what the meaning and form of Islam were in fact supposed to be;* adolescent boys exposed themselves to the *kijaji*'s learning in schools supported by the members of the entire community; adult men chanted in their *langgars* and instructed their women and young children in the bare essentials of Islam,** and contributed what they could spiritually and materially toward maintaining Islam:

> According to Islam, he (an urban Moslem who, however, grew up in a small village) said that there are rich and there are poor and there are people in between, and this is God's way; but the rich and poor have different duties to God. The rich must give money to take care of the poor.

* That most of these pilgrims actually derived their notions of orthodoxy from their experience in Javanese *pondoks* and their childhood around Javanese *langgars,* behaving in Mecca more like tourists than scholars, and that most pilgrims returned to remain mere *hadjis* and not *kijajis*—honored for having gone on the pilgrimage but not necessarily respected for their religious learning or wisdom—are true, but beside the point.
** The women, though unveiled and in no way secluded, were nevertheless but marginal participants in the religious life: they had but to do the prayers, wear head-shawls in the street, and look to their husbands for religious leadership.

They must pay the religious tax, give to charity; this is a bounden duty and they have no choice if they are good Moslems. They cannot forget the poor. They must teach them, help them, support them. It is they who must give money to build mosques, *pondoks,* and so forth. The poor have a lighter duty to God. They must pray, be patient, and accept help from those who have more money than they and work hard. But they cannot be expected to contribute to building mosques or *pondoks.* He said he himself had it easy. If a mosque was being built, he was not asked to give money, just to contribute a little labor, painting or something of that sort. Yet he wasn't so poor that he could no nothing but receive. Yes, he said, chuckling, he had it easy; and he seemed to think that was the best state to be in—not rich enough to be too heavily taxed and not poor enough to suffer want and have to accept charity. He said that all he had to be responsible for was the welfare of his wife and his children, while the rich man had to be responsible for more than that—for poor children, for example, and a really poor man received help to take care of his family.

That this *noblesses oblige* pattern operated so perfectly is to be doubted, as the same informant in almost the next breath complained of how the *kijajis* used to embezzle the religious tax, but the integration of roles within the rural *ummat* does seem to have been fairly stable and to some degree still is.

Tarékat: Traditional Islamic Mysticism

MYSTICISM, another phenomenon of rural religious life, cut across the segregation of the unmarried apprentice from the married journeyman *santri* and brought adult men, especially aged ones, back into *pondoks* of a rather special kind. Mysticism, under the banner of Sufism, was, of course, rife in Mecca until Wahhabi reformers put it to flight in the twenties; and for many Javanese pilgrims, who grew up in a society in which mysticism has always been a characteristic theme, the ecstatic practices of the Sufis were immediately attractive. There were often secret mystical societies within the *pondoks,* esoteric fraternities in which only a small minority of the *santris* participated but which seem to have had important informal power within the *pondoks* somewhat as exclusive university clubs often have. Spiced with strength testing, flesh mortification, and extended fasts, these sects within a sect must have approached in intensity some of the Arabic mystical orders in the Middle East and North Africa, but as they are extinct now and were secret then it is difficult to find out very much about them. There was also some mystical practice in the *langgars,* people counting their beads for hours at a stretch. But perhaps the main form which mysticism took was that of brotherhoods of aged men, grouped around a *kijaji* who was expert in the science, forming a kind of old man's *pondok,* although often the "*santris*" went home between sessions and some younger men participated.

I asked him (a modernist, and so quite hostile to Sufi practices) about the *kijaji* who died this morning. I said, "Why was he called a *kijaji,* and did he have a *pondok?*" He replied that the man was a mystical *kijaji* who had (in a village adjoining the town) a *pondok* not of students but of very old men (about thirty at any one time) fifty or sixty years old and up who did nothing but sit around all day and worship—praying, repeating the Confession of Faith maybe a thousand times at a sitting, just going out to the toilet and then coming back to go on again, just chanting and praying, often starting on Tuesday and going straight on till Friday with only the shortest of breaks to eat, sleep, and eliminate. He said that thus this *"kijaji"* was concerned with mystical science and headed a mystical brotherhood. He said that this man didn't know anything about the Moslem law. He, Ashari (the informant), knew more; and he had talked to the *kijaji* once and asked him what kind of a *kijaji* he was not to know about the law. He said that the old men would come there from their homes for a month or so at a time, bringing their own food, sharing everything together, and engaged in this mystical repeating, and preparing for death.

Such mysticism in Java is called *tarékat.* Although several different Sufi sects have penetrated Indonesia, the two of major importance in East Java seem to have been the *Kodirijah* (*Qadiriyya*) and *Naksabandi* (*Naqshbandi*) orders, both of which are considered orthodox because the participants do not abandon the regular pillars. They usually operate on the basis of a four-stage theory of mystical advancement: *saréngat,* the carrying out of the usual duties of Islam; *tarékat,* which means special mystical techniques; *chakékat,* which means "truth" or "reality"; and *makrifat,* which means gnosis. The typical image is searching for pearls. For the pearl-gatherer the boat is the *saréngat,* the rowing actions he performs are the *tarékat,* the pearl itself is the *chakékat,* and the knowledge he has that this is indeed a pearl—his ability to tell a true pearl from a false one—is *makrifat,* the goal of the mystic.

The method employed is the counting of beads; and I never heard around Modjokuto of any more spectacular techniques, although the bead-counting is inevitably connected with fasting and staying awake. Counting beads is done with a string of 99 beads called a *tasbéh* marked off into three groups of 33 grey beads each by an interspersed white bead. The mystic holds the *tasbéh* in his hand and moves the beads along, repeating silently in his mind a holy phrase such as *Allahu Akbar* ("God is most Great") until he has said it 33 times (i.e., arrived at the white bead), at which point he shifts to another phrase. The same thing can be done without beads by counting three counts on each finger, thus giving 30 counts on two full hands, to which one more finger is added for 33.

Mystic orders of this sort have declined in numbers since the rise of modernism, which vigorously opposed them, but they have not entirely disappeared. There was one in the village in which I lived, and there were said to be several in villages up in the mountains towards the east. There was a very large one with a reputed 900 members, around thirty miles to the north, and a new one had opened in the next district to the west since the war. But compared to the situation in the years before the rise of the modernists, when there were at least a dozen such *pondoks* in the Modjokuto area, it is clear that Sufism has been severely weakened in Java. One of the most significant factors in the loss of strength by the mystic sects in Java was the Wahhabi purification of Mecca under Ibn Saud in the twenties:

> When I asked him (an old *hadji* but not a *kijaji*) about the Sufi *kijaji* near me, he said that the purpose of this man's teachings was to help the students get it really embedded in their hearts that God exists. . . . He said that the students for their part hoped to receive blessings in return for their piety and their submission to the *kijaji,* while the *kijaji* wanted the students to fear him and be completely obedient to him. The students believed that if they committed a sin they could ask the *kijaji* to pray for them and the *kijaji* would pray to the Prophet Muhammad and Muhammad would pray to God. He said that when he was in Mecca the first time, in 1921, there was a place with a small pile of stones in the middle of the room, and men came there every Tuesday and counted beads, but when he got back there again in 1930 the Wahhabis had come in under Ibn Saud and cleaned them all out. Ibn Saud told them that their practices and beliefs were not from the Koran and Hadith, and challenged them to prove that they were, within three months, or face execution. So they fled Mecca.

Pondok to *Sekolah:* The *Santri* Educational System in Modjokuto

THE triumph of Ibn Saud gave a positive jolt to other aspects of Indonesian reform too, most particularly the school movement, which made rapid progress after 1924. Of all the reforms the modernists introduced, the idea of schools designed on a Western model was probably the most bitterly resented by the *kolot,* and the most strongly resisted; for by striking at the *pondok* system such schools were striking at the very roots of *kijaji* power. But time, youth, and the "spirit of the age" were on the side of the modernists; and by careful construction of their program they were able to weaken the effectiveness of the accusation of being "infidel" which the *kijajis* had traditionally directed at colonial "native schools" and now turned upon them. They proposed that schools be set up on the Dutch model with Western teaching methods, blackboards, rulers, textbooks and all the other appurtenances of Western education, but argued that they should still remain under private Islamic auspices. They insisted that both sexes should be educated, but agreed that they must be separated. They argued for a regularized class schedule of so many hours a day, but agreed to make Friday rather than Sunday the vacation day. And, although they insisted on teaching modern subjects by modern methods, they included Islam as a modern subject and made it an integral part of the curriculum.

As a result, in the Modjokuto of 1953–1954 the idea of the school, if not the form, had penetrated nearly everywhere, and one found a whole range of types of educational institutions: pure uncompromised *pondoks* which gave no quarter to modern educational theories; mystic brotherhoods heedless of the general disapproval of them, even by some of the milder conservatives; *pondoks* which included rough-and-ready approximations to Western-type schools within them, in which older *santris* taught arithmetic, the reading of Latin characters, and a little general science to younger ones; conservative-run schools which, although generally approximating the Western pattern, still concerned themselves with religious teaching of a fairly traditional kind for as much as three-quarters of their time; and modernist schools in which religion, although still important, took up less than half the curriculum and was taught in the same manner as any other subject.

The *Pondok* Pattern in Modjokuto

BEFORE the Second World War the Modjokuto landscape was dotted with *pondoks* large and small. Different informants give different statistics, but it seems certain that around 1930 there were at least six large *pondoks* and many small ones in the immediate Modjokuto area; and, of course, one of the largest and most famous in all Java was some twenty miles to the north. (Almost all NU leaders and a few of the Masjumi leaders have spent some time at this *pondok;* in the thirties there seem to have been twenty-five or thirty people from Modjokuto there all the time.) Now there are only two large *pondoks* and eleven smaller ones, the large ones having about two hundred and three hundred students respectively, the smaller ones averaging around sixty. The layout of the two large *pondoks,* one of which is half a mile east of town and the other, the larger, four miles west, is about the same and typifies the traditional *pondok* "campus": a large mosque in the center, surrounded by six or seven dormitories, and a *kijaji*'s house off to one side.

The dormitories are contributed by the various *ummat* around Java for the use of young men from that area (although others use them too, if there is room, and there are some "general" dormitories). At the larger of the two big *pondoks* most of the dormitories were built with contributions from *santri* communities in Central Java (Banjumas, Tjilitjap, Solo, Kedu), and, consequently, most of the students are from those areas rather than from Modjokuto. At the smaller of the two, the dormitories and the students are predominantly from East Java, but again not from the immediate Modjokuto area but from the north and east.

The dormitories, the newest of which cost Rp 10,000 and was completed while I was in Modjokuto, were built by the student *santris* themselves and are designed in a severe cloister style, with a covered porch running the whole length of the building and a series of small, bare, doorless cells opening out onto it, in each of which four or five boys sleep crowded together on mats spread on the floor. At both these *pondoks,* and evidently at most others in Java, the custom of working for one's living has largely died out, although there is still a little of it, and most *santris* are supported by contributions from home. But all housecleaning, cooking, and clothes-washing is still done by the *santris* themselves (people eating when they wish to, either alone or in groups of two or three), and the secular organization of the *pondok* is run, largely independently of the *kijaji*, by a board elected from among them. Even admission and expulsion are largely in the hands of the students themselves. It is little wonder that the main defense the *kolot* make of the *pondok* system, in the face of modernist charges that it is antiquated, impractical, and asocial, is that, although it may be all that, it is also an excellent model for that ideal to which Indonesia's revolutionary battlecry commits her—freedom.

At both of the large *pondoks* the chanting hours in the mosque (led either by the *kijaji* himself or one of his advanced students, the larger *pondok* having two *kijajis*) are from 7–12 A.M., 1–3 P.M., 4–5 P.M., and 8–11 P.M. Since the five prayers are additional, it is clear that anyone who followed all the "courses" woud be leading a very intensive religious life. In actual practice, almost no one chants all day. People just wander in and out of the mosque at will, joining in the chanting and noting the *kijaji's* comments when it suits them or when he is going over something in which they have a particular interest.

The typical subjects "taught" (i.e., chanted, with occasional commentaries or translations by the *kijaji*) are *fiqh, tasawuf, tauchid, nahwu, falaq, achlaq, tarich, tafsir,* and *hadith. Fiqh* is the study of religious duties and has two divisions: that concerned with the correct manner of performance of the pillars —the prayers, pilgrimage, fast, and so on; and that concerned with personal relationships—marriage law, criminal law, commercial law. *Tasawuf* ("Sufism") is most characteristic of mystic *pondoks* because it is concerned with Islamic mystical philosophy, with the "meaning of religion"; and many orthodox *kijajis* consider it somewhat dangerous to teach, particularly to younger students, because it is difficult and because too much philosophy or mysticism in the heads of the young tends to lead to heresy. Nevertheless, all of the *pondoks* in the Modjokuto area teach a little of it. *Tauchid* is concerned with Islamic logic and theology; *nahwu* with Arabic grammar. *Falaq* consists of astronomical methods for calculating the times of the prayers, the fast, and so forth. *Achlaq* is ethics, often included under *tasawuf. Tarich* is Islamic history. *Tafsir* is religious commentary, either on the Koran or the Hadith; and under *hadith* is included the scholarly methods by which the *hadiths* are substantiated as being valid. Modern-influenced *pondoks* sometimes add direct reading and chanting of the Koran and Hadith. Of the fourteen *pondoks* in the Modjokuto area, nine teach only *tasawuf, fiqh,* and the Koran, while the two large ones include most of the above. It is rather doubtful, however, that, except in the case of very keen students, much content of any but the most general and fundamental sort gets communicated to the *santris;* although many of them learn to chant with great skill and artistry a beautiful language of which they have no comprehension.

Both of the large *pondoks* now include schools taught by the older *santris* for the younger ones—not because the *kijajis* want them or even approve of them, but because the students themselves demand them.

Kijaji Chotib, from Pleset (a nearby village), was sitting there a while. He has a *pondok* in his place at Pleset, but it is very small. After he left, H. Zakir said: "He is very, very clever. He is the only *kajaji* around who has memorized the entire Koran perfectly. (He is also on the NU Governing Board.) But he is also very *kolot* and so he is losing out; his *pondok* isn't successful; he isn't getting anywhere with it. The trouble is he sticks to the old method exclusively—chant and echo—and does no teaching, and the youth these days won't accept this any more. You have to have the school pattern now, at least to some extent. Even the conservative youth no longer will accept the old *pondok* pattern in pure form, and so Kijaji Chotib is losing out, even though he is very clever." Zakir said that he had told Chotib this a number of times, but that the latter wanted to stick to the old pattern.

Most *kijajis* have enough contact with the altered reality of modern Java to permit at least some school-type teaching, although even such schools are rather rudimentary and irregular in their organization.

(The informant is relating his experiences during a four-year stay at a large *pondok* in the next district south of Modjokuto, but the pattern is identical with the large *pondoks* in Modjokuto.) In addition to the chanting there was a regular religious school in which only religious subjects were offered, which the older *santris* taught. One chose whether he wanted to attend the school or just chant, but if one started with the classes he was expected to stay with them or drop out altogether, not just come in and out as one could with the chanting. For those participating in the school there was a discussion hour each evening on the previous lesson in the subject to be taught the next day. E.g., if tomorrow the religious classes were in *tauchid* and *fiqh,* one would discuss the last class in each of these subjects, trying to get things straight. Problems the students could not solve themselves (the older teachers not being present at these meetings) they would ask the teacher about the next day. The school ran on an irregular schedule, information simply being passed around, say the day before, when there was going to be a class. In addition to the *pondok* (chanting) and the school (all religious), there were also some general classes given by teachers selected both from among the *santris* and from people outside who had special talents. The courses taught when he was there were civics, English, psychology, education, and arithmetic. To take the whole set one had to pay Rp 2.50. But there were no organized classes; one just took what one wished, and none of the various branches were coordinated with one another.

Madrasah: The Conservative School in Modjokuto

IT can be seen from the foregoing that the idea of the school—a graded, time-regulated, content-stressing educational institution—has penetrated, in the face of *kijaji* hostility, into the darkest reaches of the ungraded, casual, form-emphasizing *pondok*. The next interval along the scale toward the secularized school is represented by the NU schools which one now finds in almost every heavily *santri* village. These schools, independent of any *pondok* or *kijaji* connections, are typical NU compromises with modernism, and as such are still not always accepted by the most conservative. Although NU is a conservative organization, it must be remembered that in a wider context its efforts have been toward reform; the very idea of secular organization of the *ummat,* even to protect tradition, is in itself a radical idea in some *kolot* eyes; as is the notion of a school no matter how heavily religious.

> In the afternoon I spoke with Kosin, who lives on Merapi street in the big house with the *langgar* attached. He said that his father, who has been dead since the Dutch time, was a big trader in tobacco here before the war. . . . He was a *hadji* and one of the richest men in town. Everybody, said Kosin proudly, knew his father. His father was a very *kolot santri,* bitterly opposed to Muhammadijah and didn't even approve of NU. . . . His father was illiterate and opposed to school and sent all his children to *pondok,* and Kosin went to the one to the east of Modjokuto for eight years, living there all the time. The *kijaji* was the same one as now. Kosin gave the usual picture of *pondok* life—mostly chanting books and memorizing what they meant by listening to and noting the *kijaji*'s translations. Books on law, inheritance, family life, and so on were all to be memorized and their meaning noted. After a while—eight years—NU opened its school in the *kauman* in Modjokuto, and Kosin (who is now in Masjumi) went there for a few years—against his father's will. He said that in those days no *kolot santri* would think of sending his children to the government schools, and the schools of the Islamic organizations, which were just beginning, weren't very well received either. I asked him where he would send his child later (now aged two); and he said that there was a difference of opinion between him and his wife. His wife, *kolot,* wanted to send the child to *pondok,* but he, *moderen,* wanted to send him to school. He said that he didn't know how it would come out later.

NU schools are called *madrasah,* which means "religious school" in contrast to *pondok,* at least in Java. There were eleven such *madrasahs* in the Modjokuto subdistrict in 1952 with a claimed total attendance of over 1,500, of whom about a third were girls, and a teaching faculty of 37, of whom three were women. (As they often are rather fly-by-night affairs, their number is likely to fluctuate somewhat from month to month.) All but two of these were three-year schools, the other two being five years. (Government elementary schools, called *sekolah,* are three or six, mostly the latter.) Eighty per cent of the curriculum was devoted to religion, taught pretty much in the old *pondok* manner but with a little more effort to explain its meaning, and 20 per cent to "general studies," by which was meant reading and writing (in Latin characters) and simple arithmetic. Although these schools were nominally NU, they were, in line with the very loose central organization of that party, actually independent and autonomous under the direction of the leaders who supervised them and who neither asked for nor received much assistance or advice from the NU Governing Board in town. As they were almost entirely locally financed as well, their self-containment was complete and the desperate efforts of the more modern town leaders to raise their standards and improve their organization met with the usual difficulties.

In an effort to accomplish something along these lines, the Modjokuto unit of NU founded in 1953 a *mualimin* or normal school, designed to train teachers for the various *madrasahs*. Since it took its students (of which there were 24 in 1953, there being two teachers) from among the graduates of the grade-school *madrasahs,* so all the students were village boys (no girls), most of whom had been to *pondok* for a while as well. The *mualimin* course is three years, one-half religion, one-half general studies, after which the graduates can go back and teach in the *madrasahs*. The hope, obviously, is to train a group of somewhat more modern teachers who can then "bore from within" in reforming the village schools toward more "progressive" methods, undoubtedly a more effective method than putting pressure on the *kolot* supervisors of the school directly.

The *mualimin,* which is located in the Modjokuto *kauman,* gives six 45-minute classes a day for six days a week (Friday being a holiday). One of the two teachers, (a "graduate" of a five-year stay in the NU headquarters *pondok* north of Modjokuto) teaches all the religious subjects; and the other (a graduate of an evidently fairly modern NU school in the large northern port city, Semarang) teaches all the general subjects. The religious subjects include the typical *pondok* stand-bys—*fiqh, tauchid,* and so on, but no *tasawuf* because it is "too advanced"—with something of a novel emphasis on *achlaq,* or ethics, often with more of a Javanese than an Islamic quality to it.

> (The informant is the teacher concerned.) Ethics is taken from general life, from the *hadith,* and from Islamic philosophy books such as that of Ali Fikri, a classical Arab writer. This ethical teaching is concerned with "politeness" (having in Javanese a rather wider meaning than in English—more like "proper behavior") to God and between human beings. For example, one tells the students that to get angry or say something in a "hard" way to someone is wrong. About secrets—if one knows someone's secret, one should keep it to oneself. For example, if A knows B has a big debt he mustn't tell anyone about it. I asked, "Do you mean that if A knows B is going to steal, A shouldn't say anything?" He said, no, he meant things which are slightly sinful and that people wanted to keep hidden, such as debts and so forth. If a man fights with his wife and one knows it, one should not tell other people. He said that there was a *hadith* on this. A friend of the Prophet told the Prophet that he was about to commit an indiscretion with a girl. The Prophet said to him: "Are you crazy? Why do you tell me about this? You should keep it to yourself." The point is that one should not divulge either one's own secrets or those of other people; if one is going to do something wrong, one should keep it quiet. Another thing one shouldn't do is scare or startle people—for example, startling someone at night by wearing a mask. The ethics teacher also teaches that people with more than enough food should share it with those who don't have enough.

The secular subjects taught are geometry, algebra, English, Indonesian, pedagogy, physical education, general science, accounting, and geography. The total budget for the school is about Rp 150 a month, of which Rp 100 is donated by the NU Governing Board, the rest coming from the very nominal tuition paid by the students. (Officially, the fee is Rp 10.00 a month, but since none of the students can afford this they actually pay only Rp 2.50.) The entire budget goes for the salaries of the two teachers; other needs—benches, blackboards, and supplies—are met by irregular donations of the NU membership. (The building and grounds were donated to NU by two rich *hadjis* before the war, at which time it housed the first NU *madrasah* in the subdistrict.) Seventy-five rupiahs a month is not a living wage, but both of the teachers are peasants with a little land of their own, and they are given their noon meal each day by the chairman of the school board, a fairly well-off cigarette manufacturer. I attended classes now and then at this school, and the following extract from my notes gives a sense of what the *madrasahs* are like:

> I met Cholip, the "general studies" teacher of the NU *mualimin,* and went off with him to sit in on his classes. . . . There were 20 students present, mostly 18 to 20 years old, some of them perhaps a little younger. . . . Since only two or three students had books (which cost from five to eight rupiahs each and are hard to find), Cholip spent the first hour or so writing down the text of the textbooks word for word on the board, and the students copied it down. (The subject was botany.) He evidently tired of this, and so for the second hour he read word for word, slowly, so that they could copy from his dictation the content of a book on zoology (he had reached page 7 of a 105-page book) a passage about sea lions, something called "sea dogs," and so on. It was straight description of the odd animals and fish and classifications of them—nothing else, and there were no pictures. (The textbooks they were using were mimeographed and had only a very few drawings.) This rather non-functional information must have been somewhat incomprehensible to the students. The few who had textbooks had nothing to do but just sit there, which they did, sometimes chatting quietly with other students; the others just copied and copied and copied. After the zoology, the teacher read from a book a set of questions for them to answer, and then the class was over.

It is plain from this that, despite the change in external form, these educational institutions have not moved very far away from the traditional pattern in which the teacher reads from a book he only slightly comprehends to students who comprehend it less, with now and then a clarifying comment added.

The Modern Religious School in Modjokuto

THE next interval on the scale from *pondok* to *sekolah* (secular school) is occupied by the old Sarekat Islam school, now operating under the imposing title of Islamic Educational and Pedagogic Foundation (Balai Pendidikan Pengadjaran Islam) but known generally as BPPI and familiarly as "the Arab school." This is a six-year elementary school with 188 students (tuition: Rp 2.50 a month) and five teachers, headed by a nephew of H. Nazir, the old SI leader, and is located in the Modjokuto *kauman* directly behind the mosque. Only two of the teachers are graduates of teachers' schools, and salaries run Rp 60 a month. This is not a living wage, but all of the teachers have some outside source of income.

Ruslam (brother of a BPPI teacher) said that the head of BPPI got only Rp 80 a month and the teachers Rp 60, and that they taught for love, not for money; they had to have a "large spirit." He admitted that they couldn't live on this; he said the head had a little rice-land of his own and the teachers were mostly young men still living at home. Muhammadijah used to be this way, but now they were more efficient in collecting money and could pay their teachers more, although it was still far less than what the teachers in the government schools got. . . .

The course pattern is similar to that in the NU elementary schools except that instead of being 80 per cent religion and 20 per cent general, the proportions are 40 per cent religion and 60 per cent general. The teaching evidently is comparatively good, since of 16 sixth-graders who took the government final examination, seven passed. (NU *madrasah* graduates would not even attempt to take it.) As BPPI is the oldest private school in Modjokuto and was, before the revolution, one of the three seven-year elementary schools in town which taught general subjects in the Dutch language (the other two being non-*santri* private schools), it is not only deeply entrenched within the Modjokuto *ummat* but also has had a longer time in which to develop and perfect its program. It is still considered the *santri* elementary school *par excellence*.

But, as SI, now PSII, has shrunk in size, much of the vitality and spirit of the old days has disappeared and hardened into a conservative modernism, dreaming of the victories of the past, and most of the younger teachers in the group are dissatisfied.

Rasid (a teacher in the school) said there was quite a bit of strain between the teachers in the school and PSII proper, particularly its school committee (headed by H. Zakir and including all the older leaders), because the committee paid almost no attention to the school and wouldn't let go of any money. He said the committee never gave the school any money. It was hard to get them to even repair the building; and as for books—well, the school committee considered that its duty concerned just the building and the desks, and didn't worry about books, teachers, and so on. In 1951 three of the five teachers quit because the party wouldn't give them any money for the school. He denied that this action had been a strike but did admit that it had been an expression of their dissatisfaction. He said that he did not participate much in PSII itself, because it was a monopoly of the old guard; in that the "younger group" stayed around the school and had pretty much given up any ideas of doing much with PSII . . . (Rasid was about thirty.) He compared their situation with Muhammadijah, where he said the school committee people were much more understanding, and the relation between the parent organization and the teachers was pretty good.*

* It must be remembered that to a certain extent the Modjokuto situation is a particular one, so that comments about the Modjokuto branches of national organizations should not be taken to be necessarily characteristic, except in a rather broad sense, of these organizations throughout Java or on the national level. In another town, for example, one might find PSII much more active and Muhammadijah less so, depending upon the accidents of local leadership, history, and so on. The general distinctions between *kolot* and *modèren* that I have drawn would hold, I think, almost everywhere in Java, but the details of their institutionalization would naturally vary rather widely.

But the young teachers keep struggling to improve the school despite their frustration. (In order to escape from the local pressures, they have been trying to get BPPI set up independently with direct relationships to PSII's central school division in Djakarta rather than working through their own chapter, but they have not yet been successful.)

Rasid said that the teachers had introduced two reforms this year, both over opposition from the older PSII people. First, religion is now taught in Indonesian rather than in Arabic as it used to be, because the children couldn't understand the Arabic. Of course they still read the Koran in Arabic, but the language of instruction is now Indonesian in all subjects, general or religious, not Indonesian in general subjects and Arabic in religious ones as before. Second, BPPI is now closed Sundays rather than Fridays. This was very much opposed by the Arabs particularly, who said they would take their children out of BPPI if the change went in. It did go in, but they didn't take their children out of BPPI because they knew no other school would take them. (The dynamic Arab children are notorious as behavior problems in the more genteel atmosphere of Javanese schools, and, with the exception of BPPI, most schools refuse to accept them because "they behave like animals.") The argument was that if the children were off on Sundays they would be going to church and becoming Christians. Rasid thought this pretty asinine, but said it was hard to change anything in PSII in Modjokuto, the other men are so conservative.

As BPPI fairly well fulfills the *santri* elementary school need within the town (and the need of the modernist element in the villages: of the 188 students, about 130 are from the countryside), Muhammadijah's effort is mainly directed to the high school level, although they do have an elementary school which is having a fairly difficult time in the face of BPPI competition.

(This is a transcript of a report on a Muhammadijah school committee meeting by another member of the project.) The elementary school seems to be withering on the vine. First grade, 10 pupils; second, 16; third, 10; fourth, 20; and fifth and sixth, none (a function of the time when the school was reopened after the revolution—i.e., four years ago). Now there is no teacher for the first year, and also there are too few pupils in the class for a full-time first-year teacher. What to do? In general, the school is dwindling in size, and all but about twenty of the pupils are from the (Muhammadijah) orphanage, this last being a fairly stable population which is getting older. Anyway, what to do this year with the first class? They don't want to force the children into another school. In the first place, the orphanage arrangement with the people who put the children in there is that they will go to a Muhammadijah school, and they don't want to go back on this. But they don't want the few outside children to suffer for the orphans' good either. . . . Also, it wouldn't be possible to find places for them all in the government schools anyway. It would be easy to get them into BPPI, but this would involve a surrender of their principles, for that is a different "ideology" (*tudjuan*—literally, "direction") which has too much religion; Muhammadijah emphasizes general education as against the NU and PSII religious emphasis. In the end they decided to keep the school going and spread the teachers out.

Muhammadijah also runs a kindergarten for pre-school children, which, from my observation, has almost no religious character at all and is attended by children of *santris* and non-*santris* alike, and a strictly religious school, called *diniah,* with 80 students, all girls, and three teachers.

> I asked what was taught in the *diniah* and she (a teacher there) said mainly religion, . . . because the children get "general studies" in the regular Muhammadijah schools in the mornings. . . . The religious teaching is all set forth for her in a little book issued by the Central Governing Board of Muhammadijah in Djokjakarta. The parts of religion which are taught are *achlaq, fiqh,* the Hadith, and the Koran. Muhammadijah emphasizes in its teaching of the Koran that the students should understand what they read. It is better to be able to read and understand a few pages than to be able to recite the whole book with no understanding of the content. This is the big difference between Muhammadijah and other groups. . . .

But it is its high school which Muhammadijah regards as the heart of its program. The Sekolah Menengah Bawah Muhammadijah—"Muhammadijah Lower Middle School"—is comparable to our junior high school, consisting of grades seven, eight, and nine, and teaching subjects similar to those taught in our junior high schools. A summary of the distribution of the 232-hour weekly teaching load borne by the staff of nine teachers (two of them women) gives a picture of the character of the curriculum and an excellent indication of the over-all education policy under which Muhammadijah operates:

	hours
Indonesian (i.e., reading, writing, and speaking Malay, the Indonesian national language)	41
Algebra	24
Religious Ethics (i.e., moral instruction based on Islam)	21
Geometry	19
English	18
History	16
Chemistry and Physics	16
Geography	15
Biology	15
Business Arithmetic	12
Javanese (i.e., writing good Javanese, reading traditional literature, etc.)	11
Physical Education	10
Arabic	5
Handwriting	5
Drawing	4

A dedication of 11 per cent of the curriculum to religious subjects (counting Arabic as a "religious subject")—and that largely to generalized "moral instruction"*—is a far cry, not only from the 80 per cent emphasis in the NU schools on technical religious subjects, but even from the 40 per cent in the "modern" BPPI. This difference is not due to the fact that this is a high school rather than an elementary school (although the fact that Muham-

---

* When I asked the boy who taught this for some examples of the instruction he imparted, he gave such maxims as "Don't drink while standing up" and "Never enter anyone else's house without first receiving permission." He also teaches the moral significance of selected Koranic passages and *hadiths.*

madijah·has far more high schools in Java than either NU or PSII is itself indicative of the greater strength of the school idea within their group). The relative emphasis of the various education systems remains about constant at each school level.

The whole organization of the school testifies to the distance between it and both the *pondok* and the *madrasah*. Six of the teachers are full-time and can live moderately well on their salaries of Rp 200 to Rp 275 a month, especially as they are furnished free quarters either in Muhammadijah homes or in empty houses owned by the richest member of the organization, a storekeeper. Tuition for the nearly 200 students is Rp 10 a month, and Muhammadijah donates Rp 600 a month toward the budget. Six of the teachers have diplomas from senior high schools or above, and the rest either from an advanced religious school or a junior high school. Success in passing the government entrance examination for senior high school have steadily increased since the school was founded after the war; and in fact the student body managed to startle almost the entire Modjokuto populace in 1954 by having the best record in the examination of the three private junior high schools in town, although the other two had been generally considered to be academically superior. (Before the war, Muhammadijah had only an elementary school.)

Unlike the NU system, Muhammadijah's school system is patterned exactly after the government school system. Their effort has been not to set up a self-consistent Islamic school system complete in itself, but rather to organize a private system which will parallel the national system and be able to take advantage of it. An example was the founding of a new teachers' school by Muhammadijah, during the time I was in Modjokuto. The lower normal school (i.e., one which trains teachers for elementary schools) in the national system is the same as the junior high school except that the normal school is four years long instead of three, the extra time being needed for education courses. As there was a severe shortage of places in the government normal schools, Muhammadijah opened a lower normal school of its own, consisting only of the fourth year—i.e., mainly education courses—and admitted graduates from the junior high schools. Thus a pupil would have his three years of general education in the usual junior high school, either government or Muhammadijah, and his year of professional courses in the Muhammadijah normal school. The school committee talked a *prijaji* who was probably the most competent and dedicated teacher in the public school system into heading the new school in addition to his regular job, all the courses being held in the evenings. Since only about a dozen students participated and there was some question as to whether the school would continue a second year, the success of the venture was at best ambiguous. But the setting up of the school at all is indicative of the energy, imagination, and persistence with which Muhammadijah pursues its aim to educate the *santri* community along more "Western" lines.

Another example of the comparatively greater vitality of the Muhammadijah education program is the effort—first proposed by the Modjokuto chapter—of all the Muhammadijah chapters in the residency (six, one from each of the six largest towns) to form a kind of regional school system among themselves by (1) coordinating their curricula so that the same subjects in the same amount would be taught at each school, facilitating interchange of teachers, standardization of texts, and the like; (2) maintaining comparable standards at each school so that students could move easily from one to the other without either advancing or going back a grade; (3) appointing a "school inspector" to inspect the schools and give advice on how their standards could be raised; (4) holding regular joint meetings of the school committees from each chapter to coordinate policy; (5) initiating a "Muhammadijah Students' Day" at which students from all the schools would gather for sports once a year. Admittedly, this somewhat grandiose plan had hardly got off the ground by the time I left Modjokuto, and many obstacles stood in the way of its full realization. Nevertheless, even the mere conception of it is a sign that Muhammadijah thinks about education rather differently than do the other *santri* organizations.

This rather different way of thinking about education, which, except that it maintains some contact with Islamic ideology, is nearly the same as that of those who direct the secular public school system, has, from a functional point of view, some of the defects of its virtues when considered in relation to the *santri* context in general. In the first place, although the technical level of the education is no doubt higher in Muhammadijah schools than in NU schools and, of course, in *pondoks,* it is purchased by allowing a greater secularization of the curriculum, which, in turn, keeps it from reaching the conservative elements in the *ummat* as effectively as it might.

Even the more religious members within Muhammadijah itself were somewhat restive about the rudimentary quality of the religious education provided in their schools and tended to be apologetic and defensive about it. Muhammadijah schools are more or less the *terminus ad quem* of the *pondok*-to-school transformation, the point beyond which it would be seemingly impossible to go and still claim to be giving *santri* education (the normal school being, in fact, almost entirely secular). They are thus far removed from being attractive to those who are still strongly opposed to "infidel" education but, realizing the need and demand for some degree of Western-type education, are willing to go along with the school idea so long as religious teaching in a somewhat recognizably traditional form is maintained as an important part of it. There is an interesting and very marked tendency for the more progressive elements in each subgroup in the *ummat* to have their own children educated not in the schools of their own organizations but in those of the next more modern group. Thus the less inflexible *kijajis* send their children to NU schools as well as giving them *pondok* training; the urban leaders of NU seem almost always to send their children to Muhammadijah schools; and most children of Muhammadijah parents attend public schools.

The second and, to my mind, more serious functional defect of Muhammadijah's more secular approach to education is one it shares with almost all educational thinking in Indonesia in both private and public systems— a concern with financing and organization at the expense of considered reflections on general policy and educational philosophy. There is a tendency to spend so much time in trying to worm subsidies out of the central government and in planning new schools and revising the forms of old ones that little thought is being given to what kind of education is best suited to the Indonesian context or to the *santri* community they are supposedly serving.

Rachmad (head of the Muhammadijah high school, reporting to a school committee meeting) gave a report on his trip to Surabaja to the office of the Ministry of Religion. As nearly as I understand it, the same situation exists in the religious normal schools as in the secular ones: i.e., there are not enough places. The religious normal school is just like the secular—three years' general education, plus a years' professional training—except that the professional training in the religious school is in religion, not pedagogy. They thought that now they could just add a little more religious teaching to the high school course (to bring it up to 25 per cent) and stretch the curriculum out over four years and they would have a religious normal school all their own and could attract some of these students here, perhaps a few on government scholarships, which would be helpful financially. . . . So Rachmad suggested they do this. They would just keep running the high school (as well as the secular normal school) and hire another religion teacher, or ask the ones they have to teach a little more, and then just ask the students who entered whether they wanted to be high school students or religious-teaching students. High school students would get high school diplomas, and religious-teaching students would get religious-teacher diplomas, although all would have the same education in the same courses, except that the high school students could omit some of the religion courses and get out a year sooner. They would all sit in the same room and hear the same teacher, but some would be in high school, some in religious normal school. As a result the number of students could be increased because they could attract both kinds of students. (The high school has never been full.) . . . This remarkable manipulation of names pleased all immensely . . . and H. Ustaz talked about writing an article for the newspapers about the founding of a new school by Muhammadijah in Modjokuto, gleefully reciting it out ("In a meeting on June 1st at the orphanage . . ."), and they discussed the ethics of this for a while and decided that perhaps they ought to say something like "a new division." But H. Ustaz went happily on, and when I saw Ali (chairman of the school committee) the next morning he said to me: "You see, Muhammadijah is still forging ahead, we're going to found a new school"; and Ustaz said that pretty soon Modjokuto would have as many schools as Blitar. . . . This making two schools grow where one grew before by simple manipulation of the excessively complicated and specialized Indonesian educational system seems to me to be rather typical of educational efforts in Indonesia in general now, not just Muhammadijah. In all the meetings of the Muhammadijah people that I have attended they never once discussed an educational problem. This annoys Pandji (the *prijaji* head of the teachers' school); he says that the secular school groups never discuss educational problems either. They always discussed finances, manipulations—as last night, or how to get some more money out of some government bureau. . . .

Thus, although Muhammadijah has been without a doubt the most successful of the *santri* groups in providing adequate general education for the *ummat,* and has made (at least in Modjokuto) perhaps the most tireless private effort actually to do something on the local level about some of the social problems facing contemporary Indonesian society, their tendency merely to ape the dominant public school system in both its strength and its weaknesses has made their efforts rather less effective than they might otherwise have been. By imitating the secularism of the public schools they have lessened their appeal to the *ummat,* the result being that they are caught in the middle. Without the finances to raise their teaching to the level of the public schools, they are unable to attract away from those schools the non-*santri* urban students, whose interest lies in an adequate modern Western-type education; without adequate religious teaching, they tend to put off the more orthodox in their own camp who are ready to make a compromise with the modern world but not, as yet, a capitulation to it.

Moreover, by imitating the concern of the public schools with externals, necessary as some of them may be, rather than considering the problems they are trying to tackle in somewhat more fundamental terms, they have so far been unable to provide a genuine fusion between the intellectually more effective educational methods of the West and the religious-practical orientation of the old *pondoks.* The latter, for all their ideological shortcomings, were more integrated into the society of which they were a part and at least impressed upon their students the virtues of simplicity, the moral significance of honest sweat, and the necessity, in an almost entirely agricultural society, of working with one's hands either in the fields or in producing simple manufactures. Such a fusion could provide a genuine alternative to the white-collar literary-lawyer type of education to which the public school system seems committed rather than merely a somewhat weaker copy of it.

These considerations, it ought to be admitted, have not been wholly overlooked in the higher echelons of Muhammadijah leadership. When I was in Djokjakarta, the Central Governing Board of Muhammadijah for all Indonesia was engaged, in cooperation with the Ministry of Religion, in setting up an experimental school in which the students would study religion one-third of the time and general subjects one-third of the time and spend the last third working either in small industries learning commercial methods or on farms learning modern agricultural techniques. If such experiments prove successful and percolate down to the Modjokuto level, a genuinely reformed version of Indonesia's strongest scholarly tradition may eventually appear. But there is no sign of it at the moment.

Religion in the Public Schools in Modjokuto

ONE last stage on the *pondok*-to-*sekolah* continuum remains to be briefly considered—the teaching of religion in the public schools. This is a post-revolutionary innovation, made necessary by the political pressure of the *santri* parties on the national government. Grades four, five, and six in the public elementary schools receive two hours a week of instruction in Islam of a very simple sort, taught by two Muhammadijah people who are paid salaries by the Ministry of Religion for performing this task. The classes are voluntary, but most children seem to participate as a matter of course; most Javanese are too outwardly polite to insult a teacher by taking their children out of his classes no matter how little they may think of him or his religious position. The subjects taught are the most elementary—how to pray; the characteristics of God; who the Prophet was, and what he did; the correct marriage and death procedures; and simple ethics, mostly taught by means of children's stories about Javanese "Islamic heroes." There is a great deal of resentment on the part of the non-*santri* community at this religious "invasion" of the secular schools.

> When I asked her (a *prijaji* public school teacher) what the difference is between public and private schools, she said that basically, in the teaching, there is no difference. Even in the matter of religious teaching they are almost the same, for now there is religious teaching in the public schools. I asked what per cent of her class take the religious course, and she said all of them in her class. She said that many people don't want their children to take it—for example, she herself doesn't want her own children to; and she named another teacher who won't let her children attend the class. This is because it would confuse their thinking. Later, when her children have graduated from high school, she herself will teach them a little about religion. . . . I asked if she would teach her children to chant, and she said no, she would teach them just a few Arabic words and their meanings. Pak Surjo (her husband) doesn't agree with her that they ought to be taught religion at all; he thinks they ought to be left alone to find out for themselves. She says she just keeps quiet about the issue.

Chapter 15

The Administration of the Moslem Law: Islam and the State in Modjokuto

THE ISLAMIC LAW (*sarak*) is, in Gibb's phrase,* the very conscience of Islamic culture; it is through the law that the commands of God, as given in the Koran, are translated into concrete prescriptions for secular behavior. Thus, in a sense, there is no genuinely secular behavior for a true Moslem just as (as we shall see) there is properly speaking no "state" as opposed to "church." All aspects of life fall within the jurisdiction of the law; and, as the law is sacred, all aspects of life are in theory sacred. This is the real meaning of theocracy in Islam: the unreserved acceptance by the *ummat* of the prescriptions of the law as binding for daily life "in all its parts and activities."**

Since the death of Muhammad and his immediate successors, such theocracy has everywhere proved possible only of approximation. Everywhere the Moslem law has had to compromise with local custom. Everywhere the effort of the pious scholars and judges has been to extend the sacred law into the whole of a given community's secular life, to establish *Dar Ul Islam,* "the abode of Islam." And everywhere this effort has been resisted by the less pious. Thus the administration of the law is a crucial practical concern of the leadership in any Moslem country. This is no less true in Indonesia, where the compromise the sacred law has had to make with engrained tradition has, perhaps, been greater than in many other Islamic countries. So we find in Modjokuto a third social form—in addition to the party system and the network of Islamic schools—in which the *santri* religious orientation is embedded: the religious bureaucracy.

* H. A. R. Gibb, *Mohammedanism* (London, 1949), p. 10.
** *Ibid.*

The General Organization of the Ministry of Religion

BY "the religious bureaucracy" I mean the Ministry of Religion* and its subordinate bureaus and offices, which administer all government regulations concerning religion. Although there are Protestant, Roman Catholic, and "Other Religions" sections, the Ministry of Religion is for all intents and purposes a *santri* affair from top to bottom. A much simplified organization chart of the Ministry follows.**

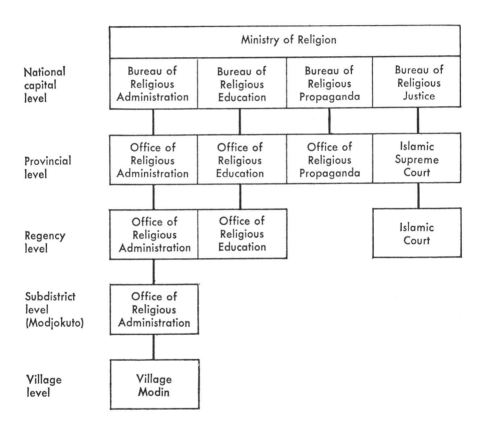

Concerning the national, provincial, and regency levels little need be said here. The Minister of Religion has been a member of either Masjumi or

* Almost every educated *santri* will tell you, "Israel is the only other country besides Indonesia which has a Minister of Religion with cabinet rank."

** Before the war, the religious bureaucracy was not nearly so elaborated as now. It lacked all of the middle-rank offices and bureaus which are now so important in its functioning and was of far less significance in the over-all governmental structure, being but a small division under the Education Department of the colonial government.

Nahdatul Ulama in all the cabinets,* and almost all the offices in the bureaucracy are occupied by members of these two parties, plus a few scattered people from minor *santri* parties such as Partai Sarekat Islam Indonesia (PSII). One of the most important informal functions of the ministry is, then, to provide jobs for deserving Moslems, a function extremely valuable in terms of patronage for *santri* party leaders attempting to build up local machines.

The Bureau of Religious Administration is the largest and most important of the four bureaus and the only one whose branches extend to the Modjokuto level. Besides the technical management of the ministry as a whole— budgeting, the arrangement of office complements, etc., the Bureau of Religious Administration is concerned with the administration of the marriage and divorce laws and laws relative to the setting up and maintenance of religious foundations (*wakap*); listing and reporting on the condition of private mosques and inspecting their finances:** the organization of the pilgrimage, which is now managed by the government in every detail; and the collection of various sorts of statistics, such as the number of religious schools, teachers, and students, the number of registered circumcisers, and the like. The Protestant, Roman Catholic, and "Other Religions" offices are under this bureau, but, except in heavily Christian areas and in "Hindu-Buddhist" Bali, such offices are confined to the national level. (Hesitancy on the part of Christians about allowing any official interference in their affairs by an almost wholly Moslem government reduces the ministry's functions in relation to them largely to counting the number of churches, registering Christian marriages for the record, and publishing a booklet on Christianity every now and again to show that the ministry is "for all religions, not just Islam.")

The Bureau of Religious Education is concerned with providing religious instruction in the public schools; awarding subsidies to private religious schools; running such government-owned religious schools as the Islamic University in Djokjakarta (Perguruan Tinggi Agama Islam Negeri) and several government-owned schools for religious judges and for religious teachers; providing Moslem chaplains for prisons, the army, police barracks, and the like; printing and distributing schoolbooks on religion, including translations of foreign books. The Bureau of Religious Propaganda is concerned with distributing pamphlets, booklets, posters, and the like concerning Islam and in providing translated sermons (*chotbah*) for use in local mosques if the directors of the mosque so desire. The Bureau of Religious Justice regulates the Moslem courts, the function of which in turn is to give

---

* It was a conflict within the unitary Masjumi over whether a Muhammadijah or an NU man was going to get the seat in the Wilopo cabinet which finally drove NU— Muhammadijah having won the intra-party struggle—out of Masjumi in 1952.

** Since mosques, especially in town, may be dedicated as *wakaps* with a proviso that the *nadjir* (official caretaker) be the head of the local religious office, this often includes the actual management of such mosques, although in theory all mosques are private.

advice to those who request it on difficult points in the Moslem law—most often centering around inheritance*—and to grant divorces to women who complain of desertion or maltreatment under the clause permitting divorce for such reasons included in every marriage contract.

The Local Organization of the Ministry of Religion

IN a subdistrict capital such as Modjokuto, where there is only an Office of Religious Administration (Kantor Urusan Agama, commonly referred to as KUA or the Kenaiban, from *naib*, the chief official in the office), whatever functions of the other three bureaus need to be performed at that level are either channeled through it or, more commonly, handled directly by the regency or provincial office. Thus the religious teachers in the government schools are supervised by the Regency Office of Religious Education in Bragang, the regency capital, and the one religious scholar in the area— a Masjumi leader—who prepares Friday sermons for government distribution works directly out of the Office of Religious Propaganda in Surabaja, the provincial capital. As for legal advice, the local *naib* will give it if he is able, which is not likely if the case is very complex, but if not he will refer the petitioners to the Islamic Court in Bragang.

The head of the local KUA is the *naib*. Under the new set-up there should be a "Head of the Religious Office" (Kepala Kantor Urusan Agama) over the *naib*, so that Christians cannot argue that the office is entirely Moslem; but in Modjokuto (and, I imagine, elsewhere on the subdistrict level) this has not yet been instituted and the *naib* heads the office as traditionally. His duties mainly concern the general direction of the office and the regulation of marriage and divorce. He is assisted by a staff consisting of the *chotib*, who has as his special duty the giving of information talks to Moslems about the requirements of the Islamic Law; the *imam*, who leads the worship in the Modjokuto mosque and is generally concerned with problems focusing around religious ritual; the *mukadin*, who assists the *imam* and who calls the *ummat* to prayer from the mosque tower; the *merbot*, who cleans the mosque, office, etc.; and the *ketib*, who is the office clerk. Actually, the table of organization, although all the jobs in it are filled, is more theoretical than actual, and in Modjokuto all the officials (except the *merbot*, who is a janitor pure and simple) do all the work of the office without any apparent division of labor among them, save for the general executive functions of the *naib*.

* One does not have to use Moslem inheritance law, however, and few people, even among the *santri* group, do. The Islamic courts have only advisory powers and may act only in cases voluntarily referred to them by petitioners who are free, so far as the civil state is concerned, to reject or ignore their decisions. Only concerning marriage and divorce are the civil and the Moslem laws fused (except for Christians and the Balinese, who are Hindus); in all other areas recourse to Moslem law is voluntary.

Marriage and Divorce

IDEALLY, the KUA should, from a *santri* point of view, be concerned with administration of the whole of the Moslem law, but in fact it is largely restricted to that surrounding marriage, divorce, and remarriage. Under Moslem law a man who wishes to divorce his wife must pronounce the so-called *talak* phrase: "*Kowé kok-talak*" ("You I divorce"). If he pronounces the *talak* only once, he may change his mind at any time within three menstruation periods and take his wife back, a process known as *rudjuk*. He then has two *talaks* left. He may, say ten years later, dismiss his wife again, and then remarry her within three menstruation periods. If after either of these first two *talaks* he does not remarry her within the prescribed three-month period, the pair is irrevocably divorced and cannot remarry unless the woman has in the meantime married and been divorced from another man. Similarly, after a third *talak* (i.e., after two *rudjuks*) the pair cannot *rudjuk* and so cannot remarry unless the woman has married and been divorced from another man in the interval. It is also possible for a man who is particularly angry at his wife to issue two or even three *talaks* at one time, making *rudjuk* impossible; but the *naib* usually attempts to discourage this latter practice as rash and unreasonable. The administration of this and of the marriage law takes up probably 80 per cent of the time of the officials of the KUA in Modjokuto.

Religious Foundations and the Pilgrimage

THE other 20 per cent of the officials' time is employed in gathering various statistics about the *ummat,* running the Modjokuto mosque, giving courses for village *modins* (a class being held each Thursday morning in the Kenaiban for these village religious officials, the instruction dealing largely with their duties and with various elementary points of Moslem law), regulating religious foundations, and, to some extent, organizing the pilgrimage.

A religious foundation is called a *wakap.* It may consist of nearly anything of value—house land, buildings, rice fields. The *wakap* is usually made over by the donor to a local *kijaji* or, sometimes, to the *naib*, who is then its executor (*nadjir*) but not its owner, for it is considered to be the property of God. It is not taxed, but the government requires that all products of the *wakap*—for example, coconuts from a *wakap* garden—be recorded by the *naib*'s office as well as all expenditures for repair of buildings and the like, to prevent misuse of *wakaps* by dishonest *nadjirs*. The *nadjir* appoints his own successor before he dies. Several mosques, *langgars, madrasahs, pondoks,* and Moslem schools in the area are *wakaps,* some with a little *wakap* rice land to help pay expenses. Large, extensive *wakaps* covering many acres or controlling great amounts of wealth, do not exist around

Modjokuto; and, although the *naib*'s supervision of it is more theoretical than actual, there is no apparent abuse of the system such as occurs in some other Islamic countries.

For the most part, the organization of the pilgrimage is handled directly from the regency office, the Kenaiban merely keeping the statistics on the number of *hadjis*,* giving out information on the process, and the like. The pilgrimage is carefully regulated from beginning to end by the Ministry of Religion. The would-be *hadji* merely pays a lump sum (Rp 7,300 in 1954) to the ministry, which takes care of everything including ship passage and room and board in Mecca, and even doles spending money out to him, the whole three-month trip being planned in every detail by the government. That this kind of regulation is, to an extent, necessary is shown by the description an old *hadji* informant gave me of the situation as it was in the Dutch period.

> He said that there were many ticket brokers, both Arabs and Javanese, who often swindled people. They sold ship tickets to the peasants about to go on the pilgrimage, and made a tremendous profit from it. If a ship ticket cost Rp 550, they would tell the peasant it cost Rp 575; and, as the peasant knew no better, he was entirely at the mercy of such dishonest brokers. Worse yet, once the peasant was in the hands of a broker like this, the latter kept milking him of more money. Thus, when the prospective *hadji* arrived in Surabaja, he might find that he had to pay five rupiahs a night to sleep there until his ship left, often not till a month or so later, the broker having deceived him about the departure date. (The elder brother of the storekeeper on the corner had to wait 26 days in Surabaja for his ship, the storekeeper told me, and just about exhausted his resources.) Then he would have to pay five rupiahs more for various services upon embarking, one rupiah for a bus to the dock, and so on. Each time the pilgrim's baggage moved around or got stored, the broker gobbled up a few more of his long-saved rupiahs. Another swindle the brokers practiced was selling time. A would-be *hadji*, for example, might give the broker Rp 500 for the trip, and the broker would buy a ticket for a ship due to leave in two weeks. However, he would hold the ticket and not tell the anxious pilgrim that he had already obtained it, telling him instead that he was still looking for a ticket. What he was actually looking for was a richer man who would pay more for the ticket in order to get a ship just about to leave. The broker would then sell the ticket for Rp 550 to the rich man and buy another for a ship sailing in a month or two. The routine would then be repeated, while the poor pilgrim out in the village waited impatiently, constantly assured by the broker that it would not be much longer. After six months or so, the pilgrim would finally get his ticket, but only after having provided free capital for the broker for half a year. After he got on the ship, his troubles were still not over, for there he would run into even more brokers trying to sell him a place to sleep in Mecca, tours to Medina, and so forth.

As there has been a severe shortage of foreign exchange since independence, the number of people allowed to make the pilgrimage has been drasti-

---

* A census made in 1952, which was probably inexact, revealed 194 persons who had gone on the pilgrimage at one time or another living in the subdistrict. Of these, 27 were women.

cally limited during the past few years. (The quota for the whole regency of which Modjokuto is a part was only 37 in 1954.) A prospective *hadji* must first convince his village chief that his family will not suffer, economically or otherwise, if he goes on the pilgrimage. He then must take a physical examination and a written or oral test on religion and on Indonesian affairs. (E.g.: "Who can go on the pilgrimage?" "Moslems who are not crazy, slaves, or children." "What happened on August 17, 1945?" "Indonesia's independence was declared.") The individuals then actually allowed to go on the pilgrimage are chosen by lot from among those eligible, except that people turned back in previous years are given priority.

Actually, the limitation on the number of *hadjis* is not felt as much of a hardship by the *ummat* because the pilgrimage is not nearly so popular as it once was. In the towns, interest in the journey to the Holy Land has practically died out altogether. There has not been a single pilgrim from the town of Modjokuto since 1930; and each year since the war all applicants for the trip in the district have been from the countryside. When I asked people why this loss of interest had occurred, they usually said that people no longer feel that they have to go to Mecca to find out about Islam, since there are good schools for it in Indonesia; that people in towns prefer to plow the money they save back into their businesses rather than "throw it away" on a trip to the Middle East; and that, anyway, going on the pilgrimage is nothing so special any more.

> (The informant made the pilgrimage in the late twenties.) When he was a child there were only about fifteen or so *hadjis* around, and they were very honored, each one usually having one or two hundred people as followers. However, as time wore on, more and more people made the pilgrimage and this reduced the homage paid to *hadjis* because they were no longer anything particularly out of the ordinary. Formerly, the pilgrims were the only villagers who had been out and seen the world; but nowadays you can get to Surabaja in two hours by car, so this doesn't count for much any more.

Religious Propaganda and Village Religious Officials

IN addition to their administrative duties, the officials of the Kenaiban are charged with the task of enlightening the rural masses as to the basic requirements of Islam and as to what the Ministry of Religion is attempting to do, a duty they fulfill by traveling around to all the villages in the subdistrict to give talks on subjects related to the work of the office.

> Hadji Arifin (the *chotib*, speaking in a village near town) talked about marriage and divorce. He said that the KUA is much interested these days in "improving marriage." He said marriage is an important problem to Indonesia, which is trying to build itself up to be a first-rate country. Divorce, he said, is tough on the women and on the children especially, for they are the ones who really suffer, grow up uncared for, uneducated, all this at a time when Indonesia is trying to build up the country. He quoted some

Arabic from the Koran and translated it to show that God is not in favor
of easy divorce; and he said that in line with this KUA is endeavoring to
bring about marriages which are "true marriages" and which last. He said
they have made some progress, but things are still bad. Last year, before
starting their propaganda campaign, they had 800 divorces per 1,000
marriages and now it is down to about 500 in 1,000. (These figures are
exaggerated, but only slightly: the Javanese divorce rate is very high.)
Obviously, he said, we need more diplomacy in marriage, and also people
who are about to marry must truly want to. . . . He seemed to place all the
blame for marriage failures (perhaps because he was speaking to an all-
male audience) on the men not knowing their duties and so forth. . . .
He gave some examples of masculine neglect culled from his experiences in
the Kenaiban as the kinds of things to be avoided. The first was about
a man who went to the movies when his wife was having a baby. He
said this is the way love gets lost. The second had to do with men who
don't help their wives with the wife's work when it gets too heavy. If
the wife's work is too heavy, this can cause divorce; and a man should
not have rigid ideas about what is properly his work and what is his wife's,
but should help the wife if she is overloaded. The third example was of a
village man who sold his harvest and then didn't take the money home but
bought himself a sarong with it, which made the wife angry because he had
not discussed it with her first. . . . Then he went on to the problem of
registering marriages with the KUA. He gave the number of the national
law involved here and said that as Indonesia is trying to become a law-
regulated state people must obey the laws. Only two religions have as
yet been accepted by the Ministry of Religion: Islam and Christianity;
the others have not yet been acknowledged. If a marriage is not recorded
in the KUA, the couple are living in sin; also, marriages which are just
a meeting of minds ("I am willing"—"I also am willing") are sinful. The
lack of registration leads to other things, such as a man having many
wives in various places because there is no way to check on him. Then who
is the victim? Our women.

But the main mediation of the interests of the Ministry of Religion
to the villages is carried on by the *modin*. The *modin* is elected for life by
his fellow villagers. (In order to stand for nomination he must take a simple
examination in Islamic law and must be literate.) He is actually subject
to two ministries at the same time: the Ministry of the Interior, as a village
civil servant, and the Ministry of Religion, as the village religious official.
(There may be more than one *modin* to a village, or one chief *modin* and
several assistants.) His religious duties are twelve: (1) to prepare corpses
for burial and to give advice to the survivors on the proper conduct of the
funeral; (2) to see that the graveyards are kept up (the actual cleaning
being done by a handyman who gets small donations from families who
have relatives buried in the cemetery); (3) to conduct people who wish to
be married to the Kenaiban after checking to make sure that everything is
as it should be—that the girl has the right *wali* (guardian), that the man
is unmarried, etc.; (4) to perform similar duties in divorce and (5) remarriage cases; (6) to give advice to people on inheritance according to
Islamic law (although usually he tries to get them to settle their differences

by customary law so as to avoid open breaches and if unsuccessful refers them to the *naib*); (7) to perform the slaughtering of oxen, goats, or sheep, which he must report to the subdistrict officer after having inspected the meat* (since people disobey with impunity the rules requiring goats and sheep to be slaughtered by a *modin*, and almost all oxen or water buffaloes are slaughtered in the town at the abattoirs, this is not of too much importance to the average *modin*); (8) to pray at *slametans* if requested to do so; (9) to give advice and consolation to people who have recently lost a relative by death; (10) to see that the religious tax is correctly gathered and not embezzled (not making the collection himself but checking on the organizations which do—at least theoretically); (11) to answer any attacks upon Islam and defend the faith against the criticism of infidels; (12) to provide an example for the villagers by himself carrying out the religious and social duties of Islam correctly and completely. The *modins*, who, naturally enough, tend today to be village political party leaders as well as traditional religious leaders, provide the main contact with Islamic law for almost all the *abangans* and many of the less educated *santris*, and as such they wield considerable power. They are paid, as are all other village officials, by a grant of land from the village rice fields, which they then work.

The Ministry of Religion
and the *Santri* Political Parties

TWO rather more general problems demand discussion in connection with the religious bureaucracy: first, the relation of the bureaucracy to the two-winged party structure which I have already described as being pervasive in *santri* life; and, second, the place of the bureaucracy in respect to the Islamic formulation of that fundamental concern of all religious political theory— the proper relation between "Church" and "State."

As for the party problem, I have already related how the prewar ideological struggle between the modernists and conservatives reached its point of maximum intensity in a fight over succession to the post of *naib* within the family which had dominated the Kenaiban since its founding in Modjokuto. With the abolition of the semi-hereditary system encouraged by the colonial regime and the substitution of a modern rational-legal bureaucracy and the ever-increasing tendency for posts to be filled in terms of party patronage, the family which had so long controlled the offices was no longer able to do so. Although the *naib* who had earned his succession by bitter intra-family maneuvering was not displaced from the bureaucracy, in 1950 he was promoted and moved to another town. The establishment of higher posts in a bureaucracy which had once been almost entirely local

* The slaughtering of animals is a duty of the *modin* because Islamic law prescribes rituals which must be performed when an animal is killed in order to make the meat lawfully edible.

means that the possibilities for mobility are made comparable to those in the civil service, with the result that the old stability of tenure, in which a man who was appointed *naib* remained *naib* until his death, has been disturbed and replaced with a system in which there is a constant turnover of personnel and a continual jockeying for position between the two major *santri* parties.

In any case, after the old *naib,* now a Masjumi member, had been transferred, Nahdatul Ulama was able, in part because its national head was Minister of Religion at the time, to take over all the posts but one in the Modjokuto KUA. (The *naib* is the chairman of Modjokuto NU; the *imam* is the party secretary.) This event very much disturbed the modernists.

> H. Husein (a Masjumi leader) said that now the NU people have just about taken over the Ministry of Religion and regard it as their province. He said that H. Muchtar (the *chotib*) is the only Muhammadijah-Masjumi man in the Modjokuto office now, and that he wouldn't be there if it were not that he is so clever and knows so much about the situation around here, having lived here all his life, that they can't do without him. If perchance H. Muchtar had been stupid, they would have kicked him out long ago and there wouldn't be any Masjumi people left.

Thus the control of the local religious bureaucracy is an important issue in party politics and tends to have significance for the organization of the *ummat* generally, determining even the choice of mosques.

> He (a young modernist and a member of the family which controlled the office of *naib* before the war) said that in the old days when his uncle was the *naib* here there were many more people who went to the mosque here on Friday—so many that they spilled over into the yard. In those days Ali (chairman of Masjumi), Iskak (chairman of Muhammadijah), and the *naib* himself gave the sermons. Now the new *naib* is not so good and is not so well liked; and so things are calmer, and nearly all of the sermons are given by NU people and are mostly about religion, with only "We must choose an Islamic State" tacked on at the end. Now many of the Muhammadijah people go to other mosques—for example, to Banjuurip (a village Masjumi stronghold about five miles from Modjokuto). . . . He said that most of the sermons are about the same nowadays since NU took over—fear God and behave yourself—and are not very interesting. They don't suit the times.

Although the NU control of the Modjokuto Kenaiban gives that party an important advantage over Masjumi, Masjumi leaders seem to do better at the regency and provincial levels (although the *penghulu,* the head of the regency religious bureaucracy, is also an NU man now, being the son-in-law of a Modjokuto NU leader, and the modernist family which used to control that post no longer does so). One Masjumi leader is employed—"part-time" —in writing sermons for the Provincial Office of Religious Propaganda (headed by a Masjumi man) to distribute to local mosques. The head of Muhammadijah is employed—"part time"—as a chaplain to the army by the Regency Office of Religious Education. And the chairman of Masjumi is employed—"part-time"—as a school inspector for all the private religious schools and *madrasahs* in the Modjokuto area which receive subsidies from the Ministry of Religion, a job which not only allows him to go around to all the villages and combine official work with party work but also provides him with a motorcycle on which to do it.

It is not necessary to trace here the manifold ways in which the religious bureaucracy and the party structures intertwine, the manner in which party interests can be served by control of various ministry offices, or the ways in which the bureaucracy responds to the tensions and pressures of party politics. But one issue—that of subsidies for religious schools—reflects the interaction between the two structures rather vividly and leads as well directly into the "Church" and "State" problem.

The response of the various groups to the idea of government subsidies for private religious schools takes pretty much the forms one would expect. *Pondok kijajis,* for the most part, want to have little to do with the government as it is now constituted because they feel that the requirements their institutions must meet to be eligible for the subsidies limit their personal freedom to run their own affairs in their own way. Moreover, they are suspicious of a secular government in which non-*santri prijajis,* occupying the great majority of the civil service posts, play such an important role. What they would like, and what they agitate for, is an "Islamic State" dominated by *kijajis* which would give subsidies to *pondoks* on the same basis as the religious tax is now given them by the populace generally: as a divinely commanded obligation of the less religiously concerned toward the more religiously concerned and with no strings attached except that the religious education must be orthodox.

Madrasah directors are willing to accept subsidies and to reform their schools slightly to get them, but are both unwilling and unable to sacrifice religious training in order to raise the level of their general education programs high enough to meet the comparatively strict technical requirements for private school subsidy applicants set by the Ministry of Education. As a result, NU leaders, as representatives of this group, have backed a policy of "something for everyone, no matter how little," in setting up within the Ministry of Religion a much smaller subsidy program for religious schools. As this party has had the dominant voice within the Ministry of Religion for most of its existence, this is the policy which has been followed. Every local religious teacher who is willing to add a course or two in arithmetic or writing Latin characters* is given something, but usually very little. One NU school in Modjokuto had a Ministry of Religion subsidy of two rupiahs per child *per year,* and the total subsidy of another for the year came to 30 rupiahs. Thus the resources of the Ministry of Religion, small enough in the first place because most of the money for education is channeled through the Ministry of Education, are so diffused through the thousands of Indonesian religious schools, good, bad, and indifferent, as to be almost entirely ineffective. NU has, of course, lobbied for a larger total budget, but in a political context where the Ministry of Religion is only barely tolerated to start

---

* *Pondok kijajis* have largely refused to meet even this requirement. In Modjokuto no *pondok* was getting any subsidy while I was there, although the *kijaji* of one of the larger *pondoks* was thinking of asking for a few rupiahs for the student-run secular school included in his program.

with by the majority of non-*santri* party leaders, this has not proved very successful.

Muhammadijah, and to a lesser extent PSII, while also interested in increasing the total budget, tend to favor a policy of fewer Ministry of Religion subsidies but larger ones. Caught between their inability to raise their standards to meet the requirements of the Ministry of Education (not always: some Muhammadijah schools do manage to qualify for the larger subsidies, and the Muhammadijah high school in Modjokuto was trying hard to raise its standards toward such an end) and a severe shortage of money which the present Ministry of Religion subsidy program does almost nothing to alleviate, they have argued for a concentration of the resources of the Ministry of Religion into a few large subsidies to be awarded to those religious schools most technically qualified to make good use of them—i.e., their own schools.

> The first point on the agenda (of a Muhammadijah school-committee meeting) was the problem of asking the government for a subsidy. This soon resolved itself into (1) asking for a subsidy for the high school from the Ministry of Religion and (2) asking for one from the Ministry of Education. The difference between the two is that the Ministry of Religion subsidy is small but quite easy to get, that ministry operating on the principle that "although only a very little, everyone is able to receive," while the Education Ministry subsidy is larger and harder to get, since it demands "results" before one gets anything. . . . H. Arifin said he thought that the subsidies given by the Ministry of Religion ought to be made about the same size as those of the Ministry of Education . . . and that maybe all the Muhammadijah people in the residency should get together and ask the government to do this. Rachmad (head of the high school) was dubious about this. He said that it would be "striking blows" at fellow Moslems in NU who had *madrasahs* in the villages, because it would mean fewer and larger subsidies in the Ministry of Religion which would be harder to get, so that these little schools, with mostly religious teaching, would be out in the cold. . . . And so the question was, "Do we want to stir up bad feeling by 'striking' our NU friends or are we willing to do so for the sake of larger subsidies from the Ministry of Religion?" There were many aggressive jokes here about "blows" etc., and they finally decided to plan a regency meeting to push the idea of fewer but bigger Ministry of Religion subsidies. . . . As for the Education Ministry application, they weren't very optimistic but felt they might as well try: "More Muhammadijah students passed the government examination this year, and all they can do is reject us again."

The Islamic State: The *Santri* Approach to the Problem of Church and State

THE problem lurking both behind this specific issue and behind the Ministry of Religion in general (which a number of non-*santri* parties wish to abolish) is the one Western political scholars formulate as the relation between Church and State. This formulation fits badly with Islamic political theory, however, because of the absence of a church and because of the theoretical ideal (if almost never the actuality) of absolute theocracy—of *Dar Ul Islam,* "the Abode of Islam," which has been present in Islam since the days when Muhammad headed his own army and state and the first four caliphs to succeed him continued to be the supreme authority in both religious and secular affairs.* Since the title-slogan *Dar Ul Islam* has been appropriated by *santri* fundamentalists in open military revolt against the established Republic in West Java, in South Celebes, and sporadically in Northern Sumatra, those *santri* parties loyal to the new national state and committed to parliamentary methods for pursuing their aims have adopted the title-slogan *Negara Islam,* "Islamic State," to indicate the "theocratic" ideal for which they are agitating.

I put "theocratic" in quotation marks because a series of interviews with *santri* party leaders in Djakarta on the subject and my experience in Modjo-kuto have convinced me that not only is the idea of *Negara Islam* an extremely vague one to just about everyone who holds it (as, admittedly, is the opposed *Negara Nasional,* "National State," of the secularist parties) but also insofar as it means anything to anyone, it means quite different things to different people. In general, more conservative people tend to conceive of a *Negara Islam* in terms of a theocracy more familiar to us— one in which *kijajis* will dominate. Even here the exact methods which can bring about such a domination in the absence of a church organization within Islam is not clear, although people suggest such notions as having a special parliament of *kijajis* to check on secular legislation passed by the regular parliament to make sure it is orthodox, placing *kijajis* in high government position or appointing the most learned one as Head of State, and introducing a great deal more religious teaching into the government schools—i.e., turning them into *madrasahs.* Presumably, it is for some such program as this that the *santri* rebels in West Java and elsewhere are fighting insofar as they are fighting for a program at all.

Modernists, on the other hand, although also committed to a *Negara Islam* tend to restrict it to a general proclamation of an Islamic State: that is, the institution of a law that no non-Moslem can be Head of State (an occurrence extremely unlikely in any case with a population 95 per cent of

---

* Not only is there no church in Islam; there is properly speaking no state either. The basic political unit in Islam is the *umma Muhammadiyya,* Muhammad's community, defined not territorially but legally, and composed of all those who follow the Moslem law: "Perhaps the greatest difficulty in the way of the new Arab countries is the necessity to overcome rapidly the traditional Islamic concept of, and attitude toward, the state as such. Islam never developed the idea of 'the State as an independent political institution,' which has been so characteristic of classical and Western thought. In Islam the State was not a [territorial] community or an institution, but the totality of those governed, *umma,* with the *imam* as their leader. As a result, the Oriental State had no conception of citizens in the modern sense. Government was not everybody's business nor even that of a privileged class. Participation in executive power was, in the public mind, as haphazard and accidental as were, apart from taxation, the contacts of the individual and government in general." (G. E. von Grunebaum, *Islam: Essays in the Nature and Growth of a Cultural Tradition* [Menasha, 1955], p. 73.)

which is nominally Moslem), and a constitutional provision stating that laws should be in accord with "the spirit of the Koran and the Hadith," leaving it up to the legislators themselves to make certain of this. (*Negara Islam* is perhaps the single most powerful slogan among the *santri* masses. Any party which came out flatly for a separation doctrine—such as the secularists support—would lose almost all its rural backing.) Obviously, such a doctrine is not much more "theocratic" in fact than the recent effort of a New England senator to get the U.S. Congress to pass a resolution declaring Christianity the official religion of the United States, although it has some of the same symbolic drawbacks in the eyes of religious minorities and those suspicious of organized religion that the proposed resolution did.

For people holding either of these positions, or just vaguely affirming the dire need for an "Islamic State," the Ministry of Religion is an embarrassment because it dramatizes the fact that the State is not in fact officially "Islamic." Both parties are caught between trying to widen the scope of the Ministry of Religion within the present secular government in order to increase their power within that government and realizing dimly that by doing this they are in part going along with a heterodox view of the relation between religion and politics. A number of religious scholars at a conference called by the ministry in 1954 tried to resolve this problem by declaring the Ministry of Religion a kind of "temporary Islamic State," an agent of the government which, at least for the time being, was legitimately to be obeyed in terms of the Moslem law. (Actually, they extended this beneficence to the cabinet as a whole and to the president, but the point of the proclamation was to give the Ministry of Religion a legitimate status according to Moslem law.) A number of party leaders and religious teachers cried havoc at this, however, evidently fearing the world-wide tendency for the temporary to become permanent in things governmental, which, in this case, would cut the ground from under the struggle for an "Islamic State."

> I talked to Fachid (a young NU shopkeeper) about the Ministry of Religion conference in Sumatra which decided that the president and cabinet are a legitimate Moslem government and which some *santri* members of Parliament have been attacking. He said that it is only a temporary compromise until the general elections can be held. The problem is that the Kenaiban, under the Ministry of Religion, is marrying and divorcing people and performing other religious functions, and there had to be clarification as to how this was legitimate since some people had questioned it in terms of religious law. The result was that some *kijajis* looked into the law books and came up with this temporary legitimization which says the government's efforts in the Ministry of Religion relative to religion are legitimate but must be reviewed again after the election. In the meanwhile, Moslems are to obey the ministry in things religious—for example, its determination of the day the Fast is to begin. . . . Fachid, evidently somewhat nonplussed at my interest in the subject and also somewhat depressed over the Church-State issue himself, said that, whereas Christians want a split between Church and State, Islam doesn't permit this. Thus the problem is very difficult.

In any case, this note shows that in identifying separation as a "Christian doctrine" and non-separation as the Moslem one the *santris* are unable to support an open split between Islam and the secular government such as has occurred in Turkey. It also shows that some compromise is possible, with *santris* settling for less than an Islamic State if the government "does not transgress the religious law," i.e., is willing to allow a certain degree of State-Church fusion to serve *santri* interests. In such a situation the Ministry of Religion may in fact turn out to be a permanent compromise which can resolve *santri* political theory with the facts of the situation, namely, that not all Indonesians by far are *santris*.

Actually, however, the type of political thinking done by people in all the parties tends to militate against this because each group—*abangan, santri,* and *prijaji*—sees the political struggle not so much as a process of mutual adjustment between their separate interests as parts of a larger society but as a naked struggle for power in which one group wins and the others lose.

> Fachid went on to say that it is natural that every group has its own ideology and wants it to triumph. The Communists want Marxism, the Nationalist Party wants Nationalism, and the *santris* want Islam. No matter what, they are interested in winning and will give the elbow to the other groups in order to gain the power to put their own foundation under the State. When in power, they will of course take care of their own followers. A man may have adopted children, but he always likes his own just a little better no matter how fair he may be. So each group tries to get its ideology and its own people into power. I agreed with this but said that maybe no one group will win such a decisive victory that the other groups can be ignored; and he said, "Well, it is so; the minority has rights. But an Islamic State will protect them." (He mentioned that, although the Christians want a separation of Church and State,* when something like the forced Islamization of Christians in the Celebes occurs they want the State to do something about it.) If two men are running for election, the one who has lost can still spread his ideology, but the man who is in is the one who rules. It is like a store. The man next to me may run his business differently than I do and that is up to him, but in my store I run things my way. So if the *santris* are in control of the country, they will run it their way: i.e., there will be an Islamic State.

This "if we win it's our country" view of politics is common to nearly all shades of party opinion, *santri* and non-*santri;* and the following transcript of a statement of it by a local Masjumi member may be compared to the NU quotation above.

> He talked a little about the Islamic State, saying that some people are afraid it will mean they can't gamble, drink, or hold *slametans,* and will be forced to pray. He said no, it won't mean this, it will just mean that the laws will be Islamic. (Like just about everyone else I talked to on this subject, he could cite as an example only that thieves' hands will be cut off.) He said that the government will be a legal Moslem government, fit to be obeyed in both reli-

* Though *santris* tend to discuss separation as a Christian doctrine, its main supporters in Indonesia in fact are the Nationalists, including the president of the country.

gious and secular matters. I asked if the Ministry of Religion was not this temporarily; and he said (wrongly) "No, not yet, it is just a ministry." He said that later in the Islamic State the Minister of Religion will be the Prime Minister (his own idea, not Masjumi policy). I said: "Well, won't the non-*santris* revolt if you try this?" he replied: "That's the way elections are. The PNI [the Nationalist Party] wants the *Pantjasila* (President Sukarno's Five Points, put forth as the ideological basis of a National State), the Communists want Communism, and the Moslems want an Islamic State; so whoever wins gets to put it in."

Chapter 16   The *Santri* Ritual Pattern

Santri RITUAL LIFE is modulated in time by the five fixed prayers—morning, noon, afternoon, sunset, and evening—repeated day after day in the same simple form. In space it is bounded by the borders of three progressively inclusive social circles defined by the three institutions in which the prayers are typically performed: the home, the neighborhood *langgar* (prayer house), and the village mosque.

The morning, noon, afternoon, and evening prayers are usually performed in the home; the sunset prayer is often carried out (by the men, the women always praying at home) in a nearby *langgar* with a few friends; the Friday noon prayer is almost invariably performed in the mosque in the company of the whole of the village *ummat*. It is the intersection of the temporally patterned prayers—for it is fidelity in performing the prayers which, ultimately, defines a *santri; prijajis* and *abangans* almost never do them—and the spatially outlined social groups of household, neighborhood, and village which organizes the elemental Islamic congregation, the individual's most immediate *ummat,* which in turn has a marked tendency to be incorporated as a unit into one of the two over-arching *santri* political parties.

Thus the religious and the social aspects of Islam lend support to one another.

(The informant is an NU shopkeeper.) It is permissible to do the prayers in one's house, but it is always better to do them in a group in the mosque or in a *langgar* than to do them alone at home. Each prayer of the five is better performed in the mosque or *langgar,* although this is compulsory only for the Friday noon prayer. The reason for this is that when the prayers are done in a group the mistakes, the good works, and the blessings are shared among all. Thus, if one is doing the prayers in a mosque or *langgar* and makes a mistake (in the ritual) or is not concentrating enough (for one never really knows how effective and pure and correct his worship is), then the punishment which comes for this can be spread thin over the whole group, who will carry it on their shoulders, and the burden will be

215

much lighter and in fact hardly felt. But if one performs the prayers in the house by himself and he makes a mistake, he gets all the punishment himself. Contrariwise, when one prays in a mosque or *langgar* one benefits from the piety of others more deeply versed in religion and better at praying, and thus gets more blessings and builds up more good works. Just going to the mosque is enough to get one something. For instance, if one goes to the mosque intending to pray but instead falls asleep, one still gets some credit in heaven for having come to the mosque with the intention of praying and also as a result of the prayers performed by the more pious present. Thus it is always better to pray with other people than to pray alone.

The Prayers

ACTUALLY, "prayer" is not an altogether accurate translation of *solat* (also called *sembahjang*) because, unlike Christian prayers, the *solats* are fixed not only in time but also in form and content, a sharp distinction being made between these obligatory acts of worship and any voluntary personal prayer (*doa*) one may wish to direct to God for various special purposes of one's own, which may be done anytime, with any phrasing, and in Javanese rather than Arabic if one wishes. Thus *solat* might better be translated "ritual incantation."

In any case, the form of the *solat* in Indonesia is the same as in any other Islamic country; and, as this has been so often described—the lustrations, the prostrations, and the chanting, I need not review the manner of their performance here except to note that, although all *santris* do the *solat* regularly, they differ somewhat in the elaborateness with which they carry out the act.

Bisri said in connection with describing the prayer that there are several optional parts. There is a part in the middle where one recites any passage from the Koran. Bisri knows about eight verses, all very short and easy. There is another place where one chooses between two prayers; he doesn't even know the longer one. After the main prayer is over many people continue to say certain phrases over and over, usually 33 or 66 or 99 times—phrases such as *Allahu Akbar* (God is most Great)—but he never does. He just gets the whole thing over with as quickly as possible.

The prayer pattern fits quite neatly with the daily round of the typical peasant. The 5:00 A.M. prayer gets him out of bed and early to work. By noon or one or two o'clock the work is done and the second prayer can be performed, to be followed by the big meal of the day and a nap in the midday heat. At three or four he is up for the afternoon prayer and then can either return to the fields if work is unusually heavy or, more commonly, visit around in the cool of the afternoon, ending up in the *langgar* for sunset prayer. Then he goes home to an evening meal, the final prayer, and bed.

In the town, the prayer pattern fits less well, although storekeepers can always take five minutes to do the prayers in back of their place of business (which is often their home as well). Other urban occupations raise problems; and I knew one *santri* who quit driving a taxi and returned to being a farmer because his taxi-driving took him on long trips during which it was impossible to do the *solat* correctly. (Strictly speaking, one can perform a *solat* in a field or along a roadway so long as one does the proper lustrations first, which is no problem in well-irrigated Java, but Javanese seem reluctant to do this; and all the time I was in Java I never saw anyone performing his *solat* in this manner.) Another *santri* claimed that *santris* often do not like to enter the army because the military routine often makes it difficult to do one's *solat*.

I doubt, however, that such considerations are very important for most people; the prayer regime is rather more flexible than it looks. In the first place, one can do the required prayer any time between the correct time for it and the correct time for the next one. Thus the noon prayer can be done from shortly after noon to 3:30, the 3:30 prayer from 3:30 until sunset, and so on. (The sunset prayer must be done while there is still light in the sky, however, and so is an exception.) In addition it is possible, for good reason, to combine certain couples of the prayers into one: e.g., if one misses the noon prayer one can do it at 3:30 along with the prayer for that time; and, conversely, if one knows he will not be able to do the 3:30 prayer, he can do it ahead of time at noon.

The brevity and simplicity of the prayers also make it easy to fit them into the daily routine. I have dozens of times interviewed a husband and wife in their home alternately through prayer time, each of them taking turns to go out back for about five minutes to do the prayer. (It is not impolite either for them to do this or for one to sit there; one is not expected to leave while people do their prayers.) Sometimes if one is talking with only one person, he will nevertheless excuse himself for a minute and go off somewhere in the house to perform the *solat*. (Although Arabs have performed their prayers in their homes in front of me—while I talked merrily on with those of the family who had completed theirs—no Javanese ever did this. They always went into a little room or out to the back of the house where others could not see them.) On long bicycle trips with *santri* informants we stopped at a wayside mosque or *langgar* for a few minutes while the informants performed the prayer, and then we went on. Thus the urban pattern of life, in Modjokuto at any rate, had not yet made the prayer-sequence awkward to fulfill for most people.

I have been told that in Surabaja, where some people must work from 8:00 A.M. until 4:00 P.M. in offices, the noon prayer is sometimes regularly skipped, even by good *santris,* and only four prayers are done a day, although strictly speaking, this is heterodox. In any case, for most *santris,* doing the *solat* is not so unrelated to such more mundane considerations as seeking one's daily bread as it might seem; like the Catholic act of crossing oneself, the daily prayers are a kind of ritual reflex, assuring one of material well-being as well as spiritual:

(The informant was a common laborer on the roads.) He asked me if I went to church on Sunday and was quite surprised when I said no. I asked him if he went to mosque every Friday and he said yes. Did he know how to pray? "Yes," he said, "since I was a child. It's better if you pray, ask for clothes, food, well-being for yourself and your children, a healthy strong body."

The Friday Service

THE Friday group-prayer represents a symbolic coming together of the *ummat* of the entire village; and the sense of having a "mosque of one's own" is strong enough so that people who move into town from nearby villages often return to the mosque in these villages for Friday prayer. (For those who live immediately around it, the mosque acts as a neighborhood *langgar* in which the evening prayer may be performed daily.) The control of the village mosques is entirely local, the director and the governing board being chosen by the people whom the mosque serves.

(The informant is an official in the Office of Religious Administration.) To set up a mosque, one first builds it either alone or in a group (or, of course, pays to have it built). Then a paper is signed surrendering it to the populace in general and the Office of Religious Administration in particular. The Office gathers together the people the mosque is to serve (i.e., the people who live around it), and they choose the *nadjir*, the man in charge and his name is entered in a book. (In fact, this is almost inevitably the man who built it himself or someone approved by him.) Here in town the head of the Office of Religious Administration is automatically *nadjir*, so the *nadjir* changes as the *naib* changes; but in the villages a man remains *nadjir* until he dies, when a new one is chosen. In addition to the *nadjir*, a general governing body for the mosque is chosen from among its *ummat*, which aids him in keeping it up.

To give a feeling for what the Friday prayer is like, I cite the following description from my notes on a mosque service I attended with an urban informant in the nearby village where he had been born and had grown up. The mosque was an NU-dominated one and thus old-fashioned in manner, as one can see from the fact that the *chotbah* (sermon) was not translated.

I went to mosque for Friday services with Amiri yesterday in the village where Amiri lived until the Japanese time. We just went in and sat down at about 11:30. The mosque, a small, square, white-plaster building with a slightly peaked red-tile roof, was just a big empty room—or rather two since there was a wall, pierced by two glassless windows and two doorless doors at the sides near the outer wall, about three-quarters of the way back, behind which Amiri and I sat. Outside on the porch hung not the usual slit gong (called a *bedug*) but a huge parade drum, which some people were engaged in beating with a large wooden club, first slowly and then faster and faster, repeating this about a half-dozen times and calling out in Arabic for people to gather for the prayer. As we squatted there on the stone floor, men and boys of all ages (the youngest perhaps six or seven) wandered in (some of them stopping to shake my hand and touch their chest, none of them seemingly surprised to find me there) and then squatted down, either on a woven mat or on their sarong or just on the bare stone floor. (Amiri rode out on the bike in trousers, but changed to a sarong when he got there.) Many of them were carrying Korans, which they left on a table near the mid-room door. Eventually there must have been 150 people there, and it was quite crowded.

When we arrived, there were already some people chanting, not in unison but individually, each at his own pace with his own rhythm. The result, some of the voices being deep and old, some high and adolescent, and all chanting at varying speeds, was an oddly beautiful cacophony. As others came in, they started chanting too, but finally at about 12 noon, they all stopped suddenly, perhaps on a signal from the *imam* (prayer leader), whom I could not see because of the wall, and then began the formal prayers. However, they still were not in rhythm, but each man went at his own speed. When one was bending over, another next to him was still standing up; and when one was bending over the other was touching his forehead to the floor. (They chanted to themselves now, moving only their lips, although the *imam* at the front was chanting aloud.)

In five minutes or so the praying was over, but the man at the front chanted on in Arabic in what I later found out was the *chotbah* but at the time thought was merely more praying while the *ummat* sat and waited. After maybe 20 minutes the *chotbah* was over, and they all prayed again; but this time they were all together in their motions. After this was over, most of the people left, others sitting there a while quietly or resuming the un-organized chanting that had gone on before the service began. Amiri sat there quietly for a while, and then in about ten minutes we went out and went across the street to see a friend of his. . . .

The problem of whether or not the *chotbah* should be translated is still a very live one, and most conservative mosques still refuse to do so, almost always using Arabic *chotbahs* written years ago by a famous Javanese *kijaji* from Semarang. (The Modjokuto mosque, now NU-dominated, continues the translated *chotbahs* introduced by Muhammadijah before the war.) The Javanese-language sermons holographed by the Bureau of Religious Propaganda are distributed to all the mosques whose officials want to use them, but few do. Those willing to give translated sermons want to make up their own more politically pointed ones, because nowadays when translated sermons are given, especially by urban modernists, they tend to be on political and social problems as much as on religious ones. (There was in fact an intense controversy in the parliament while I was in Indonesia concerning the use by Masjumi and NU of the mosques for political purposes.)

(The informant is the Modjokuto *imam*.) *Imam*, he said means the man who leads the prayers, but in the office of Religious Administration his duties are broader. In the first place he is in charge of the sermons here in the mosque on Friday. There are four sermon-givers (two NU men, one Masjumi man, and an Arab, the latter still giving his in Arabic) who alternate from week to week, and they write their own sermons. He said that the sermons are not only about religion but depend on the situation and are sometimes about politics. The one he gave last week was on Communism, warning the *unmat* not to believe the Reds when they say they are pro-religion; he said he wanted to prevent the more unlearned *santris* from being taken in by Communist propaganda. . . . He said soon there will be a sermon on Acheh (a province in North Sumatra where a Moslem revolt against the government had just broken out).

This pattern is, however, largely confined to town. Even in those more modern village mosques which accept translated sermons they are usually still mostly on religious subjects.

The village chief was copying a sermon out of an old sermon book written by a man from Surakarta. He said that he had to give one of the four monthly sermons in the Sidomuljo (a village Masjumi stronghold) mosque the next day. He said that he always copied them out of this book; he wasn't clever enough to make them up himself. He said the sermon was entirely concerned with religious things—urging people to pray, to believe in God; all quite simple. He said that he read it first in Arabic and then in Javanese. Evidently it isn't very long.

The Fast

THE droning chant of the interlocked *solat-ummat* pattern which flows along quite evenly through eleven months of the year, dividing each day into fixed segments, assembling the *santri* neighborhood each evening and the *santri* village each Friday noon, reaches a kind of crescendo in the Fast month (*Pasa*), when strictly religious activity is suddenly intensified and strictly secular sharply curtailed.

We talked about the Fast. He (a Masjumi leader) said that political activity for Masjumi and NU slows down very much in the Fast, which is used for religious reflection. He said that the Fast is not just to be viewed as a month of fasting but as a much more religious month than all the rest. In addition to fasting, one is not allowed to say evil things about other people or listen to or see evil things. Religious activity in general is much stepped up; and *Pasa* is considered the month in which a Moslem is supposed to get his religious house in order. . . . A sin in the Fast is much worse than the same sin in another month. And at the end comes the *zakat fitrah* (religious tax) to help erase the sins committed in the Fast.

After sundown each day during the Fast everyone eats a large meal and then gathers at the *langgars* (or the mosque if they live near it) to perform the evening prayer and, after it, the *trawèh* and *darus*. (Just before this begins one hears the children around each *langgar* gaily shouting TRAWÈH, TRAWÈH, TRAWÈH, in a manner somewhat akin to a football yell.) The *trawèh* consists of extra prayers (i.e., *solats*, not free prayers) as special added duties—although, strictly speaking they are voluntary—for the Fast. The *darus* is a reading of the Koran verse by verse; this also is voluntary, and evidently felt to be somewhat less incumbent than the *trawèh*.

In both these rituals there is, once more, a difference between *kolot* and *moḍèren* as to the correct manner of carrying them out. Concerning the *trawèh,* this difference is over the correct number of *solats* which should be performed. There are two legitimate *hadiths* on this matter, the first saying that one should do 23 *solats* and the other that one should do 11. Until the rise of modernism, 23 was the number accepted in Java as orthodox, and NU people still do 23; but Muhammadijah-Masjumi people mostly do 11. (The Modjokuto mosque, although now NU-dominated, has not shifted back to 23 from the 11-system introduced by the modernists when they were in control.) The NU people say the modernists are lazy and not very much interested in religion anyway. The modernists say that, although they do fewer prayers, they perform them more carefully and with greater understanding of the meaning of what they do, while the conservatives just race through their prayers super-ficially.

> (The informant is a modernist.) The 11-system is the newer and was largely spread by the modernist movements here and sharply opposed by the more old-line people when it was originally introduced. It was introduced in the Modjokuto mosque by Kijaji Nazir (the old Sarekat Islam founder) over much opposition—so much, in fact, that most NU people went elsewhere to pray, to their own *langgars* and the like. The reason that the 11-system is preferred by the modernists, in addition to the fact that it is a direct tradition from the Prophet while the 23-system is from the Companion Umar, is that it is possible to do the prayers slowly and in order, and thus to be more pious, while with the 23 they are always hurried through. The old men, who prefer the 23-system, feel that the greater the number of prayers the greater the good works credited to one's account; the younger, usually, and more pious people who prefer the 11 feel that if one does not do the prayers deeply and piously one will not get any good works on his account at all.

The *darus* conflict is over whether participants should read the Koran alternately or concurrently. The traditional system, still employed by NU, is for each individual to read one of the 30 Koran sections (*not* the chapters—*surat*—which are of uneven length; but the sections—*djuz*—which are of equal length, each $\frac{1}{30}$th of the Koran) alternately and to be corrected by the others if he makes a mistake. There is no attempt to complete the entire Koran in one night; but, since each *langgar* tries to get through the whole Koran once or twice in the month, the chanting, in this system, often lasts until three or four in the morning. (*Santris* do a good deal of sleeping during the daytime in the Fast.)

The other method is one in which the participants sit along a bench, each being given a section to read and then everyone chanting at once in a grand cacophony of mispronounced Arabic, thus completing the whole Koran in about an hour or so. (If there are less than 30 people, the man who finishes his section first runs down to the other end of the bench and starts in on one of the extra sections.)

It is not strictly accurate to describe the differences between these two systems in *modèren-kolot* terms; it is more a rural-urban difference (except for the *trawèh* difference). In town, most *santris* are either traders or small craftsmen, notably tailors. Since the end-of-Fast holiday, *Idul Fitri,* stimulates a great buying splurge (especially in clothing because, as among us on Easter, everyone gets out and parades around in new clothes if he can) business for most of these people is heavier during the Fast month than at any time during the year. In general Muhammadijah people simply do not do the *darus* at all, considering it pretty much of a *kolot* pattern anyway, but the simultaneous system is embraced by NU urbanites and the more moderate modernists who simply cannot afford to sit up all night chanting the Koran but cannot bring themselves to discard the *darus* altogether.

> He (a PSII member and urban *langgar* head) said that he doesn't like the new system but he is using it anyway in his own *langgar*. It makes it impossible to correct the reader, which is the whole point of the *darus,* and is in general more superficial. The main reason for its popularity is that in town people don't have time to sit and read the Koran and are in a hurry to be off. I asked him why, if he didn't like it, he used it. At first he said something about still being able to make the corrections even with all reading at once. (He said he lets only those people read together who he knows can do it. The ones who are not yet good readers he makes read a section by themselves.) Finally he admitted that those who frequent his *langgar* are mostly young men, and, like most young men, they want to get off in time for the second show at the movie.

The praying in the Fast reaches its climax with the prayers on the morning of the end-of-Fast holiday, *Idul Fitri*. (Only *santris* refer to it by this name. Others call it *Rijaja* in Javanese and *Hari Raja* in Indonesian.) Muhammadijah holds its prayers in the public square; NU, orthodox to the end, holds its in the mosque. More people usually turn up at the mosque than at the public square, but the prayers in the public square are usually marked by the presence of a few high *prijajis* who never go into the mosque but who turn out for the *Idul Fitri* prayers, much the way some of us turn up at church on Easter and Christmas. (Outdoor prayers are held in the public square by Muhammadijah on *Idul Adha,* "Sacrifice Day," as well as on *Idul Fitri*.) The chairman of Masjumi usually gives the sermon in the public square. (The NU mosque ceremony is about the same as any Friday prayer, only larger.) The times I heard him, he spoke on the equality of women in Islam, the need for Indonesians to study in the sciences, and the fact that all over the world members of the *ummat* were performing similar prayers.

The very fixing of the day ending the Fast (as well as the one beginning it) is a source of conflict between the modern and conservative groups. Weeks before it is to happen, Muhammadijah people receive the word when the Fast is to begin and end from their central headquarters in Djokjakarta, where it is figured out by their leaders according to the system (called *falak*) for computing the phases of the moon given in special Islamic treatises. NU, as well as the NU-dominated Ministry of Religion, since they distrust this system, are always forced to wait like so many anxious empiricists for the moon actually to appear. As the moon always appears when Muhammadijah predicts it will, this gives them something of an edge on NU in such things as gathering the *zakat fitrah* tax.

The *naib* (and chairman of NU) said that the best way is to wait until the night when the Fast is supposed to end and see if there is a moon. He said that for him and NU, both being naturally cautious, it is like when one adds up a long string of figures to see how much money one has. When one finishes adding, one still counts his money itself to see if it checks with the figures; and if it doesn't, one trusts the money rather than the figures. Muhammadijah, on the other hand, trusts the figures and so knows way ahead of time when the day will fall and doesn't have to wait to see if there is a moon or not. He thought this rather lacking in caution, but admitted somewhat sadly that they do always seem to be right. In Sumbersari (a nearby village) the head of the Masjumi told me gleefully that Masjumi got a better return on its *zakat-fitrah* efforts this year because he and the rest of the party felt assured that the moon would show when Muhammadijah had said it would and so had no problems and just went ahead and collected the *zakat;* but NU vacillated, not being sure what day it would be, with the result that they got a late start and didn't do so well.

As for the fasting itself, for the most part only *santris* keep it very well, although a few *abangans* and a number of *prijajis* also do because fasting is a Hindu-Buddhist custom as well as an Islamic one and deeply engrained in the culture generally. The great mass of non-*santris* make no attempt to keep the Fast; nor do they put up any pretense of doing so. They eat in the Fast along the street or in coffee-shops in full view of fasting *santris,* with little thought on either side that this is either unfeeling or impolite—although the *santris* naturally regard the non-fasters as rather inadequate Moslems. One pious *hadji* who fasted but ran a coffee-shop for a living told me that he tried unsuccessfully to keep his coffee-shop open during the Fast—because, after all, every nickel helps. But, he said sadly, with his reputation as a firm *santri,* people were a little embarrassed to come into his shop in the Fast because they knew he would think ill of them even if he didn't say anything and accepted their money with his usual eagerness, and so he was forced to close.

Fasting all day every day for a month is for many people quite taxing. One old NU leader of 70 or so told me that he had fasted in each Fast all his life had never gotten used to it and each year seemed more hellish than the last. He said that with some people it was easy but with others, perhaps most, it was just a month of suffering. Each evening one sees fasting *santris* sitting around nervously waiting for the slit-gong to sound signifying that it is lawful to eat. There are various compromises with their stomachs that people make, such as fasting only on the first and last days of the Fast (which one *kijaji* at an NU meeting compared rather aptly to wearing a hat and shoes but nothing in between) or fasting only until noon (legitimate for younger children, but most *santri* children can fast the whole day by the time they are twelve), which are mostly employed by people who say they work too hard to keep the Fast. But most people either fast or do not; and most *santris* do.

When one asks *santris* why one is supposed to keep the Fast, they almost invariably give three reasons: to show obedience to the commands of God, to experience what it is to go hungry so one can have greater understanding of what it is like to be poor and not have enough to eat, to steel oneself so that one will be able to take whatever suffering comes his way. It is exercising the soul the way sports exercise the body; and one young educated *santri* compared it to an examination in a school.

> He said that he always feels before the Fast as he does before an examination in school—anxious. Because it is like an exam, he is afraid he won't pass. Last year he was ill and couldn't fast, and he didn't feel right because all his friends were fasting. When the end of the Fast came he went along to the prayers as though he had been fasting, but he still didn't feel right. During the Fast one is not supposed to do any wrong things, not supposed to gossip or swear or deceive people. Every day at the end of the day he takes account of himself.

The Fast reverses the hours of eating and shifts the hours of sleeping for those who observe it. The Fast is broken at sunset with only a small bite of food, usually a date or a piece of fruit, this being called the *buka* or "opening." After evening prayer a full meal is served, and the *darus* and *trawèh* follow this, often lasting until after midnight. At 2:00 A.M. the whole family, wakened by the beating of the mosque slit-gong, rises for *saur,* the main meal in the Fast, and more pious *santris,* particularly in the villages, often sit up reading the Koran until morning, sleeping much of the day. With *Rijaja,* this upside-down month ends in a great holiday somewhat like our Easter, when everyone buys new clothes, visits friends, and prepares feasts:

> He (a young modernist *santri*) said people tend to make *Rijaja* more important than fasting. They talk about it more—about saving money for it, about the things they are going to buy. They discuss it all through the Fast. When I asked if *santris* do this too, he said yes, except those who "know." I asked for an example of someone who "knows," and he mentioned Pak Ali (Chairman of Masjumi, Vice-Chairman of Muhammadijah), who always says one shouldn't wear new clothes on *Rijaja* but should dress just in ordinary clothes that one likes to wear on every day, and who has never appeared on *Rijaja* in new clothes. Women are the worst. They always talk about clothes, money, getting ready all the special foods. . . . He said that when he was small he always liked the month of the Fast because it meant the *Rijaja* was coming.

But *Rijaja* is not merely a *santri* holiday. It is one in which every Javanese participates, regardless of his religious beliefs. As such, it will with greater appropriateness be treated in the Conclusion.

Part Three

THE "PRIJAJI" VARIANT

Chapter 17

The Background and General Dimensions of *Prijaji* Belief and Etiquette

The Development of a "Great Tradition"

IT IS Robert Redfield who has pointed out that, whereas the pre-civilized hunter or villager is preliterate, the peasant is illiterate.* When people come to live in cities and towns—and in Java they seem to have come to do this shortly after the time of Christ—there occurs a splitting (which Redfield calls a transformation) of the homogeneous cultural tradition of the self-sufficient tribe; for this cultural tradition has now to serve two social structures: that of the sophisticated city, economically dependent upon the village, and that of the rustic village, culturally dependent upon the city. Out of the confining chrysalis of inward-looking tribalism there emerges a dual tradition in which urban elaboration of aesthetic, moral, political, military, religious, and economic patterns is matched in the countryside by an increasingly effective elaboration of agricultural techniques to support such specialized efforts.

There is a cultural elite, whose ultimate basis of power is their control over the central symbolic resources of the society (religion, philosophy, art, science, and, most crucially in the more complex civilizations, writing); and there is a subordinated practical hard-working peasantry, whose ultimate basis of power is their control over the central material resource of the society, its food supply. The two become symbiotically dependent upon one another, their two variant traditions reflecting back and forth within one another as in two etched mirrors, each catching dimly the other's reflection. One cannot have a peasantry without a gentry or a gentry without a peasantry.

In such a situation whether one calls the peasant tradition a vulgarization of the gentry,** or the gentry tradition a refinement of the peasant, is not very

* Robert Redfield, *The Primitive World and Its Transformations* (Ithaca, 1954).
** Which in large part it certainly is. The folklorists have taught us that, often, what seem to be prime examples of spontaneous "people's art" are but outmoded urban traits "fallen by a peculiar cultural gravity into the lowest strata" (See G. F. Foster, "What is Folk Culture?" *American Anthropologist,* Vol. 55, No. 21, 1953, pp. 159–173).

important. What is actually the case is that there is a persistent cultural dialogue between gentry and peasantry, a constant interchange of cultural material in which fading urban forms "coarsen" and "sink" into the peasant mass and elaborated rural forms "etherealize" and "rise" into the urban elite.

The symbiotic relationship between folk (i.e., "peasant," although, as I have already pointed out, one finds "peasants" in town in modern Java) and non-folk (i.e., "gentry") here postulated as the key concept of folk culture implies that the direction of culture flow is not alone outward and downward, from city to country and from upper to lower classes. Rather, we are facing a circular phenomenon in which folk culture draws on and is continually replenished by contact with the products of intellectual and scientific social strata, but in which folk culture continually, though perhaps in lesser degree, contributes to these non-folk societies. The dance is illustrative of this process. In the 17th and 18th centuries Western European dance masters introduced folk dances to social dancing, adapting them to the needs of the courts. English country square dances played a part in the development of the French *quadrille,* which was then introduced back into London. These folk dances then became the forms around which composers, then and now, created important works. Folk dances, now become court dances, spread from Spain and France to Latin America, and the process began anew whereby little by little they became the property of the folk. The current American rage for square dancing also reflects this process: after suitable time the folk entertainment of yesteryear becomes the pastime of the artistic *avant-garde.**

In a fully developed non-industrial civilization, then, there is typically a ruling class of literates and a ruled class of illiterates (although both groups may be further internally differentiated), the two facing one another across an at best only sporadically bridgeable chasm of class. Those who can write provide the ideal model for those who cannot, and the latter ape the former as best they can from a distance which is usually great. The gentry represents the Great Tradition as the peasant represents the Little; and, although both may have been heavily stimulated by outside influences, as they were in Java by Hindu-Buddhism and Islam, they grow in time so close as to become distorted images of one another, alternately repelled by and attracted to each other. In the peasant the gentleman sees both a disturbingly barbaric parody of his own carefully controlled behavior and an attractive spontaneity and animal power which tempt him from the infinite boredom of his own constricted politesse. In the gentleman the peasant sees both a summation of all that he wishes he could be—self-controlled, polished, learned, spiritually refined—and a kind of self-important stuffiness and genteel fastidiousness which, he feels, must surely take most of the joy out of life.

Gentry and Peasantry in Java

THE *abangans* are Java's peasantry, the *prijajis* its gentry. *Abangan* religion represents the peasant synthesis of urban imports and tribal inheritances, a

* *Ibid.*

syncretism of old bits and pieces from a dozen sources ordered into a conglomerate whole to serve the needs of an unpretentious people growing rice in irrigated terraces. Nowadays there are *santri* peasants also, for the old homogeneous peasant culture is beginning to break up under the pressures of modern life; but until this century, and still for most peasants (including many of the nominally *santri* ones), the *abangan* tradition—a little native curing, a little Tantric magic, a little Islamic chanting, all clustered about a simple commensality ritual—served to define and order the basic social interrelationships of the land-bound peasantry. And it projected for them a symbolic world of meaning in which the work they did, the lives they led, and the values they held all made cosmic sense.

The *prijajis* have always been mainly of the towns; in fact, one of the most sociologically interesting characteristics of modern Java is the degree to which they have stayed in them. Partly because of the political instability of the pre-colonial kingdoms, partly because of their own inward-looking philosophies, which elevate mystical achievement over political skill, partly because of Dutch opposition to their direct encroachment upon the peasantry, the *prijajis* have not been able to turn themselves into a landed gentry. They are not, with a few exceptions (none around Modjokuto), baronial landlords working serfs or semi-serfs on huge estates. For the most part they are bureaucrats, clerks, and teachers—white-collar nobles.

The "noble" element is less important now. *Prijaji* originally indicated a man who could trace his ancestry back to the great semi-mythical kings of pre-colonial Java; but, as the Dutch, rulers of Java for over three hundred years, employed this group as the administrative instruments of their policy, the term widened to include commoners pulled into the bureaucracy as the supply of authentic aristocrats ran out. Nevertheless, even in Modjokuto, which, being but a district and subdistrict capital, represents the lowest reaches of the central bureaucracy and so could be expected to be manned by the less elevated in any case, the sense of the importance of noble descent remains.

Then I asked him (a titled *prijaji* draughtsman in the government Irrigation Office) about class. He said that there were just two: *prijaji* and non-*prijaji*. *Prijajis* are people who do "refined" (*alus*) work, those who work for the government. The other group consists of people who do "unrefined" (*kasar*) work, and includes peasants, laborers, traders, and everyone else. He said that this is an outgrowth of the old system here before the Dutch, which is still present to an extent in Bali: the Hindu system which had five groups: (1) Brahmans, or priests and teachers; (2) Satrijas, or soldiers and kings; (3) Vaisias, or traders; (4) Sudras, or peasants and craftsmen, and (5) Pariahs, who are beggars. The last three were all really set off against the top two, and the *prijajis* of today are the descendants of the Satrijas, the old kings and courtiers. (He said there were no more Brahmans.)

I asked about Sosro (the town's largest landowner, who has about eighty acres and is a former government official, also titled). He doesn't work for the government; is he a *prijaji?* "Yes," said Wiro (the informant), "because he follows the style of life of the *prijajis* and mixes with *prijajis,* and because he is descended from *prijajis.*"

How about H. Abdul (a wealthy *santri* merchant)? "Oh, no, he isn't," said Wiro, laughing. "Yes, I know," I said, "but is he really on the same class level as a carpenter out in the kampong?" And he said, yes, that from his, Wiro's, point of view, they were on the same level. He said that this is relative, though: if one asked a village man whether H. Abdul was a *prijaji* he would probably say, yes, because he is up there so high that he seems like a *prijaji* to the village man." (This, on my experience, is untrue. No village man would make the mistake of calling a rich *santri*, no matter how high up he was, a *prijaji*.) If one asked Abdul himself, he probably wouldn't say that he was a *prijaji*, but he wouldn't say that he was the same as a carpenter either, but higher. But from Wiro's point of view as a *prijaji*, Abdul, the carpenter, and the peasants are all one big undifferentiated group.

He said that there were a number of benchmarks which one could use to distingush *prijajis* from non-*prijajis:* wealth (but *prijajis* are, as a matter of fact, often less wealthy than rich *santri* traders and perhaps even than some of the richer *abangan* village chiefs); style of life—the clothes they wear, the houses they live in, the way they behave; whom they associate with, since *prijajis* associate almost exclusively with other *prijajis;* and, most important by far, descent. That is why Abdul and the carpenter are the same; their origins are the same—i.e., from commoners. . . .

I kept at him on this, asking him about a boy who was born noble and was separated from his parents, grew up in a village, and then discovered his origin. Is he a *prijaji?* "Oh yes," said Wiro, "if he is a descendant of kings he must be different; you would notice it right away. He would talk and behave in a much more refined manner than the village people around him."

I then said, "What about high government officials who haven't got the pedigree—say the regent in Bragang? (The Regent of Bragang is a Masjumi man and so a *santri*, a situation which goes down very hard with almost all the *prijajis* in town, who almost never fail to lament his politically necessary appointment as "unfitting.") Wiro guessed that the regent was considered a *prijaji* now, for the times are changing—a *prijaji* by "work" (i.e., achievement), which is more and more accepted now. However, from Wiro's point of view the *prijaji* with descent is higher than any achieved *prijaji* could ever be. For example, there are many people with the titles of Mr. (i.e., Master of Laws) and Dr. (i.e., Doctor of Laws) now, and many of them are not from the *prijaji* group but are sons of rich village people, rich village chiefs, traders, and so forth and are not people with a real title but merely an academic one. Such people must think differently and have a different inner character no matter how hard they try to copy *prijaji* manners.

I asked him just what the difference was. He said that those who have their status from riches and "work" (e.g., "study") have less of a humanitarian feeling (*rasa kemanusian*) compared to *prijajis* of the same level and education—for the most part anyway, although there may be exceptions. For example, the Sultan of Djokjakarta compared say with a *prijaji* leader has much greater "humanity" (*kemanusian*). Even though he was educated in Holland he still has his Satrija-ness. . . .

He said that *prijajis* never have stores . . . because no *prijaji* is ever really clever at trade. It is not in their "inherited duty" (*darma*), not their "cleverness." Their "inherited duty" is as soldiers and guarding the government (i.e., as officials), and thus they can't sell, and, if they try, their minds are unsettled. He knows that if he went into trade he would feel unhappy in his heart. Being clever at trade like other things is a matter of descent, but among non-*prijajis*—especially those from Solo, Djokjakarta, and Kudus. The "thought pattern" involved is lower than *prijaji*. . . . All non-*prijajis* have the same "inherited duty" and their souls are all the same. A trader thinks only about his own needs and not about society generally. . . .

He said that the *Pantjasila* (President Sukarno's Five Points, the basis of the present state) was an effort to re-establish the old Hindu system, which was very good. He said that in his view the times go in circles; history repeats in cycles and one keeps going back to the time before. This is the will of nature, the will of God. . . . What is important is not for the exact society of the past to be re-established, which is impossible, but just that people know each what his duty is according to his descent so that the descendants of peasants will be peasants, of traders traders, and so on. If not ordered so, society will be ruined. If common people keep acting like *prijajis*, who is going to hoe the fields after a while? The country will fall. However, he admitted, more and more village people are imitating *prijajis*, and he wondered who would hoe later. He said that if he, for example, were obligated to hoe, he couldn't do it.

This *prijaji* ethic, with its intense sense for status differences, its calm assertion of spiritual superiority, and its dual emphasis on the inner life of refined feeling and the external life of polite form, is the outcome of nearly sixteen centuries of urban living. The ancient Hindu-Buddhist city-states were headed by a king who was also a God, a divine monarch enthroned at the very peak of spiritual refinement upon a symbolically divine mountain set in the exact center of his squared-off capital.* They brought into being a group of religio-aesthetically concerned warrior-gentry, receivers of foreign cultural fashions and rationalizers of local ones. The city-states rose and fell, one following the next as so many unsuccessful political experiments. With the possible exception of the great fourteenth-century kingdom of Madjapahit, and the seventeenth-century Mataram, they were unable to throw roots very deep into the peasant mass. The Javanese aristocracy lacked the land-linked system of feudal obligation of Western Europe with its fief-holding agricultural gentry, or the rationalized Chinese bureaucracy drawing its officials from rural gentry as well as urban. They lacked even the solidified patron relations of the caste-organized India whence they borrowed so much of their world-view. Therefore, the Javanese aristocracy had, until the Dutch came, but two ways to hold the peasants in order to extract from them the rice and manpower they needed to support their own specialization: simple military terror and religious enthusiasm. They used both.

Basic Concepts in the *Prijaji* World-View

PEASANTS clung to gentry princes not only for military protection but also because the latter had about them that magical-mystical aura Max Weber called

* See R. Heine-Geldern, "Conceptions of State and Kingship in Southeast Asia," *Far Eastern Quarterly,* Vol. 2, 1942.

charisma. Spiritual excellence was correlated with political eminence and culminated in the immobile king, the incarnation of Vishnu or Shiva, meditating in his castle at the center of the universe. Spiritual power flowed outward and downward from its royal fountainhead, attenuating as it sank through each layer in the bureaucracy, draining weakly at last into the peasant masses. Peasant and king, center and periphery, pinnacle and base, God and animal, sacred and profane—these were, and, with some reinterpretations, are now the coordinate termini of the *prijaji*'s metaphysical and social measuring rod, termini summed up in a pair of concepts central to the *prijaji* world-view: *alus* and *kasar*.

Alus means pure, refined, polished, polite, exquisite, ethereal, subtle, civilized, smooth. A man who speaks flawless high-Javanese is *alus,* as is the high-Javanese itself. A piece of cloth with intricate, subtle designs painted onto it is *alus*. An exquisitely played piece of music or a beautifully controlled dance step is *alus*. So is a smooth stone, a dog with his hair petted down, a far-fetched joke, or a clever poetic conceit. God is, of course, *alus* (as are all invisible spirits), and so is the mystical experience of Him. One's own soul and character are *alus* insofar as one emotionally comprehends the ultimate structure of existence; and one's behavior and actions are *alus* insofar as they are regulated by the delicate intricacies of the complex court-derived etiquette. *Kasar* is merely the opposite: impolite, rough, uncivilized; a badly played piece of music, a stupid joke, a cheap piece of cloth. Between these two poles the *prijaji* arranges everyone from peasant to king.

But even to begin to understand the *prijaji* outlook, one must comprehend the meaning of another pair of concepts: *lair* and *batin*. *Batin* means "the inner realm of human experience," and *lair* "the outer realm of human behavior." The immediate temptation is to equate them with body and soul, but this would be a serious mistake. *Batin* refers not to a separate seat of encapsulated spirituality detachable from the body but to the emotional life of the individual taken generally—what we call "the inner life," or "the subjective"; it consists of the fuzzy, shifting shapes of private feeling perceived directly in all their phenomenological immediacy. *Lair,* on the other hand, refers to that part of human life which strict behavioral psychologists limit themselves to studying—the external actions, motions, postures, and speech of the individual. These two sets of phenomena, the inner and the outer, are conceived as somewhat independent realms to be put into proper order separately, or, perhaps better stated, sequentially. The ordering of the outward life leaves one free to turn to the ordering of the inward. The cultivated man needs to give form both to the naturally jagged physical gestures which make up his external behavior and to the fluctuating states of feeling which comprise his inner experience. A truly *alus* man is polite all the way through.

Of the two tasks, the ordering of the external life is easier, in support of which statement I offer the following stanza, all too literally translated, of a long poem (or song, for Javanese poems—*tembang*—may always be sung). It was composed by a Modjokuto Javanese, who, although he is actually something of a *santri* mystic too, expresses a basically *prijaji* outlook on life in this set of moral verses intended for the edification of his children:

> Politeness in outward behavior,
> Although complex, is easy to learn
> If only you wish to,
> Because it is both audible and visible.
> If you inspect it carefully and in detail, over and over again,
> You will be able in a short time
> To do the polite thing
> From the point of view of good form and customary behavior.
> Wherever you may live,
> You will be able to mix with everyone.

The contrasting task, ordering the inner life, is much more difficult:

> Now as for ordering the inner life,
> This is not something every person knows about.
> It is very, very difficult.
> One feels even more uneasy
> When one tries to know the order of the inner life.
> Because it is invisible,
> Even more than fine powder is.
> One might say it is inexplicable, or that it is unclear.
> So if you are not very thorough in searching for it
> You certainly will not find it.

By "finding" the "order of the inner life" the poet refers to that ultimate aim of *prijaji* religion in general, mystical experience; for in the truly well-ordered man the whole being is permeated by politesse, the inner and outer merge, and there is a revelation of their significance.

> Whoever knows the politeness of the inner life
> Knows also the true nobility,
> Shows the true signs of high character.
> He will be able to care for his spiritual castle,
> Indeed, a glorious place,
> Which is never further from him than his beard,
> And which will be shielded with but a curtain of light.
> Lo! Such are the teachings of extraordinary men.
> It is fitting that you should follow their advice.

The political metaphors which identify spirituality with political nobility and employ the image of the meditating king's castle for the light-shielded inner life of man (where, as we shall see, God also dwells) depend upon the more fundamental identification of religious and political status set forth in the concept of a *kasar*-to-*alus* gradation. But the combination of the *lair-batin* distinction and the *kasar-alus* continuum brings about a situation in which the ascent from the uncivilized animalistic peasant to the hyper-civilized divine king takes place not only in terms of greater mystical achievements, more and more highly developed skills of inward-looking contemplation and refinement of subjective experience, but also in greater and greater formal control over the external aspects of individual actions, transforming them into art or near-art. In the dance, in the shadow-play, in music, in textile design, in etiquette, and, perhaps most crucially of all, in language, the aesthetic formalization of the surfaces of social behavior permeates everything the *alus* Javanese does.

Prijaji versus *Abangan:* General Differences

OF course there are no sovereign courts in Java, and there have not been for centuries. The Dutch, however, not only drew their native administrators, teachers, and clerks from among the descendants of nobles and king but also permitted the two great courts of Djokjakarta and Surakarta to persist through the entire colonial period, having destroyed their military power and relieved their kings of any independent authority. Thus the cultural tradition persisted, grafted now to a progressively more rationalized colonial bureaucracy. The *prijajis* remained both the cultural leaders and, so far as the indigenous society was concerned, the political ones even though everyone was aware that the ultimate locus of power in the society had shifted into foreign hands. The gentry concern for etiquette, art, and mysticism continued, as did the peasant imitation of the forms they developed.

The *prijaji* religious orientation is more difficult to set off from the *abangan* than is the *santri,* because the change from a syncretic South Asian polytheism (or "animism," if "deity" is too elevated a term to apply to such as *danjangs, ṭujuls,* and *ḍemits*) to a Mid-Eastern monotheism is rather greater than the shift from such a religion to a Hindu-Buddhist pantheism. The traits I shall discuss under *prijaji* are not confined to them. The *gamelan* orchestra and the *wajang* shadow-play, for example, could hardly be said to be absent from peasant life; but they are included in this context because their cultivation, the elucidation of their religio-philosophical meaning, and their most elaborate variations are found in a *prijaji* context; and because they have been pulled into and integrated with a general gentry style of life toward which the whole rest of the society, even the *santri* sector, to an extent and grudgingly, looks as the very model of civilized living.

Although the *Prijaji* and *abangan* orientations, from the point of view of culture content, are in part but genteel and vulgar versions of one another, they are organized around rather different types of social structure and expressive of quite different sorts of values, a difference Cora Dubois has characterized, speaking of the entire Southeast Asian culture-area, as follows:

> Here was a class (the gentry) whose ethos was deeply at variance from that of the peasantry. It conceived of life in terms of hierarchy and power rather than in terms of simple communal democracy; in terms of privilege rather than mutual obligations; in terms of ostentation and aggrandizement rather than subsistence and communal obligations.*

Thus, as one traces *prijaji* patterns downward, they tend to shift in significance as they approach the *abangan* social context. Mystic practices tend to turn into curing techniques; a vague and abstract pantheism gives way to

* *Social Forces in Southeast Asia* (St. Paul, 1949).

a vivid and concrete polytheism; a concern for individual religious experience is replaced by a concern for group religious reciprocality. And the corollary holds too: *abangan slametans* become *prijaji* formal banquets. In any case, although the *prijajis* and *abangans* have, in many ways, very similar world-views, and although they share many concrete items of religious belief and practice, the ethics which can be deduced from these underlying world-views and which the items are arranged to symbolize differ rather markedly.

Literati versus Intelligentsia

THERE is within the *prijaji* group something of a distinction comparable to the conservative-modern division already outlined in connection with *abangans* and *santris*. Here the distinction seems to coincide with one made by Redfield, building on Arnold Toynbee and Gordon Childe, between what he calls the "literati" and what he calls the "intelligentsia":

> In emphasizing two contrasting aspects of the functions and roles of the literate in the early and later civilizations, Childe and Toynbee point to a difference that might deserve the distinguishing terms that these writers give to the two kinds of literate people. Childe is impressed with the separation between craftsmanship and literacy in the early civilizations and with the "scholastic attitude" developed by those clerks who used writing to set down traditional lore and knowledge and who came to develop the exact sciences and philosophy. Some of these became custodians and interpreters of sacred books. In this aspect of their functions, internal to the developing civilization, we might speak of the new type of men as the literati. The literate elite of China illustrate the type. These persons are enclosed within the culture that has become civilization. They carry it forward into a more systematic and reflective phase. . . .
>
>   Toynbee, on the other hand, writes of the functions of those literate persons who mediate between the society out of which they arose and some other and alien civilization which is impinging upon it. These people have learned something alien to the culture of their native community; they "have learnt the tricks of the intrusive civilization's trade so far as may be necessary to enable their own community, through their agency, just to hold its own in a social environment in which life is ceasing to be lived in accordance with the local tradition and is coming more and more to be lived in the style imposed by the intrusive civilization upon the aliens who fall under its domination." . . . These people Toynbee calls by a word which developed for them in Russia, the intelligentsia. In contrast to the literati, the member of the intelligentsia "is born to be unhappy." He belongs to two worlds, not one; he is a "marginal man."[*]

The intrusive civilization whose tricks the Javanese intelligentsia have learned is, of course, the Dutch version of the Western. In addition to the mysticism, the pantheism, and the palace etiquette there is in *prijaji* life an

[*] *Op. cit.*

all too familiar petty-bourgeois element whose provenance is not difficult to guess. It is among the *prijajis* that one finds women embroidering, giving wedding presents, furnishing their homes with heavy baroque furniture, and decorating the walls of their little box-shaped cement houses—which often would look less out of place in The Hague—with cozy landscapes. It is among them that one finds men engaged in tennis, chess, swimming, and hunting. One even still finds a few of them reading Dutch novels and magazines, although this has dropped off since the Revolution; and I even knew one or two who did pencil sketches, hardly a native Javanese custom. The peasants for such people are something of an embarrassment: they are not only ignorant and lacking in proper manners—a literati complaint—but they are also "disorderly," "dirty," and "lazy," and they bring up their children in an irregular fashion.

> When I told him I was studying children, he (the head of PNI—Partai Nasional Indonesia—the major *prijaji*-dominated political party, and Modjokuto's purest case of the intelligentsia type) gave me his opinions on this. He thought Javanese children weren't "trained"; that they were just let alone to eat what and when they wanted, sleep when they wanted; and some never bathed or got their clothes washed. *His* children get up at a certain time, bathe, eat breakfast, go to school; and only after school can they play. The old lady (a distant relative of the informant) chimed in, echoing Rekso, remarking that peasant children don't eat regularly, are dirty, have to gather wood and grasses for their mother instead of going to school.*

Prijajis at the middle and higher levels tend to speak Dutch instead of Javanese; and the higher levels do so to the point where, except for the low-Javanese they use to command their servants, they are nearly unable to speak their native language. It is the *prijajis* who before the war were the beneficiaries of what education the Dutch provided the Javanese (some of them even going to schools, with Dutch children), who worked as clerks and petty administrators in the Dutch sugar-factories, import-export firms, and transport industries; and it was from among them that the very few Javanese chosen to be educated in Holland were in the main selected *prijaji* pilgrims to a Western Mecca.

Out of all this came a new model for the Javanese aristocracy and for the commoners patterning themselves after them, a model based on white-collar Western education emphasizing Dutch language, history, and literature and Dutch manners and values. Women's clubs, credit cooperatives patterned on plans constructed by Dutch administrators anxious to raise the standard of living of the "natives," *noblesse oblige* adult education movements to uplift the masses—by teaching them to read and write, to reduce their divorce rate, and to wash their clothes—appeared alongside the dance groups, the religious training sects, and the *gamelan* orchestras.

Parallel to the social pyramid based on artistic-mystic skills and on closeness to the core of Hindu-Javanese court tradition there came to be erected another pyramid based on skill in manipulation of Western ideas and values

---

* This passage is a transcript from my wife's field notes.

and on closeness to the Dutch colonial community—an intelligentsia as well as a literati.

> He (a well-educated young *prijaji* head of a private school run by a private *prijaji* educational society) criticized the failure of many *prijajis* to participate in modern life. . . . He said that Sosro (the landowner mentioned above by Pak Wiro) was an example of this. In the Dutch times he had the highest position in the bureaucracy of anyone who ever grew up in Modjokuto, being head of the Fish Harbor in Djakarta, but now he doesn't do anything at all; he just sits home being *alus,* studying mysticism and the like. I asked if that was because he was old. Narjo (the informant) said, "No, he is only fifty, and quite healthy." In this case the passivity was mainly due to his Surakarta wife. After he married her, a *Radèn Aju* (a fairly high female court title), he changed course 180 degrees and started doing things the Surakarta way, which is very slow and *alus.* Narjo expressed strong disapproval of this and said Rekso (the PNI head) was different in this respect; he was very active in things.

The difference between the two groups is not nearly so sharp as the comparable difference among the *santris,* however. Most *prijajis* have both a literati and an intelligentsia aspect to their outlook. (Even the above informant belonged to a mystic society.) In general, as one progresses up the status ladder in the direction of the large northern port cities—Djakarta, Surabaja, and Semarang, the literati element steadily lessens and the intelligentsia element steadily increases, until in some circles in Djakarta it would be difficult, if one ignored physical anthropology, to tell that one was not in Holland. Similarly, as one goes up the status ladder in the direction of the great inland court centers, there is an increasing tendency for the literati element to grow stronger, although the intelligentsia aspect does not necessarily decrease, until in the court circles of Djokjakarta and, especially, Surakarta, it is possible, if one ignores the furniture and the electric lights, to imagine one is in a pre-Dutch Hindu-Buddhist court.

Modjokuto, in the middle geographically and socially, gets influences from both directions. If one were to wear customary court dress to the north, around Modjokuto and Surabaja, he would be laughed at, one informant told me; and he said that he knew a man who had had his traditional clothing literally torn off him. But in the Surakarta-Djokjakarta direction people prefer such dress, and many still look down on anyone who wears pants and a jacket as a Dutch imitator.

In general, however, the intelligentsia and literati elements tend to get bound into the same person, with only relative emphasis on one or the other. The current (1954) *prijaji* culture-hero is the Sultan of Djokjakarta, who, it is said, behaves exactly like a conservative, mystic, traditional king within his palace and like a progressive, modern, Dutch-educated political leader outside of it. And even in the most intelligentsia circles in Djakarta one will often run into mysticism in unexpected places:

> He (an advanced student in sociology at the University of Indonesia) asked me if I had studied philosophy, and I said, "A little." He asked if I had found there a key to life, an answer. He said that he knew very little philosophy but

that he was always looking for such a key. He said that he had made up a philosophy for himself: one part Indian philosophy, one part Islam, one part sociology, and one part psychology. . . . He had written all this down and sent it to *Siasat* (a weekly socialist magazine), but the editor said that he should send it to a theological magazine. He thought he would just keep it for a while, because if he published it people might not understand it the same way he meant it and then would be led astray.

The General Dimensions of *Prijaji* Belief

THE three major foci of *prijaji* "religious" life are etiquette, art, and mystical practice. I admit to using "religion" in a somewhat broader sense than may be typical, but there is nothing else to do when these factors are so fused as to make their separate consideration nearly meaningless. For etiquette, art, and mystical practice represent the *prijaji* effort after order as it moves from the surface of human experience toward its depths, from the outer aspect of life toward the inner. Etiquette, the polishing of interpersonal behavior into smooth decorum, lends to everyday behavior a spiritualized formality; art, a dual discipline of mind and body, provides a revelation of inner significance in outward gesture; and mystic practice, the intensive regulation of the life of thought and feeling, organizes the individual's spiritual resources for an attack upon ultimate enlightenment. The connecting link between all three, the common element in them all which ties them together and makes them but different modes of the same reality, is what the Javanese, borrowing a concept from India, call *rasa*.

Rasa has two primary meanings: "feeling" and "meaning." As "feeling" it is one of the traditional five senses (*pantjaindrija*)—seeing, hearing, talking, smelling, and feeling. It includes within itself three aspects of "feeling" that our view of the five senses separates: taste on the tongue, touch on the body, and emotional "feeling" within the "heart"—sadness, happiness, and the like. The taste of a banana is its *rasa;* a hunch is a *rasa;* a pain is a *rasa;* and so is a passion.

As "meaning," *rasa* is applied to the words in a letter, in a poem, or even in speech, to indicate the between-the-lines "looking north and hitting south" type of allusive suggestion that is so important in Javanese communication. And it is given the same application to external acts generally: to indicate the implicit import, the connotative "feeling" of dance movements, polite gestures, and so forth. But, in this second sense, it also means "ultimate significance"—the deepest meaning at which one arrives by dint of mystical effort and whose clarification resolves all the ambiguities of mundane existence. *Rasa,* said one of my most articulate informants, is the same as life; whatever lives has *rasa,* and whatever has *rasa* lives. To translate such a sentence one could only render it twice: whatever lives feels, and whatever feels lives; or: whatever lives has meaning, and whatever has meaning lives. As the first, or sensationalist, definition of *rasa* indicates both feeling from without (taste, touch) and from within (emotional), so *rasa* in its second, or semantic, definition indicates both the meaning of events in the *lair,* the external behavioral world of sound, shape, and gesture, and in the far more mysterious *batin,* the fluid inner world of life.

The changes which the Javanese ring upon this protean root are numerous and so marvelously consistent as almost to give in themselves a complete picture of the phenomenological analysis of human experience upon which the *prijajis* base their world-view. *Ngrasani* means to speak ill of someone, to gossip about them. *Ngrasakaké* means to sympathize with or "feel with" someone or something. ("My business is so bad," moaned one storekeeper to me, "you can't even *ngrasakaké* it"; and people urged to cooperate are told to *ngrasakaké* one another.) A *rerasan* (to *rasa* one another mutually) is a discussion or conversation, usually an acrimonious one. *Sarasa* (to be of one *rasa*) is to be in harmony, to agree. *Mirasa* is to reason over something, think about something. *Krasa* indicates "feeling" as an abstract noun; thus *krasa bingah* (*bingah*—"happy") means happiness. *Krasan* means to "feel at home," to feel comfortable in the situation which you are in, to be used to it. ("Are you *krasan* in Java?"—i.e., do you feel at home in Java? Are you already used to the heat, food, and customs here so that they no longer disturb your equanimity? This last is the Javanese equivalent of our perennial question to visiting foreigners, "How do you like America?") *Rasa-pangrasa* means to "feel out" one another tentatively and warily, to hold back one's feelings in untrusting concealment from one another, a typical *prijaji* pattern. *Rumangsa* means to be conscious of, to perceive, something. As J. Gonda points out in his *Sanskrit in Indonesia,*[*] the two meanings of *rasa*—"ultimate meaning" or "hidden significance," and "tactile sensation," "taste," or "inward feeling"—actually derive from two different Sanskrit roots; but, as he also points out, in modern Java "the latter . . . word . . . has, indeed, blended with the former." It is upon this blending that the *prijaji* religious analysis is based.

By taking *rasa* to mean both "feeling" and "meaning," the *prijaji* has been able to develop a phenomenological analysis of subjective experience to which everything else can be tied. Because fundamentally "feeling" and "meaning" are one, and therefore the ultimate religious experience taken subjectively is also the ultimate religious truth taken objectively, an empirical analysis of inward perception yields at the same time a metaphysical analysis of objective reality. This granted, the characteristic way in which human action comes to be considered, whether from a moral or an aesthetic or a religious point of view, is in terms of the emotional life of the individual who perceives it, whether from within or without; the more refined (*alus*) one's feeling, the more profound one's understanding, the more elevated one's moral character, and the more beautiful one's external aspect. The management of one's emotional economy becomes one's primary concern, in terms of which all else is ultimately rationalized. The spiritually enlightened man guards his psychological equilibrium well and makes a constant effort to maintain its placid stability. His proximate aim is emotional quiescence,

* Nagpur, 1952, p. 158.

for passion is *kasar* feeling, fit only for children, animals, peasants, and foreigners. His ultimate aim, which this quiescence makes possible, is gnosis, the direct comprehension of the ultimate *rasa*. To feel all is to understand all. Paradoxically, it is also to feel nothing—but we shall come to that problem later.

Emotional equanimity, a certain flatness of affect, is, then, the prized psychological state, the mark of the truly *alus* character. As the forms which life takes vary from the disordered grossness of animal existence up through the only slightly more refined peasant to the hyper-genteel high-*prijaji*, and, finally, through the divine king to the invisible, intangible, insensible (except mystically), self-sufficient Being of God, so the forms of feeling vary from the vulgar actuality of base passion, through the spiritualized placidity of the true *prijaji* to the ultimate *rasa,* where feeling is but meaning only. Happiness and unhappiness, say the Javanese, are irrevocably connected and imply one another as up implies down. "Happy now, unhappy later; unhappy now, happy later," is perhaps the most quoted *prijaji* maxim. The really good man tries to get beyond happiness and unhappiness as our mystics attempt to escape good and evil.

> If you can calm your innermost feelings
> You will be able to build a wall around them;
> You will not need to be or to feel greedy,
> To want this and that and the other thing.
> For the only things one receives in life
> Are merely happiness and unhappiness.
> In this there is no difference between the rich
> And the poor carrying burdens through the street.
> If you are happy now, you will be unhappy later.
> If you accept unhappiness, it will totally disappear.

This stanza of my informant's poem is worth comment. The word I have translated "calm" (*puntu*) really means to think seriously about, or, better, to talk yourself into not feeling about something you would normally feel deeply about. An informant, asked for an example said: "If my parents die, I am all upset; but if I say to myself, 'Oh, they were already old and everyone must die sometime,' then I will be at peace—this action is *puntu*." This kind of behavior, from my observation, is a major Javanese defense mechanism:

> When Pak Ardjo (my landlord, whose house had been robbed in his absence) got back home after the robbery, he didn't say anything to Bu Ardjo about it for quite a while. In fact, when I came in, just after he returned, he was talking to a railroad friend and said there had been a lot going on here too, but he just ignored this and went on talking about other subjects. . . . Later he told me he had resigned himself about the theft; had convinced himself by saying, "If it's gone, it's gone, and that's all there is to it." Being upset wouldn't bring the bike back, nor would getting angry at his wife. . . . He said he had kept himself from being upset about it all.

There are three main values involved in this calming of the true feelings, this flattening out of affect: *trima, sabar,* and *iklas. Iklas* I have already discussed, in connection with death, as meaning detachment from the contingencies of the external world so as not to be disturbed when things go awry in it or if something unexpected occurs. It is "not caring," on the premise that if one does not care about worldly things they cannot hurt or upset one; or, as our poet puts it in another stanza:

> Although you may own
> A house like a great heaven
> And lock it with a golden key,
> You must surely die in the end and be buried in the ground,
> And all your material things are yours but for a moment.

Sabar is usually translated patience. If one asks people what is the main quality which a leader, political or otherwise, should have, this is the characteristic they almost always mention. *Sabar* indicates an absence of eagerness, of impatience, of headstrong passion. A *sabar* man advances carefully through experience, stepping tentatively as we do when we are not certain that a plank is strong enough to hold us or that a hillside rock will not give way under our feet. His aim, as another line from our poem puts it, is to "go gingerly through life as a caterpillar inches over water."

Trima literally means to accept or receive; in value terms it means not to kick against the pricks, to accept what comes without protest and without rebellion. The three ideas are obviously very close. *Iklas* brings psychological peace through a lack of attachment to the external world; *sabar* brings such peace by an inward restraint of emotional drive, an atrophy of the will, an excess of caution; *trima* brings peace through the acceptance of the inevitable with grace: "If you accept unhappiness, it will totally disappear."

If one can calm one's most inward feelings (by being *trima, sabar,* and *iklas*), the poet continues, one can build a wall around them; one will be able both to conceal them from others and to protect them from outside disturbance. The refinement of inner feeling has thus two aspects: the direct internal attempt to control one's emotions represented by *trima, sabar,* and *iklas;* and, secondly, an external attempt to build a well around them that will protect them. On the one hand, one engages in an inward discipline, and on the other in an outward defense. Mysticism is mainly training in the first—how to be *trima, sabar,* and *iklas.* Etiquette is training in the second. At bottom, the refinement of the inner world—the *batin*—makes possible the refinement of the outer, which in turn protects one from being easily upset. The *prijaji* thus has two lines of defense against the shocks of the external world: the formalization of social behavior so that it is easily predictable, and the flattening of affect so that if the unexpected does occur it will be less likely to lead to an inward disturbance.

The Role of Etiquette

THE wall, then, is a wall of etiquette. Etiquette provides the *alus prijaji* with a set of rigidly formal ways of doing things which conceals his real feelings from others. In addition, it so regularizes behavior, his own and that of others, as to make it unlikely to provide unpleasant surprises.

In the model conversations dictated by *prijaji* informants teaching me Javanese, the same sort of situation occurs and reoccurs almost to the point of monotony. Two men are speaking. One wants something from the other (a loan, a service, his company in going somewhere), and both know it. The petitioner does not want to put his petition directly for fear of angering the petitioned; and the petitioned does not want to state his refusal directly for fear of frustrating the petitioner too severely. Both are very concerned with the other's emotional reactions because ultimately they will affect their own. As a result, they go through a long series of formal speech patterns, courtesy forms, complex indirections, and mutual protestations of purity of motive, arriving only slowly at the point of the conversation so that no one is taken by surprise. Etiquette is the transfer to the level of interpersonal behavior of the calm and muted feeling tone of the inner life.

The relation between *rasa* and etiquette often gets expressed in an incisive commercial metaphor:

> What is the aim of life? (The informant, a teacher-leader (*guru*) of a mystic sect, was giving me a kind of catechism of his group's beliefs.) The aim of life is to seek emotional peace; other than that there isn't any. No one seeks upset, disturbance; everyone just seeks peace. Now each person starts out on this search for inward peace with a certain amount of capital, as in the market, only it is not in the form of money but of *rasa*. This capital is neither more nor less than the ability to make other people feel at peace. . . . Every person has a capital of *rasa* to accomplish this. When I came to his house he emerged in proper style to meet me. This was his capital because it put me at ease; and so I was in turn polite to him, and so he was at ease and his capital of *rasa* was increased. You often see written and hung in people's houses, or hear people say: "Men must have etiquette-feeling (*rasa sopan-santun*)." This etiquette-feeling, this form of politeness, is a kind of instrument or tool for making others peaceful within, and thus yourself also; a kind of capital of *rasa*, because all movement is from *rasa* and so this politeness has *rasa*. If you meet a man on the street and you just coast by and don't say, "Where are you going, Pak?" in high-Javanese (the typical Javanese greeting), he will feel upset; and later his upsetness will react back and you will feel upset.
>
> He said that each people has its own politeness forms, and that no American, for example, would behave thus—and then he gave a perfect demonstration of the way Americans in fact do behave, clapping someone on the back and saying, "Let's go into town" while towering over him. (Having your head higher than another's is impossible manners for a Javanese.) In fact, his imitation was so good that I misunderstood and missed the point, agreeing that was the way Americans acted. He looked appalled and then said, mumbling, "Well, if you knew someone for a very, very long time."

Lest this be thought but an interpretation of the views of just one sect, I cite the following, from a conversation with a policeman who, although a *prijaji,* was not at all learned in mysticism, which points up even more sharply the unity of etiquette with the rest of the *prijaji* religious complex:

The policeman, who originally came from Surakarta but who has been here a long time, informed me of the various levels of the Javanese language and said that these were very important to the Javanese. Formal language, Javanese art, and etiquette, he said, were all of a piece. Each person has within him a capital of *rasa* which is his real riches and which is what makes for smooth relations between people and for peace among them and within people. Thus, said he, before I (the ethnographer) came here to Indonesia, I felt inside that I was going to try to be like the Indonesians and not try to feel higher than they were and try to get to know them; and so when I got here things worked out well and I was peaceful inside. This "emotional set" is what is called a capital of *rasa,* and it is very important. Etiquette, language, and art, such as the *gamelan* orchestra and the shadow-play, are all intended to build up within the individual this store of *rasa* capital.

Four major principles animate *prijaji* etiquette: the proper form for the proper rank, indirection, dissimulation, and the avoidance of any act suggesting disorder or lack of self-control. Under the proper form for the proper rank comes the all-important matter of the correct choice of linguistic form, to which we shall come in a moment; but it also includes the *anḍap-asor* pattern. *Anḍap-asor* means to humble oneself politely and is the correct behavior to adopt toward anyone who is either of approximately equal rank or higher. It is always a situation of some anxiety when two Javanese, especially *prijajis,* meet for the first time, for each must determine the other's rank in order both to employ the correct linguistic forms and to apply the *anḍap-asor* pattern correctly. (There are many cues: dress, occupation, bearing.) If the two are of the same rank or nearly the same, then both will adopt the *anḍap-asor* pattern; and I have seen many *prijaji* conversations that seemed to consist almost entirely of an attempt by each of the participants to put himself in the lower position, a kind of obsessive competition to be bottom dog. (The competition is pretense, of course. If either were to flatly acknowledge the other's inferiority in such a situation it would be a grave insult.)

If one participant is very obviously higher in rank than the other—a prince and a commoner, a high official and a low one, a master and his servant, an adult and a child, a rich man and a poor one (which is, however, a touchy situation, since many a poor *abangan* peasant will be unwilling to acknowledge inferiority to a rich *santri* trader)—the problem is much simpler. The lower man takes the *anḍap-asor* pattern and the higher takes a superior one, sometimes even a haughty one even though it is considered unseemly. The problem comes in the "about equal rank" situation—in deciding in borderline cases whether one's opposite number is clearly enough inferior to one to permit an adoption of a superior attitude or, conversely, if the other is high enough to be allowed to get away with such behavior. There seems to be a general fear on the part of many people that they will *ngrendahaké* (literally: to humble or lower) i.e., insult, someone lower than themselves and will be met with a sudden burst of unexpected aggression in return. One must always be careful in speaking to lower people, one woman said, because they are very easily insulted and once insulted they become uncontrollably angry.

As a result, the tendency is to move "like the caterpillar creeping over water"; to be doubly cautious about missteps. One gives people the benefit of the doubt; and so the mutual *andap-asor* competition pattern is perhaps the most common, at least within Modjokuto *prijaji* circles, where no one is really high enough to get very haughty with anyone else. Similar problems arise when separate rank characteristics conflict. What is an old man of no particular standing to do when dealing with a young man of high rank (or, nowadays, education); or a poor *prijaji* dealing with a rich trader? In part the problem is resolved by the fact that the *andap-asor* pattern as well as linguistic usage is not an absolute matter of either abject humility or lordly pride but can be indulged in by degrees. This, in fact, is half the fun of it. The accomplished *prijaji* can express all sorts of nuances of status (and insult), many of which escape Western perception altogether; and a true virtuoso can reduce novices to quivering immobility. As a Javanese put it, "I have a friend who is very *andap-asor* [to me], so that I feel ashamed with him because I am not capable of behaving as he does; and when I am going to reply to him I want to be *andap-asor* too, but I can't, so I feel ashamed."

In behavioral terms the *andap-asor* pattern consists in the first place of all kinds of submissive actions, for the Javanese take the physical metaphor seriously, associating height with high status. In the old days (and one still sees it occasionally in *prijaji* circles in the larger cities) servants served the family's meals on their knees, and the correct greeting of an inferior to a superior was to kneel and make the obeisance gesture (palms of hands together with thumbs at the nose and a "horizontal nod" of the head) to the superior's knee or even to his foot. I saw this done only once in Modjokuto —by an old servant who had come to visit her former mistress, the wife of a high *prijaji*. This sort of thing is considered too extreme nowadays, but the anxious effort to keep one's head lower than a superior's is still very much present. So is the custom of the host not sitting at the visiting table* when an important guest calls but placing himself on a low chair to the rear and side of the guest. Allowing others to go first to take the best seats and minimizing one's own abilities, property, and accomplishments are part of the same pattern.

Indirection as a theme of *prijaji* behavior, and of Javanese behavior generally, has been mentioned in this essay several times already. I have quoted the proverb "to look north and hit south," and related something about the magnificent beating about the bush that goes on when the family of the groom requests the bride from her family for their son; and I have quoted the Modjokuto *naib* on the fact that old-time *kijajis* (Koranic teachers) never explicitly informed people they were wrong but told little stories from which the listeners could get the point less painfully. One must get the *rasa* of what people are saying, the real content, informants are always emphasizing, because *alus* people often don't like to say what is on their

---

* A small round or square table, which nearly all Javanese seem to have, around which host and guests always sit, sipping lukewarm tea and nibbling bland cookies. It is also part of the *andap-asor* pattern for the host to insist that the food being offered is highly inadequate; the more the insistence, the better it is.

minds. Bluntness is simply not a virtue, and by the time one comes to the point in a well-modeled *prijaji* conversation everyone should be quite aware of what one is going to say. Often it is not necessary to come to the point at all—a great relief to everyone.

One of my *prijaji* informants wished to divorce his wife, but he thought it unseemly of someone of his status to go boldly into the *naib*'s office and simply dismiss her "village style." Instead, he unobstrusively exacerbated a latent conflict between his wife and the mother-in-law of his first, now deceased, wife, who lived next door. (He was living on his first wife's lands.) The conflict between the women soon got to the point where the wife, evidently sensing her husband's withdrawal of support from her (although he said nothing to her and behaved as though things were as normal as ever between them), could bear it no longer and went into town to request the divorce herself. The husband thus appeared to the *naib* and to his neighbors to be the injured party and to be doing his wife a favor by divorcing her. A triumph, he said to me, of *alus* behavior.

Another similar situation occurred in which a wife, unhappy not so much with her husband as with the in-laws with whom she was forced to live, got her husband to move away without coming right out and asking him to do so.

One day the husband suddenly found a postcard in the house which said, "I can't stand it any longer here. If my husband doesn't want to move, it would be better for me to go back to my parents." Then the husband was angry at everyone. First he went to his wife and asked her: "Did you write this?" No, she said, it wasn't her writing anyway. Then he accused his younger sister, who also denied it. Since the parents couldn't write, they were out of the question. He thought it might have been written by someone not in the household who wanted to make trouble. Nothing was done, and after a while things settled down again. Then the husband found another postcard just like the first, and again there was a quarrel. He gathered the family together and asked them one at a time about it, but no results. Five times the cards appeared. Finally the husband went to look for a house of his own, and after he moved things were peaceful again. Now everything is fine once more, but as yet no one has admitted writing the letters.

The use of go-betweens is part of the same pattern (although in using a go-between, a *prijaji* is caught between his great desire to keep his own affairs secret and his unwillingness to face issues in their naked form). Several *prijajis* in Modjokuto lend money, for example, and almost everyone knows they do; but they nearly always employ agents to do the actual loan arranging and keep their own identity as secret from the borrower as they can. As the borrower on his side will often employ a close friend as agent (or, if not, will insist anyway that he is acting as someone else's agent), the circuitousness of the process can become quite elaborate.

Dissimulation is rather close to indirection, and most of the above examples, especially the postcards, display it as well. The Javanese have a word for dissimulation or pretense: *étok-étok*. The characteristic quality of *étok-étok,* in contrast to our patterns of dissemblance, is not merely that it is far more prevalent and that it is largely approved (being sometimes called "proper lying"), but that it need not have any obvious justification, being merely gratuitous. I asked one informant to define *étok-étok:*

> He said: "Suppose I go off south and you see me go. Later my son asks you: 'Do you know where my father went?' And you say no, *étok-étok* you don't know." I asked him why should I *étok-étok,* as there seemed to be no reason for lying, and he said, "Oh, you just *étok-étok.* You don't have to have a reason."

When we tell white lies, we have to justify them to ourselves, even though the justification be weak. We tell a woman her horrible hat is pretty because it would be rude not to; if someone sees us en route to a lawyer, we may say we are going to the bank because we do not wish to advertise our troubles or have others poking into our affairs. In any case, we usually have to find some sort of reason for telling a lie. For the Javanese (especially the *prijaji*) it seems, in part anyway, to work the other way around: the burden of proof seems to be in the direction of justifying telling the truth. The natural answer to casual questions, particularly from people you do not know very well, tends to be either a vague one ("Where are you going?"—"West") or a mildly false one; and one tells the truth in small matters only when there is some reason to do so. Thus, if a Javanese is going to the movies and people ask him were he is going, he will probably tell them "to the store" unless he wants them to join him or wants to ask them if the picture is worth seeing. When I went to see a curer with my landlord about a half-dozen people asked him along the route where he was going, and each time he replied that he was going to the house of someone a half-dozen houses or so down from where they were. It was only when he finally met someone he wished to invite to accompany him that he told the truth about his destination. In general, polite Javanese avoid gratuitous truths.

In terms of etiquette proper, *étok-étok* is especially valued as a way of concealing one's own wishes in deference to one's opposite. As one informant said: "For example, you are working. Then I come to visit. . . . I come and call out at the door. Then you act as though you were not working, not doing anything. *Étok-étok* you aren't working."

The same sort of pattern is involved in the nearly absolute requirement never to show one's real feelings directly, especially to a guest. Any kind of negative feeling toward another must be dissimulated; and people are strongly enjoined to smile and be pleasant to people for whom they have very little use. Strong positive feelings are also supposed to be hidden except in very intimate situations. The effort is to keep a steady level of very mild positive affect in interpersonal relations, an *étok-étok* warmth behind which all real feelings can be effectively concealed.

Similarly, one must call out to any passerby one knows inviting him to stop in, even though he may be the last person on earth you wish to see. One must refuse food (unless the host persists in offering it) even if one is dying of hunger (and the host must offer it even if it would be great trouble to prepare and he wished the guest would go away and leave him alone). One should never refuse outright people's requests to do something for them; rather, one merely agrees even if one has no intention of going through with whatever it is, and then one never gets around to doing it, putting the petitioner off with various *étok-étok* excuses until he realizes at last that one was not serious in the first place. For this last the Javanese have a proverb: "The crocodile is quick to submerge but slow to come up," meaning: it is easy to get people to agree to do something but hard to get them actually to do it.

One result of all this is that even Javanese are sometimes not quite sure whether the other person is being *étok-étok* or serious. One hears people saying: "Come to my house. I really mean it; it's not just *étok-étok*. Please come." But the other person will still not be certain whether he is in fact expected to come or not. Just when to accept offered food in a very *prijaji* household is always a problem, for a host never quite believes the guest is serious in refusing it, and there usually has to be much backing and filling before the signals are clear.

One often hears people say in praise of someone that "one can never tell how he feels inside by how he behaves on the outside." At a village election where the candidates for village chief had to sit immobile and expressionless in full view of the voters for the entire day, including the almost unbearable tense period when the votes were counted aloud one by one, people kept saying to me in a tone of high praise: "Just look at those candidates—they may be burning up inside but they show no feeling at all on the outside." One political speaker in my village began by saying: "No one ever says what he really thinks. People always *étok-étok* when dealing with other people. I'm no different. I too never say what I really think, and you can't tell how I feel about things by what I say." This seemingly self-defeating statement for a politician was evidently but mere common sense to his audience, who listened to him for all the world as though he were actually communicating something.

Lastly, there is the avoidance of any act suggesting disorder or lack of self-control. According to the Javanese, the difference between men and animals is that the former "know order." By "order," the *prijaji* means formality of bearing, restraint of expression, and bodily self-discipline—a constant awareness of himself as being an object of perception for others and therefore obligated to present a pleasing, *alus* picture. Spontaneity or natural-ness of gesture or speech is fitting only for those "not yet Javanese"—i.e., the mad, the simple-minded, and children. "If life is disordered," writes our poet, "it has the value of a dried teak leaf," and elsewhere he has a whole stanza on the subject:

> Because if you do not yet know
> How to put things in order
> And how to use them in order,
> You will become disoriented, wandering here and there,
> Mistaking things for their opposites.
> If you do things in this disordered fashion, you will meet troubles
> And will be confused by them.
> This may be said to be a loss of humanity.
> And as humanity is God's greatest creation,
> You must not be careless with it.

Here he again emphasizes from the point of view of the individual's spiritual advancement the relation between order in the outer life and in the inner. Order in the outer life regularizes stimuli so that they will not puzzle, shock, or surprise. In the same way, following the "emotional capital" theory, one should provide an ordered picture for others so as not to upset them. Here one would point to the great concern with correct posture, with soft-colored (browns and blues mainly) abstract textile designs, with graceful gesture, with soft, slow, even speech. Care, deliberation, the careful sorting out of one thing from another is the proper mode of procedure; and behaving otherwise puts one in danger of being *diguju pitik*—laughed at by the chickens.

Linguistic Etiquette

BUT the entire etiquette system is perhaps best summed up and symbolized in the way the Javanese use their language. In Javanese it is nearly impossible to say anything without indicating the social relationship between the speaker and the listener in terms of status and familiarity. Status is determined by many things—wealth, descent, education, occupation, age, kinship, and nationality, among others, but the important point is that the choice of linguistic forms as well as speech style is in every case partly determined by the relative status (or familiarity) of the conversers. The difference is not minor, a mere *du* and *Sie* difference. To greet a person lower than oneself (or someone with whom one is intimate) one says *Apa pada slamet,* but one greets a superior (or someone one knows only slightly) with *Menapa sami sugeng*—both meaning "Are you well?" *Pandjenengan saking tindak pundi?* and *Kowé seka endi?* are the same question ("Where are you coming from?"), in the first case addressed to a superior, in the second to an inferior. Clearly, a peculiar obsession is at work here.

Basically, what is involved is that the Javanese pattern their speech behavior in terms of the same *alus* to *kasar* axis around which they organize their social behavior generally. A number of words (and some affixes) are made to carry in addition to their normal linguistic meaning what might be called a "status meaning"; i.e., when used in actual conversation they convey not only their fixed detonative meaning ("house," "body," "eat," "walk," "you," "passive voice") but also a connotative meaning concerning the status of (and/or degree of familiarity between) the speaker and the listener. As a result, several words may denote the same normal linguistic meaning but differ in the status connotation they convey. Thus, for "house" we have three forms (*omah, grija,* and *dalem*), each connoting a progressively higher relative status of the listener with respect to the speaker. Some normal linguistic meanings are even more finely divided (*kowé, sampéjan, pandjenengan, pandjenengan dalem,* for ascending values of "you"), others less (*di-* and *dipun-*) for the passive voice; but most normal meanings, taking the vocabulary as a whole, are not divided at all. Thus the word for "table" is *medja* no matter to whom one is speaking.*

A further complication is that status meanings are communicated in speech not only intentionally in terms of word selection *within* the speaker's dialect but unintentionally in terms of the dialect he uses as a whole. Not only are there "levels" of speech within the dialect which are ranked in terms of their status (or *alus/kasar*) connotations; the various dialects in the community as a whole are also ranked in terms of the *alus* to *kasar* spectrum, this latter sort of ranking being characteristic, of course, of any stratified society.

In order to clarify the relationship between the intra-dialect and inter-dialect systems of status symbolization, one voluntary and one involuntary, I offer the accompanying three charts depicting paradigmatically how a single sentence alters within each of the dialects and among them. Chart I shows the speech range in status terms for what I would call the non-*prijaji* but urbanized and at least slightly educated group, which would include the better educated *abangans,* most urban *santris,* and even some of the lower *prijajis,* particularly when they are mixing with people outside their own immediate circle. It is, then, the most common dialect in the town. Chart II shows the dialect of most peasants and uneducated townsmen, which is the most common style of all in terms of sheer numbers of users. Chart III depicts the *prijaji* dialect, which, although spoken by a relatively small group of people, provides an ideal model of correct speech for the whole society.

The English sentence selected as an example is: Are you going to eat rice and cassava now? The Javanese words (low forms first) are as follows:

Are:	*apa/ napa/ menapa*
you:	*kowé/ sampéjan/ pandjenengan*
going:	*arep/ adjeng/ badé*
to eat:	*mangan/ neḍa/ ḍahar*
rice:	*sega/ sekul*
and:	*lan/ kalijan*
cassava:	*kaspé*
now:	*saiki/ saniki/ samenika*

The numbers at the sides of the charts indicate the levels, and the sentences, on the right, derived by reading across the chart at each level, are those available to a speaker in the particular dialect concerned. This range of sentences does not represent a mere theoretical set of possibilities. All of these variations are used every day. Moreover the Javanese have names for each of the levels. Level 3a is *krama inggil;* level 3 is *krama biasa,* or just *krama;* level 2 is *krama madya,* or just *madya.* (These three highest levels are often

---

* Although in terms of the total Javanese vocabulary the number of words which show formal changes in terms of status connotations are relatively small in percentage, since they tend to be the most frequently occurring in actual speech, in word counts of common utterances the percentage of status-expression forms is quite high. In general it may be said that there is no set rule by which one can determine which words change in different status situations and which do not except a vague one that the commoner the word and the more it denotes something fairly closely associated with human beings, the more likely it is that it will have such forms.

Chart I

DIALECT OF NON-*PRIJAJI*, URBANIZED, SOMEWHAT EDUCATED PERSONS

Level	are	you	going	to eat	rice	and	cassava	now	Complete sentence
3a	menapa	pandjenengan	badé	ḍahar	sekul	kalijan	kaspé	samenika	Menapa pandjenengan baḍé ḍahar sekul kalijan kaspé samenika?
3	menapa	sampéjan	baḍé	neḍa	sekul	kalijan	kaspé	samenika	Menapa sampéjan baḍé neḍa sekul kalijan kaspé samenika?
2	napa	sampéjan	adjeng	neḍa	sekul	lan	kaspé	saniki	Napa sampéjan adjeng neḍa sekul lan kaspé saniki?
1a	apa	sampéjan	arep	neḍa	seḍa	lan	kaspé	saiki	Apa sampéjan arep neḍa seḍa lan kaspé saiki?
1	apa	kowé	arep	mangan	seḍa	lan	kaspé	saiki	Apa kowé arep mangan seḍa lan kaspé saiki?

Chart II

DIALECT OF PEASANTS AND UNEDUCATED TOWNSPEOPLE

Level	are	you	going	to eat	rice	and	cassava	now	Complete sentence
2	napa	sampéjan	adjeng	neḍa	sekul	lan	kaspé	saniki	Napa sampéjan adjeng neḍa sekul lan kaspé saniki?
1a	apa	sampéjan	arep	neḍa	sega	lan	kaspé	saiki	Apa sampéjan arep neḍa sega lan kaspé saiki?
1	apa	kowé	arep	mangan	sega	lan	kaspé	saiki	Apa kowé arep mangan sega lan kaspé saiki?

Chart III
DIALECT OF THE *PRIJAJIS*

Level	are	you	going	to eat	rice	and	cassava	now	Complete sentence
3a	menapa	pandjenengan	baḍé	ḍahar	sekul	kalijan	kaspé	samenika	Menapa pandjenengan baḍé ḍahar sekul kalijan kaspé samenika?
3	menapa	sampéjan	baḍé	neḍa	sekul	kalijan	kaspé	samenika	Menapa sampéjan baḍé neḍa sekul kalijan kaspé samenika?
1b	apa	pandjenengan	arep	ḍahar	sega	lan	kaspé	saiki	Apa pandjenengan arep ḍahar sega lan kaspé saiki?
1a	apa	sampéjan	arep	neḍa	sega	lan	kaspé	saiki	Apa sampéjan arep neḍa sega lan kaspé saiki?
1	apa	kowé	arep	mangan	sega	lan	kaspé	saiki	Apa kowé arep mangan sega lan kaspé saiki?

referred to merely as *basa* or language, although by high *prijajis* only the first two would be so considered.) Level 1a is either *ngoko madya,* or just *madya;* and level 1 is *ngoko biasa,* or just *ngoko.* Level 1b, a *prijaji* specialty, is called *ngoko sae* ("fine *ngoko*") or *ngoko alus.*

Krama, madya, and *ngoko*—or high, middle, and low—are the three main levels expressing status and/or familiarity available to speakers in the language. They represent sets of linked conjugates (*menapa . . . badé . . . samenika; napa . . . adjeng . . . saniki; apa . . . arep . . . saiki;* etc.), the occurrence of one of which for any given meaning (e.g., *menapa/napa/-apa*) will predict the occurrence of the other if the meaning concerned occurs (i.e., *badé/adjeng/arep;* or *samenika/saniki/saiki,* etc.). In some cases the *madya* conjugate is the same as the *ngoko* (e.g., *lan*); sometimes it is the same as the *krama* (e.g., *sampéjan, neḍa, sekul*); and of course, sometimes the conjugate is the same in all three cases (e.g., *kaspé*).

In addition to these sets of linked conjugates, there is a group of special words, mostly referring to people, their parts, possessions and actions, which occur independently of the first kinds of conjugates and which act to raise the level of speech indicated by the first, inevitable selection, one "notch" higher —or, better, one-half notch. *Ḍahar* and *pandjenengan* are such words in the above sentences, rasing level 3, *krama biasa* (literally: "usual" or "common" *krama*) to level 3a, *krama inggil* ("high" *krama*). In the *ngoko* level, the use of *krama* words (e.g., *sampéjan,* or *neḍa* in the above) also has an honorific effect, lifting *ngoko biasa* (level 1), to *ngoko madya* (level 1a). As these *krama* words employed in *ngoko* sentences occur in the same meanings as the special honorifics, they might be called "low honorifics," in contrast to the special "high honorifics," such as *ḍahar, pandjenengan.* Finally, the use of high honorifics in a *ngoko* context yields level 1b, *ngoko sae.* As a result, the intra-dialect system of status symbolization consists, at the most, of three "stylemes" (high, middle, and low) and two types of honorifics (high and low). The honorifics occur, at least in the dialects described here, only with the high and low stylemes, never with the middle one.*

On the basis, then, of how many stylemes and how many types of honorific are customarily employed and what combinations occur, the three "class dialects" diagrammed in the charts are distinguished. In the dialect of the non-*prijaji,* urbanized, and at least somewhat educated group (Chart I), all three stylemes are customarily used (high, middle, low) and both types of honorific (high and low). Since the high honorifics occur only with the high style and the low ones only with the low style,** a speaker of this dialect has

---

* In utterances of more than minimal length the chance that at least one *krama/madya/ngoko* style marker will occur is nearly unity. I owe the suggestion to treat the "style" problem and the "high word" problem separately to Mr. Rufus Hendon, who has also suggested that the three linked conjugate sets be dissolved into a new unit, called a "styleme," which then occurs once in (nearly) every sentence, and that the high words, which occur sporadically, be called "honorifics." The formal parts of the above discussion are heavily dependent upon his analysis.

** As the two types of honorific are in complementary distribution, high ones occurring only with high Stylemes, low ones with low, the difference between them is redundant and could be eliminated in a more elegant analysis.

five possibilities, represented by the five sentences: 3a, *krama inggil* (i.e., high styleme and high honorifics); 3, *krama biasa* (high styleme without honorifics); 2, *krama madya* (middle styleme without honorifics); 1a, *ngoko madya* (middle styleme with low honorifics); 1, *ngoko biasa* (low styleme, no honorifics).

In the peasant and uneducated townsman dialect or idiom (Chart II), two stylemes (middle and low) and one type of honorific (low) customarily occur, the honorifics occurring only with the low styleme, to raise *ngoko biasa* to *ngoko madya*.* Thus the possibilities for the expression of "status meaning" for a speaker of this dialect are only three: 2, *krama madya* (middle styleme without honorifics); 1a, *ngoko madya* (low styleme plus low honorifics); 1, *ngoko biasa* (low styleme, no honorifics).

Finally, in the *prijaji* dialect, the middle styleme—considered to be vulgar —drops out. Thus, there are two stylemes (high and low) and both high and low honorifics, the high occurring with both high and low stylemes, the low, again, only with the high. This gives five possibilities: 3a, *krama inggil* (high styleme plus high honorifics); 3, *krama biasa* (high styleme without honorifics); 1b, *ngoko sae* (low styleme, high honorifics); 1a, *ngoko madya* (low styleme plus low honorifics); and 1, *ngoko biasa* (low styleme, no honorifics).

It will be noted that sentences 3 and 3a are available to both *prijaji* and educated townsmen; sentence 2 to both educated and uneducated townsmen and to peasants; and 1 and 1a to all three groups (although, as mentioned, 1a tends to be omitted by the more *alus* among the *prijaji*); 1b is characteristically employed only by *prijajis*.

Given this brief and over-condensed formal analysis of the level problem, the sense in which Javanese linguistic behavior is but a part of their wider system of etiquette and, in fact, a simplified and summarizing model of it is more easily set forth. First, as already noted, the levels themselves reflect the *kasar* to *alus* continuum. *Ngoko*, level 1, is the basic language. People think in this, fall into it whenever the urge to express themselves overcomes the desire to maintain propriety, and generally regard it, like the peasant himself, as the rough, down-to-earth, and necessary foundation on top of which all the *prijaji* fancy work is erected. It is for this reason that all Javanese terms in this report have been given in their *ngoko* forms.

As one moves up the level ladder from *ngoko* toward *krama* (level 3) and *krama inggil* (level 3a), the manner of speaking shifts too: the higher the level one is using, the more slowly and softly one speaks—and the more evenly, in terms both of rhythm and pitch. As, on the whole, the "higher" conjugates tend to be longer than the lower ones (*kowé/sampéjan/pandjenengan*—and, for the *very* elevated, *pandjenengan dalem*—for "you"; *kéné/-ingriki* for "here"), the high language levels, when spoken correctly, have a kind of stately pomp which can make the simplest conversation seem like a great ceremony. Like the forms of etiquette generally, the patterns of linguistic

---

* As low honorifics are but high styleme "markers" occurring in low styleme contexts, a combination of high styleme and low honorifics is, of course, impossible, for the honorifics could not be distinguished from the styleme markers.

etiquette modulate, regularize, and smooth the processes of social interaction into an *alus,* unvarying flow of quiet, emotionally tranquilizing propriety.

It has already been pointed out how etiquette patterns, including language, tend to be regarded by the Javanese as a kind of emotional capital which may be invested in putting others at ease. Politeness is something one directs toward others; one surrounds the other with a wall of behavioral (*lair*) formality which protects the stability of his inner life (*batin*). Etiquette is a wall built around one's inner feelings, but it is, paradoxically, always a wall someone else builds, at least in part. He may choose to build such a wall for one of two reasons. He and the other person are at least approximate status equals and not intimate friends; and so he responds to the other's politeness to him with an equal politeness. Or the other is clearly his superior, in which case he will, in deference to the other's greater spiritual refinement, build him a wall without any demand or expectation that you reciprocate. This is, of course, but a restatement of the *anḍap-asor* pattern discussed more generally above. But in terms of language it is possible to state the exact nature of this pattern, the core of Javanese etiquette, in a rather more precise, abstract and formal manner.

If we take the six levels (or three levels and three half levels) of speech present in one dialect or another in Modjokuto, we can diagram them in terms of the "wall" metaphor as follows:

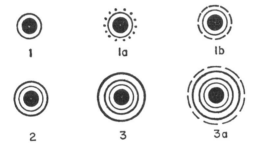

The solid center is intended to represent the *batin,* the inner life. The solid lines represent the stylemes—the low styleme taken as one "layer," the middle as two, the high as three. Low honorifics are represented by a dotted line, high by a dashed. The circles—solid, dotted, or dashed—around the solid center are thus intended to diagram the *lair,* the behavioral world of etiquette. The higher the level of language spoken *to* an individual, then, the thicker the wall of etiquette protecting his emotional life.

In such terms one can diagram nearly any relationship between two individuals of whatever rank or familiarity.* Thus, two close friends of

---

* One complication is that it is not entirely true that the status and/or familiarity relationship between speaker and hearer is the only determinant of status forms, because sometimes the status of a third person referred to, especially if he be quite high, may determine the form used: thus, in speaking to a lower-status person one will still use the high, *krama,* form of "house" when speaking of the one the District Officer lives in.

equal rank (that two close friends will be of roughly equal rank is nearly a tautology for most Modjokuto Javanese) will both speak *ngoko* to one another:

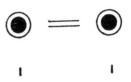

A high official, say the District Officer, and an ordinary educated urbanite will follow a sharply asymmetrical pattern:

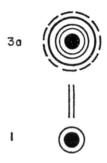

—i.e., the District Officer will speak *ngoko biasa,* the ordinary man, *krama inggil.*

Two ordinary townsmen who are not intimate friends tend to speak *krama madya* reciprocally:

Two *prijajis* who are not intimate friends tend to speak *krama biasa* (if particularly elevated, *krama inggil*) reciprocally:

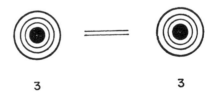

A peasant speaking to a higher status person will use *krama madya,* for the most part, for he doesn't use *krama biasa* or *krama inggil:*

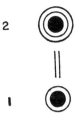

One might get a similar pattern if a "lower class" townsman were conversing with a "middle class" townsman, say a carpenter with a well-off storekeeper.

A peasant speaking to a fellow peasant with whom he is not intimate might use *krama madya,* but more commonly he will use *ngoko madya,* reciprocally:

Middle or lower ranking townsmen who are casual acquaintances might also use reciprocal *ngoko madya* or *krama madya,* depending mostly on the occasion, the content of what was being communicated, and so on.

Ngoko sae, the *prijaji* speciality, is used between *prijaji* who know one another fairly well and are of equal status but regard each other to be so elevated as to make the reciprocal use of *ngoko biasa,* or *ngoko madya,* which might sometimes be used in this context, unseemly:

The inclusion of this level in the dialect shows the *prijaji* reluctance to use very low language to anyone of much status. *Ngoko sae* is used to close friends and relatives whom one knows well enough to use familiar speech but to whom one wishes nevertheless to show proper respect. Thus sentences on this level resolve the conflict between familiarity and respect implicit in the Javanese etiquette pattern with a greater delicacy and subtlety than is possible in either the "urbanite" or "peasant" dialects.

A thorough semantic study of the contexts within which the different levels are employed would in itself be a complex and extended investigation, for the number of variables specifically determining the selection of a particular level are very numerous. They include not only qualitative characteristics of the speakers—age, sex, kinship relation,* occupation, wealth, education, religious commitment, family background—but also more general factors: for instance, the social setting (one would be likely to use a higher level to the same individual at a wedding than in the street); the content of the conversation (in general, one uses lower levels when speaking of commercial matters, higher ones if speaking of religious or aesthetic matters); the history of social interaction between the speakers (one will tend to speak rather high, if one speaks at all, with someone with whom one has quarreled); the presence of a third person (one tends to speak higher to the same individual if others are listening). All these play a role, to say nothing of individual idiosyncratic attitudes. Some people, particularly, it seems, wealthier traders and self-confident village chiefs, who tend to think the whole business rather uncomfortable and somewhat silly, speak *ngoko* to almost everyone except the very high in status. Others will shift levels on any pretext. A complete listing of the determinants of level selection would, therefore, involve a thorough analysis of the whole framework of Javanese culture.

In terms of the more general relationship between the Javanese language and Javanese culture, it is of interest to note how the three charts when taken together present a picture of how the three groups—"urbanites," "peasants," and *prijajis*—perceive the Modjokuto-wide status system, the varying form of their etiquette systems, and how they are related to each other—how, in essence, the ideal model set by the *prijajis* refracts through the rest of the social structure. The *prijaji* chart (Chart III), with its excluded middle, shows the *prijaji* tendency to put people into two categories: those to whom one speaks respectfully, equals and superiors (i.e., other *prijajis*); and those to whom one speaks familiarly, inferiors (i.e., non-*prijajis*) and very close friends and relatives. As noted, level 1b, *ngoko sae,* forms a nice compromise between respect and familiarity, and among the more refined *prijajis* in the larger towns, the omission of *ngoko madya* (1a) in their dialect would even further strengthen the dichotomous nature of their model of the status system.

The peasant chart (Chart II) shows both the peasants' lessened sense of internal differentiation of status within their own group and their view of the whole structure from the bottom, the upper reaches of the system being mostly beyond their ken. The chart, in fact, provides a concrete case in point of the relationship between gentry and peasant culture patterns outlined earlier. Gentry patterns are reflected dimly and in a somewhat distorted fashion in the peasant context, but they are reflected there. *Prijaji* speakers of (what they regard as) "correct" Javanese are continually making fun—to one another, or to the ethnographer—of "ignorant" villagers who use *tjinten* as the high form of *tjina* (Chinese), when "really" there is no higher form. Similarly for the village use of *konten* for *kori* (door) and, worst of all, their creation of high forms for place names which never should alter: *Kedinten* for *Kediri;*

---

* For a discussion of the selection of language levels within the kinship and family context, see H. Geertz's volume in this series, *The Javanese Family.*

Surobringo for *Surabaja*.* For the *abangan* peasant at any rate, *prijaji* speech, like *prijaji* etiquette, religion, art, and style of life, is the ideal form, even though they may regard it as too difficult and restrictive for their own use. For the *santri* the religion and art drop out as patterns worthy of emulation, but the speech, etiquette, and style of life remain as models.

Chart I shows the results of the jostling together of people from all walks of life in the urban context. Since the average middle rank urbanite mixes with everyone from *prijaji* to peasant, he employs whatever language level seems reasonable in the situation. To speak respectfully to a peasant, he will use *krama madya* (level 2); to a high *prijaji, krama inggil* (3a); and to people of his own rank or slightly higher he will use *krama biasa* (3). But he will have little use for the kind of subtleties represented by level 1 b, *ngoko sae*. Thus, in place of the dichotomous (gentry versus the field) view of the status structure of the *prijaji* and the relatively speaking more equalitarian view of the peasant, the urbanite sees a more even gradation of status over quite a wide range.

Lastly, a word should be said about the increasing popularity of Indonesian, the national language based on Malay, among certain groups, particularly the urban youth and the political elite of the town. Indonesian appeals to those whose sense of political nationality as Indonesians rather than as Javanese is most developed, to those who are interested in the cultural products of the new Indonesia's mass media (newspapers, magazines, movies, radio), and those who wish to take leadership positions in government and business. But the use of Indonesian, now taught in all the schools, is spreading very rapidly beyond these somewhat special groups to nearly all townspeople and to a greater and greater number of peasants. As most available reading matter is now in Indonesian rather than Javanese, literacy more or less implies Indonesian, although a reading knowledge does not, of course, imply its use in everyday life. In any case, although the use of Indonesian for everyday conversation is still mostly confined to the more sophisticated urbanites, and its use suggests something of an air of "public speaking" for most Javanese, it is rapidly becoming more and more an integral part of their daily cultural life and will become even more so as the present generation of school children grows to adulthood. That it will, in the foreseeable future, entirely displace Javanese is, of course, entirely unlikely. Rather, it seems destined, at least in the short run, to become part of the general Javanese linguistic system, to become one more type of sentence among those available, to be selected for use in certain special contexts and for certain special purposes.

> Before the meeting began, when they (the members of a mystical religious sect) were discussing language, Sudjoko said that one simply couldn't

---

* These "mistakes" are based on false analogies to types of formal alteration which are common in moving from high to low Javanese. Though there are no specific rules for such changes, a few sorts of changes occur repeatedly (lower terms given first): (1) a shift of final vowel from *a* to *i: djawa/djawi*, "Javanese"; (2) a shift form *i* to *os: ganti/gantos*, "change"; (3) a kind of "pig-latin" form in the higher term involving, among other processes, various forms of medial or final nasalization: *kena/kenging*, "hit," "may"; *karep/kadjeng*, "wish," "want"; *kari/kantun*, "left behind"; (4) a complete change of form: *omah/grija*, "house."

use Indonesian to discuss mystical philosophy. When I asked him why, he said: "Well, all the terms are in Javanese in the first place; and in the second place Javanese fits the kind of thought better. It would be very hard to express such thoughts in Indonesian; it just wouldn't feel right." Contrariwise, he said that, giving a political speech in Javanese is one of the hardest things in the world to do; it just doesn't seem to have the expressions. Someone then noted that even when one goes to a political meeting in the village and they use Javanese, many of the words are Indonesian words which, although the people in the audience perhaps cannot use them or at least cannot make them into whole Indonesian sentences, they nevertheless understand quite well.

Chapter 18 The Role of Classical Art

IN DISCUSSING non-*santri* art in Modjokuto it seems profitable to differentiate between three somewhat separate clusters, three art complexes the component forms of which not only bear an intrinsic relation to one another but also enter into the social and cultural structure I have been describing in roughly similar ways:

Cluster I: The "*Alus* Art" Complex

1. *wajang*—the shadow-play, which uses leather or wooden puppets to dramatize stories from the Javanese versions of the Indian epics, the Mahabharata and the Ramayana, or mythological versions of the history of the kingdoms of pre-colonial Java.

2. *gamelan*—the percussion orchestra which can either be played alone or can accompany the *wajang* or various other art forms.

3. *lakon*—literally "plot" or "scenario." A myth which may be dramatized in the *wajang* but is often merely related orally as myths normally are.

4. *djogèd*—Javanese court dancing, which may be autonomous or which may "dance out" *lakons* from the *wajang*.

5. *tembangs*—poems, written in various rigid forms, which may be either read or sung, with *gamelan* accompaniment if one wishes.

6. *batik*—the wax and dye method of textile decoration.

Cluster II: The "*Kasar* Art" Complex

1. *ludrug*—popular farce, involving as major features male transvestitism and low clowns.

261

2. *klèḍèks*—female street dancers, who dance both "from door to door" and as hired performers at weddings, circumcisions, and the like.

3. *djaranan*—popular dance, in which the dancers "ride" paper horses and become possessed, behaving as though they themselves were horses.

4. *dongèngs*—folktales, legends, animal stories, and so on; the main difference from *lakons* lies in the fact that *dongèngs* are always told orally and never dramatized in the *wajang*.

Cluster III: The "National Art" Complex

1. *orkès*—popular "dance bands" (although no one ever dances to them) consisting almost entirely of plucked instruments—banjos, guitars, etc.

2. *lagus*—popular songs, played almost continuously over the radio and sung at circumcisions, weddings, and other such occasions by vocalists attached to the *orkès*. Originally patterned on Portuguese-inspired folk models from various parts of Indonesia, they are now more and more approaching modern Western (i.e., American) models.

3. *kesusastraan* Indonesia—modern, Western-style novels, poems, short-stories, and plays, written in Indonesian, the national language.

4. *bioskops*—movies, Western and Indonesian (or Malayan).

With the exception of the "National Art" complex, which has not yet been widely discussed, the content, the technical analysis, and the distribution within the Javanese-Sundanese-Madurese culture area of these various art forms—as well as others not found in Modjokuto—have been thoroughly and systematically handled by generations of Dutch scholars, and so little of that need be repeated here.*

Wajang: The Shadow Play

OF the three art clusters, the first—the *"Alus* Art" complex—is at once the most widely spread throughout the culture, the most deeply ingrained, and the most philosophically and religiously elaborated, this last largely by the *prijajis*. The center of the complex is the *wajang,* the world-famous Javanese shadow-play. The shadow play is called so because the puppets, which are flat cut-outs of leather, painted in gold, reds, blues, and blacks, are made to cast large shadows on a white screen. The *ḍalang,* as the puppeteer is called, sits on a mat in front of the screen. A *gamelan* orchestra is behind him, and an oil lamp hangs above his head (traditionally: nowadays, in the towns at least, an electric lamp is used). The puppets are fastened to a tortoise-shell stick,

* For the reader interested in further detail, in either technical, historical, or distributional terms, the following two books, the first, unfortunately, still untranslated are indispensable: Th. Pigeaud, *Javaanse Volksvertoningen: Bijdrage tot de Beschrijving van Land en Volk,* 's-Gravenhage and Batavia, 1938; J. Kunst, *Music in Java, Its History, Its Theory and Its Technique,* 2 vol. (The Hague, 1949).

running from head to below their joined feet, at which point the *ḍalang* grasps the stick as a sort of handle. The movable arms, the only movable parts, also have short sticks attached to them which the *ḍalang* holds in the same hand and manipulates with his fingers. He holds the puppets up in either hand over his head and interposes them between the light and the screen. If they are nobles, as most are, he must be doubly careful never to let them get lower than his head. From the *ḍalang's* side of the screen one thus sees the puppets themselves and their shadows rising up dominant on the screen behind them. From the reverse side of the *wajang* screen, one sees the shadows of the puppets only.

Along the base of the screen, in front of the *ḍalang,* there is a banana tree-trunk into which are stuck the puppets not immediately in use. As the play, which usually lasts all night progresses, the *ḍalang* takes and replaces characters from the tree-trunk as he needs them and manipulates the puppets immediately in play. (Mostly they are either engaged in very formal conversation, in war—in which case he knocks them against one another—or, in the case of the clowns, in some kind of burlesque.) He imitates all the voices called for, sings when singing is appropriate, kicks an iron clapper with his foot to keep the rhythm and to symbolize the sounds of war, and, as he has only the bare outline of the story given to him by tradition, makes up most of the details of the plot as he goes along, particularly in the comic scenes, which often contain elements of contemporary social criticism. He does this the whole night long, sitting until the dawn with his feet folded inwards in the formal Javanese sitting posture, performing with a dexterity, a fertility of invention, and a physical endurance which are altogether remarkable.

Wajang Stories

ALMOST entirely, the stories (*lakons*) dramatized in the *wajangs* are from the Mahabharata. Ramayana stories—often referred to contemptuously as "monkey stories" because of the prominence in them of the half-monkey hero Anoman and other similar figures—are not liked in Modjokuto. I never saw one performed there (although I did in Djokjakarta) and never met anyone who had anything favorable to say for them in comparison with the Mahabharata stories. My *ḍalang* informant said that although he knew the Ramayana stories he almost never got a contract to perform them. As for the stories of Madjapahit, Kediri, and other early kingdoms, they evidently are almost never performed either in the leather-puppet or in the wooden-puppet form around Modjokuto, although one old man who lived near me sometimes performed with wooden-puppets for the casual amusement of the *abangans* in his quarter as an avocation, and the *lakons* seem still to be popular as oral traditions. There are in Java as a whole various different kinds of *wajangs,* classified according to the type of puppets used and the stories dramatized. In Modjokuto, in any case, almost all *wajangs* performed dramatize Mahabharata stories.

In the Mahabharata stories there are three major groups of characters:

1. *Déwa-déwi*—the gods and goddesses, headed by Batara Guru (Siva) and his wife, Batari Durga, and including Batara Narada, Sang Hjang Brama, and Batara Kala. As in the Greek epics, the gods are far from uniformity righteous: Batara Kala, for example, eats only-children, unless they have been protected from him by a performance of a special *wajang* depicting his birth.

2. *Satrijas*—the kings and nobles of the Javanese kingdoms of olden days. Supposedly, the "Ramayana Time" (in India) was succeeded by the "Mahabharata Time," then by the "Buddhist Time" (i.e., the Hindu-Javanese period of Kediri, Singosari, Madjapahit, etc.), and finally by the present. Thus, in theory, the *satrijas* are the ancestors of the present-day Javanese, a circumstance which has led several scholars to view the *wajang* as an ancestor cult, originally connected with dual organization initiation rites in which young men learned the secrets of the tribe. Whatever the merits of this rather speculative theory, there is no apparent trace of such a view in Modjokuto today. There are several groups of *satrija* and various mythical kingdoms involved in the *wajang*. Among the most important characters are:

a) The *Pendawas:* the five brothers who rule the country of Amarta—Judistira, Bima, Ardjuna, Nakula, and Sadéwa (the last two identical twins). The Pendawas are usually accompanied by Kresna, king of the neighboring country of nDarawati, who is an incarnation of Wisnu and general advisor to the Pendawas. The two other famous figures in this camp are Gututkatja, the powerful son of Bima, who can fly, and Angkawidaja, the son of Ardjuna.

b) The *Korawas:* the hundred *satrijas* of Ngastina, led by Sujudana, Sengkuni, Durna, and Karna, the dissident half-brother to the Pendawas. Although cousins of the Pendawas, the Korawas have usurped the country of Ngastina from them, and it is the struggle over this disputed country which provides the major theme of the *wajang,* a struggle which culminates in the great Bratajuda war in which the Korawas are defeated.

3. *Punakawans*—Semar, Pétruk, and Garèng, the great Javanese low-clowns, servants and constant companions of the Pendawas. Semar, the father of the other two, is actually a god in all too human form, a brother to Batara Guru, the king of the gods. The guardian spirit of all the Javanese from their first appearance until the end of time, he is perhaps the most important figure in the whole *wajang* mythology.

The *lakon* as the *dalang* learns it is hardly more than an outline, consisting of a bare description of what happens in each of a half-dozen to a dozen major scenes, which scenes are in fact a series of encounters in which the ruling lord of one kingdom meet those of another and either talk or fight.

He (a *dalang* who lived just outside of Modjokuto) said that in the *wajang* the same pattern recurs over and over. First the people face each other, then they talk, then they leave, then they talk again, and then they fight. He said that it is the same as now: when two countries can't get together they talk; then the talk breaks down and they fight. He said that *wajang* has meaning for today too. The thing one has to do is talk and talk; and slowly the people come to agree (*tjotjog*) and then there is peace. Otherwise, if the talk breaks off, there is war. He said: "That is the way it is with people too. If you come to me to study, we talk with each other, slowly begin to *tjotjog,* and after a while I learn from you about American art and you learn from me about Javanese art."

A sample story presented in the form in which it was dictated to me by this Modjokuto *ḍalang,* and in the form in which he had learned it, follows:

The Marriage of Angkawidjaja

SCENE (*bab*) I. Present (*djèdjèr*—literally, "standing up") in the Kingdom of nDarawati: King Kresna, his son Prince Samba, his brother-in-law Prince Sentjaki, and various courtiers.

Subject of Discussion (*ingkang dipun rembag*): The request by Prince Ardjuna of Ngamarta for the hand of King Kresna's daughter, Siti Sundali. Kresna agrees on the condition that Prince Ardjuna provide the girl with two female servants who are identical twins.

A Visit (*kasowan*): The Prime Minister of Ngastina. He also asks for the hand of Kresna's daughter and is also told to provide two female servants who are identical twins.

SCENE II: Present at the Place of Meditation, Kembangsoré: The Holy Man Sempati with his disciples.

A Visit: His granddaughters, Pregiwa and Pregiwati, who are identical twins. They tell him they are looking for their father. Sempati tells them to go to Ngamarta and look for Prince Ardjuna. They leave.

The holy man tells his disciples to follow the girls and watch over them.

The disciples meet the girls and tell them they have been instructed to guide them to Ngamarta. They walk with them to the edge of the forest.

A Hostile Meeting (*kepapagan* [whenever two groups of *satrijas* meet in the woods—i.e., outside of the protected compounds of each other's cleared kingdoms—they seem inevitably to fight]): Various Korawas from Ngastina: Prime Minister Sengkuni, Prince Kartamarma, Prince Tjitraksa, and others. The Korawas ask the girls to come to Ngamarta as servants. They refuse. The Korawas attempt to force them. The disciples defend the girls and are killed. The girls run away into the forest. The Korawas hunt and hunt for them.

SCENE III: Present in the Castle in Ngamarta: Ardjuna, with two of his wives, Sembadra and Srikandri, his son Angkawidjaja, and his nephew Gatutkatja. Also the three clowns: Semar, Pétruk, Garèng.

Subject of Discussion: The proposed marriage of Angkawidjaja.

A Visit: Samba, Prince of nDarawati. He tells them of his father's decision that they must find twin servants for his daughter in order for the marriage to occur.

Angkawidjaja, Gatutkatja, and the three clowns are ordered by Ardjuna to search for two such identical twin girls. They leave.

They go into the forest. In the middle of the forest they meet the two granddaughters of Sempati, Pregiwa and Pregiwati. Angkawidjaja asks them where they are from and they say, "From the Place of Meditation, Kembangsoré. We are seeking our father, Prince Ardjuna." Angkawidjaja then says that he is the son of Ardjuna, and if what they say is so they are his younger sisters. He offers to take them to their father.

Not long after, they meet the Korawas of Ngastina still searching for the girls. A great battle ensues. The Korawas lose, and run away to their home country, Ngastina. Angkawidjaja and his company return to Ngamarta.

SCENE IV: Present in the country of Ngamarta: The five Pendawas—King Judistira, Prince Bima, Ardjuna, Nangkula, Sadéwa.

Subject of Discussion: The prospective marriage of Angkawidjaja and Siti Sundali, and the necessity of finding two identical twin servants.

A Visit: Angkawidjaja, Gatutkatja, the three clowns, Pregiwa, Pregiwati. They announce that they have found the twin servants and that the girls are in fact daughters of Ardjuna. [Ardjuna, the masculine ideal, has many wives and countless offspring.] Everyone is very happy.

The entire company then goes in a procession to nDarawati for the wedding.

SCENE V: Present in the country of Ngastina: King Sujudana.

A Visit: Prime Minister Sengkuni, Prince Kartamarma, Prince Tjitraksa, and others of the Korawas, who are fleeing the scene of battle with the *satrijas* from Ngamarta. They tell the king they have been beaten by Angkawidjaja. The king calls his son, Prince Lesmana, and instructs him to put on his wedding clothes.

The entire company then goes in a procession to nDarawati for the wedding.

SCENE VI: Present in the country of nDarawati: King Kresna, his son Prince Samba, and his brother-in-law Prince Sentjaki.

A Visit: The Pendawa company, including the twin-girl servants.

Angkawidjaja and Siti Sundali are then married in the castle.

A Visit: The Korawas from Ngastina arrive. They request that Siti Sundali be married to Prince Lesmana. They are informed that she has already been married to Prince Angkawidjaja. They do not accept this.

There ensues a great war between the Pendawa camp and the Korawas. The Korawas are beaten and flee home to Ngastina.

SCENE VII: Present in nDarawati: King Kresna, King Judistira, Prince Bima, Prince Ardjuna, Prince Nangkula, and Prince Sadéwa.

They all eat together.

Into this general schematic outline the *dalang* weaves noble speeches, humorous episodes, and noisy wars until he stretches a story which takes only a few minutes to tell (and is usually but a very minute part of the whole Mahabharata cycle) into a performance lasting the whole night. The *wajang* is like a sonata, Western-educated Javanese intellectuals sometimes say, since it opens with an exposition of a theme, follows with a development and variations of this theme, and concludes with a resolution and recapitulation of it. From nine until midnight the political leaders of the various kingdoms confront one another and state the terms of the story: a *wajang* hero wishes to marry the daughter of a neighboring king, a colonialized country wants its freedom, or whatever. From midnight until three o'clock or so difficulties of some sort set in: someone else is bidding for the daughter's hand, the imperialist country refuses freedom to its colony. And, finally, these difficulties are resolved in the last section ending at sun-up—inevitably by a war in which the heroes triumph, after which there is a brief celebration of the accomplished marriage or the achieved freedom.

One informant had a more down-to-earth theory of why the *wajang* is subdivided so. He said that the *alus* but rather boring speeches of the great lords and diplomats are placed early in the evening before people are tired enough to be put to sleep by them; at midnight, just as some of the audience are beginning to feel drowsy, the clowns come on and initiate the development-and-complications period and liven things up with their crude humor (one of their chief functions, evidently, being to cheer up the heroes in their time of troubles); and finally, toward morning, when people are really about to drop off, the great wars begin, waking people with their great clatter and vigorous dramatics.

Prijaji versus *Abangan* Views of the *Wajang*

A *wajang* performance is at once a kind of elaborated *abangan slametan* and a refined art form subtly symbolic of the *prijaji* outlook and ethic. It is literally viewed from two angles. In the old days the women and children sat on the side of the screen where only the shadows of the puppets were visible and the men sat on the other side. But now the situation has changed, and the man giving the *wajang* (now usually a *prijaji,* not so much because the peasant interest in the form has weakened as because the cost has grown too great for most peasants to bear) along with his guests of both sexes—separated from one another—sit on the shadow side; while out in the yard, on the ḍalang side, great crowds of uninvited peasants and lower-class townsmen gather to watch. The arrangement indicated below is typical.

Key

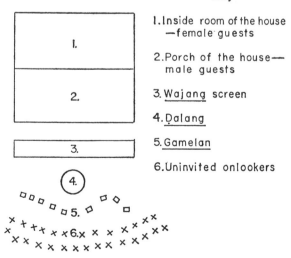

1. Inside room of the house
   —female guests

2. Porch of the house—
   male guests

3. Wajang screen

4. Ḍalang

5. Gamelan

6. Uninvited onlookers

The *wajang,* rooted as it is so deeply in Javanese culture that even the most hard-bitten *santri* modernist will admit that one ought to see one once, is a prime case in point of the futility of attempting to determine whether gentry patterns are rationalizations of peasant ones or peasant patterns corruptions of gentry ones. On the one hand, the *wajang* is part of the *abangan* ritualistic-polytheistic-magical religious pattern, although this is decreasing; and on the other hand it is part of the *prijaji* mystical-pantheistic-speculative religious pattern. This last, too, is decreasing, but perhaps less rapidly. The decrease in popularity of a once widespread art-form tends, initially, to increase its cost as lesser practitioners drop out to leave the field to the more highly trained, throwing the burden of its support more and more on those who are willing and financially able intentionally and self-consciously to cultivate it as a professional art. They may cultivate it, of course, more for reasons of prestige than of appreciation or for both. In any case, all the *wajangs* I saw while I was in Modjokuto were sponsored by *prijajis* and all the *dalangs* were imported from the larger towns elsewhere,* although I do not doubt that richer *abangans* still give them from time to time. The average fee for a competent *dalang* seems to run about Rp 500.00.

On the *abangan* side, the *wajang* is a popular drama of legendary heroes, a drama the appeal of which is, perhaps, not so very different from that of the other less pretentious popular dramas we shall consider presently; but it is also a part of the *slametan* complex. In general, a *wajang* may be given on any day on which a *slametan* may be given and for the same reasons for which a *slametan* would be appropriate. Weddings, circumcisions, births are fit occasions for *wajangs,* as is the Prophet's birthday. For weddings and births (but not for circumcisions, a non-Hindu custom) there are specially appropriate *lakons,* such as "The Marriage of Angkawidjaja" (or of Bima or Ardjuna, there being such a marriage *lakon* for nearly every major hero), related above, for a wedding, or "The Birth of Gatutkatja" (perhaps the most popular *lakon* of all) for a birth. I have mentioned the necessity of giving a special *wajang* to protect an only-child from being devoured by Batara Kala. One can also give one to prevent or cure illness. Contrariwise, some particular *lakons* are considered likely to bring misfortune and so are almost never played.

In addition, the presentation of a *wajang* is itself set in a *slametan* context:

> He (a *dalang*) said that before one gives a *wajang* one must burn incense for the spirits to eat and pray—just as at a *slametan.* Then there is a *sadjèn* (offering), which is prepared by the man who contracts for the *wajang* and includes a banana, a coconut, incense, and 18½ cents. Also, food is prepared —cooked chicken, coconut, etc., which the *dalang* takes home afterwards and eats. The *sadjèn* is placed next to the *dalang* where everyone can see it, and it remains there through the performance.

As in a *slametan,* anyone attending a *wajang* is safe from all harm at least as long as it is going on and probably longer. Thus the giving or attend-

---

* Including, in one instance, one of the first female *dalangs* in Java, who, I suspect, was more of an oddity than a portent.

ing of a *wajang* is in part the same kind of a ritual defensive act as a *slametan;* and one often sees a *wajang* going on but no one really paying much attention to it, the point being not the content of the story but the ritual efficacy of the performance. Sometimes people regard the puppets themselves as being entered by spirits during the performance; and good *ḍalangs* are often said to be entranced, which is why they have such powers of concentration and strength. As one has possessed curers (*ḍukun tiban*) as well as those whose skill comes through learning, so one also has possessed *ḍalangs* (*ḍalang tiban*) as well as the more common type who learn their skill from other *ḍalangs*.

> The groom-to-be came by again and said that there was a *ḍalang tiban* not so long ago near Kediri. Evidently a spirit came and entered him; for, although he had never *ḍalang*ed in his life, he was then able to do so without study and did so for thirty-five days without stopping and then lost his spirit and didn't know how to do it any more.

For the *prijaji* some of this ritualistic aspect of the *wajang* may still be of importance (incense being burned at court *wajangs* too) although, as he has turned the *slametan* into a nearly secular feast, in his hands the *wajang* becomes a fairly secularized art-form. But this secularization on the ritualistic side actually tends to liberate speculation about the "meaning" of the *wajang*, to encourage—its formal ritual meaning gone—interpretation of its content. And this tends to bring the shadow-play into even closer integration with the *prijaji* religion than with the *abangan*. Art, like etiquette, is seen as providing a material form for an essentially spiritual content, an outward symbolization of an inward *rasa:*

> I talked to Pak Wiro (a *prijaji* draughtsman), the head of Budi Setia, the theosophical club. (We were watching a *wajang*.) He said that the *wajang* was originally a propaganda device of the Hindus to spread their religion. (Just about as often one hears that it was originally a propaganda device of the Moslems to spread *their* religion.) He said that the people would accept it more easily than in thick books which they couldn't or wouldn't read, and that Jesus, Muhammad, and Kresna were all the same really since all ascend to heaven and all are messengers of God. . . . All religions are at base the same. One of the two younger men next to me, who were listening attentively and approvingly, said, "Yes, many are the roads." Wiro said that from the *ḍalang* side the *wajang* figures show their bodies, their outside, but from the shadow side they show their souls, their inside. The boy next to me said, "Yes, but their souls have different characters, just like people. Some are refined, some rough."

Prijaji Interpretations of the *Wajang*

WHAT, then, is the meaning of the *wajang* for the *prijaji?*

In essence, the Mahabharata is the story of a struggle between cousins, the Penḍawas and the Korawas, a struggle which culminates in the great war of kinsmen, the Bratajuda, during which the champions from each side face one another. Ardjuna kills his older half-brother Karna, Bima dispatches Sujudana, and so on. The immediate impulse is to call the Pendawas, who are certainly heroes, the "good" men and Korawas, who are not quite so clearly villains, the "bad" men; but to identify the figures in the drama as though they were characters in a medieval morality play would be a serious misunderstanding. (The Pendawas are always on the right in a *wajang,* the Korawas on the left— another reminder of those allegoric dramas of our own religious tradition.) The absolutistic dichotomous morality of Western thought is generally foreign to the pantheistic *prijaji* outlook which sees God in everything, the good as well as the bad, in pain as well as pleasure.

The struggle between the Pendawas and the Korawas is an endless one— despite its seeming ending in the Bratajuda war (an episode almost never actually played in Java, in any case). The time-bound realities of good and evil, pleasure and pain, love and hate are dwarfed and rendered meaning-less by the timeless and ultimately amoral background against which they are fought out. The feudal virtues of courage and duty are resolved with the seem-ingly antithetical religious virtues of renunciation and compassion by an invo-cation of the cosmic-comic inevitability of human actions given the divine con-text in which they are set. One does what one has to do only because the gods expect one to. Only through action unmarred by passion, a detached perform-ance of inevitable duty, does one reach peace.

In keeping with their tendency to find ultimate reality in their own feelings, to turn objective metaphysical meaning into subjective emotional experience, the *prijajis* give the Mahabharata as it appears in the *wajang,* a psychological, almost psychoanalytic, interpretation.

> He (a schoolteacher) said that the main purpose of the *wajang* was to draw a picture of inner thought and feeling, to give an external form to internal feeling. More specifically, it pictured the eternal conflict in the individual between what he wanted to do and what he felt he ought to do. Suppose one wants to steal something, and at the same time something inside tells you not to do it, restrains one, controls one. That which wants to do it is called the will; that which restrains is called the ego (literally, the word is *aku*— "I," "me," "myself"). All such wishes and tendencies threaten every day to ruin the individual, to destroy his thought and upset his behavior. These tendencies are called *goda,* which means something which plagues or teases (someone or something). He then gave another example. "You go to a coffee-shop and people are eating, and they invite you to join them. You have already just eaten at home and so are full; yet you want to eat with them, and so you have a struggle within. Should I eat with them? No, I've already eaten and I will be overfull. But the food looks so good. . . ."

This second, so very, very Javanese example, concerning food, points up that the struggle is not between good and evil, as the first example might lead one to believe, but between the old opposites of *kasar* and *alus* feelings, be-tween base animal passion and detached, effortless self-control, like Ardjuna calmly dispatching his half-brother in the Bratajuda war.

In the *wajang* the various plagues, wishes, and so on, the *godas*, are represented by the Korawas, of whom there are 100, and the ability to control oneself is represented by their cousins the five Pendawas and by Kresna, the incarnation of Wisnu. The stories are ostensibly about a struggle over land, as the abstract elements in the *rasa* can be represented in concrete external elements which will attract the audience and seem real to them and still communicate its inner message. . . . For example, the *wajang* is full of wars which are supposed to represent the inner war which goes on continually in every person's *batin* between his base and his refined impulses. In every *lakon* Ardjuna and the other Pendawas are continually fighting the giants and ogres, and, oddly, they have to keep killing them over and over again. They kill them once and then a couple of hours later they are killing them all over again. Why is this? It is because the giants and ogres represent the passions. They represent a person's inner desires to amuse oneself instead of study, to play instead of work, to wander here and there rather than sticking to a fixed course; and, since these lusts and passions keep arising again and again, one has to keep fighting them off with good impulses, represented by the Pendawas. (The Pendawas are usually held to symbolize the five senses also, the correct ordering of them.) But one can't ever defeat them once and for all. They always keep coming back and one has to keep killing them again and again.

The metaphysical doctrine of the Indian Mahabharata is here stated in a psychological rather than a socio-political vocabulary, but it remains essentially unchanged. As the king's castle becomes a symbol for the inner heart and the height of political status becomes a sign of inward refinement, so here the conflict in the Bhagavad Gita between the feudal obligation to fight and the inner compassion for other mere humans is resolved by projecting both duty and compassion against the all-encompassing background of an ever-present God. It is transformed into a conflict between the grosser sensory necessities of natural existence and the polite ideal of refined feeling which is resolved in turn by projecting both *kasar* and *alus* feelings against the all-encompassing background of the ultimate "feeling-meaning," or *rasa*.

> I asked them (a *prijaji* couple, members of a mystic sect): "What do you think of when you meditate?" They said: "You don't think of anything. What you try to do is clear your mind of any thoughts at all, so you can have direct contact with God. You have to get complete emptiness without thought; a pure, clear, serene insight." I asked them if they felt anything when this happened; and they said, "Yes and no. There is a tremendous feeling but it is not like regular feeling, and you can't explain it to anyone else. It is a purely private thing."

And the result of this kind of ultimate emotional understanding is the same as the result of the understanding Ardjuna got from Krishna—an inward serenity in the midst of an outward reality.

> I went to the market and bought some cloth from Pak Lamidjan and his wife, he being one of the ten *gurus* (teachers) of Sumarah (a mystic sect). He said that Sumarah was concerned with making one so that one does not pay too much attention to worldly things; so that you do not care too much about the things of everyday life. He said that this is very difficult to do. His wife,

he said, was not yet able to do it much, and she agreed with him. She still likes to ride in motorcars, but he doesn't care whether he does or not. It takes much long study and meditation. For example, one must get so that if someone comes to buy cloth one doesn't care whether he buys it or not. One must not get one's emotions really involved in the problems of commerce, but just think of God. He said that Sumarah wants to turn people toward God and avoids any strong attachments to everyday life.

We shall return to mysticism in greater detail later. The point here is merely to establish that the *wajang,* and hence those other arts of literature, music, and dance which cluster about it, is, for the sophisticated literati at least, part of the general religious complex constructed around the concepts of *kasar—alus, lair—batin,* and *rasa;* and that the *wajang* states in an emotionalist vocabulary the same formulation of what is perhaps the basic dilemma of Indian religious thought as it is presented in the Mahabharata—how is action possible, given compassion?

Sudjono (the school teacher) went on to say that each of the three main Pendawas has a different character. The oldest, Judistira, is very good; in fact he is too good, too free of evil. The result is that in his extreme sense of compassion he is not a very effective king, being completely unable to rule the country for himself. For example, he views all things in the world as belonging to God, and people as unimportant parts of the larger whole. Thus, if a man comes to him and asks for his land, Judistira will just give it to him, the ultimate result being that all the land be given away and the state unable to hold together. Or he will give away all his food, unthinking of himself, and then starve to death. He is compassionate, too compassionate; and so he needs his brothers to help him rule. His main difficulty, said Sudjono in conclusion is that he doesn't know the word "no." The second brother, Bima, is just the opposite. If he has an intention he follows it out straight to its conclusion; he doesn't look aside, doesn't turn aside or idle along the way. He always advances and never looks back. Once he has an idea and feels that he is capable of carrying it out, he is brave to the end and will not listen to anyone or anything. He is single-minded and fears no one. The third brother, Ardjuna, has the ability to do good and to do evil. His goodness comes from the fact that he opposes evil, that he shelters people from injustice, without caring for himself, and that, also, he is courageous in fighting for the right. His badness is that he can kill in cold blood and that he does not feel compassionate enough, sympathetic enough. He does not feel mercy enough for evil-doers and thus can be brutal in the name of justice.

The three major characters of the *wajang* (excluding, for the moment Semar) thus state the action-compassion dilemma, presenting dramatic metaphors of the several forms it takes in human experience. Judistira, his ability to act drained by his compassion, is praiseworthy but pallid—a symbol of the beauty and incapabilities of too unworldly a sensitivity. Bima, his will to action interfering with his emotional flexibility, is colorful and attractive, but in part a victim of his own somewhat immature will—a symbol of the vitality and dangers of passionate commitment. The middle brother, Ardjuna (the other two younger brothers, the twins, being minor characters only, notable for their dog-like fidelity to their elder brothers), is able to sustain action by stifling compassion through an invocation of divine order or justice into the human context, but only at the cost of leaving him a figure at once the most coldly capable and the most mercilessly just.

Judistira's sense for the negating effects of the wider frame of existence upon human actions, *tout comprendre c'est tout pardonner;* Bima's sense for the felt realities of injustice viewed in human perspective, rather than under the aspect of eternity, and the consequent need to take resolute action against such injustice; and Ardjuna's cruel insistence upon the application of a divine code to a human world, are all part of the same dilemma. And for all three the solution is the same—mystical insight. With a genuine comprehension of the realities of human situation, a true perception of the ultimate *rasa,* comes the ability to combine Judistira's compassion, Bima's will to action, and Ardjuna's sense of justice into a truly *alus* outlook, an outlook which brings an emotional detachment and an inner peace in the midst of a world of flux but yet permits and demands a struggle for order and justice within such a world. As our Modjokuto poet points out:

> Indeed the saints
> Know God directly every day
> During the time they are in the world.

In sum, the philosophy of the *wajang* stories is that insofar as one can perceive ultimate reality, which is within oneself as an ultimate feeling, *rasa,* one will be free of the distracting effects of earthly emotions—not only compassion, but anger, fear, love, hope, despair, and all. This gives one great power—either for good, as in the case of the Pendawas, or for evil, as in the case of the Korawas, who after all are *alus* too. It is not only the good who can mediate, but the evil as well; for mysticism is an amoral science anyone can employ. It brings knowledge; and, as in science generally, knowledge is power for good or for evil. Good and evil are human values only, and God is in everything—the hate and the cruelty as well as the love and the compassion; and everything is in God. It is a religion arguing that understanding of the self brings power and peace in this world, and the *wajang* stories often point this up quite sharply.

He told me a *wajang* story. Someone tells Bima that if he gets a special kind of water and bathes in it he will be invulnerable and thus will certainly win in the Bratajuda war against Sujudana. As he doesn't know where this water can be found, he goes off to see a *guru* to find out where to get it. The *guru,* however, has lately been given lots of gifts by the Korawas, and so the *guru* aids evil and tries to send Bima to his death. (There are *gurus* like that, the informant said; some use their knowledge for good, some for bad.) The *guru* tells Bima to go and get the water at the top of the mountain—although he knows that two very powerful giants are meditating there and that they will be infuriated when they are disturbed by Bima looking for the magic water to make him powerful and invulnerable. Bima goes, and indeed the giants become angry and fight with him. He is nearly beaten, but finally he manages to strike the giants' heads together, and lo, they turn into gods. Sometimes the gods themselves do evil; and these two had done something wrong and had been incarnated as giants by Batara Guru, from which state Bima removed them by knocking their heads together. Grateful, they tell him that he has been deceived and there is no water there. Angry, he goes back to the *guru* and says that he has been deceived; but the *guru* explains by saying that he had sent Bima up the mountain as a test of his bravery and strength to make sure that he was able to undergo the actual journey he must make. Then he tells Bima that he will find the water in the middle of the sea, hoping that Bima will be drowned there. Bima leaves for the sea, single-mindedly, while his older brother, Judistira, and his younger brother, Ardjuna, plead with him not to go telling him that he is being deceived again. He pays no attention to them but marches straight to the sea. When he reaches the sea, after great struggles with monsters, he finds a god who looks exactly like himself except that he is only as big as his little finger. Bima, astonished at this midget replica of himself, tells him his quest. The little god says "Enter me"; and Bima does, through the mouth, the big man entering the little. Inside, he sees that the whole world is there, contained inside the little god. Then he emerges again, the god telling him that there is no water, that his power is within himself, and that he must look into himself, for that is the source of his strength. "If God is everywhere in the world, then he is in you too, and you must look into yourself and see the world there, and then you will have the power you seek." And so Bima goes off to meditate. Sudjono (the informant) was quite conscious of the symbolism of all this and kept saying that the midget-god replica of Bima represented his inner self.

Bima's meditation brings him the knowledge he seeks, and the very form of the *wajang* puppet which represents him serves as a reminder to the audience of the main "message" of the *wajang,* the need for mystical meditation.

(The informant is a clerk in the hospital.) According to "Javanese science" (*ilmu djawi*), there are seven levels below the earth and seven levels in the sky, the earth being in between the two sets. People whose minds are clear can see down all seven and up all seven. All this is further explained in the *wajang*. In the *wajang*, Brataséna (another, far more common name for Bima) can see down all seven and up all seven. . . . His name, in fact, means to finish (*brata*) meditation (*séna*); and so this means that if people finish meditation—that is, attain mystical union—they can see all seven levels up and all seven down. Only very few people can do this, and those who can are called *gurus,* mystical teachers. One can go further into all this and look at the appearance of Brataséna in the *wajang*. First, there is the long thumbnail he has, the *pantjanaka* (five nails), which symbolizes that all his five senses (*pantjaindrija*) are sharp and acute. Second, there is the sarong he wears, which is checked in red, white, and black, the red indicating bravery, the white purity, and the black fixity of will, resolution. Next, there is the ear decoration he wears, which is called *sumping* and described as *djinaroting asem endèk arep duwur buri,* literally "the root of a tamarind which is low in front and high in back." But each of these words has a second meaning. *Djinarot,* "root," here has the force of "essence," "core," etc. *Asem,* "tamarind," has the secondary meaning *rasa* or "feeling." *Endèk arep,* "low in front," indicates the ego, the individual self in its humbleness; and *duwur buri,* "high in back," means God, because God is high and walks behind the individual. The meaning of it all then, details aside, is that the *lair,* the outer aspect of Brataséna, shows that he has already made as one his "ego," himself, and God. In more explicit terms, a man who has finished meditating has joined the outside and the inside, *lair* and *batin,* and made them as one and has also become one with God. Thus, the above aspects of Brataséna—that is, of any man who has meditated—can be summarized as follows: The thumbnail indicates that his five senses are as sharp as possible; the various colors of the squares on his sarong indicate that he is brave, pure, and fixed of will; and the ear-ornament means that he is one with God and that his *lair* and *batin* have merged. Theoretically, every man can be Brataséna—can meditate and reach this state.

It is worth noting here that this is not the radical pessimism of later Hinduism and of Buddhism, in which the tendency is to devaluate action except as a necessary evil. Bima, like the other Peṇḍawas, is no hermit and no pacifist; rather, as the Javanese most often describe him and his brothers, he is a "defender of society." For the Javanese, mystical experience is not a rejection of the world but a temporary retirement from it for purposes of increasing spiritual strength in order to operate more effectively in the mundane sphere, a refinement of the inner life in order to purify the outer. There is a time for the mountain-top (where most really advanced mythical mystics do their meditations) and a time for the city, one of my informants said; and Javanese semi-historical legends repeat the single theme of the dethroned or threatened king or the defrauded heir to the kingship retreating to a lonely mountain-top to meditate, and, having gained spiritual power in this manner, returning to lead a successful military expedition against his enemies. This theme persists. Many Modjokuto people still insist that the leader of the ill-fated revolt against the Japanese in a near-by city who disappeared when it collapsed is alive and meditating on a volcano-top, and will return to lead a crusade of purification against the present state of society. This is the warrior Kshatriya ethic before India's priestly Brahmans turned it other-worldly; it is not escape from life, but escape in life which is prized.

I asked him (another cloth salesman) about Sumarah. Why did they medi-tate? He said that it was only to make the heart peaceful; to make one calm inside so that one will not be easily upset. "For example," he said, "if you're selling cloth and you are all upset you may sell a cloth for forty rupiah when it cost you sixty, or some such thing. Suppose a person comes here and my mind is not calm; then I can't sell him anything." Why, I asked; but he couldn't explain very well, for he seemed to take it as self-evident that if one was not calm in the heart, the sale wouldn't happen. . . . "Any-way," he said, "that is all there is to Sumarah: a practice to help you calm your inner heart." I said, "Well, why do you have to have a meeting? Why not just meditate at home?" And he said, "Well, in the first place you are not supposed to get peaceful by withdrawing from society. You are supposed to stay in society and mix with people, only with peace in your heart."

But what about Semar, the native Javanese figure (who does not appear in the original Indian epics and so must have been introduced into the stories after they arrived in Java) in whom so many oppositions seem to meet, the figure who is both god and clown, man's guardian spirit and his servant, the most spiritually refined inwardly and the most rough-looking outwardly? Semar is said to be the eldest descendant of "He that is One" (i.e., God), elder brother to Baṭara Guru. Baṭara Guru became king of the other gods— Wisnu, Brama, Kala—who followed him, but Semar became a man—a fat, awkward, ugly-looking man, full of rough talk, comic stupidities, and hilarious confusions. At least this is the pure version; but syncretism, the need to account for new actualities, and the vagaries of oral tradition sometimes shift things a little.

> The son (of the ḍalang) said in the beginning Java was all woods and full of spirits. Then the people came and displaced the woods and the spirits, but there are still plenty of the latter. The ḍalang said that he couldn't tell me about spirits because he had never seen one and he could not explain that kind of thing to me. Evidently he was thinking of the scorn he had received from Westerners before on this point. When I said, "No, you can't see them, but you can see people who have been entered by them and you can feel them," he said, "If you have an opinion like that, then I can explain them to you. If you have a sceptical attitude, then you can't learn anything about them; you just won't understand what I am talking about." His son said that all people are descended from just two people and so they are all the same and shouldn't fight, but they forget this sometimes. The ḍalang agreed and gave me the following genealogy:
>
> Nabi (i.e., Prophet) Adam married Babu Kawa (Eve)
> and had children
> Nabi Sis   and   Sajang Sis (Semar)
> Nabi Sis then gave birth to all the Prophets, such as Nabi Ibrahim, (Abraham), Nabi Nur (Noah), Nabi Muhammad, and Nabi Isa (Jesus); and the various Western peoples descended from their nabis (The Arabs from Muhammad, the Dutch from Jesus, and so on). Semar gave birth to the Hindus and the Javanese. Thus all people are the same and all religions are the same.

In any case, Semar, the lowliest of the low, upon whom the Penḍawas look, as one Javanese writer puts it, as they look upon the bottoms of their feet, is at the same time the father of us all. Here is an explanation from a schoolteacher:

> Everywhere Ardjuna goes he is accompanied by Semar Garèng-Pétruk, his "parents" (metaphorically, since he has a literal father, the defrauded King of Ngastina) and servants; and even though Ardjuna is a satrija he still listens to the advice of these comical old servants. Why? Because even though Ardjuna has killed many giants, he must not be proud and think he had conquered all. Even though he is higher than his "parents" and far more brave, far more clever, far more successful than they, he must still listen to them; for they have more experience than he, more wisdom even if they appear stupid and he clever. Thus, no matter how high above them he gets, he must still honor his "parents," still ask and take their advice. For instance, young people are often extravagant and take ill-considered actions, and Ardjuna is also; and old people can hold them back from actions they would later regret the way the three clowns keep Ardjuna in tow and keep

him from rash behavior. Also, the *satrijas* must be always accompanied by Semar, because he is a representative of God. The *satrijas* guard and defend society, and they remain safe and unharmed because they are accompanied by Semar until the end of time.

A full analysis of Semar's role in the *wajang* could in itself fill a book, but it seems clear that in some sense he represents the realistic view of life as opposed to the idealistic. He calls Ardjuna back to everyday humdrum existence, cheers him up in his despair, and blunts the edge of his pride in his triumph. He tries to moderate the *satrija*'s rigid sense of cosmic justice in terms of comic reality. All in all, the closest parallel in Western art to the *wajangs* seems to be Shakespeare's chronicle plays. In considering the relationship between Ardjuna and Semar, one thinks immediately of the relationship between Prince Hal and his symbolic father, who was also fat, ugly and not a little wise. Even the form of the *wajang*—the long formal scenes in the courts with messengers coming and going, interspersed with short breathless transitional scenes in the woods or along the roads; the double plot, the clowns speaking a rough common language and full of a practical worldly-wise ethics, caricaturing the forms of action of the great nobles, who speak an elevated language full of apostrophes to honor, justice, and duty; the final war, which, like those at Shrewsbury and Agincourt, leaves the vanquished beaten but still noble—even the form of the *wajang* suggests Shakespeare's historical drama.

The world-view the *wajang* expresses is, however, hardly Elizabethan at base, although there seems a peculiar similarity between Semar and his English counterparts in the relationship in which, as clowns, they stand to the two different traditions which dominate and motivate the two separate theaters. Both Semar and Falstaff provide a rather general criticism of the very values the dramas in which they are enclosed affirm. They furnish a reminder that, despite over-proud assertions to the contrary, no completely adequate human world-view is possible; and that, behind all the pretense to absolute and ultimate knowledge, the sense for the irrationality of human life, for the fact that it is unenclosable, remains. Whether or not Semar is, as has been suggested, a master-symbol of the peasantry, a criticism of gentry values in terms of the more earthy sense of life of the villagers (and the increasingly important role the clowns play in the more popular forms of drama, until they nearly swallow the heros entirely, leaving the latter rather overbred fools than descendants of *satrijas,* would tend to support this), he does, in his *kasar* human form, remind the *alus* Ardjuna of his own humble animal origins and, most crucially, resists any attempt to make humans into gods and end the world of *kasar* contingency by a flight to the *alus* world of absolute order, a final stilling of the eternal psychological-metaphysical struggle.

He said that in that story (I had been relating a *wajang* I had seen and been largely unable to follow) Siva comes down to earth in the form of a mystical teacher in an attempt to bring the Peṇḍawas and the Korawas together, and that he is succeeding quite well except that Semar stands in the way; for Semar is really a god even though he seems to be only

a servant. Ardjuna is bewitched by Siva in his earthly incarnation as a
mystical teacher and told that if he kills Semar the Pendawas and the
Korawas will be able to make peace and the eternal struggle will end.
Ardjuna does not want to kill Semar, whom he loves, but he is bewitched,
and so he goes to Semar and is about to kill him. Semar then says, "So
this is how you treat me after I have followed you around and served
you and loved you." This is the most poignant point in the play. Ardjuna
is very ashamed, but he has given his word. Semar then says, "Well, all
right, I will burn myself"; and he builds a bonfire and stands in it. But instead
of dying he turns into his godly form and then defeats the magician. Then
the war between the Korawas and the Pendawas begins again.

The *Gamelan:* Javanese Music

SUPPORTING the *wajang* in its expression of *prijaji* values, the *gamelan* orchestra presents to the ear the picture of the inner life the shadow-play presents to the eye. Except for the occasional inclusion of a two-stringed violin-
like instrument called a *rebab,* the *gamelan* is entirely a percussion orchestra,
which may consist of as many as fifty instruments in a very large court en-
semble but usually contains about a dozen. One even meets, in Modjokuto,
orchestras made up of only three or four people. I knew many individuals
who owned only one instrument, or perhaps two, which they played solo when
the mood struck them, or, regularly or irregularly, gathered together with
others who owned an instrument or two to form a small orchestra. As the
gamelan demands rather little of the delicate adjustment between separate
virtuosi required by the Western orchestra, with its greater freedom for individual interpretation and consequently greater need for a coordinating con-
ductor, there is little need for a stability of personnel. (But people say that
the members of a really good *gamelan* orchestra must *pada rasakaké:* they
must "sympathize with," "feel with," one another.) One often sees one performer replacing another at a certain instrument right in the middle of a
piece; and any group of performers can form an orchestra on the spot, even if
they have never met one another before. (Almost every man in Java—the
players are all men—seems able to play a little *gamelan* music.) A lumber-
yard manufacturer around the corner from me bought a set of instruments
and placed them on a vacant porch for his workers, who played them almost
every night; but hardly ever was the orchestra made up of people who had
often played together as a unit.

The basic theme of the *gending,* or musical composition, quite simple and
severe in form, is usually carried on the *saron,* a kind of metal xylophone the
seven keys of which are struck one at a time with a wooden mallet and held
down with the hand immediately afterward to prevent overtones. Thus the
nuclear melody is struck out in a series of clear, distinct, and elemental tones,
following one another in an even-flowing and almost entirely unstressed
rhythm. A set of gongs of different sizes (of which the *gong gedé, kenong,*

kempul, and *keṭuk* are the most important, the first being the largest, the latter the smallest) "punctuate" the music, the largest gong marking the largest phrase, the second largest gong marking the next most gross subdivision, the smallest its basic units. Thus a *gong geḍé* musical phrase, marked by the dull boom of the big gong, may be divided into two *kenong* phrases by the sounding of this somewhat smaller and hence higher-pitched gong; the *kenong* phrase may be divided into two *kempul* phrases; and finally the *kempul* phrase may be divided into two *keṭuk* phrases.

A number of other instruments, most particularly the *gambang,* a large wooden xylophone struck with two mallets simultaneously, and the *gendèr,* which consists of a xylophone with keys strung on cords above resonating bamboo sound-tubes, play around the nuclear theme in small, delicate embellishments to enrich the starkness of the basic melodic line. The double-ended drum, one end of which is smaller than the other, the small end being played with the left hand, the large with the right, provides the beat. (There are sometimes two of these, one large, one smaller, both played by the same man.) It maintains the rhythm until the point comes for it to break into a new pattern; then it changes the rhythm, the other instruments following after. It is for this reason that the drummer is often called the "leader" of the *gamelan* orchestra and that the drum is considered the most difficult instrument to play.

Two major types of scales are used; *sléndro* and *pélog,* there being several sub-types of each. *Sléndro* has five equal-interval tones covering our octave; *pélog* has seven unequal-interval tones covering the same range. The *sléndro* scale is used in the accompaniment of *wajangs* dramatizing Mahabharata or Ramayana stories, the *pelog* scale for those dramatizing Hindu-Javanese kingdom stories; and, of course, both may be played alone.

The interweaving of the *wajang* and the *gamelan* is quite close. The three major divisions of the *wajang* noted above—the opening period until midnight, the complications period until three, and the closing section until dawn —are all marked off by the playing of special musical compositions or *gendings* (increasing, as the play itself, in noise and loudness as the evening wears on). There are *gendings* for nearly each aspect of the *wajang.* A war scene demands different *gamelan* tunes from those required by a court meeting between *satrijas;* the Pendawas have *gendings* played for them different from those played for the Korawas; there is a whole class of tunes used for announcing the arrival of guests at court; *alus* figures are accompanied by different tunes from those for *kasar.* Each of the major figures has a *gending* associated with him, perhaps the most readily recognized tune being the one played at midnight to usher in the complications period and bring Semar ambling, in his peculiar rocking gait, on to the scene.

Another way in which the *gamelan* is married to the *wajang,* and to poetry as well, is through the songs called *suluk,* which are sung by the *ḍalang* at appropriate points in the play. Again, there are special songs for special events (impending war, a king entering his castle) or special characters (for Semar's appearance, for the appearance of such a meditating *guru* as Ardjuna's grandfather), and, further, special songs appropriate to special emotions (grief over a dead *satrija,* love songs, songs of doubt and indecision). As the *suluks* are derived from ancient Javanese versions of Hindu poems, and so are in great part incomprehensible both to the *wajang* audience and to the *dalang* himself, the emphasis tends not to be on their intrinsic meaning but, as in the music generally, on the mood they suggest. They are viewed more as abstract vocal music whose significance, like that of the *gendings* themselves, is in their *rasa,* in the feeling contained in them.

Playing (or listening to) a *gamelan* is a spiritual discipline, not just a mere amusement; in Modjokuto, people will tell you that they often play on a single *gamelan* instrument for a while in the evening in order to discipline and restrain their emotions, in order to make them *alus.* On the other hand, certain *gendings* are considered to have ritual efficacy, and so are proceeded by the burning of incense and a *sadjèn* offering to the spirits.

The *Tembang:* Javanese Poetry

ON the other side, *gamelan* music connects up with Javanese literature as well as drama through its accompaniment of Javanese poetry, the *tembang.* Tembangs are both poems and songs. They may be recited in a half-singing rhythm without accompaniment or they may be sung to a *gamelan gending* appropriate to them. The *tembang* forms are quite rigid; the number of syllables the line shall have, the number of lines, and the final vowel in the line are all carefully prescribed. There are about a dozen or so such forms, but only three are very common in Modjokuto: *dandang-gula, sinom,* and *kinanti,* for which the "formulas" are as follows:

	1	2	3	4	5	6	7	8	9	10
Dandang-gula:	10i,	10a,	8e(o),	7u,	9i,	7a,	6u,	8a,	12i,	7a
Sinom:	8a,	8i,	8a,	8i,	7i,	8u,	7a,	8i,	12a	
Kinanti:	8u,	8i,	8a,	8i,	8a,	8i				

My diagram means that the *dandang-gula* form demands 10 lines: the first line must have 10 syllables and have *i* the final vowel or final syllable; the second line must have 10 syllables and *a.* It means that the *sinom* has 9 lines, the first being 8 syllables ending with an *a* syllable and so on. The poem composed for his children by a Modjokuto *tembang* maker from which I have already repeatedly quoted is in *dandang-gula.* Here I shall quote a stanza in Javanese before translating it—to serve the double purpose of displaying the form and, as the stanza concerns the *prijaji* view of language and poetry, of connecting *tembangs* into the general *alus* art complex I have been describing.

Rèhning Djawa ahli olah budi
Kudu weruh surasané basa
Kang sinandi sasadoné
Kang ,kandas djroné kalbu
Hambukaa kekeran batin
Jwa tjawuh panjurasa

Awit jèn tan runtut
Pangrembugé tanpa guna
Nora antuk munfangaté kawruh batin
Mung malah dadi wisa

As Javanese are experts in exercising their spirits,
They need to know their feelings of words;
Those whose hidden meanings are unclear,
Those which have come aground in the heart.
Unfold the secrets of the inner life;
Do not confuse your linguistic insights;
Because if you do not put them, one by one, in order,
Your talk will be without use,
You will achieve nothing of any value in the understanding of the inner life.
In fact, your confused understanding will be as poison.

Here words are held to cloud meaning as much as reveal it; they are the *lair* forms in which we cast, never directly but always obliquely, our inner feelings. Words taken literally or impressionistically lead not to knowledge but to the poisoning of the spirit. Each word, each expression must be taken one by one in its proper order so that its true meaning, always vague and elusive as the *batin* is vague and elusive, may be partially grasped. *Lair* behavior, of which language (as well as music, dance, and drama) is a part, masks the *batin;* and thus only those who study the *lair* patiently and in orderly fashion are able to sort it out and get the "feeling"* that is subtly suffused through it.

For a *sinom* example I take not a stanza from the Modjokuto informant, although he wrote a long *sinom* poem too, but what is perhaps the most famous of all *tembangs,* certainly one nearly everyone knows and one you can hear sung by everyone from pedicab drivers to district officers:

Amenangi djaman édan
Ewuh-aja ing pambudi
Mèlu édan ora tahan
Jèn tan mèlu anglakoni
Nora keduman mélik
Keliren wekasanipun
Ja talah nora salah
Bedja bedjaning sing lali
Luwih bedja kang éling lawan waspada

We have lived to see a time without order
In which everyone is confused in his mind.
One cannot bear to join in the madness,
But if he does not do so,
He will not share in the spoils,
And will starve as a result.
Yes, God; not wrong:
Happy are those who forget,
Happier yet those who remember and who have deep insight.

* *Surasa; panjurasa,* in line six, which I have translated "linguistic insights," literally means something like "the comprehension oɪ the feeling of words."

The "time without order," the *djaman édan,* has been variously identified with the depression, with the revolution, and with the present, with its motorcars, airplanes and atom bombs. In any case, a detachment born of deeper insight is again suggested as the main defense against madness within or without. (*Waspada* means to see clearly, to have clear insight into something; sometimes even in the sense of second-sight or clairvoyance.)

Finally a *kinanṭi,* one of the simplest of all *tembang* forms. This famous one is taken from the scene in the Ramayana in which Anoman, the monkey hero, hears the imprisoned Dèwi Sinet, kidnapped wife of Rama, sing of her love for her distant husband, thus proving her faithfulness:

> Ḍuh Déwa ḍuh Beṭara gung,
> Tingalana Solah mami
> Sèwu lara sèwu brangta
> Tan ana timbangé mami
> Jèn pukulun tan panggiha
> Kalawan Pangéran mami

> O God, O Great God,
> See my gesture!
> A thousand sicknesses, a thousand longings—
> There is none such as I
> If I do not meet
> My Prince.

As with us, different poetic forms are appropriate to different purposes. *Kinanṭi* poems are almost inevitably love-songs. *Sinoms* are often moral in tone, and sometimes prophetic as well, for example in the poetic predictions the 19th-century Javanese writer Rangga Warsita is claimed to have made of the coming of automobiles, airplanes, radios, and other modern wonders. The *ḍanḍang-gula* form is not so sharply defined in terms of function and may be used for various purposes, such as the didactic use above or for beginning a *wajang* dance. Of all the forms of the *alus* art complex, the *tembang* is perhaps the most widely diffused and the most often practiced, for it takes no capital to sing and not very much skill. You cannot walk from one end of Modjokuto to the other after ten at night and not hear someone singing a *tembang* somewhere along the way.

The *Djogèd:* Javanese Dance

THE *gamelan* connects drama to poetry and dance to them both. Javanese dancing is called *djogèd* as opposed to *ḍangsah,* Western dancing, which seems to appear almost obscene in many Javanese eyes. Evidently Javanese formal dance is more closely linked to the Javanese sense of their own identity, their body-image, than any other of their arts. Even people who are very Westernized in almost every other way still reject Western dancing with a shudder, using such expressions as, "When you dance *djogèd* you get lost in yourself, but when you dance Western-style, you are still conscious of what you are doing," or "*Dangsah* may be all right for Westerners who are used to it, but Easterners (of either sex) dancing so close to a partner are not able to control themselves, and so it will inevitably lead to sexual intercourse," or "I don't mind seeing Europeans *dangsah* together, but if I see a Javanese doing it, it makes me feel queasy inside." A student riot at Gadjah Mada University in Djokjakarta was set off during the time I was there by a few students daring to hold a party with Western dancing; and the death of a man in a Djakarta riot was held to have, in part, resulted from a similar situation.

There are two main types of *djogèd:* the ancient "princess" (*putri*) dances, *srimpi* and *bedaja,* performed only by young girls, and the much more recent dances (usually of both sexes) which act out the *wajang* and so are known as *wajang wong, wong* being the word for "man," "human being." The *srimpi* and *bedaja* are both group dances, the former having four dances, the latter nine. Until a few years before the war these dances were restricted to the courts; and it has only been in this century that Europeans have been permitted to watch them even within the confines of the castle. Formerly, *srimpi* was the name of an office as well as a dance, for each of the two courts (at Djokjakarta and Surakarta) had only four, chosen from among immature descendants of the ruler and replaced when pubescent. *Bedajas,* on the other hand, were pubescent but unmarried girls sometimes taken from among the common people outside the court and often serving as the sultan's concubines. Dressed bare-shouldered in velvet bodices and brown-white *batik* sarongs, a long bright-colored double sash hanging between their half-bent legs from their waists to the floor in front of them, their heads crowned with a black and gold headpiece, their faces painted with the yellow powder we have seen at Javanese weddings (for these are the "princesses" the bride is imitating), and moving with a kind of impossibly decelerated grace which made every gesture a calm defiance of anatomy and gravity, the *srimpi* and the *bedaja* summed up the Javanese theory of beauty and demonstrated it to king and court.

In practice the above costume description applies only to the Surakarta (commonly called Solo) court. The Djokjakarta dress is slightly different, as is the dance style itself. The Solo style is usually considered to be rather more "soft" and "feminine," that of Djokjakarta rather "stern" and "masculine"; but neither is likely to be considered very dynamic by our standards. This general difference runs through nearly all the arts of the two courts—music, dance, drama—as well as through the systems of manners; but to an untrained Western eye the differences are likely to be small enough to be missed entirely. In any case, since for various reasons Djokjakarta has traditionally been more conservative and encapsulated within itself than Solo, the latter has had a far wider influence on the countryside and has provided the aesthetic model for most of those outside the immediate environs of the court. This includes Modjokuto, where one sees almost no Djokjakarta style dancing at all, and where, when people say the *kraton* ("court," "castle"), they almost always mean Solo.

Interestingly enough, in the postwar period the situation has reversed in the sense that the Djokjakarta court, led by its modern-thinking sultan, has become a center of political consciousness in the new *Republik* while Solo has been left behind clinging to the relics of its old supremacy. Since the twenties, nationalism has had a greater impact upon the Djokjakarta court than upon Solo, which remained vigorously pro-colonial to the bitter end, with the result that the intelligentsia leadership of the *prijaji* group has come more and more from Djokjakarta and the literati leadership, to a great extent, has remained in Solo.

The line between Javanese gestures in the dance and out of it is not very sharp—as one realizes when a coolie on the back of a truck gestures to one to pass with an arm motion that could have come out of a court dance, although he no doubt knows no dance; or when a Modjokuto girl seats herself on the floor with the same unbelievably gradual sinking motion with which this is accomplished in a *srimpi*. The gestures seem to flow along self-contained, detached from the rest of the body, as though they were operating in a world of their own, and then suddenly break into a final twist or turn and join again into a unity with the other limbs, the trunk, and the head. Many of the most intricate gestures of the dance itself—the pointed-finger flipping of the sash in one direction or another, the kicking of the sarong train back with the foot, the bending of the hand backwards toward the wrist, or the movement of the head horizontally along the plane of the shoulders—are considered so difficult to perform with the necessary grace that only those who begin to study them very early can ever practice them with the required skill; and as soon as a dancer grows to womanhood, about twenty to twenty-five, she no longer will dance. One never sees anyone older than the middle twenties dancing *alus* dances in Java; most performers are from about ten to fifteen years old.

Both the *bedaja* and the *srimpi* have stories behind them. Some of the motions are supposed to be imitations of natural actions—such as "waves of the sea," a kind of half-rocking motion—or of such human behaviors as combing the hair, dressing, fighting, or bowing to a lord. (Djokjakarta *srimpis* involve the wielding of daggers—*kris*—and bows and arrows, for they tell the story of a struggle of two girls over one man.) These natural actions are so highly stylized that the dances are in no way realistic but starkly abstract. The girls move back and forth within a square space, always facing either north, south, east or west, never diagonally. The rhythm of the dance is slow, deliberate, controlled; and the motions have a ritualistic exactness. An absolutely correct posture is required, the shoulders in just such a place that the shoulder bones do not protrude at all. Breathing must be shallow and not noticeable. Eyes must be kept fixed in one place, directly forward and a little down, giving a trance-like effect to the dance, an effect heightened by the frequent use of the "waves of the sea" step, which is merely a gently rocking motion while standing in one spot, a motion that seems to be hypnotic for both the performers and the spectators. The set expression, the carefully controlled motions, give a feeling of inwardness, of concentration on the self, and of a conception of a perfection of self-contained grace which each dancer is trying to reach independently of the others:

> At one point he (a member of the governing board of a Modjokuto *gamelan* and *djogèd* group) talked about the *djogèd* and said that its purpose was to *njetunggalaken batin,* to make as one, to unify and concentrate the inner life. He illustrated with arm motions from a man's dance, with arms high and crooked in front and elbow rather forward, and said that the eyes must follow the point of the elbow, first on one arm and then on the other, and not just look here and there.

The *wajang wong* is less abstract. The modern *wajang wong* came into being only about the middle of the eighteenth century as part of a revival of classical Javanese art after the blows it suffered during the period of Moslem intrusion. It more or less amounts to a "dancing out" of the shadow-play *lakons,* or, more often, of sections of them. Most of the *lakons* are from the Mahabharata cycle (there being over a hundred of these, by far the largest corpus of any of the cycles, which is one reason for its popularity), and different dancers take the different parts—Ardjuna, Bima, Semar—speaking lines as well as dancing. The form of the *wajang* is somewhat simplified, each scene consisting usually of a *djedjer,* in which important persons stand facing one another and chant a few words in a kind of gruffly pompous tone; *mlaku* (literally, "to walk"), in which they dance toward and away from each other, often someone coming in and bringing news; and then *prang,* war, in which some vigorous but formalized fighting-dances take place. Some of the characters, particularly those representing giants, wear masks, and the whole thing is accompanied by the *gamelan* as usual.

Except for professional touring companies and, increasingly, on the radio, one rarely comes in contact with a performance of an entire *wajang wong.* If one does, one witnesses more a dramatic performance, a kind of opera, than a dance performance. At the court centers certain scenes or dances, which differ rather little in basic form from scene to scene and *lakon* to *lakon* in any case, are elaborated into dances complete in themselves called *peṭilan* or "excerpts," such excerpts often including hilarious slapstick pantomime clowns—Semar and his sons—mimicking the hyper-*alus* movements of the principals.

In Modjokuto one sees only such "excerpts," usually even more simplified (there almost always being no clowns), performed by amateurs, the more drama-like *wajang wongs* being left to professional companies. Thus the *wajang wong* in Modjokuto refers to two things: an opera-like rendition of a *wajang lakon* by a professional troupe, which form I shall discuss in the next section, and a set of abstract dances largely complete in themselves built generally around *wajang* themes and characters. In fact, the only difference between these latter and the *srimpi*—which, indeed, is often mixed in with them during a performance, more or less at random—is the addition of male dancers and male-type dances; they are not developed dramatic performances.

People can hear the full performances over the radio; and every few months or so a professional troupe of dancers and actors who travel about performing the *wajang wong* will come to town and perform for a few days. In both these latter cases, the *wajang* has been even more adapted away from its original form and become something like a Western opera—a mixture of semi-realistic drama mixed with music and dance, although there is not as much singing. The formal tripartite division of the *wajang wong* proper, which is essentially still a dance rather than a play, dissolves into a looser and more dramatic form approaching the freedom and realism of the popular dramas such as the *ludrug, ketoprak,* and others, to which we shall come presently. Thus, at its "bottom end"—and some of the professional *wajang wongs* which come to Modjokuto are sorry affairs indeed from an aesthetic point of view—are popular "folk plays" in which the name, the bare outline of the plot, the characters, and the *gamelan* of the *wajang* are present, but little of the *rasa*. At the upper end, however, the dance performers of *wajang wong* fragments which are performed in Modjokuto represent the same *alus* theory of art as underlies the *srimpi,* perhaps best summed up by a Djokjakarta university student, who said:

> There are three main principles of the dance, the essence of the dance:
> *Wirasa* [*rasa: wi-* is just a fancy prefix which no one but the elevated use]— the philosophy, the direction, the "mystic *Weltanschauung*" underlying the dance; the "purity" of it.
> *Wirama*—the music [literally: tempo, rhythm].
> *Wiraga*—the action, the dance itself.
> There must be a harmony between these three principles. All the actions have meaning, but you must know the *wirasa* to understand the meaning.

"You must always look at the dance," a Modjokuto informant warned me, "not at the dancer."

In Modjokuto there were four *alus* dance groups, three of them under the same leader, a public school teacher who was also a *dalang* (and headed an organization of all the *dalangs* in the area which was designed to raise standards of performance, exchange material, and so on, but which seems rarely to have met). He trained a group of young boys and girls from his school to dance the *srimpi* and *wajang wong,* contracting performances for them at occasions such as weddings and circumcisions held by *prijajis* or richer *abangan* villagers, such as village chiefs. He also taught a group of young men and women in their late teens and early twenties who were attached to the railroad union, an organization which had a lively interest in the arts, owning a *gamelan* and having a special department for "sports and culture." This group performed in the union's meeting-hall on various special occasions such as the First of May. Lastly, he found time to teach a group of small girls in an organization called Langen Putera Modjokuto (Modjokuto Recreation Society for Children) to do the *srimpi*. This organization, originally founded by a retired civil servant in Modjokuto, was run for the most part by officials from the government pawnshop and other government offices to teach children to dance, play the *gamelan,* sing *tembangs,* and so on— although by the time I left Modjokuto it was beginning to lose much of its impetus.

Lastly, there was a dance group of Taman Siswa* students who practiced weekly at the home of one of the Taman Siswa school teachers. They performed at Taman Siswa events of one sort or another and sometimes at the district officer's office on national holidays, although they had to compete with the other groups for this honor. Some, but very little, *alus* dancing seems to have been taught in the government *sekolah guru*—in teachers' school— in town. But with the new emphasis on subjects such as science, history, and Indonesian literature in the public schools, the heavy emphasis on Javanese art that marked the "native schools" before the war has disappeared.

Batik: Javanese Textile Dyeing

Batik, the final element in the *alus* art complex, is a method of resist-dye textile design which uses wax as the resistant. A design, largely abstract although sometimes there are bird or floral designs included, is drawn or stenciled in pencil on a piece of white muslin which is then hung over a rack about a yard high. The artist, always a woman, sits on a mat on the ground with the bottom part of the cloth spread out before her. (She can roll up the end on which she is not working on sticks.) Next to her she has a small charcoal stove which keeps a pan of wax molten. With the aid of a small metal instrument (*tjanting*), built on the funnel principle, she covers with wax those parts of the design which she wishes to leave free of color. This completed, the cloth is dipped in a vat of dye, most often either ink-blue or brown, sometimes yellow or reddish-brown. Then the wax is scraped off, and later one can, if that is the intention, apply more wax and dip again in a second color.

Since each of the important *batik* centers such as Djokjakarta, Solo, Pekalongan, and Surabaja has special designs and colors, one can almost always tell where a particular cloth originated or at least what style it is following. In the days before the *Republik* certain designs were reserved to royalty, and the female manufacture of *batik* was an important means of support for many *prijaji* families whose male head spent much of his time in largely unremunerative court duties. Also, like dance, music, and drama, *batik* was a spiritual discipline. Since single pieces may take months to complete, it took great inward concentration to work on such a piece of very detailed and delicate cloth painting; and a favorite symbol of mystic experience is still *mbatik manah*—"drawing a *batik* design on the heart."

Nowadays, however, probably 95 per cent of the *batik* production is *tjap* —a semi-mechanized method in which the design is cast into a lead stamp which is then dipped into wax and stamped by hand on the cloth. Although still slow compared to Western mechanical methods of textile painting, this

---

* Taman Siswa is a Java-wide private school system, with headquarters in Djokjakarta. It has devoted itself to the preservation of Javanese culture and the building up of "national feeling" among the masses.

method speeds up production tremendously—at the cost of a loss of the delicacy of the hand-drawn *baṭik*.

Baṭik production is an important industry in Java, and all married women still wear *baṭik* sarongs every day in Modjokuto. (Unmarried girls wear Western dresses.) On special occasions men still wear *baṭik* sarongs although the practice is disappearing rapidly. (They are always worn in the dances.) In Modjokuto only two women told me they ever did any *baṭik* themselves; and I never actually saw them do any. Most *baṭik* worn by Modjokuto women is *tjap* imported from Djokjakarta, Solo, Surabaja, and other large cities. In Modjokuto, hand *baṭik*-making is a lost art; but in the large cities one still sees a little of it, serving now a carriage trade which can afford to pay three or four hundred *rupiah* for a single sarong.

Classical Javanese Art: Summary

Wajang, lakon, gamelan, djogèd, tembang, and *baṭik,* then, form an integrated art-complex expressing largely *prijaji* values. Although the forms are well-known and still attractive throughout the whole of the society—but perhaps not so attractive to most as the *kasar* art-forms we shall discuss next, it is among the *prijajis* that they find their greatest strength and their most explicit interpretations. Even in the past, the heart of these *alus* forms was always in the courts, where they were cultivated and perfected and, from which center they flowed outward and downward, as political and spiritual power themselves, to the masses, increasingly ineptly performed as they descended. If anything, the tendency for these *alus* art-forms to become a gentry concern is increasing with the greater hold the popular dramas and the more Westernized forms of art are getting on the masses, leaving interested *prijajis* as the main patrons of the traditional high-art. It is at the large *prijaji* conspicuous-display rites-of-passage celebrations that one mainly sees this sort of art now in Modjokuto. The district officer gave his daughter a two-day wedding, with imported *djogèd* dancers the first evening and a shadow play with an imported *dalang* the second; a retired official of the government pawn-shop hired the town hall in which to show a *wajang* when his daughter married; and a *prijaji* politician hired dancers for his son's five-days-after-the-wedding celebration.

Chapter 19　The Role of Popular Art

Popular Drama: *Wajang Wong, Keṭoprak,* and *Ludrug*

BEGINNING in the nineteenth century and increasingly in the twentieth, a new art form has taken hold among the Javanese masses—the popular serio-comic staged drama. There are many versions of this form of art—the *keṭoprak* of central Java ("invented" as late as 1923); the *ludrug* of Surabaja; the farce-plays of West Java; and the most popularized forms of the *wajang wong*. Although each tends to dramatize a different sort of story,* they nevertheless have similarities: the half-hour prologue featuring a comedy act of low clowns and/or some *alus* dancing; a main story, always a serio-comic farce, which, whatever the mythic nature of its content, is realistically acted; the playing (usually) of female parts by male transvestites; and, lastly, a commercial form of production with professional traveling troupes, paid admissions, and a "theater" setting.

These plays are composed of items from old, sometimes extinct, art-forms—masked dancers, peripatetic rural comedians, outmoded rituals, *alus* court art—all poured into a new mold, a theatrical convention certainly heavily influenced by Western forms of drama, most especially the moving pictures. As Modjokuto lies on the edge of the *wajang wong* and *keṭoprak* areas, and within the *ludrug* area, I shall deal only with these and give most attention to the last, which, in Modjokuto, is by far the most popular indigenous art-entertainment.

Wajang wongs, keṭopraks, and *ludrugs* are presented either in the wooden theater at the south edge of town, which is owned by a Chinese, or at the

---

* The term *keṭoprak,* for example, seems to be applied to dramas which have plots with either a Persian or a Hindu-Javanese kingdom background, *ludrug* to those with a contemporary background, and *wajang wong* to those with a Mahabharata-Ramayana background.

pasar malam ("night market") traveling carnivals. These carnivals, which are very much like our own, with various types of gambling games, skill tests, side-shows, and so forth, although perhaps not quite so raucous, come to town (under Chinese sponsorship) once or twice a year. In general, since the level of performance is very low, with the exception of the *ludrug* company, which is quite skilled, they attract mostly peasants and lower class townsmen. They are usually dominated by their clowns, as the following synopsis of a *wajang wong* I saw will demonstrate, for here the *alus satrija* heroes are pushed into the background by the slapstick antics of Semar and his cohorts.

"Semar, Pétruk, Garèng, and Magic"

. . . Curtain up after the *gamelan* (all such plays being accompanied by a *gamelan*) had been going for a while. Five *srimpi* dancers who sang and danced at the same time—the seediest group I've ever seen, one being a dwarf. They were crude, mechanical, ill-trained. Solo style.

After this the story began. The King of Madura announces to a group of people that his daughter has been stolen by Duratmuka, a giant, and that whoever gets her back for him can marry her. Ardjuna takes the challenge, and he and Semar go off to look for her.

They meet the two other daughters of the King of Madura, one of whom is attracted to Ardjuna and tries to persuade him to give up his quest and stay with her. When he refuses, she curses him, saying that if he is hungry later he won't get food; if he is thirsty, he won't get drink.

The next scene is a fight with a giant who is guarding the forest where the missing girl is kept. The giant is very ferocious looking but rather stupid. The clowns approach him first, one at a time, singing to him, and he sings back and dances with them. Pétruk engages him in conversation, talking about how much the giant has traveled and how many languages he knows, with much play on words. While he is talking, Garèng creeps up and steals the giant's dagger and goes off into the wings to sell it. He comes back a little later saying the market women won't give a good price. Pétruk whispers to him to try again, while still engaging the giant in conversation. This occurs several times and finally Garèng, who is quite stupid, comes back and says that all the market women have gone home. At that point the giant discovers his dagger is missing and starts to search the clowns. As they bend over, he lifts up their shirts to look under them. With much clowning, they hand the dagger to one another, until finally they drop it and he finds it. Semar and the giant also act like clowns, Semar being chased by the giant and sticking out his posterior at the giant in ridicule. Later Semar tries the old trick of telling the giant to "look there on the ground" and hits the giant on the head. Finally Ardjuna comes in and kills the giant, but then Ardjuna faints for lack of food, a result of the earlier curse.

Semar has an idea of how to get food. Having no money, he will hold a magic show and get paid in rice. He goes to a girl who lives in the forest and performs his act. He turns a stone into a tortoise, which Pétruk throws in disgust at the girl, who promptly faints, and he turns coconut leaves into an eel, which Pétruk is also frightened of and throws at the girl. They grab the

rice and run off, frightened of their own magic. Semar brings the rice back
to Ardjuna, and they go off again in search of the girl. . . .

They go back to guard the two other sisters because they fear another
kidnapping. The three clowns go to sleep on the mat, while Kakrasana,
another *satrija* who has joined Ardjuna, sits up. In the middle of the night,
the son of Duratmuka comes by. Kakrasana knows that he is a girl-kidnaper
and tries to catch him but fails. He then wakens Ardjuna, and there follows
a long chase with more clownish humor. Finally, the kidnaper escapes.
Ardjuna and Kakrasana decide to go to the enemy castle invisibly, which
they do. Pétruk, also invisible, accompanies them and goes up to Duratmuka and smears his face and the faces of two of his henchmen with white
paint—a great joke; and they all laugh at each other's white-smeared faces.
Then there is a general war, the giants lose, and the girl is taken home. The
end.

In this performance, obviously, the clowns predominate the whole play,
and the story, such as it is, is just a frame within which to display their antics
rather than having much point in itself. Even the *alus* Ardjuna, who in the
original *wajangs* never loses his sense of proportion for an instant, is made
to engage in a clownish chase. As one informant said, in the *wajangs* the
lakon is the important thing but in the farce-plays, the story isn't much of
anything; it is only the jokes that count.

The *ketopraks* are very similar except that they have, in Modjokuto, a
Hindu-Javanese background (although the stories may be dated in the time
of the post-Islamic Mataram kingdom). The one I saw was concerned with
stealing from a rebellious lord the spear which was the magical source of his
power, this deed being accomplished by the sultan's daughter marrying him
incognito and flattering him and persuading him to leave it behind when he
goes out. ("It's just like Delilah cutting off Sampson's hair," said my informant,
who had just seen "Sampson and Delilah" in the movies.) Although the story
was more important than that of the *wajang wong* just related the play was
again clown-dominated.

In the *ludrug,* the form most often produced in Modjokuto, the story
and humor balance one another off more and the aim to entertain (and
make a profit) is fused with an aim to instruct. The *ludrug,* whatever it was
before the war, now approaches the form of modern Western drama. It is
played in *ngoko,* low-Javanese, except where *krama* or Indonesian are
necessary for realism (e.g., in the speech of a high official or at a sophisticated
big-city party), and has plots set in the present or the immediate past, with
characters from "everyday life." The female parts are played by men who
dress and act the part well enough to deceive most observers. (Every informant with whom I attended a *ludrug* pointed out to me about a dozen
times during the evening that the "girls" were really "boys," evidently un-
convinced that I believed them.) These female impersonators (who, from some
casual observation of them off stage, seem often if not typically to be overt
homosexuals) also sing "educational" songs between the acts.

The songs are modern in form, something like the *krontjongs* we shall discuss below, except that they are more distinctly Javanese in style and their subject matter is supposed to be "useful." One actor will sing a song urging the men in the audience to take good care of their families, another will insist on the necessity for education, a third will argue for the advantages of honesty. Sometimes even political content will be inserted—usually of a general type such as "Down with corruption," or "We must build up the country."

The major *ludrug* troupe which came to Modjokuto, evidently the smallest town to which it toured, grew out of a leftist youth group active in the Revolution. It was called Marhaen (roughly, "common people," "proletariat") but apparently had no specific connection with the leftist religio-political party, Permai (Persatuan Rakjat Marhaen Indonesia) even though it shared a similar orientation and was identified in part of the public mind with it. Before the war the Dutch forbade popular plays of this sort, unless licensed, on the ground that the plays were "communist" (a label applied to nationalist agitation generally); and the Japanese forbade them altogether. Even now, some *ludrug* troupes are restrained from being even more explicitly political only by the weather-eye of the government, the rumor being that companies have had their licenses suspended for referring too directly, albeit in song, to the disadvantages of the Marshall Plan.

Although its prices were high (Rp 4.00 for a first-class seat; Rp 1.00 for a fourth-class), the Marhaen *ludrug* was very popular in Modjokuto. I never attended one of its performances when the house was not packed or nearly so, and the company was a prime topic of conversation from about a week before it came until a week after it left, the general opinion being that it was excellent. (It came three times for a total of about thirty days during the fifteen months I was in Modjokuto.)

The *ludrug* always began with a solo Madurese dance, the dancer singing the audience a welcome in high-Javanese. Next followed a long prologue with no apparent connection to the plot except that the clowns who were introduced in it later played leading roles, as the same characters, in the play proper. The following describes a typical prologue:

> A clown whose name turned out to be Rukun (literally: "cooperation," "mutual help") enters and gives a short monologue (punctuated by what for the audience is a series of hilarious hiccups) on people who drink and gamble and the evils that flow therefrom. Later he is joined by a second clown, Bawa (literally: "beginner," "undertaker," in the sense of "entrepreneur," Bawa being the most important character in all the plays and acted by the director-leader of the troupe), who turns out to be the central character not as hero or protagonist but, in the manner of all such clowns, as a kind of catalyst for the rest, the thread which ties the whole together. After the two clowns have joked and chattered a while, Rukun starts talking about *urip*, which means "life" but is also the name of the third clown, who has now entered. Rukun is talking about how hard his life is, repeatedly using the word *urip*. Rukun does not see the third clown but the third clown thinks Rukun is talking about him and becomes angry at some of the things Rukun says about him. During all of this exchange Bawa tries to tell Rukun that

Urip is there, making various signals and gestures, making faces, and so on.

The three clowns then go on to talk about a fourth man who is conceited and whom they want to swindle. They have a discussion of *"persatuan."* (Literally, *persatuan* means "unity," but it is used to designate an organization in the way we use "brotherhood." Since it is a very common word in the modern nationalist political vocabulary, and is an Indonesian, not a Javanese, word, this dialogue was a political satire in part.) They talk about the pitfalls of organization and how everyone tries to get the best things for himself under the pretext of mutual help. The next scene shows a fourth man in his home. There comes a knock on the door. He goes, but Bawa comes in another door, and sits down, and when the fourth man returns Bawa pretends that he owns the house and says he is going to sell it. After some twenty minutes of talk in this vein, Bawa goes off and Rukun comes on. Rukun says that he wants to borrow some money and tells a long story of his hard luck. When the fourth man refuses to give him money, Rukun grabs himself around the neck and ostensibly chokes himself to death. Bawa now re-enters to extort money from the now terrified fourth man as the price of his silence. (Bawa accepts the money with a very humorous gesture of unwillingness, raising his left arm and receiving the money with his right under it while backing away—as though the money were tainted—precisely as the host at a *slametan* often receives, although less exaggeratedly, a guest's contribution.) Bawa then carries Rukun away—and Rukun stands up to put his arm around Bawa's shoulder, somewhat mystifying the fourth man. When they have gone, Urip enters, shakes hands with the fourth man, and promptly falls across the table as though dead. Bawa re-enters and repeats the business of accepting money as the price of silence, using similar pantomime, and carries Urip away, grabbing him gingerly by the folds of his coat. Urip really walks under his own power. There follows a scene in which the three argue about the division of money while the fourth man comes upon them unseen. Rukun and Urip finally see him and steal away, leaving Bawa to face him and give him back the money.

It should be apparent from this description that the clowns are not without skill. In the stories proper they almost always play servants, a continuation of the Semar tradition, and carry on the same kind of joking and horseplay. The stories are usually of the "soap-opera" type. Everyone concerned has many troubles of a common, recognizable sort, but all works out happily in the end—although sometimes with a peculiarly Javanese twist. In one story a boy is forced to choose between the servant he loves (and has married secretly) and the girl his Assistant District Officer father has chosen to be his bride, she being the daughter of a pensioned District Officer. After much soul-searching (while Bawa keeps packing and unpacking his master's suitcase), the boy decides to accept his father's decision and casts off his present wife, who, unbeknownst to him, is three months pregnant. Twenty years later, the boy, now a middle-aged man, is marrying off a daughter by his *prijaji* wife against the girl's will. (She wants to continue her schooling.) The daughter suddenly falls over, dead, the examining doctor says, of a broken heart. The grief-stricken father wanders around, meeting, of all people, the now grown daughter by his first servant-wife.

The girl, who looks exactly like his second daughter who has just died, has been raised by Rukun and Bawa in such sheltered circumstances that she is unaware that the great majority of people have one parent of each sex. The father, having just lost his daughter, has a happy reunion with her, and all is forgiven on all sides. So all comes out right in the end—at least for those who survive.

In another story, a girl's foster father (the clowns being his servants) dies, and his brother, actually a thief, is appointed executor and tries to deprive the girl of her inheritance. He gives her a pill which will put her to sleep for ten days and which, if she is not treated by a doctor in that time, will kill her. Bawa and Urip, who have been sent on a vacation to get them out of the way, return unexpectedly, discover the plot in the nick of time and turn the evil brother over to the police. (They bury the girl first, thinking she is dead, but dig her up again, and she recovers.)

In a third story, a boy leaves home because his father wishes him to marry a girl he doesn't love. In another house, the daughter of a widowed mother leaves her house in tears because her mother wants her to marry a man she doesn't love. After she leaves, the exiled boy comes to the house of the widowed mother and asks to stay there. The widow agrees on the condition that he marry her. Although she is no longer young and pretty, he does so because, the housing shortage being what it is, he has no other place to go. Meanwhile, at the boy's home, his father is lonely without him, and, when the exiled girl appears there the father marries her. Then the two newly formed families meet, and there is much confusion about correct kin terminology, for the wife of the son is the mother of the father's wife. The young man wants to exchange wives, but the father refuses, advising his son to be satisfied with an old wife, for as long as there is mutual understanding between husband and wife they will have a good life.

In yet another plot, things are even less *alus*. A middle-aged man sees a young girl in a restaurant and is attracted by her. He requests her in marriage from her parents, but her parents, being modern, leave the decision to her, and, seeing how old he is, she refuses him. He returns to his own city, where he is a merchant, and resumes his business, vowing to himself to get the girl as his wife somehow. Meanwhile his adopted son falls in love with the girl, marries her, and brings her home. The merchant falsely accuses his adopted son of embezzlement, and the boy is put in prison. The father then rapes the girl and, to conceal the crime, kills her. When the son gets out of prison, the father tells him the girl has left and returned home. Shortly thereafter, the ghost of the girl begins appearing, shaking the father's confidence. Then the parents of the girl come to pay a visit to see her, and, with the aid of the ghost and a servant who witnessed the murder, the story comes out. This is perhaps the most popular story of all, and is said to be based on a real case which occurred in Surabaja before the war.

The nuclear conflict in the *ludrug* seems to be the conflict of generations, the conflict between the attachment to tradition of the older generation, particularly concerning arranged marriages, and the wishes of the younger. In the first play, the father forces the son to divorce the girl he has already married in order to accept the father's choice, and then the son, twenty years later, destroys his daughter in a similar manner; in the third, both a mother and a father exile their children—or the children exile themselves rather than give in—because the latter will not marry the spouses they are supposed to; in the last, a father and an adopted son compete for the same girl. In this conflict it is the younger generation which is always right; the rights of the heart and of self-determination are being asserted against the rights of tradition and of parental authority. If the older generation is not raping the younger, it is cheating it out of its inheritance, forcing it to marry rather than continue school, breaking up its love affairs, or marrying the young women and leaving the old ones for the young men. All in all, the plays lend force to the common complaint of Modjokuto's chastened older generation. "We used to have a proverb, 'The buffalo suckles the buffalo-calf,' but now we have to say, 'The buffalo's calf suckles the buffalo.'"

There are other themes, of course, notably that of the "adopted child-problem," but all in all it is clear that, with its didactic character, its special type of comedy, and its concern with social and moral problems characteristic of a changing society, the *ludrug* is very much the child of the present. But it is also a child of the past, for if it were not it would hardly draw such crowds in a town like Modjokuto, where such problems as it dramatizes are as yet real only to the most urbanized fraction of the audience. The clowns, the female impersonators (who are never humorous objects as such, tranvestitism evidently being funny to the Javanese only in the sense of "peculiar," not in the sense of "amusing"), the dancers, and the *gamelan* all tie the play to familiar cultural forms, so that a peasant who is really only half-clear as to what the plot is all about can laugh at the clowns, wonder at the transvestites, and enjoy the dancers.

The attitude towards the homosexual aspects of the *ludrug* is, in fact, quite ambivalent. Most people say that the *ludrugs* break up many homes because the homosexuals attract the men away from their wives; and the general opinion is that there is much homosexual activity among the various members of the troupe. It is said—whether truthfully or not, I do not know—that *ludrugs* are banned in some areas because of their deleterious moral influence. *Santris* stay away from the *ludrug* almost entirely, and when I took a *santri* boy with me to see one he was distinctly uncomfortable. *Prijaji* parents regard the *ludrug* as too *kasar*. Although the parents often attend themselves, they frequently prohibit their children from attending, saying that it is bad for them to see such things at an impressionable age.* A mixture of leftist politics (somewhat dampened at the moment), simple melodrama, low comedy, and forbidden forms of sexuality, the *ludrug*'s hold on its predominantly *abangan* audience would seem nearly unbreakable.

---

* "It is *kasar*, I admit," said one woman in her defense when I taxed her with her attendance at a *ludrug*, "but it is very educational and good for building up the country." She suggested that the Ministry of Information might profitably employ the *ludrug* to get their less objectionable political message across to the uneducated masses, who are bored with and confused by the usual propaganda meeting.

Street Dancers: *Klèḍèk, Djaranan,* and *Djanggrung*

THE next element of the *kasar* art complex is the *klèḍèk,* sometimes called also *tanḍak:* female street-dancers and singers performing both as hired entertainers and, more commonly, from door to door along the streets of the town, in the market, or even in the villages. In this last capacity they are often hardly more than beggars and are viewed as such. They stand in front of a house or a store—their faces usually painted with thick white make-up, an outgrowth of the old masked dancers pattern—and wail out a song for a few moments until someone gives them ten cents to move on. Some of them are somewhat more skilled and, accompanied by one or two men playing *gamelan* instruments, dance poor imitations of the *srimpi* and the *beḍaja* with elements from folk sources mixed in. They also sing a kind of *tembang*-monologue of somewhat off-color sort and engage in some double-entendre repartee with their accompanists. The small procession, sometimes as many as two or three girls and a half-dozen accompanists (occasionally with a male dancer), but more often just a single girl and a single accompanist, moves through the streets, stopping at each house to sing. Sometimes people give them ten cents or a quarter to move on; often, however, they are ignored and move on of their own accord. Sometimes, however, people will "hire" them, paying anywhere from Rp 1.00 to Rp 2.50, in which case they put on their whole act for about a half-hour, great crowds gathering to watch. As the girls are as often as not professional prostitutes, this art is at the bottom of the *kasar-alus* ladder and is consequently almost wholly confined to *abangan* circles.

Somewhat similar to the *klèḍèk* is the *djaranan,* also a street-show of dancers. In the *klèḍèk* the dancers ride papier-mâchè horses (*djaran* means "horse") and become possessed so as to act as though they were themselves horses, prancing, neighing, eating rice husks (as well as hot peppers, broken glass, etc.), being whipped, and so on. They too are itinerant troupes wandering around from town to town playing in the streets and markets. The following is a description from my notes:

In the afternoon a troupe of wandering performers of the horse-dance came by, and I hired them to perform. There were five people in the troupe. One man carried on his shoulders a set of instruments, drums, *gambang* (*gamelan* xylophone), *angklung* (a musical instrument made of bamboo tubes which is played by shaking it), and another man carried a big drum. As they went along the street they beat the drums to attract attention. The other three, one in a clown costume of burlap bags and a mask and the other two astride hobby horses painted white and black, pranced along in front of the people, weaving back and forth among them while wearing odd smirks on their faces, collecting dimes here and there as they passed by. To hire them cost Rp 2.50. . . . The horse-dance began with a beating of the drums and a playing of very simple, not very exciting music. Two of the players, who were astride horses, began to prance slowly around like horses, weaving in and out past each other. Meanwhile the third man was getting ready a bowl of water and rice husks—which is considered proper horse-food—which we supplied. After a while the horses began to get more frisky and began a real prancing dance. Then one stopped and took a whip and began directing the first one with the whip, not hitting him at first, but just laying it on him from time to time. The first one was now in a trance and beginning to imitate a horse in great detail. While in this state he slopped up water like a horse and ate, with apparent pleasure, the dry rice husks, keeping up this action for some time—smelling the food, prancing away from it, eating it, savoring it, and so on. At the end of this time he did another prancing dance and ended with the hobby horse lifted above his head. This was the climax. He was brought out of the trance, the helper going behind him and holding him while whipping his hands loose from the hobby horse, whipping his two feet together so that he would stand straight, the man in the trance rather leaning against the man in back of him. Then the hobby horse was taken and laid lengthwise along the front of the man, symbolically covering him, then the helper hitting the tranced one a sharp crack with the whip. When the tranced one was finally touched with a black rubber ball on the chest, he came out of the trance. He seemed bewildered. Dazed, he sat down and slowly came around to himself while the helper hovered around him to keep him from wandering off or running amok.

The trance is evidently real enough, although evidently its intensity varies, for some dancers are whipped harder than others, eat glass (one I saw ate a light-bulb), and red-hot peppers, and go on longer and more vigorously than others, some of whom barely trance at all and are rather colorless. Before the performance the dancers usually burn incense to call the spirits who are supposed to enter the dancer, and the owner of the house often prepares a *sadjén* offering to protect himself against the spirits thus called. People, although sometimes a little apprehensive of these tranced dancers, are not afraid of them. They crowd around, adults and children, to watch them; and I have never heard any story of their going amok or hurting anyone while in a trance.

The *djaranan* is not the only trance dance of this kind, merely the most common. A dance called *gendruwon* (from *gendruwo*, "spirit") is often seen, and the troupe described above also danced a *gendruwon* for us, for another Rp 2.50. It went as follows:

The single dancer was dressed in a burlap suit and wore a wooden goblin mask. The drums began to beat, and he began to dance, moving his hand and his head primarily, hands in some of the *srimpi* or *wajang wong* motions, head in the "horizontal nod" motion. He also went into a trance. I don't know how the helpers knew when it had happened, but when it had, they removed the mask and gave him a plate of rice with some red peppers and a piece of soy-bean cake. The rest of the dance was a comedy built around his eating the food. He received it, examined it, ate it. He made a play on the hotness of the pepper, on taking too much in his mouth at one time—belching, breaking wind, and so on. (He just stuffed the rice in his mouth until he couldn't shut it and had to keep his hand stuffing it back in as he chewed and kept gagging.) The crowd was convulsed by this. After eating, he ran water on his plate, drank off the water, and took a mouthful of water and spit it out almost on the spectators in a big stream. There also was a long routine in which the helper offered him the food and then took it away from him, teasing him, and the dancer was very angry. The end of the trance came when, finished with eating, he danced a little, and the helper brought back the mask. As the helper came near him, from behind, the dancer reached back his hand and grabbed suddenly at the helper, at what I think was the helper's penis, just gripping it and not letting go. They made a comic scene of this. The actual release from the trance came when the mask was put on his head again, and the whip was snapped, and the little black ball was rubbed on the man's chest.

Perhaps it is doubtful that all the trances are genuine. I have seen the same dancer have two or three trances within the space of an hour. But the spectators believe they are, and the performers say they are. There are various other roving dances of this sort. (*Klèdèks* and *djaranans* may, of course, both be combined in the same troupe.) Another dance acts out an old legend of the Hindu-Javanese period in which a lion eats 144 soldiers and then is killed by the king's son. The lion dances. Girls riding horses attack him and one by one are eaten by him. (Girls sometimes are the trance subjects in the *djaranan* as well, although men are more common. In this play there are four girls to represent the 144 soldiers.) Finally a masked dancer representing the king's son dances to the tune of a flute and dispatches the lion. There is usually no trance involved in this.

In addition, one sometimes sees the *djanggrung* dances. These are roughly the same as the *klèdèk* except that the "dancing girl" involved is a transvestite man. Both female *klèdèk* and homosexual male *klèdèks* are accused of "ruining the morals" of the villagers and of being hated by village women for making off with their men. (The *djaranan* and *gendruwon,* as can be seen from the above descriptions, also show explicitly homosexual elements along with their sado-masochistic and oral themes.)

The wandering dance troupes—sometimes called *amèn* as a group—are almost wholly an *abangan* concern. *Prijajis* regard them as coarse and obscene; and the troupes do not even bother to go to *santri* villages where they might be set upon by the pious if they did. But, connected with begging, prostitution, and homosexuality as they are, they are nevertheless (or consequently) still very popular with the mass of the peasants and lower townsmen. Almost every day one sees one sort or another of these *amèn* performing in the market in the midst of a great crowd; and one would come by our house at the edge of town nearly every week. (They did not appear at all regularly; sometimes five or six would come within a few days, and then weeks would pass without one.)

All of these groups are said to originate outside of Modjokuto, mostly in Tulungagung and Ponorogo, where this form of art is said to be at its strongest. (The latter town is noted all over Java for the violence of its inhabitants, for the radicalism of its politics, and for the great amount of male homosexuality which is said to occur there.) Whether this is so or simply indicates an unwillingness on the part of Modjokuto people to admit that they would sink to such a level is difficult to say. Certainly some of the *klèḍèks,* at least, were Modjokuto girls, but I never heard of a locally based *djaranan, gendruwon,* or *djanggrung.*

The *Tajuban:* A Javanese Party

THERE is also another form of "art" in which the *klèḍèk* plays a major role and which still has some popularity in Modjokuto. This is the *tajuban,* a combination drinking and dancing party given usually on the occasion of rites-of-passage celebrations and so forth. A description of the pattern by a Modjokuto informant follows:

There is usually one *klèḍèk* (almost always a prostitute), but at fancy *tajubans* there could be two or three. The *klèḍèk* dances for a while at the beginning. When the *tajuban* itself is about to begin, the host appoints a man *pramugari* ("leader"). Now it is the *pramugari's* job to point out to the *klèḍèk* whom she is to choose to dance with her. This man must be clever in gauging the status of people because the order in which people participate is very important and must be right. If the occasion is a wedding, the groom, if a circumcision, the host, must be first. (The women are out behind and don't like the *tajubans* at all. Organizations like Perwari, the main *prijaji* women's club, hate the *tajuban* and are dead set against it.) After this the order is strictly according to status. If the subdistrict officer is there, he is obviously first, then the village chief, and so on; and the *pramugari* has to be careful not to offend anyone. The *pramugari* is in front and starts off dancing, *djogéd* style, over toward the guests, the *klèḍèk* following him with a tray in her hands which has a dance sash on it. The *pramugari* points out each time the guest whose turn it is and then goes off and sits down. The *klèḍèk* kneels and holds the tray up to the chosen one, who takes the sash and drapes it around his neck. He then places on the tray some money, which the *pramugari* then takes from her and puts in the bowl on the table. How much money the guest puts on the tray is strictly dependent upon his rank and what the host put on his tray when he gave such an affair. If the host gave 10 rupiahs, and both are about the same rank, the guest gives 10; if higher a little more, and so on. The *klèḍèk* starts dancing backwards toward the other end of the space, and the guest dances about two feet in front of her (facing her), following her, dancing a male-type *djogéd.* Now two people come forth to "honor" the man who is dancing. Usually they are the same rank or slightly lower than the man dancing. For instance, a village chief or an office clerk will come forth if the sub-district officer is dancing; but sometimes, if, say the sub-district officer is very friendly with the village chief he may come forward for the village chief. One of these men takes two glasses, the other one glass and the gin jug, and they start dancing in the other direction, from the table toward the guests.

Two glasses are for the helpers, the other for the main guest dancer. They dance this way until they pass each other and the positions are reversed (i.e., the helpers are down by the guests, the *klèḍèk* and dancer up by the table). Then they reverse and meet in the middle as the *gamelan* music stops.

At this point the man with the jug pours drinks in all the glasses and the three men drink. Then the two men take the main guest dancer by the elbows and push him up to the *klèḍèk* and make him kiss her. (This evidently is not always necessary, for I did not see it in any of the *tajubans* I witnessed.) The helpers then retire, but the guest dancer may continue dancing, depending on the number of people who are there. If two other helpers come forth immediately he may go on; if not, the *pramugari* will choose another man. Usually in the beginning a man will only have to go through the routine once or twice, but toward morning, when people have started dropping out or becoming drunk and going home, and there are fewer people, one man may go on six or seven times. As the night wears on, all the formal order tends to be forgotten, and everybody is just dancing around, kissing the *klèḍèk,* and drinking gin (and presumably tossing money in the dish) with gay abandon. . . .

In view of the remarkable sobriety of the Javanese in general, the *tajuban* seems anything but a typical occurrence.* Although at one time it was apparently fairly popular among the *prijajis,* it has become more and more the property of highly urbanized *abangans*—chauffeurs, small craftsmen, and others who see in the *tajuban* an attractive combination of Eastern and Western vices—and of certain of the richer village *abangan* peasants for whom it evidently represents the delights of urban wickedness. In Modjokuto there were several groups of generally rowdy loafers who formed a kind of circle of *tajuban*-givers, each inviting the others in turn, sometimes getting to the point where the dancing was skipped altogether and people just sat around and drank while the *klèḍèk* sang songs to them to *gamelan* accompaniment, a form of "art" known as *klenèngan.*

But *prijajis* evidently still give *tajubans* from time to time. The district officer gave one late in the evening on the occasion of his daughter's marriage—collecting Rp 1500.00 from it in the process; and a nearby village gave one for its *bersih désa* ceremony to which only town *prijajis* were invited, giving a *wajang* separately for the local folk.

In general, the *tajuban,* too expensive for the *abangans* and too *kasar* for many *prijajis,* is dying out.

Her husband (one of the more active *tajuban* givers and attenders) said that *tajubans* are rather few and far between now. There were more before the war but they have degenerated into a fairly crass money-making proposition since the war, and now people don't like them very much. Few are given; few of those which are given draw much of a crowd. He said that one reason people don't like to go is that since the money has to be given in view of all the guests some people always try to give a lot so that other people will be embarrassed. Before the war everyone at a *tajuban* gave the same amount, say fifty cents or one rupiah, and no one was embarrassed. People at any rate much prefer *wajangs* and the like, for there they can give money by the secret handshake method and no one knows what they give. . . .

* Except at a *tajuban* I have never seen a Javanese drunk. In any case, only a very small percentage of the population drinks anything stronger than fruit wine, partly because they cannot afford it, partly because of their intense dislike of the "confused" or "disoriented" feeling it gives them.

Folktales

JAVANESE folktales, stories which are not dramatized in the *wajang* but are told orally, are usually called *dongèng,* in Modjokuto. They include little moral stories and legends centering around certain sacred spots; tales about the Hindu-Javanese period which account for the existence of ruins; similar stories attributing magic power to certain objects—daggers, spears, gongs, and so forth—called *pusaka* ("heirloom") stories; and animal stories.

An example of the *pusaka* stories, of which there are literally thousands, follows:

> One of the early district officers of Modjokuto, Pringgokusumo, was very powerful. He had a spear which every night became a snake. The spear's name was "Kijaji Upas." (*Upas* means "messenger," "office boy.") It wove around the banyan trees; and all the village guards were afraid of it, for if they slept it bit them. Later this man went with his spear to Tulungagung. When he got there, he caused a big flood all over the city in order to clean it up. His snake-spear also went around among the banyans there. Now, every year in the Javanese month of Sura there are *slametans* for the spear (which is still in Tulungagung) to which people come from far and wide. Everyone who cooks for the *slametan* must be clean—with hair washed, no menses, etc. Many *ḍalangs* come, and they *wajang.* And still people who look at the spear disagree as to how big it is. One will say it is a mile long, one an inch. If one sleeps near it, it will lift one up by the feet invisibly.

Many *pusaka* stories are long and elaborate and have given rise to *pusakas* which people come for hundreds of miles to "honor"—such as the gong at Ludojo (a nearby town) which is really a transformed tiger (the boom of the gong being his roar) from the time in the past when those Ludojo people who had no crevices in their upper lips could turn at will into tigers and devour their less fortunate neighbors.

As for the animal stories, there are thousands of these too, the most famous and best loved ones still being those about Kantjil, the sly, tricky, highly intelligent, if somewhat amoral, mouse-deer who makes up for what he lacks in strength by the exercise of his wits.

> Tiger was after Kantjil, about to pounce on him. Kantjil ran in fear to a place under some bamboos. The wind blew in the bamboos and they squeaked, rubbing together, and Kantjil said to Tiger: "Hear that? It is a magic flute. If a person can blow this flute, he will be healthy forever." So Tiger wanted to blow the flute, and Kantjil told him he'd show him how to do it. He said Tiger should put his tongue between the two bamboo trees, which Tiger did, and when the wind blew his tongue got caught and Kantjil got away free.
>
> Another time, Tiger and Kantjil met under a tree where there was a bees' nest. Tiger was angry at Kantjil because he had been fooled by him. Kantjil told him that the thing hanging up there was a gong, and that if he hit it all the animals in the forest would be frightened of him; and only Kantjil could hit it. So Tiger insisted that Kantjil let him hit it. Kantjil said:

"Only if I run away first, and then when you hear me whistle three times you may hit the gong." Which he did, and then Tiger hit it and was attacked by bees.

Such stories are probably told to children in almost every Modjokuto home. Kantjil is usually taken quite explicitly to symbolize "the little man"; and peasants talking about the gentry often quote the proverb: "When the elephants fight, the *kantjil* gets crushed between them." Many animal stories make explicit value judgments, such as this one about the dangers of employing a go-between:

A dog and a cat are fighting over some meat. They meet a monkey and ask him to divide it equally between them. He agrees, but says that he must have payment. He divides the meat in two parts and puts it on the scales, but one part is heavier than the other. So he eats a little, and then the other side is heavier and he eats some off of that side. And so it goes until he has eaten it all and the dog and cat don't get anything.

The *kasar* art complex of *ludrug, klèdèk, djaranan,* and *dongèng* is admittedly not nearly so interwoven or so integrated as the *alus* art complex; but all the elements share an expression of a more down-to-earth ethos, one appropriate to a people whose world-view regards high refinement as an excellent ideal but not so attractive a practice.

Contemporary Art

WHAT I have called the "national art" complex is almost entirely confined to the town and is in any case not always regarded as art by Modjokuto people but merely as entertainment.

Then he got on to talk about the *wajang,* saying that the *wajang* was art (*kesenian*) but a movie was just entertainment (*kesenengan*), and that the reason one could tell is that it is possible to see the same *wajang* over and over again. This is because the *wajang* has content, has meaning in it whereas the movie does not. (He admitted that nowadays even many *dalangs* don't know what the meaning is and so can just play one *lakon* or something and do it automatically; but the good ones know the meaning of the *wajang.*) Therefore one can keep going back to a *wajang* over and over again and getting more and more out of it, whereas one gets all there is out of a movie by seeing it once.

Despite the reservations of the conservatives, the forms of national art— not only the movies, but the orchestras, popular songs, novels, and so forth— continue to grow in popularity. I call them national art for several reasons. They are not confined to Java; nor is there much of anything characteristically Javanese about them as compared to other areas of Indonesia such as Sumatra or the Celebes. Insofar as they are literary, they are in the national language, Indonesian Malay, rather than in the "regional" language, Javanese. They are in part presented over the mass media, which of course extend all over the islands—the radio, movies, and nationally circulated magazines. They are practiced and appreciated by the same groups, mostly the urban youth, who have always been in the forefront of nationalism. They are the forms of art common in the large port cities—Surabaja, Djakarta—where indigenous forms of art have been weakened in the general deracination of culture; and they are especially popular among the new political elite which is in power in those cities.

Orchestras and Popular Singers

ON the musical side, the national-art complex is represented by the *orkès,* the name derived from *orkest,* the Dutch word for "orchestra," and the *lagus,* or popular songs. The *orkès* consists of stringed instruments tuned to the Western diatonic rather than the *gamelan* pentatonic scale: banjos, guitars, violins, bass fiddles, mandolins, ukeleles. On one occasion at least, in Modjokuto, a trumpet was added. There were three such semi-professional orchestras in Modjokuto, one of which more or less disbanded after a while. They played at such ceremonies as weddings and circumcisions for fees ranging from Rp 50.00 to about Rp 125.00, depending upon the elaborateness of the occasion and upon whether outside talent was imported to improve the band—such as the above-mentioned trumpeter or an outside singer. Most *orkès* groups had about five or six members and a female vocalist. (Some of the musicians, usually all of them, doubled as male vocalists, there almost never being any purely instrumental numbers.) The members were not full-time musicians but tailors, chauffeurs, petty clerks, policemen, and the like; but they were not without professional aspirations.

Perhaps because of the similarity in some respects between the Arab-influenced *gambusan* orchestra discussed in the *santri* section and the *lagu* orchestras, among the most active of the *orkès* people were two or three local Arabs, younger men who formed the nucleus of the more vigorous groups. Several of the players were *santris,* and there was a tendency for such *orkès* to appear at the rites-of-passage celebrations of richer town *santris*—such as well-off traders—who wanted to engage in a moderate degree of conspicuous consumption but who would not consider giving a *wajang;* but I have seen them many times at *abangan* affairs also. They seem to be characteristic of those among the thoroughly urbanized who have some sort of a relatively steady and more-than-subsistence income.

Although the players take themselves seriously and attempt to improve their art by means of frequent practice, the level of skill is quite low and is generally recognized as being so. It was a commonly voiced complaint among the younger men in town that better orchestras did not seem to grow up in such an unimportant place as Modjokuto and that the ones which did exist did not seem ever to get any better. As the national radio network broadcast little else except *lagu* music most of every day (but a *wajang wong* on Sundays, which was very popular), and many people kept their radios going continually, there was a constant professional standard of comparison against which to measure the relatively inept efforts of the local groups.

The *lagus* (or, more properly, *lagu-lagu populèr*—"popular songs") played and sung by the ensembles are of several types. Some are in a Western (usually Latin-American) form, such as the rumba or samba, and are composed either by Western songwriters and fitted with Indonesian lyrics (which may or may not translate the original words) or composed by an Indonesian, Chinese, or Malayan composer. Sometimes Hawaiian or Chinese tunes are used as models; and sometimes Southeast Asian folk tunes—the *lagu Malaju* ("Malayan songs") of Malaya and the Western archipelago, and the *krontjongs* of East Indonesia—are so used. The *krontjongs*, which were originally based on Southern European folk music brought to Indonesia by the Portuguese in the sixteenth century—particularly to East Indonesia: Flores, Timor and the Moluccas, where the Iberian influence was at its greatest, are probably the most popular of all; and, in fact, many Modjokuto people refer to all popular songs in whatever style as "*krontjongs.*" The lyrics of most of these songs tend to be rather heavily sentimental:

The Handkerchief from South Bandung

A white handkerchief of silk, decorated with colored flowers—
A symbol of a wonderful magic love,
From the south of great Bandung [a city in West Java],
Accompanied by sweet words.
Thank you, little sister [*dik*, the term of address for a wife, and in
    general a term of endearment],
Don't forget
My tears are shining.
Your handkerchief I keep.
I kiss the end of your finger.
With a prayer I say,
Goodbye,
Fight on,
Don't forget South Bandung.

A somewhat less sentimental song is based on the traditional belief (which I heard actually invoked in Modjokuto several times) that before a girl is going to be married she will dream about being bitten by a snake. Here is a song, considered to be slightly humorous, which was tremendously popular during the first part of my stay in Indonesia, being played on the radio mercilessly from morn till night:

Night Dream

(Girl:) Last night, *bung* ["brother," "comrade"; here a term of endearment],
    I dreamed
    I met a snake, *bung*,
    Very large.

The snake bit, *bung,*
My toe.
After it bit, *bung,*
The snake went away.

My cuts, *bung,*
Bled.
I screamed, "*Aduh!*" [an exclamation of pain, disappointment,
grief, etc.]
Then woke up.

What is it, *bung,*
The meaning
Of the dream last night, *bung,*
So creepy?

(Boy:) Don't fear, *dik,*
Don't be sad.
All is fate, *dik,*
The will of Allah.

Stories in the night, *dik,*
Dispel the clouds.
The stars come clear, *dik,*
Finally certain.

A flower in the garden, *dik,*
When it has blossomed,
Before very long, *aduh,*
Is picked by someone.

That's it, *dik,*
The meaning of it.
Your dream last night, *dik,*
Was a dream of happiness.

In addition to sentimental ballads there are humorous, novelty, and political *lagus.* (One of the most popular of the *lagus* in Modjokuto was one beginning, "Let us go/ Let us go/ To the General Election . . ." Another agitated for the turning over of West New Guinea by the Dutch to Indonesia, a hot political issue in Indonesia.) All in all, tirelessly disseminated as it is by the radio and attractive as it is to the urban youth, the *lagu* is probably at present Indonesia's most pervasive art-form, no more easily escaped than "hit tunes" in America.

Contemporary Literature, Drama, and Motion Pictures

ON the literary side, national art consists of modern novels (*roman*), poems (*sjair*), short-stories (*kissah*), and plays (*sandiwara*) written in Indonesian perhaps most commonly by non-Javanese, Sumatra producing a disproportionate number of Indonesia's modern writers. The novels and stories are bought either as books or in magazines in the regency capital, after which they are passed around from friend to friend. Several national magazines have Modjokuto subscribers and are eagerly read by the younger urban set. There is a bookstore in Modjokuto but it sells mainly textbooks and, as it is *santri*-run, Islamic books.

There can be no attempt here to describe this literature except to say that much of it concerns the Revolution—heroic stories of the battles, ill-fated wartime romances, and so on; that it is extremely socially conscious, being more reminiscent of our proletarian novels of the thirties than our present psychological novels; and that it is written, for the most part, in an extremely elevated romantic style. Most commonly, this literature takes for its setting the big-city Djakarta-Surabaja-Medan asphalt jungle in which almost all of the writers live and has for its heroes and heroines young men and women—the group the Indonesians call *pemuda* ("youth")—trying to make their way in such an environment, or rather, trying to remake that environment in terms of an ideal largely drawn from Western political theory.

Since Indonesian Malay, the official national language, is taught in all the schools and almost all town children and many village children go to school for at least three years, and since the Indonesian government claims to have reduced the illiteracy rate 40 per cent since the transfer of sovereignty, this literature is almost certainly going to become steadily more important as Indonesia proceeds through her history as an independent state.

The *sandiwara,* or modern play form, grew out of the *stambul* or "Malay opera," which was a play something on the order of our earlier musical comedies or Victor Herbert-type operettas in which a kind of artificial and sentimental declamatory plot was interspersed with *krontjong* singing and popular dancing, the plots being taken from popular folk stories and such sources as the "Thousand and One Nights." With the appearance of Southeast Asian movies—Indonesian, Malayan, and Philippine, the *stambul* form shifted into that medium, leaving the *sandiwara* to develop toward greater realism, until today it displays the same general style and outlook as do the novels, short-stories, and poems—a socially conscious romantic realism.

The *sandiwara* appeals mostly to Westernized intellectuals, and, facing double competition from the *ludrug* on the one hand and movies, Western and Eastern, on the other, it almost never appears in Modjokuto. Only one *sandiwara* was produced in Modjokuto during the period of my stay. A young Modjokuto author wrote a play based upon his sister's divorce from her titled husband, also a Modjokuto man, and got the local chapter of a veterans' organization to produce it in the hope (vain, as it turned out) of getting some money for their organization, the sister herself playing the role of the wronged woman.

Indonesian moving pictures are made not only in Indonesia but also in the Philippine Islands and in Malaya. For the most part they are on the *stambul* pattern, being very stiff light operas usually built around a legendary or folk-story theme. Among the more popular of such films during my stay were one based on the folk story *Bawang Merah, Buwang Putih* about the stepmother problem and another, made in the Philippine Islands, built on the Siegfried story, both of them done in the *stambul* form. But there have been a few realistic pictures about the Revolutionary period in Djokjakarta (which was the Republican capital during the war). One movie, written by a well-known Indonesian novelist, included the first kiss ever shown in an Indonesian film and aroused such a violent reaction from various pressure groups that the kiss was eventually censored.

The attitude involved is similar to that which I have noted in connection with the dance. As one Javanese expressed it: "I don't mind seeing kissing and loving and the rest in an American movie, but in an Indonesian movie it makes me all upset." (Such actions are in fact more or less symbolic of American movies—and, in part, of America—in the Modjokuto public mind. The street in town which is lined with houses of prostitution is sometimes nicknamed "Hollywood Street.") Evidently the psychic distance of an Indonesian movie is much less for a Javanese than that of an American film, and so the fantasy fulfillment of forbidden impulses can be carried on more safely in the latter. In any case, American films are heavily preferred to Indonesian ones—usually on the ostensible ground of technical superiority—and it was one of the biggest events in years when the local motion-picture theater (Chinese-owned) brought Cecil B. DeMille's *Samson and Delilah* to town.

Many people, especially younger men and women, go to the movies several times a week; and I was continually being asked such questions as whether I knew Montgomery Clift or how much education Doris Day had before she became a movie star. For Modjokuto people, movies defined the social context out of which I had come into their lives. To convince them that most motion pictures were about as realistic a picture of American life as the *wajangs* were of everyday Javanese life was nearly impossible. In addition to presenting a picture of American life, the movies also provide a new ideal for those interested in "progress." True, Indonesians often disparage the movies, as well as other aspects of American popular art—such as comic books and popular songs—as cheap, vulgar, and materialistic, and argue that they want to combine the material skills of the West with the superior spiritual qualities of the East; nevertheless, the Indonesians are in the peculiar position of launching a social effort after a utopia which they do not have to dream up for themselves but can see played out for them every night in the local theater.

Contemporary Art and the Emerging "Youth Culture"

THE national-art complex reflects for the most part the intelligentsia values of Indonesia's emergent "youth culture," a group of restless, educated, urban young men and women possessed of a sharp dissatisfaction with traditional custom and a deeply ambivalent attitude toward the West, which they see both as the source of their humiliation and "backwardness" and as the possessor of the kind of life they feel they want for themselves (minus, of course, the gangsters, the kissing, and the materialism). They are deeply committed to altering society in the direction of their borrowed dreams but have little idea of how this is to be done.

Painfully sensitive, easily frustrated, and passionately idealistic, this group is in many ways the most vital element in contemporary Indonesian society—even more so in the large metropolitan centers than in a town such as Modjokuto. Probably they are the most unpredictable elements as well. They are the Republic's hope and its despair: its hope because their idealism is both its driving force and its moral conscience; its despair because their exposed psychological position in the avant-garde of social change may turn them rather quickly toward the violent primitivism of other recent youth movements in Europe whose inner need for effective social reform was greater than the actual changes their elders were capable of producing for them.

Chapter 20　　　　　　　　　　　　Mysticism

OUR DISCUSSION of the *prijajis* proceeds from the outer man to the inner man. Having considered their etiquette, language, and art, we turn now to mysticism, the distinctly religious aspect of their life.

In Modjokuto, mysticism is practiced both individually and in sects. The sects are small, voluntary religious groups, usually loosely connected—but very loosely indeed—to other chapters of the same sect in other towns and to a central headquarters in one of the larger cities, usually the court centers. They meet, rotating among the members' houses in most cases, weekly or monthly, to discuss and meditate. In theory, one can meditate and study one's inner life as well by oneself as with others, but to do so in a group is considered preferable because individual meditation smacks too much of a hermit-like isolation from daily life of which most people disapprove, it is easier to carry on such activities regularly and undisturbed if one belongs to a group than if one attempts to carry them out at home, and, in a sect, the more advanced people can help and train the less advanced. Nevertheless, some people, most notably a few of the highest *prijajis* who feel that the sects are not *alus* enough for them, meditate and study alone or, informally, with one or two close friends.

There are five sects of importance in Modjokuto: Budi Setia (nearly impossible to translate, but, roughly, meaning "Faithful in the Rational Search for Understanding"), Kawruh Bedja ("Knowledge of True Good Fortune"), Sumarah ("To Surrender [to God's Will]"), Ilmu Sedjati ("True Science"), and Kawruh Kasunjatan ("Knowledge of the Highest Reality"). Only the first three are mainly *prijaji* in membership, the third and fifth having a large *abangan* admixture; but even the latter are based on the teachings of high *prijaji gurus* (teachers) in the court centers and are modeled after the more elevated sects. Although the sects are independent of one another and teach somewhat different doctrines (sometimes kept jealously secret from one another), they share a basically similar philosophical mysticism and as such

309

form an interrelated structural outlet for *prijaji* religious beliefs and practices.

In essence, mysticism in Java is applied metaphysics, a set of practical rules for the enrichment of man's spiritual life, based upon an underlying intellectual analysis of experience. Although different individuals and different sects have somewhat different positions and draw somewhat different conclusions from the same analysis, none questions the basic premises of the analysis. As in, for instance, the Western dualistic tradition from Descartes to Kant, the basic metaphysical presuppositions are common to all. What differs, and much less so in Java than in the Western tradition, is the ways in which these presuppositions are arranged and explicated to account for actual experience. This being so, it is advisable to inspect the content of Javanese mystic metaphysics before going more deeply into its institutionalization, the social forms it takes, in Modjokuto.

In order to provide a framework in which the otherwise rather involved and confusing material I have to present may be seen and ordered, I should like first to state my own summary formulation of this system and then attempt to show how my postulates appear in the formulations of my informants themselves. That there are no more than the postulates which I have set forth, or that this is the most satisfactory presentation of *prijaji* thought which could be constructed, I have no wish to argue. What follows is merely an outline statement of some of the more important notions about how the world "really" is which, I think, are shared by most Modjokuto mystics.

The Theory of Mysticism

I WOULD set down my summary in the form of eight postulates, as follows:

1. In the everyday life of man, "good" feelings and "bad" feelings, "happiness" and "unhappiness," are inherently and indissolubly interdependent. No one can be happy all the time or unhappy all the time, but must vary continually between these two states from day to day, from hour to hour, from minute to minute. This variation is the same for all emotions—love, hate, fear, and so on. Further, the main aim in life is not to maximize the positive emotions and minimize the negative ones, that is, the "pursuit of happiness," which is, in the nature of the case, impossible, a maximization of one implying a maximization of the other. Instead, the aim is to minimize the passions altogether so far as possible, to mute them in order to perceive the truer "feelings" which lie behind them. The aim is *tentrem ing manah,* "peace (quiet, tranquility) in the heart (the seat of the emotions)."

2. "Underneath" or "behind" these coarser human feelings there is a pure basic feeling-meaning, *rasa,* which is at once the individual's true self (*aku*) and a manifestation of God (*Gusti, Allah*) within the individual. The basic religious truth for a *prijaji* mystic lies in the equation: *rasa = aku = Gusti.*

3. The religious aim of man should be to "know" or "feel" this ultimate *rasa* in himself. Such an achievement brings spiritual power, a power which may be used either for good or for evil in earthly pursuits. There is rather little thought about other-worldly rewards; insofar as such a thing is possible, this is a "this-worldly" mysticism.

4. In order to achieve such "knowledge" of ultimate *rasa,* one must have a purity of will, must concentrate one's inner life entirely upon this single aim, intensifying and focusing all one's spiritual resources on a tiny point— much as one focuses the sun's rays through a burning glass in order to bring their maximum heat to bear on one spot. The main means of achieving such a purity of will and such a concentration of inner effort are: first, the blunting of the individual's instinctive life, a "rising above" everyday physiological needs; and, second, a disciplined withdrawal from mundane concerns for more or less extended periods of time and concentration upon inward things. Most important among the instinctual disciplines are fasting, staying awake, and sexual abstention. The temporary withdrawal of attention from the mundane world is called *semèdi* or, in its most intensive form, almost never practiced now, *tapa,* and consists of sitting absolutely still and emptying one's inner-life, so far as possible, of all mundane content.

5. In addition to the spiritual disciplines and meditation, the empirical study of human emotional life, a metaphysical psychology, also leads to an understanding and experience of *rasa.* Such a study amounts to a phenomenological analysis of experience and is considered the "theory" corresponding to the "practice" of fasting and other observances. One range of variation of the several mystic sects—at least in Modjokuto—seems to be along this continuum: according to the amount of weight they give instinctual control and meditation on the one hand and reflection and analysis on the other; but none wholly neglects either, for they support and strengthen one another.

6. As people vary both in their ability to carry out the spiritual disciplines (and no one is really as good at it today as people were in the past)— in the length of time they are able to fast, stay awake, and meditate— and in their ability to carry out a systematic analysis of inner experience (or to understand an analysis a famous *guru* has carried out), it is possible to rank individuals according to their spiritual abilities and achievements, a ranking which gives rise to the *guru-murid* (teacher-pupil) system in which an advanced teacher instructs a less advanced pupil and is himself a pupil of a more advanced teacher.

7. At the ultimate level of experience and existence, all people are one and the same and there is no individuality, for *rasa, aku,* and *Gusti* are "eternal objects," the same in all people. Although at the level of everyday experience individuals and nationalities may be said to have different selves and different feelings (although even here there is an important element of commonality), at base they are all the same. The combination of this notion with the idea of a hierarchy based on spiritual achievement gives rise to an ethic urging an ever-increasing inclusiveness of fellow-feeling for others, starting with one's own family and proceeding through one's neighborhood, village, district, and country to the whole world (only a few saints—Gandhi, Jesus, Muhammad —are supposed to have attained such universal sympathy), and a feudal-

organic view of social organization in which individuals and groups have a place in society corresponding to their presumed spiritual abilities.

8. Since the aim of all men should be to experience *rasa,* religious systems, beliefs and practices are only means to that end and are good only insofar as they bring it about. This leads to a relativistic view of such systems in which it is held that some systems are good for some people and others good for others and all have some good in them for someone. An absolute tolerance is thus enjoined, if not always completely practiced.

1. The Inner Connection between Happiness and Unhappiness

IN the *abangan* section I quoted a young man whose wife had recently died and who emphasized the necessity of keeping one's emotions flattened out, of avoiding wide swings of feeling. He argued that the way to do this was to realize that each person always has periods of happiness and periods of un-happiness. In discussing the *prijajis* I have quoted a Modjokuto poet on the same point. This theme appears again and again in interviews with members of all the sects.

> He said that his science (which he had learned from *gurus* and from books) also taught that one cannot be happy all the time—there must be some unhappiness as well. "For example," he said, "when you were just married, you felt that everything was good now and that you would never have any more unhappiness. But you did. A man builds a big factory and says to himself, 'Now I am happy, I have what I want'; but then another, poorer man builds a little factory, and the first man begins to fear that the little man's factory may grow and eclipse his own and is unhappy again. My science teaches me to avoid such strong feelings—not to be envious, jealous, or greedy."

It sometimes seems that what the *prijajis* most fear is strong feeling, for this implies severe frustration and either the freeing of carefully inhibited aggression or the initiation of an intense depression. *Gela,* which means "disappointed," and *kagèt,* which means "startled," are two of the feeling states most to be avoided, for the one depresses and the other disorganizes. They are in fact different forms of one and the same thing, *gela* being normal, that is, not entirely unexpected, frustrated, and *kagèt* being sudden, unforeseen frustration. One might hypothesize a typical psychological sequence something like this: (1) Aggression may not be directly expressed. (2) Therefore, one in part represses it and in part dissimulates it through the various etiquette forms. (3) Severe frustration, either in the *gela* or *kagèt* form, thus puts the individual in an impossible dilemma of either expressing his suddenly accentuated aggressive feelings, which reaction tends to occur in the more severe *kagèt* situation,* or of turning the aroused hate inward against the self, bringing depression, more common in the *gela* situation and among *prijajis,* whose stimulus-weakening and stimulus-regularizing defenses against startle are better.** (4) In order to avoid this dilemma one tries to calm one's emotions entirely, to put oneself beyond both disappointment and surprise.

Whether or not this admittedly speculative sequence is actual and typical—and I think there is some evidence that it is—it is certain that the effort of the mystical schools is primarily to still the continual emotional fluctuation of every-day life and reach a state of "peace in the heart," a theory worked out (or espoused) in explicit detail by the more sophisticated—for example, as expressed by a Modjokuto *guru* of Kawruh Bedja:

"What is the nature of feelings in life?" he asked rhetorically. "From birth until death only happiness, unhappiness, happiness, unhappiness, in unending alternation. Up and down, happy and unhappy—you can't be either one all the time. If a man asks why it is that all there is to life is happiness and unhappiness, the answer is that happiness results from the fulfillment of your wishes, unhappiness from their non-fulfillment; and every day there is both fulfillment and frustration, and you can't get away from this." I asked: "Can't you avoid wishing for things?" He said, "No, not completely. The will is an inseparable part of life and to give it up altogether is to give up life. People often forget this basic necessity for happiness and unhappiness to be inwardly connected. If they are happy for a little while, they think they will be happy always; and if they are unhappy for a while, they despair." I asked if this was bad; and he said, "Well, it isn't evil exactly, but it means that the person doesn't understand. It is better to understand. For example: You lose 100 rupiah and you are very unhappy, and you are walking along the road feeling awful, and I come along and you feel happy to see me. We chat a minute, and you are glad to talk with me because you haven't seen me for a while; and then we part and you become unhappy again, thinking about your lost 100." He said that often people don't remember these small happinesses in the middle of unhappinesses and thus don't get the proper perspective on life. . . . In any case, feelings are not certain—one moment one is happy, the next sad; these are connected with one another, necessary implications of one another. This is the difference between *bedja* ("good fortune," "the feeling, sensation, experience of good fortune") and its opposite, *tjilaka* ("ill fortune"). *Bedja* means that one has order and peace within—not happiness, not unhappiness—just peace. *Tjilaka* means that one has uncomfortable feelings, disordered and coarse ones, whether they are happy ones or unhappy ones. Thus *bedja* is better than happiness, because it does not carry the implication of later unhappiness. *Bedja* is a *rasa,* but it is higher than everyday *rasa* and different in essence from them. . . . As an example of the difference between these two states, he said: "Suppose you lose something. Now a man who doesn't know 'science,' who is unen-lightened, will get angry, disappointed, and generally depressed and upset

* Four separate thieves who were caught in the act of thievery were lynched on the spot during the time I was in Modjokuto; a chauffeur in a nearby town was beaten to death by an aroused citizenry when he stopped after having nearly hit a small girl; and all these events were explained—and excused—by a reference to *kagèt*—"the people were startled."

** All the above lynchings were by village people and were attributed by the *prijajis* in town to the *kasar* characters of the peasants.

within. However, the man who knows will be peaceful." I questioned how this was possible if one lost something very important, say an heirloom which had been in one's family for a long time. He replied: "Well, you would just say, 'Yes, so it's lost, it's lost'; or you would reflect and say 'Such an object is losable; it is not eternal. Some day it had to be destroyed anyway, so why get upset about it?' Suppose you break my cup. Since it is valuable, I start to feel angry, but I am advised by my science to remain cool, and so I do. It is hard to believe that this is possible until you do it." But he added that he couldn't always do it himself.

2. The Fundamental Religious Equation

IF the emotions can be stilled—through various means to which we shall come presently—then "behind" or "underneath" or "within" them one may come face to face with ultimate reality, the reflection of God in the self; a process our poet compares to the cracking open of a coconut:

> There is another metaphor which applies:
> If, for example, you wish to make coconut oil—
> The shell of the coconut may be likened to outward forms of religious
>   discipline,
> And the white meat of the coconut
> May be likened to the inward forms of religious discipline,
> While the oil of the coconut is the truth.
> Thus the action
> Of breaking open the coconut
> Is the method by which can be extracted
> The oil which lies within.

Most commonly, the central part of one's inner life, the place wherein God resides in the individual, is called the "heart" (*manah*). Sometimes this is identified with a special organ, for example, the liver, or with the heart itself. (Some who are more superstitious will not say the word for "heart" as an organ—*djantung*—because that is where God is in the individual and to do so might anger Him and bring bad luck.) But generally it is just considered to be the core of the human individual, the deep center of his being. Thus the "heart" in this sense is a kind of spiritual location, the place in the depths of the individual where both his true self and the ultimate *rasa,* which is God, can be found.

A sect member (a storekeeper by trade) drew the following picture of the situation as he saw it:

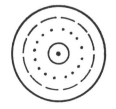

This, he said, is a picture of man. The outer, solid line represents man as a thing, as a body. People, first of all, are things, just like other things: rocks, chairs, tables, light-bulbs. Like such things they can be ruined. If one breaks a light-bulb it is ruined forever, and if one breaks a person he also is ruined. This is the same for everyone, and anyone who understands this will not want to hurt anyone else or see anyone in trouble. The second, broken line represents the five senses: seeing, hearing, smelling, talking, and feeling. At this point in just about every one of these catechisms, the informant pinches one and asks if it hurts, and when one says yes it does, he pinches himself and says that it hurts him too, which shows that people have the same sensations, *rasa*— another reason why one should not want to hurt anyone. The dotted line represents the conscious will, wish as perceived. ("I will drink this water" as a reflective thought was the example given, a conscious intention.) The inner solid circle represents the source of such wishes, the unconscious origin of desires. Wishes, he said, begin unperceived in the inner circle and proceed to the outer, where they are felt.

But we must judge such wishes and intentions, and the question is, what is it that judges?

> "*Kula* ('I,' 'me,' high Javanese for *aku*)," I answered. He laughed and said, "Where is '*kula*'? That's what the last solid circle represents, the essence of the self. Fixed and unchanging, it is always good, and it is that which judges and directs our will, or ought to. It cannot be wrong." He then went into a discourse on the difference between sensed objects and conceptualized ones. "What is 4 × 4? It is 16. If you say 15, you know it is wrong. How do you know? Because of your inner self. But if you see, say, a match, what is it that sees it? Your eyes; close your eyes and you can't see it. Or a voice, you hear with your ears; if you're deaf you can't hear it. But 4 × 4 is 16 inside; you don't have to see or hear it. Also, another difference between sensed and conceived objects is that if you ruin a sense object there is a trace. Burn the match and you have a burnt match; a corpse is left when a man dies. But after you've stopped thinking about 4 × 4 = 16 there is nothing left, no trace. Some people get far away from their real self, their *aku,* and in such a case their intelligence just aids in their doing evil. (He gave the atomic scientists as an example). . . . At any rate the real self, the *aku,* the inner solid circle on the chart is the part of the self that is the best. It is not old or young, male or female; and it is not fanatic like the Moslems. Also, it is very hard to get to. You have to *semèdi,* meditate. . . ."

Separating out the true self from the false self, the ultimate *rasa* from everyday feelings, the eternal within man from the *batin* in general, is itself a difficult task. The members of Budi Setia spent three meetings in a row discussing just which feelings could be asserted to come from the *swara ing asepi* —"the voice in the quiet." The problem seemed to be whether such premonitions as a feeling that one is going to have an auto accident or that one's child off in Djakarta has fallen ill could be said to come from the *swara ing asepi,* which, everyone agreed, was not so much a voice as a feeling and could only be reached by meditation; and whether the voice of conscience is always from this ultimate source or just from the *batin* generally, the latter being suggested by the fact that some people's consciences actually lead them astray.

It was finally decided that there were three things which are easily confused: (1) *swara ing asepi,* known only through meditation, which is the "voice" of God in the individual, the manifestation of God in the depths of the person's inner life, and therefore his ultimate "benchmark" which cannot be wrong; (2) "hunches" and "emotional predictions" of accident or good fortune, which can come to the person anytime, with or without meditation, even sometimes in dreams; and (3) the voice of conscience, which is more or less constant but which is identical with the "voice" of God, the *swara ing asepi,* only in the truly *alus* man, the man who has gained contact with his real self through meditation.

This kind of phenomenological analysis is an inward-looking but nevertheless empirical attempt to sort out the contingent and the permanent, the human and the divine, within the *batin.* A quite complex analysis was given by the *guru* of Kawruh Bedja:

> "The soul (*djiwa:* 'soul' is an unfortunate translation, although I can think of nothing better; for, as the analysis makes clear, this *djiwa* is quite unlike our 'soul,' being rather the perceived self, the 'me' as against the 'I')," he said, "is a thing, an object, but it is invisible. Although you feel it, it has *rasa.* Your name is Cliff, and (closing his eyes) you feel (*rasa*) Cliff. This is called feeling your name." I said that I didn't understand this. He said: "Suppose you come here in the dark. No one can see anything and you say, 'May I come in?' 'Who is it?' I reply. 'Me,' you say. 'Me who?' I say. 'Me, Cliff,' you say. Thus you feel 'Cliff'; this is your soul. Now, that which feels Cliff, which feels the 'feeling of Cliff,' is *aku,* 'I.' *Aku* is not the feeling 'Cliff'—the soul is that; but the feeling *aku* is the feeling which feels the feeling 'Cliff.' It is the feeling which knows. It is not the soul which knows, it is what is known; *aku* is what knows. *Aku* is an eternal object, it can never be destroyed; and some say it is God, so that God is both in the sky and in the individual. But Bedja, dealing only with actually perceived things, takes no position and just says *aku* is an eternal object." (In a later interview, however, the *guru* said that he and everyone else really thought that *aku* and God were the same, and that the former was only the latter manifested in the individual. The reason he didn't teach it was that it only confused people, especially at the beginning, and such confusion could be quite harmful and upsetting. Therefore it was better to stick to simple, perceivable things.)

In Ilmu Sedjati, this identification of the "I" in man with God is even more direct, for this semi-secret mystic cult (sometimes called Islam Sedjati, "True Islam," which infuriates the *santris*) patterns itself upon the form of Islam and has in place of the Islamic Confession of Faith ("I believe there is no God but Allah, and Muhammad is His Prophet") a Confession: "I believe God is in myself and my breath is His representative (Prophet)." The whole confession is rather long and complicated, with secret, "hidden" secondary meanings for all the major words; and a whole set of yoga-like disciplines concerned with breath regulation is built upon it. As one member explained:

> Ilmu Sedjati is based on a understanding of God and of life. . . . It says that God is in your own body, which means not that the individual is God but that one must look into one's self in order to find and understand God. It goes on to say that God is manifest in your breath, not so much that He is the

breath but that He is what makes the breathing—i.e., you constantly feel yourself breathing and then you refer to what it is that makes this breathing "go" and the answer is God, which is within you.

Thus in Ilmu Sedjati one meditates while regulating his breath (always a part of meditation since meditation involves a severe regulation of one's physical as well as psychological processes) and hears in his own breathing the mystical word which is the secret core of the "science," *u* (inhale), *rip* (exhale), *urip* meaning "life." Over and over again one breathes with perfect regularity and feels the ultimate meaning, *u, rip, u, rip.* . . . A similar discipline in Ilmu Kasunjatan leads to a different word but with roughly the same import: *hu* (inhale), *Allah* (exhale), *hu Allah, hu Allah.* . . . Thus the true self, the ultimate inward feeling, and God are one and the same, an idea the modern *santris,* at least, realize is diametrically opposed to their own basic tenets.

> I told him (a Muhammadijah member) in a lapse of caution that I had been to a Budi Setia meeting. He asked if I knew what Budi Setia was, and I said no. He said that these people thought that God and man were one, in contrast to Islam which teaches that God is God and man is man, that the Lord is the Lord and the servant the servant. I asked: "But aren't these men Moslems?" He replied: "They say they are, but they don't carry it out. They don't follow the Koran, and in fact have no book at all but merely follow their own ideas. There are many people like this in Indonesia, who say they are Moslems but really follow 'Javanese science.' "

3. The Search for Ultimate Enlightenment and "This-Worldly" Mysticism

THE knowledge of the ultimate *rasa* is the end of mystical endeavor and should be the religious aim of all men. Often this act of comprehension is considered to have two main stages: *neng,* literally "quiet," "stillness," referring to the calming of the emotions; and then *ning*—"clearness of insight," the intuition which follows upon the stillness and which may be, although it is usually described as having "no content at all, a completely empty *batin,*" quite an emotional experience.

> Sudjoko (a Budi Setia member, speaking during one of their weekly meetings) then said that he was uncertain of all these things. Most of the time one can't really feel the real self, but only now and then; most of the time one feels the individual, selfish, false self. But sometimes, in fleeting moments or in meditation, one feels the real self and feels a rush of power. "*Aduh!*" he said passionately at this point. (*Aduh* is an exclamation of deep emotion or pain.) He described a number of situations not altogether clear to me showing the difference between the false and true self; and he described the meeting of the real self as a tremendous emotional experience. . . .

As one might expect, both from the emphasis on the rush of emotion and power in the mystical experience and from mysticism elsewhere, the experience is often described in sexual terms, for example in these three consecutive stanzas from the long poem I have been quoting:

Day and night do not leave off from praying,
The result of your great effort will be a mystical experience.
In other words, the light of God will be revealed to you,
It will be felt in your heart.
That is to say, the heart is one with the soul,
That strange inner hindrance.
And you shall see it,
Opened and clear.
Clearly, such a result
Cannot be compared to anything else.

All this comes only as a blessing of God,
And it cannot be explained
Clearly and simply.
If you wish to know about it
You must know it by having experienced it
And then you will truly know it.
It is as the proverb says: a young boy and a young girl
Cannot really know the pleasures of sex
If they have not experienced them.

After you have actually carried out
Coitus, then you truly understand it.
And also you don't wish to talk about it,
To discuss your sexual experiences with others.
It is the same with mystical experiences;
Those who have already been able to come directly in touch with God
See mystically this supernatural power.
My child: memorize this!

These stanzas bring together a number of themes. First, they accent the empirical nature of Javanese mysticism: the final appeal is always to (emotional) experience which carries its own meaning. God, forms of worship, and views of the nature of man, are always validated on these grounds—never on grounds of logic or essential rationality (as in Thomistic Christianity), never on pure belief (as in Islam and Tertullian Christianity), never in terms of social consequences (for these can be good or bad—even though Javanese mystics are much concerned with the social consequences of their beliefs), but always on the quality of experience which is self-validating and empirical, no matter how much it might point beyond itself to non-empirical grounds.

The sexual metaphor is the natural one in this context, particularly since many Javanese, *alus* ones especially, regard it as almost indecent to talk about their real feelings with others. (Sudjoko, the informant above, was the only person I ever heard describe the mystical experience with any vividness. Other people were vague or embarrassed to talk about it.)

Earlier he (a high-school teacher) said that he thought the first class (in the high-school) would be best for psychological tests because the students at that age are still open a little emotionally. Javanese are very closed up emotionally, he said, and never want anyone else to know what they are really feeling, what is in their hearts. Although by the second and third high-school grades this condition is pretty well established, the first-graders are still somewhat expressive. When I asked him why they didn't like others to know what they are feeling, he said that he didn't know; that they were just ashamed to do so. . . . Another informant said that one can tell, sometimes, a man's wishes and inner feelings from his face, from how he looks. Most Javanese, he said, want to hide this. They don't want to show what they want down deep, and so they mask the face—hold it stiff so that their inner feelings and wishes are not visible to others.

In any case, mystical experience brings an access of power which can be used in this world. Sometimes the use is semi-magical, such as in curing, foretelling the future, or gaining wealth.* Boys *semèdi* before school examinations in order to pass with high marks; girls who want husbands sometimes fast and meditate for them; and even some politicians are held to meditate for a higher office. During the period of the right-wing Moslem rebellion in Acheh, in Sumatra, when many Modjokuto people thought "the crazy times" of the Revolution might be returning, Budi Setia (which opened every meeting with a report on the week's national and international news by one of the members) meditated so that the country would be safe, stable, and peaceful.

Hardjo then said that Budi Setia was . . . just concerned with the science of the inner life and with asking God for order and peace. Advancement in spiritual things is what is important. . . . He said that he had seen from the newspapers that many groups such as Budi Setia were springing up around the country; they were on the increase everywhere. Wasisto then said that he also had noted the springing up of new "inner life" groups. He said that he thought that the reason was that things in Indonesia were getting not more peaceful but less so; that all the upset gave rise to attempts to calm it through such groups as Budi Setia. He said that we must ask God that this upset stop quickly and secondly that nothing bad happen here in this area. Hardjo said that the effort was to bring peace and order in the world. Wirjo said that meditation was the most important thing in this: one's heart must be peaceful. . . . Peace depends upon the inner state of individual people; peace in the world follows upon this, but the first peace is in the inner self. But it is not just for oneself. One must carry out one's duties in life, and in doing so with an inner peace one spreads peace socially. There are those too who think that peace cannot be reached in this world, but fortunately they are wrong. . . . Modern life is lacking in peace—so much so that many people argue that one can't find peace anymore in this world because nowadays people can't stop—a moment here, a moment there—

* Both Budi Setia and Sumarah meditate en masse when one of their members is ill in order to cure him; and Sumarah claims that one crippled boy—who is still a member and still partly crippled and supports their story—was made capable of walking through their *semèdi* efforts. Kawruh Kasunjatan is considered often to make its participants capable of acting as *ḍukuns;* and it is led by one of the better known *ḍukuns* in the area.

but are always on the run. But nobody can effect our advancement toward real peace but ourselves. If the Javanese join in this mad modern rush, they will lose the way of old which their ancestors pursued to peace. The problem is really how people can live peacefully in this world. . . .

Heaven and hell are here and now within one, several sect people told me; and one of the strongest criticisms they have of the Moslems is the latter's emphasis on the afterlife, which seems to them foolish. Although certain individuals hold to a reincarnation theory, one in which individuals are incarnated higher or lower according to the ethical quality of their behavior while alive, there is little concern for a complete escape from the process as in India; and Nirvana, as a permanent state of bliss, is not very meaningful to most people. More often the incarnation theory is used mainly to buttress the ranking system and the organic theory of society much as it is used in India, although quite a bit more casually, and then only in the more intellectual *prijaji* circles. Individuals and groups are held to be at the level appropriate to their spiritual ability, like children graded in school. ("Light souls, those of people who 'know,' naturally rise," one *prijaji* informant said, counting himself among the knowers. "Dark, heavy souls, those of people who don't 'know,' naturally sink.") In any case, mystical practice is considered to be a means not of turning away from life but toward it.*

The heart of the "science" evidently is a reinterpretation of the five pillars of Islam. . . . They interpret these five pillars quite differently from the Islamic meaning used by the *santris*. He (*guru* of the Ilmu Sedjati group) said that *santri* Islam is for the future, for the afterlife, but Ilmu Sedjati is for the here and now, for securing well-being in this life. If no heaven now, no heaven later, he said. He said that the science teaches one how to recognize God. He said that this teaching is secret and that one must be a pupil to be allowed to hear it. If one did, and they told one that this is where God is, one would say, "Oh yes, I see; it is so obvious." He also said that they teach that the source of man's troubles is in himself, and teach one to recognize, face, and deal with this and unify oneself and find peace. . . .

The power gained from mystical experience can be used for good or evil. Besides giving one the ability to cure, it gives the ability to make people ill; the detachment one gets through meditation can make one a more efficient evil-doer as well as a "defender of society." (A Budi Setia member suggested in one meeting that Indonesian society in general was so unstable because not only good people but also the bandits were getting more disciplined spiritually; thus the situation instead of getting more orderly got progressively less so.) The members of one sect, despite their professed tolerance, usually accuse the adherents of the other sects of being mainly concerned with getting rich or gaining political power rather than with using their mystical knowledge for the good of society as their own sect does.

This dualism runs through the whole of the mystical philosophy. If one

---

* Not typically, at any rate. I have one contra-indicative case, a quite high *prijaji* who argued with me for a withdrawal from the world, but he is almost universally dispraised for his attitude.

meditates on the south side of a certain nearby mountain, one will gain the power to do good; if one meditates on the north side one will gain the power to do evil. People do not like to admit that they fast a good deal or *semèdi* too much for fear others will think they wish to do evil. Sometimes the increased ability to do evil is held to arise not from true mystical experience but from a false one in which the individual is actually "far away" from his true, good self although he thinks he is close to it; but more commonly people simply accept the fact that spiritual discipline leads to insight into the self which in turn leads to power which may then be used for various purposes. Further, the power itself is most often viewed ambivalently, for it is possible to have too much, to get in over one's head, and, failing to build up one's spiritual constitution step by step, be overwhelmed by the power one gets.

> We talked some about "Javanese Science," which he (a young school teacher) said is different from Islam. He said that it is "strength in the inner life," and that there are people who have science and can kill other people. He said that this power, as well as curing power, comes through fasting; and that the reason one's *batin* gets strong from fasting is that when one fasts one gets very hungry and thinks a lot about God, and then God gives one the power. People who are not strong enough to take this often go mad because the science is too much for them and they think too much about such things; the veins in their heads snap and they go crazy. Sometimes they go crazy because they have this science and it forbids them to do something —e.g., strike someone, or lie to someone, but they lose their temper and hit someone and then they go mad because they have broken the rule. One must be strong to deal with Javanese science. . . .

As spiritual "strength" is correlated with social status, lower-class people are well advised not to try too much along such lines. In any case, one must proceed cautiously. (One of the leaders of Sumarah went into a fit during a meditation session, and it took two or three men to hold him down. The collapse was interpreted as the result of his having overreached himself in mystical exercise.) An incontinence of mystic practice can easily destroy the individual totally.

> He (another informant) said that *amuk* (a temporary but very violent psychosis in which the individual runs about attacking and killing innocent bystanders isn't caused by jealousy or poverty, as common insanity often is, but by "science," by religion. . . . A person gets to thinking about religion, and he can't figure some things out. He gets to worrying about where God is: is he under the ground, is he in the sky, what does he look like, is he red, is he black, is he big, is he little, how does he order people to do things? People who are stupid, who have no religion, don't go *amuk*.

4. Mystical Discipline

IN order to accomplish the mystical state, one must *ngèsti*. *Ngèsti* means to unify all the powers of the individual and direct them toward a single end, to concentrate one's psychological and physical faculties toward one narrow goal. It stands for a kind of intense mental quest, a search for understanding which is supported by an irresistible will and a fusion into one simple whole of the different forces within the individual. The senses, the mind, the emotions, even, so far as is possible, the physical processes of the body—all are brought into a single unity and focused toward a single end.*

He (a high *prijaji* adherent of a sect which had no chapter in Modjokuto at the moment and who therefore studied by himself) said that his "science" argued that there were four parts to the individual: the body, the will, the soul, and feeling, the last including the senses and emotions. All these must be unified, made as one, in an effort called *ngèsti*. *Ngèsti* means to concentrate all these four parts, including the five senses, and to close up the nine holes in the body (two ears, two eyes, two nostrils, mouth, anus, and urethra) and really concentrate so that one senses nothing. He said that the first thing one must put in order and unify is the body, next the will, then the soul, by which he meant the inner emotional life, and finally one will reach *rasa*. . . . One must *ngèsti* every evening so that one will feel cool and peaceful.

The reason that one must *ngèsti* every night—or at least at regular intervals—is that it is a practiced skill. Javanese often compare it to sport. One must train and actually perform it quite frequently to be any good at it; and if one stops doing it for a while one gets rusty and must get into shape again before one can regain his old skill. Thus one *guru* said that he used to be a good curer by means of meditation when younger, but stopped doing it during the Japanese period and lost his skill and never has gotten back to being as good as he once was. Moreover, like sport, there is a large element of natural ability involved in it. Sect meetings, in fact, are usually called *latihan*, which means "practice sessions," "exercises"; and breath control, concentration of the senses, emptying of the mind, are all rehearsed for at least part of each meeting. In one of the sects, Kawruh Kasunjatan, people stare at a lighted lamp for long periods in order to *ngèsti;* in others they gaze at a single point, stand up and look at the floor in front of them, or just close their eyes and withdraw into themselves.

Often *ngèsti* is phrased in slightly different terms as *nuwun*, which means to ask or beg for something. The notion here is that one must ask God for insight with such a concentration of energy, beg with such a single-minded intensity, that one will reach Him despite the deterring elements of mundane feeling and sensation which obscure Him from one's view or one from His. This formulation is based on the dual idea that the way to get things from (higher-status) people is to ask them for it and that if one wants something badly enough the people whom one is importuning cannot possibly refuse. They will feel too sympathetic to resist one's demands; but if they do resist them, it can only be because one has not pleaded his case intensely enough.

* Thus the name of the most famous professional *wajang wong* troupe in Java is Ngèsti Pendawa, which, as the Pendawa are usually held to represent the five senses, has the mystical meaning of concentrating and unifying the self in an effort after ultimate meaning.

In daily life this leads to a situation whereby lower-status people get things out of higher-status ones by such petitioning and the higher ones protect themselves from being too easily exploited by the formalities of the etiquette system and the attendant "shame" lower-status people feel in dealing with higher-status people. In dealing with God, this pattern is most common in situations where people want specific material blessings—as, for example, in the mBah Buda ritual petitioning mentioned earlier, which was compared to "crying for something" as a child does to its parents. But even in purely mystical quests one often hears the formulation that what one must do is to want to know God so badly, to beg him with such importunity, that He in His infinite mercy will reveal Himself.

Whether *ngèsti,* the concentration of all one's powers toward a single end, is phrased as an intense quest or as a pleading supplication,* it is tremendously facilitated by instinctual disciplines and, in fact, cannot really be very successful in their absence. Of these instinctual disciplines, by far the most important are fasting and staying awake; for one of the most widespread beliefs in the culture is that asceticism in matters of food and rest leads to spiritual strength and intensity.

> In the evening I saw Samidjan, the carpenter, in the coffee-shop. . . . We talked about eating, and he said that many Javanese eat only a banana a day and survive; many need very little food. The same is true of sleep. He sleeps about six hours a day, and some people sleep only four or five hours. (This, incidently, is not entirely an ideal pattern. I never ceased to be amazed at how little people seemed to sleep in Java, and how deeply they slept when they did sleep.) He said that Javanese believe that if one does not eat much or sleep much but concentrates on God and works hard one can be rich. In fact, one can achieve anything by this fasting method—but one can't just fast, meditate, and then go to sleep. One must also go out and work for what one wants. He said that it is because the fasting makes the power of the mind stronger that one can get things this way. When I asked him why many people who fast this way still don't get rich, he said that it is usually because they are not of a single will. One must, he said, have just one idea: fast, meditate on God, and work—and have all this to one aim, to get rich. But often a man will not have just one aim; he will wish other things. For example, a man will fast to be rich, but inside he will also want to be handsome. This is what prevents him from being successful.

This is an *abangan,* not a *prijaji,* formulation. The belief in the relationship between instinctual deprivation and spiritual power is—with a partial exception among the *santris,* who hold that the purpose of fasting is to feel how it is to be hungry like the poor, to show one's subservience to God, and to toughen one for whatever trials life may bring—almost universal. When asked to complete the sentence "A man who doesn't eat much . . . ," about one hundred and fifty high-school students in the *prijaji*-run private high school in town gave (in addition to a number of, from our point of view, more

---

* It is also sometimes put in terms of a surrender, a humble prostration before the power of God, a submission of one's will to His, a formulation important in Sumarah, the very name of which conveys this meaning.

"expectable" responses such as ". . . he would get thin," ". . . he gets sick," ". . . he will lack vitamin B") such replies as these:

. . . that is very good.
. . . is a man whose religious discipline is very great.
. . . his health will be good.
. . . is disciplined religiously.
. . . is a man who will be an expert in meditation.
. . . will be clever.
. . . will usually also stay awake all night.
. . . will have a clear mind.
. . . will do good actions.
. . . quickly rich.
. . . that is called religious discipline in order that one's ideals may be reached.
. . . must be clever.
. . . pleasant.
. . . yes, he will be strong.

One would probably not find any such answers in a million tests in the United States.

Similarly, to the reverse question, "A man who eats too much . . . ," in addition to such answers as ". . . he'll get fat" or ". . . he'll fall sick," we got such replies as:

. . . will not be able to think easily.
. . . will become stupid.
. . . will be unable to think.
. . . his actions will not be good.
. . . will not be intelligent.
. . . his mind will be bound, he will be unable to think.
. . . must be stupid.

Many Javanese, *abangan* and *prijaji,* still fast on Mondays and Thursdays from dawn to dusk. To stay awake all night, particularly on holidays or special occasions, helps one stay young and leads to a long life. By far the most common Islamic practice to which the non-*santris* are faithful is the Fast, because, as one *prijaji* puts it, "despite the fact that it is Islamic, it is an excellent exercise both for the body and the spirit." And old men complain about the growing laxity of the younger generation in these matters:

He went on to talk about experts in fasting and people who meditate a long time. He said that this is the way to become clever quickly; one can know everything this way. He told the two children there (about eight and ten years old) that they should fast on Monday and Thursday; that it had to be on those two days. He said that fasting was the real way to power, the only way to real knowledge; that if one fasted and God received it—which wasn't necessarily certain—he would ask: "What is your wish?" and one would get what one wanted. He said scornfully that these days no one fasts any more as people used to. For example, the children were always eating something, always nibbling on tidbits. He warned that, since when one doesn't eat it makes for a purer soul, many children die now because they eat too much.

Old people knew that fasting was the best thing for one and the way to riches and knowledge, but now they don't do it as much as they used to. He said that men make money but God makes men. We should not be too interested in wealth, but realize that such things as fasting are what is good. He asked the children again if they would start fasting on Monday and Thursday, but they were non-committal.

This again is an *abangan* formulation, but on this point the *prijajis* are at one with them.

Djojo said that people say there is much advancement today—in the schools they learn mathematics, physics, and they are very clever; but he thinks that in the heart and soul they are not so good as the people in the old days. In the old days people lived to be much older, 100 years, and didn't lose their teeth or their eyesight in old age. . . . His wife added that this was because formerly people could fast for days, or go without sleep for days, and not be any the worse for it, but now if they miss one meal they catch a cold! Djojo agreed and said that in the old days people were calm and wouldn't, for example, drink coffee or tea until it was cold. He said that nowadays people are not so strong in the soul as formerly even if they are cleverer in the mind; before, they could be vegetarians, but now if there is not meat with every meal they are upset.

In sum, in order to come into contact with God one must concentrate one's entire powers toward that end and deny so far as possible one's needs to eat, drink, and sleep (also one's sexual needs, but, with their usual reticence on such topics, the Javanese do not emphasize this particularly or care to talk about it much). Such activity is called either *semèdi* or *tapa,* depending mainly on its intensity. *Semèdi* really means meditation, with or without much instinctual discipline, but as practiced in Modjokuto it is often accompanied by some cutting-down of the amount of food eaten and the hours of sleep. No one really practices *tapa* now. In fact, insofar as it involves more or less impossible feats of self-denial, it never has been practiced—although, as we have seen, it is ascribed to various mythological heroes such as the *wajang* characters. In *tapa* one places oneself in some wild place—in the deep woods or on top of a mountain—and goes into an extended trance, neither eating nor sleeping— just meditating. The result of this is tremendous magical and spiritual power and a heightened ability to get what one wants in this world.

In this, as in so many things, Sunan Kalidjaga, the great mythological culture hero, who not only was one of the founders of Islam but who invented the *wajang,* the *gamelan,* the *slametan,* and almost all the other religious *pusaka* (heirlooms) the Javanese have, provides the model. Kalidjaga was the son of a high government official. As a young man he was a thief, a gambler, a profligate, and a general no-good. One day there came to his father's town another of the founders of Islam in Java, Sunan Bonang, an Arab. Sunan Bonang wore beautiful clothes and expensive jewelry, and the head of his walking-stick was of solid gold. He walked down the street where Kalidjaga (who was then called Radèn Sa'id) was holding up people and robbing them; and he was stopped by Kalidjaga, who demanded his jewels and his cane on penalty of his life. Bonang merely laughed and said: "Why, these jewels are

as nothing; look about you!" And Kalidjaga looked about him and saw that
Bonang had turned all the trees to gold hung with jewels; and he was startled
and realized that the things of this world were as nothing next to the power of
Sunan Bonang. Kalidjaga begged Bonang to teach him the secret of his science.
Bonang said, "All right, but it is very difficult and dangerous. Do you have the
courage?" And Kalidjaga said: "I am brave to the death." So Sunan Bonang
said: "If you are brave, then wait for me here by the side of the river until
I return." Kalidjaga waited, doing *tapa.* For many years Bonang did not return, but Kalidjaga continued unmoved in one place, *tapa*-ing. Trees grew up
around him, sirens came to tempt him, demons to frighten him, but he did
not move. Finally, Bonang returned and discovered that Kalidjaga (whom he
now presented with this name: *kali,* "river"; *djaga,* "guard") was now in fact
more powerful than he, Bonang, because of his long period of *tapa.* After this
Kalidjaga never robbed or gambled again but went about spreading Islam—
the *abangan* version—throughout the country-side.

Tapa is, then, a kind of suspended animation, a continuing mystical experience. The baby is said to *tapa* in the womb, "trying to become a person,"
and the womb imagery is in general quite conscious. At a circumcision ceremony the mother will often step across the recumbent child three times so
that he will be reminded of the time of his *tapa* in her womb and so remember
the source of his strength. But the imagery, too, is often that of death.

> He who has need of knowledge about the inner life
> Cannot be hindered,
> But must be helped in his search.
> He will be continually reading books and asking questions
> Of those who are learned.
> He will always be feeling
> About the perfectness of death.
> Sometimes he will travel around
> Meditating quietly in wild places,
> Searching for a message from God.

In the less spiritually heroic present, such extremes of religious asceticism
are but unpracticed ideals, and most mystics are content with *sumèdi:* meditation, anywhere from twenty minutes to several hours in length, for which one
prepares by a certain amount of fasting, staying awake, and sexual abstinence.
But the principle is the same: absolute and intense concentration upon a single
aim, that of emptying the *batin* of mundane content in order to come into contact with the representative of the divine within one. And the result is the
same, if less spectacular: an increased spiritual strength which allows one to
pursue one's aims in this world with a fixed and unchanging will instead of
being pulled here and there by distracting elements. Tranquilly undisturbed
by the surprises of a contingent reality, inwardly peaceful and stable in a world
of flux, the man who has gained the true knowledge of what lies within him
proceeds steadily on his way, master of his own desires. If he sets out to go
north, he goes north, not east, south, or west—and he does not stop in at a
coffee-shop on the way.

5. Metaphysical Psychology

IN addition to embracing the spiritual disciplines and meditation, the empirical study of emotional life is seen as a means to the understanding and experience of God within the self. Thus Kawruh Bedja works out the phenomenological analysis of the self, already quoted; Budi Setia argues about the different kinds of "voices in the quiet," also already quoted; and Ilmu Sedjati bases a very complicated system indeed on the analysis of the four basic "drives" in Javanese metaphysical psychology: *amarah*—aggression, lust for power; *supiah* —greed, desire for property; *mutmainah*—the passion for tranquility, desire for inner peace; *aluamah*—hunger, desire for food and drink.

Around these four drives and their correct regulation there is constructed an extremely complicated metaphysical and ethical system in which each of the drives is tied to various aspects of reality: the sun, moon, earth, and stars; four kinds of spirits; the objects concerned in the birth process—the bamboo knife, birthcord, afterbirth, and navel-healing medicine; four kinds of correlated illnesses (e.g., too much greed makes you feverish); the four elements which make up the physical world—earth, fire, water, and wind; four religious groups in Javanese society (Moslems, Mystics, Christians, and "Intellectuals" —the last meaning "free thinkers"); four kinds of black magic; four political parties—Moslem, Nationalist, Communist, and Socialist; and so forth and so on. The whole system is diagramed in a spectacularly complicated chart with lines running in all directions between the various interrelated elements. This kind of arbitrary speculation, based always on inner perceptions as the basic data from which the theory departs, is endemic among *prijajis*. Almost every *prijaji* has some fantastically elaborated scheme, that of his sect if he is a member of one, which explains, usually with the help of spectacular diagrams, all aspects of experience and ties all outer reality to inner feeling. The only adherent of Ilmu Ngèsti I found in Modjokuto described his system as follows:

> According to this science there are four basic elements represented by four symbols: fire, standing for the will; earth, standing for the mother; water, for the blood; and wind, for the breath or life. Four other aspects of life are coordinated with this: the seed or sperm, the womb, birth, and death. There are thus four basic requirements for the individual: he must examine carefully and know the order in the sperm; he must examine carefully and know the order in the embryo; in life; death. Thus, all this amounts to finding order in each stage of one's life: as a sperm, as an embryo, as a living human being, and as a corpse. . . .

This reasoning goes on, as do all the other systems, at great length; but perhaps this excerpt is enough to demonstrate why the Javanese refer to this sort of thing as the "theory" corresponding to the "practice" of fasting, meditating, and other observances. There is some difference of opinion on whether the theory or the practice is more important: Budi Setia and Kawruh Bedja emphasize the speculative aspects of mysticism, arguing that intellectual understanding is as important as spiritual discipline, if not more so. Kawruh Kasunjatan and Sumarah (the leaders of which criticize Budi Setia rather severely for its "intellectualism") emphasize meditation and emotional experience. Ilmu Sedjati stresses both about equally. All, however, include both speculation and meditation, and regard the "theory" and the "practice" as mutually self-supporting.

> Another young man spoke on theosophy. He said that he had studied it seriously before the war but thought that since the war it had gotten too theoretical. He said that theosophy was theory, but Javanese science was the carrying out of it, the meditation. He thought that one needed both the intellectual theory and the concrete practice. Now these things have to be justified in terms of Western science instead of the old terms they used before the war: for example, the theory of the circulation of the blood.

6. The Teacher (*Guru*)–Student (*Murid*) Pattern

SINCE, whether "true knowledge" is accomplished mainly by means of spiritual discipline or philosophical speculation or by an even balance of both, people vary considerably in their abilities along these lines, there is a kind of natural ranking of individuals according to their presumed or proven capacity for mystical achievement.

Sumarah, for example, has a four-rank system for its members. First are the younger people, twelve to twenty years in age, who meditate by themselves separate from the rest of the membership (but under the leadership of the *guru* of the sect) so that they will not disrupt the concentration of their betters. It is held that if one is meditating and someone else in the same room is not, or is not meditating so deeply, it will disturb one. Second, there are the older regular members of no special spiritual qualifications. Third is a group of advanced mystics (about a half-dozen in Modjokuto out of a total membership of about forty) who are nominated by the local branch, their names being sent to the headquarters in Djokjakarta, where the governing board of the sect meditates upon them and, without any information about the people the names symbolize, comes to a "feeling" decision about whether they should be "promoted" or not. And, fourth, there is the highest rank, of which only the *guru,* a pawn-shop employee, is a member in Modjokuto, chosen in a similar fashion—except that, presumably, the meditation of the governing board is deeper. In all the sects there is some such ranking as this, although not necessarily so formalized as in Sumarah. At the least, there is always the idea that some of the members are more advanced than others and that one of the purposes of sect organization is to enable the more advanced mystics to help the less advanced. The common image is that of the school where the student in the first grade, even though he may have the potentiality to equal, after much time and long study, the achievement of the sixth-grader, is for the moment at least far below the latter in capacity and accomplishment.

Groups of people as such also vary in their abilities along these lines, peasants, for example, being notoriously poor at meditation when compared with *prijajis*. Women are usually inferior to men in such matters.

When I asked if women in the neighborhood study much with *gurus,* she said no, it wouldn't be of very much use. Because women have to say what is on their minds, they can't be patient (*sabar*) and accept things (*trima*) the way one must if a *guru* teaches one. The other day she had a fever and Pak Sardi (the *guru* of Ilmu Sedjati) came in and told her that it was because she was greedy. . . . She does what she can about being patient, but she's a woman and can only go so far.

Some women do fairly well, in fact; and all the sects are coeducational, the women usually sitting in among the men, in sharp contrast to both *abangan* and, especially, *santri* religious practices. In Budi Setia women contribute their opinions fairly freely, if less freely than men, and are usually listened to respectfully. In Sumarah some of the second-highest-level mystics are women. (I have never heard of a woman *guru,* however, in any of the sects.) In all the groups women are allowed to do whatever men are allowed, although the general opinion is that mysticism is more difficult for them, given their inherently less peaceful nature.

On the other hand, the old, *ceteris paribus,* are considered to be rather better at mystical asceticism than the young.

"This (a chart the informant had drawn for me) represents the ages of man *windu* by *windu* (a *windu* is eight years). When you are eight you are still a child and don't think about anything. When you are sixteen you are all wound up about girls. When you are twenty-four you are getting married. At thirty-two you are involved in the things of everyday life. But by the time you are forty you begin to reflect about life and only then can you really begin to understand it, to learn this 'science'; and as you become older you get wiser. Most people don't live eight *windus* (i.e., 64 years) but die in their early forties." The informant, who is about fifty, thinks they die early because they don't turn away from life toward this philosophy, and so wear themselves out. He has never been sick a day. He thinks that his health is due to this "science," whereby one can live to a ripe old age—more than eight *windus,* even ten or so.

It is upon the difference in spiritual talents among various individuals and groups, talents which are improvable but only to a point, that the *guru* system rests. Rank, sex, and age combine to form a fairly even gradation of spiritual status—a gradation that, despite some protestations that one cannot always tell a man's inner worth from his outer aspects, so that a beggar may really be higher than a regent, coincides in fact remarkably well with the gradation of political and social status generally. All the Modjokuto sects stem from high court mystic *gurus* who first came upon the "science" they teach in a fit of meditation such as is not possible to ordinary men. The *guru* then taught it to disciples (*murid*), and those disciples taught it to still lower disciples, and so on down the line until, in some cases, even the peasant was reached.

Thus there is a linked—but very loose—network of *gurus* and *murids* spreading outward and downward from the court centers to the countryside; a diffuse image of the power situation generally as the *prijajis* see it. It is interesting, too, that many people say, I am not certain how accurately, that before the Revolution many of the more *alus* of the "sciences" now taught were confined secretly, like the *srimpi* dances, to the courts and only now have seeped out to the masses. Similar assertions are made about certain refined systems of numerical divination, certain meditation-linked curing techniques, and so forth, with the result that, whether correctly or not, it is widely believed that the Revolution has released to the people generally much of the mystical power which was formerly confined to the ruling classes. Thus the (partial) revolution in the political sphere finds its (partial) reflection in the religious. When an old-fashioned peasant brought up in a political discussion the famous old-Javanese prophecy that Java would be peaceful only when the Ratu Adil —the Just King—came to rule, a more modern thinker rebuked him, saying that, although the prophecy, coming as it did from great mystics in the past, was true, in a democracy the people is king and so it means that Java will be peaceful when its people are just.

But culture does not change as rapidly as all that, and in Modjokuto the *guru* system is still an important pattern. Ilmu Sedjati was founded by a Radèn Mas (i.e., a court noble) in Madiun, a large city near Surakarta. Kawruh Bedja was founded by and is still headed by a Djokjakarta prince. Sumarah is led by high Djokjakarta *prijajis,* some of them high officials in the Ministry of Education and Culture. Kawruh Kasunjatan was founded by a Radèn Mas from the Surakarta court of Mangkunegara IV (and is often merely called Ilmu Suwana, after his name, R. M. Suwana). Budi Setia is more independent, but, insofar as it has been influenced by the Javanese version of the international theosophy movement, it too has been spiritually directed from the court centers. Further, most of the groups spend part of each meeting reading articles aloud from magazines published in Djokjakarta and Surakarta by the more advanced mystics, magazines such as *Dudu Kowé* and *Brahma Widjaja,* which have a strong influence upon those who read them:

> I went to see the *dalang,* and he had a copy, the latest, February 1954, of a "science" magazine from Djokjakarta named, *Dudu Kowé,* which celebrates Kawruh Bedja and is headed by Kangdjeng Ki Agung Surijomentaram from Djokjakarta. Other leaders are from Djokjakarta. Solo, Magelang, and Semarang (all large central Javanese cities). This magazine is passed around among three people and forms the basis of a discussion group of about twenty people who meet every month or so. The lead article was by Surijomentaram himself, and outlines the main principles of the science. The next, which was by the vice-chairman of the magazine and the "science," said that everyone had an animal and a divine soul within him and should try to see that the divine ruled. There was politics in the magazine too, said the *dalang* happily, and he showed me an article called "Parties in Indonesia," which described the form of the present Republik, the parties in it, and the need for them in a parliamentary state. The article declared that all the parties were good and acted only for the good of the people, but it went on to describe only one in any detail—Persatuan Indonesia Raja (the conservative party of civil servants and aristocrats; there being a loose formal connection between this party and Kawruh Bedja, as we shall see). The article explained what the letters stood for and what the party stood for

(the welfare of the people). It declares that the party is a good one which knows the value of mystical science and the like.

The *guru-murid* connection is thus the structural backbone of the sects. The sects are not so much social organizations as are the Moslem party chapters with their governing boards, standing committees, and rank-and-file membership. Rather, they are a set of dyadic relations between an individual *guru* and his individual *murid,* the terms being, ultimately, relative since when two people are studying mysticism together the higher one is more or less automatically a *guru* and the lower a *murid.*

When I told him (*guru* of Ilmu Sedjati in Modjokuto) that I was interested in Ilmu Sedjati, he said that I had to be a *murid* to learn it. I said that I just wanted to know the general features, and he agreed to explain them. He said that it was a "science," first founded by Muhammad, passed on from him to Iman Sofi'i, a man who came here from Arabia, who passed it on to Hadji Samsuddin, who then passed it on to Radèn Prawirosudarso, the popularizer of it in Java, who set up the sect in Madiun in 1925 and still heads it. Evidently it is quite a loose structure. A man studies the "science" for a while with a *guru* and, if he wants to become a *guru* himself, memorizes the "science" well and applies for a certificate to his *guru,* who forwards his request to central headquarters. When he receives his certificate the new *guru* can branch out on his own and teach the "science" to others. They evidently are very sensitive about the organizational aspect of the sect and are forbidden to use words like "organization," "member," or "chairman." They use only two words: *guru* and *murid.*

Thus, in this pure form, sect organization is almost a logical outcome of the fact that as one moves up the scale of spiritual ability the number of people at each level decreases more or less exponentially, so that the *gurus* of many lower *murids* must necessarily coincide more and more in the same man. Ilmu Sedjati's chief *guru* (as well as those of the other sects) is *guru* to all those who follow his teaching; and, as one moves down from him, fewer and fewer people are under the same *guru,* although they are studying the same science. In Modjokuto, the above *guru* is the head one for the area, but he has four other sub-*gurus* spotted around town, with small *murid* groups of their own. Others of the sects are somewhat more highly organized, but they all rest on the basic teacher-student dyad; and there are independent *gurus* in Modjokuto, linked to no larger organization, who teach only a few of their close friends as pupils.

Sutimah had said that Pak Pandu, the man who drives the hospital ambulance, was a kind of a *guru* to her husband and that Pandu and her husband had gone to a one-night "science" meeting given by Pandu's older brother near Tegowangi (a nearby village) during every Sura (the first Javanese month). Pak Pandu himself was rather reticent about the "science." He said there were three reasons he couldn't tell me much about it. Since his brother, who is the real *guru* of it around here, is not yet dead, he doesn't like to teach it himself and so has no *murids* except for a few close friends. It is supposed to be taught in detail only in Sura. One is supposed to teach it only to close friends, relatives, and people you love, and to people who are certainly going to use it.

There is a continuum from individual self-advertised *gurus* who teach and advise a few friends and neighbors, up through the minimal organization of this system in a loosely structured group such as Ilmu Sedjati, to the tighter organization of a sect such as Sumarah, where *guru* is a formalized office conferred by a central governing board; but in all, the *guru-murid* link is the basic building block. As a result, the teacher role gets a kind of religious consecration.

He (a school teacher) said that the Javanese view was that the *guru* was not like an ordinary man but was supposed to be better than the average person. He opposed the term *guru* to the term *wong* (man). A *guru* must be pure—not gamble or be dissipated or behave badly, because if he does his *murid* will be badly influenced. Thus a *guru* is something special, almost like a holy man, and is set aside from the everyday behavior of men.

The *guru-murid* relationship is emphasized in many ways. A man who is a former pupil of another man always should use high Javanese to his former teacher and receive low Javanese in return, even if the former pupil has become higher in worldly status than the former teacher. This is a sharp contrast to the typical pattern in other relationships which I observed on several occasions. *Gurus* should not accept money payment but only freely volunteered "gifts," which gifts are actually obligatory in the general sense upon the *murid*. And the rule that *gurus* should behave with more circumspection than the ordinary man actually has an at least symbolic effect in practice.

Another time she and Pak Supeno (an Ilmu Sedjati *guru;* the informant being his sister-in-law) had a quarrel which actually led to their not speaking to one another, a quarrel Pak Supeno himself made up by coming and calling on her and asking her to come and help at his wedding preparation several times. She said that he was ashamed because, when people came asking for him, she often said, "Oh, we're not speaking; I don't know anything about where Pak Supeno is." She said that it wasn't right for a *guru* to be quarreling like that.

As is the *dukun* to his patient, the guru is symbolic father to the *murid*. He is often referred to as such; and when a man says "my parent" he is often talking not about his father but about his *guru,* who, in turn, treats him as a son. Similarly, *murids* of the same *guru* often consider themselves "brothers," although this tie is much less stressed. *Prijaji* sects are composed of clustered *guru-murid* relationships of this sort, different *gurus* sometimes being loosely linked together in virtue of their common adherence to the teachings of the same "higher" *guru,* and the religious rank of a *guru* being largely determined by his class standing. Unlike the traditional *abangan,* for whom the basic social unit is the family or rather the neighborhood of independent families, and whose religious "congregation" is thus determined almost wholly by his location in space, and also unlike the *santri,* who increasingly chooses his religious primary group, his elementary *ummat,* on vaguely ideological grounds, the *prijaji* chooses a sect or a "science" mainly because he believes in its *guru*. He chooses him because he thinks: Here is a man who "knows," who is slightly higher in the social scale than I but not so high that I must tremble with respect in his presence, and who will be, consequently, both able and willing to teach me something.

7. The Underlying Identity of Individuals and the Organic Theory of Social Organization

THE sects, then, place emphasis on the kind of social relationship one finds when two people occupy (relatively) adjacent rungs on the social ladder—the father-son, teacher-pupil, leader-follower relation. It is an emphasis of which the essential consonance with bureaucracy, particularly with the kind of personal bureaucracy one finds in Indonesia—what the politicized Indonesians despairingly call *bapakisme,* "fatherism," when they see it in operation in the government ministries—is fairly obvious. Similarly, the normative social theory the sects support is congruent with the needs of a rank-conscious class of white-collar administrators with idealistic pretensions. This theory is based on two considerations. The first is the fact that, since the divine in each person is identical, at the ultimate level of experience there is no individuality because the more advanced one is spiritually, the more one has a genuine fellow-feeling for others, a comprehensive sympathy. The second is that, since people (and groups of people) differ in spiritual advancement, not only does the range of their sympathy vary but also their fitting place in society is correlated with their presumed religious status, with the result that some people are appropriately leaders and others followers, some properly till the soil, while others are traders, clerks, carpenters, or school teachers, the health of society being dependent upon the right relationships between the various groups.

Statements of the first theme, the identity of all individuals on the ultimate level of experience, are easily enough found, for this is one of the most consistently expressed beliefs. For example:

> Sudjoko (at a Budi Setia meeting) then expanded on something in the text (a reading from a "science" magazine having just been completed) about "first person," "second person," "third person," saying that they were all really one for a *prijaji* who already was *alus* in his feelings. "Last night we went to see the movie, Sampson and Delilah. My friend and I and all of us who went together were as one." Harijo said that what the reading meant was that we were all creations of God. Wirjo said that what was explained in the reading was *"aku"* and *"dèwèké,"* "I" and "he." He said that when he looks at three people he sees three forms or shapes, three people different in body and outer aspect, but in the depth of their thinking and feeling they are the same. He said: "Their outer form I see is different, but their 'insides,' their selves, are all the same; they are one." He said that the important thing to remember is that the true self was only one for all men and came from God; and Wasisto then said that individuation comes only

from "opinion" and from the existence of the individual will, but the real self is connected with God.

Often this thought is put in terms of the difference between proximate and ultimate *rasa,* between the everyday feeling of self, of nationality, and the underlying feeling of unity with all, as for example in this discussion of a passage from *Dudu Kowé,* the Kawruh Bedja magazine:

> The *guru* makes a number of points. Everyone has a feeling (*rasa*) of his own native country, and this is deep in his heart. A good example of how deep this goes is the Jews. For centuries they wandered, exiles from their own country; but the *rasa* remained and then finally they got their country back. All men are the same at base in ultimate *rasa.* It is only partial *rasa* which is different—as the handshaking and etiquette of the Javanese are different from those of the Dutch. Also, the *rasa* can be very wide or narrow, depending on the individual. For example, there are people in Djokjakarta (where the magazine is published) who are upright and polite in the Djokjakarta style, but their *rasa* is only as wide as Djokjakarta. If they go off to Solo, they start chasing prostitutes. Only one man ever really got above local *rasa* entirely and felt at one with all humanity: Mahatma Gandhi. (More commonly, Muhammad, Jesus, and Buddha, at least, are allowed within this select circle.) He had no native land. Most of us do not get that far, however, and so should just try to be tolerant.

Usually this is summed up in the ethical imperative that one should spread peace in the world from the center outwards, from the self in ever-widening circles through family, neighborhood, village, country, and world, as ripples in a pond spread circularly away from their point of origin. One calms one's heart, then orders one's family, and so on. And the reverse is true also: if one is upset or disturbed, one naturally upsets and disturbs others. Thus refinement of personal emotion, the quest for personal enlightenment and peace, is at the same time a social effort, for it eases the process of *rukun,* cooperation among different individuals with, in part at least, different feelings. A society of perfectly *alus* men would be a perfect society because it would be a perfectly polite and perfectly altruistic society, everyone feeling as one with everyone else and as sensitive to others' feelings as to his own.

In the absence of the second consideration—that resting on the actual differences in *alus*-ness among individuals—this kind of utopia would seem to imply a normative social theory stressing, as did primitive Christianity, the equality of all men when seen *sub specie aeternitatis;* but in the presence of the second consideration it leads rather to an organic view of "every man in his proper place," a clear statement of which has been cited at the beginning of our discussion of the *prijaji,* the informant being the *guru,* more or less, of Budi Setia. A similar statement is part of the involved Ilmu Sedjati creed.

> He (the *guru* of Ilmu Sedjati) said that there were five kinds of roles in the society: "chief," which may be of a family only or of the whole state, such as President Sukarno; "soldier"; "priest"; "common people"; and "teacher." There are proper feelings appropriate to each role, and people thus differ in their appropriateness to fill them. Patience and a broad view are held to be the proper characteristics of a chief. He said that a chief leads

and must deal with many different kinds of people, and so must be patient. "He deals with people who are red, who are green, who are white; those who are good and those who are bad; and what he needs in order to get them to do what he wants them to do is patience." The characteristic of the soldier is courage, and of the priest detachment. (These two roles seem a resultant of Hindu caste theory and have little importance in the system generally; and the latter has no obvious actual referent in the society, there being no priests.) The characteristic of the common people is acquiesence (*trima*). The whole duty of the people, he said, is to obey the government. Decisions are taken by people high up in the government who are clever and educated; and the duty of the people is merely to carry them out. Since the common people lack experience, they must always accept the orders given to them by the government. The government can never be wrong; and the people never make important decisions. (Individuals in the government may be wrong, but the government itself cannot be; and one may never go against it even though one may disapprove of specific people in it.) Even in a democracy, if the people want something they have to beg or request the government for it. If the government doesn't accept their request, that's all there is to it. The people must sit quietly and do what the government tells them. Lastly, uprightness is the ideal characteristic of the teacher. These five characteristics and the attendant roles are the basis of society, but there is another major mode of division according to the way people get their living: whether they are peasants, workers, or clerks. . . .

This sort of theory is common to most of the sects. In one Setia meeting a retired pawnshop clerk said that as he saw it there were three elements in the effort to make society peaceful: stability in the civil bureaucracy, adherence to one's ascribed duties in life, and uncomplaining acceptance of authority. In relation to the first he pointed out that Java no longer had a king and that the proper line of authority now descended from the president down through the resident, regent, village chief, and so on; and he said that this must be kept stable at all costs. As for the second, he said that we all have work we must do according to our station and must carry it out in order to make society peaceful. The third merely indicates that we should *trima*— receive orders and decisions from above without comment and without complaint—*kulina meneng,* to customarily keep quiet.

Admittedly, however, this pure and elitist view is somewhat ultra-montane even for a *prijaji* nowadays; and there is usually rather more of an attempt to fit old values to new situations, for example in trying to view the major political parties in organicist terms as necessary parts in an integrated state, each with its own functions.

He (the *guru* of Ilmu Sedjati) said that some people support the Communist party, some the Nationalist, some the Socialist, and some Masjumi (the Islamic party), and each person says the other is no good. But the Communist party is good; it is the defender of the country, the fort or wall of the country. The Nationalist party is good; it is for nationalism and for humanitarianism. The Socialists are good; they are interested in bettering the economy, in industrialization. And Masjumi is good; it is interested in government and religion. . . . They must all work together, *rukun;* that is what is important.

8. Religious Relativism

THIS leads into the last basic proposition I have attributed to *prijaji* mysticism: universal tolerance, a relativistic view of religious beliefs and practices. Mystics always insist, sometimes quite passionately, on their freedom from fanaticism. They argue that the ultimate *rasa* is not fanatic but calm, cool, and peaceful in feeling tone, and that no fanatic can even understand their "science." All religions are good, but none is good for everyone; "many are the roads." Perhaps the most basic conflict between the sects and *santri* Islam is the universalism of the latter, a view which goes down very poorly indeed with both *prijajis* and *abangans*. (That a *prijaji* means *santri* when he says "fanatic" is fairly clear from the answer one often gets when one asks a *prijaji* if he does the prayers or fasts in the Fast. "No, of course not," he says. "I'm not a fanatic!")

Prijajis move easily among the different sects with more or less total unconcern (which makes the effort after secrecy of a few of them—in Modjokuto, Ilmu Sedjati and Kawruh Kasunjatan—rather a mockery). One of my best informants on these matters, now a *guru* in Kawruh Bedja, was at one time or another a member of every one of the sects in Modjokuto, "sampling" them. He even spent a few months in a *pondok* to see what the *santri* "science" was like. (He didn't like it, he said; they were too "fanatic" and didn't share his relativist view.)

All religions, the head of Budi Setia said, are the same in that they concentrate on the holy power. Christianity, Islam, Hinduism, Mazdaism— all have at least a grasp on the truth. Only materialism is wrong completely. The head of Kawruh Kasunjatan said that his religion was an international one and would admit Christians, Moslems, Chinese, and Europeans without their giving up any of their beliefs. Ilmu Sedjati attempts to include four religions—Christianity, Islam, Theosophy, and Intellectual Free-thinking— within its system. Sumarah claims that any fanaticism among its members disrupts the entire meditation meeting, and that fanatics are banned from joining.

This kind of relativism is also based on the idea that at the most fundamental level of feeling everyone is the same.

> He (a high *prijaji* not a sect member) said that every nationality has its own feeling (*rasa*). There is, therefore, Javanese feeling. The trouble with Nahdatul Ulama, for instance, he said, is that since it does not want to translate the Arab-Islam feeling into Javanese feeling it doesn't mean anything to the Javanese. He said all these feelings have the same end-point, the same meaning, and that if one is a really great man, like Jesus or Muhammad or someone, he can rise above them, but most of us have to follow our own feeling and realize that others have to follow theirs. He said in conclusion that all this (that he had been telling me about a special kind of "Javanese science") would be hard for me to understand because it was Javanese feeling, but that the feeling of all people is the same underneath. All come from a sperm; all given birth to by their mothers; taken care of by

their parents; live through sorrow and happiness; and in the end die. So they are all the same. Only their surface feelings are different.

This is not to say that the ideals projected are always, or even commonly, reached. Perhaps Shaw's comment that the only trouble with Christianity is that it has never been tried is applicable to religion generally; for certainly there is much rivalry and backbiting among the various sects and a universal intolerance on their part for Islam, often on the grounds of its intolerance. But it is nevertheless true that the syncretistic, tolerant, relativistic outlook toward religious belief fits well with the whole tenor of *prijaji* mysticism.

Mudjono (principal of the *prijaji*-run high school), it turns out, is a member of Kawruh Bedja. He said that quite a few people around Modjokuto are interested in this sect, but some of them don't really follow out its spirit; they just read about it and then go out and play cards, or, at the other extreme, take it as something to force on other people. He said that such imposition isn't right; that one is supposed to follow it oneself but should not try to force others to do so. For example, if he, Mudjono, wants to sleep on the floor (because Bedja denigrates material comfort, or at least attachment to material comfort), that is all right; but if he makes his wife do it when she doesn't want to, that is wrong. (His wife said, laughing, that she just couldn't understand the "science" or really "feel" it, and that maybe she was too young. He replied that maybe she was just slow to understand but would eventually. She said, "When I am angry. I am angry; but Mudjono isn't, he is patient.") He said that he himself may have no interest in tea cups (pointing to those out of which we were drinking) or fine furniture but must provide them for others who may not agree with his "science." One must be patient and just slowly feel the "science." He said that he was probably the youngest person in Modjokuto interested as most young men were not interested in it very much. (He was about thirty.) He said that the essence of the "science" was to adjust to others and not want too much, not to have too strong desires. If one wants something and can't get it, one can just retreat without worrying about it; but if one's desires are too strong and one is frustrated, then one will be upset. He meditates now and then if the mood strikes him, but not very often or regularly. He said that if one gets rid of attachment to things one can cooperate (*rukun*) with others. Thus no one will be disappointed (*gela*); and so a wider and wider circle—house, neighborhood, village, world—can be unified, can *rukun*.

Prijaji mysticism can, therefore, be summed up in terms of a set of fundamental ideas. Behind the *kasar* feelings of everyday life lies an *alus* feeling which is at once the individual's true self and the manifestation of God within him. One can and should experience this ultimate feeling-meaning both by means of asceticism and meditation and through study and speculation; and such experience leads to personal power to accomplish one's ends, whatever they may be, in this world. People differ in their ability to carry out such discipline and thus differ as to their proper social rights and duties in a well ordered society. Despite this difference, and despite the differences in mundane feeling among individuals and among groups, at base people are identical one with the other. Therefore, by calming one's own emotions one is not only initiating a process which, depending upon the degree to which it is successful, will spread away from oneself through family, village, and nation to the whole world but also striving after the feeling one shares with everyone else. Finally, because of the ultimate identity and proximate relativity of feeling, tolerance in religious matters is the ideal; although the means differ, the end is always the same. This, in any case, is the creed—its realization is another matter.

Chapter 21   The Mystical Sects

HAVING DESCRIBED the general theme, I want now briefly to outline the particular variations upon it one finds in Modjokuto, for each of the five major sects has its own special slant on mysticism and its own peculiar mode of social organization, and each draws on slightly different types of people for its membership.* Part of one general religious movement, and cognizant of the fact that they are, they nevertheless adopt noticeably different positions within it.

Budi Setia is heavily influenced by the international theosophy movement of Annie Besant, a somewhat Westernized (in this case Dutchified) version of Eastern mysticism, and is as a result, the kind of high-thinking religious discussion group of like-minded and like-class idealists that is not entirely unfamiliar in the West. Sumarah, on the other hand, is a sharply anti-intellectual sect which decries almost any sort of "thinking" or speculation beyond the minimally necessary and confines itself almost entirely to "emotional unification" and simple meditation, its meetings being little else but collective meditation sessions. Nevertheless, this sect is the most formally organized and the most tightly integrated on the regional as well as the local level. Kawruh Bedja, also rather better organized than the others, is a very intellectualistic, almost but not quite agnostic sect which emphasizes the phenomenological analysis of experience, somewhat at the expense of meditation, and is very much concerned with erecting a social-ethical system on this speculative base. Ilmu Sedjati takes as its main theme a cabalistic reinterpretation of the five pillars of Islam as well as of various other threads from Javanese tradition; words get double (secret) meanings, arcane theories from various sources are joined together in an elaborate scheme which clarifies all for those who know the key to it, special practices lead to mystical experience. Lastly, Kawruh Kasunjatan emphasizes practice to the relative exclusion of

* Besides being called *ilmu djawi*, "Javanese science," these sects as a group are often called *kedjawèn*, which, roughly, means "Javanese-ism."

speculative theory much as Sumarah does except that its emphasis on detailed method is much greater and so includes both various secret and semi-secret means of attaining mystical experience and a somewhat animistic notion of the content of that experience.

Budi Setia

BUDI SETIA was founded during the Dutch military occupation of Modjokuto in 1949, in the midst of the Revolution, under the leadership of a half-dozen federalist civil servants,* including the district officer of the time, a pensioned *mantri polisi* (police chief),** the federalist school inspector, who before the war had been the principal of the *prijaji*-run high school, the federalist village chief for Modjokuto (now the *guru* of Kawruh Kasunjatan), and an irrigation draftsman, who still heads the organization today. The Dutch, of course, forbade all organizations on the part of the natives, but in this case it so happened that the Dutch chief of police in charge of domestic order was himself a theosophy enthusiast, and so when he met the pensioned Javanese police chief, who had been a theosophist for years, he suggested that a small group be formed to meet periodically and meditate for peace, under his, the Dutch police chief's general direction. Thus, during the whole occupation period this small band of federalist officials gathered once a week with the Dutch police chief at the police station to meditate and discuss general religious matters, out of which grew the present Budi Setia organization. Evidently the Javanese participants did not feel that they were giving aid and comfort to the enemy for, as the present leader argued, "we didn't just meditate for the Dutch to win, but for peace generally."

Whatever the merits of this argument, the feeling against the federalists, those Javanese who cooperated with the Dutch in the Revolution, has tended to subside in Modjokuto, in line with the general remarkable inability of Javanese to bear grudges over any length of time. (*Liwat, wis liwat,* they say—"What's past is past," a phrase which excuses not only collaborators with the Dutch but also forced-labor gatherers for the Japanese and pre-war recruiters for the Dutch plantations in Sumatra.) Once in a while one hears a negative comment from some of the old republicans about the collaborators, but there remains only a small amount of tension between the groups as groups; and all the federalists seem, if anything, to have raised their civil-service status since before the war, due to the severe shortage of trained personnel to man the bureaucracy. Today Budi Setia seems to bear no scars of its past; and, although it still attracts the same sort of people—clerks, pensioned civil servants, teachers, not all of them are former federalists, and one or two in Modjokuto were active republicans.

* I.e., civil servants collaborating with the Dutch in the administration of the areas the returned colonialist government had occupied.

** A *mantri polisi,* however, is not properly speaking a police officer, but rather is chief executive assistant to the Assistant District Officer.

In Modjokuto there were about twenty-five or thirty members of Budi Setia, all of them *prijajis,* for this is the "purest" of all the sects as to status. The members ranged in age from twenty-five to seventy or so, most of them being around fifty, I imagine, although one of the most active members, a Taman Siswa teacher, was only twenty-five. Only about a dozen or so of the members were regular in attendance, the others appearing at meetings only now and then. Of the members who came frequently, all were either clerks in the bureaucracy (mainly in the government pawnshop and the irrigation office), or teachers, mainly in Taman Siswa, but some were from the public schools. The group met each Thursday evening at the home of one of the members, each member taking a turn as host, and, although there was a loose formal organization with a chairman, secretary, and treasurer, the meetings were conducted in a quite casual manner. Each meeting was opened by the chairman, who usually made a short speech stating that the aim of Budi Setia is only peace in the heart and in the world generally. This was followed by a report on the week's national and international news by one of the members, after which there was much wringing of the hands over it.

Wirjo called on Wasisto for the news, and Wasisto said: "The news this week is both good and bad. As for the good: First, security has improved somewhat in West Java (where there was in progress a right-wing Moslem rebellion against the government) due to the actions of the new cabinet; many terrorist bands arrested and guns captured. Second, the government has nationalized the electric works in Ambon. Third, the Foreign Minister of Japan is coming here to discuss war reparations. As for the bad: First, West New Guinea has still not been returned to Indonesia, and the Dutch are getting more obstinate. Second, the Achehnese rebellion (also a right-wing Moslem rebellion, subsequently quelled, but then at its height). Communications are ruined, trains derailed, telephone lines cut." He reported that some documents had been found linking the rebellion to the West Java one, and that the assistant prime minister had gone there to look in on the situation personally. "Third," he said, "the political struggle grows more and more intense. The right wing, especially Masjumi, the biggest party of all, wants only for the government to fall. But, let us hope, it won't succeed. We should thank God that our country is running smoothly. We don't want that old *rasa* that wasn't comfortable (i.e., the terror of the Revolution) to return." Wirjo added to Wasisto's remarks, saying with deep seriousness that, with all the strikes, stealing, and revolts, things looked very bad, awful in fact, but seen from the point of view of the inner life, it wasn't anything.

Sometimes before the report but usually after it came the meditation period. Everyone turned his chair to the East (because that is where the sun comes up), the lights were turned off and curtains drawn, and each person drew into himself for about a half-hour, emptying his mind, regulating his breath, and striving after at least a partial mystical experience. Next came a *kursus,* a "'course," given usually by Wirjo, more or less the *guru* of the group, but sometimes by another of the members. This was a short lecture on some subject or other by the man giving the course, followed by an extended discussion of it and related topics by all the members, male and female, present. Among the wide range of subjects discussed at the ten meetings I attended were: the difference between the true self and the false self; the problem of reincarnation and whether it is possible actually to regress in the ladder of existence or is non-advancement the worst that can befall you; the nature and source of evil and the necessity for and the form of divine retribution; the nature, cause, and meaning of dreams; meditation and *tapa,* their aims and methods; the relationship between outer behavior and inner feeling; individual religious effort and its relation to social action; experiential differences between such aspects of the inner life as the imagination, the senses, the soul, the self, the will, the conscience; the inevitable connection between happiness and unhappiness; proofs of God's existence and His attributes, again in phenomenological rather than logical or simple dogmatic form; the unity of all people at base and the ethical implications of this; the differences between emotional and intellectual insight; the comparative values of study and meditation in religion; the relativity of all religions. All this discussion, which often is more a series of alternating speeches delivered to the ceiling or the floor or out the window than a true discussion, goes on in very formal high Javanese, the only proper language for such concerns.

After the discussion was completed there was usually, if it was not too late, a *watjan,* a reading, usually by Wirjo from either *Brahma Widjaja,* a mystical magazine published in Djokjakarta, or from a commentary on the Baghavad Gita, or, sometimes, from the theosophy magazine. After this, and perhaps some discussion on it, the meeting was closed.

The relation of theosophy to Budi Setia is somewhat anomalous. There are theosophy "lodges" (*loges*), as they call their chapters, all over Java, the nearest to Modjokuto being in Kediri, the regency capital some fifteen miles away. Although when Budi Setia was originally founded four or five people were theosophists, of the Modjokuto group only Pak Wirjo and his wife were officially members of the international organization. During the time I attended the meetings Budi Setia became more and more a typical theosophy club, with Wirjo giving lectures on the "science," complete with elaborate charts—in Dutch—explaining the doctrines; and he had finally gotten around to proposing that Budi Setia actually become a member of the wider organization, a theosophy *loge,* assuring the members that this would necessitate no alteration of their beliefs. This was under consideration when I left. It looked as though they might join, even though they seemed to disagree with some details of theosophy's creed, mainly those denying the possibility of regression in reincarnation (theosophy evidently holding to inevitable progress through higher incarnations, or at worst no change), the absolute goodness of the power got from meditation which could not be used for evil, and the notion that there must inevitably be retribution for evil—in other words, with the highly optimistic view of the problem of evil the Indian-English creed takes. Theosophy also has other counts against it in its "Western" air, its connection with the Dutch, some of whom evidently were quite active in the movement, and its extreme intellectualism.

Sumarah

SUMARAH, although next to Budi Setia the most *prijaji*-dominated group, is sharply different in character from Budi Setia, which it regards as much too theoretical.* In the first place, the Sumarah meetings consist almost entirely of meditation. They usually begin with a short period of absolute quiet. After a rest, there is a somewhat longer similar period; and finally there is a very long meditation, often over an hour in length and sometimes performed while standing. Supposedly when one succeeds in one's meditation one hears God chanting, in Javanese *tembang* style, the various commands and prohibitions that make up the Holy Book of the sect. In case there are some who do not achieve this, the *guru* (a pawnshop employee) chants the book himself as it was copied down from dictation by the founder and head *guru* of Sumarah. It is in low Javanese, and the more advanced members of the audience join in at the end of each sentence, so that the effect is something like that of a Javanese version of an Islamic chant. Except for a twenty-minute intermission when the *guru* and his assistants leave to "exercise" the youthful members in meditation in another room, that constitutes the entire meeting, there being no reports or discussion at Sumarah gatherings.

Sumarah is the most highly organized of the sects. Not only does it have four ranks—youth, regular members, advanced members, and *gurus,* chosen through meditation by the central governing board in Djokjakarta— but it has a written constitution, interchapter meetings where advanced students of Sumarah groups from different towns gather and meditate together, various formal divisions at both the local and national level, biannual nation-wide congresses of the local *gurus,* and such declared (but as yet unrealized) intentions as erecting schools and helping the poor. The constitution, in addition to setting down rules and regulations for membership, outlining the formal organization of the whole sect into divisions, chapters, and sub-chapters (branches), and announcing the general aim of the "congregation" to be peace in the outside (*lair*) and inside (*batin*), also sets forth nine vows which summarize the group's creed:**

(1) The members of Sumarah congregation are convinced of the existence of God who has created heaven and earth and all in it, and they acknowledge the prophets and the Holy Books.

(2) They vow to think of God and not to idolize themselves (the "I"— the lower self) and they seek truth and God and self-surrender.

(3) They vow to try to achieve bodily health, inner peace, and a pure soul and to ennoble their character, words, and deeds.

* In Modjokuto the members of Sumarah, who numbered about forty, were mostly clerks and teachers, although there were a few tradesmen and one crippled peasant, the latter the prized specimen of the group's curing power. Like Budi Setia, the group met weekly, circulating among different members' houses.
** As the original text was given in Javanese, Indonesian, and English, this is not a translation.

(4) They vow to promote universal brotherhood founded on deep love.

(5) They vow to widen life's duties as citizens leading to greatness and nobility and to promote world peace and order.

(6) They vow to do right, to submit to the laws of the country, and to respect others, not to defame others' creeds and to try with love to make Sumarah clear to all, and to make clear that all religions should be united in their aspirations.

(7) They vow to refrain from evil, hurting, hating, sinning, and all speech and action is to be unpretentious and true, and performed patiently, and accurately, without haste and without strain.

(8) They vow to widen their knowledge of wordly affairs as well as the inner side of things.

(9) They vow not to be fanatic but to rely on truth.

Thus, in intention at least, Sumarah is something more than merely an informal meditating society; it has aspirations to be a kind of "Javanese-science" Muhammadijah—a socio-religious society based on mysticism rather than Islam. However, its formal elaboration was far greater than its actual organizational complexity and it was still, in reality, little more than an informal meditating society when I saw it in operation.*

Kawruh Bedja

KAWRUH BEDJA has similar organizational aspirations to those of Sumarah, but it is more loosely organized on the local level. (It held a nationwide congress in Surabaja, which the *guru* and a few members of the Modjokuto branch attended, during my stay.) In Modjokuto, at least, Kawruh Bedja, which is largely concerned with speculation on the metaphysical bases of perceived feelings and events, was mainly held together by its publications, particularly its monthly magazine *Dudu Kowé,* published in Djokjakarta. A man can become a Kawruh Bedja *guru* mainly by studying the magazine and various other publications the group disseminates. There is a special set of books one should study, a self-study course lasting five months—but one may of course discuss the content with others studying it, for there is nothing secret about it.

The main *guru* of the "science" in Modjokuto was a former clerk in both the civil bureaucracy and in Dutch sugar factories, and he had around him a small group of older *prijajis,* about a half-dozen or so. He lived just outside of town in a village and held meetings every full moon (so that people could see their way about) to which came not only his close associates

* Sumarah took its present form in 1950, and had been going in Modjokuto for only a short time when I was there.

but also usually about thirty village people who lived near him and sometimes other townsmen. At such meetings he and his "students" discussed various topics and read articles from *Dudu Kowé*. In general his meetings were much like a Budi Setia meeting except that there was no meditation.

Kawruh Bedja members claim that they deal with nothing which is not directly experienceable and that they try to build up their system entirely on the basis of perceivable facts. Somewhat like Descartes, they try to put aside all inherited belief and start from "clearly perceived ideas"—the notion of the self, the continual alternation of happiness and unhappiness, the sex and hunger drives. Unlike him, they do not work back to discover what the metaphysical base for those ideas might be, but rather try to build an ethical system directly atop them, which ethic turns out, not so surprisingly, to be the usual *prijaji* one emphasizing rank, politesse, concealment, and muting of feeling. The result is a system which is almost agnostic about ultimate metaphysical issues and is a kind of universal speculative psychology. "It is not that we do not believe in God or in spirits," the *guru* said. "It is just that we want to get as far as we can without them, and then introduce them at the end rather than the beginning—because that way is less confusing."

I have already presented Kawruh Bedja's phenomenological analysis of the soul and the true self. As a further example of the way philosophers of this school think I quote here the Modjokuto *guru* on how this is connected with behavior in general:

> Now, to return to the point, the soul is an object which can be ruined. It begins with birth and ends with death, when individual experience ceases. The soul of man, put another way, is a result of the "notation" of the individual in everyday action, the funded experience of the individual. A man not only knows who he is but also when and where he was born and what he has done. This is all noted down. You remember, for example, when you played marbles as a child. Well, that is part of your soul; all experience becomes notation, and this is the soul. Now from this, two propositions follow: if the soul and the true self are dissolved in one another, as sugar dissolves in coffee, then the soul will be enlightened and directed by the true self, and the individual will act in an orderly and directed fashion. But if the soul and the true self are not merged, the individual will be directionless, unenlightened, and disturbed. The first man will be peaceful, the second will be upset inside. . . .

Ilmu Sedjati

ILMU SEDJATI is loosely organized in roughly the same fashion as Kawruh Bedja, except that its content is even more systematically formulated. Each *guru* (who must obtain a certificate from the head *guru,* usually upon the recommendation of his own local *guru*) must memorize a set eighteen-point agenda which contains the whole of what he is supposed to teach. This "science" is so arranged as to be teachable in a single session. Thus at each

Ilmu Sedjati meeting the eighteen points are all reviewed, almost in chant fashion, by the *guru,* the *murids* listening quietly, and, theoretically, the whole "science" can be learned in one evening. In actual fact, however, it is so complicated and obscure that it requires many times of hearing it over, memorizing it, and discussing it with the *guru* before one can really comprehend it well enough to get anything useful out of it, much less to teach it.

The Ilmu Sedjati system, which is supposedly secret but readily enough revealed by many people, is summarized below in my own version of the eighteen points:

(1) The cabalistic reinterpretation of the Confession of Faith to read "I believe God is in myself and my breath is His representative." This is mainly done by giving words secondary meanings on a generally free-association basis: e.g., *rasul,* Prophet, is said to "really" mean *rasa,* "feeling."

(2) The reinterpretation of the other pillars: e.g., the fast means not only limiting one's food and drink but also limiting one's expression of anger and one's self-seeking; the *zakat* means giving good advice to others as well as money and food; the pilgrimage is into the self.

(3) A discussion of the "correct" or "polite" behavior toward five types of people: parents, parents-in-law, grandparents, kings, teachers (i.e., to superiors).

(4) How to cultivate such desirable emotional states as patience, acceptance, and detachment.

(5) How to have fellow-feeling for others.

(6) How to keep oneself from such "bad" behaviors as gambling, stealing, drinking, and frequenting prostitutes.

(7) How to avoid such "bad" feelings as envy, selfishness, and stubbornness.

(8) How to avoid heretical practices such as worshipping wood and stones and idolatry.

(9) *Tapa:* how to regulate the outer life and the inner life. For the outer life the points covered are how to be ascetic in such things as sleep, sex, drinking, and eating; for the inner life there are various techniques of calming the emotions. (It is here evidently, that the breath-control exercises are relevant.)

(10) Various illnesses and their causes: such as sickness in the body, lassitude, upsetness in the heart.

(11) How to maintain a fixed will, not give up hope.

(12) Parts of the body and parts of the soul (five of each).

(13–18) Various proverbs and bits of moral advice: such as, do not discriminate against other nationalities or religions.

As most of this is presented in involved, elliptical language, a good deal of it depending on a play on words and on the employment of obscure, archaic "Old Javanese" terms with which most people are not familiar, it comes out more as a kind of chant than anything else.* The system may be taught any time someone requests it, always as a complete unit; and there were no regular meeting times for the sect in Modjokuto, but merely sessions every now and then (usually on Saturday evening) and a good deal of informal discussion of it. The "science" may be taught individually or to a group. Although there is no charge except Rp 2.50 to pay for the printed "reminder chart" and the diagram, one is expected to give the *guru* some sort of a gift. In terms of sheer numbers the adherents of Ilmu Sedjati are perhaps the largest of any Modjokuto sect,** but the sect is so informally organized that there is less feeling of solidarity among the different members than in the other groups.

Kawruh Kasunjatan

IN Kawruh Kasunjatan, speculation is again rather minimized and the emphasis is upon practice, upon methods of concentration. The *guru* of the sect was the former federalist village chief for Modjokuto, and actually more of an *abangan* than a *prijaji*. One can trace a descending order of status through Budi Setia, Sumarah and Kawruh Bedja, the mainly *prijaji* groups, to Ilmu Sedjati and Kawruh Kasunjatan, which are more *abangan*. It would even be possible to include Permai, the political-religious cult, which is almost wholly *abangan,* here also as the terminal point of the continuum, or to include Karwuh Kasunjatan under the *abangan* section as a non-politicized comparison to Permai. The terms *abangan, prijaji,* and *santri* indicate dimensions of cultural variation, not absolute categories; and, if one insisted on pure types, one would have little to discuss but *slametans,* Muhammadijah, and Budi Setia. The mixed cases, the great majority, one must discuss in the place which seems strategic for displaying the exact composition of their mixture.

Kawruh Kasunjatan was founded in 1925 by a Surakata aristocrat, Radèn Mas Suwana (who died in 1930), and the *guru* of the Modjokuto movement claimed to have studied with the leader-founder personally and to have set up the first chapter of the group in Modjokuto in 1927, which made it by far the oldest of the groups in town.

The sect met once every thirty-five days (on *Minggu Legi*) at the home of the *guru* in Modjokuto, and a meeting lasted the entire night. Since from eight until midnight the meeting was open to anyone, I witnessed that part.

* There is an extremely complicated diagram which goes with it and each pupil is given an outline "reminder" or "memory chart," more or less like my listing above.

** One thousand three hundred and sixty-three people had taken the course from the head *guru* in Modjokuto according to his own records.

From midnight until dawn it was secret. Most of those who came to the meetings were from outside of Modjokuto town, commonly from villages, but a few *prijajis,* local and from other towns, are also members. People came from as far as fifty or sixty miles away, on foot or riding bicycles, to attend; and as many as two or three hundred usually crowded into the *guru's* house to participate in the post-midnight mass meditation.

The pre-midnight period of Kawruh Kasunjatan meetings is reserved to the initiation of new members. The *guru* sits in front of his *sentong tengah*— the ceremonial center bedroom, and reads the creed of the organization in a chanting style to the new members, who, by and large, do not understand much of it as most of it is in elaborate literary Javanese containing many obsolete words. In any case, it is mostly made up of platitudes and general exhortations to plain living and high thinking.

The new members are responsible for feeding the entire company a rice-meal around midnight and for giving some sort of a gift to the *guru.* For most new members the food and gift mean a cost of twenty-five to fifty rupiahs. After the *guru* has chanted the book to them, initiates stare for some time at an oil lamp, supposedly without blinking; and then they see either the sun, the stars, or, more rarely but more important, their "brothers" of the umbilical cord and afterbirth. The process of meeting one's spirit brothers is called a "marriage." Supposedly the techniques of breath regulation, concentration of the inner life, and perception of the ultimate *rasa*-sounds in one's inhaling-exhaling (*hu Allah*) make it possible for one to call up these "*alus* brothers" to aid one in such activities as curing, in business, and love-affairs.

Since there are various methods employed for training the members in meditation—staring at points, different rhythms of breath regulation, and so on, which the members call self-hypnosis, Kawruh Kasunjatan is minimally organized.* It amounts to a kind of specialized training in one set of mystic practices which both the *guru* and the members agree is but one way to achieve gnosis and useful only for those whom they "fit"—whether they are Javanese, Chinese, or European; Christian, Moslem, or *abangan.* Others are advised to try other methods.

There is little inter-chapter organization. Once a year, on the Javanese New Year, the first of Sura, the Modjokuto *guru* takes about thirty of his followers to Lumadjang, a town in southeastern Java, to meditate all night on the grave of the founder of the sect. Since the other *gurus* of Kawruh Kasunjatan in the East Java area also do this, there is a kind of informal convention of the more active members of the "science." But there is no formal meeting, just a night-long meditation. *Gurus* are self-appointed or appointed by recognized *gurus,* such as the Modjokuto one, who was quite famous throughout the area and who said that he intended to appoint his son a *guru* in the science to succeed him.

* It gets somewhat more organization from the fact that one cannot perform the techniques anywhere but in the *guru's* house, of at least under the *guru's* direction in certain special places—e.g., the grave of the founder. One cannot perform them alone and at home.

The Social Implications of the Mystical Sects

THE unorganized sects—"wild" sects, as the Dutch called them—such as Ilmu Sedjati and Kawruh Kasunjatan are not new in Java, but the effort to organize—to "tame"—them is.

Ilmu Sedjati and Kawruh Kasunjatan represent the "old" form of organization of "science" movements. (Both are pre-war in origin and existed in Modjokuto before the war.) They are loose, largely charismatic groups bound only by ties between a teacher and his followers. In the "new" sects, Sumarah, Kawruh Bedja, and, to a lesser, extent, Budi Setia, all of which have appeared, in their present form at least, only since the war, there seems to be a tendency for the sects to take a more specific, almost denominational form. Over against the familialistic-geographical context of *abangan* religion and the congregational organization of the *santris,* a still only feebly organized group of mystic sects, independent from one another but loosely tied to similar ones in other towns, seems to be gaining strength. Whether these will crystallize into a well-defined religious movement or remain in their present state of moderate anarchy is difficult to say. Several such groups in Java are already demanding that the Ministry of Religion recognize them as "official" religions, coequal with Islam and Christianity; and we have seen how Sumarah, for one, has tried to formalize the *guru-murid* relation into a more stable over-all structure.

Against the inherent anti-institutional and individualistic nature of mysticism as a religious form are balanced the pressures of party politics, the increased means of communication, and the felt need for more social application of religious beliefs.

After the meditation, Wirjo (the leader of Budi Setia) said that there were some things he had been thinking about which he wanted to present to the group. He said that, with the upset in West Java and now in Acheh, Budi Setia members must think about these things in the depths of their inner life in order to understand fully that such rebellions were evil. They were the result, he said, of egoism, of making the self the important thing, of paying attention to oneself and not to the general welfare. The problem that had been bothering him, he said, was, how could Budi Setia help make its views known to the masses and not just to its own adherents so this egoism could be opposed. "Every Thursday evening we come together here to meditate," he said, "but we must all have a practical program. We need a plan whereby our ideas can spread to the egoists who need them most, so that the bad social situation can be improved. What I want to ask, then, is, how can Budi Setia really have an effect on other people's beliefs?" Sudjoko said that the problem seemed to be the problem of belief and politics, of spiritual aims and political aims, for Budi Setia. He said that it seemed to him that we must realize our values in our own lives first. He said that the rebellious bands were led by one or two leaders who had egoistic hearts. "Everybody has a leader," he said. "When the leader is egoist, the society is egoist. If the leaders are not egoist, the society will be truly social. What we need is a social (He pointed out that he didn't mean 'socialist') society—one in which we have so-

cial, non-egoistic leaders. Thus what is important is that we purify ourselves,
fellow *prijajis,* and then apply ourselves to our several tasks: Pak Wirjo in the
irrigation office, Pak Tjipto in the pawnshop, myself teaching in the Taman
Siswa school." He then asked Wirjo what he had in mind in the way of a plan
and asked him for an example of practical action. Wirjo said that he had no
example or way to offer. (About a month later, however, he offered his
proposal that Budi Setia become part of the national theosophy association.)
He just had thought, he repeated, that the cause of all the social unrest
in Indonesia was due to egoism, and he thought that the members ought
to think about this seriously: how to realize their ideas, so that peace would
be rapidly achieved.

Perhaps one of the sharpest stimulations to organization on the *prijaji*
side is the progress toward organization already made by the *santris.* The
santris threaten the *prijajis'* traditional domination—as do groups, such as
Permai, representing the politicized proletariat—in politics; and it begins
to dawn on even the most individualistic of *prijajis* that the only effective reply
to mass organization, so far as the struggle for power goes at any rate, is
mass organization on their part.

When I went over to Harijo's to say goodbye to Sulastri (an in-law of
theirs, a very highly-educated girl from Djokjakarta who happened to be
visiting Modjokuto for a few days), she asked me if I was interested in
religion, and I said yes. She said that the Harijos were involved in Sumarah,
and that they were trying to formalize it, write it down in books, in order
to turn it into a regular religion. . . . Sulastri said that for them the sect was
a stronghold against Masjumi (i.e., the *santris*); that they were more or less
non-political, but the belief had the effect and the purpose of balancing off
the *santri* parties politically; and that they were Moslems all right but opposed
to the Masjumi way of life. She emphasized that the religious organization
on the non-*santri* side makes for a balance of political power against the
strong Moslems.

The relationship between religion and politics is not, however, always
so indirect, for Kawruh Bedja is loosely joined with the party Persatuan
Indonesia Raja to form the kind of political-religious party for *prijajis* and
for others willing to follow their lead which Permai represents for the more
radical *abangans.* Persatuan Indonesia Raja, or PIR, whose slogan (in English) is "The right man in the right place," and whose major aim is usually
stated to be to "organize the society and government in a systematic manner,"
has had its ideology well summarized by George McT. Kahin:

The PIR is to be a mass-backed party without the religious orientation of
Masjumi and without being based on the Western political concepts of the
PNI (the nationalist, intelligentsia-dominated party). It is to be based
upon traditional Indonesian political and social-economic concepts partially
modified and adapted to those of the West. The present is seen as a transitional period between the old authoritarian society and the more Western-
oriented Indonesian society that is yet to come. The ballot cannot alone serve
to insure that the interests of the common people will be looked after. Not
only will many of the common people not vote, but when they do they may
well vote in a way that does not serve their interests. They are not in-

dividualistic enough to look after their own interest directly and are accustomed to and expect authority from above.

The great danger is that the peasant vote will go to irresponsible demagogues who do not understand the people and are not in a position to represent their interests. The people need and expect guidance from above; this has been ingrained in them for centuries. The people themselves are not accustomed to pushing their own interests in a politically articulate manner and cannot overnight be expected to become politically responsible individualists of the character of people living in the Western democracies.

Some means must be found for giving real representation to the agrarian population. Such representation was given them in the past by the civil servants because of the fact that they went out to and among the people and learned what their interests and desires were. Somehow this virtue must be incorporated into the structures of Indonesian government. The leaders of the government must be able to know the interests of the people and must to a very large extent depend upon themselves, rather than upon the people, to ascertain what their interests are. The character of the Indonesian government that is to be developed must allow for "fatherly authority" from above to look after the needs of the peasantry.*

In Modjokuto, Kawruh Bedja and PIR are firmly joined, and the *guru* of Kawruh Bedja is a fairly active PIR political leader. The party, however, is small, and most members of it seem also to be followers of Kawruh Bedja; and for many people, including the *guru,* the distinction between the two is not very clear.

He said that he belonged to PIR, although most people seemed to belong to Masjumi. He said that PIR was more concerned with "soul science" than with politics; it believed that what was important was the changes which went on within people; and that if everyone was made "good" inside first the country would be good too. PIR wanted to erase the strong feeling of emnity between parties so that everyone would feel "good" towards everyone else and the political problem would be solved. There was too much hate and mutual recrimination between the parties now.

The political leadership of the party, headed in Modjokuto by a young clerk in the government office regulating the market, however, had more directly political interests, with the result that, much like a Permai meeting, Kawruh Bedja meetings were a combination of "science" and politics:

When Merto (the Kawruh Bedja *guru*) held a meeting of PIR at his house, I went. It was an attempt to combine PIR politics with Kawruh Bedja, and to found a branch of the party in the village. There were about twenty people altogether, most of them from the village, plus the few *prijaji* party leaders from town. Narijo (the local head of PIR) started off by announcing the purposes of PIR. Among the points he made in addition to general remarks about democracy were the following: before the war only sons of *prijajis* went to school, but now sons of peasants can go too, and this is a sign of democratic progress here; some people want to make a state here just for their own group and say that everyone else is an infidel (referring to *santri* efforts to set up an "Islamic State"), but PIR is for nationalism and doesn't

* *Nationalism and Revolution in Indonesia* (Ithaca, 1952), p. 325.

approve of that; PIR thinks that it doesn't matter if one is a Chinese, European, Christian, or *santri,* or has no religion at all; as long as one is a citizen he has equal rights. One unnamed group wants to make a special religious state, but PIR is against this. PIR is for social justice, but, he hastened to add, he didn't mean that he thought people's land ought to be split up or people's houses divided around; not that kind of social justice. He also said that PIR was for having clever men do the high jobs. It wouldn't be fitting for Pak Samidjan (a village man present) to become a candidate for district officer. For village chief, yes; but not for district officer. That would be out of place. (People laughed, agreeing.) High government posts should go to the clever. . . . When he had finished, Merto took charge, and the rest of the meeting was on Kawruh Bedja. . . .

Even the intelligentsia party, Partai Nasionalis Indonesia, (PNI), although not directly tied to "science" groups, has developed a kind of mystique based on President Sukarno's "Five Points," *Pantjasila,* which enters some way or another into the doctrines of all the groups; and many sect members—especially in Budi Setia—belong to PNI. Whether or not this incipient religious movement will further solidify is nearly impossible to tell. It depends on what role the remains of the pre-war civil-service class come to play in the development of an independent Indonesia, whether their descendants will follow their values, whether they can recruit younger men to their ideology, and so on. One suspects that, as in so much of *prijaji* life, and especially in the mystic doctrines just reviewed, the characteristic theme of *Pantjasila* is one of an attempt to avoid the impotence of an essentially passive attitude toward life, of deeply engrained unwillingness to project themselves into *kasar* actualities of everyday life and the struggle for political power:

> He (the principle of the *prijaji* school, who although he is a Kawruh Bedja follower, belongs to PNI, mainly because his brother-in-law heads PNI in Modjokuto) talked some about the failure of *prijajis* to participate in the modern nationalist movement. He said that there was a general retreat of "those who know" because *prijajis* were, first, afraid of the sentiment directed against one when one tried to do anything these days in the way of leadership, and, second, felt that the big leaders were often men of less learning and status than they and so did not want to associate with them, the result being that they withdrew and did not participate at all. . . . Mudjono expressed strong disapproval of all this. He said that Wito (the PNI head) was different in this respect anyway; he actively participated. He said that there were many *prijajis* along Pohredjo row (the heavily *prijaji* section of town) who were not brave enough to get out into the new society, who were withdrawn.

If the *prijajis* overcome their reticence, as some show signs of doing, and engage themselves directly in the process of social reorganization now taking place in Indonesia, the sects, more highly developed and organized, may, perhaps, play something of a role in sustaining their political courage.

Part Four

CONCLUSION:
CONFLICT
AND INTEGRATION

Chapter 22   Conflict and Integration

Religion and Society in Modjokuto

ON THE BASIS of a presentation of the content of the three religious variants in Modjokuto alone, one might easily come to the conclusion that *abangan, santri,* and *prijaji* are encapsulated "pure types," and that Modjokuto community life consists of three sub-communities whose main relationships with one another are geographical and perhaps economic—a "plural society" within a plural society, so to speak. Such a notion would be totally incorrect; for the three groups are all enclosed in the same social structure, share many common values, and are, in any case, not nearly so definable as social entities as a simple descriptive discussion of their religious practices would indicate. Therefore, I wish to close this report on Modjokuto religion with a brief discussion of the interrelationships among the three world views I have set forth within the Modjokuto social system. Because, contrary to some theorists, religion does not play only an integrative, socially harmonizing role in society but also a divisive one, thus reflecting the balance between integrative and dis-integrative forces which exist in any social system, I shall discuss both the conflicts between the three religious types and the manner in which these conflicts are minimized and, in fact, turned to positive social uses.

To sum up in advance the points I wish to make, three propositions may be set forth as broadly describing the situation as one finds it in Modjokuto:

1. There is a great deal of antagonism between the adherents of the various religious orientations; and this antagonism is probably increasing.

2. Despite their differences and antagonisms, all, or nearly all, Javanese share many common values which tend to counteract the divisive effects of variant interpretations of these values. In addition, there are also various social mechanism which tend to prevent value conflict from having disruptive effects.

3. In such terms one may point out several factors tending to exacerbate conflict among the three groups and several tending to moderate it. Among those exacerbating it might be included:

(a) Intrinsic ideological conflicts resting on deep-felt dislike for the values of other groups.

(b) The changing system of social stratification and increased status mobility which tends to enforce contact between individuals and groups formerly more or less socially segregated.

(c) The sharply increased struggle for political power to fill the vacuum left by the departure of the Colonial Government, which tends to embue religious differences with political significance.

(d) The need for scapegoats upon whom to focus tensions generated by a rapidly changing social system.

Those moderating the conflict include:

(a) The sense of a common culture, including the increasing importance of nationalism, which emphasizes what all Javanese (or Indonesians) have in common rather than their differences.

(b) The fact that religious patterns do not become embodied in social forms directly, purely and simply, but in many devious ways, so that religious commitments and other commitments—to class, neighborhood, etc.—tend to balance off, and various "mixed type" individuals and groups arise which can play an important mediating role.

(c) A general tolerance based on a "contextual relativism" which sees certain values as appropriate to context and so minimizes "missionization."

(d) The steady growth of social mechanisms for a pluralistic, non-syncretic form of social integration within which people of radically differing social outlook and basic values can, nevertheless, get along well enough with one another to keep society functioning.

Religion and Social Conflict

ANTAGONISM among the several religious groups is easily enough documented. The strain is clearly greatest between *santris* and the other two groups, but significant tension between *prijaji* and *abangan* also exists. This general antagonism has almost certainly increased markedly in this century, has sharply intensified since the Revolution, and is probably still increasing. But it is by no means an entirely new phenomenon. Since the days of the struggle between the Central Javanese kingdom of Mataram and the north coast harbor kingdoms (Demak, Gresik, Surabaja), at least, i.e., since the sixteenth and seventeenth centuries,* *prijaji* and *santri* have not seen eye to eye; and the resentment of the peasantry against the more or less exploitative ruling aristocracy and the shrewd urban-centered *santri* trading class is obviously of long standing. Nevertheless, at the moment, the conflict between the various groups is probably more intense than in the past and almost universally felt to be so by the Javanese themselves.

IDEOLOGICAL CONFLICTS

THE tension between *abangan* and *prijaji* is more subtly expressed than between these two groups and the *santris,* where the strain finds a more explicit outlet:

> Talking of *santris,* Juminah (an *abangan* woman) told me of a taunting jingle the children shout at *santri* women. They just recite the first line, which has meaningless rhyming sounds, and keep the second, which carries the content, in their mind—thus not really saying out loud what they are thinking, although, as everyone knows the jingle, the intent is clear:
>
> Mendung-mendung tjap gomèk
> Kudung-kudung digawé lèmèk
>
> Clouds, clouds, a Chinese holiday
> A Moslem lady's head-shawl used as something to lie on.

The meaning is that, although they wear shawls (only *santri* women, and almost all of them, wear these shawls; they are in no way veils, however, but are merely draped over the top of the head) and make a great profession of piety, they are promiscuous.

Here the resentment is directed, as it commonly is, against *santri* holier-than-thou moralism which *abangans,* particularly, tend to resent. But another aspect of the conflict, insofar as it is focused on ideological patterns, *santri* universalism and salvationism, also draws the pragmatic, relativistic *abangan*'s fire:

> I talked the other evening to Mbok Min and her husband, who is a day-laborer in the rice fields when he finds work. They said that the *santris* say that if one doesn't chant the Koran one will end up in hell, but they, the Mins, don't believe it. As the Mins put it, heaven and hell are in the here and now. "If you don't have enough to eat, if you steal and do bad things, if you are emotionally upset, then you have hell now." . . . The village children nearby were yelling *traweh* (to announce the extra evening prayers during the Fast) and I asked the Mins innocently, what was that and they said, "O, it is just for *santris* to pray every night in the prayer-house. . . . The *santris* have 'Arab religion' but we don't hold with that. What is important

* For a review of this period, see B. Schrieke, *Indonesian Sociological Studies* (The Hague and Bandung, 1955), Part I, esp. pp. 80–82.

is not chanting and all that business but doing right, not stealing and so on. The *santris* around here are always telling us we will end up in hell if we don't do just as they do."

In *prijaji* attacks, the criticism of *santri* hypocrisy and intolerance is often combined with theoretical differences on patterns of belief:

He (an independent mystic *guru*) said that his "science" was not religion like Christianity or Islam but real "science" and so not easily to be dispensed to all comers like religion. . . . He commented on the *santris*, whom he dislikes rather intensely, saying that people spend money to go on the pilgrimage which is just throwing money away. He said: "They go to pray at the holy place and then come back here and are very honored. But the fact is that they haven't done anything to be honored for, because the real holy place is within the *batin*, the inner life. I make my pilgrimage to that. There is no need going off to Mecca when you can make a pilgrimage to God in your own inner life. Take the Mosque in Modjokuto. It can be ruined, can't it? Or fall down? Well, my mosque (pointing to his chest) cannot be ruined. It is in my heart and it is not like a building. Nothing can happen to it. And it is in there that I pray and that I come in touch with God." He said that during the Japanese period, when the big riots occurred in Modjokuto, in which the Javanese populace stripped the Chinese stores of all their goods, all his pious *santri* neighbors joined in the looting, but he didn't. He told them not to, but they went ahead anyway and considered him a fool for abstaining. But now he still has a good job, whereas many of them have lost all they stole and are poor again. "That's the way *santris* are," he concluded. "Hypocrites—all of them."

From the *santri* side the attack is no less astringent. They accuse the *abangans* of being idol-worshipers and the *prijajis* of failing to keep themselves separate from God (a mortal sin of pride) and they have a marked tendency to consider everyone outside the fold a communist:

While talking with Abdul (a *kijaji*) he said that there were a lot of "wild" religions around now, naming some of the sects in town. He said that they were all communist dominated and were a mixture of communism and "Javanese science." He said that he thought that the communist plan was to set up lots of little religions so as to generally confuse the religious situation, and then later they would say: "See, religion just disorganizes things; away with all religions!" . . . He said that he had told one man that the "native" beliefs of his sect really came from India, not from Java, and the man said he was talking like a colonialist. He told me that some time ago five communist youths came down from Surabaja and one of them said that when he became dictator all the *kijajis* would be done away with. Abdul said that there was a sect in Modjokuto called Islam Sedjati (Ilmu Sedjati)—"true Islam"—but it really was "false Islam."

On the ideological level, the differences between *abangan* and *prijaji* are rather muted, both because of the general relativism of the two groups and because the *abangans* are not much interested in dogma in any case. Many *prijaji,* especially the better-educated ones, regard many *abangan* beliefs and practices as "mere superstition"; and they generally regard the *abangans* as over-credulous. But the *prijajis* seldom express open disapproval of *abangan* beliefs and practices to the peasants directly. For the most part they deal with villagers as they always have—by minimizing direct contact with them as much as possible.

One exception to the non-interference policy is the *prijaji* attitude toward *abangan* beliefs centering around childbirth and to a lesser extent, around the role of women. Emancipated women of the *prijaji* group, organized into women's clubs, propagandize against birth practices and theories they consider unhygienic and in favor of modern Western methods as practiced by the trained midwives attached to the hospitals. Similarly, they express disapproval of certain elements in the marriage ritual which symbolize the subservience of the woman—such as the washing of the groom's feet by the bride, certain "degrading" art forms—such as the *tajuban,* and, of course, polygamy—although this brings them into sharp conflict with the *santris* rather than with the *abangans.* Their efforts are, in any case, half-hearted, and, although ostensibly directed toward the peasants and town proletariat for whose welfare they feel responsible, are actually mostly aimed at advancing the status of women within the *prijaji* group itself.

In the other direction, the *abangans* are likely to regard most *prijaji* mystic theories as beyond their comprehension. They view *prijaji* religion with much of the grudging respect with which they view *prijajis* and the *prijaji* style-of-life generally—as undoubtedly admirable, but not necessarily attractive.

CLASS CONFLICTS

THE *prijaji-abangan* tension shows most clearly in relation to problems of status. *Prijaji* often accuse "village people" of not knowing their proper place and so disturbing the organic balance of society, of having big ideas, and of unsuccessfully aping the *prijaji* style-of-life.

I asked the *prijaji* wife of the Modjokuto government animal-husbandry agent who lived in the houses around her, and she said, "Peasants." I said: "When you visit around, where do you go?" She pointed in the direction of the center of town and said: "Peasants aren't very good for mixing with. . . . They say anything they want to—just follow their impulses of the moment. They talk about people; they don't keep secrets. *Prijajis* won't tell about anyone, won't disclose secrets. . . . Village people nowadays dress like *prijajis.* Sometimes you can't tell the difference. They even do their hair in the *prijaji* way. . . . This first happened just about the time the Japanese came (1942–1945). The Japanese used a lot of village girls for nurses, and this introduced them to wearing dresses, nice sarongs, etc. They buy one nice set of clothes and don't care if they have to wear rags when they're around the house and don't care if people see them always in the same set of clothes. *Prijajis* prefer to buy many sets of clothes, which may not be of top quality, so then they can change often; they feel ashamed if they are always seen in the same clothes . . . or village people will buy a bicycle. Nowadays many have them that didn't before, and they ride their bicycle in any old clothes." Talking about the comparative situation of *prijajis* now and in the Colonial period, I asked which was a better time for them; and she said that from the point of view of those who are not "convinced" (i.e., convinced nationalists) it was better before and many people complain nowadays. But those who are "convinced" say that these times are like war times, and one cannot expect much. She said that in the Dutch time the *prijajis* who were at the level of Police Chief and above wore trousers and spoke Dutch to their superiors. Her husband, as animal husbandry agent, was in this group. Those who were below the Police Chief wore sarongs and spoke Javanese, and called the District Chief etc., "*ndoro*" (roughly: "master").

That the blurring of social demarcations began only in the Japanese period is, of course, not true; but that the blurring has been progressive and is continuing is obvious no matter at which aspect of the Modjokuto social system one looks. Although the claims of the more Jacobinic among the nationalists that sharp stratification contrasts have disappeared in Java, that the *prijaji* values system is dead or dying, and that power in Indonesia has been put into the hands of the masses—in other words, that the Revolution completely cut off Indonesia from her past—are very much over-stated, it cannot be denied that the Revolution seems if not to have begun at least to have stimulated wide-spread changes in the hierarchical patterns of prestige in terms of which Javanese society has been for so long integrated. The tracing of such changes, of their bases and their implications, cannot be carried out here; what is important to note is that such changes bring the *prijaji* and *abangan* (as well as the *santri,* who, so far as status is concerned, tends to side with the *abangans* against the *prijaji* claim to traditional privilege) world-views into more direct opposition than they have been in the past.

The traditional system of social stratification allowed mobility for individuals, as does every such system, but the system itself was stable and more or less unchanging; it was, in Schumpeter's image, like a hotel, always full but of different people. Today the system itself is changing, not just the people within it; and this changes the whole basis and perception of social mobility. It is no longer a situation in which a few favored individuals (or families) rise by a combination of luck and cunning out of the peasantry into the gentry but one in which mobility is a normal, expectable occurrence. Now, although the barrier between the governed and the governing (which was the major basis of the old system) remains real enough, it is considered crossable not merely by the extraordinarily fortunate or talented but also by anyone of normal ability and persistence. As a result, the bettering of his station is a legitimate and reasonable aim for a man to have, a meaningful goal toward which his life can be directed. Further, since whole classes are moving now, even if the individual, so to speak, stands still, his class relationships do not remain constant. It is as though the floors in Schumpeter's hotel have begun to move and rearrange themselves. In such a situation, a sharp conflict between class-linked value systems is inevitable as the old pattern attempts to maintain itself in the face of the changing bases of social evaluation.

I asked a young modernist *santri* about class. He said that the main difference is between the *prijajis* and the non-*prijajis*. Then he drew a triangle, saying, with no prompting from me, "This is the whole society—with occupational ranks:

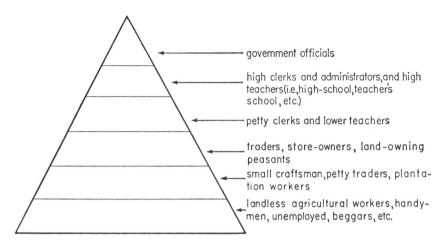

government officials

high clerks and administrators,and high teachers(i.e,high-school,teacher's school, etc.)

petty clerks and lower teachers

traders, store-owners, land-owning peasants

small craftsman,petty traders, planta-tion workers

landless agricultural workers,handy-men, unemployed, beggars, etc.

He said, in response to my question, that many of the Moslems came from the upper trading class and that most of this "class" was Moslem. . . . He said that teachers used to be somewhat higher before than they are now; in the Dutch times a teacher in an elementary school was a really big person; but now less so because there are so many. He emphasized that this was *not* a class ladder, and said that a number of other factors besides occupation determined class standing. Wealth was one, he said, and was becoming much more important now than it used to be, so that a well-off craftsman could be at the same level as a trader. Who one travels with is another factor, i.e., people who are socially conscious, who join organizations (political parties, labor unions, fraternal organizations, etc.) and mix with people are considered higher. He said Ali (the head of Masjumi) was a good example of this. Ali was not rich, he had only a fair education, and he was only a small teacher in the years before the war; but he mixed with the higher-up people, was socially conscious, joined Masjumi and Muhammadijah etc., and got along with bigger people so that now his class standing was much higher than one would expect. Education was another important factor in ranking; so was age. . . . As for family, this was much less important than before, for people looked more to the individual than to his origins now. However, it still counted, particularly on the *prijaji* vs. non-*prijaji* business. For example, when Sarta started his store in his place he was still considered higher than H. Arifin (a faintly wealthy *santri* store-owner) because he was from a *prijaji* family, and by and large he is still considered a *prijaji,* having lost no status by going into trade (he did in the eyes of some *prijaji* informants, however). . . . He repeated that he thought that the thickest line was still between *prijajis* and non-*prijajis.*

The sense that the old barriers are down, that feats of mobility are possible and extremely desirable, appears in many of the Thematic Apperception Test protocols: for example, in this one from a twenty-year-old urban *abangan* given a card showing a man ploughing and a younger woman standing nearby, the picture being redrawn with Javanese scene and figures:

> There was a man named Pak Karta. He had one child named Suprapti. Besides this he also had a servant named Mbok Sosro. Pak Karta was a peasant whose home was near the mountains, and his work every day was farming. He wanted very much to send Suprapti to school so that she would become an intelligent person and of a high rank. He worked eagerly, day and night, sweated, so that his daughter, Suprapti, could go to school.
>
> After she graduated from elementary school, Suprapti went to high school and there Suprapti was never lax in her studies. Because their village was one of the more advanced ones, many of her friends were also industrious. Suprapti was rather popular in school in comparison with her friends, because at home she didn't have to work, because she was taken care of by the servant. Then she wanted to continue (her studies) and she thought she wouldn't get married until after she carried out her wishes. After the final examination of the Junior High School she went on to Teachers School for six years. There she studied many different things concerning teaching. Suprapti was there long, and her many young friends tempted her (evidently to get married and abandon studying), but nevertheless she remained steadfast in her aim to study knowledge of a high level. After she had studied three years in the Teachers School, her parents frequently sent her letters saying that the situation at home was not good, the household economy was poor, and that Suprapti should remember that one day she would have land of her own and a household of her own. Suprapti, when she heard this, was rather let down, disappointed. But it was her fate. After graduating from Teachers School, Suprapti was given a position as a teacher in a certain city, and there she set up a household for herself and helped the income of her parents in the village. After awhile Suprapti's teaching became well-known, because she was very clever in language and mathematics, etc. But every year she had to go home, carrying things from the city which were needed by her parents. After about seven years Suprapti was married to a teacher who also taught in school, and her parents were in agreement, and they lived after that in harmony.

Thus the caste or semi-caste mechanisms which in the past isolated the *abangan* and *prijaji* value systems from one another no longer operate with the traditional effectiveness, and a forced contact between the two world-views occurs in which each is obligated to take the other into consideration in a far wider range of occasions than once was necessary. It is no longer a case of the *prijaji* being, from the *abangan* point of view, way off in the dim distance (spatially as well as socially, for there has never been a really strong rural gentry in Java), as awesome figures of power, wealth, and magical strength perched at the thin-air altitudes of the social structure. Nor of the *abangans* being, from the *prijaji* point of view, a great undifferentiated mass of animalistic peasants least painfully dealt with through a few of their more polished representatives as intermediaries. Now, instead, the *abangan* and *prijaji* world-outlooks are competing to define the same social situation. There are a great many *abangans* in town (and even village *abangans* are more directly involved in urban life than they have ever been in the past), and *prijajis* who have any grasp on present day realities know that their maintenance of traditional prerogative rests on an acceptance of their values by a wider group than that consisting entirely of noble or near-noble bureaucrats.

POLITICAL CONFLICTS

IN addition to intrinsic ideological conflicts and increased status mobility, the intensified struggle for political power is a third divisive element which exacerbates religious conflict. In a colonial regime, particularly one so conservative in policy toward changes in native social structure as the Dutch, the subject people tend to be progressively cut off from the crucial political and economic roles in the system. Indirect rule, whether motivated by ethical or administrative considerations, is postulated on the supposition that traditional native institutions serve native interest better than any other institutions, particularly Western ones, are likely to do. This, in a sense, may well be true, and proponents of such a doctrine can point to the anomic results of more direct impact of Western forms on non-Western peoples in other parts of the world, say the Indian in the United States. Nevertheless, despite the theory, what actually occurs is not the mere stabilization of native society in its pristine forms, but, rather, as the social system "naturally" grows more complex, the European ruling group takes over each new role of functional importance as it appears, either filling it themselves or permitting certain others, typically non-European immigrants, half-castes, and a few specially chosen native aristocrats, to fill it, thus "sheltering" the native society from the effects of change. In time, not only do the *loci* of all types of power shift more and more away from native hands as the "Western" sector of the "dual" (or "plural") society grows in complexity and importance, but also the ruling group has to spend more and more time merely in keeping the native society intact. Traditional forms of life no longer exist naturally, as adaptive responses to their environment, but must be consistently and consciously shored up by special efforts on the part of the ruling group in the name of "native welfare." Keeping the natives native becomes a full-time job.

When, at length, a political revolution occurs, as in Indonesia, the power vacuum suddenly revealed as almost all posts of crucial political importance are suddenly left vacant is tremendous and draws almost the whole of social life into it. (For various reasons, this occurs to a much lesser degree in the economic sectors; a fact which only magnifies the importance of the political in the eyes of the native population.) With the well- or cynically-intended deceptions of Colonial rule removed, the real distribution of power becomes apparent to all; and, with the new understanding of what the score really is—an understanding confined in the pre-revolutionary period to a few nationalist intellectuals—the scramble for power becomes intense. Such heightened political struggle naturally results in a sharpened internal conflict between various religious groups. Religious positions become political ones—almost without alteration.

Mhd Rais spoke next (Rais is one of the dozen or so most important Masjumi national leaders; he was speaking at a mass meeting at the Regency capital to which all the local Masjumi leaders went). He said that he had read some nasty comments about him in the PNI (the *prijaji*-dominated Nationalist party) press in Surabaja, but that he wasn't angry; he only laughed, because one couldn't expect politeness from the PNI. He started off on the PERMAI problem (a PERMAI leader had been reported in the press as saying that Islam was a foreign religion and Muhammad a false prophet, an event which was something of a *cause celebre* for awhile), and rose to high pitch with a rhetorical challenge to the cabinet: "Muslims are patient, but they won't be patient forever. You had better realize that they will take only so much and then they will fight. You must consider that your actions may bring about the flow of blood, that if you allow these insults to Islam to continue we may end up in a civil war." . . . Then he attacked the proposals for separation of Church and state, ridiculed the religio-ideological theories of PNI as empty of meaning, and said that the non-Islamic groups were urging marriage without going to the Naib, which would lead to a nation of bastards and Indonesia would become known as the bastard country. . . . The other speaker started off by attacking the Communists in general terms, reading off the organizations he held were Communist dominated, and rising to heights of sheer spleen. He spoke entirely at a shout, pounded the rostrum, interrupted his speech to get the audience to shout ALLAH HU AKBAR (God is most great) back at him, attacked the "half-ripe intellectuals" who were for separation of Church and State, and in fact attacked intellectualism in general, saying that the only thing one had to do was fear God and follow the Moslem law. He attacked all non-Islamic parties as infidel and said that Muslims who joined them were breaking the rules of religion. He said that the idea of a secular state was infidel; that Indonesia should not try to learn from Russia and America, but just base its country on Islamic teachings. . . .

A few comments must be made concerning this quotation. In the first place, comparable remarks could be quoted for each political group which would show little difference of intensity or rationality. Secondly, speeches of this sort are not to be taken over-literally as heralding immediate recourse to arms and violence, for they are well within the limits of permissible political hyperbole in present-day Indonesia. Thirdly, in each party there are, in contrast to foot-stompers such as the one quoted, calmer, more rational, and more thoughtful leaders to whom such men are as inherently unattractive as our Western political demagogues are to our more responsible leaders. Nevertheless, despite the qualifications, such demagogy is hardly without effect, and the quotation does indicate both the rather intense level to which political conflict has come in present-day Indonesia and the manner in which it tends, in part, to focus around ostensibly religious issues.

PSYCHOLOGICAL FACTORS

HEIGHTENED status struggle, intensified political conflict, and, although in a more indirect form, increased economic stresses have all tended to emphasize religious divisions in post-Revolutionary Indonesia. The connection between such rapidly changing social structures and the accompanying heightened feelings of anxiety and aggression and the consequent fantasy search for scapegoats to provide a rationale for the anxiety and an outlet for the aggression is well-attested in the literature of the social sciences.

The Dutch, and to a lesser extent Westerners generally, form natural objects of such aggression, around whom fantasies (not all of them necessarily unrealistic) of imperialistic exploitation can be built, but, particularly in a town the size of Modjokuto, they are at such a distance as to be largely abstract and not completely satisfying. Since the Chinese are near at hand, they make somewhat better scapegoats; but even they can't be blamed for everything, thus, the need for local, everyday scapegoats from the Javanese community itself tends to get satisfied along religio-political lines. Fantasies (again, aside from any judgment as to their realistic elements) of *santri* persecution of non-*santris* if they come to power, of the suppression of Islam and the murder of *kijajis* if the "Communists"—a term often applied with about the same degree of accuracy as it has been recently by some of the more politically primitive elements in the United States—come to power, and other similar ones tend to account for anxiety. They also legitimize rather more open expression of hostility than the Javanese value system and patterns of etiquette traditionally allow. Such anxiety and aggression arise not only out of realistic social fears, of which there are enough, but also out of the psychologically wearing process of rapid social change.

Religion and Social Integration

IF the divisive forces were the whole story, Javanese society would have fallen into a war of all against all a good while ago. It is necessary now to turn to the integrative elements in Javanese society which tend to maintain it against the divisive elements. Among the most important of these is the sense of a common culture. This takes two main forms: a denigration of the present in terms of the past, especially criticism of contemporary practices by traditional standards of judgment, a practice mainly, but not entirely, resorted to by older people; and the growing strength of nationalism which attempts to appeal to sentiments of national self-respect, solidarity, and hope for a more "modern" style-of-life in order to curb social disorganization, which is characteristic mainly, but again not entirely, of younger people.

A night-long political discussion in a heavily *santri* village some fifteen or twenty miles from Modjokuto displayed both of these themes.

> About ten or so, the *kijaji* showed up and started giving speeches of one sort or another, and a quite interesting discussion began. . . . They started by lamenting the decline of traditional religious life, saying that only a few of the larger *pondoks* were still running in the old style and putting this decline down to laziness. The *kijaji* asked me about the general election in the United States

and he said that there would be a hot time in the election here later (the election was then scheduled for early 1955). He talked about the Masjumi-NU split and said that it was too bad and then said something to the effect that he thought a 100 per cent Islamic state here was not possible because there were too many other groups; and so the Muslims should learn to get along with them. This statement met general agreement, one man saying that not all the Islamic law could be carried out in daily life; what was important was that Islam influence the State. There was some discussion then of Freedom (i.e., the post-Republican period), and the *modin* said that Djojobojo (a semi-legendary Javanese King) had predicted that when there was a Just King there would be good time for Islam and it would prosper. Then, surprisingly, he said that under the Dutch this was so—that they had just kings and Islam prospered. Someone said, "Well, we have a President now, and we can't have a king again"; but the *modin* insisted that the old days were better than now because now party politics were tearing the country up. The *kijaji* agreed that the real differences between people in Indonesia were not those, say, between Christians and Muslims, but between political parties, and that one can't go back to the old days. He said that there were two ways that this prediction of Djojobojo could be read. One way was the way the *modin* had read it: literally, as meaning that there would have to be a real king in the future who was "just" as a leader of the people, and then Islam would prosper. But another way to interpret it was that if all the people, the people as a whole, tried to be "just," Islam would prosper—in a democracy the people is king, he said. . . . The *kijaji* said that this was the Islamic view; he didn't know about the Christian view. One man then asked me, as the local expert on Christianity, I guess, if I could give them any information on this matter. I said that I thought that Christians would agree with the *kijaji*'s comment that if the mass of the people were just, religion would be well-off, hoping that this was a high enough abstraction for the purposes. But the *kijaji* suddenly changed his tune and said, "Yes, but, often men have to die to achieve justice; blood has to be shed"; and then they launched into the Communists, saying that they were anti-religion, etc. . . .

TRADITIONALISM AND THE INHERITED COMMON CULTURE

TRADITIONALISTS tend to lament the younger generation and refer to the greater stability and single-mindedness of people in the past. They invoke against the open expressions of discord the values for harmony and cooperation, for polite suppression of feeling, and for proper behavior in terms of status-values which still have some force for even the most "modern" of young men. A treatment of Javanese religion in terms of its major variants, such as I have offered, tends to obscure the common value consensus upon which these variants are based and out of which they grow.

All Javanese—*santri, prijaji,* and *abangan*—hold certain general truths to be self-evident, just as behind the division into Catholic, Protestant, and Jew, Americans cling to certain over-arching values which in many ways make, for example, an American Catholic more similar in his world-view to an American Protestant than, say, to a Spanish Catholic. The high concern for status formality; the emphasis on rigid politeness and on dissimulation of emotion and avoidance of intense external stimuli; inwardness; a view of religion as phenomenological "science" and of fasting as "applied science"; the idea that resolution and fixity of will are one of the most important elements in living an effective life; the conviction that people (particularly if they are neighbors) ought to *rukun,* that is, cooperate and help one another (almost no one completely avoids giving *slametans*), and that religious beliefs of others ought to be viewed relativistically, as suitable for them if not for everyone—all these are beliefs and values which appear throughout Javanese society, even among the *santris,* whose departure from them is most marked.

In support of the last proposition I offer my notes on a speech by the head of Muhammadijah—in theory, one of the "purer" Moslems in Modjokuto—to Aisjijah, the women's auxiliary of Muhammadijah, on the subject of the approaching general elections, a speech in which the influence of the general *prijaji-abangan* "Javanism" outlook is more apparent than the Middle-Eastern reformist Islam element.

He said that he was supposed to speak about the approaching General Election, but first he wanted to explain the intention of it. So he started out on a lecture on the nature of man. He said first that it was important to note that there was both the body and the soul. A body can't live without a soul; if it is lacking there is only a corpse. "How do you know there is a soul? You feel it. For instance, if you are pinched, it hurts, and if you try to describe the hurt you can't—it just hurts. This is the supernatural thing within you, an *alus* object." From here he went on to draw a stick figure on the blackboard, and to label the head with "mind" and the body with "heart." "The 'heart,'" he said, "is what makes you feel unhappy, makes you want to do things, while the 'mind' searches out ways for you to do it. It is the 'heart' which feels the pinch of poverty and says, 'I'll be a market-seller and get money.'; but it is the mind which shows the way. Otherwise you would just keep wanting to be a market-seller and never do it." Then he went into a sort of typing of the desires, using an Arabic classification. "First, the desire to make yourself beautiful, to decorate yourself, to please yourself. Second, the desire to be a leader, to say to others: 'Follow me, I will show you the way.' Third, a liking for your own kind, your own nationality. Fourth, courage in the face of risk of loss. Fifth, fear." He didn't say much about the first two but gave several illustrations for the third, love of one's own kind. He said, "We all like our own children best, or our own cousins. Then we all like best our own organizations. We get invited to GERWIS (a leftist women's organization), but we are reluctant to go; we get invited to an Aisjijah meeting, and we want to go because we know we will see our friends there. When we meet an Aisjijah member on the street we feel different about them because we know they too are Aisjijah. . . . We like to be with Javanese because they are *alus.* All have brownish-yellow skin, not too black, not too white, just right. If you are in a group of Chinese, everyone doesn't talk much, but in a group of Javanese, everyone is talking happily. If you talk with a Chinese, it is as if you don't 'meet the man'; you don't come in contact with the man. This is because he is from a different nationality. The fourth feeling, courage, means you have to be daring, be willing to take risks. If you go into business, you have to expect to lose as well as to make a profit. The fifth one is really not good, except as fear of God which lies behind everything, for it is dangerous to people and makes for loss. If I am selling in the market and I am afraid that everyone else is undercutting my prices, I lower mine and I lose. Actually none of these desires are good in themselves or bad in themselves. People may have a stronger concentration of one desire than of the other two. Everyone is different. The desire to please the self may be weak in one person and almost absent in another. Some people emphasize the desire to lead, and this is necessary in order to have leaders. You can have too much of one of these too (and he gave the Germans and the Italians and Hitler and Mussolini as examples of too much love of their own kind). Understanding or knowledge enters the eyes; then it goes to the head, the 'mind,' and from these to the 'heart.' This shows that understanding is not just reason but emotion." He went on to talk about ideology and said that Islam meant "*slamet*" (well-being). Thus Islam means to wish in the heart intensely so as to reach *slamet*. . . . He said: "If we want a *slamet* life, we must go by the Islamic Ideology, which is based on the Koran and the Hadith. To do this we must study and struggle. . . . We must struggle in three arenas: in the home, in society, and in politics. Politics concerns how we will be able to grasp the State. This must be done not by revolt but by election. Then if the State is in the hands of the Moslems, the fight for the *slamet* life can be carried on through the State Police, the Civil Service, the National Radio, the National newspapers (there are no State-owned newspapers, however), etc.; and obviously this will be much faster than merely struggling in the home. The changes one person can make in twenty years of effort in the home can be made in one year through politics."

There are many characteristically *santri* aspects in this—the emphasis on "business," the Fear of God and the Islamic State based on Koran and Hadith, the recourse to Arabic analysis rather than Hindu-Javanese ones, the split between "body" and "soul" rather than "inside" and "outside." But what is striking is how much of *santri* ideology gets stated here in generally Javanese terms: the emphasis on a phenomenology of feeling, on *slamet*—well-being—as an end, the relativism based on different feelings for different peoples, the emphasis on concepts like "*alus*" and "heart" (*ati*), and the like. Islam almost becomes another "Javanese Science." Only "almost" of course; but the common vocabulary and the reliance on widely shared concepts, beliefs, and values means that even if *santris* differ with their neighbors they are at least able to talk intelligibly with them and to agree on some of the ground-rules of dispute and on some of the basic truths—such as that everyone in life seeks *slamet*—upon which differences of opinion may then be elaborated. The integrative importance of such an underlying agreement is crucial. *Santris* may not like *abangans,* and *abangans* may have their doubts about *prijajis;* but they all prefer each other to Chinese or Europeans.

NATIONALISM AND THE PROJECTION OF A
NEW COMMON CULTURE

THE more nationalistically inclined among the Javanese (who, of course, may be the same concrete individuals as the traditionalists in another context or mood) also rely somewhat upon the common traditional values, for the doctrines of nationalism are, in many ways, attempts to restate those values in a somewhat more generalized form; but over and above this, the nationalistic Javanese appeal to the kinds of aspirations stimulated by contact with the world outside of Java. At nearly everyone of the almost daily meetings of one or another of the town's "organizations," a term (*organisasi,* from the Dutch) used to refer to the various modern-type political parties, women's clubs, youth groups, lending cooperatives, social and charitable organizations, labor unions, and so on which have proliferated spectacularly since the Revolution; at each major holiday, in addresses by local political officials; in the government news-reels and over the government radio; in the big-city newspapers, magazines, and the like, which are more and more read in Modjokuto—whenever and wherever the opportunity offers—the din of the nationalist ideology is un-remitting.

Rather than give an example from my notes, I translate below a newspaper report of a prospective celebration of the twenty-fifth anniversary of the women's movement which conveys a more vivid and precise sense of both the tone and content of this ideology as it is repeated day after day in Modjokuto than any summary could.

"One-Quarter Century Celebration"

Surabaja, 16 May. The Committee for the Celebration of One-Quarter of a Century of the Unity of the Women's Movement in Indonesia was set up on 24 November, 1952, by the Women's Congress of Indonesia, in order to lay plans for the celebration of this anniversary on 22 December, 1953.

As already announced by this committee, the 22nd of December marks the passage of 25 years since the Women of Indonesia united their will in support of the realization of the National Struggle. On 22 December, 1928, for the first time the various women's organizations of Indonesia met in one Indonesian-wide Congress at Djokjakarta. This Congress reflected the deep-felt struggle for freedom that had spread throughout the entire Indonesian society. In that year the youth of Indonesia had already set forth the famous revolutionary slogan:

One People: Indonesian
One Country: Indonesia
One Language: Indonesian

The Women of Indonesia were also fired by this slogan, and for the first time there occurred a unification of the Women's Movement.

Thus this day, the 22nd of December, has been proclaimed The Day of the Women's Awakening. Before this historic day the various women's organizations were interested only in general advancement, but beginning December 22, 1928, the Women of Indonesia, fully conscious of their responsibilities, merged their movement with the national struggle.

Today, 25 years later, our country has attained its freedom. The Women's struggle does not end with that. And although, perhaps, in content and form it is somewhat different, its aim is unchanged; it is the Glory of our Country and People. The form and the content of the movement will continue to progress as Indonesian society progresses. . . . (*Suara Rakjat* [Surabaja], May 18, 1953.)

This sort of intensely felt but curiously abstract kind of ideological expression, with its emphasis on the unity of all groups, on struggle, and on social morality, is in part a symbolic masking of real value conflicts within the society, a kind of cultural protesting too much, by means of which conflicts which threaten to upset the social equilibrium can to a degree be kept out of conscious awareness or at least from open expression. But, in part, it is also an attempt to work out a set of values which, while related to traditional values and developed out of them, are less concrete and specific and so more able to deal with the wide range of situations in which a modern society inevitably finds itself. Thus a traditional value such as *rukun* is freed from its explicit and concrete context in the *slametan,* in carefully specified village "public" labor on the roads and irrigation ditches, in traditionally frozen labor-exchange patterns in agricultural work, and becomes generalized to celebrate cooperation in any context. In this form it serves two functions: it hides (to a degree) the real differences of opinion which exist, and it serves as a basis for the development of genuinely effective patterns of cooperation more widely applicable.

Supported by a new, if still weak, sense of national identity, a new, but still uneasy, sense of self-confidence, nationalism is thus becoming an important integrating factor in the society, most especially for the elite, for the educated youth, and the urban masses. It is, in fact for some of the more engaged, a secular religion in the sense in which Marxism for the Soviet Union and "Free-Enterprise" success ideology for the United States serves as such a religion for certain elements in those populations. " 'Revolution' is still a holy word in Indonesia," a professor at an Indonesian university told me. "It is still a holy word in America?"

MIXED TYPES AND MARGINAL GROUPS:
SOCIAL STRUCTURAL FACTORS

IN addition to the sense of a common culture, whether expressed in the vocabulary of traditional religion or of modern nationalism, a second factor in preventing value differences between *prijaji, santri,* and *abangan* from having the full effects which seem implicit in them is the fact, universal in the articulation of culture and social system everywhere, that value patterns are not institutionalized directly, purely, and without distortion but, rather, are integrated into a differentiated social system in such a manner that the resultant social structure does not mirror the cultural organization in any simple way.

The first reason why this is true is that organizing forces arising from religion, stratification, geography, economics, and so on do not all run in the same direction. A high-status *santri* has often more in common with a *prijaji* than with a low-status *santri*. An *abangan* who, confounding the probabilities, makes good in business, is likely to find himself seeing things the *santri* way to a degree, even if he can't be bothered with praying. And for a *santri,* as for all Javanese, a neighbor is a neighbor after all, even if he does burn incense to idols.

This cross-cutting, balance-of-forces nature of social life is what allows several antagonistic social and cultural elements to be contained within the same relatively balanced system. It is, in fact, the absence of such cross-cutting which bodes ill for the future of a social system. One of the most important reasons for the extreme instability of the relations between Javanese and Chinese, for example, is just such an ominous coalescence of racial, economic, and religious factors all going in the same direction. The chances for open violence in such a situation are greater than in a case where the divisive aspects of racial and religious difference and inequality of wealth do not support but check one another.

The general failure for cultural and social forces to coincide exactly in any concrete society produces a type of individual one can only call "mixed," and whose "mixed" character lends to him a greater ability to mediate between contrasting groups. For example, one of the first-rank leaders of NU, the conservative Moslem party, in Modjokuto is in almost every other respect but the political a *prijaji*. Before the war he was a bookkeeper, belonged to such moderate *prijaji* nationalist organizations as Parindra and Budi Utomo, and did not pray, go to mosque, or know very much about Islam. In general he followed the *prijaji* variant of Javanese religion—its mysticism, aestheticism, and rank-consciousness—as, despite externals, he still does. After the Revolution it was considered certain that he would appear as a leader in PNI, the nationalist party successor to the type of organization to which he belonged in the pre-war period, but he startled the entire community by joining NU and, for the first time in his life, by beginning to pray five times a day and to attend mosque.

What was involved here was not a religious conversion; this man is still as strong a *prijaji* as he ever was. He still looks down on most *santris* as fanatic and uneducated, regards his own position as frankly anomalous, and realizes that he doesn't "fit" (*tjotjog*) where he is. The rest of his family does not even make the pretense of being *santri*. His wife does not pray; she keeps aloof from NU women's activities and continues to restrict her friendships to *prijaji* circles. We are *korbans*—"victims," "sacrifices"—both the man and his wife say, claiming that they gave up their more "comfortable" position in the *prijaji* group to provide much-needed intellectual leadership to the ignorant and over-religious orthodox Moslem group, sacrificing personal happiness to contribute to the progress of the new Indonesia. Those who take a less kind view of this man's behavior say that he joined NU because, being one of the few educated members, he would be a major leader (he is the party's representative on the Regency governing board), whereas in PNI, with its greater supply of intellectuals, he would be only second rank. The details of the matter are, however, unimportant. What is important is that this man serves as a link between two culturally defined groups otherwise rather antagonistic by the simple expedient of being a member of both of them at the same time.

There are other people of the same sort: the now-retired Sumatran doctor, a *prijaji* by status but, like Sumatrans generally, a pious Moslem and so sympathetic to the *santris;* the *prijaji* store-owner who, although he dislikes Islam, mixes more with *santris* than with non-*santris* (his store is in the Moslem Kauman); the *abangan* village clerk in an otherwise entirely *santri* village administration; the *santri* high-official—the Bragang Bupati is an example—who naturally tends to move in *prijaji* circles.

But in addition to mixed-type individuals there are also mixed-type groups, cultural "minorities," members of which are able to perform similar mediating roles. An example here is the small Protestant community in Modjokuto. Speaking broadly, there are two main types of Protestants (Catholics in Modjokuto are nearly all Chinese) within the town of Modjokuto: first, those who adhere to the Dutch Reformed Church, who are mainly *prijaji* in social status and style of life, many of them being or having been in the past white-collar employees of Dutch sugar concerns, the local HVA hospital, etc.; and second, those who adhere to the more revivalistic Protestant sects (Seventh Day Adventist, Pentacostal, etc.), who, if they are Javanese—perhaps the majority of the members of such sects are either Chinese or non-Javanese Indonesians from Ambon, Flores, Sumatra, etc.—are fairly poor *abangans.* The second group is of only marginal social importance in Modjokuto, but the first serves as an important buffer between the major religious groups. Other cultural minority groups, such as certain Chinese and the above-mentioned non-Javanese Indonesians, serve similar functions, being, as they are, more-or-less neutral with respect to the major Javanese religious variants.

Groups which are products of recent social change and Western contact, and so to an extent secularized, also tend to fall "in between" the major religious variants. The most important of these is undoubtedly the *pemuda* group, *pemuda* being an Indonesian word meaning "youth." The relatively sudden expansion of Western-type education in Indonesia in recent years has produced a "youth-culture" whose members are marked by a deep-going rest-lessness, a sharp ambivalence vis-à-vis traditional Javanese values, and an in-tense nationalism. They are often relatively free of commitment to any of the major religious systems described, a situation which leaves them both more independent of traditional constraints and more anxious and uncertain about how they ought to live—although rather unwilling to admit it. In Modjokuto, the secularization of this group has proceeded less far than in larger cities such as Djakarta and Surabaja, and most young men can still be classified as at least vaguely *santri, abangan,* or *prijaji.* But it can hardly be denied that *pemudas,* even in Modjokuto, often find much more in common with each other, irrespective of religion, than they do with adults of their own (rather attenuated) religious persuasion. This emergent Indonesian "youth-culture," made up of an intense, idealistic, and perplexed group of young men and women who have suddenly been projected into a world they never made, is an important cross-cutting force in present-day Modjokuto, tending to off-set the conflict between religious views with the war between the generations.

Another social structural circumstance militating against the simple segmentation of society along religious lines is the fact that the *prijaji* are the traditional leaders of the society, the time-honored holders of power. The result is that the elites of all groups have a tendency to include at least some *prijajis,* either because *prijajis* attracted by power-wielding possibilities have moved into them or because their own leaders have become "*prijaji*-ized" as their personal power has grown. Peasant leaders, for example, are rarely peasants; most often they are lower *prijajis;* for, though the *abangans* have the numbers to form an impressive followership, they but rarely produce from among themselves men with the social skills to lead them, even in terms of their own values. The Communist party, as all others, is largely led by town-based clerks, not agrarian radicals. In the early days of the nationalist movements, almost all the leaders, even of the *santri* groups (Tjokroaminoto, the founder of Sarekat Islam being an example), were drawn from the civil-servant class because the latter had a virtual monopoly on education and because they bore the traditional trappings of authority.

The converse proposition holds as well. As individual *abangans* or *santris* gain in power because of their leadership of effective political groups, they tend naturally to adopt *prijaji* ways, which poses something of a problem, because in so doing they lose at least part of the specific ideological attraction which gained them power in the first place. The problem is particularly acute among the *santris,* whose values are so anti-bureaucratic, "independent," and "equalitarian" in nature; for they realize that as their leaders become civil servants due to *santri* political power, they become also less *santri* in outlook. This is not entirely integrative, however, because the more "traditional" *prijajis* tend to resent such *parvenu* power holders and, as I have already remarked, some of the more conservative *literati* elements among them tend to hold aloof altogether from activity in the "new society" for this reason. In part, what is occurring is a shift in traditional leadership patterns, in which lower *prijajis* particularly, those with more of a stomach for contact with people of all types and emerging leaders from non-*prijaji* groups are forming a new elite with a culture based to a degree on the old *prijaji* patterns and in part on the newer *intelligentsia* culture connected with nationalism, more or less cutting out the purer *literati.*

TOLERANCE AND PLURALISTIC SOCIAL INTEGRATION

THE last two points making for a moderation of religious conflict—tolerance based on "contextual relativism" and the growth of social mechanisms for a pluralistic non-syncretic form of social integration—may be dealt with together, for they are, in part, merely two sides of the same coin. Relativistic tolerance has been mentioned several times in this report as being characteristic of non-*santri* religious views, but even *santris* adhere to it despite the intense concern with missionization which tends to be characteristic of

Islam. Traders and richer peasants are seen, by all groups, as more or less "naturally" *santris,* civil servants as "normally" *prijaji,* and poorer peasants and town proletariat as "typically" *abangan;* and there is really little serious thought in any of the groups that there is much possibility of "converting" the others. The *santris* may talk much about "missionary work" (*tablèg*) and rail about the heathenism of the non-*santri* group, but in fact almost all their missionary work is directed inward, toward the *santri* group itself, being designed to improve the doctrinal purity of those who are already committed rather than to gain new adherents. Most *santris* would be appalled at the idea of personally trying to talk a convinced *prijaji* or *abangan* into becoming a *santri.* Thus the three groups tend to become socially segregated to a degree and come to accept the *de facto,* if not *de jure,* existence of one another. In part, the displacement of religious conflict to the political level is based on just this deep-going reluctance of Javanese to urge their own beliefs on others who differ with them.

Thus, despite protestations to the contrary, it seems as if at least some members of each group are coming to the conclusion that a new synthesis based on the complete triumph of their own values throughout the entire society is not likely to occur, and that an open society is to replace a closed one. Such views, even in a half-concealed form, are not dominant as yet; and an American committed to a loose balance-of-interests system not only in government but in social organization generally is especially likely to over-emphasize them. Certainly the yearning for a new synthesis which will have some of the psychological and social comforts of the old syncretic unification of belief is easily to be found; it is perhaps the most widespread social sentiment and that upon which the Dar Ul Islam Moslem rebels, the Com-munists, and the more xenophobic nationalists all play. Nevertheless, the realization that such a re-establishment of an organic society is not possible or, if possible, not desirable, is becoming increasingly apparent to many people of all shades of opinion, albeit in an almost unconscious form. But if a society is to be formed in which groups of rather different outlooks on life and committed to varying basic values are mutually to co-exist, social mech-anisms in terms of which the necessary continual adjustment and readjust-ment among such groups are to take place must be constructed.

The Holidays—Ceremonies of Social
Integration and Conflict

THE analysis of such mechanisms on the Modjokuto scene, aside from those already suggested, would take us too far afield into an analysis of the political system, the proliferating system of private associations, clubs, unions, parties and the like, and, in general, into the hundreds of specific social be-haviors by means of which the Modjokuto people actually get things done. But symbolic of both the strains towards integration and the sharpened conflicts of the emerging society are the ceremonies, practices, and beliefs focused around the increasingly important national holidays and those traditional holidays which are still of importance. The holidays mirror the religious, political, status, and other conflicts upon which I have touched, reflecting the sharpened antagonisms which arise in any society which is changing its form; but they indicate also, dimly and uncertainly, something of the new forms which may emerge, presenting an indistinct and misfocused image of the value choices with which *abangan, santri, prijaji,* all three, are for the moment faced. As such, a brief treatment of them forms a useful conclusion to this description of Modjokuto religious belief and behavior.

Since the Revolution, the number of holidays has greatly multiplied, at least in theory if not in actual practice. Nationalist holidays, traditional holidays, religious holidays all crowd one another until it sometimes seems that, indeed, in Indonesia every day is a holiday. For example, there are Hari Lagu Kebangsaan (Holiday for the National Anthem), Hari Ibu Kartini (Princess Kartini's Day, Princess Kartini being a turn-of-the-century forerunner of the nationalist women's movement), Hari Peladjar Internasional (International Students Day), Hari Pelawan (Heroes Day, commemorating the victims of the Revolution), Hari Angkatan Perang (Armed Forces Day), Satu Mei (First of May; sometimes called Hari Buruh Internasional, International Worker's Day), Hari Gerakan Wanita (Women's Movement Day), and Hari Kemerdekaan (Freedom Day, Indonesia's "Fourth of July," which, as it falls on August 17th is consequently commonly referred to as *tudjuh-belas-Augustus*)—all of them being more or less nationalist holidays, as is indicated both by the events they celebrate and by the fact that they have Indonesian names. Then there are special religious holidays which only part of the population celebrates: Idul Adha (Sacrifice Day, commemorating Abraham's sacrifice), Mi'radj (the day on which Mohammed ascended to heaven to address God), Maulud (the Prophet's birth- and death-day), etc. for the Moslems; Hari Natal (Christmas) and Hari Pentacostal (the Pentacost) for the Christians; and the first of Sura, the actual Javanese New Year, for a few scattered adherents to mystical sects. But the big holiday is still the traditional end-of-fast celebration: Rijaja, the one holiday with an important significance to all Javanese.

National Holidays

WITH the exception of May First and August Seventeenth, almost all the national holidays are, so far as the mass of the people are concerned, empty formalities. Some of them, such as Princess Kartini's Day or Armed Forces Day, occasion very little celebration of any sort in Modjokuto and are known there mainly from newspaper descriptions of celebrations in the larger cities. Others, such as International Students Day or Women's Movement Day, are the concern only of that small minority of the population in the relevant special organizations, in this case of students or of "awakened" women. Even within such relatively homogeneous subgroups, however, all is not always harmonious. The Moslem student groups held aloof from Students Day because they regarded the main secularist student group—Ikatan Peladjar dan Pemuda Indonesia, or IPPI—as Communist dominated, and held their own celebration on a different day. The women managed to do better. A joint committee of representatives from all women's groups—Moslem, nationalist, and left-wing—conducted the celebration, which consisted mainly of a mass meeting with speeches in the town hall. But the whole affair nearly came to grief over the polygamy problem, leaving embittered feelings and resolutions of "never again" on all sides.

On National Anthem Day, a corps of Chinese students dressed in white uniforms marched briskly into the District Officer's yard. There was an (obligatory) competition in the singing of the anthem (which, as it is in Indonesian, is not within everyone's power) by the village officials of the eighteen village-clusters, and there were speeches by several town leaders and the District Officer. But very few people came to watch the proceedings, and those who did were, most likely, merely reminded of their prejudices against the commercially prosperous Chinese.

In general, *abangans* and *santris* tend to regard the less important national holidays as a largely *prijaji* concern and are "ashamed" or "embarrassed" to go to them.

At Bu Ardjo's credit society meeting (Bu Ardjo was our landlady, an *abangan*), Bu Merto announced, as a representative of PERWARI (Persatuan Wanita Republik Indonesia, an entirely *prijaji* women's club), that there was going to be a ceremony of flower strewing on the graves of the heroes of the Revolution on October 5, the Armed Forces Day, at 4 p.m. Bu Ardjo said on the way home that she was going. . . . On the morning of the fifth we went to the market to buy the flowers, but in the afternoon Bu Ardjo said she wasn't going, that just Supiah (her granddaughter, aged 12) would go as her representative. I asked why, and she said that women without underpants could not go in a graveyard; and I said I didn't believe it. She then said that she would have to sing, and that she doesn't know the songs. Later I asked Supiah what it was, and she gave the same reasons, but added that there were going to be a lot of *prijajis* there. When it came time to go, Bu Ardjo said that the affair was at five; so we waited until 4:30 to go. We found when we (Supiah and I) got there that it was all over, having happened at 4:00. . . . This not going to the ceremony which was run by PERWARI shows up the class position of PERWARI. When Sulastri (a *prijaji* girl from Djokja) was visiting us she asked Bu Ardjo if she belonged to women's clubs and Bu Ardjo said no, she couldn't write.

May First is rather more of an occasion. The labor unions—by-and-large "Communist dominated," parade around town carrying banners demanding the death of imperialism, the cessation of corruption, the cession of Western New Guinea to Indonesia, and so on. They end up at the town square, where a large rally is held under some huge pictures of Stalin, Lenin, Mao, and national Communist heroes and leaders (recently, the displaying of portraits of foreign leaders has been forbidden). Partly because during the field period the Communist party was supporting the Government, partly because the Government, afraid of violence, laid down rather strict rules about what could be said and done on May 1st and enforced them by the presence of a goodly number of well-armed policemen, the rallies and celebrations tended to be rather mild.

Although the influence of this holiday in the villages is undoubtedly less than it is in the town, it is not wholly absent, especially since the unions are very strong in those villages near or within the former Dutch plantation areas. *Santris,* of course, hold aloof (as do some of the more anti-Communist *prijajis*) and in fact unsuccessfully attempted to establish a new holiday—Hari Kabungan Nasional (Day of National Mourning)—to "celebrate" (on May 1st) the attempted Communist revolt against the Republic at Madiun in 1948.

In the large cities, May 1st celebrations are very large indeed and, along with the unions and such religious groups as PERMAI, form another mechanism by means of which *abangans* can be attached to left-wing causes, which in the absence of any important radical non-Communist political movements of importance means, ultimately, the Communist party. (In the large cities separate Socialist rallies are usually held on May 1st, but there are no Socialists in Modjokuto, and even in the large cities the movement seems to be crumbling.)

The largest of the nationalist holidays is undoubtedly August Seventeenth, Freedom Day, the day on which (in 1945) President Sukarno and Vice President Mhd. Hatta issued their declaration of independence from Dutch rule and so inaugurated the Revolution. The symbols in terms of which the Seventeenth of August is celebrated are, for the most part, not those of Islam nor of traditional *abangan* religion nor of mysticism, but those of modern nationalism, of *intelligentsia* culture. There is a parade of school children, complete with drum corps; there is a laying of wreaths on the graves of victims of the Revolution (there is a special cemetery for the war dead next to the District Office); there is a flower-arrangement contest for women, for which the prize is a set of dishes; there are various sports contests—badminton, volley-ball, one-o-cat, soccer—for which trophies are awarded to the winning teams; there is a baby-show at which winners are selected for health and beauty; there is a profusion of Indonesian national flags; there is a banquet and formal reception for town leaders of all groups at the District Office; and, at the climax, there is the President of the Republic's speech broadcast from Djakarta and sent out over loudspeakers to crowds of people gathered in the public square. Some more traditional symbols persist. People decorate their houses with young coconut palm leaves as for any celebration; Nahdatul Ulama holds a *terbangan* in the mosque; and there are Javanese dances, popular dramas, *wajangs* and so forth, both at the District Officer's and at the railroad union hall. But, in general, the holiday takes the forms of its expression from the vocabulary of modern nationalism.

The degree of participation, if only passive participation in the sense of mere observation of the events or displaying of a flag, of the mass of the people in the August 17th celebrations is surprisingly great, particularly, of course, in the town, but also outside of it. August Seventeenth is a genuine "new" holiday symbolizing the new forms of social and cultural integration being proposed for Indonesian society by an urbanized and educated elite; and its remarkably great importance in the minds of the people generally, many of whom have but little understanding of the political changes through which they are passing, is evidence that nationalism's hold on the average Javanese is already very extensive and gaining in strength. August Seventeenth is the "new Indonesia," with all its strength and weaknesses. It is an urban sponsored advertisement for a way of life which though still unclearly formulated is of increasing attractiveness to more and more Indonesians.

But the appeal of August Seventeenth as a truly national holiday, a general ritual form acceptable to all subgroups within the society, is still severely limited by several factors. In the first place, although participation in the holiday is certainly far more extensive than in any of the other new nationalist holidays, it is still predominantly a *prijaji* affair so far as active organization and direction of it is concerned. Baby-shows, flower-arrangement competitions, and banquets at the District Officer's are not likely to prove very meaningful even to the least tradition-bound peasant; and the centering of all planning effort on ceremonies in the town leaves the countryside with little but a passive, mass-audience role to play. As for the *santris,* although they cooperate to a degree, they do so hesitantly and passively, for they are still not entirely convinced of *prijaji* sincerity in making the holiday genuinely non-partisan in respect to religion. "We don't mind serving on the sub-committees (planning the program), say sports or something," one *santri* leader admitted uneasily, "but we don't like to get involved in the main committee. We just sort of hang back because there are so many *prijaji* involved." At a Muhammadijah regional conference, a Muhammadijah leader deplored this attitude and urged Muhammadijah people to participate more in such national holidays and accept more responsibility for them, not just stick to Moslem holidays such as Maulud, so that these new holidays will be truly national and people won't say *santris* aren't in favor of progress.

Another limiting August Seventeenth as an effective integration ritual is the fact that any event which brings together rather antagonistic groups naturally emphasizes not only their willingness to cooperate but also their differences. Thus a government sponsored Seventeenth of August meeting at which leaders of all groups spoke was notable for the suppressed tension and for the sly digs the speakers took at one another. "They didn't say much," a teacher said to me afterward, "but you could certainly feel them jabbing one another." This phenomenon of a supposedly integrative ritual symbolizing divisive elements as well as those making for harmony does not mean that the division is more genuine than the harmony, but merely that any ritual which really reflects the values of a society will reflect not only how they fit with one another but also how they don't fit. This is even more apparent in the case of what is easily Java's most important general holiday: *Rijaja.*

Rijaja: The End of Fast Holiday

IN *Rijaja* almost every theme we have discussed in this report finds its place. The holiday, coming as a gala climax of the Fast month, manages to hold within itself the whole range of religious belief and practice characteristic of present-day Modjokuto. *Abangan, santri,* and *prijaji;* ardent nationalist and subdued traditionalist; peasant, trader, and clerk; townsman and villager— all can find somewhere in this most syncretic of public festivals the sort of symbol congenial to them. This syncretism, this easy tolerance of religious and ideological diversity is, as I have repeatedly stressed, a fundamental characteristic of Javanese culture, the recent intensification of inter-group conflict to the contrary notwithstanding. But, recent or not, that conflict, too, finds its expression in *Rijaja*. In a sense, *Rijaja* is a kind of master symbol for Javanese culture, as perhaps Christmas is for ours; and, if one really understood everything one observed on *Rijaja*—a simple impossibility—one could say one understood the Javanese.

The central ritual act of *Rijaja* is a personal, individual begging of forgiveness patterned in terms of status differences. The child asks forgiveness of his parents, the young of the old, the worker of his boss, the tenant farmer of his landlord, the politician of his party chief, the former *pondok* student of his *kijaji,* the cured patient of his *dukun,* the mystical student of his *guru*. Each of these (relatively) lower status people goes to the home of the higher status one, where he is received, usually with tea and snacks, where he formally begs the pardon of the host.* The meaning of this act is that the petitioner wishes the host to forgive from the depths of his heart any injuries, intended or unintended, which the latter has done to him in the past year, so as to lighten the weight of his sins. Having theoretically expiated his sins in the Fast, he now asks those against whom they were committed to forgive him for them. *Santris* sometimes say that this pattern is mildly heterodox, for only God can forgive sins; but it is probably the most universally practiced ritual in Modjokuto today. Even many Christians do it even though, strictly speaking, the holiday is Moslem.

Because of the inherent relativity of status, the celebration usually must spread over several days; and in any case higher status people tend to remain at home so as to receive petitioners until toward the end of the period, when they journey out to the few people who outrank them. Very high individuals, such as the doctors or the District Officer, may make very few if any visits; the village chief in the semi-urban village in which I lived spent three wearying days receiving guests in his home without going out at all.

Despite the nominally religious aspect of the forgiveness ritual, the visiting around is for most people a gala, quite unserious business. Everyone almost inevitably buys new clothes for *Rijaja* as we do for Easter, and prepares the best food he can for his guests. The visiting pattern is, thus, as much an opportunity to display one's clothes and one's fancy food as it is

---

* The most common phrase—in high Javanese—is *nuwun pangestunipun sedaja kalepatan kula, lair batin:* I request your pardon for my faults, inside and outside (i.e., your genuine, undissembled, pardon). This is often shortened to *lair batin.*

a sacred ritual, and the day is both holy day and holiday. The people move in colorful throngs through the streets and roadways, passing from house to house, stopping at each for only fifteen or twenty minutes, so covering a dozen or so in the day, sometimes even two dozen.

In the more urbanized circles one often finds a replacement of the individual visiting pattern by a kind of secular party—one high *prijaji* actually held one at which beer was served—called a *halal bihalal* (Arabic for a mutual begging of pardon), which both simplifies the ritual almost to the point of disappearance and strongly emphasizes its festive aspects. Perhaps the final stage in this secularization process is the increasingly popular custom, more so in larger towns than in Modjokuto, where it is confined to the highest status levels, of not actually making the pardon-begging visit but merely sending a small card, rather like a Christmas card, with the pardon request printed on it in Indonesian.

There are, of course, other more explicitly religious rituals. As I have already mentioned, mass prayers are held at dawn in the town square and in the mosque; *santri* organizations give out the *zakat-fitrah* religious tax to the poor; there is a special *slametan* on *Rijaja* (as well as one five days after). Also, simply because it is such a universal holiday, one in which absolutely everybody participates (it is the one day in the year when the market closes down), *Rijaja* reflects the religious strains, conflicts, and readjustments I have been discussing. Perhaps the most striking example of this is the fact that one cannot properly speak, in Modjokuto at least, of one single *Rijaja* day, for the various groups do not agree on the proper date. In 1954 some people celebrated the *Rijaja* on Wednesday, some on Thursday, and some on Friday, each holding that the other people were incorrect.

The immediate cause of this conflict is the different modes of calculating the day. We have already seen that there is a conflict over the proper mode of calculating the date between modernist and conservative *santris:* the modernists calculate ahead of time by means of astronomical data; the conservatives wait, with true caution, to see the moon appear. But they both agree that the proper day *is* the day the moon appears, and in 1954 this was Wednesday, June 2. *Abangans* and *prijaji,* however, use the so-called *abogé* system of calculation, which is, in essence, but another *pétungan* numerological system like those described in the *abangan* chapter above.* The lunar year drifts,

---

* In the *abogé* system, the "a" stands for Alip, one of the eight years in the *windu* cycle (i.e., eight years, each with a different name, make up one *windu*), "bo" stands for Rebo, one of the days of the week (Wednesday), and "gé" stands for Wagé, one of the five market week days. This means that the year Alip always starts on Rebo Wagé, and knowing this, one can figure the day on which *Rijaja* falls in any year merely by extended, though simple, calculation. A shorter method is to take the day on which the year began and apply the *waldjiro* formula to calculate *Rijaja*. "Wal" is Sawal, the month; "dji" is *sidji*, "one", "ro" is *loro*, "two." This means that *Rijaja* (which falls on the first of Sawal) is calculated by counting one from the week day and two from the market day on which the year began. For example, if the name of the year is Éhé, it must have begun (i.e., the first of Sura) on Ngahad Pon. The first of Sawal, or *Rijaja,* then falls on Ngahad Wagé eight cycles (of thirty-five days each; seven times five) and 22 days later, because Wagé follows Pon in the five day cycle and you count: "Ngahad-one"; "Pon-one, Wagé-two."

of course, in relation to this rigid mathematical calendar; so in 1954 this day came out to Friday, June 4 (actually, *Djumaat Wagé*). Now *Djumaat Wagé,* it just so happens, is an unlucky day generally, so that many *abangans* made their beg-pardon calls on Thursday, while many *prijaji,* regarding the unlucky notion as mere ignorant superstition, did their visiting on Friday, the proper day. The result was that the *santris* held *Rijaja* on Wednesday, the *abangans* (and a few *prijaji*) on Thursday, the *prijaji* (and a few *abangans*) on Friday, a phenomenon which gave rise to a tremendous amount of discussion and a sharp highlighting of some of the religious strains in contemporary Modjokuto life.

Despite all the disharmonies it reveals, *Rijaja,* simply because it is the most catholic, the most festive, and the most genuinely collective of their ceremonies, reveals even more clearly, though less explicitly, the underlying unity of the Javanese people, and, beyond them, of the Indonesian people as a whole. With the exception of Hindu Bali and a few Christian and pagan areas, it is everywhere a major holiday. In a broad, diffuse, and very general way it stresses the commonalities among all Indonesians, stresses tolerance concerning their differences, stresses their oneness as a nation. It is, in fact, the most truly nationalist of their rituals, and, as such, it indicates the reality and the attainability of what is now the explicit ideal of all Indonesians—cultural unity and continuing social progress.

Appendix: A Note on
Methods of Work

THE WORK on this report on Javanese religion has been conducted in several phases.

In the first phase, from September 1951 to July 1952, intensive preparation in the Indonesian language (i.e., Malay) was undertaken at Harvard, first under Professor Isadore Dyen and then under Mr. Rufus Hendon, later director of the project, with the assistance of native speakers. July to October of 1952 was spent in the Netherlands interviewing Dutch scholars on Indonesia and making use of the unparalleled library resources on Indonesia at the University of Leiden and at the Tropical Institute in Amsterdam.

The second phase, from October 1952 to May 1953, was spent mainly in Djokdjakarta, a central Javanese court town, where a study of Javanese language, using students from Gadjah Mada University, was undertaken, and a certain amount of general familiarity with Javanese culture and urban life gained. A month and a half was also spent, during this period, in Djakarta, the capital of the country, interviewing religious and political leaders, collecting statistics, and investigating the organization of the government bureaucracy in general and the Ministry of Religion in particular.

The third phase, from May 1953 to September 1954, comprised the field work period proper, and was spent in Modjokuto. My wife and I lived during this whole period with the family of a railroad worker at the northern edge of the town, the house actually being located not in the village of Modjokuto itself, but in a neighboring one which was only urban in its southeastern quarter.

This family consisted of the worker, a man of about sixty-five, his wife, perhaps five years younger, an adult married, but now divorced daughter, probably in her late thirties, a son of about twelve years of age, and a daughter and son of the adult daughter—i.e., grandchildren of the householders—about ten and four years of age. Two other older married sons lived in Djakarta and returned once or twice for stays during this time. We had one-half of the house more or less to ourselves, and built a wooden "office" in the main room for additional privacy.

All work with informants, formal or informal, was conducted in Javanese, with the exception of a few young, highly nationalistic students who preferred Indonesian (Malay). No interpreters were ever used, and although during the early months of research, communication was both awkward and not wholly reliable, this total sink-or-swim commitment to Javanese fairly soon led to at least a relatively high degree of fluency and comprehension, and the knowledge of the language thus attained proved to be by far the most important single research tool in the investigation of religious beliefs and practices.

Despite the focus of this report on religion, and despite the formal division of labor among the six field workers taking part in the project, all aspects of Modjokuto culture and society were given some attention in the actual process of research, and work on religion as such occupied a good deal less than one-half of my total time.

Various procedures of research were employed. I did a good deal of extended and systematic work with particular informants on particular topics, either in their own homes or in our wooden "office." These informants represented every major religious stream in the local society, the major occupational types, the main political affiliations. They were also scattered as to place of residence, class standing, regional background, and age, as well as being of both sexes (the bulk of formal interviewing of women was done, however, by my wife). It cannot be claimed that as a group my informants were a representative sample in the specific sense, for the practical problems of securing informants in the field and the lack of a wholly reliable and detailed quantitative description of the population as a whole, made this impossible. But the group was at least neither heavily loaded in any one direction nor lacking in representatives of any major social and cultural category. With one or two exceptions, I did not explicitly pay informants, but rather periodically gave them gifts as expressions of gratitude.

The bulk of the period of research was actually not spent in the formal interviewing of specialized informants however, but in more informal "participant observation" activities. I attended dozens of public events, organizational meetings, rituals, and so on. Hours were spent in "idle" conversation or informal interviewing in coffee shops, in stores and market stalls, in the fields, in the office of the village, in the mosque yard, etc. Trips with informants—to their parents' home, to the city, to see some ruin or other, etc.—were taken. I sat in school rooms, watched soccer games—even in the movies one does not escape one's work, because one finds oneself more interested in the pattern of audience reaction than in the movie, particularly as the movie is usually "Tarzan's Savage Revenge."

Finally, a good deal of statistical and other data were gathered from the various government offices in the town; Thematic Apperception Tests were given (by my wife) to thirty-five subjects; sentence completion tests were administered to high school students, who also wrote short "life history" compositions for us (in Indonesian). Together with other members of the project, most notably Donald Fagg who planned and directed the work, a map of the urban area was prepared showing house types, business, public buildings and areas, etc., which was then correlated, as well as possible, with voting lists, to give at least a rough household and occupational census of the town.

I represented my role, as did the other members of the project, in a simply straight-forward way for what it was: I described myself as a university student come to Java to gather material on "the Javanese way of life" in order to write a dissertation for a university degree. Not all my informants, of course, understood very precisely what I meant—though a rather surprising number did—but the fact that I was *murid,* a student, was a fully comprehensible and readily accepted role, for reasons which should be apparent from the text.

Though attitudes toward me and assessments of my "real" motivations naturally varied, the overwhelming majority of the people with whom I came in contact seemed willing to accept me as more or less what I said I was, and to assist me in my work. During the whole period I never met with an outright rejection, a simple refusal to have anything to do with me at all, a reflection of Javanese etiquette rather more than my own social skills, and a great many people responded with genuine enthusiasm—or at least as much enthusiasm as the Javanese feel it proper to permit themselves to feel—to my requests for aid. Despite the fact that there were, altogether, eleven of us Americans in and around Modjokuto, no incident, political or personal, occurred and no member of the project experienced any unusual difficulties in carrying out his research plans.

The single space quotations in the text are from my field notes, with at most a few grammatical and syntactical repairs, the removal of some unprofessional editorial comments, and a translation of a great number of words and phrases, sometimes whole sentences or paragraphs, from Javanese. I took notes in English, translating what I and my informant were saying as I went, but left expressions which were either peculiarly apt, peculiarly difficult to find English equivalents for on the spur of the moment, or were of technical importance to record, in Javanese. The result was a kind of field note pidgin which became rather more Javanese and less English as the period wore on, so that ultimately the notes become unreadable for anyone who does not know Javanese; a defect I have, I hope, removed in the text excerpts.

In formal informant interviews, and in many other cases, notes were taken at the moment. When, especially in certain kinds of informal contexts and certain kinds of meetings, etc., note-taking would alter the social situation, I wrote notes only afterwards, usually within an hour or so. Handwritten notes for one or two days were then typed, mainly at night, in a chronological fashion. A tape recorder was used for TAT's and some other material, but because it is so much easier to put material on to such a recorder than to transcribe it off again, I did not use it very much in interviews as such.

As a result of this method of work there is perhaps less verbatim material in the notes than in those cases where the anthropologist works with an interpreter and records, electrically or by hand, the text and its translation, or demands a "literal" account from the interpreter. Much of my material is thus a paraphrase, or at least a somewhat catch-as-catch-can translation, of what the informant said rather than his exact words. When, however, quotation marks are put around an informant's statement in the notes quoted above, it is, at least more or less, a literal, or close, translation of what he actually said, for I wrote down the Javanese. My own opinion is that whatever loss of accuracy is involved in non-verbatim translation it is more than compensated for in the increased quantity and variety of material one gets and the greater degree of naturalness and free-flow quality of the interview situation (it also has the virtue of not presenting as verbatim what is really paraphrase). But this is a debatable point, and for some sorts of material—myths, folktales, linguistic texts, etc.—verbatim transcription is of course essential, and was used here as well.

The final phase of the report was, then, the writing of it, a full-time occupation from October 1954 to August 1955, when I was employed as a research assistant at the Center for International Studies, at the Massachusetts Institute of Technology, the sponsors of the project. Because of the joint nature of the project, and the division of labor into "aspects" for purposes of reporting, as well as because of the paucity of specific data of a modern anthropological sort on Java, it was decided by the members of the research team to write reports which were basically descriptive, rather than either comparative or explicitly theoretical in nature.

The above report, with a different introduction and conclusion, was submitted as a doctoral thesis to the Department of Social Relations at Harvard University in the Spring of 1956.

Subject and
Author Index

387

Index of Javanese and Indonesian Terms

[Only the more important terms appearing in the text are listed, each with a single reference to the place where it is most completely explicated. Terms followed by (I) are Indonesian; the rest are either Javanese or both Javanese and Indonesian.]

MAPS

KEY TO MAP OF THE
TOWN OF MODJOKUTO

SCHOOL BUILDINGS

Government Schools

1 Secondary School for Teachers
2 Technical Secondary School
3 Elementary schools (six grades)

Private Schools

4 "Ngèsti Tunggal," a local foundation and secondary school
5 Taman Siswa elementary and secondary school
6 Muhammadijah elementary school, secondary school and secondary school for teachers
7 PSII elementary school
8 Nahdatul Ulama religious teachers school
9 Typing school
10 Catholic elementary school
10A Chinese school

GOVERNMENT BUILDINGS

11 District Office (*Kewedanan*)
12 Subdistrict Office (*Ketjamatan*) and Information Office
13 Village Office of Modjokuto (*Kelurahan*)
14 Village Office of Sumbersari (*Kelurahan*)
15 Regency Police Headquarters
16 Regency Police Barracks
17 Army Training School
18 Regency Hospital
19 Post Office and Telephone and Telegraph Office
20 Electricity Office
21 Department of Public Works: Roads and Buildings
22 Department of Public Works: Irrigation Office
23 Market Office and Bank
24 Pawn House
25 Abattoir
26 Poor House
27 Forestry Office
28 Agricultural Extension Service
29 Railroad Office
30 Department of Health Office

RELIGIOUS INSTITUTIONS

31 Mosque and Office for Religious Affairs
32 Village shrine at banyan tree
33 Dutch Reformed Church
34 Pentacostal Church
35 Cemetery
36 Memorial Cemetery for Heroes of the Revolution
37 Private cemetery, "Ngèsti Tunggal"
38 Chinese cemetery
38A Bethel Church

OTHER BUILDINGS

39 Private Dutch hospital
40 Motion picture theater
41 Theater (*Wajang Wong* and *Sandiwara*)
42 Rice mill
43 Public Meeting Hall (*Gedung Nasional*)
44 Railroad Union Hall
45 Bus and Jitney Station
46 Orphanage (Muhammadijah)
47 Ethnographers' houses
48 Federation of Chinese Associations (CHTH)

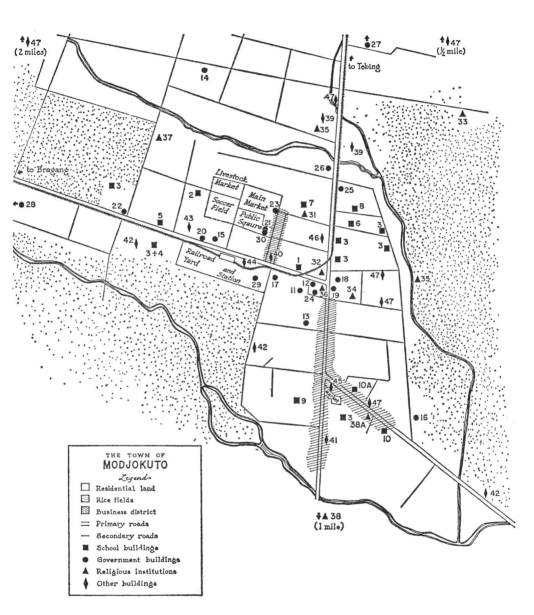

THE TOWN OF
MODJOKUTO
Legend

☐ Residential land
▦ Rice fields
▨ Business district
═ Primary roads
— Secondary roads
■ School buildings
● Government buildings
▲ Religious institutions
♦ Other buildings

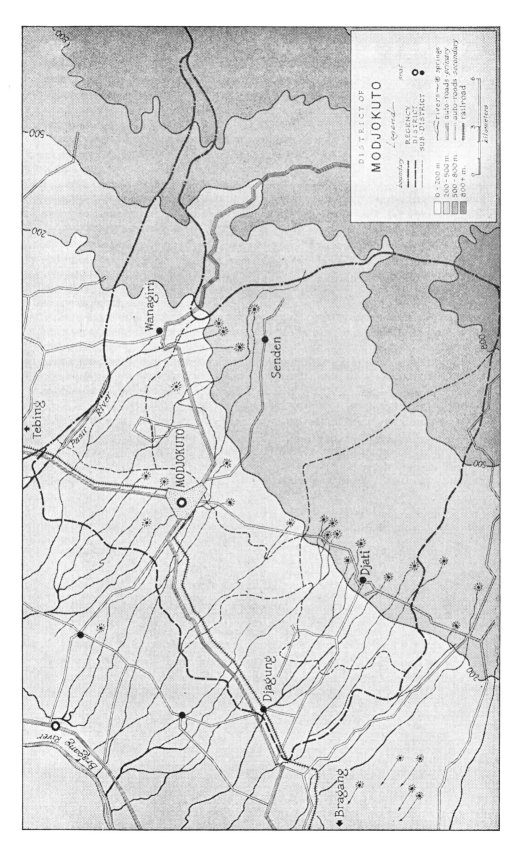

DISTRICT OF

MODJOKUTO

Legend

REGENCY
DISTRICT
SUB-DISTRICT

boundary

○● seat

⌖ springs
rivers
auto roads - primary
auto roads - secondary
railroad

0 - 200 m.
200 - 500 m.
500 - 800 m.
800+ m.

0   3   6
kilometers

Tebing

Wanagiri

Senden

MODJOKUTO

Pasir River

Brantas River

Djati

Djagung

Bragang